Baseball with a Latin Beat

Also by the author

The Baseball Scrapbook
The History of the NBA
The Brooklyn Dodgers
Baseball's Great Dynasties: The Dodgers
Baseball's Great Dynasties: The Reds
The Toronto Blue Jays
Roberto Clemente, Baseball Legend
Duke Snider, Baseball Legend
Ernie Banks, Baseball Legend
Warren Spahn, Baseball Legend
The Encyclopedia of Pro Basketball
Team Histories
Slam Dunk Superstars
Shaq: The Making of a Legend
Big Ten Basketball
Hoopla: A Century of College Basketball

As editor

Encyclopedia of Major League Baseball
(Team Histories): National League
Encyclopedia of Major League Baseball
(Team Histories): American League
Baseball and the Game of Life:
Stories for the Thinking Fan
Baseball and the Game of Ideas:
Essays for the Serious Fan
The Inter-National Pastime

Works for juveniles

Top 10 Basketball Slam Dunkers
Top 10 Baseball Base Stealers
Reggie Miller, Star Guard
Sports Great Dominique Wilkins
Sports Great Scottie Pippen

Baseball with a Latin Beat

A HISTORY OF THE LATIN AMERICAN GAME

by

Peter C. Bjarkman

McFarland & Company, Inc., Publishers
Jefferson, North Carolina, and London

British Library Cataloguing-in-Publication data are available

Library of Congress Cataloguing-in-Publication Data

Bjarkman, Peter C.
Baseball with a Latin beat : a history of the Latin American game / by Peter C. Bjarkman.
p. cm.
Includes bibliographical references (p.) and index.
ISBN 0-89950-973-8 (sewn softcover : 50# and 70# alk. paper) ∞
1. Baseball—Latin America. 2. Baseball players—Latin America—Biography. 3. Baseball—United States. I. Title.
GV863.155.B53 1994
796.357'098—dc20 94-3526
CIP

Manufactured in the United States of America

McFarland & Company, Inc., Publishers
Box 611, Jefferson, North Carolina 28640

For Luís Rodríguez-Mayoral of Puerto Rico, the truest voice and spirit of Latin American baseball, and José de Jesús Jiménez, M.D., of the Dominican Republic, who kept the fires burning until the rest of us finally got there! And for the conscience of Cuban baseball, Jorge Figueredo, of Tampa, Florida. Amigos, may all your summer days be glorious doubleheaders!

Acknowledgments

Chapter 1 was earlier published in a different form in *The Perfect Game* (edited by Mark Alvarez), Taylor Publishers, Dallas. It is republished here with permission of the publisher and the Society for American Baseball Research.

Chapter 5 first appeared in *Dodgers Magazine* volume 3, number 4 (1990). It reappears here with permission of the Los Angeles Dodgers Baseball Club.

Chapter 8 originated in a shorter version in *The International Pastime: A Review of Baseball History*, number 12 (1992). It is being reprinted here with the permission of the Society for American Baseball Research.

Invaluable assistance in locating and acquiring photographs and other materials was provided by all the following: Brent Shyer and John Olguin of the Los Angeles Dodgers; Sally O'Leary of the Pittsburgh Pirates; Patricia Kelly of the Photo Department at the National Baseball Library in Cooperstown; Mark Rucker (Transcendental Graphics) of Boulder, Colorado; Mark Alvarez of the Society for American Baseball Research; Jorge C. Menéndez of the Yucatán Leones (Mexican League) Baseball Club; Dr. José de Jesús Jiménez of Santiago, Dominican Republic; and Luís Alvelo of Caguas, Puerto Rico.

Contents

Introduction

> Had Abner Doubleday seen the sort of baseball we played, he might well have given up the game and taken up quoits. Rarely did we have the luxury of a baseball to play with. Instead we used lemons. They were green and sort of sweet and, most important, they were plentiful around Haina. They also broke easily when we hit them with our hands, which we used in place of bats.
>
> —Felipe Alou

First they were hopelessly forgotten, a sprinkling of lost Caribbean stars (Perucho Cepeda, Cristóbal Torriente, Martín Dihigo, José Méndez) buried far out of sight in the renegade black leagues seldom visited or acknowledged by America's majority white fans. When Jackie Robinson belatedly broke through the odious color line at the close of the Second World War, dark-skinned Latins soon followed, all too often only to be buried in their assigned roles as journeymen infielders, low-profile bullpen tenders, or half-complete stars seemingly without the mental wherewithal (such was the rap in the popular press) to master the American national pastime.

It was a fact conveniently ignored by light-skinned fans and press alike that many Latins had already starred for decades in outlaw black leagues alongside giants of the game like Satchel Paige, Judy Johnson, Buck Leonard, and Josh Gibson. Or that some less talented and almost invisible "blacks" from Cuba (Tomás de la Cruz, Armando Marsans, and Rafael Almeida), Puerto Rico (Hiram Bithorn), and Venezuela (Alex Carrasquel) had already sneaked past the hate-inspired barriers of the "gentlemen's agreement" ahead of Jackie Robinson and debuted briefly if unspectacularly in the white man's big leagues. Or that Abner Doubleday's sport of "rounders" had long been as much the reigning national pastime and unrivaled people's passion in Caribbean nations as it was in metropolitan centers and farmlands across North America.

Finally, once the Latin American ballplayer did become entrenched in the mainstream big leagues during the carefree Eisenhower years of the

1950s, his true stature and onfield importance always seemed somehow overshadowed by long-familiar stereotypes. Roberto Clemente could hit, true enough, but after all was said and done, wasn't he merely a hot-tempered badball hitter with plenty of luck and very little heart? Juan Marichal, like Rubén Gómez before him, was acknowledged to be a loose cannon as well as a hard thrower, more ready to avenge a perceived slight or settle a personal score than win a pennant. And so it has continued to the present: George Bell can hit and field when he puts his mind to it, but public opinion has long dismissed the Dominican slugging hero as the owner of an oversized set of Latin rabbit ears. Pete Rose, it is widely held, scrapped and clawed his way across the diamond simply because he was baseball's beloved Charlie Hustle—but Orlando Cepeda, public opinion mandates, always did so only because of an outrageous lack of ballplaying ethics. Such distorted and discrediting images of the Latin ballplayer ignore all evidence to the contrary.

The plight of the Latin ballplayer in the professional leagues (majors and minors) operating on North American soil has been a particularly tragic affair from the outset. First tapped in large numbers by Clark Griffith's penny-pinching Washington Senators during the early 1940s, Cuban and later Puerto Rican and Dominican and Venezuelan athletes were soon being hired on as big-league "indentured servants"—fastball-flinging migrant workers brought in boatloads to tend outfield pastures and harvest base hits rather than tobacco, coffee, or sugarcane. When their summer's employment was done for another season, their visas would expire, and they would return to winter-league employment on their native islands, a practice that would keep batting and hurling skills sharp but worked against any progress with English language skills or North American cultural adaptation. The itinerant Caribbean, South American, and Mexican ballplayers continued to arrive on the scene in increasing numbers throughout the decades of the fifties, sixties, and seventies, attracting ballpark customers in Philadelphia, Chicago, or New York, yet their strangeness of language, behavior, and cultural attitude kept them locked firmly outside America's melting-pot culture. Ballplayers who sported overbearing Latin macho egos, stood proudly aloof from fans and teammates, or proved impossibly bad interviews in the press and on the airwaves were always a giant leap away from full-fledged baseball stardom.

Today, despite years of neglect and a monsoonlike storm of stereotypes, these ballplaying sons of the Caribbean have now at last emerged as baseball's biggest story of the past and current decade. The tiny island nation of the Dominican Republic today seems to produce shortstops as Yankee Stadium used to produce championships and Kansas City has always poured out rhythm and blues. José Canseco, Juan González, Julio Franco, and Dennis Martínez are among the game's most celebrated superstars. Books and articles now treat (even exploit) the story of the Latin ballplayer with boring regularity, chronicling his struggles with language and cultural adjustment, explaining away the knack of ballplaying that seems to come naturally with being born in the land of sugarcane and endless sunshine, speculating on whether Latin American athletes may someday dominate a game that originally grew up with white-skinned farmboys from the hills of Missouri and Appalachia. Latin ballplayers are now as hot in the pages of North America's sporting press as they have long been on the diamonds of big-league play.

But if they have gained a measure of recognition, it seems that Latin American baseball players nonetheless still suffer from an insidiously unfortunate brand of ongoing neglect. For it is their heritage itself in large part that has been hopelessly lost. While hordes of writers and historians have recently turned their belated attention to the Latin American baseball story, most wordsmiths have focused almost exclusively on the narrow if important chapter that chronicles the Dominican Republic's remarkable baseball pipeline. José Canseco (Cuba), Ozzie Guillén (Venezuela), Dennis Martínez (Nicaragua), Fernando Valenzuela (Mexico), and Robbie Alomar (Puerto Rico) are nowadays lionized by fans, to be sure. But pioneering stars like Miñoso, Marichal, and Cepeda remain highly undervalued in the retrospective view of history. Luís Aparicio draws far less fond recollection among Windy City fans from his perch inside Cooperstown than his old keystone mate Nellie Fox from far outside the hallowed shrine. Clemente is a full-blown idol (especially in his native Puerto Rico and throughout the Caribbean nations) yet an idol with an asterisk. José Méndez, Martín Dihigo, and Dolf Luque, sadly enough, are now all but forgotten.

The Dominican baseball saga is indeed one of our greatest success tales from the modern era of American sport. But the Horatio Alger–style tales involving San Pedro de Macoris and its cornucopia of shortstops during the eighties and nineties are no larger a story, perhaps, than the record of those first talented Latin superstars of the post–Robinson and postintegration years. Few ballplayers in any generation have exerted a greater sociological impact on the game than a handful of Latins—Miñoso, Power, Clemente, Marichal—who arrived in the wake of Jackie Robinson but also in the vanguard of the present Spanish-speaking superstars.

And lurking behind the inspired story of pioneering Latin big-leaguers is the lesser-known and less well documented account of baseball as it has long been enthusiastically played in the homelands of these dark-skinned Spanish-speaking diamond superstars. The glorious Caribbean Series, for example, contested annually for national bragging rights between rival winter-league champions from four Hispanic nations, remains a full-fledged (if little documented) chapter of baseball history, one that has few rivals for raw excitement and rare legend. And there are endless tales of colorful Caribbean batting and hurling stars unknown to the once all-white big leagues as well as epic winter-league feats that demand their full page in baseball's expansive chronicle. Each passing year, while baseball naps in Beantown and Tinsel Town and the Queen Cities of Cincinnati and Toronto, it roars with rare energy in San Juan, Santo Domingo, Hermosillo, and Caracas.

Perhaps the true tragedy of the Latin baseball story is that no detailed history may be feasible. That singular chapter of blackball history involving winter barnstorming across island ports of call during the decades between the two world wars is even more incomplete and less carefully documented than blackball feats performed here in the United States. Winter-league records from Puerto Rico, Venezuela, and the Dominican Republic are today hopelessly scattered and partial, and many of the historical accounts from several decades back are unfortunately more apocryphal than historical in their flavor. Pre–Castro baseball documentation is buried in a dozen or so rare Spanish books inaccessible to the monolingual North American baseball buff, while post–Castro play has been long shrouded by a steel curtain of secrecy and misinformation.

But countless legends and gripping stories fortuitously remain, all waiting to be collected and retold for a new generation of fans and *fanáticos* for whom names like Torriente, Dihigo, Tiant the Elder, and Ramón Bragaña might again become something more than a distant memory. The tales are inspiring and always instructive: Luque obscurely building the first great Latin big-league legend behind the veil of hopeless stereotype; Marichal carving out Hall of Fame numbers that in the end even the most unfortunate incident from Latin baseball history could not expunge; Sandy Amoros spearing Yogi's sinking liner and frozen in an indelible postseason image surpassed only by the magic of Bobby Thomson's immortal swing; Clemente the inspired ballplayer and Clemente the inspired humanitarian standing tall side by side in a story that remains more the stuff of myth than history; Miñoso and Vic Power and Tony Oliva meeting head-on and overcoming through sheer willpower the challenge of still-prevalent racism directed at Latin players in the decades following Jackie Robinson; Tony Pérez and Orlando Cepeda stoically awaiting an inevitable call from Cooperstown; Valenzuela spinning his unhittable screwball and single-handedly creating a wave of "Fernandomania" that was the freshest phenomenon of baseball's 1980s revival; Carew and Concepción and Tiant and Cuellar constructing piecemeal their own lasting diamond legends. Nowhere in baseball's vast literature is found a collection of tales more inspired than these.

Big-league ballplayers represent a diverse and complex family, one drawn from at least three of the four corners of the globe. One useful measure of the true sociological significance of baseball's colorful history is the successive waves of European, Mediterranean, and (most recently) Caribbean immigrant athletes who have regularly enriched the professional game over the course of its past eight decades.

For each of these new ethnic groups, the national pastime quickly became a broad avenue into the promised land of a fleeting American dream. If one could hit a curveball, dash the basepaths, and toss a horsehide skillfully enough to earn a living, untold fame and riches always seemed to be there simply for the taking. First came Central and Western European refugees, who filled up an expansive young nation at the end of the past century – the Irish, German, and Slavic strains from the farmlands and industrial belts of middle America. Names like McGraw, Keeler, Kelley, Ewing, Schaefer, and Donovan fill the bulk of early entries in Macmillan's *Baseball Encyclopedia.* Next to arrive on the scene were second-generation Jews from northeastern urban ghettos, strong-armed "he-men" like Hank Greenberg, Ed Reulbach, Buddy Myer, Dolly Stark, and slugging Sid Gordon. Soon appeared the hard-nosed and broad-shouldered Italians – DiMaggio (Joe, Dom, and Vince), Lazzeri, Crosetti, Rizzuto, Cavaretta, Lombardi, Cuccinello, Lavagetto, and Garagiola. Finally Afro-Americans emerged at the close of the Second World War, their baseball achievements speeding the process of integrating an entire North American nation of sportsmen and workaday citizens alike. And most recently we have witnessed a much-publicized Latin American invasion of the North American national pastime – Cubans, Puerto Ricans, Venezuelans, Mexicans, Virgin Islanders, and especially those diminutive and speedy Dominicans from the impoverished sugar-mill town of San Pedro de Macoris.

The Latin baseball invasion is unlike all earlier ones in substance and impact. Here for the first time it is truly "foreigners" taking the field as replacement players for indigenous Iowa or Arkansas farmboys and California and Connecticut phenoms. These are no longer the nativized sons of past-generation immigrants, Americanized converts who by inheriting our native game thus shed the last vestiges of ties with their parents' Old World culture. The stakes have now been altered drastically. This is true internationalization at work on the ballfield and no longer simply the homogenizing force of a rampant (and for some, healthy) Americanization.

One small measure of baseball's change in sociological structure is the fact that our most frequently encountered big-league name is no longer Smith, Johnson, or Kelley (or even Sisler, Page, or McCarthy). At the beginning of the 1993 baseball season, the foreign-sounding name of Martínez (with seven active rostered players) would boast the largest number of major-leaguers answering to a single family moniker: Carlos with Cleveland, Tino with Seattle, Dave with San Francisco, Dennis with

Montreal, Chito with Baltimore, and brothers Pedro and Ramón with Los Angeles. No higher than second place in the baseball name census would come more familiar Anglo surnames like Davis (six individuals), Smith (six), and Clark (five). Baseball, by this measure as well as by others, finally sports a truly international flavor.

In this sense, then, we have been witnessing in the past two decades the most significant evolution in the history of a cultural institution that has been constantly and irrepressibly changing its shape, flavor, and superficial ethnic tone. Baseball makes much of its vaunted traditions, yet it has always been best characterized by ceaseless evolution. Day ball to night ball; white players to black players; colorful radio play-by-play accounts to colorized television reportage; urban East Coast venues to suburban West Coast venues; outdoor parks to indoor stadia; organic to plastic playing fields; and now "American flavor" to "international flavor."

While dark-skinned Caribbean ballplayers were noteworthy when Minnie Miñoso, Vic Power, and Roman Mejías first came upon the scene—at the dawn of the television age in the early fifties—they have been truly commonplace only over the past decade. Nearly 40 percent of the 600-plus Caribbean and Hispanic ballplayers who are now major-leaguers would first don their big-league flannels only after the flamboyant Cuban Luís Tiant had starred in the unforgettable Boston-Cincinnati World Series of 1975.

It seems only yesterday that Tony Pérez starred for the Big Red Machine, that "Beto" Avila of Mexico first won a batting title, that Miñoso and Clemente and Vic Power established a looser and flashier style of infield and outfield play. Yet even Tony Oliva and Juan Marichal are today relative old-timers in the time line of big-league Hispanic ballplayer history.

Mere mention of baseball's rich Latin American flavor today conjures up three subjects of acute scholarly interest: Latin American influence on big-league history, the lost annals of Caribbean winter-league play, and those intimate connections between Latin stars of yesteryear (especially dark-skinned Cubans like Martín Dihigo and Cristóbal Torriente) and the once thriving world of Negro league baseball. While the major league aspects of baseball's far-reaching Latin American connections are impressionistically far more familiar to casual fans and serious baseball researchers, relatively little information about pioneering Latin big-leaguers has yet been codified and committed to print. How many Latin-born players have reached the big leagues? Who was the first recognizable Hispanic star, and who was the best Cuban or Dominican or Mexican ballplayer of all time? Who was the first Latino slugger to win a league batting title or to pace the circuit in homers or (among hurlers) to win 20 games in a single season or 100 over a pitching career? Which Caribbean countries have historically produced the greatest number of big-leaguers? What National League and American League teams have maintained the most productive Latin American scouting connections? Who are the greatest heroes among the earlier Latin ballplayers, and how would they compare (statistically and in myth and legend) with our grandest North American major league stars of a similar epoch?

In the end, baseball is the ultimate game of statistical analysis, and with the subject of Latin American player recruitment, the numbers clearly exposed the game's most dominant immigration trends by the mid–1980s. *Baseball America*'s 1985 survey of major league farm systems revealed that 349 professional ballplayers under contract to major league teams (as of June 1985) claimed a Latin birthright. Among that lofty number were 163 Dominicans, 93 Puerto Ricans, 52 Venezuelans, 18 Mexicans, 10 Panamanians, 9 Cubans, 3 Colombians, and a single Nicaraguan. Toronto's Blue Jays, with 34 Hispanics (including 23 Dominicans), led all 1985 ballclubs in Latin American recruitment, followed by the Pittsburgh Pirates with 25 (including 18 Dominicans). The much-ballyhooed Dominican connection (first highlighted by George Bell's 1987 MVP season) has for nearly two decades been the unrivaled showcase of the Latin American talent pool and the modest-sized city of San Pedro de Macoris (125,000) has supplied more than 270 talented prospects (plus a dozen established big-league shortstops alone) over the past two decades. When State Department officials in Washington effectively closed down access to Fidel Castro's Communist nation during the early sixties, they would unwittingly open up a new and totally unexpected export trade business for the resource-thin nation of Hispaniola (the half known as República Dominicana) located only a horsehide's toss due east.

For most casual observers, the belief may persist that Latin America's baseball saga begins in the shadow of Jackie Robinson with a flock of flashy shortstops sporting difficult names like Carresquel, Aparicio, Miranda, Cárdenas, Valdivielso, Pagán, and Versalles, or perhaps an entire Washington Senators pitching staff consisting of Pascual, Ramos, Consuegra, Moreno, Fornieles, Aloma, and Marrero. Latin American immigration into the big leagues did not actually begin with Clark Griffith's low-budget and high–ERA Washington Senators mound corps, of course, and certainly not with the present Toronto Blue Jays of Pat Gillick or Clemente's Pittsburgh Pirates (some of the story of Latin players with the Toronto and Washington teams is detailed in Chapter 4 and in my individual histories of those clubs).

While it may now almost defy belief, the first recorded Hispanic major-leaguer actually took his initial strides plateward long before the World Series became a national passion—a full generation before an upstart junior circuit had even been born to challenge the granddaddy National League for big-league supremacy. This all but forgotten Latin diamond pioneer had banged out base hits and shagged flies even before the present mound distance of 60 feet, 6 inches had become the standard of big-league play.

His name was Esteban Enrique Bellán, though he played as "Steve" Bellán during the three summers (1871–1873) he patrolled several infield positions for two National Association clubs now long defunct, the Troy Haymakers and New York Mutuals. Bellán would later be recognized as a true father of Cuban baseball, a claim based on his role in organizing the first recorded game in his native Havana in 1874. It was a contest in which he anchored third base for the Havana club, which trounced Matanzas by an unlikely 51–9 score. The Fordham-educated Bellán compiled a .236 big-league batting mark over a brief 59 games while laboring as a second baseman, third baseman, shortstop, and outfielder in baseball's first true professional league.

In the century and a quarter since Bellán opened new athletic horizons for his Spanish-speaking countrymen, a total of 613 Latin American major-leaguers (by completion of the 1992 season) have followed in the footsteps of the pacesetting Cuban outfielder-infielder. This Latin ballplayer inventory skyrockets with each passing season and now stands as follows: 166 Dominicans, 147 Puerto Ricans, 129 Cubans, 64 Venezuelans, 58 Mexicans, 27 Panamanians (with 4 from the Canal Zone, including recent Hall-of-Famer Rod Carew), 8 Virgin Islanders, 5 Nicaraguans, 3 native-born Spaniards, 3 Colombians, and one active performer each from Honduras (Houston Astros' outfielder Gerald Young), Belize (Chito Martínez with the Baltimore Orioles), and Curaçao (Hensley Meulens of the New York Yankees, who left the big leagues for Japan at the close of the 1993 season). Perhaps the most significant number of all, however, is the present census tally: above one-quarter of the total 613 Latin player population (1871–1992) consists of current major-leaguers occupying positions on 1993 active rosters.

While the tradition of Latin players is thus long and proud, any survey of Latin American statistical leaders (top Latin American hitters or sluggers, top Latin pitchers, etc.) indicates shamefully few stars before the official breaking of the modern major league color barrier in 1947. Pitcher Dolf Luque (1919–1935) was indisputably the first genuine Latino hero, the first Latin-born athlete, in fact, to appear in World Series play (pitching for the Cincinnati Reds against the ill-fated 1919 Chicago Black Sox) or to lead a league in any statistical category. Luque is also the only pre–1950s player still appearing in composite listings of all-time Latin career leaders (see Appendix D) in pitching (wins, shutouts, ERA, etc.) or hitting (BA, hits, homers, RBI, etc.). One effective measure of the long paucity of true Latin stars is that among all such lists of career pacesetters, only Camilo Pascual, Pete Ramos, Juan Pizarro, Minnie Miñoso, Felipe and Matty Alou, Orlando

Cepeda, and the incomparable Roberto Clemente appeared in major league games before the escalation of the Vietnam conflict.

At first glance, baseball's onfield and front-office leadership seems equally devoid of rhythmical Latin names and mestizo-looking Latin faces. This is especially so when one considers the numerical impact of Latin ballplayers on the game over four decades. Yet the Hispanic world has not been entirely without its figures of authority, at least among those men who fill out the lineup cards and direct field strategy from the manager's hotseat.

Seven men of Caribbean birthright have now filled the manager's slot at the big-league level holding either a temporary appointment (González, Virgil, Martínez) or a more legitimate full-time assignment (Gómez, Rojas, Alou, Pérez). Cuba's Miguel "Mike" González was the long-forgotten pioneer in this field, breaking in as journeyman player and part-time skipper when Latins were a big-league rarity. González managed but 22 games as a substitute benchman for the National League Cardinals in 1938 and 1940, yet his greatest claim to fame is the single moment he fearlessly stood his ground as third base coach for St. Louis while Boston's Johnny Pesky inexplicably held the ball and "Country" Enos Slaughter dashed from first to home, carrying the dramatic winning tally of the 1946 World Series. Fellow Cuban Preston Gómez has served the longest managerial term and is the only Hispanic to date (excluding U.S.-born Hispanic ethnics like Hall-of-Famer Al Lopez of Tampa, Florida) to take the helm with more than one ballclub. Ossie Virgil (the first Dominican big-league player) and Marty Martínez served the briefest of temporary terms, the former calling plays with the Padres over nine games in 1984 (a substitute for suspended skipper Dick Williams) while the latter filled out a Seattle Mariners lineup card on a single substitute occasion. With the 1992 and 1993 appointments of established stars Felipe Alou and Tony Pérez (and despite a brief 44-day tenure that was to await the quickly fired Pérez), Latin ballplayers now seem to be getting more serious consideration for important bench jobs and crucial spots in the everyday batting order and weekly pitching rotation. Old myths die hard, and the one about the ineptness of poorly educated Latin ballplayers with broken English and poor communication skills has been one of the hardest to overturn.

As indicated in the following table, Latin managers outnumber all others of foreign birth who have piloted big-league teams — not a surprising fact, given the dominance of Latin players among foreign-born baseballers. A full 28 percent of foreign-born skippers have hailed from the Caribbean countries (54 percent if we consider the 20th-century managers alone and 86 percent among managers debuting after World War II). Perhaps the numbers should be higher. Certainly it remains an embarrassment for those directing the national game that there has yet to be a single Latin American citizen anywhere in high-ranking front-office positions (general manager,

Baseball's Foreign-Born Managers (25 managers)

Latin America (Dominican Republic and Cuba) (7 managers); * = Interim manager

Miguel (Mike) González (Cuba)	1938, 1940	St. Louis Cardinals*	(9-13, .409)
Pedro (Preston) Gómez (Cuba)	1969–1972	San Diego Padres	(346-529, .395)
	1974–1975	Houston Astros	
	1980	Chicago Cubs	
Ossie Virgil (Dominican Republic)	1984	San Diego Padres*	(4-5, .444)
Marty Martínez (Cuba)	1986	Seattle Mariners*	(0-1, .000)
Octavio "Cookie" Rojas (Cuba)	1988	California Angels	(75-79, .487)
Felipe Alou (Dominican Republic)	1992–1993	Montreal Expos	(164-123, .571)
Tony Pérez (Cuba)	1993	Cincinnati Reds	(20-24, .455)

Canada (5 managers)

George Gibson	1920–1922	Pittsburgh Pirates	(413-344, .546)
	1925	Chicago Cubs	
	1932–1934	Pittsburgh Pirates	
Vedie Himsl	1961	Chicago Cubs	(10-21, .323)
Arthur Irwin	1889–1899	Washington (N)	(416-427, .493)
		Boston (AA)	
		Philadelphia Phillies	
		New York Giants	
Fred Lake	1908–1909	Boston Red Sox	(163-180, .475)
	1910	Boston Braves	
Bill Watkins	1884–1899	Indianapolis (AA)	(452-445, .504)
		Detroit (N)	
		Kansas City (AA)	
		St. Louis (N)	
		Pittsburgh Pirates	

Ireland (5 managers)

Tommy Bond	1882	Worchester (N)*	(2-4, .333)
Patsy Donovan	1897–1911	Pittsburgh Pirates	(684-879, .438)
		St. Louis Cardinals	
		Washington Senators	
		Brooklyn Dodgers	
		Boston Red Sox	
Jack Doyle	1895, 1898	New York (N)	(40-40, .500)
		Washington (N)	
Fergy Malone	1884	Philadelphia (UA)	(21-46, .313)

Ireland (*continued*)

Ted Sullivan	1883, 1888	St. Louis (AA) St. Louis (UA) Kansas City (UA) Washington (N)	(132-132, .500)

England (3 managers)

Tom Brown	1897–1898	Washington (N)	(64-72, .471)
Harry Wright	1876–1893	Boston (N) Providence (N) Philadelphia (N)	(1000-824, .548)
Jimmy Austin (Wales)	1913, 1918	St. Louis Browns	(31-44, .413)

Scotland (2 managers)

Jim McCormick	1879–1882	Cleveland (N)	(106-137, .436)
Hugh Nicol	1897	St. Louis (N)	(8-32, .200)

Germany (1 manager)

Chris Von Der Ahe	1895–1897	St. Louis (N)	(3-14, .176)

Australia (1 manager)

Joe Quinn	1895, 1899	St. Louis (N) Cleveland (N)	(23-132, .148)

Czechoslovakia (1 manager)

Hugo Bezdek	1917–1919	Pittsburgh Pirates	(166-187, .470)

chief scout, etc.). Yet for all of baseball's foot dragging on affirmative action, the picture is slowly beginning to change for the better. The 1993 season represented the first ever with two Latins (Alou and Pérez) and three blacks (Cito Gaston, Hal McRae, and Don Baylor) drawing manager's paychecks. The gloom of stereotypes may finally be lifting somewhat from the big-league baseball horizon, and it is Latin players who stand in the forefront most ready to benefit from such healthy and long overdue social change.

The inexorable charm of our national pastime resides in baseball's unabashed mix of documented fact with overblown legend and insubstantial myth. Today's fans are well schooled that Jackie Robinson was an unprecedented and lonely racial pioneer, that Fred Merkle is the sport's biggest bonehead, that Johnny Vander Meer's 21-straight hitless innings remain an unmatched milestone, that George Herman Ruth once "called his shot" and on another occasion promised (and thus predicted) a lifesaving home run for a dying urchin. None of these events ever happened, of course, at least not in anything like the manner repeated time and again by the history books. Baseball's very "birth legend," set in the idyllic pastures of Cooperstown, is now universally dismissed as shameless fabrication. Yet we baseball fans love our lore and our history spiked with a strong and almost lethal dose of hyperbolic mythology.

The extensive history of major league baseball's deep-seated Latin American connections now comprises a bulky tome, one containing numerous chapters detailing those initial painful struggles for recognition (especially among early Cuban black-skinned pioneers like Miñoso and Oliva), flamboyant heroes (from Vic Power to Roberto Clemente to José Canseco), and glorious triumphs (like Bobby Avila's unprecedented 1954 league batting title and Clemente's unforgettable World Series performance of 1971) that mark the four decades since superscout Joe Cambria first tapped a rich mine of burgeoning Caribbean baseball talent. And like any such historical tome, this one maintains its inviolable dimensions of myth and legend, entwining fact with fancy and enlivening the Latin baseball story at every turn. Buried behind recent accounts of the Latin big-league phenomena (especially as reported in the popular press) are some surprising "facts" and some surprising "pseudofacts." Thus there is crying need at the outset simply to set the record straight.

Many of the best of these tales involve the Brooklyn Dodgers and their masterful front-office magnates Branch Rickey and Walter O'Malley, incomparable executives who together drastically reshaped the face of diamond play during the golden era that was the 1940s and the 1950s. For starters, modern scholarship now reveals that a small handful of Latin ballplayers, both obscure and celebrated, played sizable roles in that most dramatic event of modern sporting history—the bold integration plan of Branch Rickey and its immediate aftermath of long-awaited color-blind baseball.

Had the fickle wheel of fortune spun with a slightly different twist, Rickey's gripping drama might well have found a different hero to stand at center stage. Perhaps a pioneering Cuban player and not Jackie Robinson might have brought down the game's troublesome racial barriers. Had Mr. Rickey only followed his original course without detour, baseball's first black martyr may have worn a very different game face and carved out a far different legacy. When Rickey first opened his search for the proper integration hero, it was a living Cuban legend of 1930s and 1940s winterball, Silvio García, who waited at the head of the line. García's talented infield play was sufficiently without peer, apparently, to tease Mr. Rickey into dispatching his right-hand man O'Malley on a preliminary Havana scouting mission. After all, there was something altogether attractive about cracking the big league doors with a Cuban since dusky Latins had already intruded ever so slightly on the major league scene during seasons past. They had often prompted questions and some slight alarm, but rarely (especially if not too dark-skinned) did they inspire all-out rebellion. Garcia just might have been Rickey's perfect answer had the heavy-drinking prospect not turned out to be battling twin handicaps of age and a dissipated personal life.

One unsubstantiated report suggests that Rickey interviewed Garcia personally and that the Cuban search was quickly terminated when the Spanish-speaking ballplayer swore through his translator that he would kill any white man who dared lay a fist or pair of spikes anywhere near his olive skin. The more reputable account has O'Malley's Havana mission failing when he was unable to locate García, supposedly drafted into the Cuban military but more likely lost somewhere on a weekend drinking binge. García was not exactly the end of the Brooklyn integration search throughout the Caribbean region, however. On the heels of the Rickey-Robinson revolution, Dodger front-office unwillingness to move too fast in integrating Ebbets Field also kept Roberto Clemente (a hot rookie prospect with the 1954 Montreal Royals) out of the Brooklyn lineup. More than four black players (Campanella, Robinson, Gilliam, and Newcombe) in the starting lineup, even in Brooklyn, seemed to be unnecessarily risking a white backlash. The decision to hide Clemente in the minors (and therefore lose him to Pittsburgh) thus robbed fans of what might have been one of the greatest fly-chasing trios (imagine Snider, Furillo, and Clemente together) ever assembled.

Rickey's Dodgers and the pioneering Jackie Robinson are also featured in yet another mysterious tale whereby baseball history is seemingly shot through with apocryphal legend. Not only did dark-skinned Silvio García perhaps miss by only the length of a rum bottle from leading Robinson into the majors as integration's true standard bearer, but fickle history has buried the fact that at least one and perhaps several Cuban and Puerto Rican blacks actually did cross the color line (in considerable obscurity it must be noted) several seasons before the most famous of North America's black athletes. It can be fairly well documented (once the shifting definition of true "blackness" is somehow reasonably settled) that at least one unheralded ebony-skinned Cincinnati pitcher of Cuban birth (Tommy de la Cruz) did precede Robinson in crossing baseball's twentieth-century racial barriers during the 1944 National League season. Even before Rickey's plan had materialized in 1945 and 1946, other Cubans (Jack Calvo and José Acosta with the 1920s Senators) and Puerto Ricans (Hi Bithorn with the 1942–1944 Cubs and perhaps Luís Olmo with the Dodgers from 1943 to 1945) had also slipped behind the racial barriers quietly and almost unnoticed.

Tommy de la Cruz and Silvio García have thus been condemned to the chafe and flack of diamond history by the persistent influences of blatant racial prejudice. It is a little harder to explain the obscurity surrounding still another long-forgotten Latin star of the interwar period, one who once played a major role in the infamous 1919 Black Sox World Series and who pioneered as the first true Caribbean star to showcase his considerable talents in a big-league venue. For a short time during the final-hurrah years of Ty Cobb's dead-ball era and in the initial seasons of Ruth's lively-ball epoch, Cuban Adolfo Luque stood supreme as one of the most feared hurlers in baseball. The Luque big-league portfolio is indeed impressive: one 27-win season and sub-2.00 ERA marker (27-8 and 1.93 ERA in 1923); a first-ever World Series appearance by a Latin or Caribbean player; nearly 200 career wins over a two-decade major league career. Yet Luque is now all but forgotten, though he does stand firm in the record books as the most dominating single-season pitcher of Cincinnati Reds history.

If Latin America's racial and ethnic pioneers have been lost to history, this is unfortunately not the case for its handful of reputed hotheads and hooligans. Bright as ever shines the undying legend of the hot-tempered Latin sorehead who squanders his talents for lack of mental discipline. Unfortunately, this stereotype is just enough of a tasty mixture of outrageous bigotry and documented example to have remained alive and well for decades. It is an image fostered as much by the regrettable onfield behaviors of a few misguided ballplayers as by blatant headline-grabbing racist remarks such as those of 1960s-era San Francisco Giants manager Alvin Dark.

Luque himself implanted the popular image, first by charging defenseless Casey Stengel on the Giants bench and then by sprinkling his career with macho threats and pugilistic displays that always demanded bigger headlines than his pitching prowess. Rubén Gómez and Juan Marichal clinched the case with sensational onfield assaults of rival hitters—Gómez once chasing Joe Adcock of the Milwaukee Braves with a deadly switchblade and Marichal nearly wrecking his Cooperstown credentials during the infamous Roseboro incident. Alvin Dark thus spoke for more than just a small corner of the baseball establishment when he accused Hispanic ballplayers of being selfish and unreliable: "We have trouble because we have so many Spanish-speaking and Negro players on the team [and] they are not able to perform up to the white ballplayers when it comes to mental alertness," barked the outspoken Dark.

The harmful stereotype always seemed to revert to the mislabeled and underappreciated Dolf Luque. One isolated incident involving the colorful Casey Stengel would capture the public imagination and thus erase almost everything else in the career of one of the game's best pitchers from the early live-ball era. And Luque was doomed as much by playing in the hinterlands of Cincinnati, shining only dimly at first in the dark shadow cast by the Black Sox scandal, and then lost altogether in the relentless glare of Babe Ruth's era. Luque's 1919 World Series landmark debut went largely unnoticed. His spectacular 1923 season drew fewer raves still. But one always remembers the colorful man of temper just as one remembers Merkle's "boner" and not his steady everyday play for more than a decade in McGraw's lineup or Carl Mays's lethal beanball (the one that felled Ray Chapman) but not his dozen years of Hall-of-Fame performance.

Luque thus set the tone for all other Latins seemingly primed by circumstance and cultural miscommunication to foster a disarming stereotype. Most visible perhaps was the Giants' fireballing Rubén Gómez, who repeatedly reinforced his reputation as an *hombre loco* even in his own native Puerto Rico and always overshadowed fine moundsmanship with outrageous onfield and clubhouse conduct. And while Giants teammate Orlando Cepeda was less of a flaky hothead, he was another proud individualist prone to macho behavior that was easily misinterpreted, almost always for the worse.

More recent media mishandling of a young and sensitive George Bell, especially during struggling minor league summers in cowtown outposts like Helena and Spartanburg (Chapter 8), goes far toward explaining at least one contemporary Dominican all-star's justified disdain for booing fans and a harping media. Bell's penchant for continued tantrums in the Toronto and Chicago outfields (he once "flipped the bird" toward 50,000 local fanatics from his left-field post in Toronto's SkyDome) or before the newsreel cameras (where he blasted his Chicago skipper, Gene Lamont, during the 1993 ALCS playoffs) has further stirred an already boiling caldron. On one hand, Bell has often seemed justified in turning a cold shoulder toward a press corps that has warped most of his words into a disrespectful parody of the uneducated and "foreign-sounding" buffoon; on the other hand, his own insensitivities to cultural differences have served to widen a perceived gulf between the Latin superstar and an unappreciative white fandom that pays his megasalary and therefore demands his conformity.

Other stories—often short on historical detail and long on mythic overtones—flesh out the drama of Latin America's big-league heritage. Even the raw facts sometimes take on the proportions of a well-conceived piece of surrealistic baseball fiction. It is ironic if not incredible, for example, that the greatest single-day hitting performance by any Latin ballplayer was turned in not by Clemente, Cepeda, Oliva, Carty, or Carew but by the quintessential "good field, no hit" broken-English shortstop, Venezuelan utilityman César Gutiérrez. Gutiérrez would eventually own an anemic lifetime .235 ledger without a single big-league home run or a single season of batting 100 points above his feathery weight. On June 21, 1970, however, "Cocoa" Gutiérrez shocked himself and the remainder of the baseball world when he banged out six singles and a double in seven trips to the plate during a 12-inning doubleheader nightcap. It remains a major league record for hits in one ballgame without making a single out at the plate.

The same brand of irony cheapens the fact that the greatest Latin American batsman of all time, newly elected Cooperstown resident Rod Carew, is not a native Latin American ballplayer at all, either by birthright or sandlot apprenticeship. It turns out that Carew was born not in Panama but in the American territory of the Panama Canal Zone, the son of a Panamanian father and North American mother. It was Carew's mother who transported her son to New York City ate age 17 and thus initiated events spawning the young man's outstanding professional ballplaying career. Like the transplanted Dominican Ossie Virgil a decade earlier, Carew learned his baseball on the high school diamonds of New York and not in the surgarcane fields of some tropical paradise.

The intriguing case of Rod Carew enjoys a further ethnic complexity, to spice the story a bit further, considering that the slugging Hall-of-Famer reportedly converted to Judaism late in his baseball career (a fact reported in his autobiography) and thus could boast back-door credentials as the leading all-time Jewish hitter to boot. In the end, however, Carew's Jewish conversion never materialized, leaving open to question the legitimacy of his claim to either ethnic batting title.

And if one prefers baseball history soaked in irony, perhaps nothing can top those tragic circumstances surrounding a forgotten idol many still dub the greatest Latin American star of all time. Here is a man enshrined in Cooperstown (as well as the "halls" of Mexico City, Caracas, and Havana) who nonetheless never actually played a single inning in the major leagues. Of all the dark-skinned Cubans who faced bitter rejection from baseball's hypocritical barons of the pre–World War II epoch, none had more reason to grieve than mountainous Martín Dihigo – the Babe Ruth, Christy Mathewson, and Ty Cobb of Cuba rolled into one massive black-skinned frame.

The 6′3″, 200-pound Cuban giant was perhaps the most versatile player ever – in any country, any epoch, or any league! Dihigo was already a Mexican, Cuban, and Venezuelan Hall-of-Famer long before Cooperstown came calling, a three-decade star who not only played at eight of the nine positions (catching was his only weakness) but shone brilliantly at every one. Not only did racial pressure bar Dihigo from fame and wealth in the big leagues; it also assigned him to Negro league and winter-league play where statistical records were so poorly kept that future generations will never know the magnitude of his domination in a sport whose very lifeblood is its statistical records.

Known primarily as a fastballing pitcher in Latin America (he threw the first no-hitter in Mexican League history), Martín Dihigo was a dominating hitter as well during a dozen seasons of North American Negro League play (several times home-run champ and batting leader in those seasons, where statistics do exist) and in Mexican League play (where he hit .317 over a 10-year Mexican career). Elected posthumously to the North American Baseball Hall of Fame (Cooperstown) in 1977, Dihigo would never live to see his career formally recognized by the major league establishment that so long rejected him and his entire race. The true losers, of course, were the two generations of big-league fans robbed of seeing the versatile Cuban perform alongside the likes of Babe Ruth, Lou Gehrig, or Ted Williams.

Yet of all the tales of Latin ballplayers that blend fact with fancy and cloud real event with musty legend, none is better known—or more preposterous—than a familiar and apocryhal story about the Senators' (or Giants' or Yankees'—teams differ with each account) near signing sometime in the early 1940s of a hot Havana University pitching prospect named Fidel Castro. How many times have you heard this one as a trivia question on radio sports talk shows? "What famous dictator might have pitched for the New York Yankees if only some bush-league scout had been a better judge of pitching talent?" That is how the question is most often phrased. The truth is that popular legend about Castro's prodigious hurling talent has little basis in fact. It is well documented that Castro was an arch *fanático* who later appeared regularly at Havana Sugar Kings games during the years surrounding his rise to power, often donning the uniform of his informal club, the Barbudos (bearded ones) and tossing a couple of exhibition innings preliminary to Havana's International League contests of the late fifties (Chapter 9). Scattered references in the literature repeatedly mention Cambria's scouting of Castro, yet no documented or believable account suggests that any scout assessed the future dictator as a legitimate prospect. Two reputable sources (Kerrane, 1984; Oleksak and Oleksak, 1991) both report Cambria rejecting Castro at least twice as an amateur pitcher and Clark Griffith acknowledging that "Uncle Joe scouted Castro and told him he didn't have a major league arm" (Oleksak and Oleksak, 1991, p. 45).

Beyond this, Latin baseball scholars are stone silent on Fidel Castro, failed rookie pitching prospect of the 1940s. One respected Cuban authority—former Havana sports journalist Jorge Figueredo of Tampa, Florida—perhaps comes closest to the truth in speculating that Castro (and certainly his followers and henchmen) likely fostered the popular legend simply to add luster to the dictator's public image. Like his island neighbor and strong-arm forerunner Presidente Rafael Leonidas Trujillo Molina in the Dominican Republic, Castro apparently recognized a near-certain public-relations victory to be gained from hitching his rising star to a baseball culture. Baseball, after all, was the national passion of not only his subjugated countrymen but his political enemies and his bothersome gringo rivals.

Such are the hopelessly intertwined episodes of myth transfused with documented fact that compose much of the Latin American baseball saga—both the shadowy winter-league saga and its better-known yet nonetheless often sketchy big-league counterpart. In the 10 chapters of this book many of these well-worn myths will be reopened, recounted, and even celebrated. At the same time, much of documented Latin baseball history will be enlightened for readers new to the subject while being rescued and preserved for more serious baseball historians.

While no attempt has been made to be comprehensive in coverage or exhaustive in detail, it is hoped that these pages capture much of those distinctive onfield rhythms and those colorful, flamboyant athletes that provide the heart and soul of baseball played and nurtured "south of the border."

This book is thus not a true encyclopedia of Latin diamond lore, but it does aim to expand the focus of the Latin baseball story. Sufficient statistics (many never before available in any single English-language source) provide enough documentary records to satisfy most numerically oriented fans nurtured on Bill James and sabermetrics. Outlines of year-by-year Caribbean winter-league pennant and playoffs winners are offered for five countries alongside annual individual winter leaders in major hitting and fielding categories. Five appendices at the end of the book will thus hopefully flesh out much of the poorly documented Latin big-league and winter-league record.

Chronological and alphabetical listings of all major-leaguers from 13 Latin nations—including abbreviated career statistics and accurate information on births, deaths, and big-league debuts—are featured, as well as a valuable chronology of more than 200 landmark moments and events in Latin baseball history. But the intention is as much narrative as documentary. Early chapters attempt to capture the character and contributions of some of the most legendary Latin ballplayers—Luque, Marichal, Clemente, and dozens of lesser stars. And later chapters fill in details for at least a vital part of the blackball and winter-league components that are also a staple of Latin American and Caribbean baseball history.

The book is divided into three parts. Part I (five chapters) aims at capturing the essence of Latin America's big-league contributions. Familiar stars like Clemente (Chapter 3) and Marichal (Chapter 2) are placed in proper career perspective. Slightly lesser talents like Dolf Luque (Chapter 1, Chapter 5) and Vic Power (Chapter 4) are recognized at length for their special contributions in establishing proud big-league traditions to be emulated by today's Hispanic and Caribbean ballplayers. On a far darker note, painful struggles of pioneering Latin players to achieve full acceptance in the face of severe racial and linguistic barriers are documented and discussed (Chapter 4, Chapter 8). If Cuban, Dominican, and Puerto Rican blacks were to become a permanent fixture of the game in the two decades following Robinson and Rickey's "noble experiment" in integration, it is commonplace that they were often, especially in the early going, tolerated as a nuisance rather than celebrated as a boasting point.

Part II summons up memories of the blackball era as it was once celebrated and enjoyed for three decades throughout Cuba and other Caribbean baseball-playing nations. Along with the tale of barnstorming Negro teams both north and south of Florida's ports of entry comes the rich but often poorly documented history of Caribbean winter-league play. Here is the joyous celebration of a true Pan-American national pastime, sampled in chapters devoted to baseball's nation-by-nation Caribbean origins (Chapter 9) and the glorious four-decade extravaganza of the Caribbean Series (Chapter 10)—winterball's showcase of postseason championship play. Throughout these final chapters it is hoped that a new panoply of diamond heroes and a new treasure trove of exciting diamond events will open to the serious baseball researcher and the interested casual fan. Alongside household Spanish-flavored big-league names like Canseco, Cepeda, Javier, and Rijo will emerge a new lineup of wintertime ballplaying heroes (Agapito Mayor, Nap Reyes, Jesús Cabrera, Pedro Formental, Narciso Elvira, Héctor Espino, Fermín Guerra) largely lost to North American fandom but of true legendary stature in their baseball-crazed native islands and coastal nations. José Méndez, Martín Dihigo, Tommy de la Cruz, Tommy Fine, and Willard Brown, among so many others, are recognized for the truly legendary feats they authored across five decades in distant ballparks a lifetime away from the big-league diamonds in Chicago, New York, Houston, or Anaheim.

This reference work is intended to supplement and extend the fine work of recent academic baseball historians like Rob Ruck (University of Pittsburgh), Alan Klein (Northeastern University), Milton Jamail (University of Texas), and a number of Spanish-language authors, all of whom have aimed at telling in more detail other aspects of the complex Caribbean baseball story. As a resource for scholarship, Part III (Appendices) thus provides further guidelines for ongoing research on the topic. Finally, an extensive Bibliography (partly annotated) points to numerous English and

Spanish resources basic to the subject of Latin-born ballplayers and Latin American baseball history. Complete player lists (Appendix B, Appendix C) and partial winter-league statistics (Chapter 9, Appendix E) should be sufficient basis for further building of the archival records for Latin American baseball history.

Many have contributed in large and small measure to the chapters that follow. I have benefited in manifold ways from the written records provided by Rob Ruck, Alan Klein, and John Krich, as well as those from the pens and typewriters of the Dominican Republic's José de Jesús Jiménez and California's Angel Torres. Jerry Vaughn, a dedicated SABR researcher, has expanded my knowledge of Mexican baseball, as have Jorge Figueredo regarding Cuba and Tony Piña Campora regarding the Dominican Republic. And no one who has ever shared a friendship or an interview with Luís Rodríguez-Mayoral has come away without a wealth of novel information and insight into Latin ballplayers and the unbounded Hispanic love for the game of baseball. My work has been an attempt to add one more chapter to all that these colleagues and so many others have done.

Of the dozen books and numerous essays on baseball history I have written in the past four years, this volume has most nearly approximated a true labor of love. The first time I saw Clemente run the base paths with fire and gun down opposing baserunners from his right-field post with merciless accuracy, I was inspired by the special flair of the Latin American ballplayer. In more recent years, when professional duties have taken me onto the batting-practice field and into the locker rooms and clubhouses of numerous major league stadiums, it has been dignified men like Manny Mota, Juan González, Julio Franco, Dickie Thon, Robbie Alomar, Juan Samuel, Andrés Galarraga, José Offerman, and Dennis Martínez, among so many others of their countrymen, who have treated our interactions and interviews with the greatest respect, good humor, and endless goodwill. This is their story and that of their 600 and more compatriots who have tasted sometimes glory and sometimes disappointment on the unforgiving stage that is major league baseball. All have in their own ways enriched the game beyond measure.

Open up these chapters, then, and hear for yourself the distinctive rhythms of our Pan-American international pastime as it has now been played on countless diamonds for over a full century—from Havana to Hermosillo, from Caguas to Caracas, and from Redlands Field and Ebbets Field to Anaheim's "Big A" and Toronto's futuristic SkyDome—ennobled by names like Clemente, Marichal, Luque, Alou, Carrasquel, and Aparicio and enlivened by resounding strains of an ever-present and relentless Latin beat.

References Cited

Bjarkman, Peter C. *The Toronto Blue Jays.* New York: Gallery, 1990; Chapter 6: "El Béisbol North of the Border."

________. "Toronto Blue Jays: Okay, Blue Jays! From Worst to First in a Decade." Chapter 12 in *Encyclopedia of Major League Baseball: American League (Team Histories).* 1993 edition. New York: Carroll & Graf, 1993, 445–486.

________. "Washington Senators–Minnesota Twins: Expansion-Era Baseball Comes to the American League." Chapter 13 in *Encyclopedia of Major League Baseball: American League (Team Histories).* 1993 edition. New York: Carroll & Graf, 1993, 487–534.

Kerrane, Kevin. *Dollar Sign on the Muscle: The World of Baseball Scouting.* New York: Beaufort, 1984.

Oleksak, Michael M., and Mary Adams Oleksak. *Béisbol: Latin Americans and the Grand Old Game.* Grand Rapids, Michigan: Masters Press, 1991.

PART I

Peloteros in Paradise
The Latin American Invasion of the Major Leagues

Honors, like impressions upon coin, may give an ideal and local value to a bit of base metal; but Gold and Silver will pass all the world over without any other recommendation than their own weight.

—LAURENCE STERNE,
The Life and Opinions of Tristram Shandy

CHAPTER 1

Dolf Luque, Baseball's First Hispanic Star

> In race-conscious North America, at a time when dark-skinned Latinos had trouble breaking into baseball, Luque's light skin was to his advantage. A newspaper story of the period describes him as "looking more Italian than a full-blooded Cuban."
>
> —Jill Barnes

Perhaps the most spurious of apocryphal tales in the ample catalog of legends that often substitute for serious baseball history is the one surrounding the fiery-tempered Cuban hurler Adolfo Luque, who pitched a dozen seasons for the Roaring Twenties Cincinnati Reds. Legend has it that Luque, after taking a severe riding from the New York Giants bench, stopped in midwindup, placed the ball and glove gingerly alongside the mound, then charged straight into the New York dugout to thrash flaky Giants outfielder Casey Stengel within an inch of his life.

This tale always manages to portray Luque as a familiar Latin American stereotype—the quick-to-anger, hot-blooded, and addle-brained Latino who knows little of North American idiom or customs of fair play and can respond to the heat of combat only with flailing fists. The image has been reinforced over the lengthy summers of baseball's history by the unfortunate (even if largely uncharacteristic) real-life baseball events surrounding Latin hurlers. Juan Marichal once brained Dodger catcher John Roseboro with his Louisville slugger when the Los Angeles receiver returned the ball to his pitcher firing too close to Marichal's head. The Giants' Rubén Gómez was infamous for memorable brushback incidents involving Carl Furillo and Frank Robinson. Gómez also plunked heavy-hitting Joe Adcock on the wrist, released a second beanball as the enraged Braves first sacker charged toward the mound, then retreated to the safety of the dugout to return moments later wielding a lethal switchblade.

The oft-told story involving Luque's kamikaze mission against the

Giant bench seems, in its most popular version, either a distortion or an abstraction of real events. Neither the year (it had to be between 1921 and 1923, during Stengel's brief tenure with McGraw's club) nor circumstances are often mentioned when the legend is related, and specific events are never detailed with care. The true indiscretion is that this story always seems to receive far more press than those devoted to the facts and figures surrounding Luque's otherwise proud and productive 20-year big-league career. This was, after all, a premiere pitcher of the live-ball era, a winner of nearly 200 major league contests, the first great Latin American ballplayer ever, and the first of his countrymen to pitch in a World Series, win 20 games in a single summer or 100 in a career, and lead a major league circuit in victories, winning percentage, and ERA. Dolf Luque was far more than the hot-spirited Latino who once, in a fit of temper, silenced the loquacious Charles Dillon Stengel.

For the record, the much ballyhooed incident involving Luque and Stengel has a basis in fact. And like the Marichal-Roseboro affair four decades later, it appears to have contained events and details infrequently (if ever) properly reported. The setting was Cincinnati's Redland Field (later Crosley Field) on the day of a rare packed house in midsummer 1922. The overflow crowd—allowed to stand along the sidelines, thus forcing players of both teams to take bench seats outside the normal dugout area—added to the tensions of the afternoon. While the Giant bench, as was their normal practice, spent the early innings of the afternoon disparaging Luque's Latin heritage, these taunts were more audible than usual on this particular day, largely because of the close proximity of the visiting-team bench, only yards from the third-base line. Future Hall-of-Famer Ross Youngs was reportedly at the plate when the Cuban pitcher decided he had heard enough from offending Giant outfielder Bill Cunningham, a particularly vociferous heckler seated boldly on McGraw's bench. Luque at this point left ball and glove at the center of the playing field as he suddenly charged after Cunningham, unleashing a fierce blow that missed the startled loudmouth and landed squarely on Stengel's jaw instead. The unreported details are that Luque was at least in part a justified aggressor and that Stengel remained a totally accidental and unwitting victim.

The infamous attack, it turns out, was something of a humorous misadventure and more the stuff of comic relief than the product of sinister provocation. While the inevitable free-for-all that ensued quickly led to Dolf Luque's banishment from the field, the enraged Cuban soon returned to the battle scene, again screaming for Cunningham and brandishing an ash bat like an ancient warclub. It took four policemen and assorted teammates to escort Luque from the ballpark a second time. Thus the colorful Cincinnati pitcher had managed to foreshadow Marichal and Gómez—later club-wielding Latin moundsmen—all within this single moment of intemperate action. Yet what passed for comic interlude had dire consequences. Luque had suddenly and predictably played a most unfortunate role in fueling the stereotype that has since dogged his career and those of many of his countrymen. Yet like Marichal, he was in reality a fierce competitor who almost always manifested his will to win with a blazing fastball and some of the cleverest pitching of his age. He was also a usually quiet and iron-willed man whose huge contributions to the game are unfortunately remembered only by a diminishing handful of his aging Cuban countrymen. So buried by circumstance are Luque's considerable pioneering pitching achievements that reputable baseball historian Lonnie Wheeler fully reports the infamous Luque-Stengel brawl in his marvelous pictorial history of Cincinnati baseball, *The Cincinnati Game* (Orange Frazer Press, 1988), then devotes an entire chapter of the landmark book to the "Latin Connection" in Reds history without a single mention of Dolf Luque or his unmatchable 1923 National League campaign in Cincinnati.

It is a fact now easily forgotten in view of the near tidal-wave invasion of Latin players during the 1980s—especially the explosion of talent flooding the majors from the tiny island of the Dominican Republic—that before Castro shut down the supply lines in the early 1960s, Cuba had dispatched a steady stream of talented players to the big leagues. The first and perhaps least notable was Esteban Bellán, an average infielder with the Troy Haymakers and New York Highlanders of the National Association in the early 1870s. The earliest National-Leaguers were Armando Marsans and Rafael Almeida, who toiled over a few brief seasons with the Cincinnati club beginning in 1911. After the color barrier was bashed in 1947, the 1950s ushered in quality players from Cuba as widely known for their baseball abilities as their unique pioneering status—Sandy Amoros of the Dodgers, Camilo Pascual, Pete Ramos, Connie Marrero and Julio Becquer with the Senators, Minnie Miñoso, Mike Fornieles and Sandy Consuegra of the White Sox, Chico Fernández of the Phillies, Roman Mejías with the Pirates, Willie Miranda of the Orioles, and stellar lefty Mike Cuellar, who launched his illustrious pitching career with Cincinnati in 1959.

The best of the early Cubans was Luque, a man who was both fortunate beneficiary and ill-starred victim of the racial and ethnic prejudices that ruled major league baseball in his era. While dark-skinned Cuban legend Martín Dihigo was barred from the majors, the light-skinned Luque was welcomed by management, if not always warmly accepted by the full complement of southern mountain boys who staffed most big-league rosters. Ironically, Havana-born Luque had been raised only a decade and a half earlier and less than 50 miles from Dihigo, who hailed from the rural village of Matanzas. Yet while Luque labored at times brilliantly in the big leagues during the second, third, and fourth decades of the century, his achievements were always diminished in part because he pitched the bulk of his career in the hinterlands that were Cincinnati, in part because his nearly 200 big-league victories were spread thinly over 20 years rather than clustered in a handful of 20-game seasons (he had only one such year). And in the current revisionist age of baseball history, when Negro leaguers have at last received not only their rightful due but a huge nostalgic sympathy vote—Martín Dihigo is now widely revered as a cult figure and enshrined in Cooperstown for his Cuban and Mexican League play, while Luque lies obscured in the dust and chaff of baseball history.

The memorable pitching career of Dolf Luque might best be capsulated in three stages. Most prominent were the glory years with the Cincinnati Reds throughout the full span of the Roaring '20s, baseball's first flamboyant and explosive decade after the pitching-rich dead-ball era. But first came the formative years of apprentice moundsmanship in two countries. Beginning professional play in Cuba in 1912 as a pitcher and hard-hitting infielder, Luque displayed considerable talent at third base and on the mound. A mere six months later the talented youngster was promptly recruited by Dr. Hernández Henríquez, a Cuban entrepreneur residing in New Jersey and operating the Long Branch franchise of the New Jersey–New York State League. A sterling 22-5 record that first New Jersey summer along with a strange twist of baseball fate soon provided the hotshot Cuban pitcher with a quick ticket to big-league fame. This was the epoch when professional baseball was not played in New York City on the Sabbath, and thus visiting major league clubs often supplemented sparse travel money by scheduling exhibition contests with the conveniently located Long Branch team on available Sunday afternoon dates. It was this circumstance that allowed Luque to impress Boston Braves manager George Stallings sufficiently to earn a big-league contract late in the 1914 season, the very year Boston surprisingly charged from the rear of the pack in late summer to earn lasting reputation as the "Miracle Braves," unexpected winners of a National League flag. In his debut with Boston, Dolf Luque became the first Latin American pitcher to apear in the American or the National League, preceding Emilio Palmero of the Giants by a single season and Oscar Tuero of the Cardinals by a full four campaigns.

Brief appearances with Boston in 1914 and 1915 provided little immediate success for the Cuban import, who soon found himself toiling with Jersey City and Toronto of the International League and Louisville of the American Association in search of much-needed minor league seasoning. A fast start (11 wins in 13 appearances) in the 1918 campaign, however, brought on stage two for Luque: a permanent home in Cincinnati that would span the next 18 seasons. The Cuban fastballer was an immediate success in the Queen City, winning 16 games in the combined 1918–1919 seasons, throwing the first shutout by a Latin pitcher, and playing a major role out of the bullpen as the Reds copped their first-ever National League flag during the last year of the century's second decade. Luque made history that fall of 1919 as the first Latin to appear in World Series play. He tossed five scoreless innings in two series relief appearances as his underdog Cincinnati Reds edged Charlie Comiskey's Chicagoans and Shoeless Joe Jackson during the infamous Black Sox fall classic.

But it was Luque's 1923 campaign that provided his career hallmark and was one of the finest single campaigns ever by a National League hurler of any epoch. Few moundsmen have so thoroughly dominated a league for a full campaign: Luque won 27 while losing but 8, leading the circuit in victories, winning percentage (.771), ERA (1.93), and shutouts (6). The 6 shutouts could well have been 10; he had four scoreless efforts erased in the ninth inning. His 1.93 ERA was not matched by a Latin hurler until Luís Tiant registered an almost unapproachable 1.60 in the aberrant 1968 season. That same summer, Luque also became the first pitcher among his countrymen to sock a major league homer, while himself allowing only two opposition roundtrippers in 322 innings, the second-stingiest home-run allowance ever for a pitcher in the senior circuit and close on the heels of the 1921 standard of one homer in 301 innings pitched recorded by Cincinnati Reds teammate and Hall-of-Famer Eppa Rixey.

Next in the evolution of Luque's career came the dozen waning seasons as a role player yet significant contributor with the Reds, Dodgers, and Giants. After losing 23 ballgames with the second-place Reds in 1922 and then pacing the league in victories with the runner-up Cincinnati club of 1923, Dolf Luque would never again enjoy a 20-victory season, though he did come close on both ends of the ledger with a 16-18 mark (plus a league-leading 2.63 ERA) during the 1925 campaign. He won consistently in double figures, however, over a 10-year span extending through his first of two brief seasons with Brooklyn at the outset of the next decade. It is one of the final ironies of Luque's career that while he was not technically the first Latin ballplayer with the Cincinnati Reds (following Marsans and Almeida in that role), he did hold this distinction with the Brooklyn Dodgers team, which he joined in 1930. And while it was with the Reds that he made his historic first World Series appearance, it was with the Giants a decade and a half later that he made a truly significant World Series contribution at the twilight of his career, gaining the crucial fifth and final game victory of that series with a brilliant four-inning relief stint against the powerful Washington Senators in the nation's capital.

The third and final dimension of Luque's lengthy career is the one almost totally unknown to North American fans—his brilliant three decades as player and manager in the winter-league play of his Caribbean homeland. As a pitcher in Cuba, Luque was legendary, compiling a 103-68 (.602) career mark over 22 short seasons of winter play, ranking as the Cuban League's leading pitcher (9-2) in 1928-29. In 1917 he was the league's leading hitter (.355), and he also managed championship teams on eight occasions (1919-20, 1924-25, 1934-35, 1939-40, 1941-42, 1942-43, 1945-46, 1946-47).

Perhaps Luque's most significant contribution to the national pastime was his talent for developing big-league potential in the players he coached and managed over several decades of winter-league play. One of Luque's brightest and most accomplished students was future New York and Brooklyn star hurler Sal "the Barber" Maglie, who learned his tough style of "shaving" hitters close from his famed Cuban mentor. Luque (who had developed his own "shaving" techniques with senior-circuit hitters two decades earlier) was Maglie's pitching coach with the Giants during the latter's rookie 1945 season as well as his manager with Cienfuegos in the Cuban League that same winter and at Puebla in the Mexican League in the winter seasons of 1946 and 1947. Maglie has often credited Luque above all others for preparing him for the major leagues. So did Latin America's first big-league batting champion, Bobby Avila, who played for Luque in Puebla during the Mexican League campaigns of 1946 and 1947. It was this talent for player development in the end that perhaps spoke most eloquently about the falseness of Luque's widespread popular image as an emotional, quick-tempered, untutored ballplayer during his big-league playing days.

In selecting a descriptive term to summarize Luque's career, "explosive" has often been the popular choice. For many commentators, this is the proper word to describe his reputed temperamental behavior, his exaggerated onfield outbursts, his infrequent yet widely reported pugilistic endeavors (Luque never shied away from knocking down his share of plate-hugging hitters, but neither did most successful moundsmen of his era). For still others, it characterizes a career that seemed to burst across the horizon with a single exceptional year, then fade into the obscurity of a forgotten journeyman big-leaguer.

But both notions are wide-of-the-mark distortions, especially the one that sees Luque as a momentary flash on the baseball scene. "Durable" would be a far more accurate epithet, for Dolf Luque was a tireless warrior whose pitching career seemed to stretch on almost without end. His glorious 1923 season was achieved at the considerable age of 33; he again led the senior circuit in ERA (2.63) two summers later at 35; he recorded 14 victories and a .636 winning percentage in 1930 while laboring for the Dodgers at the advanced age of 40; his two shutouts that season advanced his career total to 26, a mark unsurpassed among Latin pitchers until the arrival of Marichal, Pascual, Tiant, and Cuellar in the 1960s. Referred to widely as the rejuvenated "Papa Montero" by 1933, he recorded eight crucial wins that summer and the clinching World Series victory at 43. His big-league career did not end until he was 45 and had registered 20 full seasons, only one short of the National League longevity standard for hurlers, held jointly by Warren Spahn and Eppa Rixey.

Luque's unique claim to durability and longevity is further strengthened when one takes into consideration his remarkable winter-league career played over an incredible 34 summers in Cuba. Debuting with Club Fe of Havana in 1912 at 22, the indefatigable right-hander registered his final winter-season triumph at 46 in 1936, then returned a full decade later to pitch several innings of stellar relief work in the 1945-46 season at the age of 55. Luque's combined totals for major league and winter-league baseball, stretching over almost 35 years, total 297 wins, a figure still unrivaled by all his Latin countrymen. And for those critics who would hasten to establish that longevity alone is not sufficient merit for baseball immortality, it should also be established that Luque's 20-year ERA of 3.24 outstrips such notable Hall-of-Famers and all-stars as Bob Feller, Early Wynn, Robin Roberts, Nolan Ryan, and Lew Burdette, to name but a few of baseball's most unforgettable moundsmen.

Perhaps the greatest irony surrounding Dolf Luque's big-league career is the misconception that he was a cold, laconic, hot-tempered man, on the field or off. Upon the occasion of the Cuban hurler's premature and largely unnoticed death at age 66 (of a heart attack in Havana in July of 1957), legendary sportswriter Frank Graham provided the final and perhaps most eloquent tribute to this "Pride of Havana" who had reigned so stoically as the first certified Hispanic baseball star:

> It's hard to believe. Adolfo Luque was much too strong, too tough, too determined to die at this age of sixty-six. . . . He died of a heart attack. Did he? It sounds absurd. Luque's heart failed him in the clutch? It never did before. How many close ball games did he pitch? How many did he win . . . or lose? When he won, it was sometimes on his heart. When he lost, it was never because his heart missed a beat. Some enemy hitter got lucky or some idiot playing behind Luque fumbled a ground ball or dropped a sinking liner or was out of position so that he did not make the catch that should have been so easy for him.

No claim should be made that Luque was a ballplaying saint. As player, manager, and ballclub owner (the latter two roles in the winter leagues of his homeland), the redoubtable Luque was not free from displays of fiery temper and volcanic outbursts that fleshed out his colorful reputation. One incident recorded by Negro-league historian Donn Rogosin is likely as typical as it may be apocryphal. As manager of his old Havana Almendares club in the mid–1940s, Luque reportedly established instant dominance over Negro-leaguer Terris McDuffie when the imported star refused to take the mound for a pitching assignment with but two days' rest. Summoning his reticent hurler into his pigeonhole dressing-room office, the menacing skipper calmly pulled an oversized pistol from his desk drawer and patiently repeated his lineup assignment. The frightened McDuffie is reported to have seized the offered ball without further protest, then tossed a brilliant two-hitter against the far less threatening opposition.

Luque's career now lies largely buried, yet not so buried that a careful reader of the *Baseball Encyclopedia* does not find the full measure of his greatness. New focus on Latin players in recent years has also brought Luque's name (if not full memory of his career) back into our collective baseball consciousness. Any proper list of all-time Latin American hurlers reveals him as surpassed in accomplishment only by that "Dominican Dandy" Marichal and his modern alter ego and fellow countryman Luís Tiant, Jr. Even today, Luque still outdistances all other Latin hurlers, including such memorable figures as Mike Cuellar, Camilo Pascual, Juan Pizarro, Fernando Valenzuela, and Dennis Martínez (the latter did surpass Luque's career victory total in 1993). And in the now-forgotten category of hitting by pitchers, Dolf Luque stands in a class by himself, having once led the Cuban winter circuit in batting, posting a career .252 average in winter-league play and batting over .227 during 20 major league seasons, an achievement unrivaled by all other weak-sticking Hispanic hurlers. He will perhaps never receive his full due in the hindsight of a big-league history so filled with flashy Hispanic players of the past two decades. Yet for the educated fan who has pored religiously over the game's rich archives, Dolf Luque is a presence ummatched by all other Hispanic heroes of sport's golden decades between the two great wars.

Luque was far more than the man who courted baseball legend by once belting the loudmouthed Casey Stengel. It would surely be an exaggeration to argue for Luque's enshrinement in Cooperstown solely on the basis of his substantial yet hardly unparalleled big-league numbers, though some have grabbed immortality with far less impressive credentials. It would equally be a failure of historical perspective to dismiss him as a journeyman pitcher of average talent and few remarkable achievements. Few other hurlers have enjoyed such dominance over a short span of a few seasons. Fewer still have proved as durable or maintained their dominance over big-league hitters at so hoary an age. Almost none have contributed to the national pastime so richly after the door slammed shut upon an active big-league playing career. Almost no other major league pitcher did so much with so little fanfare.

And this was a pitcher, let it not be forgotten, whose numbers for decades stood unmatched by any of his countrymen, one who today still outstrips all Latino pitchers with exception of the immortal Marichal, the legendary Tiant, and the upstart Dennis Martínez. In the often falsely attributed phrase of the very Casey Stengel who once was accidental recipient of one of Dolf Luque's most torrid knockout pitches, "You can look it up!"

Dolf Luque's Almost Forgotten Major League Record

Year	Team	Record	Pct.	ERA	G	GS	GC	IP	BB	SO	ShO
1914	BOS N	0-1	.000	4.15	2	1	1	8.2	4	1	0
1915	BOS N	0-0	.000	3.60	2	1	0	5	4	3	0
1918	CIN N	6-3	.667	3.80	12	10	9	83	32	26	1
1919	CIN N	10-3	.769	2.63	30	9	6	106	36	40	2
1920	CIN N	13-9	.591	2.51	37	23	10	207.2	60	72	1
1921	CIN N	17-19	.472	3.38	41	36	25	304	64	102	*3*
1922	CIN N	13-*23*	.361	3.31	39	32	18	261	72	79	0
1923	CIN N	*27*-8	*.771*	*1.93*	41	37	28	322	88	151	*6*
1924	CIN N	10-15	.400	3.16	31	28	13	219.1	53	86	2
1925	CIN N	16-18	.471	*2.63*	36	36	22	291	78	140	*4*
1926	CIN N	13-16	.448	3.43	34	30	16	233.2	77	83	1
1927	CIN N	13-12	.520	3.20	29	27	17	230.2	56	76	2
1928	CIN N	11-10	.524	3.57	33	29	11	234.1	84	72	1
1929	CIN N	5-16	.238	4.50	32	22	8	176	56	43	1
1930	BKN N	14-8	.636	4.30	31	24	16	199	58	62	2
1931	BKN N	7-6	.538	4.56	19	15	5	102.2	27	25	0
1932	NYG N	6-7	.462	4.01	38	5	1	110	32	32	0
1933	NYG N	8-2	.800	2.69	35	0	0	80.1	19	23	0
1934	NYG N	4-3	.571	3.83	26	0	0	42.1	17	12	0
1935	NYG N	1-0	1.000	0.00	2	0	0	3.2	1	2	0
Totals		194-179	.520	3.24	550	365	206	3,220.1	918	1,130	26

Italics=League Leader

World Series Record:

Year	Team	Record	Pct.	ERA	G	GS	GC	IP	BB	SO	ShO
1919	CIN N	0-0	.000	0.00	2	0	0	5	0	6	0
1933	NYG N	1-0	1.000	0.00	1	0	0	4.1	2	5	0
Totals		1-0	1.000	0.00	3	0	0	9.1	2	11	0

Dolf Luque's Winterball Statistics

The following Cuban winter-league statistics for Adolfo Luque are provided with the assistance of reputable Cuban baseball scholar and journalist Angel Torres and have previously appeared in their most complete form (including yearly batting statistics omitted here) in Torres's self-published, heavily illustrated, and little-circulated book *La Historia del Béisbol Cubano, 1878–1976* (Los Angeles, 1976).

Year	Team	Appearances	Complete Games	Wins-Losses	Pct.
1912	Club Fe	7	2	0-3	.000
1913	Club Fe	2	0	0-2	.000
1913-14	Havana	6	3	2-3	.400
1914-15	Almendares	16	6	7-4	.636
1915-16	Almendares	20	11	12-5	.706
1917	Orientales	9	6	4-4	.500
1918-19	None	Did not play	------------	------------	------------
1919-20	Almendares	15	9	10-4	.714
1920-21	Almendares	10	6	4-2	.667
1921	Almendares	Did not play due to injury		------------	------------
1922-23	Havana	23	12	11-9	.550
1923-24	Havana	11	5	7-2	.778
1924-25	Almendares	3	3	3-0	1.000
1925-26	None	Did not play	------------	------------	------------
1926-27	Alacranes	16	13	10-6	.625
1927-28	Almendares	13	6	6-4	.600
1928-29	Cuba-Havana	17	9	9-2	.818
1929-30	Havana	15	7	4-8	.333
1930–32	None	Did not play	------------	------------	------------
1932-33	Almendares	6	2	2-2	.500
1933-34	Season cancelled	------------	------------	------------	------------
1934-35	Almendares	10	6	6-2	.750
1935-36	Almendares	7	5	4-2	.667
1936-37	Almendares	7	1	2-2	.500
1937-38	Almendares	1	0	0-1	.000
1938-39	Almendares	1	0	0-1	.000
1945-46	Cienfuegos	1	0	0-0	.000
Totals	22 Seasons	216	112	103-68	.602

It might be noted that during approximately the same period (the 19 seasons between 1923 and 1947) Negro league Hall-of-Famer Martín Dihigo compiled a comparable pitching record in the same Cuban Professional Baseball League, posting 262 game appearances, 120 complete games, and a slightly superior won-lost record of 106-59 (a .642 winning percentage).

Latin America's Top Big-League Pitchers

Eleven pitchers (on next page) compose a select list of Latin American-born hurlers who have won a minimum of 100 big-league games. This listing of all-time greats among Latino pitchers is arranged on the basis of total

Pitcher	Wins-Losses	Pct.	ERA	IP	SO	BB
Juan Marichal (Dominican) 1960–74	*243*-142	*.631*	*2.89*	*3,509*	2,303	709
Luís Tiant Jr. (Cuba) 1964–82	229-172	.571	3.30	3,486	*2,416*	*1,104*
Dennis Martínez (Nicaragua) 1976–93	207-164[a]	.558	3.64	3,369	1,821	987
Dolf Luque (Cuba) 1914–35	194-*179*	.520	3.24	3,220	1,130	918
Mike Cuellar (Cuba) 1959–77	185-130	.587	3.14	2,808	1,632	822
Camilo Pascual (Cuba) 1954–71	174-170	.506	3.63	2,930	2,167	1,069
Fernando Valenzuela (Mexico) 1980–93	149-128	.538	3.45	2,535	1,842	997
Juan Pizarro (Puerto Rico) 1957–74	131-105	.555	3.43	2,034	1,522	888
Joaquín Andújar (Dominican) 1976–88	127-118	.518	3.58	2,154	1,032	731
Pedro Ramos (Cuba) 1955–70	117-160	.422	4.08	1,643	1,415	629
Mario Soto (Dominican) 1977–88	100-92	.521	3.47	1,731	1,449	657

[a]Dennis Martínez surpassed Dolf Luque in games won during the 1993 season, becoming only the third Latin American big-league hurler with 200 victories.

wins, with career leaders in other statistical categories indicated by italics. Though the all-time leader in career losses, Dolf Luque otherwise ranks well, standing fourth in victories, fifth in ERA (now trailing Marichal, Alejandro Peña, Cuellar, and José Rijo), and fourth all-time in innings pitched (behind only Marichal, Tiant, and Dennis Martínez).

Hispanic Pitchers as Hitters

Among hard-hitting Hispanic pitchers, Adolfo Luque stands supreme, having led other Latinos in almost all lifetime batting categories, including runs scored, hits, triples, RBIs, and batting average. And sufficient proof that "The Pride of Havana" knew how to wield his bat against more than just the raucous bench jockeys of the New York Giants dugout derives from the fact that Luque also won a Cuban League batting title in 1917 (.355 during a 25-game season) and compiled a lifetime .252 BA over 22 seasons of Cuban winter-league play (in 671 career at-bats).

Pitcher	AB	Runs	Hits	2B	3B	HR	RBI	BA
Dolf Luque (1914–35)	*1,043*	*96*	*237*	*31*	*10*	*5*	*90*	*.227*
Camilo Pascual (1954–71)	977	71	198	32	5	5	81	.203
Juan Pizarro (1957–74)	658	72	133	18	2	8	66	.202
Rubén Gómez (1953–67)	477	58	95	11	1	3	22	.199
Fernando Valenzuela (1980–91)	672	37	130	15	1	7	55	.193
Jesse Flores (1942–50)	304	18	55	7	2	0	22	.181
Sandy Consuegra (1950–57)	218	15	37	2	0	0	18	.170
Mike Fornieles (1952–63)	308	25	52	7	1	1	16	.169
Juan Marichal (1960–74)	1,219	73	202	29	2	4	75	.165
Luís Tiant Jr. (1964–82)	495	36	81	12	1	5	40	.163

CHAPTER 2

Juan Marichal, Latin America's Unmatched Hall-of-Fame Hurler

Dandy, Sandy, and the Summer of 1966

> Most of baseball is invisible—truly invisible—to the untrained eye. The non-fan, after watching fifteen minutes of a game, will bray that baseball is boring because "nothing is happening." But in fact the poor sap simply can not see the vast sea of pure information that shifts meaningfully with every single one of the 600,000 or so pitches thrown in a major-league season, let alone realize (as a true fan does) that all this pure information bears a beautiful and mystical link to the Great Truths.
>
> —Dick Dahl

In the best of all possible views, they were two of baseball's greatest individual phenomena—two rubber-armed hurlers who struck constant fear into the hearts of National League hitters across an entire pitching-rich decade. Perhaps no two Hall-of-Fame moundsmen from a single modern era sport more brilliant credentials or more fearsome reputations than Sandy (Braun) Koufax, rare Jewish southpaw, and Juan Antonio Marichal, flamboyant Dominican right-hander.

Koufax possessed the most flaming fastball and most fearsome strikeout delivery ever known in a century of modern big-league play. Marichal was a hard-nosed craftsman with unsurpassed flair, owner of a high-kicking delivery and bulldog competitiveness sufficient to baffle a generation of hitters. And for a dozen seasons they stood as bitter rivals—annual contenders for league pitching honors as well as staff aces for two teams, Dodgers and Giants, locked in the eighth decade of one of baseball's most legendary intercity rivalries.

But there was inevitably another, darker side to the legends of Koufax and Marichal. Baseball is, after all, primarily a sport of relentless tragedy, an endless repetition of loss, defeat, waning powers, and encroaching impotency. The braggart Casey of Mudville, immortalized by his game-losing and crowd-silencing colossal whiff, remains baseball's richest archetype. Thus it is Ralph Branca and Ralph Terry as much as Bobby Thomson and Bill Mazeroski who epitomize the game's bittersweet drama.

Thus Koufax saw his star shoot unthinkably high, then flame out suddenly in almost predictable early self-destruction. Marichal, less favored by fandom or fickle fortune, was widely misunderstood by North American press and fans alike and always underappreciated when stacked up against rival hurling stars in either circuit. His reputation was persistently more hot-blooded renegade ("loco Latino") than unrivaled mound ace. With his showboating ways and second-fiddle status, this "Dominican Dandy" even seemed to provide the perfect rationale for disparaging comments by his manager, Alvin Dark, that these dark-skinned Spanish-speaking types couldn't play the game with heart, courage, or even the proper dose of native intelligence. Not surprisingly, then, the Dominican Dandy (a nickname in itself at least partly pejorative) was always destined to perform in the long shadows of more celebrated and more fortune-kissed rivals like Koufax, Bob Gibson, even Don Drysdale, who labored simultaneously in his league.

In this second sense, these two great National League rivals were the perfect archetypes (even stereotypes) for the races and the ethnic cultures whose banners they so nobly carried. Koufax was the brilliant but tarnished and flawed Jewish baseball star. Cultural stereotype appeared (as it inevitably does) to provide a ready excuse for expecting Koufax's premature fall from grace. The handsome and refined Brooklyn southpaw at first seemed to wipe away a common notion about Jewish athletes as essentially inferior, second-rate, and feeble; then his sudden retirement at the pinnacle of glory seemed to confirm a popular conception and also certify a time-worn myth. Koufax was truly great—unhittable, an overpowering force not known since Matty and Old Pete Alexander—yet suddenly he was not only human but suspiciously cowardly at that. Did the doubts not linger? Was the Jewish phenom not, after all, sickly and thus suspect? Did he not chuck it all away in the face of mere arm pain that could not have been all that severe for a guy capable of winning three Cy Young trophies over the past four seasons? (At least so the popular line of reasoning might have gone in the mind of any fan who never threw a fastball or felt the shattering pain of a dead pitching arm.) Could anything but such cowardice have been expected from a man whose tribe historically provides scholars and clerics but never athletes and warriors?

Several years before he walked away from the glare of fame in Dodger Stadium, Koufax was already all too sensitive to the misinterpretations that legions were eager to heap upon his career. At the height of his ballplaying stardom the great Dodger hurler was thus prompted to open his autobiography with a plea for burying "the myth of Sandy Koufax"—a misshapen but popular notion that the talented hurler didn't really want to give his mind or soul to baseball but would much rather have been an architect or perhaps Brahms or Mendelssohn, certainly never a strikeout king. "The way the fantasy goes," complained the disillusioned baseball hero, "I am really a sort of dreamy intellectual who was lured out of college by a bonus in the flush of my youth and have forever regretted—and even resented—the life of fame and fortune that has been forced upon me." No matter what magic Koufax wove on the pitcher's mound, the notion of the weak and unathletic Jew could never be quite expunged.

Such blatant racism also provided plenty of rationale for downplaying Marichal's brilliant achievements. Marichal, of course, was an ideal inheritor of the mantle of unappreciated Latin athlete, forevermore discounted like Dolf Luque before him and Clemente alongside him. It would seem today hard to believe that a moundsman who owned such a lengthy resume of milestones and records would not have been automatically elected to Cooperstown in his first or second year of eligibility. Of course, the revolutionary sabermetric analyses now found in Thorn and Palmer's *Total Baseball* (1993, third edition) had not until most recently informed us that a new type of statistical record keeping would rank Marichal surprisingly high among the game's mound greats: second over the past three decades in fewest walks per game; tied for ninth all-time (with Koufax) in lowest hits–walks-allowed ratio (10.0 per 9 innings); seventeenth lowest all-time in opponents-allowed-on-base percentage (one slot behind Koufax); fifteenth all-time in percentage of wins above his team (weighted formula for determining how many more games a pitcher has won annually than might have been expected from an average hurler on his team); thirty-second all-time on Thorn and Palmer's "Total Pitcher Index" of career efficiency (Koufax ranks seventy-eighth, Roger Clemens twenty-sixth, Nolan Ryan sixty-ninth). In the end, however, it seems that the gruesome image of Marichal's enraged attack on John Roseboro would likely have clouded even this newest set of impressive career-measuring numbers.

But it was not the single outburst in the Roseboro incident that tarnished Marichal. The image of a less than complete moundsman (despite 243 career wins) was firmly etched in the popular imagination before the regrettable incident. In his revealing autobiography, *A Pitcher's Story*, with sportswriter Charles Einstein, the Dominican Dandy would perhaps rightly place some of the blame on the inconsistency of manager Al Dark, who in one mood praised his ace as an athlete who "thrives on competition" and "always rises to the occasion," then in another humor blasted him as being "without guts" and careless with his talents. (Dark once complained loudly to his bench that if Marichal continued to strike out opponents with his screwball, he would soon be unable to lift his arm and thus of no use to his teammates.) If Marichal's arm seemed to stay surprisingly healthy throughout his long career, he was plagued by numerous other small injuries that (as with Clemente) brought the label of soft ballplayer who failed to look after his health.

Most damaging perhaps was Marichal's approach to the game, one that was hard to knock for its efficiency but almost guaranteed to turn off most fans and a handful of traditional by-the-book managers alike. Frank Robinson, Cincinnati Reds slugger, once complained that you couldn't appreciate Marichal (who threw his arsenal of varied pitches unpredictably and in all situations) as you could Koufax (who relied on only a fastball and curve, yet still overpowered most batters). And this was a complaint shared by fans, who prefer powerhouse strikeout displays to hidden or subtle mound craftsmanship (just as they prefer the .240-hitting home-run slugger to the boring .330 singles hitter). While Sandy Koufax was a strikeout king, Marichal simply wasn't interested in how he got batters out so long as he did. His strategy was to throw the ball over the plate with uncanny accuracy, make hitters put the horsehide into play, avoid walks at all cost.

This was the approach that allowed Marichal to arrive in the majors with one of the most stunning minor league records of all time: 131 walks over 655 innings (1.80 walks per nine-inning game). "It takes three pitches to strike a man out," Marichal once announced to the press, "but only one to get a man out with a ground ball." This, of course, was infinite pitching wisdom from a staff workhorse expected to hurl several hundred innings over the course of a long summer. But in the broken English of an easygoing Dominican, it seemed to smack too much of the merely lackadaisical.

In the end, then, these two marvelous ethnic moundsmen provided many of the seeds of their tragic outcomes. Koufax was at best undisciplined throughout his early career, an unfulfilled "bonus baby" plagued by persistent control problems. He squandered six early seasons, compiling but 36 victories (against 40 losses) over that span (1955–1960) and winning in double figures but once (11-11 in 1958). He was seemingly nothing extraordinary upon the hill until veteran catcher Norm Sherry advised the hard-throwing southpaw to "slow things down a bit" and trade raw speed for at least a smattering of pure pitching savvy. And Koufax was willing to mold his lasting legend of unfulfilled promise by walking away at the very height of an altogether unparalleled career. It is hard to convince the average fan that a man who has just won 27 games and copped back-to-back unanimous Cy Young honors suddenly cannot lift an arm or hurl a baseball plateward as he had done so brilliantly only weeks before. Was Koufax not a spoiled goldbricker after all? Not that Sandy had much choice. His arm was truly dead from years of abuse. His pain could never be known or appreciated by the grandstand fan or the Sunday softballer. Yet no other all-star had abandoned his career so dramatically and by his own choice and never at the moment of reaching such dizzying heights of achievement and stardom.

Marichal was an even more obvious author of his own tarnished image. Juan Marichal also fostered a proud personal baseball legend, though one of darker consequence than that earlier shaped by the misunderstood yet martyred Clemente. Marichal's fate was thus a tragedy of a far different order. The lanky Dominican would successfully carve out a true Hall-of-Fame career, becoming the first of his race to be legitimately elected to Cooperstown by the standard route (in Clemente's case, the normal election process and five-year waiting period had been waived). But Marichal also fostered a legend that had its roots embedded in the myths surrounding Dolf Luque and Rubén Gómez. What fans today remember most about Marichal is unfortunately neither the blazing fastball nor the high-kicking delivery that intimidated National League hitters for more than a dozen seasons. Burned into our collective memory instead is an ugly image of Juan Marichal attempting to brain Dodger catcher John Roseboro with a Louisville slugger in one of baseball's most notorious displays.

A moment of poor judgment provided sufficient excuse for those looking to condemn and discount him. Marichal seemed to fit a familiar pattern, after all. The first great Latin pitcher, Dolf Luque of the Cincinnati Reds, had authored the lasting stereotype when he charged from the mound in 1922 to thrash Casey Stengel on the New York Giants bench in old Crosley Field. It had taken a host of helmeted officers to subdue the enraged bat-wielding Luque when he charged back upon the diamond after an initial ejection from the field. A nearly contemporary San Francisco forerunner of Marichal's, Puerto Rico's Rubén Gómez, had sullied the whole race of dark-skinned Spanish-speaking pitchers with a recent series of beanball encounters during the mid–1950s, especially with an infamous moment involving Joe Adcock of the Milwaukee Braves. Chased off the mound after beaning Adcock, Gómez (then with the New York Giants) had fled in panic to the Giant clubhouse to return to the field brandishing a deadly switch-blade knife. Gómez cemented a personal reputation as well as a Latin stereotype by becoming baseball's most widely recognized "beanball king" of the 1950s. Other Gómez head-hunting incidents involved Brooklyn's Carl Furillo in 1953 (sparking Furillo's famous charge at manager Leo Durocher in the New York dugout), Cardinal hurler Sad Sam Jones in 1957, and Cincinnati slugger Frank Robinson (hospitalized by a Gómez fastball) in 1957.

But it was fate and timing that were even more a Marichal nemesis than the behaviors of some of his temperamental countrymen. Whenever Marichal was truly hot, someone else was always just a bit hotter; when he was indescribably brilliant, the luster of his performance was usually tarnished by his team's late-season fade from pennant contention; some rival hurler always had the good fortune of playing on a better ballclub. A brilliant 1963 campaign (25-8, 2.41 ERA, third-place Giants finish) might have brought a first Cy Young trophy for the Dominican Dandy, but Koufax (25-5, 1.88 ERA, Dodgers pennant victory) shone somewhat brighter. Each of Koufax's Cy Young years (1963, 1965, 1966) outmatched and eventually buried a nearly comparable Marichal performance (second in ERA and complete games and first in shutouts in 1965; second in victories and complete games and first in winning percentage in 1966). And when his Los Angeles rival was finally removed from competition and a last-hurrah glory season was strung together in 1968, there was yet another rival in the way to steal his thunder. Marichal seemed to outdo himself in 1968, leading the league for the first time in three major categories—wins (26), complete games (30), and innings pitched (325.2). But this was the "year of the pitcher" in the senior circuit, and Bob Gibson posted a remarkable 1.12 ERA that summer (alongside 268 strikeouts and 13 shutouts) while leading his club on a successful pennant charge. Four potential Cy Young seasons, yet never a coveted Cy Young trophy for the ill-starred Marichal. And what was most painful was that thrice Koufax and once Gibson swept to their Cy Young honors by unanimous voting of the league's sportswriters. Throughout his four most masterful career seasons, Juan Marichal thus was not named on a single Cy Young ballot.

If Koufax and Marichal in the end never quite reached the career zenith many expected of them, the facts of their achievement nonetheless stand etched in the rock tablet of baseball history. Together they dominated an era renowned for its superb pitching. No other head-to-head mound rivalry ever seemed more destined to fire the fan's imagination. Here was a one-on-one pitching rivalry fueled by the most intriguing opposites. They toiled for baseball's two greatest century-long rivals (the Bums and the Jints), still at the peak of zealous competition in their newly revamped West Coast homes; one epitomized the strikeout wizard, the other the arch hurling craftsman; one was the greatest right-hander of an era, the other the most renowned southpaw.

Yet if Koufax versus Marichal provided unmatched elements of *mano a mano* baseball drama, in the end their personal rivalry was distinguished more than anything else by its rarity of occurrence. Over the seven years they occupied the league together (1960–1966), they met face-to-face but three times. A closer examination of box scores suggests that Marichal and Koufax faced off on nine occasions, though only three involved both men as final pitchers of record. It was Marichal who appeared to hold the upper hand, though a slim upper hand indeed. Twice the Dominican came out on top; Koufax triumphed on a single dramatic occasion (May 11, 1963) with his second career no-hitter. The celebrated August 1965 Roseboro game found Koufax again the loser, while Marichal (ejected in the third inning) went without a decision. (Another memorable 16-inning 1–0 shutout, which biographer John Devaney describes in his *Juan Marichal: Mister Strike,* did not involve the Dodgers and Sandy Koufax, as Devaney contends; in that game Marichal actually bested Milwaukee's ace southpaw, veteran Warren Spahn.) The final tally: Marichal 2-1, Koufax 1-3. But if the rivalry was brief, it was explosive. Perhaps nowhere else in baseball annals can be found such a short-lived head-to-head pitching rivalry in which only four meetings with both pitchers at peak form resulted in two more memorable individual games (a Koufax no-hitter and a bitter beanball brawl).

Marichal is today an unmatched diamond hero in his native Caribbean land, if sometimes a soiled star in his adopted North American one. There is little doubt that the Dominican Dandy would have reached Cooperstown much earlier, despite his transgressions against Roseboro, had it not been for the presence of the unbeatable Koufax. Brilliant as was the record of the Dominican Dandy, his best was always overshadowed by his southpaw Dodger rival. Koufax always seemed to master Marichal (despite the 1-3 head-to-head ledger) and his Giants in the heat of pennant competition, just as he spun webs over the rest of the league during his short span of unmatched brilliance.

Nowhere was this influence of Koufax over Marichal more prominently witnessed than in the tension-packed 1966 season, celebrated more than 25 summers ago. It was to be Marichal's finest year by almost any measure. It was by all rights the season Juan Marichal should finally have reached his long-anticipated apex of career achievement. Never had he enjoyed such a season: 25 wins (equaled only by his league-best 25 in 1963 and his pacesetting 26 in 1968); a league-top winning percentage of .806, almost unheard of from a pitcher winning 25 or more games in the modern era; a strikeout total of 222, matched only by his 248 in 1963. And it was a career year in other aspects for the Giants ace bent on redeeming his tarnished career. At the plate the usually weak-sticking Dominican began using his lumber as an offensive weapon of a more appropriate kind. He belted one of his four career homers that summer, compiled 28 hits, and rang up a respectable .250 batting average.

Instead of personal glories and a long-awaited San Francisco pennant, however, 1966 would yield yet another second-place finish and another year of playing second fiddle to the Giants' pesky Los Angeles rivals. Despite such brilliant numbers, Latin America's pride and joy would again labor in the long shadow of Koufax, now stoically masking his pain while posting his banner swan-song year. More disappointing still, Marichal continued to labor (in more ways than one) under another more ominous shadow, that still being cast by his darkest moment, one summer earlier.

It is largely forgotten today what impact the 1965 Roseboro-Marichal affair had upon the final weeks of the pennant chase that fateful summer and on a dramatic 1966 campaign soon to follow. John Roseboro may have suffered more immediately, but it was Marichal who would carry the long-term scars. Soon after (June 1966), the embarrassed pitcher would issue a formal apology plus a long-winded explanation in print (in the pages of *Sport* magazine, aided by Harry Jupiter of the San Francisco *Examiner*) for all the world to see and to debate. Later he would use the forum of his autobiography (polished by Charles Einstein) to discuss several immediate fallouts from the devastating affair.

For one thing, the Giants pitching staff was dangerously thin late in the 1965 season. The team carried two "bonus rookies" occupying vital roster spots, and Marichal's suspension therefore meant severe and even crippling hardships for the San Francisco pennant challenge. (So thin was the Giants staff during Marichal's suspension that manager Herman Franks was forced to use outfielder Matty Alou on the hill when a rainout forced an unscheduled doubleheader in Pittsburgh.) Furthermore, the league did not want to risk a Marichal appearance at Dodger Stadium in Los Angeles during the final month of the season (the Watts riots had also just occurred during preceding weeks), and his suspension was thus rigged to prevent such a potentially explosive occurrence. But what might have worked toward public safety in the City of Angels also worked against the Giants' pennant hopes. And finally, Marichal was quick to admit that the entire affair did not fail to have a noticeable impact upon his mental state and thus his late-season pitching efficiency. He found it difficult to keep hitters like Ernie Banks at bay, for example, and would later recount in his autobiography how teammate Mays was furious with him in subsequent weeks of the pennant stretch drive for failing to throw inside against potent plate-hugging sluggers like Banks.

It has often gone generally unnoticed in accounts of the Roseboro incident that Koufax occupied center stage in the entire ugly mess. Intimately involved as well was Marichal's most famous teammate, future Hall-of-Fame immortal Willie Mays. The rival clubs were locked in a tight pennant race when they met for a crucial late August four-game series in the Bay City. San Francisco hopes had already been dealt a severe blow by two extra-inning losses during the first three matchups of this titanic late-season clash. Now it was game four with Koufax and Marichal going head-to-head in the heat of pennant battle. It seemed something simply had to give, and on August 22 it finally did.

Tension was thick enough to cut with a knife after Marichal knocked down Maury Wills with a high hard one in inning two, then again when Koufax responded with a pitch that sailed over the head of Willie Mays and reached the backstop on the fly. The stage was thus set for baseball's most infamous fight, the Dodgers leading 2–1 in inning three and Marichal standing in the batter's box. Roseboro reportedly called for a brushback (another retaliation for the earlier pitch that sent Wills scrambling), but the mild-mannered Koufax apparently refused to deliver. Roseboro therefore took matters into his own hands by firing the ball back so close to the batter's head that it nicked the rival pitcher's ear. The rest is baseball history of the most unglamorous sort. Marichal took offense at the toss that had singed his ear, and angry words were promptly exchanged. Suddenly and unpredictably enraged, Marichal violently applied his lumber to the defenseless catcher's skull, and a bloody bench-clearing battle ensued.

It was Marichal's teammate Willie Mays who rescued both Roseboro and the moment at hand with his quick intercession in the affair. It was Mays who first reached the felled Roseboro and thus defused tensions by cradling the head of the bleeding catcher in his hands. But once play continued after a lengthy delay and a calming of spirits, Mays immediately stepped back into his role as traditional Dodger-killer and promptly rescued the Giants as well, striking a three-run homer off the now-shaken Koufax and delivering a 4–3 San Francisco victory.

John Roseboro would later admit within the pages of his 1978 autobiography (*Glory Days with the Dodgers and Other Days with Others*, with Bill Libby) his rather ignoble role in the affair. "I meant for him to feel it," Roseboro reflected on the throw he had whizzed by Marichal's ear and nose. "I was so mad I'd made up my mind that if he protested, I was going after him!" But it would also be the large-hearted Roseboro who would first plead for fan support when Marichal eventually joined the Dodgers at career's end in 1975 and later campaigned for his Dominican rival when Marichal's Hall-of-Fame election seemed about to collapse for a final time during his third year of Cooperstown eligibility.

One final upshot of the Roseboro-Marichal affair was the negative impact on the 1966 pennant race to follow. That upcoming season, Marichal's best chance for redemption, would find the two aces withheld from head-to-head competition. As the Dodgers and Giants again battled to the wire in a tension-packed pennant summer, Marichal three times faced rival Drysdale (all complete game victories) but never rival Koufax. Marichal stood 3-0 against Los Angeles that summer, failing to go the distance only once, during a 10-inning no-decision loss (Marichal was removed in the tenth) in which the victory went to Los Angeles reliever Phil Regan. Koufax in turn stood 4-0 against the Giants in six starts, hurling complete games in all four victories.

Thus it was in 1966 that Marichal lost yet another chance to redeem himself fully against the Dodgers and his greatest rival, Koufax. Not that the Dominican ace did not exact some measure of reputation-boosting revenge. Marichal shot to a 9-0 start against the league with nine complete games and a 0.59 ERA in his first 10 starts. He bore down and maintained his concentration that spring despite a flood of hate mail and a ceaseless chorus of boos resulting from the still-fresh Roseboro incident. Before the summer was out, however, last year's villain was being featured on the cover of *Time* magazine with a banner headline touting "Baseball's Best Righthander." And the nation's sportswriters (if not always the fans) were beginning to be true believers. One *Sporting News* scribe soon pointed out that with his current .685 lifetime winning percentage (115-53 midway through the 1966 season) Marichal was now in a position "to joust for the all-time leadership with the all-time masters."

But even such dawning recognition from a scattered handful (along with a 1966 25-6 record and 2.23 ERA) was not sufficient to eradicate the widespread image of Marichal as a brilliant but flawed moundsman, an image that would pursue him in coming years all the way to the doorstep of Cooperstown. When the Cy Young ballots were tallied at the end of the 1966 season, Sandy Koufax had once again been given all 20 votes for baseball's "best pitcher of the year."

Marichal by the Numbers

Juan Antonio Marichal Sánchez, it would seem from the numbers alone, is undisputably the greatest pitcher in the history of Latin American baseball, at least the greatest Latin American–born pitcher, based strictly on performances carved out in big-league arenas. Legendary feats by a handful of stellar Hispanic pitchers witnessed throughout the long years of Caribbean winter-league play or in the Mexican triple A–level leagues are certainly not admissible for comparison with major league performances. There are as many as a dozen star pitchers originating from Latin countries who have achieved outstanding major league careers: Camilo Pascual with 2,167 strikeouts; Dolf Luque boasting 194 victories; Luís Tiant with 229 career wins and Cuba's Mike Cuellar with 185 (plus a 1969 Cy Young trophy); Dennis Martínez quietly surpassing all but Marichal and Tiant as he hurdles the 200-victory plateau. But it is only Marichal who has been duly enshrined in Cooperstown's hallowed archives.

From the earliest innings of an auspicious major league debut, the Dominican Dandy established his relentless domination against National League batters. A truly unfortunate aspect of the overhyped Marichal-Roseboro incident is that it so nearly scuttled the Dominican Dandy's otherwise impeccable Cooperstown credentials. In Marichal's first major league outing he would twirl a most memorable seven innings of no-hit ball, recording a one-hit shutout against the basement-dwelling Philadelphia Phillies. Over the next 15 seasons (1960–1975), he would toil in 13 campaigns with the San Francisco Giants and one each with the Red Sox and Dodgers, winning more than 25 games three seasons, enjoying 12 consecutive winning summers, and recording over 200 strikeouts six times. While Sandy Koufax was indisputably the premier left-hander during the 1960s, Marichal was beyond a doubt the game's top right-hander of the same era. In total performance, no other Latin American pitcher has ever come close to the career records (243 wins, .631 winning percentage, 2.89 career ERA) of the high-kicking and always dominant fastballer from the Dominican Republic.

For some, it would seem that Bob Gibson of the Cardinals might better deserve that distinction. The final three seasons of the decade, taken alone, may at a glance seem to support an argument of that type. And a more feeble case might be made for Koufax's roommate, Don Drysdale. Yet any numerical comparison based on the entire 10-year span leaves little doubt about consistent superiority, thus making the point altogether moot.

Juan Marichal in the 1960s				Bob Gibson in the 1960s				Don Drysdale in the 1960s			
Year	Record	ERA	SO	Year	Record	ERA	SO	Year	Record	ERA	SO
1960	6-2	2.66	58	1960	3-6	5.61	69	1960	15-14	2.84	246
1961	13-10	3.89	124	1961	13-12	3.24	166	1961	13-10	3.69	182
1962	18-11	3.36	153	1962	15-13	2.85	208	1962	25-9	2.83	232
1963	25-8	2.41	248	1963	18-9	3.39	204	1963	19-17	2.63	251
1964	21-8	2.48	206	1964	19-12	3.01	245	1964	18-16	2.18	237
1965	22-13	2.13	240	1965	20-12	3.07	270	1965	23-12	2.77	210
1966	25-6	2.23	222	1966	21-12	2.44	225	1966	13-16	3.42	177
1967	14-10	2.76	166	1967	13-7	2.98	147	1967	13-16	2.74	196
1968	26-9	2.43	218	1968	22-9	1.12	268	1968	14-12	2.15	155
1969	21-11	2.10	205	1969	20-13	2.18	269	1969	5-4	4.43	24
	191-88		1,840		164-105		2,071		158-126		1,910

Juan Marichal	Bob Gibson	Don Drysdale
20 wins = 6 times	20 wins = 4 times	20 wins = 2 times
200 K = 6 times	200 K = 7 times	200 K = 5 times

When the 1960s ledgers of Marichal, Gibson, and Drysdale are laid side by side for careful inspection, there can be little dispute about the first-place ranking of the Dominican Dandy. Marichal won the most games by far (more than 25 ahead of either rival), held the best winning percentage (.685 to .610 for Gibson and .556 for Drysdale), and lost the fewest times (16 percent less than Gibson, 31 percent less than Drysdale). He owned the most 20-win seasons as well as the most seasons (eight) with a sub-3.00 ERA.

He is headed by Gibson on only two fronts: total strikeouts and 200-strikeout seasons; Drysdale fails to lead in a single category. What Marichal lacked were the World Series spotlight that was Gibson's in 1967 and in 1968 and the individual Cy Young awards that graced both his rival moundsmen (Drysdale in 1962, Gibson in 1968 and 1970). When it comes to counting Cy Young plaques as a final measure of superiority, it might not be unfair to speculate that where Juan Marichal truly lost out was perhaps only in the intangible arena of politics.

Among his countrymen – those who performed in the same decade or any other decade – the case is even more open-and-shut. In total number count, no other Latin American pitcher has ever rivaled the records of the high-kicking dominant fastballing right-hander hailing from the Dominican Republic. For foolproof verification, one need only scan the chart of top Latin moundsmen found at the end of this chapter. American Leaguer Tiant is the only rival Spanish-speaking pitcher who reached anything near the same heights, yet Tiant falls far short in all categories save strikeouts. Nicaragua's Dennis Martínez now mounts a distant challenge, but time seems stacked against the Nicaraguan's effort to approach the 250-victory plateau. No other potential Latin 200-game winners are currently in sight.

Yet when compared to non–Latin pitchers, especially Hall-of-Famers, the case for Juan Marichal has never been quite so clear-cut. If it remains (as it should) impossible to demonstrate without heated emotion and telltale signs of bias that Juan Marichal's Latin heritage measurably damaged his career estimation (in the eyes of hundreds of reporters and baseball commentators, and perhaps thousands of fans), it certainly might be more calmly argued that Marichal's Latin birthright never helped him very much. A reputation as a sullen and hot-blooded Latino ballplayer seemed to dog Marichal's professional career (as it has more recently dogged fellow Dominicans like George Bell, Pascual Pérez, and Joaquín Andújar), and Marichal's onfield antics often did little to dissuade the view.

It is admittedly difficult to overlook altogether the sometimes excessive antics of the Dominican trio just cited, although their excesses are perhaps more unfairly publicized than those of white-skinned North American ballplayers. Bell's constant sulking and flareups with management are felt by many to have cost Toronto serious pennant contention in 1988 (as did his inexplicable 1987 batting slump in the final weeks of a deadlocked pennant battle). Pérez's tantrums and unexcused absences from the Atlanta Braves clubhouse almost ruined a promising career before it was launched (and have been muted in New York only by a two-year sojourn on the disabled list). And Andújar faltered badly in the two seasons immediately following his equally infamous and unfortunate onfield explosions during the final 1985 World Series game. What is unfortunate is the popular stereotypes that accompany such incidents. Ted Williams, for example, was as badly behaved during portions of his stormy career, a common knowledge that is either conveniently forgotten by most fans or conveniently swept under the protective cloak of "colorful baseball character" by most baseball historians.

For the bulk of the nation's fans, there was nothing remotely "colorful" about Marichal's bat-wielding 1965 attack on a defenseless Dodgers catcher. The most severe penalty ever dealt a ballplayer for an onfield offense ($1,750 in fines and nine days' suspension) drew few enough cries of protest. Nor was the protest from most quarters more than barely audible when Cooperstown gates remained sealed to Latin America's greatest moundsman during three initial summers of eligibility. Today, despite his earned Cooperstown immortality, the question is still repeatedly raised in hot stove league discussion: How good was Juan Marichal? Does he truly rank up there alongside more recognizable and touted Hall-of-Fame reputations?

In the end there seems to be only one reasonable solution to the paradox of Juan Marichal, tainted Hall-of-Fame pitcher. Perhaps the only foolproof way to find out something substantive about Marichal's career-long achievement is through exhaustive comparison of a wide range of his pitching statistics with those of other, more cherished Hall-of-Famers. This is the advantage and the beauty of baseball. Our national pastime is, after all, a game of implacable numbers, each angle and subtle aspect of the sport being permanently recorded and quantified for minute dissection and ruthlessly balanced assessment. And the numbers rarely if ever seem to lie. *Sabermetrics* (named for its practitioners from the Society for American Baseball Research) during the past decade has brought fresh focus on baseball numbers by appealing to an advanced technology that facilitates all manner of rapid and efficient computerized statistical review.[1] But baseball's numbers have always been there for discussion and review, and knowledgeable fans have always as a last resort turned to them (to standard measures, at least, like ERA, BA, RBI, OBP, or SLG) to resolve baseball argument and dispute.

One appealing method is to compare Marichal's career statistics from several revealing angles with those of Hall-of-Fame pitchers appearing in the major leagues after the somewhat arbitrary cutoff date of 1920.[2] This particular cutoff year is not an unprincipled choice, it should be noted, since after 1920 the supposed introduction of the lively cork-centered baseball (reputed but probably apocryphal) and the free-swing batting style pioneered by Babe Ruth (more obvious and documented) radically altered hitting performance and thus pitching statistics forever. Furthermore, many of the commonplace pitching statistics relevant to a thorough comparison (ERA, BB, etc.) were not regularly (or accurately) tallied during the first two decades of the present century. Thus, eliminated from further consideration here are the following Hall-of-Fame pitchers (ranked above and below Marichal in career victories) of the early modern (pre–1920) baseball era, pitchers who enjoyed the bulk of their major league careers before 1920.

Old-Time Hall-of-Famers Outranking Marichal in Total Victories

1. Denton True "Cy" Young, 1890–1911 (511-313, .620)
2. Walter "Big Train" Johnson, 1907–1927 (416-279, .599)
3. Christy Mathewson, 1900–1916 (373-188, .665)
4. Grover Cleveland "Pete" Alexander, 1911–1930 (373-208, .642)
5. Jim "Pud" Galvin, 1879–1892 (361-310, .538)
6. Kid Nichols, 1890–1906 (360-202, .641)
7. Tim Keefe, 1880–1893 (344-225, .605)
8. Eddie Plank, 1901–1917 (327-193, .629)
9. John Clarkson, 1882–1894 (326-177, .648)
10. Mickey Welch, 1880–1892 (311-207, .600)
11. Charles "Old Hoss" Radbourn, 1880–1891 (303-191, .613)
12. Joe "Iron Man" McGinnity, 1899–1908 (247-144, .632)

Old-Time Hall-of-Famers Not Outranking Marichal in Total Victories

13. Amos Rusie, 1889–1901 (243-160, .603)
14. Mordecai "Three-Finger" Brown, 1903–1916 (239-129, .649)
15. Charles "Chief" Bender, 1903–1925 (210-126, .625)
16. Rube Marquard, 1908–1925 (201-177, .532)
17. Jack Chesbro, 1899–1909 (198-132, .600)
18. Ed Walsh, 1904–1917 (195-126, .607)
19. Rube Waddell, 1897–1910 (191-145, .568)
20. Addie Joss, 1902–1910 (160-97, .623)

Examination of won-lost records or the number of total victories suggests, superficially at least, that several pitchers from the premodern era may well rank far ahead of Marichal on some sort of unofficial "all-time-greatest" list. Consider especially the following: Clarkson, Galvin, Johnson, Keefe, Mathewson, Nichols, Plank, Radbourn, Welch, and Cy Young all won over 300 games, a much less approachable number in the modern era. Certainly no argument is made here that Marichal is superior in overall accomplishment to Walter Johnson, Cy Young, Christy Mathewson, or even perhaps Rube Marquard. The claim is only that the game changed so significantly in favor of hitters after 1920 that comparison of pre–1920s and post–1920s pitchers, certainly by statistical analysis alone, is almost totally meaningless.

More meaningful comparisons can be made with pitchers assigned to the modern baseball era. And such comparisons reduce themselves cogently to a collection of charts and tables collected at chapter's end. Thirty-two Hall-of-Famers from the modern era are compared in first-order (won-lost percentage, SO-BB ratios) and second-order (hits, ERA, innings pitched, etc.) numerical categories. Such comparison allows us to appreciate in broader perspective the details and highlights (especially numerical highlights) of Juan Marichal's overall pitching career. The reader wishing to extend this analysis beyond the space allotted here (e.g., by rank-ordering 32 pitchers for each category) may easily do so by employment of such tables. A detailed analysis of statistical rankings for each of the other 31 Hall-of-Famers, each compared painstakingly to Marichal, might well prove an insightful and rewarding exercise for devoted fans of sabermetrics.

Careful analysis of recorded achievements for the game's outstanding pitchers thus lends new support to those who have argued less formally that Juan Marichal's position in Cooperstown is well earned and that his stature as premier pitcher (if not premier player) of Latin American origin is unchallenged. Careful comparisons of career totals for all 32 modern-era Hall-of-Fame hurlers (see charts on pages 54–55) appear to place Marichal, by the measures chosen, in tenth position among the game's greatest moundsmen. Feller, Ford, Grove, Koufax, Roberts, Seaver, Spahn, Palmer, and Gibson alone seem to merit higher rank by almost any imaginable combination of statistical standards. This honor roll of immortals consists of five right-handers and four lefties, leaving us with the conclusion that by loose statistical measure alone, Marichal remains one of baseball's six greatest right-handed pitchers from the post–1920 era.

Raw numbers can be twisted to demonstrate almost anything, and baseball analysis is no exception to this fundamental truth. Yet a careful examination of raw pitching data such as the one proposed here is never designed to achieve final and unchallenged rank-order of absolute greatness. It is intended only to underscore weighty evidence for the patently obvious: Juan Marichal was indisputably one of the dozen or fewer greatest hurlers ever to toil on a major league mound.

Several remarks are necessary about Marichal's relative stature when compared with the likes of Spahn, Hubbell, Dean, Grove, and a host of other immortals. In the crucial area of ERA (which for some is admittedly baseball's most overrated statistic, yet for others still a sacrosanct measure), only Ford, Koufax, Palmer, Seaver, Wilhelm, and relative unknown Stan Coveleski boast a better career number (the latter by a mere .01). Marichal's strikeout frequency rate (5.91 per nine innings pitched) is better than 21 of the 31 rival pitchers in the charts below; his ratio of 8.10 hits per nine innings worked again outpaces 19 of the 31 rival immortals; his superb walks ratio (fewest walks allowed per nine innings pitched) is matched only by Carl Hubbell and bested only by Robin Roberts. In shutouts, only Warren Spahn and Bob Gibson can equal or outstrip Marichal's stellar achievement; his feat of winning 20 or more games in six seasons again makes him superior to 24 of the 31 listed. And finally, as a strikeout artist of remarkable consistency, Marichal boasts six seasons of mowing down 200 or more batters; only Bob Gibson did any better (Koufax tied the Dominican Dandy for second).

Juan Marichal rates by this loosest of informal measures in tenth place among all Hall-of-Fame pitchers of the modern era – among those pitchers with whom he might be most reasonably compared. By the same loose measures, Sandy Koufax would seem to rank exactly one slot ahead of Marichal, ninth on the same all-time list. Little could fans have realized during that exciting National League summer 25 seasons ago that they were witnessing something more than two evenly matched wizards of the mound as they led their rival West Coast teams in a head-to-head pennant charge for the final time. They were also seeing two immortal titans that history would someday rank equally among the true elites, despite their comparably ill-starred careers and despite their respective losing battles against racial stereotype and nagging career misfortune.

Juan Marichal's inflammatory personality ("competitive" would perhaps be a more justifiable label) has long branded one of baseball's finest pitching artists with the burden of a hopelessly devalued reputation. One infamous baseball incident spawned by flawed judgment and forever symbolizing poor sportsmanship stands today more deeply engraved in the minds of many fans than years of impressive diamond achievement. This is truly the downside of baseball's amazing facility for collective memory and its resulting glorification of the isolated incident and the legendary single event. And to the degree that Marichal's career was not buried totally under this sheer media mountain of one unforgivable moment, his years of triumph and achievement were equally dimmed by the relentless glow of his surrounding teammates and rivals – the legendary Willie Mays, the imposing Willie McCovey, the implacable Bob Gibson, and the incomparable Sandy Koufax.

Comparison of Latin America's Best Pitchers

Leading Latin American Hurlers (32 Latin American pitchers winning 50 games or more, ranked by total games won) **through 1992 season only**

Pitcher	Yrs (Seasons)	W-L	Pct.	ERA	IP	SO	BB
Marichal, Juan[a]	1960–75(16)	243-142	.631	2.89	3,507.1	2,303	709
Marichal's Rank		**1st**	**1st**	**1st**	**1st**	**2nd**	**1st**
Tiant, Luís	1964–82(19)	229-172	.571	3.30	3,486.1	2,416	1,104
Luque, Adolfo	1914–35(20)	194-179	.520	3.24	3,220.1	1,130	918
Martínez, Dennis[b]	1976–92(17)	193-156	.553	3.62	3,159.1	1,693	926
Cuellar, Mike	1959–77(15)	185-130	.587	3.14	2,808	1,632	822
Pascual, Camilo	1954–71(18)	174-170	.506	3.63	2,930.2	2,167	1,069
Valenzuela, Fernando[b]	1980–91(12)	141-118	.544	3.34	2,355.1	1,764	918
Pizarro, Juan	1957–74(18)	131-105	.555	3.43	2,034.1	1,522	888
Andújar, Joaquín	1976–88(13)	127-118	.518	3.58	2,153	1,032	731
Ramos, Pedro	1955–70(15)	117-160	.422	4.08	2,355.2	1,305	724
Soto, Mario	1977–88(12)	100-92	.521	3.47	1,730	1,449	657
Higuera, Teddy[b]	1985–91(7)	92-56	.622	3.37	1,291.1	1,019	391
Seguí, Diego	1962–77(15)[c]	92-111	.453	3.81	1,807.2	1,298	786
Rijo, José[b]	1984–92(9)	83-68	.550	3.26	1,287.1	1,096	498
Figueroa, Ed	1974–81(8)	80-67	.544	3.51	1,309.2	571	443
Gómez, Rubén[b]	1953–67(10)	76-86	.469	4.09	1,454	677	574
DeLeon, José[b]	1983–92(10)	75-113	.399	3.73	1,697	1,422	745
Hernández, Guillermo	1977–89(13)[c]	70-63	.526	3.38	1,044.2	788	349
Borbón, Pedro	1969–80(12)[c]	69-39	.639	3.52	1,026.2	409	251
Berenguer, Juan[b]	1978–92(15)[c]	67-62	.519	3.90	1,205.1	975	604
Pérez, Pascual[b]	1980–91(11)	67-68	.496	3.44	1,244.1	822	344
Guzmán, José[b]	1985–92(6)	66-62	.516	3.90	1,013.2	715	395
Fornieles, Mike	1952–63(12)[c]	63-64	.496	3.96	1,156.2	576	421
López, Aurelio	1974–87(11)[c]	62-36	.633	3.56	910	635	367
Sosa, Elias	1972–83(12)[c]	59-51	.536	3.32	918	538	334
Pérez, Melido[b]	1987–92(6)	58-62	.483	3.90	971	791	398
Peña, Orlando	1958–75(14)[c]	56-77	.427	3.71	1,202	818	352
Martínez, Ramón[b]	1988–92(5)	52-37	.584	3.32	739.2	586	268
Consuegra, Sandy	1950–57(8)[c]	51-32	.614	3.37	809.1	193	246
Leal, Luís	1980–85(6)	51-58	.468	4.14	946	491	320
Carrasquel, Alex[b]	1939–49(8)	50-39	.562	3.73	861	252	347
Peña, Alejandro[b]	1981–92(12)[c]	50-48	.510	2.95	969	743	301

[a] = Hall-of-Famer; [b] = active pitcher; [c] = relief pitcher.

Primary Pitcher Statistics (post–1920 Hall-of-Famers)

Name	Yrs (Seasons)	Games	W	L	Pct.	SO	K/9	BB	BB/9
Marichal	1960–75 (16)	471	243	142	.631	2,303	5.91	709	1.82
Marichal's Rank		**26th**	**17th**	**10th**	**7th**	**11th**	**11th**	**3rd**	**2nd-T**
Coveleski	1912–28 (14)	450	215	142	.602	981	2.85	802	2.34
Dean	1930–47 (12)	317	150	83	.644	1,155	5.32	458	2.11
Drysdale	1956–69 (14)	518	209	166	.557	2,486	6.52	855	2.24
Faber	1914–33 (20)	669	254	212	.545	1,471	3.24	1,213	2.67
Feller	1936–56 (18)	570	266	162	.621	2,581	6.07	1,764	4.15
Fingers	1968–85 (17)	944	114	118	.491	1,299	6.87	492	2.60
Ford	1950–67 (16)	498	236	106	.690	1,956	5.55	1,086	3.37
Gibson	1959–75 (17)	528	251	174	.591	3,117	7.21	1,336	3.09
Gomez	1930–43 (14)	368	189	102	.649	1,468	5.28	1,095	3.90
Grimes	1916–34 (19)	615	270	212	.560	1,512	3.26	1,295	2.79
Grove	1925–41 (17)	616	300	140	.682	2,266	4.52	1,187	2.71
Haines	1918–37 (19)	555	210	158	.571	981	2.75	871	2.43
Hoyt	1918–38 (21)	675	237	182	.566	1,206	2.90	1,003	2.40
Hubbell	1928–43 (16)	535	253	154	.622	1,677	4.20	725	1.82
Hunter	1965–79 (15)	500	224	166	.574	2,012	5.25	954	2.49
Jenkins	1965–83 (19)	664	284	226	.557	3,192	6.38	997	1.99
Koufax	1955–66 (12)	397	165	87	.655	2,396	9.28	817	3.17
Lemon	1941–58 (15)	460	207	128	.618	1,277	4.27	1,251	3.94
Lyons	1923–46 (21)	594	260	230	.531	1,073	2.30	1,121	2.41
Newhouser	1939–55 (17)	488	207	150	.580	1,796	5.40	1,249	3.75
Palmer	1965–84 (19)	558	268	152	.638	2,212	5.04	1,311	2.98
Pennock	1912–34 (22)	617	241	162	.597	1,227	3.10	916	2.32
Perry	1962–83 (22)	777	314	265	.542	3,534	5.94	1,379	2.31
Rixey	1912–33 (21)	692	266	251	.515	1,350	2.70	1,082	2.17
Roberts	1948–66 (19)	676	286	245	.539	2,357	4.53	902	1.73
Ruffing	1924–47 (22)	624	273	225	.548	1,987	4.12	1,541	3.20
Seaver	1967–86 (20)	656	311	205	.603	3,640	6.85	1,390	2.61
Spahn	1942–65 (21)	750	363	245	.597	2,583	4.43	1,434	2.46
Vance	1915–35 (16)	442	197	140	.585	2,045	6.19	840	2.55
Wilhelm	1952–72 (21)	1,070	143	122	.540	1,610	6.40	778	3.11
Wynn	1939–63 (23)	691	300	244	.551	2,334	4.60	1,775	3.50

K/9 = strikeouts per nine innings pitched.
BB/9 = walks per nine innings pitched.

Secondary Pitcher Statistics (post–1920 Hall-of-Famers)

Name	Hits	Hits/9	ShOs	ERA	20W	200K	100BB	300+In	Inns
Marichal	3,153	8.10	52	2.89	6	6	0	4	3,506
Marichal's Rank	**13th**	**13th**	**6th**	**7th**	**6th-T**	**4th-T**	**1st-T**	**5th-T**	**19th**
Coveleski	3,055	8.87	38	2.88	5	0	0	3	3,092
Dean	1,921	8.85	26	3.04	4	0	1	3	1,966
Drysdale	3,084	8.09	49	2.95	2	6	0	4	3,432
Faber	4,104	9.04	29	3.15	4	0	0	3	4,087
Feller	3,271	7.69	46	3.25	6	5	9	3	3,828
Fingers	1,474	7.79	2	2.90	0	0	0	0	1,701
Ford	2,766	7.85	45	2.74	2	1	3	0	3,171
Gibson	3,279	7.59	56	2.91	5	9	3	2	3,884
Gomez	2,290	8.24	26	3.34	4	0	3	0	2,503
Grimes	4,406	9.49	35	3.52	5	0	2	5	4,179
Grove	3,849	8.74	35	3.06	8	1	2	0	3,940
Haines	3,460	9.71	23	3.64	3	0	0	2	3,207
Hoyt	4,037	9.66	25	3.59	2	0	0	0	3,762
Hubbell	3,461	8.67	36	2.98	5	0	0	4	3,591
Hunter	2,958	7.72	42	3.26	5	0	0	2	3,448
Jenkins	4,142	8.28	49	3.34	7	6	0	5	4,500
Koufax	1,754	6.79	40	2.76	3	6	2	3	2,325
Lemon	2,559	8.07	31	3.23	7	0	6	1	2,844
Lyons	4,486	9.65	27	3.67	3	0	1	1	4,162
Newhouser	2,674	8.04	33	3.06	4	2	7	2	2,993
Palmer	3,349	7.63	53	2.86	8	0	3	4	3,948
Pennock	3,990	9.87	35	3.60	2	0	0	0	3,558
Perry	4,938	8.30	53	3.11	5	8	1	6	5,350
Rixey	4,633	9.28	39	3.15	4	0	0	3	4,494
Roberts	4,582	8.79	45	3.40	6	0	0	6	4,689
Ruffing	4,294	8.40	47	3.80	4	0	3	0	4,342
Seaver	3,971	7.47	61	2.86	5	10	0	0	4,782
Spahn	4,830	8.28	63	3.09	13	0	2	2	5,246
Vance	2,809	8.51	30	3.24	3	3	1	1	2,967
Wilhelm	1,757	7.03	5	2.52	0	0	0	0	2,254
Wynn	4,291	8.46	49	3.54	5	0	8	0	4,566

Hits/9 = hits allowed per nine innings pitched.
ShOs = shutouts.
20W = number of seasons with 20 wins or more.
200K = number of seasons with 200 strikeouts or more.
100BB = number of seasons with 100 walks or more issued.
300+In = number of seasons with 300 or more innings pitched.
Inns = total innings pitched.

Cooperstown Pitcher Rankings (post–1920 Hall-of-Famers)

Modern Hall-of-Fame Pitchers with Better Records Than Marichal

(Ranked by total wins; all pitchers included here rank higher than Marichal in total wins, or [in the cases of Ford, and Koufax] in won-lost percentage.*)

1. Warren Spahn (363-245 .597)
2. Tom Seaver (311-205 .603)
3. Robert "Lefty" Grove (300-140, .682)
4. Robin Roberts (286-245, .539)
5. Jim Palmer (268-152, .638)
6. Bob Feller (266-162, .621)
7. Bob Gibson (251-174, .591)
8. Whitey Ford (236-106, .690)*
9. Sandy Koufax (165-87, .655)*
10. **Juan Marichal (243-142 .631)**

* = fewer wins but higher pct.

Modern Hall-of-Fame Pitchers with Lesser Records Than Marichal

(Ranked by total wins; all pitchers on this list rank below Marichal in total wins and/or won-lost percentage.**)

11. Gaylord Perry (314-265, .542)**
12. Early Wynn (300-244, .551)**
13. Ferguson Jenkins (284-226, .557)**
14. Red Ruffing (273-225, .548)**
15. Burleigh Grimes (270-212, .560)**
16. Eppa Rixey (266-251, .515)**
17. Ted Lyons (260-230, .531)**
18. Urban Faber (254-212, .545)**
19. Carl Hubbell (253-154, .622)**
20. Herb Pennock (241-162, .598)
21. Waite Hoyt (237-182, .566)
22. Jim "Catfish" Hunter (224-166, .574)
23. Stan Coveleski (215-142, .602)
24. Jesse Haines (210-158, .571)
25. Don Drysdale (209-166, .557)
26. Bob Lemon (207-128, .618)
27. Hal Newhouser (207-150, .580)
28. Dazzy Vance (197-140, .585)
29. Lefty Gomez (189-102, .649)***
30. Dizzy Dean (150-83, .644)***
31. Hoyt Wilhelm (143-122, .540)
32. Rollie Fingers (114-118, .491)

** more wins but lower pct.
*** slightly higher pct. but many fewer wins

Top Thirteen Hall-of-Famers (All Eras) by Winning Percentage

1.	Whitey Ford	.690
2.	Robert "Lefty" Grove	.682
	(Juan Marichal*	**.670**)
3.	Christy Mathewson	.665
4.	Sandy Koufax	.655
5.	Three-Finger Brown	.649 (tie) (239 wins)
5.	Lefty Gomez	.649 (tie) (189 wins)
7.	John Clarkson	.648
8.	Dizzy Dean	.644
9.	Pete Alexander	.642
10.	Kid Nichols	.641
11.	Jim Palmer	.638
12.	Joe McGinnity	.632
13.	**Juan Marichal**	**.631**

*Marichal (221-109) before 1972 back injury

Notes

1. "Sabermetrics" is simply a new coinage for the long-practiced statistical analysis of baseball. Followers of Bill James who have popularized the term and in the process brought new respectability to baseball "figure filberts" are thus inheritors of a tradition that stems back as far as Henry Chadwick, inventor of the box score. What distinguishes the **sabermetrics** movement is replacement of more traditional measures of performance (e.g., batting average for hitters, earned run average for pitchers, fielding average for defensive players, etc.) with more sophisticated and (perhaps) more revealing yardsticks: run productivity average, pitching runs (determining the run contributions of pitchers), fielding runs, pitcher park factors, relative batting average, batting runs, adjusted batting runs, batting wins, and total player rating, among numerous others. The best introduction to the topic is John Thorn's defining essay ("Sabermetrics") in *Total Baseball* (1993, third edition).

2. Tables of comparison for Hall-of-Fame pitchers and methods employed in this chapter for assessing Marichal's career performance were first suggested to me by Dominican baseball expert Dr. José de Jesús Jiménez. The precise tables and methodology have been expanded and altered from those originally prosed by Dr. Jiménez; nonetheless, I remain indebted to this long-active SABR member for the foregoing approach and for numerous other insights and materials regarding Marichal and Dominican baseball history.

Selected Marichal Reading List

Bjarkman, Peter C. and José DeJesus, Jr. "Marichal the Magnificent." In *The National Pastime: A Review of Baseball History* 11 (1992), 83–84. (The coauthor of this article is actually José de Jesús Jiménez, whose name was inadvertently printed incorrectly by the journal's editor.)

*Devaney, John. *Juan Marichal, Mister Strike.* New York: Putnam, 1970.

Einstein, Charles. "The Juan Marichal Mystery." *Sport* 35 (June 1963): 48–51.

________. "Juan Marichal at the Crossroads." *Sport* 45 (April 1968): 58–61.

Jupiter, Harry. "Juan Marichal's Hard Fight to Redeem Himself." *Sport* 41 (June 1966): 30–33.

Lauletta, Michael. "Juan Marichal: A Man in Many Shadows." In *Baseball Digest* 29 (June 1970): 31–36.

Marichal, Juan (as told to Charles Einstein). *A Pitcher's Story.* Garden City, New York: Doubleday, 1967.

Ruck, Rob. "Juan Marichal: Baseball in the Dominican Republic." In *Baseball History 3: An Annual of Original Baseball Research,* edited by Peter Levine. Westport, Connecticut: Meckler, 1990, 49–70.

Stump, Al. "Juan Marichal: Behind His Success." *Sport* 38 (September 1964): 84–95.

* = Juvenile Biography

CHAPTER 3

Roberto Clemente, Hero of an Island Nation

> Now it's too late to tell him there were things he did on a ball field that made me wish I was Shakespeare. —Phil Musick

He may have been the most exciting baseball player ever. The sight of Roberto Clemente tearing headlong around the base paths legging out an extra-base hit was as thrilling an image as any moment from baseball's long and drama-filled history. Clemente played the outfield with pure recklessness yet also with incomparable grace and unique style. His cannonlike throwing arm, the arm that had first attracted legions of big-league scouts to the barrios of San Juan when Clemente was a youngster of 17, is unmatched in the game's history. Only Jackie Robinson ran the bases in comparable fashion, and perhaps only Willie Mays played the outfield with the same flair. Yet neither of these other two great black heroes of the same diamond era—the fabulous 1950s and tumultuous 1960s—was as mysterious or transfixing a figure as Roberto Clemente Walker, baseball star from the island nation of Puerto Rico.

Some fans and baseball historians may even argue that Clemente was the best natural ballplayer ever to play the game, clearly the best among a new and exciting breed of Latin American athletes entering baseball in record numbers during the two decades immediately following World War II. Certainly his brilliant achievements lend considerable weight to such an argument. He was, after all, only the eleventh player in baseball history to reach the magic total of 3,000 career base hits, and only eight more (Kaline, Rose, Yastrzemski, Carew, Brock, Yount, Winfield and Brett) have scaled this lofty peak since Clemente disappeared from the scene almost two decades ago. At the time his marvelous career tragically ended, he was the all-time Pittsburgh Pirates leader in games played, at-bats, hits, singles, total bases, and RBIs. And this was for a proud baseball franchise that had boasted such Hall-of-Famers and immortal batsmen as Honus Wagner, Clarence Beaumont, Paul and Lloyd Waner, Arky Vaughan, Ralph Kiner, Matty Alou, and Willie Stargell. He had won four National League batting titles, including the first-ever by a player born in Latin America. He had starred in two World Series triumphs and dominated all hitters in the 1971 series with a .414 batting average. He had played in more than a dozen All-Star Games (still holding a record for most putouts by an outfielder in a single All-Star Game with six in 1967) and achieved countless other awards and distinctions during the forgotten baseball decade that seemingly played second fiddle to Vietnam and the British rock invasion.

No other Latin American player before or since has achieved such numbers or demanded such recognition, though Clemente himself always thought the personal recognition he achieved was all too slow in coming, as it always seemed to be for those of his race and Hispanic background. By the time a brilliant playing career was over, however, Clemente would undeniably make them all take more than just passing notice—those devoted fans and those skeptical critics alike. Eleven short weeks after his untimely death in a tragic plane crash on December 31, 1972, it was announced that Roberto Clemente had become the first ballplayer of Latin American birthright to achieve the special brand of immortality garnered by election into baseball's most honored circle—the big-league Hall of Fame in Cooperstown, New York.

Some baseball fans today remain less than fully informed about the career achievements and special qualities of this exceptional man who was Latin America's first true baseball hero. For it was one of the many misfortunes of Roberto Clemente's baseball career that he played most of his years during a decade largely lost to baseball history. The sixties had ushered in a 10-year span when baseball for the first and perhaps only time fell from unrivaled prominence as the nation's favorite pastime. Television and national attitudes during the Vietnam years conspired to elevate the more warlike game of football as the nation's favored sport. Baseball (at least for those who did not watch Clemente play) had become too slow for the people's taste. And after baseball's offensive explosions of the 1950s, when home runs in record numbers sailed out of tiny ballparks like Ebbets Field in Brooklyn and Crosley Field in Cincinnati, pitchers seemingly took over the game lock, stock, and barrel as the decade of the 1960s evolved. Once defense began to dominate and runs were few, fan interest seemed to disappear just about as quickly as home runs and high scores had vanished from the scoreboard.

An additional element has worked to diminish somewhat unfairly the baseball legend that was Roberto Clemente. From the beginning, rightly or wrongly—and often, in part at least, of his own doing—this proud man carried with him an undeserved reputation as a moody ballplayer, an uncooperative athlete in his dealings with both press and public, and even something of a hypochondriac, one who fakes illness and pretends injury to avoid the challenges of competition. In his relationship with the working baseball press, some even saw Roberto Clemente as an often sullen man, one prone to spurning and even antagonizing those baseball writers assigned to follow the Pittsburgh team. The injuries that plagued Clemente's career were real enough, however, and they made his playing achievements even more spectacular over the long haul. And a penchant for moodiness had its clear and justifiable causes. In joining the big leagues, the young Clemente had walked unsuspectingly into a brave new world that showed little tolerance for a black man from Puerto Rico, especially one who spoke only hesitating English and was often confused by North American customs. His fierce pride and burning drive to excel were predictably met time and again by what the young and naive athlete could only assess as a lack of attention, perhaps motivated (at least as Clemente saw it) by racial prejudice and stereotype.

Yet Clemente battled against all these obstacles ceaselessly throughout his two-decade baseball career, almost always demonstrating unmatched grace and dignity. In the end this proud son of the islands would not be repelled from displaying for all the world his great athletic skills and rare compassion. Roberto Clemente would finally etch his star into the firmament, clearly visible to everyone both stateside and at home who would make the effort to see.

But the struggle was never easy for this poor son of a Puerto Rican sugarcane worker, and Clemente's life was as marred by tragedy as it was graced by the glories he would achieve on the baseball diamond, even from the earliest days in his humble native village of Carolina, Puerto Rico. There was, first, the painful death of a beloved brother at the very moment when his big-league career was about to leave the launching pad. There was, almost simultaneously with the shocking loss of his brother, the near-disastrous auto accident that left Clemente alive and uncrippled yet saddled with an unnecessary injury that would slow and plague his career in future years. There were, time and time again, the misunderstandings with management surrounding his lack of playing time, first in the Puerto Rican winter leagues and then in his debut minor league season at Montreal. On several occasions Clemente even came dangerously close to giving up the game he loved and played with such passion. There was also the nagging physical pain he constantly played with—first the ceaseless back problems which stretched across his entire career, then a career-threatening arm injury in April 1958 that left his cannonlike right limb limp and useless, then a debilitating leg injury during winter-league play in 1965, followed almost immediately by bouts with malaria and a paratyphoid infection that same spring. And there was always the emotional pain of a sensitive ballplayer who was isolated from his teammates and opponents by language barriers and skin color throughout his early big-league years, then pained repeatedly by a seeming lack of deserved recognition throughout his latter seasons.

Finally, for all those fans and admirers and friends who remained after he was gone, there were the tragic realities surrounding his seemingly unnecessary and shocking death. It was the latter set of tortuous circumstances that remained the most difficult to accept for so many of his admiring countrymen and friends inside and outside the baseball community. For Roberto Clemente would ironically die as he had lived, sacrificing his personal energies and private off-season hours to the cause of helping less fortunate Latin American countrymen he would never know yet felt compelled to champion. Each winter, when the grueling baseball season was over and the exhausted megastar had returned to his native Puerto Rico to nurse a multitude of injuries and rest for the coming season, there were endless demands that accompanied his status as a national hero – charity events to attend, winter-league games before the hometown fans of San Juan who longed to see him play, thousands of visitors who crowded his home night and day as though it were a public museum. Thus it was no different on the New Year's weekend of 1972–1973 when Clemente had taken it upon himself to direct personally a relief mission of mercy to the earthquake-torn nation of Nicaragua, an ill-fated exercise in charity that would snuff out his life in a still-unexplained plane crash from which his body would never be recovered.

The "Boys of Summer" Brooklyn Dodgers teams of the late 1940s and early 1950s had a reputation as lamentable losers – a lovable ballclub the local faithful dubbed "Bums" and one that for years made a habit of losing World Series battles with the crosstown rival Yankees. But baseball legends are often more the stuff of myth then reality, and this was a Brooklyn team that was anything but a lamentable loser. This Brooklyn ballclub of Reese, Snider, Robinson, Campanella, and Hodges was perhaps the most successful decade-long juggernaut in senior-circuit history. The Dodgers of this era simply did not make many errors, either on the field or in the front office. It is one of baseball's rich ironies, therefore, that it was these Brooklyn Dodgers who would commit perhaps the single biggest front-office blunder of the entire baseball epoch, an error in judgment involving their handling of a young Puerto Rican superstar to whom they had won bidding rights in the winter of early 1954. And it was an even more delectable irony that the beneficiary of this management error would be none other than the floundering Pirates of Pittsburgh, at the time baseball's most hapless franchise, a ballclub that until young Roberto Clemente came along, couldn't seem to do much of anything right.

It was the local Brooklyn bird dog Pedrín Zorrilla who first spotted young Clemente's unlimited baseball talent and signed the precocious youngster to play winter-league baseball in his native Puerto Rico. A gangly youth from the San Anton barrio of Carolina, Clemente had first learned his baseball skills as a shortstop with the local rice factory softball team, organized and managed by part-time high school teacher Roberto Marín. Soon he had been recruited by the local Juncos team for the island's AA amateur baseball league. Marín, sensing how marketable might be the raw athletic skills of this extraordinary local teenager, had approached Zorrilla, owner of the winter-league Santurce ballclub and one of the most respected baseball men in Puerto Rico. Zorrilla had first balked at Marín's glowing reports about Clemente, even passing up several trips to see the young phenom play. When he finally did observe Clemente, somewhat by accident, however, in an exhibition game against the local Manati ballclub near Zorrilla's plush country home, it took the veteran part-time Dodger scout only moments to recognize his sudden good fortune. Clemente banged out a long triple and two doubles and impressed as well with an eye-popping throw that nailed an enemy runner at third—easily enough fireworks to convince the astute Zorrilla to offer a winter-league trial contract (reportedly for a $400 bonus and $45 a week). But the underaged 16-year-old would be officially signed up only when his father, Don Melchor Clemente, could be convinced that this was indeed a fair enough offer for his son's precocious ballplaying talents. With Don Melchor holding out for a slightly better deal, the Santurce club finally agreed to part with a $500 bonus, a $60 weekly salary, and a spanking-new fielder's mitt as well for its sterling prospect.

The winter-league seasons of 1952 through 1954 with the Santurce Crabbers offered the first opportunity for young Roberto to test adequately his apparently extraordinary baseball skills. Yet Clemente's maiden winter seasons with Santurce were certainly not ones of limitless success and joy; if anything, they were the first true test of patience for a rising young star who would constantly meet frustration and rejection along the rocky road to major league baseball stardom. At first the raw youngster had to wait his turn in line, and Roberto was not at all comfortable with waiting. Zorrilla was unwilling to insert a 17-year-old fresh from the amateur league into a lineup boasting not only young New York Giants star Willie Mays but outfielders like Bob Thurman and Willard Brown, two of the big leagues' earliest black players. Clemente silently fumed at so much inactivity during his first professional season, and it was his friend and earliest coach, Roberto Marín, who had to dissuade the talented benchwarmer from brashly quitting on more than one occasion.

Yet when Clemente did play, he played brilliantly, and big-league scouts were not long in beating a well-worn path to his doorstep. Most ardent were the Dodgers of Brooklyn and the Giants of New York, followed a mere half step by the Braves of Milwaukee plus the National League Cardinals and American League Yankees. Zorrilla, perhaps inspired by visions of Mays and Clemente remaining in the same outfield together, quietly urged Giants owner Horace Stoneham to bid wildly for the youngster, but Stoneham reportedly turned a deaf ear, contending that his scouts feared Clemente would strike out too much against disciplined big-league pitching. Dodger scouting director Al Campanis had done his homework far more thoroughly than Stoneham, however, and thus rushed in to offer a $10,000 signing bonus, to which the stunned and ecstatic Clemente immediately made a verbal commitment. No Latin player had been offered such a bonus before; future Dominican Hall-of-Famer Juan Marichal would later be given only $500 to sign with the Giants. Once committed to Brooklyn, there was no looking back, despite the fact that the Milwaukee club was willing to offer as much as $30,000 for his services only hours later. Roberto had promised his signature to Brooklyn, and even as an untutored teenager, the youngest son of Don Melchor and Luisa Walker Clemente was an honorable man of his word. Soon Clemente would have the chance to prove what he was already confident of, that he could play professional baseball with the best of them and that he belonged next to his heroes Willie Mays and Monte Irvin, patrolling the same outfields and smashing base hits in the big leagues.

Clemente's experience with manager Max Macon, skipper of the Dodgers' top farm club in Montreal, which began in the spring of 1954, was only more of the same, however. For the impatient Puerto Rican *wunderkind*, determined that he was now ready to play on an everyday basis in the big time, Montreal provided perhaps the greatest "character trial" in a career filled with continual crises and setbacks. The Dodgers, it turned out, had no intention of playing their raw recruit regularly in Montreal because of a complex "bonus baby rule" then in effect throughout the major leagues. This rule provided that any first-year player signed for a bonus of more than $4,000 and sent directly to the minors had to remain with his minor league club a full season. To keep such a prospect tied to its organization, the parent club then had to promote him directly to their major league roster at the end of his rookie campaign. Otherwise, the prospect would be available for drafting by other major league clubs. Since Brooklyn did not foresee having a space for Clemente by spring 1955, their only hope for retaining the rookie was to keep his play hidden from other talent-thin ballclubs. Yet as one writer has observed, how could the Dodgers ever realistically hope to hide such a rare diamond in a field of broken bottles?

Pittsburgh's superscout Clyde Sukeforth and Bucs general manager Branch Rickey were soon shadowing Clemente's every action in Montreal, even if the youngster was not getting much playing time and even if there was little hope of his awesome talents being showcased on the Brooklyn farm team. The strange bonus rule was in large part responsible for the actions of the Brooklyn team in not playing Roberto. So, more than likely, were the subtle racial factors that still marred the game of baseball. The Dodgers already sported a number of black regulars (Campanella, Robinson, Amoros, and Gilliam plus pitchers Newcombe and Joe Black) in their everyday lineup and were probably loath to risk promoting still another. But whatever the reasons, Clemente was quickly benched when he hit, then ironically kept in the lineup when he slumped badly. He got into 87 games over the full summer, and in many of those his role was limited to late-inning pinch-hitting stints or brief defensive appearances.

Another Pirate official, Howie Haak, a veteran talent bloodhound who had long recruited Latin American players and spoke fluent Spanish, was also assigned to tail Clemente in Montreal and around the International League circuit. Haak at one point even talked young Clemente into not quitting the Montreal team, thus blowing his only true opportunity for escaping the grip of the Dodger organization and opening up the possibility of an eventual big-league career. When Clemente's frustration boiled over at season's end and he threatened to leave the Montreal ballclub on the eve of the International League playoffs, it was Haak who visited the youngster's hotel room and reminded him that quitting would violate the provisions of the bonus rule and allow the Dodgers to hold on to his contract for yet another season. Thus Clemente would forfeit his best opportunity at regular play in the majors, and the Pirates would see their golden moment slipping away. That moment for the Pittsburghers came at last on November 22, 1954, the annual winter draft of bonus players left unprotected by big-league clubs. The Pirates, who had once again finished last, had thus earned their expected first pick and did not hesitate in snatching the Puerto Rican outfielder they had coveted all summer long.

The tactical move went little noticed and created little stir in the press at the time, yet it was one of truly earthshaking proportions. Rickey's tenacious scouting would henceforth rob the Brooklyn faithful, and National League fans in rival cities everywhere, of seeing what might well have been the best outfield ever assembled. Brooklyn's fans could now only dream wistfully of cheering the graceful Duke Snider, the nimble Bob Clemente, and the rifle-armed Carl Furillo, together in Ebbets Field outfield pastures and all dressed proudly in royal Brooklyn Dodger blue.

Brooklyn's lost gamble was seemingly Clemente's fortuitous gain. News of his good fortune came swiftly to Puerto Rico, but Clemente's apparent upswing in luck was quickly dimmed by deep personal tragedy. In mid-December 1954 Roberto's oldest brother Luís lay gravely ill in a San Juan hospital suffering from what had been diagnosed as an untreatable brain tumor. Only days later, on New Year's Eve, the eldest Clemente son would suddenly expire from his illness. The early passing of Luís Clemente fell with horrible irony 18 years to the day before the youngest child of the clan, Roberto, would lose his life to untimely tragedy. Then there was the career-threatening and even life-threatening automobile accident in which Roberto was involved. Barely more than a week after the close of the 1954 baseball season, the young ballplayer had visited his dying brother's bedside for the first time in months. As he left the hospital that day, his car was struck broadside at 60 miles an hour by an automobile with a drunken driver at the wheel. While Roberto miraculously escaped this near-fatal incident with life and limb intact, he suffered the severe and persistent spinal damage that would haunt the remainder of his baseball playing career over the next two decades.

Opening day of the baseball season is always a time for renewed hope. Spring is the season of rebirth and reawakening, and for the local big-league team and its fans there is always fresh anticipation of an exciting pennant race. When the 1955 baseball campaign began in Pittsburgh, however, long-suffering Bucco fans had little reason to expect any great changes in what had become an unbreakable legacy of regular losing and uninspired baseball play. For three consecutive seasons (and four summers out of five) the Pittsburghers had been buried deep in the league cellar. The team had not risen above fourth since 1944 when they had finished second, and the last Pittsburgh pennant had come way back in 1927, the year of the Murderer's Row Yankees and of Babe Ruth's 60 home runs, long before most current Pirate fans were born.

Yet one bright spot at the outset of the 1955 baseball summer—perhaps the only one to be anticipated in Pittsburgh that season—was the dramatic debut of 20-year-old Puerto Rican sensation Roberto Clemente, an unknown and untested outfield talent only recently spirited away from the Dodger organization through the mysterious 1954 fall minor league player draft. When the young Clemente first stepped into the batter's box at Forbes Field on Sunday, April 17, facing promising Dodgers left-hander Johnny Podres, he rapped out a sharp infield grounder too hot to be cleanly handled by Brooklyn shortstop Pee Wee Reese. Moments later he would score on Frank Thomas's long triple, and before the Sunday doubleheader was over, the novice Clemente would register three base hits (one a double) in his stellar National League debut. To prove that his first afternoon's work with the lumber was no fluke, Clemente smacked an inside-the-park homer against veteran hurler Don Liddle the very next day at New York's storied Polo Grounds, a decisive blow he followed with a resounding triple in his third Pittsburgh outing the following day.

Clemente's major league debut was one of the most impressive in the long memories of veteran Pittsburgh baseball watchers. By week's end, the promising rookie had recorded eight base hits and several fine fielding gems in six game appearances, and he was still smashing the ball at a lofty .360 clip, seventh best in the league for the week-old season. It was indeed an auspicious beginning, even if the most significant features of young Clemente's batting style had already immediately become apparent to the league's opposing pitchers. Like many free-swinging Latin American batsmen of the decade, Clemente would apparently swing at nearly any pitch, and more often than not he somehow connected. Rarely before had the big leagues seen such a notorious badball hitter. But Clemente displayed another weakness in the batter's box beyond his wide strike zone, which seemed to extend (in the words of one wag) from the first-base to the third-base dugouts; he also bobbed his head so violently when he swung that he took his eyes completely off the ball.

Thus despite the promise of his first full week in the big leagues, Clemente's batting style exposed glaring weaknesses, and his legend as a direct consequence was to be painfully slow in blossoming. He would hit only .255 by the time his first season was over, and as exciting as his free-swinging style might be for untutored bleacherites, it was a constant source of travail for the Pirate brain trust. The Buccos soon had Hall-of-Fame hitter George Sisler (then a Pittsburgh batting instructor) assigned to work overtime with Clemente to improve his untutored approach to hitting. At first the experiment proved moderately successful, and Clemente's sophomore campaign saw his average soar to .311 and his strikeouts sharply decline. But the real culprit for the fleet-footed outfielder seemed to be personal injuries, and a stellar second season was followed by a disastrous and frustrating third summer for the struggling young Clemente. While he had shown flashes of brilliance, he had hardly moved into a class with his idol and old winter-league teammate, Willie Mays, or his childhood hero, Monte Irvin. At the end of three full seasons (the very winter when the Dodgers and Giants both moved west), Roberto Clemente was anything but an established big-league star.

The Pirates team Bob Clemente joined in spring training of 1955 was a ballclub desperately needing a lifesaving transfusion of new baseball blood. Skippered by soft-spoken Fred Haney, this team would finish dead last in 1955 and 1956 and then improve only enough (after Haney's departure) to tie the hapless Chicago Cubs for the bottom rung in 1957. Clemente's team also experienced a revolving turnstile of managers during his first few seasons in the Steel City. First there was veteran Haney, who directed the bench briefly (1955) during Roberto's rookie campaign; next came the erratic Bobby Bragan for only a slightly longer spell (1956–1957); and finally Danny Murtaugh arrived on the scene 104 games into the 1957 pennant chase. None of these regular managerial changes had noticeable impact on the Pirates' predictably inept play, however.

The disasters that pockmarked the first few Clemente summers in Pittsburgh were about to take a sudden and unexpected turn for the better. The young star was soon called to military duty at the conclusion of the 1957 season, and a six-month stay with the U.S. Marines had one quite unexpected payoff. The stint on active military duty, among other things, seemingly did wonders for Clemente's ailing back. And when the 1958 baseball campaign got under way, the Pirates team was also somehow miraculously revived for its continuing tour of duty in the National League. In one of the tightest pennant races in league history, the inspired Pittsburgh team held fast to the pace set by the San Francisco Giants and Milwaukee Braves, refusing to fold down the stretch. By summer's end the talented Braves behind Spahn, Aaron, and Mathews had finally prevailed, but the Bucs were solidly entrenched in second, a legitimate pennant contender for the first time in almost a full generation of baseball seasons.

Clemente still battled repeated injury and persistent pain. In an April 30 game against Los Angeles a snap throw from deep in the outfield brought immediate pain to his arm, and suddenly a new injury was born. For the next several seasons the arm seemed to "hang to the ground," and Roberto threw hard only when he absolutely had to. Early in the 1959 chase an errant pitch would strike the elbow of the same arm, further incapacitating the injury-plagued outfielder. But despite these new and debilitating physical trials, Clemente remained in the lineup for 140 games during the 1958 season, perhaps inspired as much as anything by the Buccos' sudden and unexpected newfound successes in the won-lost column. And a continuously sore arm did not prevent him from throwing accurately enough to record a league-leading 22 outfield assists.

The excitement Roberto Clemente generated in his earliest National League seasons was in the end not simply a matter of his explosive bat and his daring base-path play. Few players had ever created such excitement while playing the outfield. Clemente loved to throw as much as he lived to hit, and upon his arrival in Pittsburgh he had quickly developed a pet play that would terrorize league runners from the mid–1950s on. When batters ripped singles to right and then incautiously swung too widely around first base, Clemente would suddenly rifle throws to first baseman Dale Long (later to Dick Stuart), nailing the embarrassed base runner far off the bag. He also specialized in cutting down runners who dared to attempt advancing from first to third on base hits into Clemente's right-field territory. If not yet an established offensive star, which he would become soon enough during the upcoming 1960s, by the conclusion of the resurgent 1958 Pittsburgh campaign Roberto Clemente had already supplanted Dodger Carl Furillo as the most feared outfield arm in baseball.

Roberto Clemente's personal performance during his first five major league seasons—spread across the second half of one of baseball's most glorious decades, the 1950s—was a display of considerable glory and accomplishment. This was the unforgettable era of such fence-busting sluggers and flawless flychasers as Willie Mays, Mickey Mantle, Duke Snider, Stan Musial, and Hank Aaron, yet none displayed more flash than the young strong-armed Puerto Rican outfielder who performed valiantly for Pittsburgh. Clemente was a major factor, if not the sole factor, in reviving a moribund Pirates team, one of the worst in baseball when he arrived. In but half a decade he was leading his rejuvenated teammates to the top of the National League standings. He had quickly proved one of the most dramatic young stars of a star-filled era, had led both leagues in assists for outfielders in 1958, already batted at or around .300 for three of his five seasons, and proved one of the most dangerous if streaky hitters in professional baseball.

But the glories that came Clemente's way during his earliest seasons did not quite measure up to what this proud Puerto Rican ballplayer had hoped for or expected from his flashy style of play. Personal triumphs seemed always to be dulled by private tragedy; hot streaks were interspersed like clockwork with frustrating batting slumps; the cheers of fans were more than matched by the resounding silence of the baseball press and Pirate team officials; unlimited adulation back home in Puerto Rico was balanced with lukewarm reception in Pittsburgh and around the National League circuit. Roberto Clemente was clearly driven from his first winter-league seasons in Puerto Rico with a burning desire to prove that he not only belonged in the big leagues but could play this game as well as any of the white-skinned superstars of North America, the heroes of his baseball childhood who had once intimidated him as a child on the streets of Carolina but did so no longer when he lined up alongside them in the National League ballparks. But for all his base hits and brilliant fielding plays, no one seemed to pay that much attention to the young and talented Bob Clemente.

This mixture of frustration and triumph, hot victory and cold disappointment, adulation and misunderstanding, that seemed to plague Clemente's personal life and early baseball career was nowhere more evident and more distressing (for Clemente at least) than in those events that surrounded the 1960 National League season in Pittsburgh. On the surface and certainly in the hindview of history, 1960 was a true banner year for the Pittsburgh franchise and everyone associated with it. After a near miss at the pennant in 1958 (eight games behind Milwaukee, in second place) and a slight falter in 1959 (fourth place but only nine games out), the 1960 Pirates edition accomplished nothing short of a miracle—the return of baseball glory to a city that had not enjoyed a winner in 33 long summers. The 1960 Pirates, keyed by the brilliant hitting of their now well-established Puerto Rican star right-fielder and the offensive prowess of stellar shortstop

Dick Groat, burst from the gate in April and May and coasted the rest of the way to their first National League flag since the distant summer of 1927, the season a full generation earlier when Babe Ruth had socked out his immortal record of 60 home runs.

Clemente played a major role in the newfound successes of a revamped champion Pirates club that charged home at season's end with 95 victories, seven full games ahead of the runner-up Milwaukee Braves. He enjoyed his most productive offensive year to date, recording the Bucs' second-best batting average (.314, behind Dick Groat's league-leading .325) and second most home runs (16, behind Dick Stuart's 25), and leading all Bucco batters with 94 crucial RBIs. He also continued to shine brilliantly on defense, again pacing the circuit in assists for outfielders (19) and repeatedly making spectacular plays that turned near losses into miraculous hard-fought victories.

But all was not celebration for a disillusioned Puerto Rican star playing for a championship team in the Steel City. If Clemente's brilliant career was somewhat lost to the decade he played in, it had also been diminished by another factor. It was his lot to play out an entire baseball career in the sleepy industrial town of Pittsburgh and not in the celebrity-rich media meccas that were New York, Chicago, or Los Angeles. And he played for a team that labored throughout much of the decade buried in the middle of the National League pack, drawing little media following and sparse fan attention.

Only twice, for example, did Clemente have an opportunity to showcase his talent on the glitzy stage that is baseball's World Series. The first of these occasions, at the beginning of the decade, was one he was all too ready to exploit, yet the events of October 1960 surrounding the Pirates' first World Series visit in over three decades were destined to be as much a personal disappointment for Roberto Clemente as they were an unbounded joy to local Pittsburgh fans and his Pirate teammates. While Roberto continued to do everything with bat and glove that could be expected of him, it was seemingly not enough to attract the attention he richly deserved. He batted .310, fielded flawlessly, and hit safely in every game, yet these were quiet feats overshadowed in the media by Bill Mazeroski's team-leading .320 average and especially Maz's dramatic series-winning homer during a seven-game upset of the vaunted New York Yankees. This World Series, in the public eye at least, clearly belonged to the clutch-hitting Mazeroski, not the flashy Clemente.

A second chance, at the outset of the following decade, would therefore be one Clemente would have to seize with a burning passion and even a reckless desperation in the face of one final opportunity to make good. By the end of the 1971 World Series, the whole world would finally know of Roberto Clemente and his remarkable talents. At the close of that second series, one of the most memorable and dramatic of baseball history, the Clemente legend had been finally and forever born. But at the conclusion of the 1960 fall classic, things were far different. Pittsburgh deliriously celebrated its first world title in a generation. Far away in San Juan, however, a confused young Pirate outfielder struggled to understand what increasingly seemed to be a mixed fate.

And despite the first flush of true success, wintertime in balmy Puerto Rico was to bring only further disappointment on the heels of Clemente's most successful baseball campaign to date. When league honors were announced for Most Valuable Player, an award Clemente seemed to covet as a symbol of his acceptance and success in a world seemingly hostile to those of dark skin who spoke with a Spanish tongue, it was not Roberto but Pittsburgh teammate Dick Groat who was the runaway winner. Groat, of course, was arguably a reasonable choice as the league batting champ, yet Pirate Don Hoak with a brilliant glove but lackluster .282 average was a shocking surprise with his second-place finish in the balloting. That Clemente was all the way down in eighth place was the biggest shock of all, however. It was not so much that Clemente had not won the award. Far more disappointing to the proud Pirate as he read the results of the sportswriters' tally in the local San Juan press was the fact that he received so few votes and finished so far out of the running. All in all, it could only be taken as yet another signal that no one seemed to be paying much attention to a black ballplayer from the islands.

Characteristically, Clemente's personal reaction to such a snub was simply to return to the baseball wars in Pittsburgh with a renewed (even hypercharged) dedication and determination to excel. He would simply make the fans and press sit up and take notice once and for all if it was the last thing he did and at whatever the cost to his battered and injury-prone body. And what followed (a deserved payoff seemingly for such bitter determination) was the most brilliant stretch of his career, or perhaps just about any National League career in decades past or future. For it was in 1961, while Maris assaulted Ruth in the junior circuit, that Roberto finally established himself as a true senior-circuit superstar. His average soared to a lofty .351, and he became the first Latin American to capture a National League batting crown. He scored 100 runs and rapped over 200 hits for the first time in his career. He was among the league pacesetters in both hits (seven behind Vada Pinson of Cincinnati) and total bases (he stood fifth). If the Pirates sagged badly to a sixth-place finish in 1961 immediately on the heels of their surprising 1960 successes, it certainly was not Roberto Clemente's doing.

The best news for Pirate fanatics was that this was only the explosive beginning of Clemente's revenge upon his critics and naysayers. A renewed onslaught on league hurlers would bring six more consecutive seasons of batting averages above .300 (10 of 11 between 1960 and 1970); three more batting titles in 1964, 1965, and 1967; and long-overdue recognition as National League MVP in 1966 (ironically, the only season in a run of four that found the Pittsburgh slugger without a hitting title). That Clemente won but one MVP crown during a decade he dominated so thoroughly (no other National Leaguer has won four batting titles in a decade save Rogers Hornsby in the 1920s, Stan Musial in the '50s and Honus Wagner in the first decade of the century) has perhaps almost as much to do with the sagging Pirates ballclub and the brilliance of rival players like Koufax, Mays, Frank Robinson, Orlando Cepeda, and Bob Gibson as with any conspiracy against underrated Latin talent. Yet no player performed any more consistently throughout the entire stretch of baseball's most forgotten era.

And ironically if not tragically, none of the decade's superstars were more overlooked when it came to selecting a consensus "Player of the 1960s." The award went easily to Sandy Koufax, Clemente receiving but a handful of ballots. At the end of a 10-year span that will always be remembered as baseball's "roaring and revolutionary sixties," Bob Clemente of the Pittsburgh Pirates remained one of the best-kept secrets of baseball's least-remembered decade. "The best right fielder in the business," shrewdly observed general manager Joe L. Brown, "a ballplayer who has never been fully appreciated."

The young Roberto Clemente who burst upon Forbes Field in April 1955 inspired at least two distinctive mental images for baseball fans everywhere over the course of the next several seasons. One was a flashy and exciting ballplayer who would swing away at just about any pitch remotely near the plate, driving most deliveries to distant corners of the ballpark, and who ran the base paths with nothing short of graceful abandon. The most exciting play in baseball arguably is the triple, and the three-base hit was Clemente's personal trademark. In nine seasons (six in a row between 1965 and 1970) he reached double figures in triples, a truly rare feat in the modern baseball age of speedy outfielders, astroturf, and symmetrical ballparks. The lost art of the three-base hit combines that special blend of pure foot speed and outlandish daring with raw hitting power. No baseball moment across the 1960s was more exciting then one featuring Bob Clemente rounding second, arms flying, charging headlong into third with another three-bagger.

Yet despite this colorful flamboyance, there was another Roberto Clemente, a "false Clemente" who loomed large in the popular imagination. This second image was a shiftless malingerer, one who fakes injury and shows little true desire to play. This was the media's manufactured image of Clemente, time and again portrayed in the popular press as a crybaby and a goldbrick, and it was an unfortunate and largely preposterous image that was to plague the Puerto Rican star's entire baseball career.

Clemente's injuries were certainly real enough. Few players have performed with such pain over the course of a career lasting nearly 2,500 big-league games. And fewer still perhaps have spoken so honestly about it. It was the young Puerto Rican ballplayer's frank openness with management and the press that contributed as much as anything to the negative side of his public image. When Clemente was racked with pain or slowed by frayed muscles, he would speak only the truth about his circumstance. One lesson that Bob Clemente the ballplayer never learned about his North American fans was their strange admiration for the stoic athlete who played hurt and hid his injuries from public view. Clemente's stark frankness about his inability to perform up to par would detract considerably from his flashy image as a high-priced foreign sports star. That, and an unfortunate stereotype, one that was seemingly fostered, consciously or perhaps accidentally, by certain glib-tongued members of the Pirates' front-office management.

One likely apocryphal story (to cite a single example) circulated by the Pirates had manager Bobby Bragan recounting an incident that concerned his frustrations with Clemente as an erratic if talented hitter. The circumstance was simply that Clemente, third-best batter in the league at the time, once bunted into an out, thus ending a nip-and-tuck game with his team trailing by one run. As the story goes, when skipper Bragan berated his star hitter for not doing the obvious and swinging away for a homer that would have tied the game, Clemente reportedly retorted (as Bragan tells it): "Boss, me no feel like home run today!" It made exceptionally good press, an excellent locker-room story to be savored by newspaper readers with their morning cup of coffee and a snide chuckle. But it did little good for Roberto Clemente's fragile and much maligned reputation as an inconsistent and even unintelligent baseball player.

The distortion here was not necessarily in the pristine facts surrounding the bunting incident. Clemente most likely did unwisely bunt when circumstances and traditional baseball wisdom might have dictated swinging away for the fences. Injustice lies rather in the stereotypical reportage of the Latin ballplayer speaking in broken English that sounds more like a bad comic-strip parody of Tarzan than the measured words of a big-league athlete. While his English was admittedly flawed and hesitant, Clemente did not speak as childishly as reported in this colorful story. And such accounts could only have added to his personal frustration with treatment by the press corps as well as his later growing suspicion of reporters and team officials who always seemed to present him to disadvantage. This was the expected fate of the Latin American ballplayer throughout the 1950s and 1960s, if not today.

Somehow, nonetheless, injury (to both body and reputation) was always in the end overshadowed by brilliant play from the talented if streaky all-star Pittsburgh outfielder. The 1960s, taken as an episode in Clemente's brilliant career, contain the bulk of his most storied achievements. While the Pirates in years immediately following the 1960 world championship slid all the way to sixth, then rebounded to fourth, then slumped again to eighth and sixth, Clemente simply tore up the league, pocketing four batting titles over the next seven seasons and never posting an average that dipped below .312 over the entire stretch. Still, the unfulfilled expectations and bitter realizations of the 1960 World Series were somehow to be played out over and over again through much of what transpired for the Pirates and their Puerto Rican superstar during the painfully long years of a revolutionary and unpredictable decade. By the end of the 1960s, Clemente had established himself, despite the odds, the injuries, and the resistance that seemed to await players from his Caribbean homeland, as a baseball superstar. He was, it can be claimed without fear of contradiction, the very first true Latin American baseball superstar. Yet Clemente's drive for success remained largely unsatiated, and his struggle for recognition—for himself and his island people—was yet largely unfulfilled. There were still new bridges to be crossed and considerable mountains to be scaled. There was still the role of World Series hero to be filled.

Throughout all the frustrations of the up-and-down seasons that were the Pirates' lot in the 1960s, Clemente chafed most especially at the playful new nickname his teammates had adopted for him around the Pittsburgh clubhouse. Expecting more obvious and spontaneous recognition for his spectacular achievements, especially during the 1960 pennant season and the World Series of that fall, Clemente burned inwardly at having received almost no notice from sportswriters who were supposedly the game's expert judges and recorders of talent. To tease their sulking teammate good-naturedly about his obvious distress, a handful of insensitive fellow Pirates were soon referring to their young outfielder playfully as "No Votes." The new label, harmless as it may have seemed to some on the ballclub, was a constant thorn in the side of the brooding Clemente. Yet the barb only seemed to inspire its recipient to try that much harder to impress skeptics and earn his just due.

That Puerto Rico's first big-league superstar should chafe so quickly at mere oversight is hardly a mystery. For if there is any single word to capture best the perplexing figure that was Clemente, that word would have to be "pride." There was Roberto's always evident pride in his performance on the field. There was an equally deep-seated pride in his native people and his Puerto Rican heritage. But above all else there was his pride in himself as a man. It was a lesson learned from his father, Melchor, himself a man with considerable pride in his assigned craft, even if that craft had been no more than overseeing fieldhands in the sugarcane plantations on the outskirts of San Juan. Don Melchor had always carried about him a prideful look of what the Spanish call *aguioso*, and the story circulates that he once pointed at a passing car carrying plantation owner Don Pepito Rubert and told his young son, "Always remember that he is no better than you!" It was a lesson the young Roberto Clemente would never forget.

Nowhere did that pride show more clearly than in the three seasons that were destined to be Clemente's final baseball summers. While Clemente had reached a peak achievement with his MVP award of 1966, personal victory had been largely muted by team failures for this proud-spirited athlete. The Pirates had once again come on lean times in the late 1960s, sliding to .500 and two sixth-place finishes in 1967 and 1968, then resurging only slightly in the first summer of divisional play a year later. But by 1970, the Pirates were on fire once again, and it was the veteran Clemente who was still silencing critics with his familiar role as emotional leader and field leader for the newly revamped Bucco team.

Injuries again kept Clemente out of 54 ballgames (a full third of a season) during the summer of 1970, yet he made vital contributions. When the Buccos inaugurated their state-of-the-art new stadium on July 16, 50,000 partisans turned out for a special Roberto Clemente Night to honor the veteran leader of their beloved ballclub. Clemente's leadership, however, had hardly been reduced to a mere ceremonial and inspirational one. In late August he had proved there was still strength in his veteran bat and aging legs when he tied a major league record with 10 hits in two consecutive games against the Dodgers at Los Angeles. Then, in the divisional clincher against the New York Mets in late September, Clemente again provided the crucial game-tying hit on the way to the season wrap-up 2–1 victory.

Thus the aging outfielder was still demonstrating beyond a shadow of a doubt in 1970 and 1971 that he was capable of leading by onfield example. It was fitting enough, then, when the Pirates grabbed their first league pennant in a decade at the conclusion of the hard-fought 1971 season, that only one star from the 1960 team remained in the starting Pittsburgh lineup. Groat, Hoak, Law, Skinner, and Friend were now mere fading memories, replaced in the Pittsburgh batting order by the youthful faces of Willie Stargell, Al Oliver, and Manny Sanguillen. Bill Mazeroski still wore the Bucco gold and black, but only as a part-time player. A veteran Clemente was still showing the way, however, just as he had 11 summers earlier.

The 1970 season was by most obvious measures the best all-around campaign of Clemente's remarkable 18-year career. Admittedly, the ever-present bugaboo of injury cut his game appearances to barely over 100 and his at-bats (412) to the fewest in any big-league season but his very last. His batting average (.352), by contrast, soared above his marvelous 1961 batting-title season, though only by a fraction, and although he did not enjoy enough at-bats to compete for the league title, he outhit all qualifiers but the torrid Rico Carty of Atlanta. While nagged with repeated injury and illness, Clemente was revived time and again throughout the summer by the thrill of a pennant race. No moment could have been more inspirational for the Pirate batting leader than that opening night of spanking-new Three Rivers Stadium in mid-July, a night officially designated by club officials as Roberto Clemente Night. As part of the evening's festivities, Clemente was presented with a parchment petition several yards in length and containing the signatures and official well-wishes of more than 300,000 Puerto Rican countrymen.

Like so much else in Clemente's roller-coaster career, however, this sweet summer of 1970 all came to a most disappointing end, this time in the form of a disastrous three-game playoff sweep at the hands of the powerful Cincinnati Reds team that featured Pete Rose, Johnny Bench, and Cuban standout Tony Pérez in its Big Red Machine lineup. Clemente batted only .214 for the short series, with only three tame singles and but a single run scored in 14 plate appearances, the worst postseason performance of his proud career. The decade of the 1960s thus closed out for Roberto Clemente as it had begun. Despite team successes and apparent personal achievement, there was a bitter taste of disappointment at season's close. Personal dreams of World Series glory had once again not been reached. Despite a personal stash of batting titles, Clemente had still not been able to lead his team to another cherished league or world title. And despite a spate of all-star years, he was still not quite the recognized star (at least this was his viewpoint) that he had long expected to be.

But the Pirates were not quite done with their most recent revival at the dawn of the 1971 campaign; this 1970s edition of the Buccos was seemingly not so prone to be dismantled overnight as the championship team of Mazeroski and company 10 years earlier. What had been a tight pennant race in 1970 – the Pirates pulling away from both the Cubs and Mets only in the season's waning days – was followed by an almost too-easy Pittsburgh cakewalk in 1971. Clemente apparently was healthy once again, appearing in 132 games and performing brilliantly once more at the plate and in the field, batting .341, clubbing in 86 runs, and turning in his highest fielding average to date with but two errors and a .993 fielding percentage. Roberto had started slowly, as he so often had in the past, and he even heard scattered boos for the first time in the usually friendly hometown ballpark. Yet by playoff time, Clemente was again virtually on fire, which was also his usual late-season pattern, again carrying the ballclub on his shoulders throughout the short playoff series against San Francisco that won the long-coveted National League flag.

It was apparent as the 1971 season wore down that Clemente was a man again possessed by his zealous mission – a still unfulfilled dream to showcase his superior hitting and fielding talents in a public forum where all the world could clearly see them. Clemente still sought a stage big enough to prove what he had so long burned to prove – that he was indeed one of the game's premier players, an equal to Aaron, Mays, Mantle, or any Cooperstown legends of the past. "When the papers describe all the Pirates," Clemente had complained back in 1960, "you know what they say about me? 'Good fielder and runner.' That was supposed to be my contribution. What about my hitting and runs I batted in?" Later he would boast, "I believe I can hit with anybody in baseball. Maybe I can't hit with the power of a Mays or a Frank Robinson or a Hank Aaron, but I can hit." It was certainly not an idle boast, yet that much sought-after showcase would be time and again delayed until it now finally seemed reachable as postseason play again rolled into view after the runaway 1971 season.

The 1971 playoff series with San Francisco at first provided little omen of what was shortly to unfold. Again Clemente took a postseason backseat to less distinguished teammates as Bob Robertson stroked three long homers in game two and Rich Hebner provided all the necessary Pittsburgh firepower in games three and four. Yet despite all the playoff heroics of journeymen like Robertson and Hebner, it is usually the World Series alone that evokes lasting October memories, and the World Series of 1971 will always be remembered as the series owned exclusively by Roberto Clemente of Puerto Rico. Never has a fall classic been more the personal showcase for a single star player, and never has one ballplayer so thoroughly dominated both offensive and defensive ends of championship play.

Clemente was seemingly always at his best in October play, and the World Series consecutive-game hitting spree he began in 1960 was now routinely continued 11 autumns later. While the underdog Bucs slumped badly against the heavily favored Orioles in two opening contests at Baltimore, Clemente nonetheless exhorted his teammates with a bevy of hits, two in the first game (a 5–3 loss) and two more in the second (a more lopsided 11–3 defeat). He equally showed the way with flawless fielding, at one point uncorking an outfield throw later described by Baltimore catcher Andy Etchebarren as "the greatest throw I ever saw by an outfielder." Clemente then spurred a huge comeback effort in Pittsburgh, registering nine hits, several crucial, after the first five series games. In game seven it was Clemente who smacked a vital home run in the fourth inning, putting his underdog team once more in the lead. This roundtripper would provide the final margin of victory as the Bucs held on 3–1 to celebrate a second world championship of the Clemente era.

Clemente's numbers for the 1971 World Series were only short of phenomenal. He batted at a .414 clip, registered 12 hits, along with two homers and four crucial RBIs. He fielded flawlessly, handling 15 outfield chances with flair and near perfection. Thus no one was surprised this time when the often-overlooked Clemente was an expected unanimous choice to receive the flashy sports car presented by *Sport* magazine in honor of his role as series MVP. And the Pirates, at long last, after a full decade of uphill battle, held another championship flag firmly in hand. Clemente had now been a winner in both of his World Series appearances, successful bookends to the sixties. But more importantly still, this time the whole world had been watching via the magic of television as Roberto Clemente of Puerto Rico played as well as any World Series hero ever had. At long last, his considerable talents as both hitter and fielder, and as proven World Series winner, could be fairly and widely acknowledged throughout the baseball world.

Now only one final glory moment remained, though none could have fully anticipated this when dusk first settled on the World Series of 1971. The drama of Clemente's final base hit, achieved during the final at-bat of what was destined to be his last big-league game, was tinged with a special dramatic irony. Much pressure had built up internally for Roberto as he chased down what would prove to be one of the final great trophies of his marvelous career. The 3,000th career base hit would mean a new legitimacy; it would rank him as one of baseball's very best. Only 10 men in baseball's storied history had reached such a lofty number; only four had been National Leaguers. It all meant so much to Roberto, and the pressure became so great by season's end that he almost let the occasion wait for a 1973 season. Willie Stargell has often told of how he pushed Roberto to play that last game of September 1972 and the relief he later felt for having done so, especially in the light of subsequent tragic events. Play Roberto did, of course, and in the fourth inning of the season's finale, against New York Met lefty Jon Matlack, he blasted a drive deep against the left-field wall, a hit that would remain as the crowning achievement of 18 long summers of National League baseball. An inning later Clemente would remove himself from the field, never again to play in a regular-season big-league game.

The 1972 playoff series with Cincinnati that followed Clemente's final regular-season curtain call was disappointing and anticlimactic, but somehow it did not really matter. The Big Red Machine again eked out a three-games-to-two victory, nipping the Pirates 4–3 with a ninth-inning rally in the finale. The Bucs simply ran out of gas, and what should have been a dramatic defense of their world title against Charlie Finley's renegade Oakland ballclub never came about. Painfully, the pennant was lost on a wild pitch, when usually reliable pitcher Bob Moose uncorked an errant fastball in the final frame of the final NLCS game. But throughout the playoff series the Pirates' adept batsmen simply failed them, hitting .190 as a team for the hotly contested five games. In his final postseason appearance, what would prove his final moment in baseball, Robert Clemente slumped badly and collected but four hits, one of them a homer, for a .235 series average. Thus there would be no World Series encore for Roberto Clemente or his teammates in 1972. Yet for a tired Clemente who had already achieved so much, it seemed only another minor setback. There were few if any baseball horizons remaining to be conquered. The dream of building a Youth Sports City in San Juan now seemed a far worthier personal preoccupation, and retirement plans loomed foremost in Clemente's mind.

The marvelous baseball events that transpired in Pittsburgh's Three Rivers Stadium in 1971 and 1972 are only the final superficial elements of the Roberto Clemente story. When the pieces of the complex puzzle that was Clemente the man are carefully assembled, what emerges is a remarkable human being, a proud and dedicated athlete, and an always uncompromising patriot. Roberto Clemente was a true pioneer for his race and his island countrymen. He was a larger-than-life hero in an age almost completely devoid of flesh-and-blood heroes. He was a committed humanitarian as well, whose many contributions to bettering the conditions of his fellow man far outstrip in importance whatever he may have achieved on a baseball diamond. He was a loving family man who insisted that his three children be born on his native island; he was a devoted friend who chose his companions painstakingly and stood by them with unwavering loyalty. He was a man of ceaseless action who would never rest and seemingly could never sit still. The dozen or more fine adult and juvenile books (reading list at chapter's end) about Clemente's life and career are filled from cover to cover with glowing testimonials from those who knew him most intimately.

Such books (Wagenheim's and Musick's are perhaps the best) are also filled with elaborate explanations concerning the man (versus the ballplayer) named Clemente. They try to enumerate the odds he had always struggled against and articulate the passion with which he faced such odds. They strive to capture what it was like being a Latin American ballplayer in the fifties and sixties, a disadvantaged though never poverty-stricken youngster from a rural barrio in Puerto Rico whose father labored in the cane fields and at numerous odd jobs so that his family of seven children would never have to go hungry, or a pioneering black player in the big leagues a mere decade after Robinson's shattering debut, when the integration of professional baseball was still in its infancy and black players were still treated as outcasts and thus plagued by constant stereotype and regular rejection.

The best portrait of the position of the major league Latin American ballplayer in Clemente's day was perhaps that provided by Clemente himself in a candid interview with journalist Howard Cohn for *Sport* magazine in the winter following the 1961 season. "Latin American Negro ballplayers are treated today much like all Negroes were treated in baseball in the early days of the broken color barrier," wrote Cohn, paraphrasing Clemente.

"They are subjected to prejudices and stamped with generalizations. Because they speak Spanish among themselves, they are set off as a minority within a minority, and they bear the brunt of the sport's remaining racial prejudices. They have been stripped in many baseball minds of individual identities. Some ballplayers and managers lump together the Latin American Negroes with a set of generalized charges as old as racial-religious prejudice itself: 'They're all lazy, looking for the easy way, the shortcut' is one charge. 'They have no guts,' is another. There are more."

But all such racial tensions that tear men and women apart seemed momentarily forgotten in the wake of the terrible tragedy that was Roberto Clemente's unexpected death in December 1972. Clemente's off-seasons had always been filled with endless public service and personal appearances across his native island, and this despite the rash of yearly injuries that demanded rest and inactivity for his battered body at the end of each seven-month baseball campaign. Thus when a devastating earthquake shattered the countryside of neighboring Nicaragua on December 23, 1972, it was predictably Roberto Clemente who sprang into immediate action, hoping to exploit his status as a national sports hero as a focal point for marshaling the necessary relief effort. Clemente had no official obligation in Nicaragua, but he felt a passion for all the poverty-wracked citizens of Latin America. He had also been an honored guest in the capital city of Managua only a year earlier, managing the Puerto Rican team in the world amateur championships and visiting hospitals crammed with local indigent youth. Thus only hours after the earthquake struck Roberto Clemente threw himself headlong into the relief effort as honorary chairman of the Nicaraguan Relief Committee formed by San Juan television personality Luís Vigoreaux.

Clemente's role was at first to be one of heading the drive to solicit money and desperately needed clothes and food for the disaster victims, arranging for the storing of the relief supplies in San Juan's Hiram Bithorn Stadium and chartering trucks to collect and transport the items there, and chartering an airplane to fly the relief supplies across the Gulf of Mexico to the needy victims in Managua. Clemente at first had no plans to go to Nicaragua. But then reports began reaching Puerto Rico that early shipments of earthquake aid had fallen into the hands of enemies of the Nicaraguan government, that cash and clothes were not reaching their intended earthquake victims. It was at this point that Roberto decided it was necessary to accompany the mercy flight scheduled to depart from San Juan airport on New Year's Eve, even if it was a holiday he had hoped to spend with his wife, Vera, and his three small sons, Roberto, Luís Roberto, and Enrique Roberto; even if the rented DC-7 was dangerously overloaded and had already suffered several flight-delaying mechanical breakdowns.

Circumstances surrounding the crash that took Clemente's life have remained mysterious to this day. His wife, Vera, a hometown girl he had married only eight winters earlier in 1964, had pleaded with Roberto to accept as a bad omen the mechanical failures that had already delayed takeoff and postpone departure until after the holiday. Roberto had promised that any further delays would mean temporary cancellation of the mission. Yet shortly before midnight the old DC-7—ominously retired from service by a Florida airline a year earlier—rumbled down the runway and into the night air, carrying Roberto Clemente, its crew of three, and its heavy load of blankets, food, and clothing. Moments later, the plane was to begin losing altitude, to swerve back toward the airport in a desperate attempt at an emergency landing, and then to plunge out of sight into the sea several miles from the San Juan coastline.

Days of searching for remains and mourning for Clemente followed. Thousands of citizens in Puerto Rico's capital city poured onto the beach shortly after dawn as word of the crash spread; the city maintained a vigil which lasted for days, until all hope of finding their hero had been lost. It was seven days before the plane's tail section was finally located; for 11 days the beach near the airport remained roped off as Coast Guard boats and aircraft searched for pieces of wreckage and bodies of the victims. A pair of eyeglasses, believed to be the pilot's, and a small black briefcase known to be Roberto's were all that was recovered. No bodies were ever found. In the aftermath of this loss of their most favored son, a saddened island nation and a saddened baseball world continued to mourn in shock and disbelief. In San Juan, the governor's inaugural ceremonies were canceled. In Pittsburgh, local sportswriter Phil Musick captured the sentiments of millions of fans across North America when he spelled out his own helpless response to such loss: "Now it's too late to tell him there were things he did on a ball field that made me wish I was Shakespeare."

In the end, it seems we pay most attention to a great man's dreams only when that man is no longer with us. It is not surprising, therefore, that what Roberto Clemente could not accomplish while living, he was able to bring into reality with his untimely death. Clemente's often-frustrated dream of building a San Juan Sports City, a sanctuary where poor youngsters from the island's many barrios could gather to be trained in athletic contests as well as reading and other life skills, now began to move toward reality on a grassy 600-acre site located ironically only a few miles from San Juan Airport. Despite giving its earlier approval to the project, the government had long been stalling its commitment of resources. Once its national hero had fallen so tragically, however, the Puerto Rican government was prompt in donating land for the inspirational project and petitioning the U.S. government for operating funds. Donations from baseball fans everywhere also poured in, perhaps as much as $500,000 in the weeks immediately following Roberto's death. Today the completed Sports City stands proudly in urban San Juan and serves as many as 1,200 disadvantaged youngsters at a time in a full range of athletic and educational activities. It is a perfect and lasting fulfillment of the final dreams of Roberto Clemente. And it is perhaps the only mortar-and-brick monument the selfless Roberto Clemente would have wanted or allowed.

Baseball is a game of endless statistics, numbers, records—arcane facts and figures left to cement a reputation and fix immortality for hero and goat alike. Ballplaying heroes have found myriad ways to implant their legacy on generations to follow, often by a matchless cumulative achievement like Gehrig's iron-man streak, a single moment of dominance as with Vander Meer's double no-hitters, or an indelible overall impression like Campanella's quiet competitiveness and Jerome Dean's or Babe Herman's disarming daffiness. Occasionally a single mythic player like Joltin' Joe DiMaggio, with his 56-game hitting streak, Yankee Clipper moniker, and matchless grace afield combines all these elements into a single larger-than-life hero. These legacies may be built strictly on heroism (like Bobby Thomson's home-run blow) or even upon bonehead blunders (recall Bill Buckner, Fred Merkel, or Mickey Owen), yet they confer an immortality available in almost no other corner of popular American life.

Players thus live on in the records and numbers they leave behind. Ruth is immortalized by 60 homers, Cobb and Rose by 4,000 base hits, Vander Meer by back-to-back no-hit mastery, Ted Williams by the sweet sound of .400, DiMaggio by a 56-game streak, and Aaron by 755 round-trippers. For a much smaller handful of highly exceptional stars, an award or trophy or monument may be established that fixes forever in fans' minds the essence and spirit of a true ballplaying great. This is a rare event indeed for the sport of baseball, a game of unwavering tradition that persists in naming its conferences for geographical proximity (even when geography could not explain divisional assignments of the Braves, Cubs, Cardinals, or Reds) and its championship trophy and postseason awards by the simple designations (MVP, Rookie of the Year) they unambiguously carry. Baseball thankfully has no Vince Lombardi or Lord Stanley championship cups, no Adams or Wales or Pete Rozelle conferences, no Lady Bing or Con Smythe player awards. Yet in two rare cases alone has a single player seemed to merit such special name recognition. Thus the designation Cy Young remains the universal mark of pitching excellence. So too the name of Roberto Clemente now stands synonymous with flawless sportsmanship and uncompromising dedication to the pursuit of sport's richest ideals. So much so that not one but three separate prestigious trophies now bear the name of the incomparable Clemente. And these awards are perhaps one tireless humanitarian athlete's most fitting legacy.

First came the Commissioner's Trophy, renamed the Roberto Clemente

Trophy in its third year. For two decades this prestigious award has honored the game's greats for their positive labors toward the betterment of baseball and the surrounding community. Each winner is not only a ballplayer of considerable onfield stature (six of the first seven honors went to eventual Hall-of-Famers) but also an outstanding citizen active in the betterment of his community in a manner that reflects Clemente's exhaustive humanitarian labors. The most recent award, for example, has honored ironman shortstop Cal Ripken, Jr., for his ceaseless efforts to promote literacy in the greater Baltimore inner-city region. A second Clemente award was instituted by major league baseball in 1973, this one presented by the Pittsburgh chapter of the Baseball Writers of America. Its honorees each season are those members of the Pittsburgh Pirates who have performed in a manner that captures the essence of Clemente's dedication to one of baseball's oldest and proudest franchises.

A third Roberto Clemente Award, however, is perhaps the honor that would have made Clemente most proud. First established in 1973 by Luís Rodríguez-Mayoral and still organized each new season by that distinguished Puerto Rican baseball journalist, promoter, and front-office executive (today assistant public relations director with the Texas Rangers), this final Roberto Clemente Award is presented each summer as the highlight of the special Latin American Players Day sanctioned and sponsored by the baseball commissioner's office. Each recipient (some years have featured multiple award winners) is an active Latin American big-leaguer who has proudly carried on Clemente's tradition.

Below is a listing of the numerous ballplaying heroes who have enjoyed selection as recipients of three prestigious Roberto Clemente awards. The career of each—all-stars in their own right—is living testimony to the greatest baseball hero ever to emerge from the island nations of the Caribbean. No testimony could have pleased Roberto more. And for each recipient of a cherished Clemente trophy, this association with the name of Cooperstown's first Latin American resident has been a special highlight and inspiration along the bumpy road to baseball stardom. Cooperstown hopeful Tony Pérez thus spoke for a generation of Latin American ballplaying stars when he once referred to his own 1972 Latin American Day Clemente Award as "the most important honor of my entire baseball career."

Roberto Clemente Statistical Record

Big League and Minor League Hitting Record

Year	*Club*	*G*	*AB*	*R*	*H*	*2B*	*3B*	*HR*	*RBI*	*B.A.*
1954	Montreal (IL)*	87	148	27	38	5	3	2	12	.257
1955	Pitts (NL)	124	474	48	121	23	11	5	47	.255
1956	Pitts (NL)	147	543	66	169	30	7	7	60	.311
1957	Pitts (NL)	111	451	42	114	17	7	4	30	.253
1958	Pitts (NL)	140	519	69	150	24	10	6	50	.289
1959	Pitts (NL)	105	432	60	128	17	7	4	50	.296
1960	Pitts (NL)	144	570	89	179	22	6	16	94	.314
1961	Pitts (NL)	146	572	100	201	30	10	23	89	*.351*
1962	Pitts (NL)	144	538	95	168	28	9	10	74	.312
1963	Pitts (NL)	152	600	77	192	23	8	17	76	.320
1964	Pitts (NL)	155	622	95	*211*	40	7	12	87	*.339*
1965	Pitts (NL)	152	589	91	194	21	14	10	65	*.329*
1966	Pitts (NL)	154	638	105	202	31	11	29	119	.317
1967	Pitts (NL)	147	585	103	*209*	26	10	23	110	*.357*
1968	Pitts (NL)	132	502	74	146	18	12	18	57	.291
1969	Pitts (NL)	138	507	87	175	20	*12*	19	91	.345
1970	Pitts (NL)	108	412	65	145	22	10	14	60	.352
1971	Pitts (NL)	132	522	82	178	29	8	13	86	.341
1972	Pitts (NL)	102	378	68	118	19	7	10	60	.312
Totals	18 Seasons	2,520	9,602	1,443	3,038	445	169	242	1,317	.317

*Italics = League Leader; * = minor-league*

World Series Hitting Record

Year	*Club*	*G*	*AB*	*R*	*H*	*2B*	*3B*	*HR*	*RBI*	*B.A.*
1960	Pitts (NL)	7	29	1	9	0	0	0	3	.310
1971	Pitts (NL)	7	29	3	12	2	1	2	4	.414
Totals	2 Series	14	58	4	21	2	1	2	7	.362

National League Championship Series Hitting Record

Year	*Club*	*G*	*AB*	*R*	*H*	*2B*	*3B*	*HR*	*RBI*	*B.A.*
1970	Pitts (NL)	3	14	1	3	0	0	0	1	.214
1971	Pitts (NL)	4	18	2	6	0	0	0	4	.333
1972	Pitts (NL)	5	17	1	4	1	0	1	7	.235
Totals	3 NLC Series	12	49	4	13	1	0	1	12	.264

Roberto Clemente Statistical Record, *cont.*

All-Star Game Hitting Record

Year	*Club*	*G*	*AB*	*R*	*H*	*2B*	*3B*	*HR*	*RBI*	*B.A.*
1960	National	2	1	0	0	0	0	0	0	.000
1961	National	2	6	1	2	0	1	0	2	.333
1962	National	2	5	0	3	1	0	0	0	.600
1963	National	1	0	0	0	0	0	0	0	.000
1964	National	1	3	1	1	0	0	0	0	.333
1965	National	1	2	0	0	0	0	0	0	.000
1966	National	1	4	0	2	1	0	0	0	.500
1967	National	1	6	0	1	0	0	0	0	.167
1969	National	1	1	0	0	0	0	0	0	.000
1970	National	1	1	0	0	0	0	0	1	.000
1971	National	1	2	1	1	0	0	0	1	.500
Totals	11 Seasons	14	31	3	10	2	1	0	4	.323

Puerto Rican Winter League Hitting Record

Year	*Club*	*AB*	*R*	*H*	*2B*	*3B*	*HR*	*RBI*	*B.A.*
1952-53	Santurce	77	5	18	3	1	0	5	.234
1953-54	Santurce	219	22	63	13	2	2	27	.288
1954-55	Santurce	273	65	94	9	4	6	38	.344
1955-56	Santurce	278	45	85	11	3	7	30	.306
1956-57	Santurce-Caguas	225	36	89	17	3	2	29	.396
1957-58	Caguas	32	0	8	2	0	0	1	.250
1958-59	Did Not Play	---	---	---	---	---	---	---	---
1959-60	Caguas	215	38	71	9	6	4	42	.330
1960-61	San Juan	109	12	31	5	1	1	14	.284
1961-62	San Juan	66	9	18	3	0	0	8	.273
1962-63	Did Not Play	---	---	---	---	---	---	---	---
1963-64	San Juan	177	27	61	11	2	4	39	.345
1964-65	San Juan	39	6	15	3	2	2	7	.385
1965-66	San Juan	2	0	0	0	0	0	0	.000
1966-67	Did Not Play	---	---	---	---	---	---	---	---
1967-68	San Juan	68	15	26	4	0	4	15	.382
1968-69	Did Not Play	---	---	---	---	---	---	---	---
1969-70	San Juan	135	20	40	9	1	3	14	.296
1970-71	San Juan	4	1	1	1	0	0	0	.250
Totals	15 Seasons	1,919	301	620	100	25	35	269	.323

Roberto Clemente Awards

Year	Commissioners Trophy	BBWAA Trophy[a]	Latin American Day Trophy
1971	Willie Mays	Not yet awarded	Not yet awarded
1972	Brooks Robinson	Not yet awarded	Not yet awarded
1973	Al Kaline[b]	Willie Stargell	Luís Aparicio
1974	Willie Stargell	Al Oliver	Luís Tiant and Juan Marichal
1975	Lou Brock	Dave Parker	Manny Sanguillen
1976	Pete Rose	Bill Robinson	Orestes "Minnie" Miñoso
1977	Rod Carew	Dave Parker	Dave Concepción
1978	Greg Luzinski	Dave Parker	Jorge Orta
1979	Andre Thornton	Willie Stargell	Ed Figueroa
1980	Phil Niekro	Mike Easler	José Cruz and Rod Carew
1981	Steve Garvey	Bill Madlock	César Cedeño
1982	Ken Singleton	Jason Thompson	Manny Trillo and Tony Pérez
1983	Cecil Cooper	Tony Peña	Pedro Guerrero and Aurelio Rodríguez
1984	Ron Guidry	Lee Lacy	Iván de Jesús and Aurelio López
1985	Don Baylor	Rick Reuschel	Tony Peña and Dámaso García
1986	Garry Maddox	Johnny Ray	Fernando Valenzuela and Juan Beníquez
1987	Rick Sutcliffe	Andy Van Slyke	Sandy Alomar, Sr. (and Reggie Jackson[c])
1988	Dale Murphy	Andy Van Slyke	Candy Maldonado and Ozzie Guillén
1989	Gary Carter	Don Landrum	Dennis Martínez
1990	Dave Stewart	Doug Drabek	Julio Franco and Rubén Sierra
1991	Harold Reynolds	Barry Bonds	Sandy Alomar, Jr.
1992	Cal Ripken, Jr.	Andy Van Slyke	Rafael Palmeiro

[a] = Pirates Players [b] = Renamed in 1973 [c] = Special Non-Hispanic Player Award

---

Roberto Clemente Chronology

August 18, 1934	Born Roberto Clemente Walker in Carolina, Puerto Rico, son of Don Melchor Clemente and Dona Luisa Walker Clemente.
October 9, 1952	Young Clemente signs first professional contract for $500 bonus payment and $60 weekly salary to play with Santurce Crabbers in Puerto Rico's winter league.

February 19, 1954	Brooklyn Dodgers sign 19-year-old Clemente to $10,000 bonus contract plus $5,000 salary for the 1954 season with their Montreal Royals (AAA) farm club.
November 22, 1954	Pittsburgh Pirates make Clemente their selection with first pick in 1954 major league draft of unprotected minor league bonus prospects.
December 1954	Driving home from visit to his hospitalized brother in San Juan, Clemente is hit by a drunken driver, resulting in a spinal disk injury that plagues the Pirate star throughout his career.
December 31, 1954	Luís, Roberto's older brother, dies unexpectedly in San Juan hospital of cancerous brain tumor.
April 17, 1955	Clemente singles off Brooklyn Dodgers left-hander Johnny Podres in his first major league at-bat in Forbes Field, Pittsburgh.
September 8, 1958	Clemente records first big-league batting record by stroking three triples in a single game versus Cincinnati at Forbes Field, Pittsburgh.
October 1960	Pirates capture World Series over the New York Yankees, and Clemente stars yet is overlooked in both World Series and league Most Valuable Player voting.
May 16, 1961	Clemente reaches the 1,000-hit plateau with a right-field single against left-hander Curt Simmons of the St. Louis Cardinals.
September 1961	Clemente closes season with .351 BA, thus becoming the first Latin American player ever to win a National League batting championship (and second to capture a big-league hitting title).
November 14, 1964	About 1,500 well-wishers and fans attend wedding of Clemente and childhood sweetheart Vera Cristina Zabala in their hometown of Carolina, Puerto Rico.
September 2, 1966	Clemente homers for his 2,000th major league hit in game at Forbes Field versus Chicago Cubs and right-hander Ferguson Jenkins.
September 1967	Clemente closes season with career-high single-season average of .357, earning his fourth and final league batting title.
July 16, 1970	Pittsburgh's new Three Rivers Stadium inaugurated with special Roberto Clemente Night, and the Puerto Rican star receives scroll of congratulations signed by 300,000 of his island countrymen.
August 22–23, 1970	Thirty-six-year-old Clemente enjoys finest two-day

	batting spree of modern baseball era, collecting 10 base hits in two consecutive games versus the Dodgers in Los Angeles.
October 13, 1971	In the first night contest of World Series history, played in Forbes Field, Clemente strokes three hits to pace Pittsburgh to 4–3 victory over Baltimore.
October 21, 1971	World Series MVP Clemente returns as national hero to his native Puerto Rico on heels of his single most memorable career performance during which 12 hits, .414 BA, and flawless outfield play lead Pirates to dramatic comeback victory over favored Baltimore Orioles.
January 29, 1972	Clemente presented with an eleventh Golden Glove award for outstanding defensive play, the last official league honor received while alive.
September 30, 1972	Clemente's final base hit of 1972 season and last of a brilliant 18-year big-league career is also his 3,000th, making him only the eleventh player in major league history to achieve this rarest batting feat.
December 31, 1972	Clemente dies in plane crash off coast of San Juan, Puerto Rico, while flying supplies to earthquake victims of Nicaragua.
March 20, 1973	National Baseball Hall of Fame selection committee waives normal five-year waiting rule to elect Clemente unanimously for enshrinement in Cooperstown, a mere 11 weeks after his funeral; only once before (1939, Lou Gehrig) had the mandatory retirement period been suspended.
April 6, 1973	Pittsburgh Pirates retire Clemente's uniform number 21 at opening-day ceremonies in Three Rivers Stadium before 51,695 tearful fans (the first such honor ever accorded a Latin American ballplayer).
August 6, 1973	Clemente posthumously inducted into U.S. National Baseball Hall of Fame in Cooperstown, New York, becoming the first Latin American player honored.

Selected Clemente Reading List

*Bjarkman, Peter C. *Roberto Clemente.* Philadelphia and London: Chelsea House, 1991.

*Brondfield, Jerry. *Roberto Clemente, Pride of the Pirates.* Champaign, Illinois: Garrard, 1976.

Chastain, Bill. "Right Field Rifle (Roberto Clemente)." *Sports History* 2 (January 1989): 32–39.
*Christine, Bill. *Roberto! Número Uno.* New York: Stadia Sports, 1973.
Feldman, Jay. "The Legend and Legacy of Roberto Clemente." *Smithsonian* 24(6) (September 1993): 128–142.
*Hano, Arnold. *Roberto Clemente, Batting King.* New York: Putnam, 1973.
________. "Roberto Clemente, Man of Paradox." *Sport* 39 (May 1965): 68–84.
Izenberg, Jerry. "Clemente: A Bittersweet Memoir." In *Great Latin Sports Figures: The Proud People.* Garden City, New York: Doubleday, 1976, 11–25.
Kahn, Roger. "The Children of Roberto Clemente." In *A Season in the Sun,* by Roger Kahn. New York: Harper and Row, 1977, 115–126.
McDaniel, Douglas. "Flight to Glory: The Wife of Roberto Clemente Recalls the Hero and the Humanitarian." *The Diamond: The Official Chronicle of Major League Baseball* 1(1) (June 1993): 32–40.
*Mercer, Charles. *Roberto Clemente.* New York: Putnam, 1974.
Miller, Ira (with "Foreword" by José Torres). *Roberto Clemente.* New York: Grosset and Dunlap (Tempo), 1973.
Musick, Phil. *Who Was Roberto? A Biography of Roberto Clemente.* Garden City, New York: Doubleday, 1974.
Newton, Clarke. "Roberto Clemente." In *Famous Puerto Ricans* (Clarke Newton, series editor). New York: Dodd, Mead, 1975, 41–53.
*O'Connor, Jim. *The Story of Roberto Clemente, All-Star Hero.* New York: Dell, 1991.
*Olsen, Jack. *Roberto Clemente, The Great One.* Chicago: Childrens Press, 1974.
Peters, Jess. "Roberto Clemente: Mr. Pittsburgh Pirates." *Black Sports* 2 (November 1972): 20–25.
Rodríguez-Mayoral, Luís. *Roberto Clemente: Aun escucha las ovaciones* (Roberto Clemente: Now Hear the Applause). Carolina, Puerto Rico: Ciudad Deportiva Roberto Clemente, 1987.
*Rudeen, Kenneth. *Roberto Clemente.* New York: Thomas Y. Crowell, 1974.
Wagenheim, Kal. *Clemente!* New York: Praeger, 1973.
*Walker, Paul R. *Pride of Puerto Rico: The Life of Roberto Clemente.* New York: Harcourt Brace Jovanovich, 1988.

* = *juvenile biography*

CHAPTER 4

Send In the Scouts: Big-League Teams Exploit the Caribbean Connection

> With the possible exception of Jonas Salk, John Foster Dulles, and Annette Funicello, no one public figure so personified the fifties as did Vic Power. —Brendan C. Boyd and Fred C. Harris, *The Great American Baseball Card Flipping, Trading, and Bubble Gum Book*

Luque was long the forgotten and unacknowledged pioneer of Hispanic baseball. Marichal was certainly the finest hurler who ever emerged from the sun-drenched tropics—if one makes the necessary allowances for those disenfranchised blackballers like José Méndez, Ramón Bragaña, and Luís Tiant, Sr. And Clemente stands unchallenged as Latin baseball's first true big-league superstar.

There were others, most of them dark-skinned and thus new to the big-league scene, paving the way for their countrymen in the wake of Jackie Robinson's 1947 revolution. And none was more typical of the first wave of Latin ballplayers than fiery Victor Pellot (pronounced "pay-oat") from Puerto Rico. His very name was a source of deep-seated mystery. The French-sounding surname by which he had already become a diamond celebrity throughout his native Caribbean island in the early fifties was not the same catchy handle he would soon carry proudly in northern cities like Philadelphia, Kansas City, and Minneapolis. Just as north-of-the-border fans would adopt Orestes Miñoso as "Minnie" or Pedro Oliva as "Tony" so would Victor Pellot be forced to don the colorful made-for-baseball moniker "Vic Power" as soon as he pulled on his Philadelphia A's pinstriped flannels.

The whole name-changing affair proved something of an embarrassment to the ballplayer. Power would soon have to defend himself against critics back home (Arecibo) who mistakenly assumed that he had opted for a more Anglo-sounding name simply to hide his Puerto Rican heritage. Yet the whole silly business had been nothing more than a matter of cultural misunderstanding, just as Vic Power's whole career would seemingly come to symbolize the raw-edged and inevitable clash between two largely incompatible baseball-playing worlds.

More important than the recast name, however, was the paradoxical image of the unorthodox ballplayer himself. Here was a spirited athlete who oozed gobs of flamboyance (a showboating style featuring one-handed catches in the field) and tons of excitement (seven Gold Gloves for fielding excellence plus potent clutch power at the plate). But here also was a ballplayer who threatened the baseball establishment with his flashy darkness (of behavior as well as skin tone), his open and even flaunted individuality, and his often unconventional off-field behavior.

While Anglo teammates guzzled beer and devoured country music, ebony-skinned Vic Power dated white women, frequented nightclubs to savor haunting jazz, and cruised the streets of Kansas City in flashy convertible automobiles. (The Kansas City Athletics brass once okayed Power's request to bring a white friend to a ballclub picnic, then threw a fit when that friend turned out to be blond and female.) Not since boisterous heavyweight boxer Jack Johnson in the World War I era had a black athlete dared to display such a brazen disregard for what white fans, press, and ballclub management took to be his proper place far from the limelight.

But most unsettling of all was his bold style of diamond play. Here was a hitherto unseen type of brazen ballplayer, one seemingly molded by the free-spirited tropics themselves. And once this new carefree mold of ballplayer arrived on the scene, major league baseball would never be quite the same.

For such pioneers themselves, of course, the media spotlight was unfortunately often merely a focal point for distrust and thinly veiled antagonism. Didn't the sporting press always tell us (usually after gushing about their hell-bent enthusiasm) that ballplayers like Puerto Rico's Vic Power and Cuba's Minnie Miñoso were overly "rebellious in the clubhouse" and essentially selfish (not team players) in the batter's box and in the outfield? Here were the earliest prototypes of the goldbricking and unreliable (but so exciting) Roberto Clemente. Vic Power seemed to pave the way, set the stage, for the even lustier ballplaying countrymen who would follow immediately on his heels. With the arrival of Victor Pellot "Power" on the big-league scene in 1954, we were indeed, as writer Danny Peary has so deftly phrased it, emerging from baseball's earlier innocent Light Ages into the more enlightened Dark Ages of the Pan-American national pastime.

The Puerto Rican Minnie Miñoso

Of all those writers enthralled with the ballplaying magic of Vic Power, it was film critic Danny Peary who best captured the essence of Puerto Rico's flashiest diamond all-star: "With a defiantly independent attitude and an unbridled flamboyance that hadn't been so openly displayed by a black sports figure since Jack Johnson, Vic Power outraged owners, antagonized sportswriters (who unfairly labeled him a 'showboat' and 'clubhouse lawyer'), scared opponents, excited fans, and came to represent the tension, entertainment, and color (in more ways than one), if not the false innocence, of fifties baseball."

No heftier (or more accurate) tribute has been paid to a "background" ballplayer of the glorious "Golden Age Fifties" than the one Dan Peary penned about his childhood ballplaying idol. Victor Power was a unique phenomenon during an age of relentless big-league conformity. He was also a first true signpost of those great changes now sweeping pell-mell across the national pastime. A career destined to be played out in such big-league backwaters as Philadelphia, Kansas City, and Cleveland perhaps robbed this talented first sacker of true superstar status and thus assigned him to "cult ballplayer" status for future generations of baseball historians. But for those who remember the glories of major league baseball during the decade of Sputnik, "I Love Lucy," imagined Russian invasions and nightmare-inducing fallout shelters, few if any can fail to recall the entertaining American League sideshow that was once aptly named Vic Power.

Power himself always seemed to have the best answers to charges his critics would levy against him. To the claim that he was a clubhouse lawyer, for example, he would respond that his English was so bad that he could never have inspired an audience to take up anything more than derisive laughter, certainly never something like serious locker-room revolt. As proof positive, Power would cite one disastrous radio interview in which he was asked to comment on rival American League pitchers; his phrase "some of their pitches" came out sounding more like "sons of bitches," and his thickly accented Hispanic voice was instantly pulled from the air. And to those sportswriters who praised his dextrous fielding and clutch hitting yet often criticized his choices in flashy autos and light-skinned girlfriends, he had a quick-witted response as well: "Maybe if I had driven a Volkswagen and told them I was after a big, fat colored girl, they would have said, 'Oh, he's a nice guy, see how beautiful he is!'" (quoted by Danny Peary, *Cult Ballplayers*).

It was inevitable that Power would remain a sideshow phenomenon, just as Hall-of-Famers Al Kaline, Robin Roberts, Warren Spahn, and even Ted Williams and Stan Musial remained largely "sideshows" during the talent-drenched decade of the fifties. Baseball of that era reduced itself to a main stage that was New York City (this was true of both the American and National Leagues) and a colorful if irrelevant backdrop that was played out everywhere else. The Yankees and Dodgers were always seemingly the main fare (except for once or twice, when the Giants horned in on the party); for fans of other cities, the best that could be hoped for was a significant if brief scene or two stolen from the Yankees-Dodgers annual pennant-race pageant.

Vic Power had missed his chance to stand on center stage in New York City precisely because of the ballplaying talents and unabashed style that would soon make his indelible mark upon the big-league game. The staid New York Yankees under owners Dan Topping and Del Webb were apparently not ready to have a black man donning the hallowed Yankee pinstripes; and if they did have a black in uniform, it would certainly not do to have one who called such attention to himself and his individualistic style of play. Let the Dodgers boast of Robinson and Campanella, and let the Giants claim the daring Willie Mays. The Yankees would wait instead for the soft-spoken American black Elston Howard (whose role would be largely to understudy Yogi Berra) and then for the hardly more charismatic Héctor López, lead-footed and lead-fisted infielder from Panama. Neither Howard nor López could "carry Vic Power's glove" according to most knowledgeable scouts hovering around the American League scene.

Power was never surprised that his minor league roommate Elston Howard would soon get the call to "the Show" for reasons far removed from pure ballplaying talent. "There wasn't much competition," observes Power when he reflects on their jockeying for a Yankee roster spot, "because he [Howard] didn't have the numbers." (Nor did Howard ever match Power's hitting totals in the big leagues.) But before Elston Howard could come to New York, Vic Power had to be shipped elsewhere. Black and Puerto Rican New York fans, not an unsubstantial contingent, were already pressuring the ballclub and would not have tolerated promotion of the mediocre Elston Howard with the colorful Vic Power still buried somewhere in the minors. On December 16, 1953, New York packaged their promising Puerto Rican prospect along with five other journeymen and never-to-be's as part of an unheralded deal that secured veteran first sacker Eddie Robinson and four other no-names from the cellar-dwelling Connie Mack Athletics.

If Vic Power was not (in the eyes of Topping and Webb) a fine-hewn image of Yankee greatness, he was certainly baseball flamboyance personified. Never before or since has a first baseman played the game with quite the same inventive flair. During an era of two-handed defensive baseball, Power scooped ground balls and infield throws with a sweeping one-hand motion that was as ostentatious as it was deadly effective. Entrenched in the batter's box, he crouched from his patented stance and menacingly wagged his bat at rival hurlers in bold pendulum style. Giving no quarter to hecklers or umpires, he seemed to breathe pure fire at anyone who would dare challenge his manliness. His line-drive slugging, impassioned base running (he once stole home twice in a game) and one-handed glovework were all flashy enough to have guaranteed huge celebrity status with New York's blacks and Hispanics, had he been allowed to perform regularly in "the house that Ruth built" and alongside a supporting cast of Mantle, Berra, Ford, and Kubek. What Brooklyn exploited with Jackie Robinson, the Yankees let slip through their fingers with Vic Power.

And if ever there was a ballplayer born well before his time, that ballplayer was Puerto Rico's Vic Power. It seems obvious that in today's celebrity-oriented media market Power would have been a priceless phenomenon indeed. He was also a modern journalist's ultimate dream come true. Few players have enjoyed more controversy constantly swirling around their heads, and few have been so consistently quotable concerning their real and manufactured troubles. Even in his candid interview with journalist Danny Peary three decades after his big-league sojourn had come to an end, the quotable lines flowed from Power as easily as grass-burning grounders once leaped from his potent bat.

On his reputation as a troublemaker off the field: "In baseball there were many black players like Willie Mays and Roberto Clemente who dated white women, just as there were white players who went out with black women, and it would get me mad that they had better reputations than me only because they did it secretly."

On his relationship with Kansas City police: "The editor of the black paper in Kansas City wrote that he saw fifty policemen while driving by the ballpark; two blocks later he spotted a man beating his screaming wife, but there were no police around, he wrote, because they were at the ballpark waiting for Vic Power, so they could make a routine investigation."

On segregation in the South: "I went into a restaurant in Little Rock, Arkansas, and the waitress said, 'We don't serve Negroes,' and I said, 'That's okay, I don't eat Negroes. I want rice and beans.'"

Vic Power distilled in his onfield play and off-field words and actions the essence of a new uninhibited baseball style, though it was an unconventional style that Power and his countrymen would soon pay dearly for time and time again. But it was also a style that never failed to thrill 1950s ballpark patrons. Power, of course, was hardly a mere showboat—not if "showboat" meant trading fielding efficiency for the occasional spectacular if somewhat risky play. He was almost always spectacular, but he was also almost always nearly flawless. When sportswriters first began handing out Gold Glove awards for fielding prowess in the junior circuit, Puerto Rico's Vic Power was a hands-down winner at the first-base position for each of his first seven seasons (1958–1964). Significantly, no American League first sacker has ever won that many in a row in 30 seasons since. And when he once admitted to manager Jimmy Dykes that perhaps he should give up his flashy one-handed fielding style and his exaggerated batting stance and thus court the goodwill of critical teammates and opponents, the Cleveland field boss would hear nothing of it. "Don't ever argue with success" was the warning from manager Dykes. The sage skipper had rightly assured Power that others carped about his playing style simply because he usually beat them with it.

It is inevitable, perhaps, to compare Vic Power with his Cuban alter ego, Minnie Miñoso. And surprisingly, Power hardly suffers by such a comparison, especially when one looks at the overlapping five best seasons of their nearly simultaneous big-league careers:

Vic Power Versus Orestes "Minnie" Miñoso During Peak Seasons (1955–1959)

	Games	*BA*	*AB*	*H*	*R*	*HR*	*RBI*	*SB*	*FA*
Power	695	.299	2,778	831	416	73	321	17	.996
Miñoso	740	.303	2,756	837	467	88	433	71	.978

Only in RBIs and stolen-base totals does Miñoso boast a wide edge. But Power seems to make up handily for these offensive shortcomings on the defensive side of the ledger where he was undeniably the best at his position in either league. It should also be noted that for such a free-swinging batsman, Power stands remarkably close to Miñoso in the universally acknowledged prime yardstick — batting percentage. Power, of course, was a free swinger by necessity as much as chosen style. As he would later explain, if he did not swing at any pitch within arm's length of the plate, it was inevitably called a strike. Some umpires even told pitchers they would legislate all strikes against the less than popular (with umpires) Puerto Rican showboat ballplayer. Apparently a fan-pleasing flashy style was no more endearing to arbiters of the era than it was to club owners or field managers.

Such credentials make it somewhat surprising that history has so overlooked slick-fielding first sacker Vic Power of the Cleveland Indians and Kansas City Athletics. Power, like so many other early Latins, saw his career achievements (seven Gold Gloves, three .300 seasons at the plate, and over 1,700 career hits) largely buried under his negative (and always quite ill-deserved) reputation for excessive showmanship. Miñoso too was an ostentatious showman (and an off-field carouser who equaled Power's womanizing escapades). Yet Minnie was more successful at keeping his personal life away from the press and thus away from his detractors. For all such detractors, Power and Miñoso enjoyed equally widespread cult followings among fifties fans who marveled at their stylish and revolutionary defensive play and their aggressive offensive onslaughts (especially Minnie's "go-go" base running and Power's pendulum-swinging warclub). But cult followings were always the best to be hoped for in an era when tradition-bound baseball was at its most straight-laced and conformist. The age was one designed for clean-cut figures like Banks or Mays (or for those, at least, who fostered such public impressions), not self-anointed rebels like Miñoso or Power.

Vic Power was weaned on misunderstanding and misappreciation from almost his earliest days on a North American baseball diamond. Born Victor *Pollet and Pove* (the second family name in Spanish-speaking countries is the mother's), the young Power would have his "second" last name callously changed by a monolingual English-speaking teacher in his native Puerto Rico. The teacher assumed that Power's illiterate mother was simply spelling her name incorrectly (the teacher changed the *v* to *w* and added the *r*). When he later arrived in Canada as a teenage minor-leaguer, Power found the press picking up on his mother's recognizable (if incorrect) family name rather than his father's less pronounceable one.

Power himself best relates the story of the unusual name change: "I used to write *Victor Pollet Power*, but at Drummondville I was called Victor Pollet. But the French Canadians would say 'La Pollet' with an *l* sound, rather than a *y* sound. That sounded similar to a French sexual term and everyone would laugh. So they started calling me *Vic Power* instead" (Peary, *Cult Ballplayers*, 354).

Of course, this was only the first of numerous misunderstandings that would promote and retard the flamboyant Puerto Rican's budding probaseball career. Exhibiting a method of play that was deemed unfitting of the conservative image fostered by the proud Yankee ballclub, Power was first buried in the New York minor league system until traded away to cellar-dwelling Philadelphia (soon to be Kansas City). Once on the bigleague scene, however, he outraged owners and managers, shocked sportswriters (who regularly labeled him a showboat and a clubhouse lawyer), intimidated opponents, yet excited and entertained fans. The reason was simply that no black athlete since boxer Jack Johnson (not even Jackie Robinson, who had agreed to Rickey's requests to turn his other cheek) had shown such independence and flashed such colorful lust for freewheeling play.

A single perhaps apocryphal incident captures the rare wit and classy independence that were the final measure of Power's big-league career. Arrested for jaywalking in a rural Florida town during minor league days, the wisecracking Power reputedly retorted the judge's charges with a truly priceless jab: "I try to go to a bar or a movie house, or drink from a water fountain or use a bathroom, but I see that sign, 'For Whites Only.' So when I saw white people crossing the street when the green light came on, I figured that colored people could only cross when the light was red!" (Shatzkin, *The Ballplayers*, 881).

Adored by fans who appreciated flashy showmanship, Power was never an equal favorite with ballclub brass. And bad timing as well as unappreciative ownership always seemed to dog an unfulfilled career. Dumped by the Yankees in favor of the politically appropriate Elston Howard, Power languished in Kansas City during the worst of lean years with the American League's most lackluster franchise. His arrival in Cleveland (just like Miñoso's earlier) was a tad too late to enjoy the Indians' one glory season (1954) of the decade. Entrenched in Minnesota just in time to spark the Twins' upsurge of the early and mid-sixties, Power was nonetheless given his walking papers on the very eve of a first Minnesota pennant (released in favor of an inferior ballplayer, Bob Allison, who was moved into the first-base slot solely because of his home-run power). Finally getting one last chance at playing for a winner with the 1964 front-running Philadelphia Phillies, Vic Power was predictably injured in the very midst of the stretch drive. The hard-luck Puerto Rican was destined to be the most significant loss in the truckload of tragedies that stuck like glue to the self-destructing "Phutile Phils" of manager Gene Mauch. Power again sat on the sidelines in September while Mauch's men authored perhaps baseball's biggest late-season collapse.

But even such frustrations and disappointments were never quite enough to dim the fire that burned in baseball's most colorful flaming comet of the otherwise somnolent fifties. Few players have left the game behind them with a better philosophy of ballplaying or offered a better handle on the larger game of life: "Baseball was never everything. . . . I got to combine work with pleasure. . . . I had marvelous careers in Puerto Rico and the major leagues. . . . People remember me" (Peary, 373). Perhaps no other player of any era (Bo Jackson might be the only exception) will in the end be remembered quite as much for the style with which he played the game, nor does any other ballplayer (save perhaps Pete Reiser or Dizzy Dean) maintain an image that looms so much larger than the victories or the numbers he was able to post in the game's archives.

There are ballplayers' ballplayers. There are owners' ballplayers. And there are even fans' ballplayers. Vic Power was in every sense a true fans' ballplayer. Few have brought more enjoyment to the nation's pastime; perhaps none has ever enjoyed playing it more.

First Waves of the Latin Invasion

> We have trouble because we have so many Spanish-speaking and Negro players on the team. . . . They are not

able to perform up to the white ballplayers when it comes to mental alertness. . . . You can't make most Negro and Spanish players have the pride in their team that you get from white players.

—ALVIN DARK, SAN FRANCISCO GIANTS MANAGER

View it any way you wish, the sixties was truly baseball's lost decade. Not the least important residual of this unfortunate reality is the fact that a first significant wave of Latin American big-league immigration was also lost to our collective sense of baseball history. Americans simply weren't paying as much attention to the national pastime during a decade of turmoil that fostered the Vietnam War and tidal waves of political and social upheaval everywhere on the home front.

More in tune with the distancing realities of television and the rampant violence of the times, football (especially professional football) had suddenly occupied preeminence as the nation's newest sporting passion. For the first and perhaps only significant span during the past century, baseball, for a brief while at least, was pushed to the back pages of the nation's consciousness.

The tumultuous 1960s nonetheless launched two of our greatest Latin stars onto the nation's baseball diamonds—Clemente and Marichal—however little attention we may have paid them at the time. There had earlier been noteworthy Latin hitters and hurlers, to be sure. Luque had performed in a memorable World Series and had enjoyed one spectacular National League season during the heyday of Ruth and of Gehrig in the offense-oriented 1920s. Mexico's Bobby Avila was the first Latino to capture a league batting title when he paced the 1954 American League with his .341 average (trailed, ironically, by another Spanish-speaking phenom, Minnie Miñoso). But Luque was inconsistent (with only one 20-win campaign over a two-decade career) and branded (however undeservedly) as a hopeless hothead. And Avila was unspectacular, no matter how steady, hitting barely .300 in only two other seasons and far outshone on his power-laden team by legitimate superstars like Larry Doby, Al Rosen, and the fence-bashing Rocco Colavito.

Clemente and Marichal were admittedly a different breed altogether, far more illustrious than these other olive-skinned interlopers on the Anglo-American game. Roberto suddenly flashed in Pittsburgh as perhaps the most remarkable and colorful right fielder the game had seen. Topping .300 only once in five tries during the 1950s, Clemente soon staked out the 1960s as his personal center stage with eight consecutive .300-plus seasons. And if it were not for a single rival, Koufax, Marichal would assuredly have remained the dominant pitcher in baseball for at least a full decade after his 18-11 coming-out party in 1962.

And there were other bold diamond pioneers spilling from the barrios of San Juan, Puerto Rico, and the sun-drenched sugarcane plantations of Dictator Rafael Leonidas Trujillo's Dominican Republic. The Dominicans, for example, today so noticeable at the vanguard of baseball's ongoing Latin invasion, were already making their first widespread appearance during the decade otherwise devoted to the Beatles, San Francisco flower children, unprecedented home-front political assassinations, and the divisive nationwide antiwar movement.

First and most notable of this Dominican group was Felipe Alou (owner of 206 career homers and twice National League pacesetter with over 200 hits), followed almost immediately by his smart-hitting middle brother, Matty (a lifetime .307 hitter and 1966 National League batting champ with Pittsburgh), then younger brother Jesús (skilled contact hitter and author of over 1,200 career hits as well as a longtime journeyman outfielder of considerable defensive skill for all his slowness of foot). This single family of talented flychasers would make baseball history of the most arcane sort in New York's venerable Polo Grounds on September 10, 1963, appearing together for the first time as baseball's only all-brother outfield. The trio of sibling ballhawks even batted consecutively during the same inning on that historic day, yet failed to deliver a true Frank Merriwell script as all three made quick harmless outs.

The arrival of the Alou brothers would represent the first true success story from a small unheralded island nation that would eventually boast Caribbean baseball's most remarkable talent supply line. Today even the most casual Johnny-come-lately fan seems to know that the Dominican Republic (especially the sugar-mill town of San Pedro de Macoris) is a veritable bat-and-ball plantation that ceaselessly grows an endless supply of shortstops, hurlers, and muscular home-run bangers. This popular image of the Dominican talent font is filled with myths, to be sure, just as much of baseball lore is chock-full of myths and exaggerations. There is the myth of the Dominican shortstops. The truth is that the Dominican half of Hispaniola has produced just as many outstanding pitchers (Marichal, Andújar, Soto, José Rijo, Ramón and Pedro Martínez, and Juan Guzmán for starters) as it has middle infielders. And slugging outfielders (Alou, Carty, Guerrero, George Bell), wizardlike batsmen (Franco, Mota, Cédeño), and skilled backstops (Tony Peña, Luís Pujols, annual prospect Gilberto Reyes) have not been entirely lacking either.

The first bumper crop of Dominicans, however, were all outfielders named Alou. Felipe, the eldest, would make the biggest and most lasting splash. Felipe was the first Dominican import to reach a big-league diamond. Ossie Virgil is today universally acknowledged as the first Dominican big-leaguer. But Virgil had reached the majors from his boyhood home in New York City (where he had moved as a youngster) and not directly from distant Dominican shores. Virgil debuted with the New York Giants in 1956 after attending high school and learning sandlot baseball skills in the nearby Bronx. Virgil even attained U.S. citizenship and served a short spell in Uncle Sam's marines before joining the professional baseball wars.

It was Felipe Alou and not Ossie Virgil, then, who carried the full burden of a lonely baseball pioneer. Alou was fresh from his distant homeland and knew almost no English when he first donned a San Francisco jersey in 1958. Ossie Virgil was a streetwise kid from the Bronx and thus a Dominican in name but a New Yorker by cultural experience. (Virgil's more legitimate pioneering achievement was his appearance as the first black ballplayer to suit up for Detroit during the same 1958 campaign.) A few seasons later, Mateo ("Matty") would have his moment in the sun as well, joining Felipe in San Francisco in 1960 and hitting .310 over a full rookie season the following summer. While the spray-hitting Matty would never quite match his older brother in overall achievement, he would nonetheless be immortalized as a onetime league batting champion and posted a lifetime .300-plus batting mark. Jesús (called "Jay" by broadcasters and the press, who were apparently squeamish about his "religious-sounding" name) would always be diminished by comparison with his two more talented siblings. Yet the youngest Alou also had his boasting points: a 15-year career, three part-time seasons as a .300-plus batsman, and two World Series rings earned with the Oakland Athletics under Charlie Finley.

Thus in Vic Power's wake in the late fifties and early sixties came a boatload of other dark-skinned Spanish-speaking heroes who were fast becoming a recognized and much-loved dimension of the game. Clemente would quickly succeed Power as Puerto Rico's prime import north of Miami and its special national hero back home. Hard on Miñoso's heels out of Cuba would come pitchers Camilo Pascual and Pedro Ramos in the late 1950s and finally slugger Tony Oliva and hurler Luís Tiant once the Eisenhower era transformed into the Kennedy era. Talent flow also increased dramatically from the pipeline linking big league clubs with the land of puppet dictator Trujillo. And once Dominican doors flew open, there was yet another big-league team now rivaling the Washington Senators and Pittsburgh Pirates as prime importers of Hispanic American talent. The Giants—transported to San Francisco and stocked with the likes of Marichal, several Alous, Pagán, Cepeda, and Rubén Gómez—would be the first ballclub seemingly able to find enough recruits in the land of palm trees, sugarcane, and coconuts to provide local fans with true team glory (and some serious pennant runs to boot) and not a mere handful of individual Hispanic talents.

And this was but the starting knell for a legacy of Latin stars and superstars who filled the years between Sputnik and the Woodstock generation. Gone was an earlier day of scattered second-rate Spanish-speaking utility players found only in Washington and Pittsburgh. The Giants could boast

Cepeda and Marichal and Felipe Alou as household names. Cuban lefty Mike Cuellar would anchor the first potent Baltimore pitching staffs of the middle and late 1960s. A recognizable prototype, the glue-fingered Latino shortstop, which had been born in Chicago's Comiskey Park in the mid-1950s with first Venezuelan Chico Carrasquel and then his countryman Luís Aparicio, was now proliferating with similar models spread across both leagues—José Pagán and Tito Fuentes in San Francisco, Zoilo Versalles in Minnesota, Bert Campaneris in Kansas City, Willie Miranda (and later Aparicio again) in Baltimore, and Leo Cárdenas in Cincinnati. The dike was about to burst fully open.

Camilo ("Little Potato") Pascual and Pedro ("Pete") Ramos, a pair of colorful Cuban flamethrowers long shipwrecked in Washington, were among the earliest imports to turn the heads of many North American fans. Yet the careers of both these underappreciated hurlers were unfortunately as checkered as they were diverse and disparate. Pascual suffered humiliation as the league's most ineffectual hurler for half a decade before he suddenly and surprisingly dominated the same circuit for a second half-decade after 1961. And Ramos eventually supplanted his career traumas (earned as an always welcome target for rival league sluggers) with a much larger dose of real-world trauma, a postcareer stretch in Miami prisons after convictions for pistol toting and drug dealing.

One of my favorite baseball historians, Donald Dewey, once stumbled upon the perfect turn of phrase for it when he wrote tongue-in-cheek of anemic "toothpick companies" collapsing wholesale under otherwise respectable pitching staffs while hefty "lumber companies" were often enough to shore up even the feeblest big-league mound corps. Such was certainly the case during the 1950s reign of some altogether erratic ballclubs like the Pirates, Phillies, Cardinals, Cubs, and Senators. And such was certainly the fate of Camilo Pascual and Pedro Ramos once the lackluster Senators of Washington transformed themselves almost overnight into the potent Twins of Minneapolis–St. Paul.

It certainly did not help Pascual or Ramos, of course, that they first earned their meager major league paychecks with Clark Griffith's basement-dwelling Washington Senators. Although Pascual would eventually develop a wicked sidearm curve, making him nearly unhittable in the early 1960s, such was not the case at the outset. Few hurlers have survived a rockier debut in the big time and then rebounded to pitching fame and fortune. (Koufax, of course, immediately comes to mind.) "Little Potato" (his brother Carlos was "Big Potato" during his brief big-league trial) seemed at first to own exclusive rights to the loser's column in the morning newspaper box scores, posting an embarrassing 28-66 ledger over his first five summers. No one had a clearer claim to the title of "best losing pitcher" in the junior circuit between 1954 and 1958.

Ramos fared even worse. Pistol Pete always appeared more potent on the base paths and in the batter's box than on the hurler's hill, where his only remarkable achievement was leading the league in losses four straight seasons (1958–1961). Ramos often boasted that he was the fastest man afoot in the entire American League—a rare boast for a pitcher—and he would publicly challenge Mantle to foot races on several occasions though he was never granted a trial. And as a potent batsman (he was often used as a pinch batter), Ramos could boast of 15 lifetime homers, a performance which did little to compensate for the fact that as a moundsman he generously surrendered a league-record (since eclipsed) 43 circuit blasts.

Pete Ramos did eventually experience a remarkable career upsurge once he moved on to the powerhouse New York Yankees during the pennant stretch run of 1964, but only after his arm had already logged almost all of its ordained allotment of lifetime innings. And Pascual would finally enjoy a reputable team behind him when Griffith relocated his lackluster franchise into Minnesota. But what if this ill-starred pair had enjoyed a lineup consisting of the mature Killebrew, the flashy Versalles, and the clutch-hitting Earl Battey hitting and fielding behind them only half a decade earlier? Would Camilo Pascual, with his sidewinder curve and smoking straight ball, not have won 200, perhaps even 300 games? Would not Pete Ramos perhaps have been the Luís Tiant or Juan Marichal of the American League during the era of Stengel's Damn Yankees?

Pascual was a prototype workhorse who labored ceaselessly with a truly mediocre team in Washington, then belatedly blossomed with an equally exceptional ballclub in Minnesota. Each 10-year span of the past half century has unexpectedly showcased a single dominant Latin American hurler: Marichal in the 1960s, Tiant in the 1970s, and Valenzuela in the 1980s. And each of these pitching imports has in turn reflected the special ambiance of his own particular decade. The 1950s thus featured the yeomanlike Camilo Pascual, who labored nobly in futile pursuit of a confidence-shattering .297 winning percentage (1954–1959) strapped to a hapless Washington team that could neither knock out base hits from the batter's box or knock them down in the outfield. Despite his fabulously futile record, Pascual was nonetheless respected by fans and ballplayers alike as one of the most fearsome right-handers on the circuit. And once the lowly Senators donned a new disguise as the much-improved Minnesota Twins, Camilo Pascual performed a chameleon act largely unmatched in baseball history. Newly ensconced in the Twin Cities and revived by a legitimate pennant contender, the once haplass Pascual now turned in sterling 20-11 (1962) and 21-9 (1963) campaigns, also leading the league in strikeouts for three straight seasons (1961–1963).

Had Pascual labored in Yankee Stadium rather than Griffith Stadium during the epoch of Yogi Berra and Mickey Mantle, his name and not

Marichal's might well have been toasted regularly in hot-stove discussions of Latin America's original pitching hero—to say nothing of likely enshrinement in Cooperstown. Ill-starred teammate Pedro Ramos presented quite another somber saga, however. While Pascual's career coalesced with the arrival of a more talented supporting cast in Minnesota, Ramos instead drew new blood from a late-career transition into the bullpen. In the end, however, Cuba's second-best power pitcher of the 1950s, despite nearly parallel potential, somehow never quite escaped the treacherous pitfalls always built into the joyride of sudden athletic fame.

If the maturing of Killebrew had saved Pascual, it was the trade wire that eventually salvaged Pete Ramos. Only briefly did Ramos enjoy his single shot at true glory with the frontrunning Yankees, and handed such a rare career break so late in life, the Cuban Cowboy performed admirably well. By the time he had arrived in Yankee Stadium, however, both he and the invincible Bronx Bombers were dangerously near the end of a fragile prosperity. Acquired by manager Yogi Berra's Yanks at considerable cost (Ralph Terry, Bud Daley, and $75,000 cash), Ramos initially proved to be well worth the investment, especially during the pennant dash of September 1964. Ramos shored up a sagging New York staff by posting a sterling 1.25 ERA along with eight crucial saves. The "Ramos revival" could not have been better timed for Berra's outfit since a record-tying fifth-straight pennant was squarely on the line for the New Yorkers. Two final seasons in New York would also bring 32 additional saves from the Cuban Cowboy Ramos, yet the Bronx Bombers' sudden tumble from contention after 1964 soon made their aging relief ace quite expendable.

Once his brief joyride was over in New York, Ramos nosedived rapidly into almost total obscurity (drifting from Philadelphia to Pittsburgh to Cincinnati and then back to Washington during three unsuccessful swan-song seasons). And postbaseball life brought only an endless spell of further downward spiral. A lengthy string of arrests in the late 1970s and early 1980s for such egregious offenses as carrying concealed weapons, possessing and dealing marijuana and cocaine, aggravated assault, and drunken driving and parole violation eventually landed a three-year term at a Florida federal correction center. Life had at long last knocked Pete Ramos from the box even more effectively than a decade or more of uncooperative American League hitters.

If Pete Ramos was not nearly so effective over his total career as his Washington sidekick Camilo Pascual, winning nearly 60 fewer games and never approaching a 20-victory season, he was every bit as unforgettable. Most memorable about Ramos, off-field criminal antics aside, was his generous personal contribution to baseball's long-ball slugging of the fabulous 1950s. Indeed no pitcher in baseball history has allowed home runs in a more charitable fashion.

A chart comparing the game's most generous and most stingy providers of the long ball (adapted from research by Raymond González) will easily suggest the Cuban Cowboy's uniqueness as an unparalleled dispenser of the popular circuit blast. Ramos, owner of the highest number of homers allowed per innings pitched (one homer in every 7.48 frames), stands at the furthest end of the spectrum from dead-ball ace Big Ed Walsh. Working in the pre-Ruthian era and owning a truly "heavy" fastball, Walsh dispensed only about half as many roundtrippers (24) across a full 14-year career as Ramos provided for Mantle, Williams, Zernial, Colavito, and company during the 1957 season alone. Almost outdoing himself with a career-high 48 gopher balls in 1957, Ramos matched or surpassed Walsh's career totals in each of eight straight seasons (1956–1963) during one of baseball's most homer-happy epochs. Ramos pitched the bulk of this period in two of the league's most spacious arenas – Washington and Cleveland. Cozy ballparks around the rest of the circuit may have brightened each 1950s season for sluggers like Mantle, Zernial, and Williams, but no more than did a generous Washington hurler named Pistol Pete Ramos.

If the decade of Vietnam obscured Latin baseball heroes, the subsequent decade of Watergate exposed them in all their unfolding glory. The 1970s replaced time-worn stereotypes (the Latin ballplayer as hothead and goldbricker) with a legitimate class of colorful and productive Latin heroes. The mere number of new bat-and-glove-toting immigrants from south of the border now ensured an even greater impact than was possible during any previous era.

While Clemente, Cepeda, Marichal, and Camilo Pascual stood head and shoulders above several dozen of their utility-role countrymen throughout the sixties, the field was more crowded with Spanish-speaking "franchise players" by the mid-1970s. At the forefront of this new invasion were two talented, even dominant hitters playing on the same Minnesota team – Cuba's Tony Oliva and Panama's Rod Carew.

Oliva (the last impact player to escape Cuba after Castro and the last recruit for Washington Senators superscout Joe Cambria) had begun with a burst in the mid-1960s, wresting two batting titles and leading the league in base hits four times during his first big-league decade. By the early 1970s, Tony Oliva was a well-established American League star, having earned a third batting title in 1971 and knocking out a league-best 204 safeties to launch the new decade a season earlier. As that new decade progressed, however, Oliva was by and large overlooked by fans and media and thus experienced some of the unwarranted rejection that earlier had plagued San Francisco's slugging Orlando Cepeda. If Pete Ramos was Latin baseball's biggest disappointment of the 1950s and Cepeda held legitimate claim to that dubious distinction in the tumultuous 1960s, Oliva would own it outright across the less volatile decade to follow.

Baseball's Most Generous and Most Stingy Home-Run Pitchers

(Adapted from data provided by Raymond González, "Pitchers Giving Up Home Runs," *Baseball Research Journal* 10 (SABR, 1981): 18–28.)

Baseball's Ten Most Generous Home-Run Pitchers

Pitcher	*HRs Allowed*	*Innings*	*Innings/ HR Allowed*
1. Pedro Ramos (1955–1970)	*315*	*2,355*	*7.48*
2. Denny McLain (1963–1972)	242	1,886	7.79
3. Jim "Mudcat" Grant (1958–1971)	292	2,441	8.36
4. Don Newcombe (1949–1960)	252	2,155	8.55
5. Jim "Catfish" Hunter (1965–1979)	374	3,449	9.22
6. Ferguson Jenkins (1965–1983)	484	4,500	9.30
7. Robin Roberts (1948–1966)	502	4,689	9.34
8. Preacher Roe (1938–1954)	201	1,914	9.50
9. Jack Morris (1977–1993)	357	3,530	9.89
10. Luís Tiant (1964–1982)	*346*	*3,486*	*10.1*
10. Jim Bunning (1955–1969)	372	3,760	10.1
10. Murry Dickson (1939–1959)	302	3,052	10.1

Baseball's Ten Most Stingy Home-Run Pitchers

Pitcher	*HRs Allowed*	*Innings*	*Innings/ HR Allowed*
1. "Big Ed" Walsh (1904–1917)	24	2,964	123.5
2. Addie Joss (1902–1910)	19	2,336	122.9
3. Eddie Plank (1901–1917)	42	4,513	107.5
4. Eddie Cicotte (1905–1920)	32	3,224	100.8
5. Rube Waddell (1897–1910)	37	2,961	80.8
6. Al "Chief" Bender (1903–1925)	38	3,028	79.7
7. Jack Chesbro (1899–1909)	37	2,897	78.3
8. Joe "Iron Man" McGinnity (1899–1908)	50	3,459	69.2
9. Walter Johnson (1907–1927)	97	5,924	61.1
10. Vic Willis (1898–1910)	66	3,996	60.5

Oliva's plight after his initial half-dozen seasons is easy enough to explain on the surface of it. Never has a player burst on the scene with loftier performance or greater immediate impact. Nothing short of another Babe Ruth would have satisfied the Minnesota faithful. There can be little argument that Camilo Pascual's sudden successes in Minnesota resulted from increased offensive support for his efforts and that a large dose of that support came as much from his newly arrived countryman Oliva as from Killebrew or other established Washington holdovers like Jim Lemon and Bob Allison. The chunky Cuban youngster with little advance billing was almost overnight recognized throughout the baseball world as a rare natural-hitting wonder. Just about everyone had misjudged Tony Oliva in the earliest going despite brief .400-hitting trials with the Twins in 1962 (nine games) and 1963 (seven games), but no one made a more misguided judgment than those august *Baseball Digest* editors who authored the following scouting report: "Fair hitter, can make somebody a good utility outfielder."

The baseball brass of the Minnesota Twins organization had initially misjudged their Cuban prospect just as badly as the pundits of the pressroom. The ballclub promptly cut the new recruit, who had been recommended and signed by Cambria only three days after his arrival at his first U.S. tryout camp. Passed on to the Houston Colt '45s, Oliva was promptly rejected there as well. Snubbed again after a third tryout with Minnesota's Charlotte affiliate, Oliva finally landed a slot in the lineup with Wytheville of the D Rookie League. It was an opportunity he exploited to the fullest, posting an attention-grabbing .410 BA during his initial 1961 minor league campaign. Once their previously unwanted prospect proved he could smack the ball above a .400 clip, the Minnesota braintrust reluctantly decided perhaps they had better take a second and longer look after all.

If Oliva arrived like a flaming comet, the downside was that he would also soon author one of baseball's saddest stories of unremitting over-achievement and sustained underrecognition. Perhaps no rookie has burst upon the scene with more intensity and more offensive firepower than Tony Oliva. Here is the only player in all of baseball history to lay claim to league batting titles in each of his first two big-league campaigns. For at least half a decade after his record-setting rookie campaign of 1964 Oliva looked like the next great hitting superstar, a magical batsman cut straight in the mold of Ty Cobb, Joe DiMaggio, perhaps even Ted Williams. Cooperstown seemed an iron-clad certainty for a fluid hitter who posted 593 total base hits in his first three summers and averaged an incredible 185 safeties over his first half-dozen campaigns.

But Oliva's meteroic rise was soon dimmed by another bright comet and tarnished by his personal handicaps with the media during the heart of baseball's newly emerging television age. Poor English in the long run jettisoned his career more than enemy pitching could. And eventually teammate Rod Carew would ironically also take a huge bite out of Oliva's quickly diminishing star. Just when Oliva's batting performance began to dip from superhuman to merely mortal (with hit totals of only 161 and 136 for the injury-shortened seasons of 1967 and 1968), newcomer Rod Carew would go on his own batting tear in the same Minnesota lineup, racking up four 200-hit seasons, 10 straight .300-plus averages, and a record seven league batting titles between 1969 and the close of the seventies.

It was the injury bug, of course, even more than teammate Carew that lay at the heart of Oliva's sudden tailspin in achievement and related fan and media popularity. Severe finger damage, resulting from a reckless slide into home plate in Boston during Minnesota's 1965 pennant chase, was not quite enough to derail Oliva's second-straight batting title, but it was seemingly enough to launch the early downward spiral. A dislodged knee took its toll as well before World Series time that fall. While the knee continued to plague him over the next several campaigns, it did not prevent a regular appearance in the lineup. The 1968 campaign came to an abrupt early end in late summer, however, when Oliva next separated his shoulder while diving in the outfield to rob an opponent's base hit. A more serious knee injury (his third requiring surgery) finally reduced the Minnesota star's role to that of a part-timer during his pursuit of a third and final batting title in 1971. From 1971 to the end of his career, Oliva, like Mantle, played in such pain due to weakened knees that every swing was torture and each day's game required that he take a handful of pills and as many as 10 pain-killing shots before assuming his position on the field.

Today Oliva bitterly complains in rare interviews that he did everything that could be expected for Cooperstown immortality—posting a 15-year lifetime .300 average, grabbing Rookie-of-the-Year honors and eight league all-star selections, becoming multiple-year batting champion and league hits leader on five occasions, and remaining a consistent Gold Glove outfielder to boot. Only an MVP season (he was second to Brooks Robinson during his rookie campaign) and serious Hall-of-Fame consideration seem to have escaped this brilliant Cuban batsman, who still ranks second only to Carew as the all-time Minnesota leader in nearly every important hitting category outside long-ball production.

Yet if Oliva has been somewhat overlooked at career's end by the balloting baseball press, his 10-year Minnesota roommate Rod Carew has remained a potent presence impossible to dismiss or deny. The Canal Zone native has earned lasting fame over a two-decade career as perhaps the greatest contact hitter the sport has known, at least since the dead-ball days of Ty Cobb, George Sisler, and Tris Speaker. A magician at batsmanship, Carew pocketed seven league batting titles in Minnesota, chased a .400 average for much of the 1977 season, compiled a 19-year .328 career mark, knocked out 3,053 base hits, and ultimately earned Cooperstown enshrinement through balloting of the Baseball Writers' Association of America in January 1991. Whereas the unfortunate Oliva will perhaps always live somewhere in the shadows of Cooperstown, Carew has now become only the fourth native Latin star to enter baseball's most hallowed halls.

Carew is sometimes today thought of as the ultimate singles hitter, the American League version of Pete Rose. Yet there was far more to his versatile offensive arsenal than place hitting in the fashion of, say, Wee Willie

Keeler, Cobb, or Rose. His totals in doubles and triples were consistently high, due in part to an outstanding display of base-running savvy and natural foot speed. Carew's stolen-base totals were also substantial, even if they did not represent his true hallmark. And at times his bat supplied a surprising pop. Carew was never the legitimate long-ball threat that Oliva (220 career homers) always represented. Twice he did reach double figures, with 14 in 1975 and again in 1977, the year he scored 128 runs and flirted with .400 for much of the summer. And he holds a unique distinction of being the first Latin ballplayer ever to register baseball's rarest feat of hitting for the cycle in a big-league game.

Five Earliest Latin American Big-Leaguers to "Hit for the Cycle"

(Hitting homer, triple, double, and single in same ballgame, one of baseball's rarest batting feats)

Rod Carew (Minnesota Twins)	May 20, 1970	American League
César Cedeño (Houston Astros)	August 2, 1972	National League
César Tóvar (Minnesota Twins)	September 19, 1972	American League
César Cedeño (Houston Astros)	August 9, 1976	National League
Iván DeJesús (Chicago Cubs)	April 22, 1980	National League

While most of the Spanish-speaking heroes following on the heels of Miñoso and Clemente were slugging outfielders or infielders like Cepeda, Oliva, and Carew, the pitching side of the game was hardly unrepresented among the new imports. Marichal was busy in the senior circuit seeing to it that the inconsistent American League reputations of Pascual and Ramos were not the single holdover from glorious Latin mound legends (Luque, Méndez, Tiant the elder, and Dihigo) of long-lost blackball and barnstorming days. And there were other talented Caribbean moundsmen on the horizon.

Another Cuban ballplaying refugee was already carving personal baseball fame for himself against the backdrop of the political tragedies besetting his beloved island homeland, Cuba. Luís Tiant the younger came to the big leagues boasting a largely lost but nonetheless impressive family baseball heritage. The elder Tiant, his father, had been an unmatched hero for an earlier generation of Cuban fans. The diminutive lefty had long since carved out a substantial niche in black-league and winter-league play. Luís Tiant, Sr., had been a legendary blackball star, banned from major league arenas but not from immortality in island baseball lore. (The best story surrounding the elder Tiant's career is one involving his incredible pick-off technique. Once a befuddled batsman reputedly swung at a ball delivered to first rather than to home plate, a mistake that brought little sympathy from the home-plate umpire. "If you're dumb enough to swing, it's still a strike," bellowed the amused arbiter.) Tiant the elder was to be remembered by generations of Latins and blackball fans as the prototype junkball hurler, a master of changing-speed deliveries, famed for his herky-jerky motions and his lethal pick-off moves. But the name Tiant meant little to white fans of the big leagues until it began appearing in American League box scores during the sixties first in Cleveland and later in Boston.

In the 1960s it was Marichal who reigned supreme, finding true rivals only in Koufax and Bob Gibson for the undisputed title of "best" during one of pitching's finest eras. The 1980s was the decade of Fernandomania, and the 1990s seem already staked out by the young phenoms Juan Guzmán and Ramón Martínez. As much as Marichal owned the 1960s and Valenzuela would dominate the 1980s, so did Cuban Luís Tiant seize the 1970s as his personal stage for excellence.

"Looie" Tiant's baseball career was sealed by birthright and family heritage, yet marked by an agonizingly slow start and dogged after retirement by an unfortunate set of persistent ironies. The younger Tiant flashed early brilliance just as his famous father had three decades before. Signed to a first professional contract in the Mexican League by former Cleveland Indians batting star Bobby Avila, he quickly established a Pacific Coast League record for winning percentage (15-1, .938) before joining the parent Cleveland club midway through the 1964 season. His big-league debuts in Cleveland and Minnesota were a sad tale of unfulfilled potential, however. Tiant won 20 games but one time for the Indians (during the 1968 season, when he paced the AL with a brilliant 1.60 ERA) but then lost 20 the following summer and was promptly peddled to Minnesota. Tiant's earliest claim to fame was the dubious distinction of having duplicated an unwanted feat of his famed Cuban predecessor Adolfo Luque. His hallmark achievement seemed destined to be the embarrassing fact that like Luque, he had somehow managed to dovetail seasons in which he first won and then lost 20 games.

Then came a fateful stop in Boston, one that led to true stardom and a niche as one of that history-rich franchise's most popular players ever. Tiant was assured a prominent place in diamond history by his memorable 1972 and 1975 seasons alone. During the former campaign, he again reigned as ERA champ, fashioning a 1.91 standard; during the latter, he paced a pennant-winning Bosox team with 18 victories, then earned a crucial series-tying complete-game win in game four of the fall classic. Tiant was also immortalized (like only Stengel and Berra before him) by his colorful language ("Ees great to be weeth a weiner") and eccentric cigar puffing, albeit in this case the image most assuredly carried some negative racial and ethnic overtones. Distinguished by a twisting mound delivery that rivaled his father's and never separable off the field from his huge Havana cigar, Luís Tiant, Jr., was exactly the kind of colorful and flamboyant figure on which the dominant myth of the eccentric Latino player has always thrived.

His playing days ended, Luís Tiant, Jr., settled back to endure an arduous wait for the Cooperstown recognition earlier denied his father. But that wait will likely be a long and largely unjust one for the younger big-league Tiant because, for one thing, his timing was hopelessly bad. When the Cuban hurler first became eligible for Cooperstown election in 1988, he received only 47 votes from a panel seemingly disposed more in recent winters toward balloting for long-ball slugging stars. And in the stretch of years that have followed, Tiant has faced a glut of pitching immortals (first Palmer, Gaylord Perry, Jenkins and Seaver; now Carlton, Phil Niekro, Fingers, and Sutton) stacked up for Cooperstown consideration. And the endemic lack of respect often facing Latin players has perhaps also once again played a most unfortunate role.

Immortality will almost certainly be his some day, of course, although it may well take the baseball writers (or perhaps members of the Veteran's Committee) – those who ultimately confer glory at the ballot box – a few additional years to sanction what most fans already know in their collective wisdom. Statistically as well as artistically, only Juan Marichal (who alone leads Tiant in total victories, yet trails the Cuban as all-time Latin strikeout king) was indisputably a greater all-around Latin pitcher. Arguments might well be made for Cuellar, Luque (see Chapter 1), Dihigo (Chapter 8), or even Dennis Martínez. But only Tiant has the total numbers to approach within a shout and a yell of Marichal's otherwise unchallenged throne.

While Tiant and Marichal were busy stringing up victories and logging strikeouts across the junior and senior circuits, an exceptional Venezuelan speedster left over from the previous decade was continuing to burn up the base paths and comb the infields of the American League with an equal ardor. Fellow countrymen Chico Carrasquel and Luís Aparicio today stand center stage in any saga of the first wave of Latin speedsters who would defend the infields and swipe bases around the big-league circuit during the early and mid-fifties. But Chico Carrasquel's career was indeed short-lived (he lasted as a regular for only seven seasons after his all-star debut in 1950), thus Carrasquel was never able to escape the unfortunate label of "journeyman" ballplayer. Aparicio, on the other hand, continued to run and run until he had run himself all the way to the very doorstep of Cooperstown.

Aparicio, especially, might well be extended the bulk of the credit for reviving base running as a central offensive weapon of the game. Willie Mays and Jackie Robinson had terrorized rival pitchers once they reached base, but not nearly as much as they did with their power-packed bats. As respectable as was his hitting and as brilliant as was his fielding, it was as a base stealer that Aparicio left his lasting mark upon the national pastime. Here was the first true base-thieving specialist by trade since the passing of Ty Cobb and Eddie Collins three decades earlier. Aparicio was the bridge between Cobb of the dead-ball period and other bold base-running threats to follow in the modern era of plastic grass and indoor play. First Maury Wills, then Lou Brock and Rickey Henderson, eventually ran in Aparicio's shadows. But unlike Cobb, Brock, or Henderson, Aparicio was a magician on the base paths in an era altogether undistinguished for base-running wizardry.

For nine straight seasons (1956–1954) Aparicio led the American League in steals, all during a decade and a half when long-ball slugging (and thus conservative base running) was the only sanctioned style of offensive play. Outdistanced in steals by National Leaguer Mays during his first three seasons, Aparicio doubled the totals of his nearest challengers in both leagues by 1959 and was rivaled only by National Leaguer Maury Wills during the early sixties. Unlike his followers—Wills, Brock, and Henderson—when Aparicio began tearing up the base paths in the mid-fifties, he ran not only against enemy pitchers and catchers but also smack against the grain of the game itself.

Two final larger-than-life Latino athletes from the sixties and seventies seem to remain forever linked by fate, despite their huge differences in personal history and personal style. Orlando Cepeda (1958–1974) was a raw rebel slugger from Puerto Rico who knocked down stadium fences with his ceaseless barrage of extra-base blows. Yet Cepeda always somehow seemed to be waging war against hometown management as much as against enemy pitchers. Cuba's statuesque Tony Pérez (1964–1986) was equally threatening with a Louisville slugger; Pérez, however, was from the beginning the very prototype of an ultimate team player and thus also the ideal franchise man.

Of all the emerging Latin superstar ballplayers of the 1960s who managed to foster reigning stereotypes as much as unchallenged baseball reputations, none did so more consistently (or more infuriatingly) than slugging first baseman Orlando "Baby Bull" Cepeda, slugging star with the 1962 NL champion San Francisco Giants and later valued role-player for the 1967-1968 champion St. Louis Cardinals. Son of a famed Puerto Rican blackball idol (Perucho "Bull" Cepeda) whom many still consider the island's greatest *pelotero* of a bygone era, the younger Cepeda signed his first North American pro contract at the tender age of 17. Proving his mettle as an untutored youngster, Cepeda immediately tore up minor league pitching while still a teenager, pounding out a .393 average with the 1955 Salem (Virginia) D club. Adjustments to the realities of U.S. baseball were not so easy off the field as on for a dark-skinned Latin teenager who spoke almost no English, however, and Orlando Cepeda's budding career was marked from the outset by incidents of racial prejudice and more than a little cultural misunderstanding.

Raised in ethnically tolerant Puerto Rico and therefore quite unprepared for the deep-seated racial hatreds still haunting the American South, Cepeda soon suffered a rude awakening visited upon so many of his ball-playing countrymen during the same era.[1] First came a nightmare overnight bus trip from Florida through Georgia and the Carolinas, which provided the first rude lessons about segregated seating. Arriving in backwater Salem, Cepeda innocently enough strolled through a downtown shopping district only to be strong-armed by shotgun-toting police as soon as he stopped to stare through a local shop window. Black males, it turns out, were not permitted to walk the streets of downtown Salem after dark in 1954. The terrified youngster could only repeat *"béisbol!"* over and over until someone at the local lockup finally phoned team officials to bail him out of a frightening set of circumstances.

After striking out four times in one early game at Salem, Cepeda suffered yet another rude awakening when an infuriated manager screamed what would soon become a familiar epithet: "You fuckin' Puerto Ricans are all alike!" Able to recognize only the words "Puerto Rican," the naive rookie mistakenly assumed a compliment and even further enraged his intolerant skipper by stammering, "Sank you very much," the only English phrase he knew.

Cepeda's big-league sojourn soon served to illustrate the rampant racism found even on the San Francisco Giants ballclub for which he played. The Giants clubhouse of the early 1960s fostered a bitter undertone of intolerance that would also severely plague Dominican ballplayers Felipe and Matty Alou, star pitcher Juan Marichal, and another Puerto Rican athlete of considerable natural skill, shortstop José Pagán. All were eventual victims of vitriolic skipper Alvin Dark (who took over in San Francisco in 1961) and a Giants management that strongly discouraged "fraternization" between the half-dozen Latin Americans filling out the team roster. Dark actually forbade Spanish in the clubhouse and on the ballfield, and frequently blamed team losses on the reputed lackadaisical attitude of dark-skinned Cuban and Puerto Rican ballplayers. Manager Dark became infamous in particular for his slanderous remarks to the press about his black and Latin players, once going so far as charging that "we have trouble because we have so many Spanish-speaking and Negro players on the team. . . . They are not able to perform up to the white ballplayers when it comes to mental alertness" (Dark and Underwood, *When in Doubt, Fire the Manager*, 95).[2] And Dark found a particularly vulnerable target in his proud, boisterous, and carefree slugging first sacker, often accusing Cepeda of being lazy in his approach to the game and lacking all-out enthusiasm on the field.

One thing that especially hassled Dark was Cepeda's practice of carrying his portable record player on road trips (an unusual event in 1965, if commonplace among ballplayers in the 1980s or 1990s). The manager subsequently complained to the press that his slugger often slumped at the plate because the stereo unit was obviously wearing out his arms in airport lobbies. But Cepeda's onfield style brought the most persistent heat. "You don't want to play this game, you never wanted to play this game!" Dark reportedly bellowed on numerous occasions when Cepeda (slowed by painful knee problems after 1963) showed anything less than Pete Rose hustle.

Cepeda was merely mystified. Wasn't he slugging the ball consistently at a .300 clip? Didn't he top the circuit in 1962 in both homers and RBIs, far outdistancing any of his teammates? Was a certain style of serious "game face" more important than a ringing bat? Couldn't a ballplayer have fun while he was being so productive? Dark's "born-again" Christian work ethic and Cepeda's carefree Latin spirit seemingly stood at opposite poles of the universe.

Like his teammate Marichal, Cepeda seemed largely immune to countless off-field distractions. Despite his manager's unprovoked taunts, he nonetheless rose above such constant bickering to amass a set of Cooperstown credentials beyond reproach. At the same time, however, he remained haunted off the field by a reputation for unmotivated play and uncooperativeness with the mass media. Like any athlete in the then-small minority whose native language was not English, the proud Cepeda was usually a most reluctant interview. And unquotable players were usually dismissed as unfriendly players by those who made their living writing about the game.

Eventually the ax would fall one final time on the ill-starred Cepeda, this time in the form of a single unfortunate incident at career's end that shattered the embattled slugger's fragile public image. His soiled onfield reputation may have been largely manager Dark's doing, but the postretirement slip that slammed the doors of Cooperstown was one for which the former ballplayer could only blame himself. Having retired to Puerto Rico in 1974 as a public hero second in stature only to the martyred Clemente, Cepeda shocked critics and champions alike when he was arrested at San Juan's airport with a trunkload of marijuana hidden in his car's boot. For his latest transgressions, the fallen idol received a five-year jail sentence (of which he served but a single year) and a blow to his public stature that was even more severe than prison time. In the end, nearly 400 career homers and a reputation as one of the sixties' greatest long-ball sluggers may not now be enough to expunge Orlando Cepeda's postcareer transgressions from the hypocritical and ever-watchful public eye.

An instructive contrast with Cepeda in playing style and career reputation is provided by Cuban slugger Tony Pérez, an equally heavy-hitting infielder with the Big Red Machine Cincinnati Reds teams of the early and mid-1970s. Pérez slugged baseballs throughout the 1970s in Cincinnati just as Cepeda had done on the West Coast during the 1960s, and in the end Pérez and Cepeda stood alone, deadlocked as all-time Latin American home-run pacesetters. Yet if Cepeda was largely fortune-plagued in his assigned role with the unappreciative San Francisco ballclub (as well as in his destined fate to perform within the baseball-poor decade of the less-glamorous 1960s), Tony Pérez was comparably blessed by his fated association of team and playing era.

For half a dozen glorious summers at career's height, Pérez showcased his heavy-hitting wares in the constant media glare created by Hall-of-Fame teammates Johnny Bench and Joe Morgan as well as the incomparable (if now banished) Pete Rose. His personal-best season of 1970, with high-water marks in four major hitting categories (40 HR, 129 RBI, 107 runs, .317 BA), was sufficient to pace a National League championship year for his ballclub. Five times he appeared in World Series play with Cincinnati or Philadelphia. And in the end Tony Pérez outstripped Cepeda in all major hitting departments save homers and batting average.

In the end it is the image of a true winner, a more than cordial relationship with the working press and media, and an irreproachable personal lifestyle that have left the Hall-of-Fame credentials of Tony Pérez immaculate (if somewhat obscured by the glitter of several Big Red Machine teammates) as he approaches another round of eligibility for Cooperstown enshrinement. Pérez's Cooperstown votes totalled 215 of the needed 323 in 1992, then 233 of the required 318 in 1993. By contrast, Cepeda remains a tarnished candidate in the public perception despite the fact that he has actually outpolled Pérez in each of the past three Cooperstown headcounts (192 ballots in 1991, 246 in 1992, and 252 in 1993). With the public image of a Tony Pérez, Orlando Cepeda would doubtless be a Hall of Fame shoo-in; with the candidacy of Cepeda already decided (thus eliminating the vote-splitting factor), Tony Pérez would seemingly be a lock for immortality as well.

In the end Cepeda was cursed more than anything by career assignment with a ballclub and manager that at best only tolerated his considerable baseball skills and clubhouse contributions. It seemed that Cepeda's worst enemy was his manager, Alvin Dark, and not opposing hurlers or rival bench bosses. It didn't start out that way, of course, as Cepeda's first big-league skipper, Bill Rigney, had nothing but praise for his prize rookie in 1958, calling his Baby Bull "the best young right-handed power hitter I've ever seen." Cepeda rewarded his first manager's trust with Rookie-of-the-Year honors during his freshman campaign (25 HR, 96 RBI, .312 BA, league-best 38 doubles) and an even more spectacular sophomore season (27 HR, 105 RBI, .317 BA).

Cepeda, of course, was soon battling himself as well as Alvin Dark, and a wrecked knee in 1964-1965 only led to further charges of malingering and an eventual trade to St. Louis in mid–1966 for journeyman hurler Ray Sadecki. There would be one great "rebound" season that brought a league-leading 111 RBI total, a .325 BA, and a pennant for St. Louis. But well-publicized late career gaffes (like carping to the press about uncooperative and unappreciative management) plus one colossal postcareer mistake have cost Orlando Cepeda a much greater share of baseball recognition, a lion's share that once might have been his merely for the asking.

Whereas Cepeda had the misfortune of playing several seasons under Al Dark and the insensitive Giants regime, Tony Pérez was truly blessed with a slot on the Big Red Machine. Playing alongside Hall-of-Famers Joe Morgan and Johnny Bench and eventual Hall-of-Famer Rose, Pérez was assured every possible crack at postseason heroism. One recalls, however, that Pérez did as much as Morgan, Bench, Rose, Griffey, Concepción, and company to put the true muscle into the Big Red Machine lineups that terrorized senior-circuit rivals at the end of the 1960s and onset of the 1970s. At career's end, the versatile Cuban ranked as the fourteenth-best RBI man in baseball history. For a full decade (1967–1976) he anchored a Big Red Machine batting order almost without parallel, six times topping 100 RBIs (Bench also registered six 100-RBI seasons during this period). Throughout his decade in the Cincinnati infield, Pérez and the Reds managed four pennants; his greatest single season (1970) matched Bench's (also 1970, with 45 HR, 145 RBI, .293 BA) and thus provided the champion Redlegs with one of the greatest single-season slugging tandems ever suited up in the same lineup.

It is difficult, perhaps pointless, to debate who owned the final edge between these two premier Latin sluggers of the 1960s and 1970s. Appropriately they finished lengthy careers tied with exactly 379 homers each, the Latin standard that will someday likely be challenged by José Canseco or Juan González but has nonetheless stood as unapproachable for almost a decade since Pérez retired in 1986. Pérez perhaps boasts slightly superior Hall of Fame credentials in the eyes of an untutored fandom that mainly recalls pennants and World Series appearances as well as home run and RBI totals. Pérez arguably also maintains a slight edge in rosy public image (an edge established as much by absence of off-field scandal and freedom from rumors of clubhouse agitations as by postseason heroism or hair-thin edge in slugging totals). Yet overall, Cepeda does seem to merit a faint nod in yearly batting numbers, especially when one considers efficiency (BA, HR, and RBI percentages, .300 seasons, and seasons with league-leading totals) and not mere amassing of raw power numbers.

It is only part and parcel of the hidden tragedy of modern Latin ballplayers that so much controversy now swirls around the Cooperstown

Pérez Versus Cepeda in Batting Production and Efficiency

Category	*Pérez*	*Cepeda*	*Advantage*
Career length	23 years	17 years	Pérez (+6 seasons)
Games played	2,777	2,124	Pérez (+653 games)
At-bats	9,778	7,927	Pérez (+1,851 at-bats)
Runs scored	1,272	1,131	Pérez (+141 runs)
Base hits	2,732	2,351	Pérez (+381 hits)
Doubles	505	417	Pérez (+88 doubles)
Triples	79	27	Pérez (+52 triples)
Home runs	379	379	*Even*
Home-Run percentage[a]	3.87	4.78	Cepeda (+0.91 HRs)
Runs batted in	1,652	1,365	Pérez (+287 RBI)
RBI per game	.59	.64	Cepeda (+0.05 RBI/Game)
RBI per 100 ABs	16.9	17.2	Cepeda (+0.3 RBI)
Total bases	4,532	3,959	Pérez (+573 Total Bases)
Batting average	.279	.297	Cepeda (+0.018)
.300-plus seasons	3	9	Cepeda (+6 seasons)
Slugging average	.463	.499	Cepeda (+0.036 SLG)
On-base percentage	.344	.353	Cepeda (+0.009 OBP)
Batting runs[b]	272	337	Cepeda (+65 BR)
Bases on balls	925	588	Pérez (+337 walks)
Strikeouts	1,867	1,169	Cepeda (−698 Ks)
Strikeouts per 100 ABs	19.1	14.7	Cepeda (−4.4 Ks)
Stolen bases	49	142	Cepeda (+93 SB)
World Series years	5	3	Pérez (+2 World Series)

[a]Home Runs per each 100 At-Bats (see Thorn and Palmer, *Total Baseball*, 1993 edition).
[b]Linear weights measure of runs contributed beyond what a league-average batter might have contributed (for explanation, see Thorn and Palmer, *Total Baseball*, 1993 edition).

candidacy of Cepeda and Pérez. The discredited San Francisco slugger remains tarnished by a single off-field escapade, while the backbone of Cincinnati's Big Red Machine has simply fallen victim to happenstance—playing on a team where he was but one among a half-dozen candidates for canonization. Pérez suffers precisely as Brooklyn's Gil Hodges has long suffered in the eyes of Cooperstown voters. With Robinson, Reese, Snider, and Campanella already ordained as Cooperstown legends, how true a giant could Gil Hodges have been? It was either Robbie or the Duke or Pee Wee or Campy—each more colorful than the silent and stoic Hodges—who carried Brooklyn on his shoulders. So stands the reasoning for many who now debate the legacy of Tony Pérez, a workmanlike hero similarly buried by an avalanche of Big Red Machine sympathy for flashier stars named Pete Rose, Joe Morgan, and Johnny Bench.

But in the end it is also the stereotypical Latin American ballplayer image—"good hit, no field" by birthright, "fiery but undisciplined and even unsportsmanlike"—that perhaps contributes to the Cooperstown woes of Pérez and especially Cepeda.[3] When Pete Rose scampered the bases and crashed into infielders with a raging fire inside, he was widely lionized by fans everywhere as the unsurpassed hustler. When Tony Pérez or Orlando Cepeda did the same, they were quickly branded as insufferable "hotdog" or cocky rebel. Racism and damning stereotype have never quite expired from North America's sporting scene.

Of the bevy of underappreciated Latin American stars, Cepeda and Pérez are not the only jilted Cooperstown candidates, to be sure. Clemente's tragic death while an active player removed any agony surrounding several potential rounds of Cooperstown balloting. But Marichal and Aparicio stood hopefully on the outside far longer than perhaps they should have. And today Oliva and Tiant are perhaps more unjustly overlooked than any other recent Hall of Fame rejects save perhaps Brooklyn's Gil Hodges, Whiz Kid hero Richie Ashburn, and Cepeda and Pérez. Such is the fate of the displaced Latin American ballplayer caught between two cultures and two ballplaying worlds.

Yet for those millions of *fanáticos* who call Caribbean cities and villages home and who have thus been weaned on winter-league legends like Méndez and Dihigo or big-league heroes like Clemente, Tiant, and Miñoso, the nationalistic pride generated by a dozen or more true Latin superstars of the past four decades seems once again to outstrip any measure by mere Cooperstown approbation.

Go South, Young Man, Go South

Perhaps a modern Horace Greeley would cry, "Go *south*, old bird dog, go *south*!" (Leave aside the fact that it was not Greeley but the less celebrated author John Basbone Soule who first penned the injunction that fortune indeed lay on the new frontier.) Yet it was not the dozen or so stars of the fifties and sixties (Clemente, Miñoso, Power, Pascual, and Ramos) that constituted a true Latin invasion in the years between Jackie Robinson's revolution of the 1940s and baseball's fullfledged westward expansion of the late 1950s or the birth of divisional play by the end of the 1960s. Every bit as responsible were the exploding waves of role-players, journeymen, and just plan solid ballplayers filling out everyday lineups around the expanding major league circuit. For every Clemente, there were a dozen

Carlos Paulas, Willie Mirandas, Nino Escaleras, and José Santiagos. A new talent font had now sprung wide open, and a few ballclubs especially would soon tap it in the most significant ways.

And while stars like Marichal, Clemente, Power, Oliva, and Cepeda were prominent everyday reminders of this new Latin talent explosion, other less visible baseball men (scouts, coaches, and front-office executives) were feverishly at work behind the scenes constructing a somewhat quieter baseball revolution. The stories of several such figures and their exhaustive recruiting efforts are also central to the story of baseball's modern Latin flavor.

No team has exploited this new Caribbean baseball talent pool as efficiently and with as much foresight as has the expansion Toronto ballclub under the leadership of General Manager Pat Gillick and his handpicked Latin American scouting coordinator, Epy Guerrero. Gillick's reliance on Latin American scouting reflects a long-standing policy of the Toronto organization to build quickly by circumventing the traditional amateur draft of U.S. college and high school talent. This normal drafting procedure early proved a major disappointment for the Toronto franchise, providing only Lloyd Moseby (number one pick in 1978) through the more conventional channels of recruitment. Gillick has returned instead to a long-standing working arrangement with Guerrero, a skillful talent sleuth who works from his home base of Santo Domingo in the Dominican Republic and was an important former associate during Gillick's earlier player-development assignments with the Houston Astros and New York Yankees. As a front-office team, Gillick and Guerrero first made their mark in Latin America with the discovery and signing of phenom César Cedeño for the Astros. A handful of early coups in Houston later turned into a full-blown talent raid once the two were established in Toronto.

The marriage of Pat Gillick and Epy Guerrero has been remarkably successful in talent procurement and public relations. For more than a decade, the Jays have held regular Dominican clinics, built modern if modest training facilities, and taken other concrete steps to maintain high visibility and increasing popularity with the baseball-crazed Dominican youth. And the unmatched popularity of the Blue Jays (*Los Azulejos*) in the Dominican Republic has received its greatest boost from the onfield successes in recent seasons of such overachieving native sons as Alfredo Griffin, Manny Lee, Tony Fernández, Juan Guzmán, and the lionized muscleman George Bell.

When Toronto's Jays finally reached the pinnacle of championship baseball as World Series winners in 1992 and 1993, many of the franchise's early building blocks (Bell, Manny Lee, Nelson Liriano, Junior Félix, Venezuela's Luís Leal, and Puerto Rico's Otto Velez) had long since departed. Ultimately the Jays had constructed a consistent winner more with high-priced mercenaries known as free agents than with homegrown farm-system talent from the tropics. But the old Latin fixtures were still there. Roberto Alomar (acquired from San Diego in 1992) anchored the championship infield and iced a first American League title with his dramatic 1992 American League Championship Series home run. Tony Fernández missed out on a first World Series appearance in 1992 but returned in time to spark the Toronto offensive onslaught of the 1993 series. And the club's newest pitching star, Dominican Juan Guzmán, was perhaps the essential key in finally achieving a pair of world championships, compiling a remarkable 40-11 record (.784 winning percentage) and an even more spectacular post-season performance over his first three big-league outings.

George Bell (all-time club home-run and RBI leader but since departed to the Chicago Cubs and Chicago White Sox) and Tony Fernández (flashy all-star shortstop who still holds the team career batting mark despite being peddled to San Diego at the end of the 1990 campaign and then returning to Toronto in 1993) have remained the most visible and productive Latin recruits to ply their wares in the American League's Canadian city. Other impact players for Toronto have included Jorge Orta (whose single season with the club sparked a franchise-first .500 ledger), Luís Gómez (the ball-club's first free-agent signee), Dámaso García (a fixture at second base for seven seasons), Alfredo Griffin (American League Rookie of the Year in 1979), Juan Beníquez (a major force in the Jays' ill-fated pennant drive of late-season 1987), Manny Lee (heir apparent to Tony Fernández before being dealt to the Texas Rangers in 1993), Junior Félix (a major surprise of the 1989 season but subsequently peddled to California), and Nelson Liriano (former regular second sacker now playing for the expansion Colorado Rockies). Among this past and present batch of notable Latin Blue Jays, all boast Dominican heritage with the exception of Orta (Mexico), Gómez (Mexico), and Beníquez (Puerto Rico).

If the expansion Toronto Blue Jays under the administration of GM Pat Gillick and superscout Epy Guerrero have fostered the largest recent pool of Latin players, it was the old Washington Senators of the late 1940s and early 1950s that first exploited the rich mother lode of Caribbean and South American baseball talent. A Cuban tradition fitfully spawned by Cincinnati's dark-skinned Marsans and Almeida, then continued single-handedly by Luque in the Black Sox era, was finally turned up a notch several decades later with the Washington Senators and their pioneering talent sleuth, "Papa Joe" Cambria.

Cambria pioneered at opening up the "Cuban connection" for Clark Griffith's lowly Senators (also known from time to time as the Washington Nationals, despite their American League home) during the immediate postwar period. Yet it was Griffith who remained the motivating force behind Cambria's now famous expeditions into dictator Fulgencio Batista's pre–Castro Cuba. A young Clark Griffith had become enamored of Cuban baseball talent more than two decades earlier while finishing out a stint as manager of the Cincinnati Reds, and Griffith took his pioneering steps when he inked Armando Marsans and Rafael Almeida for the sluggish Reds in 1911 (see Chapter 7). Griffith was already gone from Cincinnati by 1912, having departed for a remarkable half-century career as Washington's bench manager, club owner, and franchise icon. It would be a mild assessment to say that things did not always run smoothly for Griffith in his subsequent years as owner of a languishing second-division ballclub in the nation's capital. When the Depression years set in full force after a rare Washington pennant climb in 1933, the always tight-pocketed Griffith found himself especially strapped for player resources and much-needed gate receipts. Cambria (who had worked his way from sandlot player in his native Massachusetts to controversial minor league club owner in Albany, New York, and finally to Griffith's back-room assistant in Washington) was soon dispatched to Cuban shores in search of some inexpensive but serviceable prospects.

Cambria's first signee, Bobby "Tarzan" Estalella, a legendary long-ball slugger in his native Cuba's winter leagues, was an immediate fan favorite who opened the door for further Cuban imports. Estalella was in reality a lead-fingered third sacker who managed but 44 roundtrippers (alongside 41 errors) and a respectable .282 BA over parts of nine big-league campaigns (half of those with Connie Mack's Athletics during the talent-thin war years). But Washington fans of the late 1930s had so much fun watching the gritty Estalella knock down enemy grounders with every part of his anatomy save his glove hand that they often phoned the park in advance to find out if the Cuban was in the lineup before making the trek to the Griffith Stadium grandstands.

By the time Griffith's personal bird dog, Cambria, had completed his work—which resulted in signing over 400 Cuban prospects during the quarter century between 1934 and 1959—the Senators maintained only six farm clubs and three full-time scouts (by far the lowest numbers in the majors) and chose to recruit seriously only along the U.S. eastern seaboard and throughout the Caribbean basin. While Griffith's penny-pinching plan for garnering cheap talent won few ballgames for the hapless Nats of the Golden Fifties, the influx of colorful Latino players like Camilo Pascual, Pete Ramos, José Valdivielso, Julio Becquer, Carlos Paula, Sandy Consuegra, Mike Fornieles, and dozens more not only salvaged the ailing Washington franchise but opened the eyes of competing general managers to a rich and untapped pool of Latin American player talent seemingly ripe for the picking.

Latin American ballplayers began appearing in force on Washington rosters in the years immediately preceding the Second World War. Mexican

The Honor Roll of 1940s and 1950s Cuban-born Washington Senators

(Sources: *Washington Senators 100th Anniversary Yearbook* (Washington, D.C., 1959); John Thorn and Pete Palmer, editors, *Total Baseball*, third edition (New York, 1993).

Nonpitchers	*Position*	*Years*	*BA*[a]	*Games*	*HR*	*RBI*	*Hits*
Alvarez, Oswaldo	Infielder	1958–59	.212	95	0	5	42
Becquer, Julio	First Base	1955–63	.244	488	12	114	238
Campos, Francisco[b]	Outfielder	1951–53	.279	71	0	13	41
Delis, Juan[b]	Infielder	1955	.189	54	0	11	25
Estalella, Roberto	Infielder	1935–49	.282	680	44	308	620
Fleitas, Angel[b]	Shortstop	1948	.077	15	0	1	1
Gómez, Preston[b]	Infielder	1944	.286	8	0	2	2
Guerra, Mike	Catcher	1937–51	.242	565	9	168	382
Miranda, Willie	Shortstop	1951–59	.221	824	6	132	423
Paula, Carlos[b]	Outfielder	1954–56	.271	157	9	60	124
Suarez, Luís[b]	Third Base	1944	.000	1	0	0	0
Torres, Gil[b]	Outfielder	1940–46	.252	346	0	119	320
Valdes, Rogelio (Roy)[b]	Pinch Hitter	1944	.000	1	0	0	0
Valdivielso, José	Infielder	1955–61	.219	401	9	85	213
Versalles, Zoilo	Shortstop	1959–71	.242	1,400	95	471	1,246

Pitchers	*Threw*	*Years*	*W-L*[a]	*ERA*	*IP*	*Games*
Consuegra, Sandalio	Right	1950–57	51-32	3.37	809	248
Fornieles, Mike	Right	1952–63	63-64	3.96	1,156	432
García, Ramón[b]	Right	1948	0-0	17.18	3	4
González, Julio[b]	Right	1949	0-0	4.72	34	13
Gonzáles, Wenceslao[b]	Left	1955	0-0	27.00	2	1
Hernández, Evelio[b]	Right	1956–57	1-1	4.45	58	18
Marrero, Conrado[b]	Right	1950–54	39-40	3.67	735	118
Martínez, Rogelio[b]	Right	1950	0-1	2.25	1	2
Monteagudo, Rene	Left	1938–44	3-7	6.42	168	46
Moreno, Julio[b]	Right	1950–53	18-22	4.25	336	73
Ortiz, Baby[b]	Right	1944	0-2	6.23	13	2
Pascual, Camilo	Right	1954–71	174-170	3.63	2,930	529
Pascual, Carlos[b]	Right	1950	1-1	2.12	17	2
Ramos, Pedro	Right	1955–70	117-160	4.08	2,355	582
Roche, Armando[b]	Right	1945	0-0	6.00	6	2
Sánchez, Raul	Right	1952–60	5-3	4.62	89	49

[a] = Complete record with Washington and all other ballclubs.
[b] = Played for Washington only.

Mel Almada (a rare player *not* signed by Cambria) was the first, as full-time center fielder with a .309 BA in 1937. Cuban Bobby Estalella (who first joined the club in 1935) was also an outfield fixture of this vintage, and Venezuelan right-hander Alex Carrasquel (winner of 50 games in eight big-league seasons) made 40 mound appearances on the eve of the war. Other notable Latino players wearing Senators colors in the late 1940s and early 1950s included Rene Monteagudo (Cuban pitcher whose son Aurelio would also pitch seven major league seasons during the sixties), Gil Torres (Cuban-born third baseman), Roberto Ortiz (Cuban outfielder), "Baby" Ortiz (pitcher and brother of Roberto Ortiz), Pedro (Preston) Gómez (Cuban infielder and later big-league manager), Chile (José) Gómez (Mexican infielder), and Mike Guerra (slick-gloved Cuban catcher).

The onset of wartime conditions soon worked to increase dramatically Clark Griffith's growing stockpile of Latin players. The fact that such non-citizens were altogether free from wartime draft callups must have had a certain appeal for the financially strapped and minor-league-thin Washington owner. And the increased proportion of Latin players on Griffith's league roster actually worked to improve Senator fortunes ever so slightly in the early forties (see Vaughn, 1984). While other clubs inevitably faded amid the exodus of top talent drained by the war effort, Washington slid past normally stronger teams like Boston, New York, and Cleveland for two surprising second-place finishes in 1943 and 1945. The 1945 club actually won 87 games and finished within a whisker of a pennant by closing to within a final game and a half of champion Detroit.

It was a sudden rise in league stature that would not be long maintained by the imbalanced franchise. A return to peacetime conditions saw Washington slump back to a more comfortable nest near the league basement. Penurious by nature and reeling from the inevitable wartime falloff in ballpark attendance, Clark Griffith had trimmed the Senators' already inadequate farm system to a mere six clubs before two more seasons had passed. In what seemed to be a direct result of such drastic cutbacks, by the late 1940s the Washington Senators had been reduced to scouting the Caribbean region almost exclusively. Griffith maintained only three full-time scouts during 1947 and 1948 and restricted his skeleton crew of bird dogs to a narrow beat along the nation's eastern seaboard and the tropical climes of Havana and other largely infrequented (by other big-league teams) Latin ports of call.

The controlling reason for Clark Griffith's interest in Latin America as a primary source of player talent therefore appears to have been largely financial from the outset. Even when a decade-long improvement in the Washington farm system was finally launched with the 1947 appointment of former manager Ossie Bluege as farm director, maverick scout Joe Cambria (finally named official scout for Cuba and Puerto Rico in 1949, then for the West Indies and South America in 1954) continued to comb Latin American soil for potential big-leaguers to serve his boss Clark Griffith in Washington. "Papa Joe" (as he was known by the locals, who even named a popular cigar brand after him) is widely reported to have scouted and nearly signed a promising young Havana University pitching prospect of the early 1940s named Fidel Castro (see Kerrane, 1985: 278; see also the Introduction to this volume).

While Castro was soon called to his date with history by other pressing career aspirations and (perhaps most unfortunately in retrospect) never did don a Washington Senators uniform, the following considerable cache of Cambria signees all eventually made appearances for the Senators in the early 1950s, performing with varying degrees of big-league success: pitchers Sandy Consuegra (Cuba), Mike Fornieles (Cuba), Connie Marrero (Cuba), Julio Moreno (Cuba), Camilo Pascual (Cuba), Carlos Pascual (Camilo's older brother), and Pedro "Pete" Ramos (Cuba); outfielders Francisco Campos (Cuba), Pompeyo Davalillo (Venezuela), Juan Delis (Cuba), and Carlos Paula (Cuba); infielders Ossie Alvarez (Cuba), Julio Becquer (Cuba), Willie Miranda (Cuba), and José Valdivielso (Cuba). If Joe Cambria's legendary scouting activities did not turn Clark Griffith's ballclub into an instant winner (or even an eventual challenger), it did supply a continuous cheap supply of adequate big-league talent to keep the often foundering ship barely afloat.

The considerable honor roll of Latin American ballplayers housed in Washington in the 1950s begins with the solid pitching of "Pete" Ramos (67-92 for the Senators between 1955 and 1960) and sidekick Camilo Pascual (53-77 over the same period). Other strong-armed Latin pitchers rounded out the bulk of Griffith's always-undermanned mound staff throughout the final Washington seasons. Sandy Consuegra was 20-16 over three summers before being dealt to Chicago in 1953; Connie Marrero compiled a 39-40 career mark in the first six seasons of the decade; Mike Fornieles registered an impressive rookie 1.37 ERA in brief action before departing for future service with the White Sox (in fortuitous exchange for eventual Washington ace left-hander Chuck Stobbs). And then there were utility players like José Valdivielso, Carlos Paula, and Julio Becquer. In all, almost two dozen Latin American–born ballplayers appeared in major league action for the Senators during the cellar-dwelling club's final topsy-turvy decade in the nation's capital.

Washington's Senators of the post–World War II era also helped launch a tradition of sure-fingered and light-sticking Spanish-speaking shortstops, a handful of whom first flourished at the outset of the 1950s and thus branded the decade with an image of memorable and flashy infield play. The entire stretch of years seemed crammed full of such unforgettable figures as Alfonso "Chico" Carrasquel (White Sox, Indians, Athletics, and

Orioles), Luís Aparicio (White Sox, Orioles, and Red Sox), Willie Miranda (Senators, White Sox, Browns, Yankees, and Orioles), Chico Fernández (Dodgers, Phillies, and Tigers), Ossie Alvarez (Senators), Félix Mantilla (Braves), Mike de la Hoz (Indians), Rubén Amaro (Phillies) and José Valdivielso (Senators and Twins) – mostly American Leaguers and all ballhawking wizards who truly revolutionized our concept of glove work around the keystone position.

While Miranda and Valdivielso were never more than mere fill-ins on a handful of also-ran ballcubs, Aparicio and Carrasquel enjoyed more distinguished center-stage roles. Carrasquel (a native of Venezuela who today still handles play-by-play broadcasts for the Chicago White Sox Spanish-language radio network) was the first of his countrymen to appear in All-Star Game action, earning a spot in the Comiskey Park midsummer classic during his 1950 rookie season. And Carrasquel's countryman Aparicio, who succeeded him as White Sox shortstop in 1956, would eventually earn legendary status as the third Latin big-leaguer enshrined at Cooperstown. Aparicio's Hall of Fame election by the Baseball Writers of America in 1984, alongside Killebrew and Drysdale, was at the time a larger landmark than we now recall. Coming finally in his sixth year of eligibility, it was but the second (after Marichal's in 1983) achieved by normal induction procedures. Clemente's unanimous selection a decade earlier in the immediate wake of his tragic death had been achieved through suspension of normal operating procedure.

Willie Miranda and José Valdivielso in the nation's capital were hardly ever a match for Aparicio and Carrasquel in Chicago, but by the time the heart-wrenching Senators had donned new flannels as the fence-busting Twins of Minnesota, Clark Griffith's franchise had finally come up with a Spanish-speaking shortstop to dazzle his way through American League cities like no other keystoner anywhere in the league. Zoilo "Zorro" Versalles arrived in Washington from the baseball-rich shores of Cuba in midsummer 1959, the summer when Fidel Castro was closing off for good the once-rich pipeline of Cuban diamond talent. One of the last of Papa Joe Cambria's promising imports would therefore prove to be one of the very best.

His start was not particularly auspicious, as two summers in Griffith Stadium provided only part-time play (44 games, 15 hits, and an anemic .142 BA) and little showcase for the flashy Cuban, who would soon prove a defensive rival for even Aparicio. By 1965, however, Zorro Versalles was a major star trapped in a minor baseball market. In that one glory season he sparked Griffith's ballclub to its first AL pennant since the Joe Cronin era 32 years earlier, in the process copping AL MVP honors, and leading the junior circuit with 45 doubles, 12 triples, 126 runs scored, and 666 at-bats. There were other moments for Versalles as well – a Gold Glove in 1963 and another in 1965, two All-Star Game selections, and a single vote for league MVP in 1967 (a vote that blocked Carl Yastrzemski's much-deserved unanimous selection for the coveted award). Yet this fiery catalyst of a Minnesota Twins baseball revival was also destined to be plagued by crippling back problems before the decade was out. Soon Versalles disappeared ingloriously into the Mexican League before attempting one final unsuccessful comeback stint with the transplanted Atlanta Braves.

While Cambria was busy filling American League ballparks with a host of Cuban ballplayers wearing Washington uniforms and enlivening play if not winning pennants, another old-school bird dog was soon hot on his heels in the service of a rival National League employer. And, it must be said, with even greater results, if one measures such things by superstar talent and a ballclub's ability to make a serious run at the ultimate prize, a World Series trophy. That ultimate judge of baseball talent, Branch Rickey, was now freshly transferred from Brooklyn to Pittsburgh where one of the Old Mahatma's first bold projects was to send a young talent snoop into Latin America. It was a fateful mission that would revolutionize baseball in a manner perhaps second only to an earlier Branch Rickey experiment involving Jackie Robinson and racial integration.

One of the most mismatched but nonetheless influential partnerships in baseball's behind-the-scenes history thus began when Rickey dispatched young Howard Haak on the trail of a reported superstar-in-the-making named Roberto Clemente. It was Haak who pursued the young Clemente and eventually played the crucial role in stealing him from under the noses of the rival Brooklyn Dodgers (as detailed in Chapter 3). The event would play no small role in dismantling a baseball powerhouse of the fifties (Brooklyn) and jump-starting another (Pittsburgh) for the sixties.

Haak's career in Latin America thus began with Clemente, but it certainly did not end there. Over the next two decades it would be Haak who would truly open up Latin America to the big leagues. Here was the man instrumental in building the great Pirates teams of the sixties and seventies. As Cambria mined Cuba, Haak was soon tapping Puerto Rico and the Dominican Republic with even more startling returns. First he inked Ed Bauta, Roman Mejías, Manny Jiménez, and Julián Javier from Dominican shores for less than $1,000 in total bonus money. Over the next three decades he would also sign Diomedes (Guayubín) Olivo, Carlos Bernier, Felipe Montemayor, Rennie Stennett, Omar Moreno, Tony Armas, Tony Peña, Luís Sálazar, Luís DeLeón, and finally Cecilio Guante. Down through the years, Haak relentlessly conducted the same old-style tryout camps with the same time-worn methods, even though by the 1980s other ballclubs were moving into his well-worked territory to compete head-on with large training complexes and newer recruitment strategies. Perhaps the most remarkable fact about the venerable Howie Haak, however, was the force and charm of his personality. All that he accomplished from the 1950s through the 1990s he had managed with only enough broken Spanish to get by.

Howie Haak's biggest catch, save Clemente, would be catcher Manny Sanguillen, a Panamanian diamond in the rough who could team up with Clemente to provide the heart of those solid Pittsburgh title teams at the dawn of the seventies. Sanguillen would eventually become one of the few backstops in the game's history who could effectively combine potent offense and reliable defense. Only four backstops in baseball annals (Hall-of-Famers Cochrane, Dickey, Lombardi, Hartnett) who played more games than Manny Sanguillen hit for a higher average than the congenial catcher.

Now well into his eighties, Haak continues to ply his trade with the Houston Astros organization, which he joined in 1989 after nearly four decades in the employ of the Pittsburgh Pirates. A onetime catcher in the Cardinals organization, Haak has enjoyed a half-century behind-the-scenes baseball career filled with countless thrills and personal satisfactions, perhaps none greater than the Pirates championships garnered by Clemente, Sanguillen, and company. It was Haak who was recipient of baseball's first Scout of the Year award in 1984, an honor bestowed in tribute to his long-time contributions to the game. Late in his career Haak would also tell author Kevin Kerrane something about the secrets of his early success. In Haak's view, the true key seemed to be the fact that he was the first Latin bird dog to extend his sharp eye beyond the scope of a single country. Joe Cambria had opened the door on Cuba, but Howie Haak had kicked down the barn door on the entire Caribbean stable.

The Blue Jays under Gillick have been arguably the most successful at raiding hidden talent from the sugar-mill towns and sprawling urban slums of the Caribbean. With a narrow focus on Cuba in the years before Fidel Castro, the Washington Senators with Joe Cambria in the trenches and the Pittsburgh Pirates with Howie Haak pounding the hinterlands were the earliest foragers into this newly opened baseball flesh market. But it is perhaps the Texas Rangers who now sport the most productive Caribbean scouting pipeline. While it has not yet translated into a sharp jump in the standings or a bevy of American League pennants, it is hard to argue with the successes of the Texas Rangers' Latin scouting program.

When the 1992 season opened at Arlington Stadium, six of eight starting position players were Latins. The Rangers today sport perhaps the most decidedly Latin look anywhere in the big leagues, in both mere numbers and name-recognition players of genuine star status. The Ranger lineup features names like José Canseco (today's most glamorous Latin slugging star), Julio Franco (1991 AL batting champion), Rafael Palmeiro (an underrated star destined to be baseball's biggest free-agent prize during the 1993-94 off-season), Juan González (undoubtedly a home-run hero of the future), Iván "Pudge" Rodríguez (everywhere acknowledged as the best young catcher in the game), and a host more, including recently acquired shortstop Manny Lee from the Toronto organization and rookie infield prospects Benji Gil and Cris Colon.

And this commitment to a Latin baseball movement in Texas is not seen on the field alone. The team sports an active scouting program that concentrates its full-time efforts on Venezuela and the Dominican Republic. It has now hired a full-time Latin American public-relations director (veteran baseball personality Luís Rodríguez-Mayoral, who joined the club from Puerto Rico in 1992) and carries (as of 1992, with KXEB of Dallas) a full schedule of home-game Spanish-language radio play-by-play broadcasts.

The Rangers have slowly built up their emerging Latin American image over the past two decades. The first significant Hispanic talent did not appear until the arrival of Bert Campaneris (an American League all-star with the club in 1977) and Juan Beníquez (with three solid outfield seasons between 1976 and 1978) a full half-dozen years into franchise history. And José Guzmán (at 66-62 before departing via free agency in 1993) remains the only Latin hurler to win more than 20 *career* games in a Texas uniform. The most visible player before Canseco was Rubén Sierra, still owner of club career offensive records for triples, extra-base hits, RBIs, and total bases, and team MVP in four of his five full Texas seasons. The late-season 1992 blockbuster trade that sent Sierra packing to Oakland in exchange for Canseco was perhaps the grandest big-league deal ever consummated involving an exchange of two or more Latin American superstars.

The Rangers front office under GM Tom Grieve appears firmly committed to its Latin American player-development program. Ballclub representatives have spoken freely of their long-range dedication to the plan. Sandy Johnson, the club's assistant GM, sounds the keynote: "If you are going to have a quality organization and quality players, you better be heavily involved in Latin America, and get your share of players from there." While Texas boasts nothing that can compare with the Dodgers' plush 12-month training facility under the direction of team vice president Ralph Avila in Campo La Palmas, Texas stresses quality and not quantity in its modest camp at Ingenio Consuelo outside San Pedro de Macoris. With only 19 Dominicans and 8 Venezuelans under contract for 1992 (most of these playing professionally in the United States), the Rangers nonetheless maintain an entry (its roster partially filled with older released players from other organizations) in Dominican rookie summer-league play. Former manager Bobby Valentine was in the process of learning Spanish before a two-year slump brought his dismissal in the midst of the 1992 campaign. Dominican-born Omar Minaya heads an 11-man Caribbean scouting unit as the ballclub's first full-time Latin American scouting coordinator.

Texas Rangers All-Time Latin American Roster (1972–1993), 41 Players

(Alphabetical listing; career statistics through 1993)

Nonpitchers (29 players)	*Home*	*BA*	*AB*	*R*	*H*	*HR*	*RBI*	*POS*
Sandy Alomar (1977–1978)	PR	.250	112	24	28	1	12	IF
Juan Beníquez (1976–1978)	PR	.261	1,375	166	359	21	133	IF-OF
Jerry Browne (1986–1988)	VI	.263	692	95	182	2	58	IF
Bert Campaneris (1977–1979)	Cuba	.230	830	109	191	6	63	SS
José Canseco (1992–1993)	Cuba	.250	304	38	76	14	61	OF-DH
Leo Cárdenas (1974–1975)	Cuba	.253	194	20	49	1	12	IF
Rico Carty (1973)	DOM	.232	306	24	71	3	33	OF
Cris Colon (1992)	VEN	.167	36	5	6	0	1	SS
Mario Díaz (1991–1993)	PR	.266	418	50	111	3	47	SS
Julio Franco (1989–1993)	DOM	.307	2,358	388	725	55	331	2B-DH
Pepe Frías (1980)	DOM	.242	227	27	55	0	10	IF
Bárbaro Garbey (1988)	Cuba	.194	62	4	12	0	5	OF-DH
Benji Gil (1993)	MEX	.123	57	3	7	0	2	SS
Juan González (1989–1993)	PR	.274	1,815	277	497	121	348	OF-DH
José Hernández (1991)	PR	.184	98	8	18	0	4	SS
Manuel Lee (1993)	DOM	.220	73	31	45	1	12	SS
Fred Manrique (1989)	VEN	.288	191	23	55	2	22	IF
Marty Martínez (1972)	Cuba	.146	41	3	6	0	3	C
Mario Mendoza (1981–1982)	MEX	.224	246	19	55	0	22	IF
Orlando Mercado (1986)	PR	.235	102	7	24	1	7	C
Willie Montañez (1979)	PR	.319	144	19	46	8	24	1B-DH
Nelson Norman (1978–1981)	DOM	.225	422	42	95	0	25	SS
Rafael Palmeiro (1989–1993)	Cuba	.296	2,993	471	887	107	431	1B-DH
Luís Pujols (1985)	DOM	1.000	1	0	1	0	0	PH
Iván Rodríguez (1991–1993)	PR	.266	1,173	119	312	21	130	C
Rubén Sierra (1986–1992)	PR	.280	4,043	571	1,132	153	657	OF-DH
Sammy Sosa (1989)	DOM	.238	84	8	20	1	3	OF
Dickie Thon (1992)	PR	.247	275	30	68	4	37	IF
César Tóvar (1974–1975)	VEN	.277	989	131	274	7	86	IF-OF

Pitchers (12 players)	*Home*	*W-L*	*ERA*	*G*	*SV*	*IP*	*BB*	*SO*
Wilson Alvarez (1989)	VEN	0-1	---	1	0	0.0	2	0
José Cecena (1988)	MEX	0-0	4.78	22	1	26.1	23	27
Edwin Correa (1986–1988)	PR	15-19	5.09	47	0	272.1	178	250
Victor Cruz (1983)	DOM	1-3	1.44	17	5	25.0	10	18
Héctor Fajardo (1991–1992)	MEX	0-2	5.68	4	0	19.0	4	15
Ed Figueroa (1980)	PR	0-7	5.90	8	0	39.2	12	9
Tony Fossas (1988)	Cuba	0-0	4.76	5	0	5.2	2	0
Cecilio Guante (1988–1989)	DOM	6-6	3.79	57	3	73.2	40	73
José Guzmán (1985–88, 91–92)	PR	66-62	3.90	159	0	1,013.2	395	715
Danilo León (1992)	VEN	1-1	5.89	15	0	18.1	10	15
Ramón Manón (1990)	DOM	0-0	13.50	1	0	2.0	3	0
Horacio Piña (1972)	MEX	2-7	3.20	60	15	76	43	60

Statistics courtesy of the Texas Rangers Baseball Club

The Rangers' future thus looks bright on the Latin American front. Puerto Ricans Juan González and Iván Rodríguez should be league stars for at least a decade to come. Other youngsters also show great promise. Cris Colon, Venezuelan nephew of Chico Carrasquel, is the club's projected second baseman of the future. Héctor Fajardo from Mexico remains the top pitching prospect in the organization. José Oliva, another shortstop from San Pedro de Macoris, will almost certainly count in the Rangers' future plans as a third baseman. José Hernández of Puerto Rico was until his release another hot shortstop prospect. These players suggest that the Texas Rangers' Latin scouting effort is reaching into every corner of the Latin baseball world.

Latin American scouting and player development are today a primary focus of nearly every successful big-league ballclub. The Los Angeles Dodgers, Toronto Blue Jays, and Oakland Athletics in particular now maintain expensive year-round talent camps in the heart of the talent-rich Dominican Republic. It has become necessary for the majors to begin patrolling (formally albeit somewhat loosely) highly competitive recruiting activities throughout the Dominican backwater. And from Joe Cambria and Howie Haak in the 1940s and 1950s to Epy Guerrero and Omar Minaya in the 1980s and 1990s, it has been the unsung bird dogs in the trenches and in the dusty local ballparks of rural Caribbean villages who have begun changing baseball's ethnic flavor forever.

A Baker's Dozen of Latin America's Finest Idols

Vic Power (Puerto Rico) 1st Base, Infield

Year	*Club*	*G*	*AB*	*R*	*H*	*2B*	*3B*	*HR*	*RBI*	*BA*
1954	Phila (AL)	127	462	36	118	17	5	8	38	.255
1955	KC (AL)	147	596	91	190	34	10	19	76	.319
1956	KC (AL)	127	530	77	164	21	5	14	63	.309
1957	KC (AL)	129	467	48	121	15	1	14	42	.259
1958	KC-Clev (AL)	145	590	98	184	37	10	16	80	.312
1959	Clev (AL)	147	595	102	172	31	6	10	60	.289
1960	Clev (AL)	147	580	69	167	26	3	10	84	.288
1961	Clev (AL)	147	563	64	151	34	4	5	63	.268
1962	Minn (AL)	144	611	80	177	28	2	16	63	.290
1963	Minn (AL)	138	541	65	146	28	2	10	52	.270
1964	Minn-LA (AL)	87	266	23	65	8	0	3	14	.244
1964	Phila (NL)	18	48	1	10	4	0	0	3	.208
1965	Cal (AL)	124	197	11	51	7	1	1	20	.259
Totals	(12 seasons)	1,627	6,046	765	1,716	290	49	126	658	.284

Career Highlights:

1. Led American League in triples (10) in 1958.
2. Three-time league leader in fielding percentage at first base (1957, 1959–1960).
3. Four-time American League All-Star (1955–1956, 1959–1960).

Camilo Pascual (Cuba) RHP

Year	*Club*	*W-L*	*Pct.*	*G*	*CG*	*ShO*	*SV*	*BB*	*SO*	*ERA*
1954	Wash (AL)	4-7	.364	48	1	0	3	61	60	4.22
1955	Wash (AL)	2-12	.143	43	1	0	3	70	82	6.14
1956	Wash (AL)	6-18	.250	39	6	0	2	89	162	5.87
1957	Wash (AL)	8-17	.320	29	8	2	0	76	113	4.10
1958	Wash (AL)	8-12	.400	31	6	2	0	60	146	3.15
1959	Wash (AL)	17-10	.630	32	*17*	*6*	0	69	185	2.64
1960	Wash (AL)	12-8	.600	26	8	3	2	53	143	3.03
1961	Minn (AL)	15-16	.484	35	15	*8*	0	100	*221*	3.46
1962	Minn (AL)	20-11	.645	34	*18*	*5*	0	59	*206*	3.32
1963	Minn (AL)	21-9	.700	31	*18*	3	0	81	*202*	2.46
1964	Minn (AL)	15-12	.556	36	14	1	0	98	213	3.30
1965	Minn (AL)	9-3	.750	27	5	1	0	63	96	3.35
1966	Minn (AL)	8-6	.571	21	2	0	0	30	56	4.89
1967	Wash (AL)	12-10	.545	28	5	1	0	43	106	3.28
1968	Wash (AL)	13-12	.520	31	8	4	0	59	111	2.69
1969	Wash (AL)	2-5	.286	14	0	0	0	38	34	6.83
1969	Cinc (NL)	0-0	.000	5	0	0	0	4	3	8.59
1970	LA (NL)	0-0	.000	10	0	0	0	5	8	2.57
1971	Clev (AL)	2-2	.500	9	0	0	0	11	20	3.09
Totals	(18 seasons)	174-170	.506	529	132	36	10	1,069	2,167	3.63

Italics = League Leader

Career Highlights:

1. Three-time American League leader in complete games (1959, 1962–1963).
2. Three-time league leader in shutouts (1959, 1961–1962).
3. Three-time league strikeout leader (1961–1963).
4. Three-time American League all-star (1961–1962, 1964).

Pedro ("Pete") Ramos (Cuba) RHP

Year	*Club*	*W-L*	*Pct.*	*G*	*CG*	*ShO*	*SV*	*BB*	*SO*	*ERA*
1955	Wash (AL)	5-11	.313	45	3	1	5	39	34	3.88
1956	Wash (AL)	12-10	.545	37	4	0	0	76	54	5.27
1957	Wash (AL)	12-16	.429	43	7	1	0	69	91	4.79
1958	Wash (AL)	14-18	.438	43	10	4	3	77	132	4.23
1959	Wash (AL)	13-19	.406	37	11	0	0	52	95	4.16
1960	Wash (AL)	11-18	.379	43	14	1	2	99	160	3.45

1961	Minn (AL)	11-20	.355	42	9	3	2	79	174	3.95
1962	Clev (AL)	10-12	.455	37	7	2	1	85	96	3.71
1963	Clev (AL)	9-8	.529	36	5	0	0	41	169	3.12
1964	Clev (AL)	7-10	.412	36	3	1	0	26	98	5.14
1964	NYY (AL)	1-0	1.000	13	0	0	8	0	21	1.25
1965	NYY (AL)	5-5	.500	65	0	0	19	27	68	2.92
1966	NYY (AL)	3-9	.250	52	0	0	13	18	58	3.61
1967	Phila (NL)	0-0	.000	6	0	0	0	8	1	9.00
1969	Pitt (NL)	0-1	.000	5	0	0	0	0	4	6.00
1969	Cinc (NL)	4-3	.571	38	0	0	2	24	40	5.16
1970	Wash (AL)	0-0	.000	4	0	0	0	4	10	7.56
Totals	(15 seasons)	117-160	.422	582	73	13	55	724	1,305	4.08

Career Highlights:

1. Led American League in games lost four consecutive seasons (1958–1961).
2. Led American League in games started in 1958 and again in 1960 with Washington.
3. Posted 1.25 ERA and 8 saves for New York Yankees during 1964 late-season pennant drive.

(Pedro) Tony Oliva (Cuba) Outfielder, DH

Year	*Club*	*G*	*AB*	*R*	*H*	*2B*	*3B*	*HR*	*RBI*	*BA*
1962	Minn (AL)	9	9	3	4	1	0	0	3	.444
1963	Minn (AL)	7	7	0	3	0	0	0	1	.429
1964	Minn (AL)	161	672	*109*	*217*	*43*	9	32	94	*.323*
1965	Minn (AL)	149	576	107	*185*	40	5	16	98	*.321*
1966	Minn (AL)	159	622	99	*191*	32	7	25	87	.307
1967	Minn (AL)	146	557	76	161	*34*	6	17	83	.289
1968	Minn (AL)	128	470	54	136	24	5	18	68	.289
1969	Minn (AL)	153	637	97	*197*	*39*	4	24	101	.309
1970	Minn (AL)	157	628	96	*204*	*36*	7	23	107	.325
1971	Minn (AL)	126	487	73	164	30	3	22	81	*.337*
1972	Minn (AL)	10	28	1	9	1	0	0	1	.321
1973	Minn (AL)	146	571	63	166	20	0	16	92	.291
1974	Minn (AL)	127	459	43	131	16	2	13	57	.285
1975	Minn (AL)	131	455	46	123	10	0	13	58	.270
1976	Minn (AL)	67	123	3	26	3	0	1	16	.211
Totals	(15 seasons)	1,676	6,301	870	1,917	329	48	220	947	.304

Italics = League Leader

Career Highlights:

1. Only player in major league history to win batting titles in his first two full seasons.

2. Set American League rookie record in 1964 with 217 base hits.

3. Three-time batting champion and five-time league leader in hits (1964–1966, 1969–1970).

4. Named American League Player of the Year in 1965 by *The Sporting News*.

Rod Carew (Panama Canal Zone) 1st Base, DH (**Hall of Fame, 1991**)

Year	*Club*	*G*	*AB*	*R*	*H*	*2B*	*3B*	*HR*	*RBI*	*BA*
1967	Minn (AL)	137	514	66	150	22	7	8	51	.292
1968	Minn (AL)	127	461	46	126	27	2	1	42	.273
1969	Minn (AL)	123	458	79	152	30	4	8	56	*.332*
1970	Minn (AL)	51	191	27	70	12	3	4	28	.366
1971	Minn (AL)	147	577	88	177	16	10	2	48	.307
1972	Minn (AL)	142	535	61	170	21	6	0	51	*.318*
1973	Minn (AL)	149	580	98	*203*	30	*11*	6	62	*.350*
1974	Minn (AL)	153	599	86	*218*	30	5	3	55	*.364*
1975	Minn (AL)	143	535	89	192	24	4	14	80	*.359*
1976	Minn (AL)	156	605	97	200	29	12	9	90	.331
1977	Minn (AL)	155	616	*128*	*239*	38	*16*	14	100	*.388*
1978	Minn (AL)	152	564	85	188	26	10	5	70	*.333*
1979	Cal (AL)	110	409	78	130	15	3	3	44	.318
1980	Cal (AL)	144	540	74	179	34	7	3	59	.331
1981	Cal (AL)	93	364	57	111	17	1	2	21	.305
1982	Cal (AL)	138	523	88	167	25	5	3	44	.319
1983	Cal (AL)	129	472	66	160	24	2	2	44	.339
1984	Cal (AL)	93	329	42	97	8	1	3	31	.295
1985	Cal (AL)	127	443	69	124	17	3	2	39	.280
Totals	(19 seasons)	2,469	9,315	1,424	3,053	445	112	92	1,015	.328

Italics = League Leader

Career Highlights:

1. American League rookie of the year in 1967 and league MVP in 1977.

2. Seven-time league batting champion and three-time league hits leader (1973-1974, 1977).

3. Elected to Hall of Fame in first year of eligibility (1991).

4. Fifteen-straight seasons with .300-plus average, surpassed only by Cobb, Musial, and Wagner.

Luís Tiant (Cuba) RHP

Year	*Club*	*W-L*	*Pct.*	*G*	*CG*	*ShO*	*SV*	*BB*	*SO*	*ERA*
1964	Clev (AL)	10-4	.714	19	9	3	1	47	105	2.83
1965	Clev (AL)	11-11	.500	41	10	2	1	66	152	3.53

Luís Tiant, *cont.*

1966	Clev (AL)	12-11	.522	46	7	*5*	8	50	145	2.79
1967	Clev (AL)	12-9	.571	33	9	1	2	67	219	2.74
1968	Clev (AL)	21-9	.700	34	19	*9*	0	73	264	*1.60*
1969	Clev (AL)	9-20	.310	38	9	1	0	129	156	3.71
1970	Minn (AL)	7-3	.700	18	2	1	0	41	50	3.40
1971	Bos (AL)	1-7	.125	21	1	0	0	32	59	4.85
1972	Bos (AL)	15-6	.714	43	12	6	3	65	123	*1.91*
1973	Bos (AL)	20-13	.606	35	23	0	0	78	206	3.34
1974	Bos (AL)	22-13	.629	38	25	*7*	0	82	176	2.92
1975	Bos (AL)	18-14	.563	35	18	2	0	72	142	4.02
1976	Bos (AL)	21-12	.636	38	19	3	0	64	131	3.06
1977	Bos (AL)	12-8	.600	32	3	3	0	51	124	4.53
1978	Bos (AL)	13-8	.619	32	12	5	0	57	114	3.31
1979	NYY (AL)	13-8	.619	30	5	1	0	53	104	3.91
1980	NYY (AL)	8-9	.471	25	3	0	0	50	84	4.89
1981	Pitt (NL)	2-5	.286	9	1	0	0	19	32	3.92
1982	Cal (AL)	2-2	.500	6	0	0	0	8	30	5.76
Totals	(19 seasons)	229-172	.571	573	187	49	15	1,104	2,416	3.30

Italics = League Leader

Career Highlights:

1. Twice led American League with sub-2.00 ERA (1968, 1972).
2. Three-time 20-game winner for Boston Red Sox (1973–1974, 1976).
3. Set major league record (July 1968) for strikeouts (32) in consecutive starts.
4. American League "Comeback Player of the Year" in 1972 with Boston Red Sox.

Felipe Alou (Dominican Republic) Outfielder, Manager (1992-93, Montreal)

Year	*Club*	*G*	*AB*	*R*	*H*	*2B*	*3B*	*HR*	*RBI*	*BA*
1958	SF (NL)	75	182	21	46	9	2	4	16	.253
1959	SF (NL)	95	247	38	68	13	2	10	33	.275
1960	SF (NL)	106	322	48	85	17	3	8	44	.264
1961	SF (NL)	132	415	59	120	19	0	18	52	.289
1962	SF (NL)	154	561	96	177	30	3	25	98	.316
1963	SF (NL)	157	565	75	159	31	9	20	82	.281
1964	Mil (NL)	121	415	60	105	26	3	9	51	.253
1965	Mil (NL)	143	555	80	165	29	2	23	78	.297
1966	Atl (NL)	154	666	*122*	*218*	32	6	31	74	.327
1967	Atl (NL)	140	574	76	157	26	3	15	43	.274
1968	Atl (NL)	160	662	72	*210*	37	5	11	57	.317
1969	Atl (NL)	123	476	54	134	13	1	5	32	.282

Year	*Club*	*G*	*AB*	*R*	*H*	*2B*	*3B*	*HR*	*RBI*	*BA*
1970	Oak (AL)	154	575	70	156	25	3	8	55	.271
1971	Oak (AL)	2	8	0	2	1	0	0	0	.250
1971	NYY (AL)	131	461	52	133	20	6	8	69	.289
1972	NYY (AL)	120	324	33	90	18	1	6	37	.278
1973	NYY (AL)	93	280	25	66	12	0	4	27	.236
1973	Mont (NL)	19	48	4	10	1	0	1	4	.208
1974	Mil (AL)	3	3	0	0	0	0	0	0	.000
Totals	(17 seasons)	2,082	7,339	985	2,101	359	49	206	852	.286

Italics = League Leader

Career Highlights:

1. Twice National League hits leader (1966 and 1968).
2. Three-time American League all-star (1962, 1966, 1968).
3. First Dominican manager in the big leagues with Montreal Expos (1992-1993).

Matty Alou (Dominican Republic) Outfielder

Year	*Club*	*G*	*AB*	*R*	*H*	*2B*	*3B*	*HR*	*RBI*	*BA*
1960	SF (NL)	4	3	1	1	0	0	0	0	.333
1961	SF (NL)	81	200	38	62	7	2	6	24	.310
1962	SF (NL)	78	195	28	57	8	1	3	14	.292
1963	SF (NL)	63	76	4	11	1	0	0	2	.145
1964	SF (NL)	110	250	28	66	4	2	1	14	.264
1965	SF (NL)	117	324	37	75	12	2	2	18	.231
1966	Pitt (NL)	141	535	86	183	18	9	2	27	*.342*
1967	Pitt (NL)	139	550	87	186	21	7	2	28	.338
1968	Pitt (NL)	146	558	59	185	28	4	0	52	.332
1969	Pitt (NL)	162	698	105	*231*	*41*	6	1	48	.331
1970	Pitt (NL)	155	677	97	201	21	8	1	47	.297
1971	St.L (NL)	149	609	85	192	28	6	7	74	.315
1972	St.L (NL)	108	404	46	127	17	2	3	31	.314
1972	Oak (AL)	32	121	11	34	5	0	1	16	.281
1973	NYY (AL)	123	497	59	147	22	1	2	28	.296
1973	SD (NL)	11	11	1	3	0	0	0	1	.273
1974	Cal (AL)	48	81	8	16	3	0	0	3	.198
Totals	(15 seasons)	1,667	5,789	780	1,777	236	50	31	427	.307

Italics = League Leader

Career Highlights:

1. Led National League in batting (.342) in 1966 with Pittsburgh.
2. League leader in both hits (231) and doubles (41) in 1969 with Pittsburgh.
3. Two-time National League all-star (1968–1969).

Luís Aparicio (Venezuela) Shortstop (**Hall of Fame, 1984**)

Year	*Club*	*G*	*AB*	*R*	*H*	*2B*	*3B*	*HR*	*RBI*	*BA*
1956	Chi (AL)	152	533	69	142	19	6	3	56	.266
1957	Chi (AL)	143	575	82	148	22	6	3	41	.257
1958	Chi (AL)	145	557	76	148	20	9	2	40	.266
1959	Chi (AL)	152	612	98	157	18	5	6	51	.257
1960	Chi (AL)	153	600	86	166	20	7	2	61	.277
1961	Chi (AL)	156	625	90	170	24	4	6	45	.272
1962	Chi (AL)	153	581	72	140	23	5	7	40	.241
1963	Balt (AL)	146	601	73	150	18	8	5	45	.250
1964	Balt (AL)	146	578	93	154	20	3	10	37	.266
1965	Balt (AL)	144	564	67	127	20	10	8	40	.225
1966	Balt (AL)	151	659	97	182	25	8	6	41	.276
1967	Balt (AL)	134	546	55	127	22	5	4	31	.233
1968	Chi (AL)	155	622	55	164	24	4	4	36	.264
1969	Chi (AL)	156	599	77	168	24	5	5	51	.280
1970	Chi (AL)	146	552	86	173	29	3	5	43	.313
1971	Bos (AL)	125	491	56	114	23	0	4	45	.232
1972	Bos (AL)	110	436	47	112	26	3	3	39	.257
1973	Bos (AL)	132	499	56	135	17	1	0	49	.271
Totals	(18 seasons)	2,599	10,230	1,335	2,677	394	92	83	791	.262

Career Highlights:

1. American League rookie of the year in 1956 with Chicago White Sox.
2. Ten-time American League all-star (1958–1964, 1970–1972).
3. Holds lifetime shortstop records for games, double plays, and assists and AL record for putouts.
4. Led junior circuit in stolen bases nine straight seasons (1956–1964).
5. Elected to Hall of Fame in sixth year of eligibility (1984).

Zoilo ("Zorro") Versalles (Cuba) Shortstop, Infield

Year	*Club*	*G*	*AB*	*R*	*H*	*2B*	*3B*	*HR*	*RBI*	*BA*
1959	Wash (AL)	29	59	4	9	0	0	1	1	.153
1960	Wash (AL)	15	45	2	6	2	2	0	4	.133
1961	Minn (AL)	129	510	65	143	25	5	7	53	.280
1962	Minn (AL)	160	568	69	137	18	3	17	67	.241
1963	Minn (AL)	159	621	74	162	31	*13*	10	54	.261
1964	Minn (AL)	160	659	94	171	33	*10*	20	64	.259
1965	Minn (AL)	160	666	*126*	182	*45*	*12*	19	77	.273
1966	Minn (AL)	137	543	73	135	20	6	7	36	.249
1967	Minn (AL)	160	581	63	116	16	7	6	50	.200
1968	LA (NL)	122	403	29	79	16	3	2	24	.196

Year	*Club*	*G*	*AB*	*R*	*H*	*2B*	*3B*	*HR*	*RBI*	*BA*
1969	Clev (AL)	72	217	21	49	11	1	1	13	.226
1969	Wash (AL)	31	75	9	20	2	1	0	6	.267
1971	Atl (NL)	66	194	21	37	11	0	5	22	.191
Totals	(12 seasons)	1,400	5,141	650	1,246	230	63	95	471	.242

Italics = League Leader

Career Highlights:

1. American League MVP in 1965 with Minnesota Twins.
2. Twice Gold Glove defensive standout at shortstop (1963 and 1965).
3. Two-time American League all-star (1963 and 1965).

Bert Campaneris (Cuba) Shortstop, Infield

Year	*Club*	*G*	*AB*	*R*	*H*	*2B*	*3B*	*HR*	*RBI*	*BA*
1964	KC (AL)	67	269	27	69	14	3	4	22	.257
1965	KC (AL)	144	578	67	156	23	*12*	6	42	.270
1966	KC (AL)	142	573	82	153	29	10	5	42	.267
1967	KC (AL)	147	601	85	149	29	6	3	32	.248
1968	Oak (AL)	159	642	87	*177*	25	9	4	38	.276
1969	Oak (AL)	135	547	71	142	15	2	2	25	.260
1970	Oak (AL)	147	603	97	168	28	4	22	64	.279
1971	Oak (AL)	134	569	80	143	18	4	5	47	.251
1972	Oak (AL)	149	625	85	150	25	2	8	32	.240
1973	Oak (AL)	151	601	89	150	17	6	4	46	.250
1974	Oak (AL)	134	527	77	153	18	8	2	41	.290
1975	Oak (AL)	137	509	69	135	15	3	4	46	.265
1976	Oak (AL)	149	536	67	137	14	1	1	52	.256
1977	Tex (AL)	150	552	77	140	19	7	5	46	.254
1978	Tex (AL)	98	269	30	50	5	3	1	17	.186
1979	Tex (AL)	8	9	2	1	0	0	0	0	.111
1979	Cal (AL)	85	239	27	56	4	4	0	15	.234
1980	Cal (AL)	77	210	32	53	8	1	2	18	.252
1981	Cal (AL)	55	82	11	21	2	1	1	10	.256
1983	NYY (AL)	60	143	19	46	5	0	0	11	.322
Totals	(19 seasons)	2,328	8,684	1,181	2,249	313	86	79	646	.259

Career Highlights:

1. Led American League in base hits (177) in 1968 with Oakland A's.
2. Third player in history to hit two homers in first game, one on first major league pitch.
3. Six-time American League all-star (1968, 1972–1975, 1977).

Orlando Cepeda (Puerto Rico) 1st Base, DH

Year	*Club*	*G*	*AB*	*R*	*H*	*2B*	*3B*	*HR*	*RBI*	*BA*
1958	SF (NL)	148	603	88	188	*38*	4	25	96	.312
1959	SF (NL)	151	605	92	192	35	4	27	105	.317
1960	SF (NL)	151	569	81	169	36	3	24	96	.297
1961	SF (NL)	152	585	105	182	28	4	*46*	*142*	.311
1962	SF (NL)	162	625	105	191	26	1	35	114	.306
1963	SF (NL)	156	579	100	183	33	4	34	97	.316
1964	SF (NL)	142	529	75	161	27	2	31	97	.304
1965	SF (NL)	33	34	1	6	1	0	1	5	.176
1966	SF (NL)	19	49	5	14	2	0	3	15	.286
1966	St.L (NL)	123	452	65	137	24	0	17	58	.303
1967	St.L (NL)	151	563	91	183	37	0	25	*111*	.325
1968	St.L (NL)	157	600	71	149	26	2	16	73	.248
1969	Atl (NL)	154	573	74	147	28	2	22	88	.257
1970	Atl (NL)	148	567	87	173	33	0	34	111	.305
1971	Atl (NL)	71	250	31	69	10	1	14	44	.276
1972	Atl (NL)	28	84	6	25	3	0	4	9	.298
1972	Oak (AL)	3	3	0	0	0	0	0	0	.000
1973	Bos (AL)	142	550	51	159	25	0	20	86	.289
1974	KC (AL)	33	107	3	23	5	0	1	18	.215
Totals	(17 seasons)	2,124	7,927	1,131	2,351	417	27	379	1,365	.297

Italics = League Leader

Career Highlights:

1. National League rookie of the year in 1958 with San Francisco and MVP in 1967 with St. Louis.
2. Paced senior circuit in homers (46) and RBIs (142) in 1961 with San Francisco.
3. Seven-time National League all-star (1959–1964, 1967).
4. Retired as all-time Latin American home-run leader (379).

Tony Pérez (Cuba) 1st Base, 3rd Base, Manager (1993, Cincinnati)

Year	*Club*	*G*	*AB*	*R*	*H*	*2B*	*3B*	*HR*	*RBI*	*BA*
1964	Cinc (NL)	12	25	1	2	1	0	0	1	.080
1965	Cinc (NL)	104	281	40	73	14	4	12	47	.260
1966	Cinc (NL)	99	257	25	68	10	4	4	39	.265
1967	Cinc (NL)	156	600	78	174	28	7	26	102	.290
1968	Cinc (NL)	160	625	93	176	25	7	18	92	.282
1969	Cinc (NL)	160	629	103	185	31	2	37	122	.294
1970	Cinc (NL)	158	587	107	186	28	6	40	129	.317

Year	Club	G	AB	R	H	2B	3B	HR	RBI	BA
1971	Cinc (NL)	158	609	72	164	22	3	25	91	.269
1972	Cinc (NL)	136	515	64	146	33	7	21	90	.283
1973	Cinc (NL)	151	564	73	177	33	3	27	101	.314
1974	Cinc (NL)	158	596	81	158	28	2	28	101	.265
1975	Cinc (NL)	137	511	74	144	28	3	20	109	.282
1976	Cinc (NL)	139	527	77	137	32	6	19	91	.260
1977	Mont (NL)	154	559	71	158	32	6	19	91	.283
1978	Mont (NL)	148	544	63	158	38	3	14	78	.290
1979	Mont (NL)	132	489	58	132	29	4	13	73	.270
1980	Bos (AL)	151	585	73	161	31	3	25	105	.275
1981	Bos (AL)	84	306	35	77	11	3	9	39	.252
1982	Bos (AL)	69	196	18	51	14	2	6	31	.260
1983	Phila (NL)	91	253	18	61	11	2	6	43	.241
1984	Cinc (NL)	71	137	9	33	6	1	2	15	.241
1985	Cinc (NL)	72	183	25	60	8	0	6	33	.328
1986	Cinc (NL)	77	200	14	51	12	1	2	29	.255
Totals	(23 seasons)	2,777	9,778	1,272	2,732	505	79	379	1,652	.279

Career Highlights:

1. Retired as 14th best RBI man in major league history.
2. Belted three home runs in 1975 World Series for Cincinnati Reds versus Boston Red Sox.
3. Seven-time National League all-star (1967–1970, 1974–1976).
4. Tied with Cepeda as all-time Latin American home run leader (379).

Notes

1. No better examples are found in print of the intolerant conditions encountered by Latin American ballplayers on the U.S. mainland than those detailed in Cepeda's two autobiographical books. Minor league days and his San Francisco experiences are treated in Chapter 3 of *High and Inside* (by Bob Markus); the incidents at Salem are recounted in Chapter 2 of *My Ups and Downs in Baseball* (with Charles Einstein). The latter book also provides the most detailed commentary on Cepeda's tenuous relationship with manager Alvin Dark, especially in Chapter 9 (see also Chapter 3 of the Markus book). Cepeda's position on Dark does not pull any punches:

> When I first met him I thought Alvin Dark was an angel. He came on like a saint and fooled everybody. But it didn't take long for me to find out that he was the most vicious man I would ever meet in baseball (and I've met a few). Without mincing words, I can easily and honestly say that Alvin Dark was a liar and a bigot. (*My Ups and Downs*, 33)

2. The attacks by Dark are now a somber chapter of baseball legend, and the most infamous statement is the one attributed to him in a 1964 Long Island *Newsday*

article penned by veteran reporter Stan Isaacs. The full text of the oft-quoted statement:

> We have trouble because we have so many Negro and Spanish-speaking ball players on this team. They are just not able to perform up to the white ball players when it comes to mental alertness. You can't make most Negro and Spanish players have the pride in their team that you can get from white players. (Dark, quoted by Issacs)

In fairness to Dark, he would later claim to have been taken largely out of context with those ill-considered remarks; the beleaguered veteran manager would also suggest that Isaacs had slanted the piece as part of a covert effort by a group of New York sportswriters bent on sabotaging his big-league management career. Dark's postcareer explanation is outlined in his book (with John Underwood) and is largely as follows. The manager had harmlessly recounted to Isaacs an incident several days earlier in Philadelphia where Del Crandall had grounded into a triple play; Cepeda and Jesús Alou were base runners at the time. Dark contends that he referred to the players involved (one white and two Hispanics) as "dumb" and that had led to a further discussion of his frustrations with getting his 1964 ballclub (with the exception of Willie Mays) to want to win. Since he was starting seven blacks and Hispanics at the time, Dark contends that his remarks were unfairly twisted and construed by the reporter as an attack on an entire race of athletes, something he hadn't really intended. But it certainly seems fair to contend that Alvin Dark's overall attitude toward his Hispanic ballplayers was in the long run anything but friendly or supportive.

3. It is perhaps worthy of passing mention that the phrase "good hit, no field" has a double connection with Latin ballplayers. Not only did this pithy observation become a stereotypical label for a bevy of sure-handed yet punchless Latino middle infielders of the 1950s, but the phrase was coined ironically by a Latin American baseball figure in the first place. Invention of this popular diamond cliché is now widely attributed to Mike González, who reportedly wired this assessment in a scouting report on multilingual catching prospect Moe Berg.

4. As Canadian journalist Larry Millson notes in a chapter on Toronto's "Latin Connection" (*Ballpark Figures*, 220), these government restrictions have yet to show any significant or even tangible impact. While the U.S. State Department has long limited the number of foreign professional ballplayers to 500 for all 26 (now 28) major league teams (the number that can be employed at all levels of minor league and major league play), only 1 in 17 major-leaguers was Latin-born in 1965. Two decades later the number had more than doubled. The number of "visa slots" (major and minor league rosters) allotted to each ballclub currently varies between 20 and 24 and includes players from the Dominican Republic, Venezuela, Mexico, Canada, Australia, Europe, and the Far East (but not Puerto Rico).

5. The full incident surrounding Almeida and Marsans is reported in detail in Bruce Brown's *Atlantic Monthly* account (1984, 109–114). Much racial controversy surrounded the brief major league appearances of two additional Cubans of the same era – outfielder Jacinto "Jack" Calvo and pitcher José Acosta. Calvo appeared briefly with the Washington Senators in 1913 and again in 1920 (33 games, .161 BA, 1 HR); Acosta hurled for the same ballclub and for the Chicago White Sox between 1920 and 1922 (10-10, 4.51 ERA). While Almeida and Marsans were apparently light-skinned enough to find brief acceptance in the majors (though not without many raised eyebrows), Calvo and Costa were dark enough to play as well in the professional Negro leagues (thus being the only two pre–Robinson players to appear in both white and black major leagues). See Chapter 7 for further elaboration.

References and Suggested Readings

Alou, Felipe (told to Herm Weiskopf). *My Life in Baseball*. Waco, Texas: Word, 1967.

Bjarkman, Peter C. *The Toronto Blue Jays*. New York: Gallery, 1990; Chapter 6, "El Béisbol North of the Border."

________. "Washington Senators—Minnesota Twins: Expansion-Era Baseball Comes to the American League" (Chapter 13). In *Encyclopedia of Major League Baseball: American League (Team Histories)*, 1993 edition. New York: Carroll and Graf, 1993, 487–534.

Brown, Bruce. "Cuban Baseball." *Atlantic Monthly* 253(6) (June 1984): 109–114.

Cepeda, Orlando (with Charles Einstein). *My Ups and Downs in Baseball*. New York: Putnam, 1968.

________ (with Bob Markus). *High and Inside: Orlando Cepeda's Story*. South Bend, Indiana: Icarus Press, 1984.

Dark, Alvin, and John Underwood. *When in Doubt, Fire the Manager*. New York: E. P. Dutton, 1980.

Jamail, Milton. "The Latin Connection." In *Texas Rangers 1992 Official Yearbook*. Westport, Connecticut: Professional Sports, 1992, 56–60.

Kerrane, Kevin. *Dollar Sign on the Muscle: The World of Baseball Scouting*. New York: Beaufort, 1984; Howie Haak interview, 75–84.

Millson, Larry. *Ballpark Figures: The Blue Jays and the Business of Baseball*. Toronto, Ontario: McClelland and Stewart, 1987.

Oleksak, Michael M., and Mary Adams Oleksak. *Béisbol: Latin Americans and the Grand Old Game*. Grand Rapids, Michigan: Masters Press, 1991.

Peary, Danny. "Vic Power." In *Cult Baseball Players: The Greats, the Flakes, the Weird, and the Wonderful*. New York: Simon and Schuster, 1990, 344–373.

Ruck, Rob. *The Tropic of Baseball: Baseball in the Dominican Republic*. Westport, Connecticut: Meckler, 1991; New York: Carroll and Graf, 1992.

Shatzkin, Mike, ed. *The Ballplayers: Baseball's Ultimate Biographical Reference*. New York: William Morrow (Arbor House), 1990.

Vaughn, Gerald F. "Building the Pre-1961 Washington Senators Farm System." Unpublished manuscript, Washington, D.C., 1984.

CHAPTER 5

Dodgers with a Latin Beat

> The Brooklyn Dodgers are the first team owned solely by their fans.
> —WILLIAM HUMBER

Unheralded Sandy Amoros stretching rubber-armed across the low left-field Yankee Stadium barrier in the eternal autumnal sunshine of October 1955 plucking Yogi Berra's sinking line drive from the outstretched arms of fans and preserving a first and only Brooklyn world title; youthful Roberto Clemente recklessly dashing the base paths in a Montreal Royals uniform about to burst upon the Brooklyn scene as part of the greatest Dodgers outfield ever assembled; pudgy yet formidable Fernando Valenzuela blowing down legions of National League hitters in the early summers of the past decade. These are the composite images that immortalize for latter-day Brooklyn and present-day Los Angeles fans a rich and lengthy Dodger connection with baseball "south of the border"—a four-decade relationship with the plentiful talent fonts of the national pastime as it has long been played throughout tropical islands of the Caribbean basin and in coastal nations spread across northern Latin America.

An astute Dodger front-office executive braintrust, at least from the earliest days of the O'Malley family reign, has always seemed to recognize the immense untapped potential of burgeoning Latin American baseball talent. And yet the story of at least this one proud ballclub's considerable Latin American connections seemingly gains momentum with some strange twists and hidden intrigues. And these peculiar intrigues all cluster simultaneously around seasons preceding and following one of baseball's most celebrated hours—Jackie Robinson's pioneering appearance in Brooklyn during the immediate post–World War II years. Later still, the Dodgers' Hispanic ties would explode full force upon the 1980s, a period in which the Los Angeles ballclub stood steadfastly at the vanguard of the new Latin American invasion.

What might be termed the Dodgers' "Latin American connection" first takes tentative root a full six decades ago. It coincides with the arrival in Brooklyn of the original Cuban big-league pitching star Adolfo Luque, who took up only the briefest residence in Ebbets Field during the 1930 and 1931 seasons. Nonetheless, the Dodgers never fully exploited the earliest waves of Latin American (especially Cuban) baseball talent prevalent during the 1950s and 1960s—at least not to the same degree as their nearest National League rivals, the New York Giants (with Orlando Cepeda, José Pagán, Rubén Gómez, and the fleet-footed Alou brothers) and Pittsburgh Pirates (featuring Clemente, Roman Mejías, Carlos Bernier, and Luís Arroyo), or Clark Griffith's economy-minded American League Washington Senators, who stocked their postwar rosters with dozens of seemingly average yet inexpensive Cuban hurlers and weak-sticking but glue-gloved middle infielders. Only Luque and Mexico's Melo Almada appeared in Brooklyn uniforms during the thirties; Puerto Rican outfielder Luís Olmo boarded for a single season as the token Dodger Hispanic of the war-torn forties; outfielder Amoros, shortstop Chico Fernández (34 games) and relief hurler Rene Valdes (5 games) alone spiced Brooklyn rosters during the sizable Cuban invasion of the glorious fifties.

Thus the story of Dodger Latin American ballplayers actually begins in the mid–1950s and continues by fits and starts down to the present. Fifty-two Latin-born ballplayers have proudly worn Dodger Blue, a figure that represents nearly 9 percent of all Latin-born ballplayers to don big-league uniforms and compares favorably with other big-league clubs known for their Spanish-speaking talent. Despite their slow start at recruiting from the Latin talent pool, today's Los Angeles ballclub is as Latin-flavored as any of its rivals. Numerical comparison clinches the point: 47 Latin American players have appeared in uniform for the New York and San Francisco Giants, 68 for the Pittsburgh Pirates, 79 for the Washington-Minnesota ballclub, 46 for the Chicago White Sox, and 32 for the Toronto Blue Jays, today's most thoroughly Latin-flavored major league franchise.

For many cynical baseball fans, the 1980s was without debate the decade of unwelcomed excesses: big bucks, big labor actions, big egos among players and owners alike, and big disappointments on the field. This was especially so for the most nostalgia-driven fans, those who now pine for baseball's simpler golden days, for a time when the grass was still real; the sky remained uncovered; pitching in the guise of Warren Spahn, Whitey Ford, and Sandy Koufax seemed the game's truest art form; and huge lead-footed sluggers like Ted Kluszewski, Wally Post, Gus Zernial, or Frank Howard provided high-powered long-ball action. Yet for less backward-looking fanatics, those enamored of a modern television game, this decade was an era for exciting new superstars, dramatic divisional pennant races, and a speedier brand of baseball that provided a thrill per minute in the nation's luxurious multipurpose pleasure-dome stadiums.

And it was a decade when baseball was transfused and transformed by a rare new breed of fleet-footed and flashy superstars as well as showy and even reckless utility players, most from island nations of the Caribbean. A showcase for such Spanish-speaking stars as José Canseco, Julio Franco, Pedro Guerrero, George Bell, Rubén Sierra, and Tony Fernández, the 1980s will perhaps best be remembered as the decade that fully unleashed baseball's relentless and thrill-packed Latin American invasion.

Latin ballplayers and their dramatic impact on the American national pastime certainly did not begin with the 1980s, of course. For at least four decades now, the Spanish-speaking ballplayer has been making his influence felt in ever-increasing numbers. From the honor roll of brilliant fielding shortstops in the 1950s (Chico Carrasquel, Luís Aparicio, Leo Cárdenas, Willie Miranda, Chico Fernández, José Valdivielso, Rubén Amaro, José Pagán, Zoilo Versalles) to the strong-armed hurlers (Marichal, Cuellar, Tiant) and adept batsmen (Clemente, Cepeda, Miñoso, Rico Carty) of the 1960s, to the current crop of Hispanic superstars (Canseco, Valenzuela, Juan González, and George Bell), the Latin American impact on the majors has been inescapable over the lifetime of most middle-aged fans. Yet it was only during the 1980s that the flow of baseball talent from "south of the border" reached near floodtide proportions, and this floodtide would be far greater if not for restrictive U.S. immigration policies that today limit current foreign-born players to a maximum total of 500 roster regulars and farmhands throughout organized baseball.

To set the record straight, Latin American ballplayers in the majors extend far back into the dim prehistory of the game, long before Jackie Robinson first broke the odious color barrier in Brooklyn in 1947 and thus opened the national game not only to North American blacks but also to dozens of talented Cuban, Puerto Rican, Venezuelan, and Mexican ballplayers previously destined to perform only with shadowy barnstorming Negro-league clubs. Before Robinson, only a handful of light-skinned Latins (Luque and Bobby Estalella) and medium-toned Latins (Hiram Bithorn and Alex Carrasquel) had found a shaky big-league acceptance.

The most noteworthy, of course, was Cincinnati Reds hurler Dolf Luque, who once compiled a sterling 27-8 mark with a 1.93 ERA (in 1923), still the best-ever hurling season in rich Cincinnati history. Luque earned his immutable spot in history as the first Latin American to pitch in a World Series game, tossing five shutout relief innings for the victorious Redlegs during the now infamous Black Sox Series of 1919, and later made token appearances with the New York Giants and Brooklyn Dodgers. As the first recognizable Latin baseball star and first Latin World Series performer, Luque blazed a pioneering trail that would be rarely imitated by his country-men (most of whom were black-skinned, thus shunned by big-league clubs) for almost three decades to follow.

Yet while Luque was a point of pride for his Cuban countrymen, he was hardly a household name for run-of-the-mill baseball rooters. For the historical record, no Latin-blooded all-star performer was seen in the midsummer classic until Chico Carrasquel quietly appeared in the second Comiskey Park gala of 1950. Mexico's Bobby Avila belatedly claimed special distinction as the first native Latino to capture a big-league batting title, hitting .341 in Cleveland as late as 1954. Juan Marichal (who quietly closed his spectacular career with the Dodgers) was the first among his countrymen to hurl a no-hitter, but not until a full decade later, in 1963. And Roberto Clemente (once painfully close to becoming Brooklyn Dodger property) was the initial Latin-born National League batting champion (1961) and the first Hispanic ballplayer to earn immortality through enshrinement a mere 20 years ago in the hallowed halls of Cooperstown.

Unfortunately, Dolf Luque's indelible baseball legacy (despite 194 career wins, which trails only Marichal, Luís Tiant, and Dennis Martínez in this category among Hispanic hurlers) remains little more than a racial stereotype often attached callously to the bulk of Latin players—the hot-blooded, fiery Latin battler whose flailing fists demand more attention than his flaming fastball. It was Luque (as detailed in Chapter 1) who once unfortunately laid his glove upon the mound in Cincinnati and charged a Giants bench that had been unfairly heckling him, venting such irrational fury in the process that it took four Cincinnati constables and assorted teammates to escort him kicking and screaming from the ballpark. Latin America's first legitimate big-time ballplayer was also its first illegitimate full-blown folk legend.

Dolf Luque was nonetheless the only true Hispanic star between the inaugural appearance of his countrymen in the major leagues (Cuban Esteban Bellán made the first Latin big-league appearance in 1871 with the Troy Haymakers of the National Association, then considered a full-fledged major league) and the later full-scale invasion of dark-skinned Latins like Minnie Miñoso, Vic Power, and Bob Clemente during the 1950s. And Luque, albeit in the very twilight of his career, was also fittingly the first Brooklyn Dodger Latin-grown player. This hard-throwing and often misunderstood Cuban enjoyed something more than a mere cup of coffee with Brooklyn teams of the Daffiness Dodgers era, recording two fine seasons of stellar clutch pitching. "The Pride of Havana" was 14-8 in 1930 and hurled 301 innings over the two-year period, all at an age (41) when most hurlers are merely fading memories for the local faithful of any baseball city.

The summer of 1930, the year of Luque's arrival in Ebbets Field, provided one of the most action-packed campaigns in the history of the legendary Brooklyn club. Certainly this was a summer season that, at least in retrospect, stands among the most colorful and drama-laced in the long and event-filled annals of the tradition-proud National League. It was a year when the entire circuit (over 150 batsmen on eight ballclubs) slugged baseballs at a logic-defying .303 pace, every club in the league hitting above the magic .300 level save Boston and Cincinnati. League pitchers were truly an endangered species as Brooklyn's Babe Herman rattled the nearby Ebbets Field fences at a .393 clip, yet still fell short of a league batting title due to Bill Terry's prodigious .401 mark, pounded out in the neighboring Polo Grounds. If this was the height of the Depression era in America at large, there certainly was no economy of slugging or paucity of thrills to be found in the National League ballparks.

The thrill-packed season that entertained Brooklyn faithful that summer was one of the more memorable in club annals, though it was not a year destined to receive much ink in the numerous literary histories subsequently devoted to the Brooklyn franchise. Headline chapters are always reserved for the 1920 and 1941 pennant chases or the Robinson-Snider-Reese-Campanella-led "Boys of Summer" clubs of the fabulous fifties. Yet it is hard to surpass the 1930 Dodger summer for sheer excitement or colorful character and event. This was the peak encore and final curtain call for the bumbling ballclubs of the Wilbert Robinson era, today known fondly as the Daffiness Dodgers and always more touted by baseball historians for base-running bungles and outrageous fielding gaffes than anything approaching inspired pennant contention. (This was not the season, it should be noted, of that famous yet always misconstrued event that found Babe Herman sliding into a third-base sack already occupied by two of his confused teammates; it was actually four summers earlier that Babe Herman had "doubled into a double play" in typical Daffiness Boys style.) Yet behind the slugging of potent if unpredictable Herman, first sacker Del Bissonette (.336), and outfielder Johnny Frederick (.334), the usually also-ran Brooklyn Robins (so dubbed after their colorful manager "Uncle Robbie") rode the new league-wide hitting craze to dizzying heights. A team that had been the league's laughingstock for a decade suddenly broke a string of five straight sixth-place finishes by charging into a fourth-place first-division berth in the league's hectic hit-packed scramble for a pennant. And it was a respectable fourth, 18 games above .500, only 6 games off the pace at summer's end. Wilbert Robinson's recharged team had led the entire pack throughout most of the summer's action before fading at September's close. Brooklyn fans warmed quickly to the excitement of so much slugging and the unusual stimulation of a pennant race tussle, joyfully packing the Ebbets Field grandstands with a club record 1.1 million turnstile count.

Much of the glamour of one of Brooklyn's most unheralded glory seasons, it should be added, was provided by the club's distinctively novel Latin American flavor. Dolf Luque was an immediate success for Uncle Robbie's ballclub, earning 14 wins, a total surpassed only by staff ace Dazzy Vance's slightly superior 17 victories. Luque was one of six Brooklyn moundsmen to appear in more than 30 games, and he posted a club third-best 199 innings of work. And when Luque took the mound for Brooklyn, he formed half of a notable rarity on the big-league diamond—an all-Hispanic battery anchored by Tampa's Alfonso Ramon Lopez as the dependable Brooklyn rookie backstop. While Lopez was not technically Latin American (the Chicago Cubs would boast the first true Latin battery in 1942 with Puerto Rican hurler Hi Bithorn and Cuban part-time receiver Sal "Chico" Hernández), the team of Luque and Lopez (widely known as "that Spanish kid from Tampa" and bearing the popular moniker "Señor") was Hispanic enough in the public mind to receive considerable journalistic mention. And in honor of this closest thing to a true salsa-flavored battery, La Tropical Brewery of Havana would get into the act with a proud show of corporate sponsorship. It was the Havana-based firm that willingly underwrote a considerable transportation and hotel bill for the Brooklyn team's week-long barnstorming tour of Cuba during spring-training exhibition action earlier that 1930 season.

Brooklyn baseball historian Tommy Holmes, who long covered the Dodgers for the hometown press, recalls the impact of "Little Ay-dolph" (Wilbert Robinson's favored manner of addressing his veteran hurler) on the 1930 season in Brooklyn. Luque was fiercely independent and still an authentically tough character, even in the twilight of his career. When the Giants' Frankie Frisch once tripled off Havana's proud moundsman, the combative Cuban reportedly screamed from the pitcher's hill toward the breathless Frisch at third, offering a no-holds-barred warning of things to come: "Next time I keel you," screamed Luque in Holmes's standardized if stereotyped rendition. It is further reported that Frisch had a tough time remaining on his feet in several subsequent trips to the batter's box against a fiery and vengeful Luque.

Luque's stay in Brooklyn was all too brief. He was soon released, following seven more 1931 victories, the ax falling during a general housecleaning at the end of Uncle Robbie's tenure in the spring of 1932. Beloved Babe Herman and promising if unheralded Ernie Lombardi were both dealt to Cincinnati at approximately the same time. Unfortunately for Brooklyn fans and ballplayers alike, the move was perhaps altogether premature, as Luque was far from finished as a big-league moundsman. Pushing his mid-forties, he would nonetheless capture 19 more victories for the rival Giants over the next four seasons, including a World Series clincher during game five of the 1933 fall classic. Yet Luque's impact on Dodger history was not quite finished when the seemingly ageless hurler took his spirited pitching act to the Polo Grounds in early 1932. Two decades later, the Brooklyn ballclub would again unexpectedly benefit (fittingly with an assist by the rival Giants) from the tough-as-nails mound artistry of another fearsome master of the knockdown pitch—former Polo-Grounder Sal "The Barber"

Maglie. And it would be during two years of apprenticeship in the Mexican League of the 1940s, under manager and master tutor Dolf Luque, that Maglie would learn the pitching trade and develop the trademark style that would one day author a no-hitter and seal a 1956 pennant drive in historic Ebbets Field.

Ballpark fans are generally figure filberts (fans of the game's endless numerical dimensions), and baseball's magical statistics in the end always speak most clearly for themselves. Mileposts like 755 and 61 are the true touchstones of home-run dominance; the magic ring of .400 speaks of hitting greatness, just as 4,000 signals a strikeout milestone for hurlers. And the raw numbers are just as eloquent when it comes to tallying the full dimension of today's Latin influence on the recent major league scene. While highly visible heroes like Clemente, Tiant, Cepeda, and Rico Carty (1970 National League batting champion) graced the seventies, rosters were increasingly jammed solid with legions of Spanish-speaking players by the mid-eighties.

When 1989 spring training began, for instance, a total of 156 Latins (15 percent of the 1,040 player head count) stocked 40-man rosters for the 26 major league clubs. Toronto's Blue Jays boasted the largest number of spring-roster Hispanic players with 14, while the Dodgers and the Texas Rangers checked in with 10 apiece. Altogether, 475 Latin ballplayers had competed in the majors by the opening of the 1989 season, a century-long total that would soar above 500 before the close of the 1990 campaign and above 600 by the conclusion of 1992 play. While Cuba had been the unrivaled talent source throughout the Eisenhower fifties (raided most heavily by the Washington Senators and Pittsburgh Pirates), it was the Dominican Republic that would soon more than compensate for Castro's closing of the Havana pipeline in the aftermath of the Kennedy sixties.

While the Washington Senators first fully exploited cheap Cuban reinforcements in the years shortly after Jackie Robinson and the Toronto Blue Jays are perhaps best known today for seeking their hottest prospects in the sugarcane fields of the Dominican Republic, the Dodgers—from Branch Rickey and Leo Durocher to Peter O'Malley, Al Campanis, and Tommy Lasorda—have also maintained a storied and high-profile connection with talented Latin American ballplayers. The Los Angeles edition of the Dodgers, like the American League champion Blue Jays, turned increasingly to Latin-bred stars throughout the eighties to build consistently exciting and winning ballclubs. And the numbers of Caribbean and Mexican products pulling on the Dodger uniform more than favorably compare with those of other franchises (Toronto, Minnesota, San Francisco) often more touted for their Latin American flavor.

Admittedly the Twins-Senators may boast the largest all-time contingent of Latin-born and Spanish-speaking talent, yet this is only because of better than 50 Cubans (mostly journeyman players who appeared in but a handful of major league games) all crammed onto Washington rosters during the late 1940s and early 1950s. Only pitchers Camilo Pascual and Pete Ramos and first baseman Julio Becquer contributed significantly to Clark Griffith's lackluster ballclub during that decade. The Toronto Blue Jays, who admittedly boast a highly visible and constantly shifting contingent of Dominican stars (George Bell, Tony Fernández, Nelson Liriano, Domingo Martínez, Juan Guzmán, Manny Lee) have actually utilized fewer Dominicans (16) than the Dodgers (25) in official big-league game action. The Giants, on the other hand, despite the visibility of such sixties stars as Marichal, Cepeda, and Alou, have totaled five fewer players (47 altogether) claiming Latin birthright than the O'Malley-led Dodgers.

The Dodgers' Latin element perhaps made its most noticeable splash during the recent 1990 campaign. Dominican product Ramón Martínez lit up the 1990 season with burning promise, tying the single-game record of Hall-of-Famer Sandy Koufax by striking out 18 batters during a June Dodger Stadium game against Atlanta. The 1990 ballclub was filled with fresh Latin American talent, and the Dodgers at the turn of the new decade were capable of fielding a starting lineup top-heavy with Hispanic players— Martínez or Valenzuela on the mound, Carlos Hernández behind the plate, José Vizcaíno anchoring third, Juan Samuel and Alfredo Griffin as the keystone combination, and Stan Javier and José González patrolling the outfield pastures. At the dawn of the previous decade, Fernando Valenzuela had suddenly burst on the scene as the hottest Dodger pitching prospect since the immortal duo of Koufax and Drysdale. And between latter-day Fernandomania and present-day "Martínez Fever," Pedro Guerrero (with over 200 lifetime roundtrippers and a career .300 average) also carved out a deserved reputation as one of the most feared sluggers in the National League.

While Latin stars have often shown brightly in Los Angeles in the 1980s, however, the Latin baseball invasion was every bit as slow developing in the City of Angels during the two previous decades as it was throughout the remainder of big-league cities. And while the Brooklyn Dodgers of the 1950s had expertly utilized newfound black talent (Robinson, Newcombe, Campanella, Gilliam, Joe Black) to build one of the most fearsome teams in National League history, Latin ballplayers were not as much in evidence on the "Boys of Summer" Dodgers as on some other big-league teams (especially the rival Giants of Leo Durocher and Horace Stoneham). Yet the first faint impact of Latin players in the fifties did result in a few shocking and memorable twists for Brooklyn Dodgers history, especially that sad final chapter of Brooklyn baseball history that transpired over the course of several farewell years of play in storied Ebbets Field.

There is the little-known and often garbled tale of a mysterious Cuban ballplayer who (according to apocryphal tale) might well have been Jackie Robinson's replacement as the first black major leaguer during the modern era of big-league play. Few baseball historians and even fewer casual fans know that it was a now-forgotten Latin American prospect who nearly preceded Robinson as the original chosen martyr for Branch Rickey's "noble experiment" to circumvent organized baseball's twentieth-century color line.

What Branch Rickey needed to bring his plan for racial integration to full fruition was a perfect man for the job, someone driven with competitive spirit, yet patient enough to carry stoically the full burden of hatred that was to be the inevitable lot of baseball's first black pioneer. Ironically, Robinson might not have been Rickey's man had history conspired a bit differently. A popular Cuban infielder, Silvio García, had caught Rickey's attention by 1943, and the Mahatma that very winter dispatched his personal representative Walter O'Malley directly to Havana with a letter of credit for $25,000 and instructions to sign García at any cost. Destiny seemingly had authored a contrasting script of its own, however, and O'Malley (popular legend has it) arrived in Cuba only to find that the aging black star had recently been drafted into the Cuban army and was no longer available for civil employment. García, who according to this version of the tale might well have been immortalized as the first black big-leaguer of the modern era had O'Malley arrived in Cuba a scant week earlier, was later to play out his long career in relative obscurity as an unheralded veteran star for the New York Cubans of the invisible Negro Professional League. More careful research suggests, however, that Cuba did not maintain military conscription during 1943 and that Rickey was more likely dissuaded from the project by circulating reports of García's inconsistent play and his considerable affinity for night life and the hated demon rum.

While many have dismissed Silvio García as a much-overrated Cuban "legend" who possessed neither the talent nor mental makeup required of a big-league ballplayer, at least one reputable Cuban baseball historian has recently shed a far more illuminating light on the mysterious figure from Cuba's lost Negro league and barnstorming era. In the view of Angel Torres, writing recently in the pages of a popular Los Angeles Spanish-language daily, the long-forgotten García was more than talented enough to have reached big-league stardom. Here was a rifle-armed fielder who hit with power to the opposite field and like Dihigo before him was often as comfortable on the mound as in infield or outfield positions. Only a handful of Cuban blacks from the pre–Robinson era would rate above García in the view of journalist Torres—certainly Dihigo and famed black hurler Ramón Bragaña. And pehaps a half-dozen others: Cristóbal Torriente, José Méndez, Alejandro Oms, certainly the elder Luís Tiant, Bombín Pedroso,

Pedro Formental, and Cando López. García was born in 1914 at Matanzas (birthplace as well to Dihigo and Miñoso), threw and hit from the right side, and by his teens already possessed a formidable stature of six feet and nearly 200 pounds. Starring in the 1930s and again in the 1940s at the amateur and semipro levels as well as in professional winter- and black-league play, García earned his reputation as a deadly opposite-field hitter (hitting .314 with Santa Clara in 1941 Cuban winter-league action and .293 with Almendares in 1939). Nearly 30, he was clearly approaching the end of his career when O'Malley came calling. Nonetheless, the now obscure case of Silvio García, especially placed alongside the equally forgotten case of Roberto Clemente, suggests a cruel irony. The two greatest Latin ballplayers connected with Dodger history seem to be the very two that never donned a Brooklyn uniform.

If the story of Silvio García and the Brooklyn Dodgers' first tenuous connections with Latin American scouting is perhaps largely apocryphal, as it generally appears to be, the often buried circumstances of the Brooklyn club's involvement with future Hall-of-Famer Roberto Clemente are today both more real and more poignantly painful for those old-time Dodger fans who recall events in Montreal during the summer months of 1954. For it now seems that in the mid-fifties, at the very zenith of "Boys of Summer" glory days, an uncharacteristically poor management plan authored by the staff of Dodgers owner Walter O'Malley robbed Brooklyn fans of a chance to see what might have turned into the greatest outfield of modern baseball history.

Today one can only imagine the glories of a trio of flychasers consisting of Duke Snider and Carl Furillo playing alongside the flashy young Puerto Rican phenom Roberto Clemente. Having signed the phenomenal 19-year-old Puerto Rican prospect for a then-hefty $10,000 signing bonus and a promised $5,000 in 1954 salary, the Brooklyn braintrust decided to hide their future franchise player on the roster of the International League Montreal Royals, keeping Clemente on the bench of Montreal manager Max Macon whenever scouts might visit in search of needed outfield talent. Already blessed with an outfield of Jackie Robinson and Sandy Amoros sharing left, Snider in center, and Furillo in right, and with clutch-hitting George Shuba in reserve, the Dodgers saw little need for rushing along their touted prospect. Indeed, the prospect of yet another black star residing in Brooklyn may have weighed heavily in O'Malley's decision. The Dodgers under Rickey had been bold integration pioneers, true enough, but this was still the fifties, and the prospect of allowing black faces to populate more than half the lineup (Robinson, Campanella, Gilliam, Newcombe, Clemente, Amoros) may simply not have seemed like sound box-office business, even in Brooklyn.

The difficulty for O'Malley was that league rules at the time dictated that any ballplayer offered a "bonus contract" of more than $4,000 was subject to an irrevocable draft by other clubs during the following winter if not retained on the parent club's roster throughout an entire first season. Branch Rickey, whose hoarding of talent in St. Louis and Brooklyn had fostered such a rule, was at the time still smarting at having been forced out of the general manager's seat in Brooklyn (by none other than Walter O'Malley) a few short seasons earlier. Rickey saw in the Clemente situation a chance to strike back in aces at his old Brooklyn nemesis. Thus, while Clemente chafed at playing only sporadically in Montreal, Rickey quietly awaited his appointed time. And that time soon came after the Pirates finished dead last in 1954, thus claiming the cherished first draft slot and nabbing the hotshot Clemente as the very first selection of that winter's minor league lottery. Embarrassed Dodger officials later sought to rationalize the loss with the slim consolation that by signing Clemente and then letting him go to the lowly Pirates, they had at least blocked a more unsettling prospect—the fabulous Puerto Rican flychaser turning up in the outfield of the rival New York Giants. The Polo-Grounders (who had also heavily recruited the Puerto Rican wonderboy) had envisioned a young Clemente entrenched in their lineup nestled alongside the incomparable Willie Mays.

Although Clemente remains today only a distant dream for old-time Brooklyn and Los Angeles fans, another Caribbean outfielder did provide a handful of brief thrills and one unsurpassable moment for Dodger diehards everywhere. This was no Clemente, yet the stunted figure of Sandy Amoros is one that will never be long forgotten whenever Brooklyn fans gather to reminisce about those final seasons of their beloved Bums and their intimate Flatbush ballpark. On October 4, 1955, in the bottom of the sixth inning of the seventh game of the World Series, little-heralded Edmundo Amoros trotted out to his position in left field in Yankee Stadium as a defensive replacement for Jim Gilliam and in a flash turned in the most memorable outfield play of storied Dodger history. Snagging Yogi Berra's slicing drive along the left-field line, then firing a perfect relay throw to Reese to execute a rally-killing double play that nipped Gil McDougald at first, Amoros seemingly single-handedly clinched for Brooklyn its only world title in seven decades of Flatbush play. When besieged at game's end by reporters wanting to know what Amoros thought about the miraculous catch, the soft-spoken and shy Cuban outfielder uttered in halting English one of baseball's most truly memorable lines: "I dunno," shrugged Brooklyn's hero of the hour, "I just run like hell."

Amoros played a few final disappointing seasons in Brooklyn after 1955 and enjoyed a brief sojourn in Los Angeles (appearing in 15 games between 1959 and 1960) before two final unproductive years with the Tigers. Yet his career was largely over after his single momentary brush with World Series destiny in 1955, and later life on and off the field would be filled with pain and tragedy beyond the due of any 10 men. Inconsistent hitting kept Amoros shuttling back and forth between Brooklyn and Triple-A Montreal throughout much of the 1950s, and eventually his erratic play meant a last brief cup of coffee in Detroit, then a permanent ticket to the Mexican League where salaries were even more anemic than the batting averages of the numerous former big-leaguers who toiled there. But catastrophic disappointment was just beginning to toy with Brooklyn's greatest World Series hero. Amoros was soon detained by baseball-crazy Fidel Castro in his native Cuban homeland, stripped of his considerable household possessions and personal property, and held under house arrest for over five years for refusing to manage a team in Cuba's Castro-sponsored semiprofessional league. By the time Amoros finally escaped Cuba in late 1967, his playing days were done, his health was considerably weakened, and he was doomed to live out the next quarter century in considerable poverty and loneliness, first in New York City and later in the Cuban ghetto of Tampa, Florida. In some ways the sad tale of Sandy Amoros ironically foreshadows, admittedly on a dimmer stage, the tragic overtones of Clemente's unsettled life and aborted playing career. If Roberto Clemente remains the missing chapter in the Dodgers' unfolding Latin American saga and Fernando Valenzuela would someday write an unduplicated epic of brilliant overnight success, the life adventure of Sandy Amoros remains a depressing and tragic saga of failed career and misspent youth, salvaged only by a single brilliant moment indelible in the memories of baseball fans throughout the land.

After Amoros was gone from the National League scene and Clemente had been spirited away by a shrewd and perhaps revenge-minded Branch Rickey in Pittsburgh, there seemed to be little significant Latin American connection for Walter O'Malley's baseball franchise, at least until the glorious summers of the 1980s. Yet 13 Latin ballplayers did pull on a Brooklyn uniform at one time or another, although most of these made appearances lasting only a few innings or a few games. Perhaps the most interesting Hispanic player of the lot was Humberto Pérez "Chico" Fernández, a glue-fingered Cuban-born shortstop who broke in briefly with Brooklyn in 1956 before becoming the first black to integrate baseball for the longtime racially pure and change-resistant Philadelphia Phillies. Fernández had little chance of replacing such a fixture as Pee Wee Reese in Ebbets Field, and the talent-thin Phillies were quick to swap five players (including Canadian Tim Harkness and veteran outfielder Elmer Valo) to spirit him away from Brooklyn in the season's opening week of 1957. Feeling considerable pressure as the last National League team to integrate its roster, a full decade after Robinson's debut, the recalcitrant Phils had purchased the contract of shortstop John Kennedy (the last man to jump from the Negro leagues to the majors) during the winter months of 1957, and Kennedy's strong spring-training performance had earned a roster spot that would make him the Phillies' reported first player of color. When Kennedy suffered a career-ending injury after only two at-bats in his April 22 historic debut, however, it was left to Fernández to step in as the first regular black ballplayer on the senior circuit's most notoriously racist ballclub.

Chico Fernández was a stellar glove man but a painfully weak hitter (.242 in 342 games with the Phillies); thus he lasted only three summers in the City of Brotherly Love before finishing out a journeyman's career with Detroit and the 1963 expansion Mets. It was during this penultimate big-league stop in the Motor City that Fernández also once again hooked up with his old Brooklyn roommate and countryman Sandy Amoros during the swan-song seasons of both men's abbreviated big-league careers. Again cast in the role of racial pioneers, Fernández and Amoros closed out their playing days in the tense environment of another big-league city that had long resisted baseball integration. Less than two seasons before their arrival, Detroit had become but the second-to-last American League franchise to feature a black big-leaguer when Dominican third baseman Ossie Virgil first cracked the Tiger lineup.

The 1960s and 1970s witnessed only a small parade of Spanish-speaking role players as well as a few veteran stars who had shone brightly elsewhere, then closed out their big-league years with a brief stopover in Los Angeles. Most noteworthy, of course, was the Dominican Dandy, Juan Marichal, baseball's greatest Hispanic pitcher and second among his countrymen to find a spot alongside Clemente in Cooperstown. Another was Cuban hurler Camilo Pascual, longtime ace of the Washington Senators and Minnesota Twins, whose career 174 victories remain sixth best on the all-time list of Latin American pitchers. That Marichal (who earned all but 5 of his 243 career victories in a San Francisco Giants uniform) would close out his career with a token Los Angeles appearance was about as strange as Duke Snider playing his final 91 games in the flannels of the hated rival Giants a decade earlier. Juan Marichal was during his brief two games and six innings of work for the Bums in 1975 perhaps a whimsical reminder to Dodger fans everywhere of the extent to which the rival Giants had exploited such formidable Latin talent throughout the 1960s—slugging Orlando Cepeda, Marichal, the three brilliant-fielding Alou brothers, wildman hurler Rubén Gómez (winner of the first West Coast big-league game), and flashy shortstop José Pagán—while the Dodgers had found few if any Spanish-speaking stars during the epoch that closed out the Walter Alston years and ushered in the long tenure of Tom Lasorda.

One bright Latin star, however, did shine proudly for the Dodgers of Alston and Lasorda in the 1970s—the irrepressible Manny Mota. Mota became in his Los Angeles tenure perhaps the greatest pinch hitter in baseball history, recording across a decade of bench duty an unmatched 150 pinch-hit safeties. The standard line about the soft-spoken Mota was that he could wake up on Christmas morning, step sleepily into the batter's box, and promptly rip a single into the gap. But the Dominican native was much more than a reserve player, blossoming in the fourth of his first six seasons in Pittsburgh with a .332 average, his first of seven .300 seasons over the next eight years. While possessing little power and only average fielding ability, Mota registered over 400 at-bats in only one of his 13 seasons in Los Angeles (1970). His .304 career average, however, stands as fourth best (tied with Tony Oliva) among all Latin big-leaguers. He retired owning a spectacular .297 career pinch-hitting average, and his .315 career BA under Alston and Lasorda is the best lifetime mark (1,800 or more plate appearances) in Los Angeles Dodgers annals. No other Latin American native performed as many seasons with the Dodgers as the clutch-hitting Mota, and only Pedro Guerrero has appeared in more games. The popular Mota remains very much an integral part of the Dodger scene, having returned in 1993 for his thirteenth season as special-assignments coach and part-time hitting instructor.

Baseball's golden era of the 1950s launched a subversive Latin invasion dressed largely in Washington Senators pinstripes yet spiced by unflappable showboaters named Power and Miñoso; the insidious sixties gave quiet birth to our greatest Hispanic diamond heroes – Clemente, Marichal, Alou, and Cepeda; and the seditious seventies earned legitimacy for the new breed of Latin superstars through the unmatched performances of Tiant, Pérez, Oliva, and Carew. The 1980s will most surely be remembered by Latino and North American baseball fans alike for a novel excitement known as "Fernandomania," which swept uncontrolled across the early summers of the most recent decade.

For it was with the arrival of Fernando Valenzuela that thousands of Spanish-speaking residents of southern California were finally able to identify fully with their own true homegrown superstar and ethnic folk hero. A 20-year-old native of Sonora, Mexico, and a veteran of two competitive Mexican League campaigns, Valenzuela burst upon the National League scene in the strike-torn 1981 season like a blast of fresh Gulf Stream air, turning Dodger Stadium into a Mexican fiesta on nights when he pitched and spellbinding rival hitters with a screwball (Fernando's fadeway) unlike anything since the immortal Carl Hubbell served them up for the New York Giants a half century earlier. Valenzuela had never heard of Hubbell and had learned his potent delivery from former Dodger hurler Bobby Castillo, often mistaken for a Latin American (but in reality a homegrown native son of the City of Angels).

No one else had ever hit the National League scene with quite the same dramatic impact as the young Valenzuela; this was the first rookie in baseball's long history to cop a Cy Young Award and be named *Sporting News*

Player of the Year simultaneously. Valenzuela was the nation's foremost baseball story in 1981, winning his first 10 major league decisions, hurling eight shutouts to tie a rookie record in a season shortened by a full one-third due to the odious labor dispute that nearly wrecked the Dodgers' world championship campaign, and pacing the senior circuit in starts, complete games, innings pitched, strikeouts, and shutouts. A phenomenal rookie season was prelude to a brilliant decade for Valenzuela, one that saw him become the first player awarded a $1 million arbitration settlement (1983), then set a new big-league standard of 44.1 consecutive innings without allowing an earned run at the outset of the 1986 campaign. Fernandomania of the early 1980s was one of the most wondrous stories in the Dodgers' long and colorful history. Few players in club annals (at least since the Ebbets Field days in the more expressive borough of Brooklyn) have been so popular with adoring fans. Valenzuela indeed ranks alongside Zack Wheat in the twenties, Babe Herman in the thirties, Dixie Walker ("the People's Cherce") in the forties, and Gil Hodges and Pee Wee Reese of the 1950 Boys of Summer as one of the most colorful and popular all-time Dodger favorites.

Fernando Valenzuela was not the only Hispanic star to shine brightly in the Los Angeles firmament during the 1980s. Pedro Guerrero – a slugging outfielder–third baseman–first baseman whom popular baseball writer Bill James once labeled "the best hitter God has made in a long time" – was in many respects the Dodger "player of the decade," at least over the span from World Series confrontations with the Yankees in 1977-1978 to the dramatic Kirk Gibson World Series heroics 10 seasons later. Signed by the Cleveland Indians in 1976 and thus rescued from the stark poverty of his native San Pedro de Macoris, hometown to dozens of successful big-league-bound Dominicans, Pete Guerrero was stolen from Cleveland by the Dodgers in exchange for failed pitching prospect Bruce Ellingsen. He first burst on the L.A. scene with five RBIs in the final triumphant game of the 1981 World Series, a feat that earned the talented Dominican a share of the first three-way partition of a series MVP award. Guerrero's most memorable season was 1985 when he tied a major league record with 15 roundtrippers in June, reached base 14 consecutive times during one torrid stretch, and led the senior circuit in both slugging and on-base percentage. A stretch of similar torrid campaigns would soon leave Guerrero third on the all-time Los Angeles home-run ledger (trailing only Cey and Garvey) before he was dealt away to St. Louis for pitcher John Tudor in late August 1988.

After Guerrero's departure from the Dodger clubhouse, the 1989 and 1990 seasons would witness a number of new and promising Latino faces to fill the void left by the departed slugger and continue the special Dominican flavor that so marked Dodger ballclubs of the 1980s. Ramón Martínez, signed out of the Dominican Republic (Santo Domingo) as a free agent in 1984, the very year he starred as a member of the Dominican Olympic team, has quickly established himself as the new Dodger ace with 52 victories spread across three full-time seasons, including a 20-win campaign and league-best 12 complete games during his 1990 rookie tour. Juan Samuel, another native of San Pedro de Macoris, was obtained from the New York Mets over the 1989 off-season and saw regular service as a starting centerfielder and second baseman during his three-year Los Angeles tenure. Steady reserve outfielder Stan Javier—son of former Cardinals great Julian Javier, who anchored second base for the powerhouse 1960s St. Louis championship teams—was brought to Dodger Stadium from Oakland to provide some much-needed base-running and defensive skills between 1990 and 1992. And a fourth Dominican, flashy Alfredo Griffin, anchored the Dodger infield at shortstop for three consecutive summers, often displaying renewed flashes of the defensive brilliance that earned him American League Rookie-of-the-Year honors for Toronto in 1979. The Dominican pipeline continued into the 1993 pennant campaign with pitchers Pedro Astacio and Pedro Martínez (Ramón's younger brother), infielders José Offerman and Rafael Bournigal, and outfielders Henry Rodríguez and Raul Mondesi all promising inspired play in the well-established tradition of Guerrero, Samuel, Martínez, and Griffin.

The Dodgers' Latin American connection has now come full cycle since those early Branch Rickey days when Roberto Clemente was inadvertently lost to the grateful Pirates, Silvio García was forgotten by an accident of baseball history, and Sandy Amoros was wildly cheered for a brief moment of World Series heroism. Buried deep in the Dodgers' productive farm system at that time, the early 1950s, was a promising young left-handed pitcher who was unfortunately never to amount to much in Brooklyn as a successful big-league hurler. An affable Tom Lasorda would do his most memorable pitching in the course of winter-league play held annually in Cuba during the final years before Castro's revolution. Such was Lasorda's apparent fame on the baseball-crazed island that his single Topps baseball card of 1954 boasts (in its flipside "Inside Baseball" cartoon strip) of the promising lefty's apparent abilities to outwit supposedly hot-tempered and slow-witted Latin sluggers. The card is a superb reflection of 1950s stereotypes about Latin ballplayers in general. It is also, however, a fitting piece of irony connected with the man who decades later would manage so skillfully a big-league team filled with dozens of great Latin stars.

Lasorda has long fostered his Latin American connections, having regularly taken part as celebrity guest at an annual Cuban old-timers game staged in Miami in recent winters. And over the past decade no other manager has been more blessed with a stable of Latin sluggers and rubber-armed pitchers, a proud group of Hispanic stars stretching from Pedro Guerrero and Fernando Valenzuela to Ramón Martínez and José Offerman, who have brought surprising new glories to the always proud Dodger tradition.

All-Time Roster of Dodger Latin American Players

A total of 52 players from Latin American nations and the Caribbean islands appeared in action for the Dodgers over a period stretching from 1930 through the opening months of the 1993 season. The first was the pioneering Cuban Dolf Luque, who appeared in 50 games for the Brooklyns in 1930-31. The briefest Dodgers career was that of Juan Marichal, who pitched but six innings in two games; the longest (in years of service) was registered by Manny Mota and stretched from the final season of the 1960s through the first of the 1980s (13 full seasons). It is not surprising that the Dominican Republic has supplied the most Latin Dodgers; it is perhaps a surprise that the Republic of Panama has yet to supply a single Dodger player, however, and that the talent font found in Cuba before 1959 has been birthplace to only 6 former Dodgers down through the years. By decades, 2 Latin Dodgers (Luque and Almada) appeared but briefly in the 1930s, but 1 (Olmo) in the 1940s, 3 (Amoros, Chico Fernández, Rene Valdez) in the 1950s, 6 in the 1960s, 15 in the 1970s, and 32 throughout the 1980s and 1990s (with several ballplayers overlapping decades, a fact that explains why the composite total of players by decades surpasses the expected total of 52). By position, Latin infielders (17) have been greatest in number (with one player, Juan Samuel, counted at two positions), followed narrowly by outfielders (15), pitchers (14), and catchers (7).

Cuba (6 players)	POS	Years with Dodgers (Total Games Played with Dodgers)
Amoros, Edmundo (Sandy)	OF	Brooklyn 1952, 1954–57; LA 1959–60 (452 games)
Fernández, Humberto (Chico)	SS	Brooklyn 1956 (34 games)
Luque, Aldolfo (Dolf)	RHP	Brooklyn 1930–31 (50 games)
Pascual, Camilo	RHP	LA 1970 (10 games)
Valdez, Rene	RHP	Brooklyn 1957 (5 games)
Versalles, Zoilo	SS	LA 1968 (122 games)

Puerto Rico (9 players)		
Alcaraz, Luís	IF	LA 1967-68 (58 games)
Alvarez, Orlando	OF	LA 1973–75 (10 games)
DeJesus, Iván	SS	LA 1974–76 (88 games)
Maldonado, Candy	OF	LA 1981–85 (296 games)
Mercado, Orlando	C	LA 1987 (7 games)
Olmo, Luís	OF	Brooklyn 1943–45, 1949 (372 games)
Rivera, Germán	3B	LA 1983-84 (107 games)
Rodríguez, Eliseo (Ellie)	C	LA 1976 (36 games)
Valle, Héctor	C	LA 1965 (9 games)

Mexico (7 players)	POS	Years with Dodgers (Total Games Played with Dodgers)
Almada, Melo (Mel)	OF	Brooklyn 1939 (39 games)
Orta, Jorge	IF	LA 1982 (86 games)
Peña, José	RHP	LA 1970–72 (55 games)
Robles, Sergio	C	LA 1976 (6 games)
Romo, Vicente	RHP	LA 1968, 1982 (16 games)
Treviño, Alejandro (Alex)	C	LA 1986-87 (161 games)
Valenzuela, Fernando	LHP	LA 1980–90 (298 games)

Dominican Republic (25 players)		
Astacio, Pedro	RHP	LA 1992-93 (40 games)
Bournigal, Rafael	SS-2B	LA 1992-93 (12 games)
Cedeño, César	OF	LA 1986 (37 games)
Duncan, Mariano	SS	LA 1985–87, 1989 (376 games)
Frías, Jesús (Pepe)	IF	LA 1980-81 (39 games)
Galvez, Balvino	RHP	LA 1986 (10 games)
González, José	OF	LA 1985–91 (379 games)
Griffin, Alfredo	SS	LA 1988-91 (481 games)
Guerrero, Pedro	OF	LA 1978–88 (1,036 games)
Javier, Stan	OF	LA 1990–92 (281 games)
Landestoy, Rafael	OF	LA 1977, 1983-84 (132 games)
Marichal, Juan	RHP	LA 1975 (2 games)
Martínez, Pedro	RHP	LA 1992-93 (64 games)
Martínez, Ramón	RHP	LA 1988–93 (144 games)
Martínez, Teodoro (Teddy)	IF	LA 1977–79 (202 games)
Mota, Manny	OF	LA 1969–80, 1982 (816 games)
Offerman, José	SS	LA 1990–93 (379 games)
Peña, Alejandro	RHP	LA 1981–88 (228 games)
Reyes, Gilberto (Gil)	C	LA 1983–85, 1987-88 (35 games)
Rodríguez, Henry	OF	LA 1992 (53 games)
Samuel, Juan	OF-IF	LA 1990–92 (343 games)
Sosa, Elias	RHP	LA 1976-77 (68 games)
Soto, Mario	RHP	LA 1988 (on roster, but no game action)
Taveras, Alejandro (Alex)	IF	LA 1982-83 (21 games)
Viscaíno, José	IF	LA 1989-90 (44 games)

Venezuela (3 players)		
Davalillo, Vic	OF	LA 1977–80 (135 games)
Hernández, Carlos	C	LA 1990–93 (141 games)
Hernández, Enzo	SS	LA 1978 (4 games)

Virgin Islands (2 players)		
Cruz, Henry	OF	LA 1975-76 (102 games)
Morales, José	IF-DH	LA 1983-84 (69 games)

Dozen Latin American Dodgers with Longest Career Service

Pedro Guerrero	1,036 games	(1978–1988)
Manny Mota	816 games	(1969–1980)
Alfredo Griffin	481 games	(1988–1991)
Sandy Amoros	452 games	(1952, 1954–1957, 1959-1960)
José Offerman[a]	379 games	(1990–1993)
José González	379 games	(1985–1991)
Mariano Duncan	376 games	(1985–1987, 1989)
Luís Olmo	372 games	(1943–1945, 1949)
Juan Samuel	343 games	(1990–1992)
Fernando Valenzuela	298 games	(1980–1990)
Candy Maldonado	296 games	(1981–1985)
Stan Javier	281 games	(1990–1992)

[a]Still active with Los Angeles Dodgers.

All-Time Dodgers Latin American Team

While it would perhaps have been inconceivable to fantasize about a Dodgers all-time Latin American team before the 1980s, the current Los Angeles Dominican and Puerto Rican talent pool has swelled to a point that allows a respectable all-star team, one that would represent the Dodgers proudly on any field. The ballplayers from this mythical team were selected largely on the basis of their performances as Dodgers (thus excluding Dolf Luque or Juan Marichal from the pitching positions and César Cedeño and Candy Maldonado from the outfield). Some allowances for overall career performance had to be made for players like Jorge Orta and Alex Treviño, however, to fill out a full representative lineup. What follows may not quite be a roster of Cooperstown Hall-of-Famers, but it is a respectable enough ballclub to give any present big-league opponent plenty of fits on any warm summer afternoon in Dodger Stadium.

Pos	*Player and Country*	*Years with Dodgers (Major League Totals)*
1B	Pedro Guerrero (Dominican)	LA 1978–88 (1,536 G, 215 HRs, .300 BA, through 1992)
2B	Juan Samuel (Dominican)[a]	LA 1990–92 (1,310 G, 1,338 H, .260 BA, through 1992)

Pos	*Player and Country*	*Years with Dodgers (Major League Totals)*
3B	Teddy Martínez (Dominican)	LA 1977–79 (657 G, 355 H, .240 BA)
SS	Alfredo Griffin (Dominican)[a]	LA 1988–91 (1,916 G, 1,668 H, .250 BA, through 1992)
OF	Sandy Amoros (Cuba)	Brooklyn 1952, 1954–57; LA 1959–60 (517 G, 334 H, .255 BA)
OF	Manny Mota (Dominican)	LA 1969–82 (1,536 G, 1,149 H, .304 BA)
OF	Vic Davalillo (Venezuela)	LA 1977–80 (1,458 G, 1,122 H, .279 BA)
C	Alex Treviño (Mexico)	LA 1986-87 (939 G, 604 H, .249 BA)
RHP	Ramón Martínez (Dominican)[a]	LA 1988–92 (52-37, 3.32 ERA, through 1992)
LHP	Fernando Valenzuela (Mexico)[a]	LA 1980–90 (141-118, 3.34 ERA, through 1992)
Relief	Alejandro Peña (Dominican)[a]	LA 1981–89 (50-48, 2.95 ERA, 67 Saves, through 1992)
Utility	Jorge Orta (Mexico)	LA 1982 (1,755 G, 1,619 H, .278 BA)
Utility	Luís Olmo (Puerto Rico)	Brooklyn 1943–45, 1949 (462 G, 458 H, .281 BA)

[a]Still active player in 1993.

Suggested Reading

Allen, Lee. *The Giants and Dodgers: The Fabulous Story of Baseball's Fiercest Rivalry.* New York: Putnam, 1964.

Bjarkman, Peter C. *Baseball's Great Dynasties: The Dodgers.* New York: Gallery, 1990.

________. *The Brooklyn Dodgers.* New York: Chartwell, 1992.

________. "Brooklyn Dodgers—Los Angeles Dodgers: From Daffiness Dodgers to the Boys of Summer and the Myth of America's Team." In *Encyclopedia of Major League Baseball: National League (Team Histories).* New York: Carroll and Graf, 1993, 72–136; Westport, Connecticut: Meckler, 1991.

Cohen, Stanley. *Dodgers: The First One Hundred Years.* New York: Birch Lane Press, 1990.

Durant, John. *The Dodgers: An Illustrated Story of Those Unpredictable Bums, the Brooklyn Baseball Club.* New York: Hastings House, 1948.

Holmes, Tommy. *Dodgers Daze and Knights: Enough of a Ballclub's History to Explain Its Reputation.* New York: David McKay, 1953.

Honig, Donald. *The Brooklyn Dodgers: An Illustrated Tribute.* New York: St. Martin's Press, 1981.

________. *The Los Angeles Dodgers: The First Quarter Century.* New York: St. Martin's Press, 1983.

Schoor, Gene. *A Pictorial History of the Dodgers: From Brooklyn to Los Angeles.* New York: Leisure Press, 1984.

PART II

Tales from the Tropic of Baseball

History is a myth agreed upon. —Napoleon Bonaparte

CHAPTER 6

Doubleheaders on the Dark Side of the Moon: Negro-League Barnstorming and Caribbean Heroes of the Blackball Era

> All along they were playing, yet so far as the white world was concerned they were playing in the shadows, playing doubleheaders on the dark side of the moon, running out triples on the outskirts of town, playing on fields of their own or using the white man's field when he was away on the road.
>
> —Douglass Wallop

Over the four decades from the dawn of the First World War through the first icy stalemates of the Eisenhower-era cold war, as many as 400 drama-filled ballgames were contested between touring teams of blackball all-stars and their better-known major league counterparts. These games thrilled backwater crowds but nonetheless remained a well-kept secret to the remainder of the nation. They were little publicized and rarely reported in the national press, yet they brought to those fortunate enough to see them some of the most exciting baseball witnessed in this or any other era.

In their latter-day rediscovery of these games, revisionist blackball historians have made much of the apparent onfield successes of touring blackball outfits. John B. Holway, the most active scholar of the lot, has searched exhaustively through contemporary newspaper accounts and compiled revealing if still incomplete Negro-league baseball records. For baseball purists with a penchant for accuracy, unfortunately, Holway's numbers and conclusions are largely one-sided and blatantly contentious. Holway's steadfast position is that these lost games clearly demonstrate unarguable superiority for the touring Negro-leaguers. Holway would have us accept that these incomplete and scattered press accounts are by themselves sufficient ammunition to underscore the hypocrisy of blackball's long exclusion from the hallowed halls of Cooperstown.

Holway's argument is not entirely without merit. A majority of these barnstorming matchups were apparently won by the black all-star outfits (Holway tells us there were 436 interracial contests between 1900 and 1950, and the record stood 268-168 in favor of the expelled blacks). The historical record seemingly reveals that blacks held their own and then some in these contests. Black pitchers like Satchel Paige were often unhittable against the major-leaguers, and Paige thus seems to have had undocumented fact on his side when he often boasted, "If I had been pitching to Ruth and Gehrig, you could knock a few points off those big lifetime batting averages." And black batters (to take Holway's numbers as prime evidence) seemed to pound white all-star hurlers with regularity, almost as if they were bush-league rookies.

All this is only to say that one of the flaws in a good piece of our recent baseball history writing is the sudden replacement of blind ignorance with equally blind enthusiasms. The game's blackball scholars have torn down the entrenched myths long accepted by gullible fans only to supplant them with equally bogus legends of their own construction. Largely gone (like natural grass and daylight baseball) is the comfortable notion that Abner Doubleday was an American folk hero of the first rank and sole inventor of a nation's pastime. Quashed forever are the fabrications that Fred Merkle was an inexcusable "bonehead" goat, that Babe Ruth predicted home runs and used them to restore the health of bedridden teenagers, that Jackie Robinson was a single-handed destroyer of baseball's racism, that .400 hitters have disappeared simply because players were bigger, stronger, and fleeter of foot and far more dedicated during some "golden age" existing in the sportsworld of our long-lost youth. But newer myths are now quick to fill the void—that long-ignored Negro-leaguers like Josh Gibson, Judy Johnson, Buck Leonard, Biz Mackey, and Pop Lloyd were superior to Cobb, Speaker, Walter Johnson, and Babe Ruth.

No attempt is made here to deny that John Holway's dedicated detective work (especially in *Blackball Stars* and *Black Diamonds*) has performed a great service for baseball historians as well as literate fans in setting the record straight. Yet Holway's interpretive conclusions about the significance of black-white barnstorming games and their sparsely recorded results have not always been so sound. There are many immediate alternative explanations for Holway's reported successes by black stars competing against whites, even if the statistical record as he reports it is largely accurate. First there is the motivational factor: excluded black stars had far more at stake in such games. For a Josh Gibson or a Buck Leonard, such exhibitions were their long-overdue World Series, All-Star Game, and pennant race rolled into one. Black-league ballplayers had far more to gain by beating big-leaguers, the whites knowing in the long run that big-league fans back home would likely never see the results.

When it comes to comparing batting and pitching marks set by white and black ballplayers, there is a second strong caveat to be posted here: the relatively small numbers reported for these unofficial exhibition games. That Josh Gibson batted .424 over 16 games or Mule Suttles blasted 11 homers in 23 contests (the latter noted by author Bruce Chadwick in *When the Game Was Black and White* to be a pace of 77 homers for a 162-game season) is not very useful information for judging Gibson against Ruth or measuring Leonard against Gehrig. Many a career minor-leaguer has enjoyed such a stretch against the "big boys" during a week or two of spring training, then crashed and burned when the teams headed north for official league games. Is it not just as reasonable to assume that big-league (white) pitchers would have found Gibson's weaknesses and limited his output after a few more times around the circuit (as has always happened with even the best of slugging big-leaguers)? Would white big-leaguers not have increased their batting output against Paige if they had seen him on a more regular basis (just as talented Cubans and Negro-leaguers apparently did in the late 1920s when they ganged up on Satchel to defeat him in 5 of his 11 starts over two winters in the Cuban league)?

The 1993 season might provide the freshest example of the dangers in such selective sampling of statistics. To project career batting prowess for either of our two recent .400 challengers (John Olerud and Andrés Galarraga) based solely on the first 100 games of baseball's latest expansion season would seem pure folly, despite the fact that Olerud's or Galarraga's projections would be based upon even larger numbers of games and at-bats than Holway's projections for Josh Gibson's home runs or Satchel Paige's pitching victories. No matter what 300 plate appearances might suggest to the contrary, Olerud, like Galarraga, is still (until a much greater career span proves otherwise) closer to a .280 hitter than a .400 hitter. Baseball, more than any other sport, works out its judgments on hitting and hurling proficiency over lengthy stretches of continuous pressure-filled challenge. There are few instant stars in baseball and no instant residents of Cooperstown.

At this point we might explore Holway's projected home-run numbers as one telling example of a flawed methodology. In a delightful dual biography of Satchel Paige and Josh Gibson (*Satch and Josh*, 1992) Holway offers an appendix of statistical tables that relate reconstructed career and seasonal statistics for Negro-league games of the era between the two world wars. For the moment we will assume that the numbers can be taken at face value. (Why this is so we are not so certain. There is no scholarly documentation of where these numbers came from, how they were compiled, how well trained the compilers were, or even who they were, or how accurate the original sources—box scores?—might have been. But let all of that lie and extend faith by accepting the numbers as they are given.) What is bothersome is Holway's desire to include projected home-run tallies based on an assumed major league average of 550 at-bats per season. From these numbers we seem to learn some startling things about Josh Gibson's home-run prowess (i.e., that given the chance to bat the normal 500-plus times, he would have slugged 81 roundtrippers for the Homestead Grays in 1936, 92 in 1937, and 122 in 1939). But such numbers are without clear meaning and rationale.

The same reasoning, for example, might suggest that Milwaukee's famed phenom Bob Hazle—who actually batted daily against major league hurlers in important league games, not in exhibitions or against unknown Negro-league talent—was also a potent home-run slugger based solely on his cameo big-league career of 1957. (During his single incredible late-season stretch run in 1957 Hazle banged out 7 homers in 134 plate appearances, suggesting that he should slam 30 or more in a normal summer; yet 127 additional big-league at-bats produced only 2 more roundtrippers, and Hazle's career total stalled dead at a mere 9). Or similar projections could be made on the basis of the fast starts of dozens of players over the early weeks of any big-league season (or perhaps better still, spring-training exhibitions). It is all aimless number crunching in the end. There is enough other weighty evidence that Josh Gibson was a powerful slugger (the anecdotal accounts of so many who saw him play, for example) without resorting to such numerical sleight of hand.

The most significant factor in the documented slugging successes of Josh Gibson and company against big-league barnstorming aces like Bob Feller and Dizzy Dean might have been the nature of the Negro-league pitching. One black star, Gene Benson, has made this point while alluding to the ease of facing major-leaguers stripped of such weapons as the lethal spitter and the life-threatening beanball. "Hitting major league pitchers was a picnic," bragged Benson. "If I could have hit them all year, every year, with no knockdowns and spitters, I'd have hit .400 lifetime. . . . All I had to do was just sit there and hit it" (Chadwick, 141).

The evidence is that it was certainly tougher to bat in the wild and woolly black leagues. (And when Satchel Paige pitched against big-leaguers in October, he undoubtedly brought his own assortment of semilegal tricks with him.) But given equal playing conditions, the stars of both leagues were likely to be on a fairly equal footing. As another Negro-leaguer has observed, the best of white and black baseball continued their expected mastery throughout these highly charged yet unofficial encounters. Bruce Chadwick quotes blackballer Stan Glenn of the Philadelphia Stars:

> The black players will tell you those games proved how good the blacks were. I say it proved to the white players how good they were. A star in the majors might hit .330 for the season and play a twelve-game barnstorming tour against black players. On that tour, against top black pitchers, he might hit .250. He's going to say to himself, perhaps I wouldn't have that high average if I had to hit these guys all the time. But a guy like Jimmy Foxx or Lou Gehrig would hit just as well against us as against the whites, so he knew, and everybody in the country knew, that he was a good ballplayer. We kind of proved things. The major leaguers appreciated where on the spectrum they were and where we were. I think that talk is talk, but when guys, black and white, mix it up on the field a lot—and there were hundreds of these games—then everybody knows who's good and who's not so good [Chadwick, 142].

The bottom line is that blackball players were neither superior nor inferior to rival big-leaguers (it would certainly be no more accurate to make claims about their inferiority than it is to subscribe to Holway's bold contentions of numerical superiority). The point seems to be that these long-forgotten autumn games were a unique moment in time, an athletic celebration from which little could be drawn but the thrill of exceptional baseball for those who witnessed it. It is the joy of these games themselves, for both players and fans, that remains inescapable in the reports.

Recalling an exhibition between the white Brooklyn Bushwicks and the Negro-league Black Yankees, veteran New York City fan Robert Eisen summed up the indelible impression of a delighted few who saw baseball at its secret best: "When the game ended, the crowd—must have been a good 15,000—just stood up and gave both teams a standing ovation for the game they gave us. . . . I never saw baseball like that in my life, not Yankee Stadium, not the Polo Grounds, not Ebbets Field, not anywhere" (Chadwick, 142).

Three defensible conclusions can be drawn from the 400-odd games that matched black and white barnstormers between the nation's two great wars. Foremost, these were the only contests of that era that could actually boast of the world's best ballplayers aligned head-to-head on the same field of play. It is also clear that black stars held their own and then some against their more publicized white counterparts. And it was with precisely these games and only these games that the glorious tradition of Latin baseball, the version long played in the Caribbean islands, finally made its true and measurable mark upon the North American baseball landscape, at least in the long dark baseball age that came before integration.

For those big-leaguers and Negro-leaguers alike who sought an off-season locale for earning cash and enjoying at the same time an innocent world of racially open sporting competition, the Caribbean islands of Puerto Rico, Cuba, and Hispaniola (today the Dominican Republic and Haiti) once provided a paradise of almost unlimited opportunity. From the sandy beaches outside San Juan to mountain-rimmed Havana and the endless cane fields surrounding Ciudad Trujillo (Santo Domingo), baseball in the 1920s, 1930s, and 1940s reigned as true kingpin of the Hispanic sporting scene. Here was a land of passionate fandom mixed with tantalizing tropical breezes and lush Caribbean landscapes, a place of unrivaled pastoral dreams justly labeled by one recent blackball historian as a true "*béisbol paradiso*."

Here blackball's greatest stars from the North, especially, could enjoy true baseball heaven. Here they could compete unfettered against the best from all three corners of baseball's segregated kingdom. Blackball stars like Cool Papa Bell, Sam Streeter, Bullet Rogan, and Biz Mackey earned huge salaries to compete on teams with off-season big-leaguers. White major-leaguers honed their skills by facing the best smoke-throwing moundsmen the rival black leagues had to offer. And for the Caribbean players (especially those of dusky-hewed skin), here was the ultimate chance to prove their worth against a mix of crack Negro-leaguers and touted white professionals that the baseball capitals of North America universally considered the very cream of the diamond world.

Caribbean and Mexican stars were, by ironic contrast, often the true litmus test against which major-leaguers and Negro-leaguers most often privately measured their true merit and mettle. Existing records (sparse as they are) and anecdotal accounts today sketch only the broadest outlines of one of baseball's most glorious international episodes. Such sporadic written and oral testimonies are seemingly sufficient, however, to leave largely unquestioned the high quality of yearly winter-league play during these three lost decades.

Visible measures of baseball paradise throughout the Caribbean islands in the years between 1920 and 1940 were not hard to come by. Blackballers conditioned to starvation wages could suddenly make salaries that were high even by big-league standards. Negro-leaguer Wilmer Fields reported making more than major-leaguers—$12,000 or more after combining Negro-league, barnstorming, and winter pay—while moonlighting winter months in Mexico, and this phenomenon was common.

Lofty salaries were further supplemented by luxury accommodations, underwritten by the host ballclubs and free from any hint of racial segregation. Black stars roomed in the plushiest hotels and penthouse apartments that Havana and the Dominican cities had to offer. Racial harmony, however, was the key to the bliss of dark-skinned players heading south for the winter. Here there were no parking-lot meals on rattletrap buses or bare cots in black-only back-alley hotels. Wilmer Fields recalls being pleasantly shocked by the absence of "all that segregation crap," and some touring blackballers were so taken with the color-blind conditions of Mexico City or Havana that they eventually opted for postcareer retirement there.

And if off-field conditions were superior, onfield playing conditions were often even more dreamlike. First, the schedule of games was a breeze. Barnstormers who regularly crammed broken-down buses on endless summertime road trips across the hinterlands of the Deep South and Midwest now could relax with two or three games a week (Cuban play featured Thursday-night venues and Sunday doubleheaders only). And those ballgames were played in first-rate stadiums of undisputable major league quality before huge and enthusiastic crowds. A typical stateside Negro-league game might draw 10,000 or 15,000 with competitive teams; here throngs of up to 40,000 jammed the downtown ballparks of Havana and Ciudad Trujillo. And a winning hit or game-saving snag often promised to bring extra cash to its author when these enthusiastic partisans would "pass the hat" throughout the grandstand at game's end to reward their instant heroes.

No single winter or summer season in blackball's lost Caribbean history looms larger in legend than the Dominican season that transpired in Ciudad Trujillo (later Santo Domingo) during the early months of 1937. The events that surround that season read like an early draft of William Brashler's popular novel *The Bingo Long Traveling All-Stars and Motor Kings*, the basis for a popular Hollywood film providing epic comic treatment of the woes and glories of Negro-baseball barnstorming. It was with those events that late winter of 1937 that baseball and politics became hopelessly intertwined, perhaps as they could only become intertwined in the land of tropical breezes, machine-gun politics, and pristine Caribbean beaches.

The misadventure began with dictator Rafael Leonidas Trujillo Molina enticing Satchel Paige and a host of other black stars, essentially the entire roster of the Pittsburgh Crawfords, to head south and win him a much-needed pennant. It seems that Jefe Trujillo's political rival had not only forced a popular election but was sponsoring a ballclub (Estrellas Orientales) that was winning regularly over Trujillo's personal favorites. Trujillo had only recently combined the nation's two best clubs, Licey and Escogido, and renamed the amalgam the Ciudad Trujillo Dragones (after the nation's capital, which he had also just finished rechristening in his own image). Winning baseball games was serious business in a country where the citizens took diamond play more passionately than almost anything else.

Thus the story of Paige's recruitment (perhaps best outlined in Holway's *Satch and Josh*, 89–91) is the pure stuff of novelistic invention. It turns out that self-styled blackball promoter Gus Greenlee was losing money hand over fist in Pittsburgh even as a new political regime seemed bent on cutting into his handsome illegal profits in the numbers game. (The new reform-minded city fathers had taken to raiding Greenlee's gaming parlors before illegal profits could be banked, and things had gotten so bad that Greenlee had already informed his prized ballplayers that they would have to handle their own spring-training expenses.) Now feeling the pinch, many in Greenlee's considerable stable of barnstorming players were looking for greener pastures to ply their ballplaying trade. Here was a real-flesh version of Bingo Long and his barnstorming mates drawn straight from Brashler's novel, yet transpiring almost 40 years before Brashler's retelling of the familiar tale.

Satchel Paige was the best pitcher to be had anywhere on the open market, and Negro-leaguers were a particularly ripe target since nothing like formal player contracts stood in the way of wholesale talent raids. Paige was also a man reputed to be most easily moved by the sight of a stack of greenbacks, and thus it was that Greenlee's ace was approached by Trujillo's boys in his New Orleans hotel room shortly after reporting for spring training. Legend has it that Satch accepted his "travelin' money" ($30,000 in one account) stacked neatly in a black suitcase—something right out of popular gangster films. The talented pitcher was told to take what he needed for himself and spend the remainder to entice eight other recruits. Within days, Paige had contacted Josh Gibson in Puerto Rico and brought a prized battery mate along to Ciudad Trujillo.

Once in the Dominican Republic, the great black stars (Sammy Bankhead, Papa Bell, Bill Perkins, and Leroy Matlock were among those who played alongside Paige) experienced a tense pennant race such as they had never known before. The tale involves stories of street gunfire, midnight intrigue, and even a dash of island voodoo thrown in for good measure. The visiting players (the rival Aguilas had recruited Chet Brewer and Bertram Hunter from Negro ball as well as Cubans Dihigo and Tiant) soon learned that Trujillo did not have much patience for losing baseball games, especially when political prestige was squarely on the line on the eve of the upcoming national elections. And in Trujillo's land it seemed that people could actually be shot or simply disappear over matters transpiring on the baseball diamond just as easily as for matters transpiring anywhere else in the lawless country. One of the most colorful stories involves Paige receiving a lucky charm (a *wanga*) from a voodoo priest slipped into the country from Haiti especially for the occasion. Or was it perhaps an evil charm designed by Trujillo's enemies to ensure a Paige defeat? Whatever the facts, in a land filled with black magic such stories seem highly plausible if not probable.

In the end, the drama came down to one final game for the Dominican championship. Paige and his mates were locked up under house arrest the night before the big game to ensure that they would be "in proper playing shape" to win the title on which Trujillo's political fortunes seemed to ride. On game day, soldiers supporting each side occupied the opposing grandstands with the appearance of heavily armed firing squads.

The contest itself, by all accounts, proved most dramatic. Paige trailed 3–2 in the seventh, but Sam Bankhead rescued the game and perhaps his mates' lives with an eighth-inning roundtripper. Paige then calmly recorded the final six crucial outs from the hill (five on strikeouts) in typical ice-water fashion. In a final touch of delightful folk legend, historian Holway reports that Paige breathed a large sigh of relief, apparently much relieved that in this land where baseball was a spiritual experience he had not ended up a "spirit" by coming out on the losing end of what may have truly been a life-and-death struggle. Other accounts cited by Holway, however, suggest that perhaps these cloak-and-dagger retellings of the big Dominican game may have been a bit exaggerated for later narrative effect.

The legendary Dominican season of 1937 had other important elements often lost in accounts focusing on Trujillo and his strong-arm tactics. Satchel Paige and Josh Gibson took on some of the best among Latin stars – Dihigo, Luís Tiant (the elder), Santos Amaro, and Rodolfo Fernández – and were thus able to demonstrate their dominance through tension-packed head-to-head competition. Josh Gibson for the short season batted more than 100 points above all rivals. Satchel Paige posted an 8-2 mound record to outdistance Martín Dihigo, who finished the same campaign 6-4.

More significant still, this would be the final time that Paige and Gibson would play together on the same team. When the two veteran stars and the rest of their truant mates returnd to Pittsburgh in late spring, it was Gus Greenlee who again took control of the blackball purse strings by shipping Gibson off to the Homestead Grays. Gibson's trade was indeed the biggest deal in Negro-baseball history with a price tag for the slugging catcher of $2,500 in cold cash. The Dominican campaign of 1937 was thus a fittingly symbolic end to one of the most glorious chapters of the blackball barnstorming saga, a saga in which Paige and Gibson had long been the biggest celebrities and the biggest drawing cards.

When dramatic winter seasons like that of 1937 closed down in the Dominican Republic, Cuba, and Puerto Rico, some of the greatest stars of the local islands headed north each spring and summer to become part of the underground black leagues and barnstorming scene thriving far to the north. Numerous native Cuban stars, especially, found their way into Negro-league play: Luís Tiant, Sr., the crafty left-hander; Martín Dihigo, a one-man ballclub who hit and pitched like Babe Ruth; Cristóbal Torriente, with the heft and power of a left-handed Hack Wilson; José Méndez, surviving a dead arm to prove a crafty manager with the powerhouse Kansas City Monarchs; Silvio García, who flashed over three decades as pitcher and infielder; Rodolfo Fernández, mesmerizing Bill Terry's New York Giants from the hill during 1937 spring training in Havana; Ramón Bragaña, owner of a flashy gold tooth and an unhittable fastball and one of the Caribbean's first legendary moundsmen.

Such Caribbean stars were popular enough on the Negro-baseball scene to cause promoters to exploit their presence with team names like Cuban Stars, Cuban Giants, and New York Cubans. Often these teams were anything but all-star squads of native Cubans (though most had a Cuban or two featured somewhere on the roster for at least partial legitimacy). But the existence of such team names was a fitting tribute to the romance of island wintertime diamond play and the legendary status of little-known Cuban baseballers.

And such legendary status was not without its merit. There are accounts and rumors of many major league managers and scouts admitting their lust to have some of the finer dark-skinned Cubans dot their big-league lineups. No lesser judge of talent than John McGraw was convinced of the star status of a handful of such players: on the heels of his 1911 barnstorming tour of Cuba, McGraw reportedly announced that he would give $50,000 apiece for José Méndez and his catcher Mike González (who turned up a year later anyway with the Boston Braves) if only the duo were white. Ditto for McGraw's protégé Frankie Frisch, who a decade later drooled over Cristóbal Torriente, a slugger almost light enough to pass had it not been for his giveaway kinky red hair. And scouts who roamed the Caribbean soon marveled at what they saw. Joe Cambria, for one, eventually took the fullest measure of untapped black Cuban baseball talent.

i. José Méndez is better than any pitcher except Mordecai Brown and Christy Mathewson—and sometimes I think he is better than Matty.

—John McGraw

Of the legendary dark-skinned Latino stars, none has greater mythic stature than Cuba's Martín Dihigo, present resident in Cooperstown's and Cuba's hallowed halls (plus those of Mexico and Venezuela). But Dihigo is far from a lonely star in the rich Caribbean firmament. Other Cuban stalwarts of the barnstorming era were equally revered at home and respected on blackball and exhibition diamonds stretching far to the north.

Perhaps the most mysterious (and thus to historians the most attractive) of the early Cuban baseballers was a lithe black pitcher named José Méndez, who stood 5'9", tipped the scales at a mere 155 pounds, and hurled a remarkable fastball that seemingly weighed more than he did. John McGraw of the champion National League Giants was quick to note the talents of the unhittable Cuban Méndez.

Méndez amazed the baseball world almost overnight in the winter of 1908 when he was first discovered by baseball's white establishment, much to the dismay of one set of big-league batsmen who performed for the Cincinnati Reds. When the touring National League club arrived in Havana that winter for their whirlwind tour, they hardly anticipated the rude greeting they would receive from an unheralded set of island blackball strikeout artists. First came Méndez's 1908 exhibition contests versus the bedazzled Cincinnati ballclub. In November of that year, the diminutive Cuban first shut down the big-leaguers with a 1–0 one-hit masterpiece. To prove that the first encounter was no fluke, Méndez hurled another seven shutout innings of relief two weeks later. He then twirled a second complete-game 4–0 shutout four days later. "El Diamante Negro" had suddenly thrown 25 straight scoreless frames against the Cincinnati team. He would then continue his miraculous string of outings with a reported additional 20 consecutive runless frames, though now admittedly against somewhat lesser competition: a nine-inning shutout against a touring semipro team from Key West; a no-hitter in a return engagement against the same ballclub back in Key West (perhaps the first integrated game ever played in Florida); and two more shutout innings in Cuban-league play.

The magic Méndez began against the shell-shocked Cincinnati club in 1908 was miraculously continued against four additional big-league visitors over the course of the next three winters. Things started a bit roughly for the celebrated Cuban the following winter when the Detroit Tigers (sans Ty Cobb) drubbed him 9–3. Returning to form against Tigers Ace Ed Willett (29-8 that summer in the American League), Méndez fell again 4–0 yet yielded only six hits and one earned run and was undone by four fielding errors behind him. Méndez also managed a single victory against the Tigers in 1909, a 2–1 five-hitter in his third and final outing (Holway, 51–55). The 1909 series against Detroit also saw a second Cuban ace, Eustaquio Pedroso, dazzle the humiliated big-leaguers with his own 11-inning no-hitter.

On the heels of a 7-0 Cuban League record in 1910 (where Holway claims opponents batted only a measly .172 against him) Méndez would survive his third winter of matchups with touring big-league outfits by finishing 2-2 in five outings against the returning Tigers and the Philadelphia Athletics of Connie Mack. The two Méndez victories came against eventual Hall-of-Famer Eddie Plank, the first outing resulting in a blown shutout when Méndez's mates committed six errors behind the brilliant Cuban hurler.

The opposition in 1911 was composed of the other Philadelphia team (the Phillies) and their National League rival John McGraw's powerhouse Giants. After a 2-1 mark against the Phils (including yet another shutout), Méndez would find McGraw's club the roughest opponent of all, one he could not beat. After Pedroso and Dolf Luque opened the series with victories against the New Yorkers, a much-heralded Thanksgiving Day matchup of Méndez and Christy Mathewson found the Cuban brilliant in allowing but five hits and the great Matty even more so as he spun a victorious three-hitter. Méndez did salvage a single save in a final contest that fall against Mathewson.

José Méndez Versus Big-League Clubs in Cuba

(Source: *Blackball Stars: Negro League Pioneers*, by John B. Holway [New York, 1992])

Year	Team	Score	Decision	Opponent	Méndez Highlights
1908	Cincinnati	1–0	**Winner**	Jean Dubuc	One-hitter
	Cincinnati	2–3	No Decision	Billy Campbell	7 innings (relief), no runs
	Cincinnati	3–0	**Winner**	Jean Dubuc	Another shutout
1909	Detroit	3–9	Loser	Ed Willett	Socked for 11 base hits
	Detroit	0–4	Loser	George Mullin	Only one earned run allowed
	Detroit	2–1	**Winner**	Bill Lelivelt	Five-hitter
	All-Stars	3–1	**Winner**	Howie Camnitz	Two-hitter
1910	Detroit	0–3	Loser	George Mullin	Complete-game five-hitter
	Detroit	2–2	No Decision	Ed Summers	Wasted three-hitter
	Detroit	3–6	Loser	Ed Summers	Cobb goes one for two
	Phila. Athletics	5–2	**Winner**	Eddie Plank	Five hits allowed, but six errors
	Phila. Athletics	7–5	**Winner**	Eddie Plank	Both aces hit hard in this one
1911	Phila. Phillies	3–1	**Winner**	Dut Chalmers	Méndez slugs a triple
	Phila. Phillies	4–0	**Winner**	Eddie Stack	Three-hit shutout
	Phila. Phillies	1–8	Loser	Dut Chalmers	Chalmers turns the tables
	N.Y. Giants	0–4	Loser	C. Mathewson	Five-hitter for Méndez
	N.Y. Giants	3–6	Loser	Doc Crandall	11 innings, 11 hits, 11 K's
	N.Y. Giants	7–4	Save	C. Mathewson	4 innings, 1 hit, 0 runs

Méndez Record: 8 Wins, 7 Losses, 1 Save, 2 No Decisions

Thus, when the four-year saga of big-league visits to Cuban shores ended in 1911, Méndez stood at a respectable 8-7 against the best professional competition the sport had to offer (the Cubans as a whole were 32-32, with one tie game). Legend has it that Méndez was by 1911 the most popular man on the Cuban island. All he had to do was appear in public to receive a standing and nearly endless ovation from his delirious countrymen.

Méndez was quick to demonstrate that his debut performance against major-league players was no fluke. Over the course of that winter and the next the diminutive Cuban would dominate the lineups of a number of big-league visitors to Cuba. And soon he would take his one-man hurling act on the road to the North against the best competition baseball had to offer.

José Méndez thus carved out one of the most remarkable legends of Caribbean baseball's wealthy lore. His record against touring North American professional competition during 1908 and 1909 was a sterling 44 wins and 2 losses. And over the next couple of seasons that record was hardly diminished. Holway reports that over seven seasons Méndez would pace the Cuban league in winning percentage, five times in shutouts (*Blackball Stars*, 57). He would stand 25-13 in subsequent seasons against touring U.S. major- and minor-leaguers; overall his Cuban and blackball record was a marvelous 62-15 (an unthinkable .805 percentage).

But like many legendary figures of fact and fable, José Méndez was destined to be a comet who would burn brightly and briefly in the baseball firmament and then crash in a sudden blaze of glory. Almost overnight in 1915 his arm suddenly and mysteriously went dead. His pitching days were apparently finished even more suddenly and unaccountably than they had begun. But his baseball-playing career was not even then completely over. In the early 1920s this phenomenal Cuban athlete remained on Negro-league rosters as a manager and part-time infielder, serving first as skipper of J. L. Wilkinson's touring All-Nations team (where he doubled as a coronet player for the ballclub's postgame musical entertainments) and then as bench boss and part-time player for the same owner's touted Kansas City Monarchs. Stories circulated widely of his all-around prowess as an ultimate utility player with the Monarchs, which included part-time hurling despite his now ineffectual arm. Brooklyn Dodgers star Babe Herman would later recall having seen Méndez play all nine positions in a single contest, amazing onlookers with a credible one-inning performance behind the plate.

Méndez would eventually suffer a tragic fate. For a while he continued to manage and occasionally to pitch in Negro-league contests for the Kansas City Monarchs, despite a dead and often ineffective arm. Press reports had him appearing "grey, gaunt and grim" when only 36, yet several times he nonetheless inserted himself on the hill to save crucial games as Kansas City battled the Philadelphia Hilldales in the first modern black World Series of 1924. Méndez was the pitcher of record when the Monarchs eventually clinched the title, despite a reported recent surgery and doctor's orders that he sit out the postseason contests.

Yet despite a slide in his prowess and his health, Méndez remained an unmatched star throughout his native homeland. While no longer the on-field star he had been a decade earlier, his cardboard photograph appeared in Havana cigarette packs along with the other popular players of the Kansas City Monarchs team he managed. Those brave pitching exploits in a Monarchs uniform had been only a final futile hurrah, however. Less than two years later the first true Cuban pitching giant was reported dead, likely a victim of tuberculosis.

Yet one poignant incident at the very end of his short but colorful life suggests the true stature of José Méndez in his Cuban homeland. Cuba's other pitching hero, Dolf Luque, was in the midst of his own triumphant

Cuban-League Career Records of José de la Caridad Méndez

(Source: *Béisbol Cubano (Records y Estadisticas), 1878–1955*, by Gambino Delgado and Severo Nieto [Havana, 1955])

Symbols: NA = no available record; parentheses indicate incomplete totals for this category

Pitching Record

Year	Team	G	CG	W-L	Pct.	IP	SO	BB	Hits
1908	Almendares	15	6	9-0	1.000	NA	58	38	NA
1909	Almendares	28	18	15-6	.714	NA	106	56	NA
1910	Almendares	7	7	7-0	1.000	66	51	16	39
1911	Almendares	18	12	11-2	.846	129	68	41	91
1912	Almendares	19	NA	9-5	.643	138	92	36	115
1913	Almendares	7	2	1-4	.200	41	17	21	47
1914	Almendares	12	7	10-0	1.000	85	38	25	67
1915	Almendares	2	1	2-0	1.000	13	3	1	14
1916		Did Not Pitch							
1917–1920		Did Not Play							
1921	Almendares	5	1	1-2	.333	NA	NA	NA	NA
1922–1923		Did Not Play							
1924	Santa Clara	9	1	3-1	.750	NA	NA	NA	NA
1925	Santa Clara/ Matanzas	19	2	2-3	.400	NA	NA	NA	NA
1926	Havana	6	1	1-1	.500	32	5	8	34
1927	Alacranes	10	1	3-1	.750	NA	NA	NA	NA
Totals	13 years	157	59	74-25	.735	(504)	(438)	(242)	(407)

Batting Record

Year	Team	G	AB	R	H	2B	3B	HR	SB	BA
1908	Almendares	18	38	6	5	0	0	0	0	.132
1909	Almendares	34	90	NA	14	3	0	0	NA	.156
1910	Almendares	11	35	6	7	1	0	0	6	.200
1911	Almendares	20	50	6	7	1	0	0	2	.140
1912	Almendares	24	70	5	16	1	1	0	4	.229
1913	Almendares	26	67	16	11	1	1	0	9	.165
1914	Almendares	17	41	2	4	1	0	0	5	.097
1915	Almendares	34	119	18	31	2	3	0	6	.260
1916	Almendares	38	113	15	22	2	0	0	0	.195
1917–1920		Did Not Play								
1921	Almendares	21	65	5	10	0	0	0	3	.154

Year	Team	G	AB	R	H	2B	3B	HR	SB	BA
1922–1923		Did Not Play								
1924	Santa Clara	10	30	2	3	1	0	0	0	.100
1925	Santa Clara/ Matanzas	18	20	6	7	3	0	0	0	.350
1926	Havana	11	25	5	5	1	1	0	0	.200
1927	Alacranes	10	16	2	5	0	0	0	0	.313
Totals	14 years	292	779	(94)	147	17	6	0	(35)	.186

1923 homecoming, having just led the National League with 27 victories and thus become the unrivaled toast of a baseball-crazy nation. A formal ceremony was in progress in the downtown Havana Stadium, and Luque had just been presented with a new car by the city's adoring public. It was then that the light-skinned big-leaguer sadly spotted Méndez sitting quietly in the grandstand. Approaching his black countryman at the end of these festivities, Luque spoke from his heart: "This parade should have been for you. You're a far better pitcher than I am."

Here was a fitting final acknowledgment from the humble Luque that skin color and not the lack of an unhittable fastball was the single factor that had struck down José Méndez. Race alone had robbed Cuba's greatest moundsman of a lasting place in big-league history, perhaps pioneering enshrinement in Cooperstown's hallowed halls.

ii. In those days Torriente was a hell of a ballplayer. Christ, I'd like to whitewash him and bring him up. —Frankie Frisch

Méndez and Dihigo were perhaps the brightest stars—one short-lived, the other seemingly immortal—who planted themselves in the pre–Jackie Robinson Cuban baseball firmament. There were dozens of others whose dark skin all but obscured their legends in cities to the north. Of these, none steps more directly out of the pages of island mythology and folklore than Cristóbal Torriente, the Cuban Strongboy. If Méndez fashioned his legend seemingly overnight in Havana against an astonished lineup of touring Cincinnati Reds, Torriente built his day-in and day-out over several seasons of sensational Negro-league play. The huge left-handed hitting outfielder was the biggest run producer in the potent lineup of Rube Foster's powerhouse Chicago American Giants throughout most of the Roaring 1920s.

Holway tells us (*Blackball Stars*, 125–126) that experts on Negro-baseball history are unanimous in placing Torriente squarely among the three greatest Negro-league outfielders of all time (alongside Papa Bell and Oscar Charleston). His reported batting averages in Cuba and in the States tell much of the story of Torriente's relentless slugging: his reported lifetime mark of .352 in Cuba is the third highest; his career Negro-league average stood at .339; he is documented as hitting .311 in exhibitions against big-leaguers (including a .359 clip and several mammoth homers over 11 games in Cuba in 1919). And these raw numbers are supplemented by a lengthy series of glowing reports concerning the Cuban Strongboy's superhuman blasting of the baseball. Holway (125) quotes a young man of the 1920s named Jay Wiggins: "Torriente wore bracelets on his wrist, and when he'd shake those bracelets, look for the ball up against the fence; that's where he was going to hit it."

No assessment of Torriente's prowess is more laudatory, however, than the one that accompanied the Pittsburgh *Courier*'s selection of the all-time all-black team in 1952: "A prodigious hitter, a rifle-armed thrower, and a tower of strength on defense . . . deceptive speed and the ability to cover worlds of territory, from the right-field foul line to deep right center. He was one of the best bad-ball hitters in baseball and could hit equally well to all fields" (Holway, 125).

Much of Torriente's legend is founded not upon Negro-league play but a brief encounter with John McGraw's touring team of big-leaguers (mostly New York Giants) in Cuba during the winter following the 1920 season. And no greater figure played a key role in this memorable encounter than Babe Ruth himself, fresh from his miraculous 54-homer debut with the Yankees and enticed to perform in Havana by an incredible offer of $1,000 per game from Cuban promoter Abel Linares.

Present Tampa resident and pre–Castro Cuban sports reporter Jorge Figueredo has sketched the showdown encounter between Torriente and Ruth in considerable detail (Holway, 128–129). With regular Giant first sacker George "Highpockets" Kelly taking the mound for the big-leaguers' third Cuban exhibition contest and first with Club Almendares, Torriente took immediate advantage by smashing back-to-back opposite-field homers over the fence in left-center in the second and third innings. After Ruth had failed at the plate three times, the Bambino (only a year past his marvelous pitching feats in the uniform of the Boston Red Sox) elected to take the hill to dispose of the pesky Torriente in the fifth frame. The result was a ringing double to left that almost removed a leg from Giants third sacker Frankie Frisch. With Kelly back on the hill in later innings, the Cuban Strongboy finished his onslaught with a weak tap to the box and then a third ringing homer to left. The final count saw Torriente going four for five with three roundtrippers and six runs batted home; Ruth stood zero for two, having walked twice and reached once on an error. The onslaught was not quite over, either, as the hot-hitting Cuban proceeded to lace seven more hits (including one triple) over the final four exhibitions against Giants pitching (and in these additional games Torriente faced only legitimate major league hurlers—Pol Perritt, Jesse Barnes, and Rosy Ryan).

Torriente's Cuban stature rests not just on those three homers off substitute hurler Highpockets Kelly but the total impression he left upon several of the big-leaguers who faced him in the winter of 1920 and later barnstorming campaigns. Frankie Frisch would lionize the Cuban slugger when he remembered the smash that nearly amputated his leg: "That clout dug a hole about a foot deep on its way to left field. And I'm glad I wasn't in front of it! . . . He could really hit a ball! . . . In those days Torriente was a hell of a player. Christ, I'd like to whitewash him and bring him up" (quoted by Holway, 129). Highpockets Kelly was equally generous if somewhat laconic in his praise of the slugger who had once tattooed him: "He was simply the best hitter down there!" And the Los Angeles *Times*, reporting the great single-game performance of 1920, saw Torriente fittingly as nothing less than the "Babe Ruth of Cuba."

Torriente's moment of glory in Havana in 1920 was hardly the apex of his considerable career. That career continued in glory back in Chicago with Foster's American Giants for several seasons. He belted the ball at a .396 clip for Foster the next summer and missed out on a batting title by a scant three points. He would pace the Negro National League in hitting in 1923 with a .389 mark, then sock a league-best 21 doubles the following campaign. Unfortunately, as with all blackball exploits, the white press never again took notice.

Perhaps this lack of praise away from his Cuban homeland was in the long run a major part of Torriente's eventual tragic demise (although perhaps no greater part than his fondness for night life and his ongoing affair with strong drink). For strongboy Torriente, like his countryman José Méndez, would all too soon meet a most unfortunate and bitter demise. Only a few short seasons after his triumphs with the American Giants, Cristóbal Torriente would drift into obscurity, later to be found in a dismal state by Rodolfo Fernández and Martín Dihigo, down and out and battling the bottle in the streets of Chicago. It was Dihigo who temporarily rescued Torriente and brought him to New York. Yet his death soon came, in 1938, in poverty and obscurity with no friend but a liquor bottle—one of the unaccountable tragedies of the traveling circus that was once Negro-league baseball in the days before Branch Rickey and Jackie Robinson.

Cuba produced other stars during the great barnstorming and blackball era of the 1920s, 1930s, and 1940s. None had the good fortune of major league exposure, like Luque. And none quite reached the ironic heights of blackball legend achieved by Dihigo, Méndez, or Torriente. One did come tantalizingly close, however. Luís Tiant, Sr., was a diminutive left-handed pitcher of remarkable talents. Negro-league star Gene Benson

Career Batting Records of Cristóbal Torriente

Cuban League

(Source: *Béisbol Cubano (Records y Estadisticas), 1878–1955,* by Gambino Delgado and Severo Nieto [Havana, 1955].)

Symbols: NA =no available record; parentheses indicate incomplete totals for this category.

Year	Team	G	AB	R	H	2B	3B	HR	SB	BA
1913	Havana	28	102	11	27	1	3	1	6	.265
1914	Almendares	30	104	12	35	5	2	2	13	.337
1915	Almendares	34	124	33	48	5	5	0	19	.387
1916	Almendares	39	139	41	56	5	6	2	28	.402
1917–1918		Did Not Play								
1919	Almendares	25	100	19	36	5	5	1	10	.360
1920	Almendares	27	98	19	29	3	4	1	3	.296
1921	Havana	5	20	3	7	0	1	0	0	.350
1922		Did Not Play								
1923	Havana	46	174	37	61	9	6	4	15	.350
1924	Havana/ Marianao	43	162	28	56	9	1	2	7	.346
1925	Havana	46	163	30	62	13	2	4	6	.380
1926	Havana	32	122	17	43	7	4	1	0	.352
1927	Almendares	3	8	1	3	0	0	0	0	.375
1927	Havana Red Sox	3	9	1	2	0	0	0	0	.222
Totals	12 years	361	1,325	252	465	62	39	18	107	.351

Negro Leagues

(Source: *Blackball Stars: Negro League Pioneers,* by John B. Holway [New York, 1992].)

Symbols: NA = no available record; parentheses indicate incomplete totals for this category; * = league leader.

Year	Team	G	AB	H	2B	3B	HR	SB	BA
1919	Chicago	4	16	4	NA	NA	NA	NA	.250
1920	Chicago	25	93	37	7	3	1	2	.398
1921	Chicago	64	199	66	5	10	7	18	.332
1922	Chicago	NA	120	42	1	2	3	3	.350
1923	Chicago	58	216	84	15	3	5	6	.389*
1924	Chicago	68	239	79	21*	4	7	9	.331
1925	Chicago	NA	278	67	7	6	6	2	.241
1926	Kansas City	70	254	86	17	5	4	5	.339
1927	Detroit	84	297	95	18	2	4	6	.320

Year	Team	G	AB	H	2B	3B	HR	SB	BA
1928	Detroit	37	107	36	5	3	2	3	.336
1934	Cleveland	1	4	1	0	0	0	NA	.250
Totals	11 years	(411)	1,823	597	(96)	(38)	(39)	(54)	.327

reports that Tiant (owner of what Benson called a devastating screwball that broke wickedly at lefty swingers) was genuinely the toughest hurler of all those great blackballers he was called upon to face. During the 1930s and 1940s Tiant mastered the spitball to boot and became one of its most skillful practitioners in Negro-league play while performing for the Polo Grounds–based Cuban Stars of New York promoter Alessandro Pompez. The senior Tiant also carved out a matchless hurling legend in his native homeland and the Dominican Republic before his arm finally gave out (perhaps due to that unhittable screwball) at the considerable pitching age of 42.

The elder Tiant is the frequent subject of the perhaps apocryphal story concerning the most astounding pick-off move in baseball history. The tale reports that the Cuban Stars ace once snapped his disguised pick-off throw toward first with such complete deception that a confused batsman (rumored to be Goose Curry of the Baltimore Elite Giants) actually waved helplessly at a phantom pitch that never arrived in the catcher's mitt. "If you're dumb enough to swing it's still a strike!" reportedly intoned the bemused home-plate umpire. Ironically, however, Louie Tiant's true lasting baseball heritage would soon be a right-handed-hurling son destined to become the greatest Cuban big-league moundsman of all time and close rival to Juan Marichal as Latin America's most celebrated big-league pitching hero.

And in neighboring Puerto Rico there were further blackball legends from the barnstorming epoch. "Perucho" (Pedro) Cepeda, muscular shortstop and first baseman, was another shadowy giant whose first-born son would eventually eclipse and recall his father's considerable homeland baseball legacy. When the Puerto Rican winter league launched its inaugural season in 1937-38, Perucho Cepeda was its first batting champion, and it is the elder Cepeda who still holds the highest single-season batting average (.464 in the winter of 1938-39) recorded on Puerto Rican soil. Francisco "Poncho" Coimbre, free-swinging outfielder, followed on the heels of Perucho Cepeda as one of the most robust of Puerto Rican slugging stars, soon owning the highest native lifetime batting mark (.337) posted during two-plus decades of island winter-league play. And jet-black Luís Angel "Canena" Márquez not only built a similar legendary career as batsman in his native homeland but was young enough (a fate denied both Cepeda and Coimbre) to taste a brief major league trial (99 games and an anemic .198

average in two seasons with the Braves, Cubs, and Pirates) after integration had finally come to major league baseball.

The great Latin stars from the three decades dividing the two world wars thus suffered a truly ironic fate. In their homelands, a handful built legends of incomparable achievement by competing against touring blackball stars and white major-leaguers. They played out their heroic careers in an altogether unique baseball paradise, one that allowed black stars from the North to compete as equals in a relaxed and racially tolerant atmosphere, one that allowed white big-leaguers to experience the only genuine testing ground that featured the greatest players from all three of baseball's divided worlds—the white major leagues, blackball leagues, and racially mixed Caribbean leagues.

These pioneering Caribbean baseballers also performed joyously before fans more fanatical and dedicated than those found anywhere else on the entire planet. And yet throughout the mainstream of North American baseball culture their achievements often went unnoticed and unrecorded, and thus were soon lost to that only true touchstone of baseball history, the collective memory of the game's fans (largely white fans). Only in the most recent decade has painstaking historical research at last resurrected the awesome legends of some of the sport's greatest early Hispanic stars.

Negro-League Players in Cuban Baseball (1903–1960)

Negro-leaguers barnstormed throughout the Caribbean region over the decades preceding Jackie Robinson and the sudden demise of the black leagues in North America during the 1940s and 1950s. The story of blackball play in the Dominican Republic during this lost baseball era (especially Trujillo's 1937 recruitment of almost an entire roster of loose-footed Pittsburgh Crawfords) is rich indeed, if largely obliterated for modern historians. But it was Cuba from the first that drew the largest blackball participation and spawned the greatest diamond legends.

The following statistics for black ballplayers performing in Cuba have been supplied by the dean of Cuban baseball historians, Jorge Figueredo of Tampa, Florida. These composite tables are the painstaking work of several devoted Society of American Baseball Research (SABR) scholars (especially Jorge Figueredo, Augusto José Tuya, and Charles Monfort) and provide the most complete record of Cuban blackball hitting and pitching statistics.

All-Time Career Batting Statistics for Black Players* in the Cuban League

(Symbols: NA = no stats available for this category [as determined by Jorge Figueredo]; ** = major league player; # = U.S. Negro-league star; parentheses indicate incomplete statistics for this category.)

Player	Years	AB	R	H	2B	3B	HR	RBI	BA
Newton Allen	1924–38	223	20	62	5	3	1	(25)	.278
Toussaint Allen	1920–21	9	1	2	0	0	0	NA	.222
George Altman**	1959–60	219	41	55	5	1	14	32	.251
Jabo Andrews	1936–37	234	37	66	11	5	5	37	.282
Walter Ball	1908–11	(111)	(9)	(29)	(1)	(2)	(0)	NA	(.262)
Sam Bankhead**	1937–41	802	139	238	24	10	10	123	.297
Jess Barbour	1910–16	179	15	40	5	1	0	NA	.223
Marvin Barker	1935–36	141	12	39	3	4	0	10	.277
Pepper Bassett	1946–47	61	4	11	3	0	0	0	.180
Harry Bauchman	1915–16	56	5	12	0	0	0	NA	.214
Cool Papa Bell#	1928–41	569	131	166	30	16	10	NA	.292
Jerry Benjamin	1940–41	46	6	7	0	0	0	1	.152
Gene Benson#	1947–48	239	22	57	9	2	1	20	.238
Chas Blackwell	1920–23	95	11	30	2	4	1	NA	.316
Bob Boyd**	1949–57	647	85	194	21	6	9	79	.300
Phil Bradley	1908–09	70	8	18	0	1	0	NA	.257
John Brazelton	1915–16	11	1	0	0	0	0	NA	.000
Barney Brown	1935–40	(329)	(50)	(94)	(10)	(1)	(1)	(33)	(.286)
Larry Brown	1924–31	500	62	126	10	10	0	NA	.252
Ray Brown	1936–48	(353)	(51)	(94)	(9)	(5)	(6)	(64)	(.266)
Willard Brown**	1937–38	55	5	8	1	0	0	3	.145
Harry Buckner	1907–09	98	9	25	3	4	0	NA	.255
Pee Wee Butts	1947–48	285	26	71	8	3	0	28	.249
Joe Caffie**	1957–58	104	7	23	4	1	0	3	.221
Roy Campanella**	1943–44	128	15	34	9	3	0	27	.266
Walter Canady	1926–40	142	17	32	6	1	0	NA	.225
Tank Carr	1926–27	125	21	52	NA	NA	NA	NA	.416
Billy Cash	1947–48	224	23	48	10	2	1	24	.214
John Cason	1924–25	28	1	8	0	0	0	NA	.286
Oscar Charleston#	1920–31	996	219	360	(44)	(25)	(19)	NA	.361
Thad Christopher	1936–37	51	5	10	3	0	0	7	.196
Dell Clark	1920–21	32	3	13	1	0	0	NA	.406
Robert Clarke	1929–30	19	3	6	1	0	0	NA	.316
James Clarkson	1947–48	106	12	21	5	0	1	14	.198
George Crowe**	1953–54	75	3	12	2	0	1	10	.160

All-Time Career Batting Statistics, *cont.*

Player	Years	AB	R	H	2B	3B	HR	RBI	BA
Ray Dandridge#	1937–53	2,129	269	601	(69)	(14)	(10)	187	.282
Lloyd Davenport	1943–48	907	113	249	34	12	1	74	.275
Johnny Davis	1946–48	297	29	83	(5)	(4)	(0)	(19)	.279
Walter Davis	1927–28	82	10	22	2	1	2	NA	.268
Rap Dixon	1929–30	175	36	46	10	6	5	NA	.263
Eddie Douglass	1923–25	172	19	42	(3)	(3)	(1)	NA	.244
Solly Drake**	1956–57	770	125	200	24	12	11	59	.260
Ashby Dunbar	1908–09	133	21	41	4	2	1	NA	.308
Frank Duncan	1923–38	604	83	164	(21)	(14)	(1)	NA	.272
Pete Duncan	1915–16	58	5	20	2	0	0	NA	.345
Donald Eaddy	1959–60	266	37	68	7	1	6	24	.256
Frank Earle	1908–09	36	8	12	3	1	1	NA	.333
Mack Eggleston	1923–24	99	6	21	3	0	0	NA	.212
Buck Ewing#	1929–30	112	23	34	2	3	0	NA	.304
Hooks Foreman	1928–29	5	0	1	0	0	0	NA	.200
Billy Francis	1908–13	123	13	17	1	1	0	NA	.138
Jude Gans	1908–16	(188)	(40)	(64)	(7)	(4)	(0)	NA	(.340)
Jelly Gardner	1924–25	118	22	34	0	1	0	NA	.288
Josh Gibson#	1937–39	224	61	79	10	5	14	52	.353
George Giles	1930–31	50	6	13	0	0	0	NA	.260
Junior Gilliam**	1948–49	1	0	0	0	0	0	0	.000
Charles Grant	1907	70	4	13	0	0	0	NA	.186
Leroy Grant	1912	10	1	1	1	0	0	NA	.100
Bill Handy	1914–15	97	11	25	4	1	0	NA	.258
Nate Harris	1909–10	134	4	26	3	0	0	NA	.194
Vic Harris	1939–40	116	18	30	1	0	1	7	.259
John Hayes	1938–39	32	2	4	1	0	0	2	.125
Joe Hewitt	1920–21	16	1	4	0	0	0	0	.250
Pete Hill	1907–16	661	158	203	9	16	2	NA	.307
Crush Holloway	1924–29	252	44	73	10	6	1	NA	.290
Sammy Hughes	1939–40	175	19	43	9	2	0	15	.246
Monte Irvin**	1947–49	358	66	95	16	7	11	61	.266
Louis Jackson	1958–59	48	4	11	3	0	0	6	.229
Sam Jethroe**	1947–55	663	126	192	22	17	10	62	.290
Chappie Johnson	1907	99	10	17	0	0	1	NA	.172
Grant Johnson	1907–12	549	116	175	11	8	4	NA	.319
Judy Johnson#	1926–31	386	55	129	(16)	(5)	(2)	NA	.334
Oscar Johnson	1923–24	55	10	19	4	1	1	NA	.345
Newt Joseph	1928–30	(110)	(16)	(30)	(2)	(3)	(1)	NA	(.273)
Henry Kimbro	1939–49	942	181	277	24	13	1	77	.294

Player	Years	AB	R	H	2B	3B	HR	RBI	BA
Clarence Lamar	1940–41	73	6	14	2	0	0	10	.192
Buck Leonard#	1936–49	236	35	67	7	1	3	33	.284
John (Pop) Lloyd#	1908–30	(1,327)	(210)	(436)	(45)	(33)	(5)	NA	(.329)
Dick Lundy	1920–31	876	146	299	(31)	(10)	(6)	NA	.341
Jimmie Lyons	1912	118	19	34	5	4	0	NA	.288
Tully McAdoo	1915–16	50	5	10	1	0	0	NA	.200
Dan McClellan	1907	42	5	6	0	1	0	NA	.143
Biz Mackey#	1924–25	152	29	47	11	5	0	NA	.309
Ghost Marcell	1922–30	(957)	(148)	(292)	(24)	(12)	(6)	NA	(.305)
Sam Mongin	1908–09	134	4	26	3	0	0	NA	.194
Bill Monroe	1907–08	123	30	41	2	2	1	NA	.333
Dobie Moore	1923–24	281	38	100	(9)	(6)	(1)	NA	.356
Dink Mothell	1930–31	47	8	9	0	2	0	NA	.191
Buck O'Neil#	1946–47	116	12	25	3	1	0	14	.216
Leonard Pearson	1946–51	1,299	160	340	54	5	28	218	.261
Charles Peete	1956–57	39	5	5	1	0	0	3	.128
Jim Pendleton**	1952–53	227	33	66	9	3	6	30	.291
Art Pennington	1947–48	77	6	18	3	1	0	10	.234
Bill Perkins	1935–41	902	146	260	25	10	9	135	.288
Zack Pettus	1912	92	17	25	1	2	0	NA	.272
Bruce Petway	1908–16	385	43	81	7	0	0	NA	.210
Bill Pierce	1910–12	82	8	19	2	0	2	NA	.232
Spot Poles	1910–15	383	79	122	9	12	1	NA	.319
Alex Radcliffe	1938–39	169	14	45	5	1	1	24	.266
Larry Raines**	1957–58	165	16	42	2	4	4	21	.255
Orville Riggins	1924–30	266	40	80	7	10	1	NA	.301
Curt Roberts**	1955–57	560	74	143	17	6	7	53	.255
Neil Robinson	1946–47	12	1	0	0	0	0	0	.000
Branch Russell	1928–29	114	24	35	2	3	1	NA	.307
Louis Santop#	1912–21	33	4	8	3	2	0	NA	.242
George Scales	1927–30	375	63	112	12	8	3	NA	.299
William Serrell	1945–47	342	44	92	(14)	(3)	(2)	(29)	.269
Suitcase Simpson**	1954–55	132	13	28	10	0	1	8	.212
Chino Smith	1926–31	565	83	189	(35)	(14)	(3)	NA	.335
Milton Smith	1955–59	705	104	189	27	11	11	75	.268
Felton Snow	1939–40	166	14	37	1	2	0	22	.223
Clyde Spearman	1936–40	774	121	211	20	4	4	105	.273
Henry Spearman	1939–40	127	15	35	3	0	0	24	.276
Turkey Stearns#	1924–25	58	13	13	0	2	3	NA	.224
Edward Stone	1937–48	352	52	93	19	4	4	42	.264
Mule Suttles#	1928–40	460	65	128	14	5	12	NA	.278
Willie Tasby**	1958–60	397	45	99	14	0	11	38	.249

All-Time Career Batting Statistics, *cont.*

Player	Years	AB	R	H	2B	3B	HR	RBI	BA
Clint Thomas	1923–31	697	135	216	(12)	(10)	(5)	NA	.310
Dave Thomas	1936–37	253	32	79	8	4	0	36	.312
Hank Thompson	1946–47	789	148	252	31	24	12	126	.319
Quincy Trouppe*	1944–51	307	46	78	13	6	5	37	.254
Felix Wallace	1908–12	13	0	2	0	0	0	NA	.154
Frank Warfield	1922–30	(583)	(123)	(177)	(17)	(8)	(4)	NA	(.304)
Jap Washington	1928–29	106	7	28	3	2	0	NA	.264
John Washington	1939–41	374	44	95	13	5	0	34	.254
Speck Webster	1914–15	106	12	35	5	2	0	NA	.330
Willie Wells#	1928–40	1,099	189	352	47	20	16	(113)	.320
Edgar Wesley	1923–24	101	14	24	1	1	0	NA	.238
Chaney White	1927–30	337	59	117	6	6	2	NA	.347
Charles Williams	1924–25	112	21	26	5	0	0	NA	.232
Chester Williams	1939–41	362	35	108	7	3	0	47	.298
Clare Williams	1910–11	15	0	2	0	0	0	NA	.133
Harry Williams	1936–39	597	79	186	27	4	6	84	.312
Jesse Williams	1946–47	121	11	32	4	1	1	11	.264
John Williams	1935–36	180	16	51	11	2	3	25	.283
Marvin Williams	1947–48	42	5	12	1	0	0	4	.286
Bob Wilson	1952–53	225	28	61	7	2	5	22	.271
Jud Wilson	1925–36	769	165	286	38	27	18	NA	.372
Ray Wilson	1907	36	3	7	0	1	0	NA	.194
Bobby Winston	1908	177	41	47	0	2	0	NA	.266
Parnell Woods	1947–48	62	5	16	1	1	0	5	.258
Tom Young	1930–31	7	2	4	1	0	0	NA	.571

* = North American Negro-league player only

All-Time Career Pitching Statistics for Negro Players* in the Cuban League

Symbols: NA = No statistics available for this category (as determined by Jorge Figueredo); ** = major league player; # = U.S. Negro league star; parentheses indicate incomplete statistics for this category.

Player	Seasons	Years	G	CG	W-L	Pct.
Emery (Ace) Adams	1940–1941	1	14	3	2-6	.250
Cliff (Crooks) Allen	1929–1931	2	21	12	10-6	.625
Walter Ball	1908–1911	3	26	20	9-16	.360

Player	Seasons	Years	G	CG	W-L	Pct.
Bud Barbee	1940–1941	1	9	5	3-6	.333
Dave (Impo) Barnhill#	1947–1950	3	54	30	23-19	.548
Cliff Bell	1927–1931	4	58	27	25-17	.595
Joe Black**	1950–1952	2	43	17	20-13	.606
John Branahan	1922–1923	1	3	0	0-1	.000
Chet Brewer#	1930–1931	1	6	3	2-2	.500
Barney Brown	1935–1940	4	59	21	16-23	.410
Dave (Lefty) Brown	1922–1925	3	(31)	(15)	17-12	.586
Ray Brown	1936–1948	5	89	57	46-20	.696
Harry Buckner	1907–1909	2	12	7	1-7	.125
Walter (Lefty) Calhoun	1940–1941	1	14	2	2-5	.286
Ernest (Spoon) Carter	1937–1938	1	4	0	1-2	.333
Phil Cockrell	1920–1921	1	2	0	0-0	.000
Andy (Lefty) Cooper	1923–1929	3	(37)	(13)	15-17	.469
Willie (Sug) Cornelius	1939–1940	1	10	2	3-2	.600
Harry Cozart	1939–1940	1	4	0	0-1	.000
Reuben (Rube) Currie	1923–1924	1	(11)	(6)	10-5	.667
John Davis	1908	1	1	0	0-1	.000
Leon Day#	1937–1948	2	19	7	8-4	.667
William (Dizzy) Dismukes#	1914–1916	2	7	2	0-4	.000
Charles (Pat) Dougherty	1912	1	2	1	0-2	.000
Ed Dudley	1925–1926	1	13	6	2-6	.250
Louis Dula	1936–1937	1	21	4	5-8	.385
Frank Earle	1908–1909	1	3	2	1-1	.500
Jack Emery	1910–1911	1	1	1	0-1	.000
Felix (Chin) Evans	1937–1938	1	6	1	0-5	.000
Pud Flournoy	1920–1927	3	19	5	1-8	.111
Andrew (Rube) Foster#	1907–1916	4	34	24	17-12	.586
Willie (Bill) Foster	1927–1928	1	16	8	6-8	.429
Jonas Gaines	1946–1953	2	12	0	2-2	.500
Robert (Jude) Gans	1908–1909	1	5	3	1-4	.200
Willie (Lefty) Gisentaner	1926–1927	1	9	1	0-2	.000
Jim (Mudcat) Grant**	1957–1960	2	23	4	3-8	.273
Bill (Willie) Greason	1950–1951	1	7	2	2-2	.500
Claude (Red) Grier	1926–1927	1	14	6	5-3	.625
Bob Griffith	1937–1939	2	35	18	16-11	.593
Arthur (Rat) Henderson	1924–1925	1	14	7	8-5	.615
Bill Holland	1922–1939	4	(50)	(23)	27-22	.551
Len Hooker	1946–1947	1	3	0	0-1	.000
Willie Jefferson	1947–1948	1	8	0	1-0	1.000
Gentry Jessup	1946–1947	1	16	4	5-3	.625
Cliff (Connie) Johnson**	1954–1955	1	32	11	12-11	.522

All-Time Career Pitching Statistics, *cont.*

Player	Seasons	Years	G	CG	W-L	Pct.
Tommy Johnson	1939–1940	1	2	0	0-1	.000
Cecil Kaiser	1945–1946	1	15	2	3-3	.500
Jim LaMarque	1946–1948	2	53	7	18-13	.581
Rufus Lewis	1947–1949	2	55	16	19-11	.633
Dan McClellan	1907	1	3	2	0-2	.000
Bob McClure	1926–1927	1	14	6	3-8	.273
Booker McDaniels	1945–1948	3	49	10	15-14	.517
Terris McDuffie#	1937–1953	8	135	38	37-43	.463
Henry McHenry	1930–1945	3	30	3	8-7	.533
Max Manning	1946–1950	4	88	27	27-33	.450
Jack Marshall	1922–1923	1	4	0	1-0	1.000
Leroy Matlock	1938–1939	1	18	7	6-8	.429
Henry Miller	1948–1949	1	3	0	0-1	.000
Percy Miller	1924–1925	1	4	0	0-3	.000
Squire (Square) Moore	1924–1925	1	8	2	2-3	.400
Barney Morris	1939–1940	1	25	15	13-8	.619
Don Newcombe**	1946–1949	2	(9)	(1)	(1-4)	(.200)
Leroy (Satchel) Paige#(**)	1929–1930	1	15	8	6-5	.545
Roy Partlow#	1939–1940	1	13	10	7-4	.637
Andy (Pullman) Porter	1939–1941	2	23	11	9-9	.500
William Powell	1949–1953	2	21	4	4-6	.400
Willie (Wee Willie) Powell	1927–1928	1	18	4	3-7	.300
Ted (Double Duty) Radcliffe#	1938–1940	2	35	12	12-11	.522
Connie Rector	1927–1930	2	13	5	3-3	.500
Dick (Cannonball) Redding#	1912–1923	5	62	32	18-23	.439
Wilbur (Bullet) Rogan#	1924–1925	1	18	5	9-4	.692
Merven (Red) Ryan	1920–1927	5	39	12	12-10	.545
Harry Salmon	1929–1931	2	16	5	4-5	.444
Ford Smith	1949–1950	1	19	6	8-6	.571
Hilton Smith	1937–1940	2	23	9	10-5	.667
Robert Smith	1913	1	1	1	1-0	1.000
Theolic (Fireball) Smith	1938–1948	2	19	8	5-9	.357
Sam Streeter#	1924–1930	5	39	11	10-10	.500
John (Steel Arm) Taylor	1912	1	1	0	0-0	.000
John Taylor	1936–1939	2	25	6	4-14	.222
Art Terrell	1924–1925	1	3	0	0-1	.000
Al Thomas	1908–1909	1	2	0	1-1	.500
Harold Treadwell	1922–1923	1	3	0	0-0	.000
Ted Trent	1928–1931	2	23	9	6-10	.375
Bill (Steel Arm) Tyler	1925–1926	1	6	2	1-2	.333

Player	Seasons	Years	G	CG	W-L	Pct.
Frank Wickware	1912–1916	2	24	14	12-8	.600
Smoky Joe Williams#	1912–1916	3	48	26	22-15	.595
Johnny Williams	1946–1947	1	9	(0)	2-3	.400
Charles (Lefty) Williams	1928–1930	2	35	14	10-12	.455
Al (Apple) Wilmore	1950–1951	1	9	0	1-1	.500
Ray Wilson	1907	1	9	4	3-6	.333
Jessup (Nip) Winter	1923–1926	2	(27)	(8)	4-12	.250
Lamon Yokeley	1929–1930	1	11	4	2-4	.333

Modern Records of Selected Cuban League Stars (1940–1955)

Cuba provided its own cast of legendary diamond heroes during the three-quarters of a century marking Cuban League winter play before the advent of Castro's regime. Some of these stars enjoyed quality careers in the U.S. Negro leagues. Others would appear intermittently in the major leagues. Some, however, were legends on Cuban shores alone.

The following statistics are largely adapted from a classic and rare volume, *Béisbol Cubano, Records y Estadisticas, 1878–1955* (see Bibliography at end of this volume). These records have never appeared in another English-language baseball history volume.

Career Batting Statistics of Selected Modern Native Cuban-Leaguers

Symbols: * = major league player; # = U.S. Negro-league star; NA = no available record.

Player (Years)	AB	R	H	2B	3B	HR	RBI	BA
Pedro Almenares (1953–1955)	267	35	90	11	5	6	47	.337
Edmundo Amoros (1950–1955)*	951	163	314	49	14	20	149	.330
Asdrubal Baro (1951–1955)	200	36	53	5	2	3	31	.265
Julio Becquer (1951–1955)*	537	82	163	32	8	11	67	.304
Herberto Blanco (1940–1951)	1,519	186	392	25	5	2	151	.258
Emilio Cabrera (1943–1955)	512	43	113	11	5	1	50	.221
Lorenzo Cabrera (1942–1955)	1,905	232	585	99	30	12	199	.307
Francisco Campos (1944–1953)*	667	82	171	14	11	2	42	.256
Avelino Canizares (1942–1954)	1,371	204	344	38	12	3	112	.251
Clemente Carreras (1936–1944)	735	84	177	NA	NA	NA	90	.242
Alejandro Crespo (1939–1954)	2,535	321	701	66	19	22	362	.277

Career Batting Statistics, *cont.*

Player (Years)	AB	R	H	2B	3B	HR	RBI	BA
Juan Delís (1953–1955)*	359	51	102	15	3	5	42	.284
Carlos Desouza (1949–1955)	395	64	102	9	5	0	21	.258
Fernando Pedroso (1943–1955)	450	64	110	15	2	2	40	.244
Mario Díaz (1944–1955)	753	78	194	23	5	6	72	.258
Claro Duany (1942–1955)	1,590	197	448	77	10	33	240	.282
Humberto Fernández (1951–1955)	783	107	224	40	5	6	64	.285
Roberto Fernández (1949–1955)	417	29	105	9	1	2	48	.252
Andrés Fleitas (1942–1955)	1,796	185	485	81	18	9	223	.270
Pedro Formental (1942–1955)	2,720	431	746	98	38	54	362	.274
Francisco Gallardo (1947–1954)	172	26	44	4	6	2	23	.256
Pablo García (1946–1954)	832	96	219	32	6	11	98	.263
Hiram González (1947–1955)	559	62	127	17	4	0	40	.227
Ramón Heredia (1937–1948)	878	78	211	13	5	0	123	.240
Manuel Hidalgo (1940–1955)	1,478	168	353	40	11	10	146	.239
Amado Ibáñez (1946–1955)	1,025	146	264	26	19	7	87	.258
Roman Mejías (1954–1955)*	113	18	33	5	2	0	6	.292
Orestes Miñoso (1945–1954)*	1,764	300	510	75	40	33	225	.289
Guillermo Miranda (1948–1955)	1,271	146	321	32	17	2	88	.253
Louis Morales (1953–1955)	162	39	36	7	1	3	18	.222
Rafael Noble (1942–1955)	1,819	235	469	65	23	50	261	.258
Roberto Ortiz (1939–1955)*	1,998	269	552	67	25	51	310	.276
Carlos Paula (1952–1955)*	108	17	28	5	1	4	21	.259
Patricio Quintana (1953–1955)	172	17	36	6	2	5	21	.209
Héctor Rodríguez (1942–1955)	2,873	363	763	75	50	8	344	.266
Oscar Sardinas (1951–1955)	174	22	52	8	2	0	23	.299
Angel Scull (1951–1955)	545	96	177	21	9	5	73	.325
Oscar Sierra (1949–1955)	711	78	182	30	4	9	73	.256
José Valdivielso (1953–1955)*	61	4	11	0	1	0	3	.180
Orlando Varona (1950–1954)	204	24	47	2	0	3	18	.230

Career Pitching Statistics of Selected Modern-Era Native Cuban Leaguers

Symbols: * = major league player; # = U.S. Negro-league star; NA = no available record.

Player	Seasons	G	CG	W-L	Pct.	SO	BB	IP
Luis (Witto) Aloma*	1943–1953	131	16	24-28	.461	170	204	420.1
Fidel Alvarez	1953–1955	25	1	1-2	.333	14	12	44

Player	Seasons	G	CG	W-L	Pct.	SO	BB	IP
Vicente Amor	1954–1955	18	1	5-3	.625	24	28	64
Sandalio Consuegra*	1945–1955	104	29	41-42	.494	209	215	560
Virgilio Contreras	1952–1955	44	2	5-4	.556	41	52	97.1
Aristonico Correoso	1946–1955	65	6	8-8	.500	74	64	213.2
Lino Donoso	1946–1955	93	5	12-14	.462	162	148	279.2
Miguel Fornieles*	1952–1955	61	12	15-15	.500	140	103	181
Antonio García	1948–1955	50	0	4-3	.571	35	41	91
Rene Gutiérrez	1953–1955	34	0	2-1	.667	47	45	67.2
Alfredo Ibáñez	1952–1955	59	0	1-4	.200	54	71	120.1
Vicente López	1948–1955	120	9	17-13	.567	146	162	340.1
Conrado Marrero*	1946–1955	181	59	68-46	.596	478	295	1,036.1
Rogelio Martínez	1945–1953	135	9	16-18	.471	142	88	351.1
Agapito Mayor	1938–1953	309	54	68-64	.515	300	341	963.2
Julio Moreno*	1945–1955	191	28	38-46	.452	340	356	707.1
Gonzalo Naranjo	1952–1955	30	1	2-4	.333	31	43	96.2
Oliverio Ortiz	1943–1954	106	18	19-13	.594	119	231	314.1
Camilo Pascual*	1952–1954	28	4	5-5	.500	57	52	89
Carlos Pascual*	1950–1955	78	4	14-5	.737	93	121	211
Eusebio Pérez	1951–1954	41	2	4-4	.500	66	30	92
Pedro Ramos*	1954–1955	3	0	0-1	.000	2	1	4.1
Octavio Rubert	1947–1954	159	6	27-14	.659	246	190	407.2
Raul Sánchez*	1951–1955	102	4	12-11	.522	101	125	237.1
Rene (Tata) Solis	1947–1955	58	7	9-10	.474	28	85	165.1
Armando Suarez	1952–1955	46	2	5-4	.556	25	53	86.1
Santiago Ulrich	1941–1955	140	14	34-22	.607	108	179	333.1

Pre-Modern Records of Legendary Cuban League Stars

(Source: *Béisbol Cubano, Records y Estadisticas, 1878–1955,* by Gambino Delgado and Severo Nieto [Havana, 1955].)

Symbols: * = major league player; # = U.S. Negro-league star; $ =Cuban Baseball Hall of Fame; NA = no available record; parentheses indicate incomplete statistics for this category.

Career Batting Statistics of Legendary Native Cuban-Leaguers (pre–1940)

Player (Years)	AB	R	H	2B	3B	HR	RBI	BA
Rafael Almeida (1904–25)$*	1,273	(103)	322	23	11	8	NA	.253
Alfredo Arcano (1887–1909)$	1,273	NA	352	22	24	11	NA	.276

Pre-Modern Records, *cont.*

Player (Years)	AB	R	H	2B	3B	HR	RBI	BA
Bernardo Baro (1915–29)$	936	145	293	30	14	3	NA	.313
Luís Bustamente (1901–12)$	855	NA	190	11	6	2	NA	.222
Alfredo Cabrera (1901–20)$	1,457	(42)	327	26	17	3	NA	.224
Jacinto Calvo (1913–27)$*	1,110	144	344	41	30	6	NA	.310
Ramón Calzadilla (1888–1902)$	722	NA	181	8	9	0	NA	.251
Juan Castillo (1901–13)$	1,201	NA	372	55	32	8	NA	.310
Pelayo Chacón (1908–32)$	1,879	258	463	56	28	6	NA	.246
Manuel Cueto (1912–33)$*	1,652	268	492	66	19	8	NA	.298
Martín Dihigo (1922–47)#$	2,018	339	529	(33)	(9)	(8)	(188)	.262
Valentin Dreke (1919–28)$	1,015	186	312	32	15	5	NA	.307
José Fernández (1915–43)*	1,879	174	520	35	15	3	99	.277
Antonio García (1882–1905)$	831	NA	263	24	12	5	NA	.317
Regino García (1902–13)$	1,065	NA	318	24	10	2	NA	.299
Silvio García (1931–54)#	3,168	417	891	61	24	18	351	.282
Gervasio González (1902–19)$	1,598	(174)	398	22	19	7	NA	.249
Miguel González (1910–36)*	1,679	260	487	55	20	12	NA	.290
Valentin González (1890–1911)$	1,607	NA	431	26	27	10	NA	.268
Fermin Guerra (1934–55)	2,778	337	694	57	13	12	299	.250
Rafael Hernández (1885–99)$	560	NA	139	10	8	0	NA	.248
Heliodoro Hidalgo (1901–16)$	1,427	(129)	329	27	13	4	NA	.231
Bienvenido Jiménez (1913–29)*	845	142	225	30	10	6	NA	.266
Adolfo Luque (1912–46)*	671	94	169	14	13	2	NA	.252
Armando Marsans (1905–28)$*	1,632	(193)	426	36	22	2	NA	.261
José Méndez (1908–27)$	763	92	142	17	6	0	NA	.186
Agustín Molina (1894–1909)$	487	NA	80	3	3	0	NA	.164
Carlos Morán (1900–16)$	1,115	NA	316	24	7	0	NA	.283
Alejandro Oms (1922–46)$	1,531	328	537	74	28	15	(89)	.351
Regino Otero (1936–53)*	2,068	185	499	42	20	0	177	.242
Luís Padrón (1900–19)$	1,428	(118)	358	31	25	15	NA	.251
Napoleón Reyes (1941–52)*	1,018	114	277	21	12	5	107	.273
José Rodríguez (1913–39)$	1,597	170	400	39	20	7	NA	.251
Oscar Rodríguez (1918–39)	957	97	226	9	3	3	NA	.236
Pablo Ronquillo (1884–91)$	117	45	40	7	1	0	NA	.342
Carlos Royer (1890–1911)$	911	(8)	208	10	8	2	NA	.228
Emilio Sabourín (1878–87)$	(72)	(11)	(15)	(1)	(1)	(0)	NA	(.208)
Gilberto Torres (1934–53)*	2,434	245	652	37	10	3	268	.268
Cristóbal Torriente (1913–27)$#	1,316	251	463	62	39	18	NA	.352

Career Pitching Statistics of Legendary Native Cuban-Leaguers (pre–1940)

Player	Seasons	G	CG	W-L	Pct.	SO	BB	IP
Martín Dihigo#$	1922–1947	262	120	106-59	.642	(94)	(122)	(150.1)
Silvio García#	1934–1947	36	20	13-12	.520	NA	NA	36.1
Adolfo Luján$	1882–1891	47	36	34-9	.791	NA	NA	NA
Adolfo Luque*	1912–1946	210	99	93-62	.600	NA	NA	NA
José Méndez$	1908–1927	153	58	72-26	.735	(438)	(242)	(504)
José Muñoz$	1900–1914	171	117	81-57	.587	NA	NA	NA
Luís Padrón$	1900–1919	83	51	39-23	.629	NA	NA	NA
Emilio Palmero$	1913–1929	163	71	55-53	.509	NA	NA	NA
José Pastoriza$	1888–1895	100	83	59-40	.596	NA	NA	NA
Carlos Royer$	1890–1911	144	114	87-40	.685	NA	NA	NA
Gilberto Torres*	1934–1953	173	58	45-52	.464	NA	NA	(341)
Adrian Zabala	1935–1955	331	73	90-83	.520	(386)	(413)	(1,119)

Suggested Readings

Bjarkman, Peter C. Introduction (with references and blackball reading list) to *The Bingo Long Traveling All-Stars & Motor Kings* (a novel by William Brashler). Urbana: University of Illinois Press, 1993, xvii–xxxiii.

Chadwick, Bruce. *When the Game Was Black and White: The Illustrated History of Baseball's Negro Leagues.* New York: Abbeville Press, 1993.

Dixon, Phil, and Patrick J. Hannigan. *The Negro Baseball Leagues: A Photographic History.* Mattituck, New York: Amereon House, 1992.

Holway, John B. *Black Diamonds: Life in the Negro Leagues from the Men Who Lived It.* New York: Stadium, 1991; Westport, Connecticut: Meckler, 1989.

________. *Blackball Stars: Negro League Pioneers.* New York: Carroll and Graf, 1992; Westport, Connecticut: Meckler, 1988; Chapter 4, "José Méndez: Cuba's Black Diamond," pp. 50–60.

________. "Cuba's Black Diamond." *Baseball Research Journal* (Society for American Baseball Research) 10 (1981): 139–145.

________. *Satch and Josh: The Life and Times of Josh Gibson and Satchel Paige.* New York: Carroll and Graf, 1992; Westport, Connecticut: Meckler, 1991.

________. *Voices from the Great Black Baseball Leagues.* New York: Da Capo Press, 1992; New York: Dodd, Mead, 1975.

Peterson, Robert W. *Only the Ball Was White: A History of Legendary Black Players and All-Black Professional Teams.* New York: McGraw-Hill, 1984; Englewood Cliffs, New Jersey: Prentice-Hall, 1970.

Rogosin, Donn. *Invisible Men: Life in Baseball's Negro Leagues.* New York: Atheneum, 1983.

Tygiel, Jules. *Baseball's Great Experiment: Jackie Robinson and His Legacy.* New York: Oxford University Press, 1983.

CHAPTER 7

Cuban Blacks in the Majors Before Jackie Robinson

> For awhile I thought that Hi Bithorn, a Puerto Rican who pitched for the Cubs, 1942–43 and 1946, and for the White Sox in 1947, might be entitled to be called the first black player to appear in a big league uniform.
>
> —FRED LIEB, *Baseball as I Have Known It*

Perhaps the greatest difference between Jackie Robinson, acknowledged pioneer of baseball's integration, and Hiram Bithorn, forgotten journeyman pitcher for the lowly wartime Chicago Cubs, was the "color" of their linguistic inflections, the distinctive rhythms of their speech patterns. There was little enough to set apart their skin tones or the heritage of their racial gene pools. There was, of course, the matter of considerable baseball talent to boot. Yet to baseball's rough-hewn ballplayer stock and its gentlemanly establishment of owners as well as its hordes of paying patrons, one man (Robinson) remained anathema, an upstart descendant of slave stock who dared challenge baseball's long-cherished "gentlemen's agreement." The other (Bithorn) was merely a quaint distraction, another quirky "foreigner" of suspicious appearance and discordant language who lurked on the fringes of the sport and could not be taken seriously. And therein lies one of baseball's darkest untold tales.

It is a revealing if somewhat whimsical indictment of our American national character that we like our national history tainted with a strong dose of patriotic myth. In the arena of societal history and politics, certainly, this axiom has held fast for generations of American schoolchildren and serious adult readers. A recent generation nurtured on World War II and weaned on the four-decade cold war has eagerly adopted Esther Forbes's fanciful *Johnny Tremain*, for example, as their most vivid image of the Revolutionary War era (despite this novel's spurious historical treatment and thinly veiled flag-waving thesis that colonial patriots had genuinely found an American ideal worth fighting and dying for). More recently, social historian Michael Kammen has argued deftly in his *Mystic Chords of Memory* (1991) that almost all American popular history is a depoliticized version of events and always carries a doctrinaire message. Our popular history texts offer "revisionist history" written with a clear and heavy-handed social lesson in mind—"history" the meek servant of didactic purpose and never the true reflection of documented reality. And it is precisely in this respect that our national character is most ironically reflected in our passions for the game of baseball.

Baseball fans are indisputably the most historically aware of all sports fans. Our love for the game of our childhood feeds as much upon the memory of past events and past heroes as upon the thrill of contemporary contests. Yet the most cherished historical memories sustaining the game for its collective fandom (Ruth's gigantic home-run blows or Walter Johnson's blazing fastball) are often embellished fictions—at the very least elaborately woven legends tapping the roots of fiction.

What fan does not know, for example, that Doubleday invented baseball in the pastures of nineteenth-century Cooperstown; that Jackie Robinson broke the color barrier as big-league baseball's first black ballplayer; that Fred Merkle's boneheaded failure to touch second base directly cost the Giants a 1908 pennant; that Merkle's equally ill-fated teammate Fred Snodgrass soon outdid his fellow bonehead by personally losing the 1912 World Series with his ninth-inning dropped fly ball; that Joe Jackson and his 1919 White Sox cronies nearly ruined the nation's sporting spirit by successfully conspiring with gamblers to fix that season's World Series against Cincinnati; and that Joe DiMaggio stroked clean base hits in 56 straight games of the 1941 season, compiling baseball's greatest consecutive batting run? And what careful and astute historian of the game should not also know that every one of these sacred baseball legends is not exactly true as it is always related? Each is an embellished myth, and each contains at least one significant historical distortion. Several, especially Jackie Robinson's fortuitous role in baseball's integration and Joe Jackson's onerous role in the 1919 Black Sox series, are patently incorrect as they are traditionally reported.

The Jackie Robinson legend in particular is glossed over with the rosy hue of romanticism and muddled with the inaccuracies of oftentimes sloppy journalism. The idea that Robinson was a sole crusader who boldly set the first black foot on a professional baseball diamond, that with his dashing style of play Robinson single-handedly swept aside all vestiges of prejudice and racial hatred on America's athletic fields, is as firmly ingrained in the popular psyche as, say, the notion that Abner Doubleday concocted the rules of baseball out of thin air in 1839 in the pastures of Cooperstown, that Babe Ruth pointed to the exact spot in the bleachers where he would seconds later deposit a memorable 1932 World Series roundtripper, or that

Fred Merkle irrationally threw away a Giants pennant victory in 1908 with a thoughtless bonehead play. Ruth did not point; Merkle neither committed an atrocity of judgment nor lost a pennant; and Robinson was assuredly *not* the first black big-league ballplayer! This is not to belittle the enormity of the Rickey-Robinson experiment in Brooklyn in 1947, nor to discount Robinson's legitimate Hall-of-Fame career, nor to suggest for a moment that Robinson was not *perceived* by his peers and fans as a racial pioneer and thus subjected to unimaginable pressures, harassment, and abuse. It is simply to suggest—and this is quite a different matter—that the circumstances and events of Robinson's debut in the National League in 1947 have from the first been muddled and that the full story of baseball's gradual and fitful racial integration has never been accurately told or popularly accepted.

Much has been accomplished recently by a handful of serious scholars of black baseball to help set the record straight regarding Branch Rickey's plan for integrating major league baseball at the close of the Second World War. Most controversial in the Robinson emancipation story are the motive and method of Branch Rickey's integration plan. And nowhere are this story and other aspects of the integration saga more accurately and entertainingly told than in Jules Tygiel's landmark study *Baseball's Great Experiment: Jackie Robinson and His Legacy* (1983). Tygiel recounts in exacting detail how Rickey's moves not only opened big-league fields to black players but also had devastating effects on the Negro leagues and thus upon the black communities which had long sustained Negro baseball (just as black baseball had long sustained those communities). In Tygiel's view, something quite vital and distinctively American died with the passing of black baseball. The Negro leagues had once represented a thriving $2 million empire, one controlled by blacks, employing blacks, and providing crucial forms of cultural identification for millions of minority fans. After Robinson, more blacks were playing in the big leagues, and none would have it any other way, yet fewer blacks were making their living at baseball, and black communities had lost an important life force that could never be replaced. And Tygiel, along with prolific baseball chronicler John Thorn, has recently presented persuasive new evidence that Rickey intended originally to bring three or more blacks to the big leagues simultaneously, a plan stymied by a convoluted course of events that Tygiel and Thorn have now unraveled (see "Signing Jackie Robinson," *The National Pastime*, no. 10, 1990). It was thus apparently only an accident of history that Robinson has long held the spotlight of racial integration so exclusively.

But there is another side of the Jackie Robinson legend that to this day remains underreported. This is the persistent notion that Robinson was the first black man of any ethnic background to don the uniform of a big-league ball club. The notion is, of course, patently false on several counts. Any devotee of baseball lore worth his weight in dusty volumes of Putnam team histories knows that a black catcher named Moses Fleetwood Walker, out of Oberlin College in Ohio, was a regular backstop with the Toledo ballclub when it first gained admittance to the American Association (then a legitimate big-league circuit) in 1884. Fleet Walker also formed a colored tandem with pitcher George Stovey of the International League's Newark club in 1887, the very season when Chicago manager Cap Anson (already well on his way to instituting the "gentlemen's agreement" that would bar "coloreds" from the senior circuit) staged a boycott of a scheduled exhibition match with the Newark team and its dark-skinned battery. Moses Fleetwood Walker was for over 60 years the proper answer to a pair of obscure trivia questions: Who was the first black major-leaguer? Who was the last?

Reams have been written about the odd plight of Cuban ballplayers between the two great wars, especially by such eloquent scholars of "colored baseball history" as John Holway, Jules Tygiel, Jerry Malloy, and Rob Ruck. While fair-skinned Havana hurler Adolfo Luque was able to pass unchallenged through the unwritten racial barrier to become the first true Latin big-league star—appearing in the 1919 and 1933 World Series, compiling 27 victories during a fabulous 1923 campaign, and gaining nearly 200 career wins over 20 seasons with the Reds and Giants—dark-skinned legend Martín Dihigo (born a decade and a half later and raised only 50 miles from the home of Havana-born Luque) was doomed by his race to suffer a far different fate. Allowed no more than a barnstorming career that would lead him through backwater winter-league seasons stretching across three decades and eventually into the baseball halls of fame in his native Cuba and Mexico as well as belatedly in Cooperstown, Dihigo remained nonetheless a celebrated outcast unknown to big-league fans of his own and subsequent eras. Like Martín Dihigo, numerous other bronze Cuban and Puerto Rican stars were unacceptable to major league teams, whose managers could only salivate privately upon seeing the likes of Cristóbal Torriente, Poncho Coimbre, Perucho Cepeda, the elder Luís Tiant, and José Méndez performing brilliantly during barnstorming off-season games with Caribbean and black-league all-star squads.

Meanwhile another scenario was being played out in the clubhouses and front offices of some of baseball's less successful and less glamorous big-league ballclubs. Readers of Paul Hemphill's entertaining novel *Long Gone* (1979) will recall the bold gamble of fictional Sally League manager Stud Cantrell, who bolsters his weak-hitting Graceville Oilers club with slugging black catcher Joe Brown and then passes off the unacceptable black as José Guitterez Brown just off the banana boat from Venezuela. To management and fans starved for winning baseball, a little flirtation with the "gentlemen's agreement" might indeed be okay, provided the swarthy ballplayer in question could pass as a "foreigner" and hit well enough to distract attention from the hue of his skin. On more than one occasion (as with Bill Veeck's midget in St. Louis) baseball reality has followed meekly a full step behind baseball fiction. The history of our national pastime between closure of the dead-ball era (after World War I) and the demise of the "gentlemen's agreement" (after World War II) is replete with more than one incident of big-league management passing off dark-skinned Latinos as "Cubans" or "Castilians" but certainly not "Negroes."

First came the once-celebrated and now largely forgotten saga of two olive-skinned flychasers discovered in the lost outposts of the Eastern League by Cincinnati manager Clark Griffith. Armando Marsans and Rafael Almeida enjoyed short-lived but historically important careers for the Cincinnati Reds of the immediate pre–World War I period. The Reds had stumbled upon the duo when manager Clark Griffith offered a tryout to a touted Cuban (Almeida) playing with the Class B New Britain (Connecticut League) team in the spring of 1911. Almeida spoke almost no English and thus brought along a teammate as his interpreter; the teammate (Marsans) impressed Griffith as much if not more than the original invitee, and soon both were ensconced in the outfield back at Cincinnati's Redland Field (Oleksak and Oleksak, 1991, 25).

Almeida would hit only .270 over three short seasons of National League play. Marsans stretched out his own career until 1918, compiling only a .269 lifetime average but bashing the ball at a .317 clip during a stellar 1912 season. Yet both were the center of controversy resulting from their prominent olive-colored skin, and a worried Cincinnati management was soon forced to send off to Cuban officials for documents to certify that the two imports were of Castilian and not black heritage. Cincinnati historians Lonnie Wheeler and John Baskin report that even manager Griffith experienced mild concern when hearing of club president Garry Herrmann's original plans to sign the Cuban prospects ("We will not pay any Hans Wagner price for a pair of dark-skinned islanders"), and when Herrmann arrived to pick up the imports upon their arrival at the Cincinnati train station, he suffered near heart seizure when a couple of brown Pullman porters disembarked moments ahead of the expected ballplayers (see Wheeler and Baskin, 1988, 174–175). Soon enough, however, Cincinnati newspapers were boasting that the two dark-skinned Cubans were "two of the purest bars of Castilian soap ever floated to these shores" once the needed documentation had arrived. Writing in the season of Robinson's cataclysmic debut, Lee Allen, dean of Cincinnati baseball historians, puts the whole matter in perspective by suggesting the tensions surrounding the Cubans' arrival in town. "Today [1947] it is almost impossible to realize what a furor the signing of two Cubans caused in 1911" (Allen, 1948, 96). Yet Lee Allen was writing his baseball history in a far different age and thus makes little speculation about what it was that so disturbed the league's fans about these "foreigners" of swarthy skin color. Certain weighty sociological questions apparently did not yet get asked in popular-press sports books.

If Marsans and Almeida had once caused something of an uproar in the conservative midwestern frontier town of Cincinnati, there was soon to be similar upheaval on the professional diamond of the nation's capital. Racial questions soon greeted the brief major league appearances of two Cubans of the same era—outfielder Jacinto "Jack" Calvo and pitcher José Acosta. Calvo appeared briefly with the Washington Senators in 1913 and again in 1920 (33 G, .161 BA, 1 HR). Acosta hurled for the same ballclub as well as the Chicago White Sox between 1920 and 1922 (10-10, 4.51 ERA). While Almeida and Marsans were apparently light-skinned enough to find brief acceptance in the majors (though not without comment and controversy), Calvo and Acosta were dark enough to play simultaneously in the professional Negro leagues. Both men teamed on the Long Beach Cubans and New Jersey Cubans for Negro-league play between their several big-league stints, and in one 1920 winter-season exhibition in Cuba Acosta is reported to have fanned the mighty Babe Ruth three times. Thus this second pair of swarthy Cubans became the only two pre–Robinson players to appear in both segregated white and ostracized black major leagues. And if the appearance of Calvo and Acosta in full-fledged Negro-league play seems to give one pause concerning the percentage of black blood each carried in his veins, one might well speculate as well about the status of Acosta's brother Mérito Acosta, who also appeared briefly (175 games between 1913 and 1918) in the outfield of the Washington Senators and Philadelphia Athletics.

Jack Calvo and José Acosta were not the only dark-skinned Washington Senators to walk perilously on a racial tightrope across the American League during the decades after ragtime and Shoeless Joe Jackson and before wartime rations and one-armed Pete Gray. They were followed a decade later on the same Washington ballclub (which was now flooding its roster with low-salaried and often marginally talented Cubans and Latinos) by a Venezuelan pitcher who stirred every bit as much doubt and consternation around the cities of the junior circuit. Venezuelan hurler Alejandro "Patron" Carrasquel was signed on for Griffith's Senators by superscout Joe Cambria and passed only tolerably well for a white player from 1939 through 1945, winning 50 games for the cellar-anchored Nats ballclub. Seemingly, the nation's capital was a slightly less hostile environment for "borderline whites" than the heartlands of southern Ohio. Yet Carrasquel was nonetheless heckled for his dark complexion (as was the more pale-skinned Dolf Luque) by fans and opponents alike, and when he tried to avoid attention by Anglicizing his name to Alex Alexandra, the beat writers around the league were hardly to be taken in by such a ploy and never flagged from calling him simply "Carrasquel the Venezuelan."

If the cataclysms of World War II would eventually throw open heretofore bolted big-league doors for the nation's black athletes, it would be that same war that would crack those doors for racially questionable Cuban, Puerto Rican, and other assorted Caribbean athletes even sooner. Clark Griffith continued his policies of penny pinching in Washington, policies that leaned upon the Cuban scouting of former Baltimore laundryman Joe Cambria, who, Washington baseball historian Morris Bealle carpingly claimed, "would do even better if he could get over his predilection for Cubanolas" (Bealle 1947, 162). In the two decades following 1935, Griffith and Cambria imported 31 native Cubans to the diamond at Griffith Stadium, most for only predictably brief big-league appearances, and in spring 1940 Cambria reportedly trucked so many Cubans into camp that Griffith "had to find a special farm for them in Williamsport, Pa." (Bealle 1947, 163). (For more detailed accounts of what might be called the Washington Senators' Cuban era, a period which Bealle compares to "the daffiness era" in Brooklyn, see Bjarkman, 1993, American League volume, 501–509.)

The thin pool of wartime baseball talent made Cuban athletes all the more attractive. They were not subject to the military draft, and they demanded small wages, and a floodtide (18 total between 1940 and 1945) would appear in the uniforms of big-league clubs during the first half of the 1940s. At least two of these imports were, like Calvo and Carrasquel in Washington during previous decades, of dubious racial stock. Tommy de la Cruz (1944) apparently stirred almost as much undercurrent in Cincinnati as Marsans and Almeida years earlier, though the patriotic spirit of wartime America seemingly kept most of the strongest disapproval out of the city's press. And up in Chicago there was the case of Hiram Gabriel Bithorn (1942), hefty right-handed hurler from Puerto Rico.

Tommy de la Cruz was a pitcher of distinctly mediocre talents who would experience all the triumphs and traumas of a single abnormal big-league season in Cincinnati's Crosley Field during the final war-interrupted campaign of 1944. As baseball's oldest and most traditional franchise, Cincinnati's Redlegs are known widely to baseball historians for their unmatched string of rare diamond firsts—such pioneering moments as the nation's first professional team (1869), first uniformed manager (1869), first fielder's and catcher's mitts (1869 and 1890), first National League left-handed pitcher (1877), inaugural farm system (1887), first Ladies Day (1886), first big-league night game (1935), first all-synthetic playing surface (Riverfront Stadium in 1970), and dozens more (Bjarkman 1993, National League volume, 181–238).

Yet perhaps the most explosive first in club annals remains buried from sight by the selective view of revisionist history. The wartime summer of 1944 in Cincinnati is enthusiastically remembered for a rare if unimportant pitching debut—the two-thirds of an inning hurled by 15-year-old high-schooler Joe Nuxhall, baseball's youngest performer ever. Yet another landmark mound debut of that same summer has received almost no commentary despite its unparalleled ground-breaking nature. Ebony-hued Cuban right-hander Tommy de la Cruz took the hill for manager Bill McKecknie's Reds 34 times that summer of his single big-league campaign and fashioned a record of 9-9 across 191 innings of midsummer work. The Reds steadfastly insisted that their Cuban journeyman was merely "Hispanic" and not black, yet enough doubt existed among rival club owners that young Tommy de la Cruz was never to be invited back for a second season's swing around the league. He would show up instead the following summer toiling in Jorge Pasquel's rebel Mexican League, one of the handful of big-leaguers Pasquel was able to lure south of the border during his ill-fated effort to compete economically with the big-league boys up north. That race and not mound talent was a motivating force in Cincinnati's release of Tommy de la Cruz is perhaps cued by the fact that the pitching-thin Cincinnati club (despite wartime returnees) would boast only three 10-game winners during the following campaign.

Others in baseball were most certainly aware that Tommy de la Cruz was something of a threat to the game's sanctioned racial purity. Veteran Pittsburgh Pirates scout Howie Haak, who followed Joe Cambria across Cuba in the 1940s and 1950s, reports sarcastically on the policy of having Cuban ballplayers of that era sign phony forms claiming that their ancestry was unquestionably Hispanic, thus acceptably white. But, concludes the insightful Haak, "Hell, Tommy de la Cruz (for one) was as black as they came!" (Krich, 1989, 157).

It should be noted here that if Tommy de la Cruz did not receive proper recognition as "baseball's first true black" pioneer, he set an unfortunate precedent that would die hard in Cincinnati. A full decade later a former University of Toledo basketballer named Chuck Harmon would appear on Opening Day 1954 as a token pinch hitter and officially claim the distinction in popular histories (and thus in the memories of local fans) as the first black Cincinnati Reds player. Ironically, however, Harmon was preceded in the batting order (by exactly one batter) by another pinch hitter who perhaps better deserved this history-making accolade. Saturnino (Nino) Escalera, a native of Santurce, Puerto Rico, launched his one-year big-league career with a pinch-hit single only moments before Harmon, who followed him in the lineup by tamely popping out. Nino Escalera was labeled by local writers at the time as "a Puerto Rican" import despite the fact that his Latino skin was equally as dark as Harmon's.

A bold claim for Tommy de la Cruz as baseball's true first twentieth-century black was recently made before a national television audience by the producers of a special documentary on the history of Latin American ballplayers ("Baseball with a Latin Beat," produced by WNBC-TV, New York, October 1989). The claim was probably moot, however, not so much in light of Robinson's celebrated career but in view of Hi Bithorn's totally obscure sojourn on the big-league diamond in Chicago. Another Latin pitcher of only modest talents, Bithorn preceded de la Cruz by three full seasons and outlasted him by that many. He showed promise with a 9-14 (3.68 ERA) 1942 rookie campaign, was the staff ace (18-12, 2.60 ERA) for the fifth-place Cubbies during the war-cheapened season of 1943 (pacing the senior circuit in shutouts that year), then lost two seasons to wartime naval service (Puerto Ricans, unlike Cubans, were not draft-exempt). While sustained on navy chow, Bithorn unfortunately ballooned to 225 pounds, developed a sore arm, and kissed good-bye his promising big-league career. Perhaps the most noteworthy events marking the career of Hiram Bithorn were that he teamed with Cuban backstop Sal Hernández to provide the 1942 Cubs with baseball's first all-Latino battery and that he was gunned down under mysterious circumstances by a police officer in Mexico City on New Year's Day 1952. But not that many fans or baseball historians ever noticed either obscure event.

One baseball historian and scribe did lift his racial blinders long enough to take note, however, and that scribe was one of the game's most celebrated and respected – none other than venerable Fred Lieb. Pausing in his marvelous 1977 autobiography to comment on baseball's rich ethnic mix, Lieb recalls a personal puzzle he once faced regarding the swarthy Puerto Rican pitcher with the wartime Cubs. Lieb's full account is eye-opening for its candor:

> Late in the winter of 1946-7, when I was working in St. Louis, I was invited to see a performance of Katherine Durham's all-black dance troupe. I did not know the man who had arranged for me to sit in the wings throughout the performance. During the intermission he brought over one of the women dancers and introduced her to me. "She is a first cousin to Hi Bithorn, the pitcher," he explained to make conversation. "Yes," the girl volunteered immediately. "My mother and Hi's mother are sisters."

Lieb then continues with a speculation that the conversation had been arranged "to tell me something" (given his advantageous position in the baseball press), reporting that "it had been rumored among baseball writers and in clubhouses when Bithorn came up in 1942 that he was part black" (Lieb, 1977, 260). Lieb, for all his candor, was still a company man, however, and could only conclude, "I have been assured by a Puerto Rican baseball authority that Bithorn was *not* black, despite my curious experience."

If the greatest of the Cuban black ballplayers who sprang forth in the decades between the two wars were fated to live out their careers in the relative obscurity of island winter ball and hidden Negro-league play, at least their image was not totally obliterated by the winds of fate. They would indeed emerge eventually among the game's great legends, thanks in large part to the work of literary champions like John Holway and Jules Tygiel. Of course, it is still arguable that Dihigo and Torriente and Luís Tiant, Sr., and others of immortal stature in their native Cuba and Puerto Rico were robbed by long delays of reputations that might have rivaled Cobb's or Walter Johnson's. And their eventual enshrinement came too late for their personal savoring. But it was some of their dark-skinned compatriots who (perhaps due to their lesser talents) sneaked briefly through baseball's loose racial barriers who suffered what now seems an even crueler fate. Why is it that Robinson was deified and vilified while Hi Bithorn and Jack Calvo and Alex Carrasquel provoked more mild amusement and stifled yawns than any threats of banishment? Is it merely that the latter were mysterious island swarthy princes while the former was an upstart who did not know his place? Was it that those black Cubans who enjoyed brief cups of espresso in the big time were simply never good enough ballplayers to receive much notice? Was it that fans and owners, perhaps like characters in Hemphill's novel, were actually fooled by protestations of local management that these dark-skinned "foreigners" were not really black men? More than likely, it was some shifting combination of all the above.

If any claim that Jackie Robinson's integration of the big-league scene was neither unprecedented nor unanticipated seems too outrageous, it should be pointed out that plenty of respectable voices have earlier suggested as much. Renowned black sportswriter and editor Art Rust, Jr., was one of the earliest to question a well-established historical myth: "I have always been convinced that Jackie Robinson was not the first black man in the modern major leagues," wrote Rust. "The Washington Senators in the mid-thirties and forties were loaded with Latin players of darker hue, who because they spoke Spanish got away with it" (quoted by Rogosin, *Invisible Men*, 159). Negro-league historian Donn Rogosin struck a similar note in suggesting that big-league scouts bypassed the "Black Babe Ruth," Cristóbal Torriente, only because of unacceptable kinky hair and a flat African nose and that Negro-leaguer Quincy Trouppe was once told by scouts that he might be signable if only he would learn Spanish so that he might pass for a "foreigner" instead of an American black.

Rogosin cites further examples. Art Rust referred to Mike González (a Cuban who managed the Cardinals in 1938 and 1940) in print as "a light-skinned black man," while Washington outfielder John Welau admitted that the bulk of his teammates in the 1940s considered Bobby Estalella to be a black man. Negro-leaguer Willie Wells, who played under Mike González on the Almendares (Cuba) winter-league team, reported that his skipper's mother was completely black.

But perhaps the most luminous testimony comes from the most surprising source of all—Robinson's partner in the great integration experiment, Branch Rickey. In his outstanding book on the black leagues, historian Rogosin reports that Rickey was dismayed when Clark Griffith, boss of the Senators, objected to Brooklyn's 1947 integration efforts (which promised to destroy the Negro leagues and thus Griffith's lucrative business arrangement with the Homestead Grays, part-time tenants of the Washington ballpark). According to Rogosin it was the beleaguered Rickey who snickered to famed sportswriter Red Smith that Griffith was hardly one to object to Jackie Robinson, given his known propensity for hiring Cuban blacks. Red Smith later reported that the comments of Mr. Rickey "seemed to imply that there was a Senegambian somewhere in the Cuban batpile where Senator timber is seasoned" (Rogosin, 159–160).

No serious baseball historian would contend that Jackie Robinson does not deserve every bit of his huge and still-growing legend as baseball superstar—as an athlete of incomparable grace, skill, and magnetism and a bold racial pioneer of incomparable courage and integrity. It should not be forgotten that once Robinson left the playing field, he carried on still another crusade (one that most likely cost him his health and his life) against racial bigotry across the land, dedicating himself to the battle with an intensity shown by few Americans of any color. During the course of his decade-long big-league career, Robinson enjoyed the perfect forum for his conquest of sport's racist traditions: playing in the New York baseball capital, wearing the uniform of the colorful Dodgers, dancing his magic upon the base paths at the very moment when television's magical eye first captured images of the World Series. With the notoriety and exposure he enjoyed, Robinson took upon his shoulders the full burden of racial hatred and the full weight of the integration struggle; as a result, he enjoyed in large measure the full (and perhaps somewhat unmerited) credit for dismantling baseball's most unforgivable tradition. While Robinson wore his rebellion on his sleeve, other quiet pioneers like Campanella, Doby, and Newcombe undoubtedly did as much for the cause simply by sustaining their cheerful and infectious enthusiasms for the sport.

Yet in an era when baseball's historians (especially those who wear the label of sabermetricians) quibble at length over whether fine-tuned adjustments in rule interpretation or record keeping might justify taking away a batting title earned four decades ago or devote their labors to adjusting the statistical measures of some bygone player's relative impact upon the game, it would seem appropriate that factual inaccuracies of more far-reaching consequence for baseball's sociological history need to be set

Dark-Skinned Latin Big-League Players Before Jackie Robinson

Outfielders	Years	Debut Team	Games	BA	Hits	HR	RBI
Armando Marsans*	1911–1918	Cincinnati	655	.269	612	2	221
Rafael Almeida*	1911–1913	Cincinnati	102	.270	77	3	46
Jacinto "Jack" Calvo*	1913, 1920	Washington	33	.161	56	1	4
Mérito Acosta*	1913–1918	Washington	175	.255	111	0	37

Pitchers	Years	Teams	Games	W	L	Pct.	ERA
José Acosta*	1920–1922	Washington	55	10	10	.500	4.51
Alex Carrasquel#	1939–1949	Washington	258	50	39	.562	3.73
Hi Bithorn@	1942–1947	Chicago (NL)	105	34	31	.523	3.16
Tommy de la Cruz*	1944	Cincinnati	34	9	9	.500	3.25

Country Key: * = Cuba, # = Venezuela, @ = Puerto Rico.

straight. Should there not be a place in our narratives to recognize the historical significance of a handful of men of color who crossed baseball's racial barrier (however tentatively and obscurely) before Jackie Robinson?

References and Suggested Readings

Allen, Lee. *The Cincinnati Reds.* New York: Putnam, 1948.

Bealle, Morris A. *The Washington Senators: The Story of an Incredible Fandom.* Washington, D.C.: Columbia, 1947.

Bjarkman, Peter C. "Cincinnati Reds: Cincinnati's Hometown Game, from the Red Stockings to the Big Red Machine." In *Encyclopedia of Major League Baseball: National League (Team Histories)*, revised edition. New York: Carroll and Graf, 1993; Westport, Connecticut: Meckler, 1991, 181–238.

________. "Washington Senators – Minnesota Twins: Expansion-Era Baseball Comes to the American League." In *Encyclopedia of Major League Baseball: American League (Team Histories)*, revised edition. New York: Carroll and Graf, 1993; Westport, Connecticut: Meckler, 1991, 487–534.

Hemphill, Paul. *Long Gone.* New York: Viking Press, 1979.

Holway, John B. *Blackball Stars: Negro League Pioneers.* New York: Carroll and Graf, 1992; Westport, Connecticut: Meckler, 1988.

Krich, John. *El Béisbol: Travels Through the Pan-American Pastime.* New York: Prentice-Hall Press, 1990; New York: Atlantic Monthly Press, 1989.

Lieb, Fred. *Baseball as I Have Known It.* New York: Coward, McCann and Geoghegan, 1977.

Oleksak, Michael M., and Mary Adams Oleksak. *Béisbol: Latin Americans and the Grand Old Game.* Grand Rapids, Michigan: Masters Press, 1991.

Rogosin, Donn. *Invisible Men: Life in Baseball's Negro Leagues.* New York: Atheneum, 1985.

Thorn, John, and Jules Tygiel. "Jackie Robinson's Signing: The Real, Untold Story." *The National Pastime: A Review of Baseball History* 10 (1990): 7–12.

Tygiel, Jules. *Baseball's Great Experiment: Jackie Robinson and His Legacy.* New York: Oxford University Press, 1983.

Wheeler, Lonnie, and John Baskin. *The Cincinnati Game.* Wilmington, Ohio: Orange Frazier Press, 1988.

Negro league stars (l to r) Bill Byrd, Josh Gibson and Dick Seay in uniform for Santurce during 1939 winter season (photo courtesy of Luís Alvelo).

Josh Gibson, demonstrating the famous swing that terrorized Puerto Rican winter baseball (photo courtesy of Luís Alvelo).

Martín Dihigo, winter leagues and blackball great (top); Hi Bithorn, pioneer Latin moundsman with the '40s-era Chicago Cubs (middle) (photos: National Baseball Library and Archive, Cooperstown, N.Y.); Perucho Cepeda, Puerto Rican winter league legend (bottom); huge Luke Easter slugged homers for Mayagüez in 1948 as well as for the Cleveland Indians in the early '50s (standing) (photos courtesy of Luís Alvelo).

Adolfo (Dolf) Luque of Cuba, with New York Giants in early '30s (photo: National Baseball Library and Archive, Cooperstown, N.Y.).

Dolf Luque with the Cincinnati Reds, circa 1925 (top left); Camilo Pascual, Minnesota Twins (top right); Orlando Cepeda, Latin America's first major league home run and RBI champion (bottom left); Matty Alou, Pittsburgh Pirates 1966 (bottom right). (Cepeda photo: Transcendental Graphics; all other photos: National Baseball Library and Archive, Cooperstown, N.Y.)

Luís Rodríguez Olmo, Puerto Rican winter league hitting star in 1939-40 (photo courtesy of Luís Alvelo).

Francisco "Poncho" Coimbre, Puerto Rico winter league star, 1939-40 (photo courtesy of Luís Alvelo).

Orestes "Minnie" Miñoso, "The Cuban Comet," Chicago 1956 (photo: National Baseball Library and Archive, Cooperstown, N.Y.).

Vic Power of the Cleveland Indians (photo: National Baseball Library and Archive, Cooperstown, N.Y.). Authors Brendan Boyd and Fred Harris note that—with the exception of Jonas Salk, John Foster Dulles and Annette Funicello—perhaps no public figure so personified "the flashy fifties" as did baseball's Vic Power.

Cuba's Tony Taylor of the Philadelphia Phillies battled racial prejudice on National League diamonds in the '50s (top left); Felipe Alou of the San Francisco Giants (top right); Pepe Frías, one of the earliest sure-handed Dominican shortstops (bottom left); and Cuba's fleet-footed Bert Campaneris, first to play all nine positions in a single big league game (bottom right). (Frías photo courtesy of the Los Angeles Dodgers Baseball Club; all other photos: National Baseball Library and Archive, Cooperstown, N.Y.)

Juan Marichal of the San Francisco Giants (photo: National Baseball Library and Archive, Cooperstown, N.Y.). The "Dominican Dandy" was both the winningest Latin American big-league hurler of all-time, and also the most frequent victim of cruel racial stereotypes.

Davy Concepción (top), Venezuela's candidate for Cooperstown (author's collection); Ramón Martínez (bottom), pride of the Dominican Republic, unleashes his fastball in Dodger Stadium (courtesy of the Los Angeles Dodgers Baseball Club).

Alejandro Peña (top), the Dodgers' Dominican relief specialist and Ramón Martínez (bottom) also of Dodgers' fame (photos courtesy of the Los Angeles Dodgers Baseball Club).

Manny Mota (top left), the Dominican pinch hitting phenomenon with the Los Angeles Dodgers; Luís Aparicio (top right), Chicago White Sox; Roberto Clemente (bottom left), Pittsburgh Pirates; and Orestes "Minnie" Miñoso (bottom right), the "Black Cuban Comet." (Mota photo courtesy of the Los Angeles Dodgers Baseball Club, all other photos: Transcendental Graphics.)

Fernando Valenzuela demonstrates pose that launched "Fernandomania" in the early 1980s (courtesy of the Los Angeles Dodgers Baseball Club).

Luís Tiant, the Younger, with the Boston Red Sox (photo: Transcendental Graphics). "Little Looie" is the all-time strikeout leader among Latin hurlers, the second-winningest Latin big league hurler ever, and Cuba's most colorful gift to the North American national pastime.

CHAPTER 8

"The Comet" and "The Maestro": Legacies of Blackball's Lost Caribbean Stars

> One of baseball's prize Horatio Alger tales is that of a player whose parents were so poor he didn't start school until he was ten, who had to quit four years later to go to work, cutting sugar cane with a machete. —A. S. "Doc" YOUNG

May 1, 1951, was a date of great significance in the history of the usually lackluster Chicago American League ballclub. For diehard Chicago fans, it was a rare moment of proud triumph for the franchise long known as Chuck Comiskey's ill-fated and much-cursed Chicago White Sox; and it would be a date pregnant with considerable import for the history of Latin American baseball as well. May Day of 1951 would also unfortunately remain a day robbed of a large chunk of this significance by a rude twist of fate and bad timing. It was the kind of terrible timing that seems to be found everywhere across the career of a flashy Cuban outfielder known by the adopted moniker Orestes "Minnie" Miñoso.

On that afternoon in tradition-rich Comiskey Park, the 29-year-old jet-skinned rookie outfielder from Cuba was destined to become the first black ballplayer to don a Chicago White Sox uniform for official American League play. He was hardly a normal rookie, given his advanced age and his two earlier trials (he played 17 games in 1949 and during the previous month of 1951) at the big-league level in Cleveland. To the unrestrained joy of long-suffering Sox supporters crammed into the bleachers as well as those glued to their radios throughout the Windy City, this pioneering "rookie" was also destined to debut with a bang and a flair rarely seen during three dark decades of South Side baseball that had followed the curse of the 1919-1920 Black Sox World Series scandals. And the castoff rookie did not disappoint. In his first at-bat for his new Chicago team Saturnino Orestes Armas Arrieta "Miñoso" ("Minnie" for short) pounded out a bullpen home run off Yankee ace Vic Raschi.

But the inescapable irony that plagued and often diminished almost every step of Miñoso's brilliant career was to saturate this glorious debut moment as well. Few baseball historians, it turns out, today point to May Day of 1951 as the watershed date of baseball integration for Chicago. Unfortunately for Miñoso and his fans, in the sixth inning of that contest future Hall-of-Famer and 1950s legend Mickey Mantle would blast his very first career roundtripper for the visiting New York Yankees. And to add further insult to injury for Chicagoans, it would be Miñoso, stationed at third base, who would let a Mantle grounder escape through his legs, giving the Yankees a lead which they would never relinquish that day. The error and the loss would soon enough disappear into baseball's endless cycles. It would be Mantle's debut homer, however, not Miñoso's, that would etch this particular date into the bedrock of baseball history.

This knack for inadvertently playing second fiddle on the baseball diamond would somehow become something of a hallmark of Miñoso's otherwise brilliant big-league sojourn. Miñoso was not only the first black to perform for a hometown club in Chicago – Sammy Hairston would be the first North American black, debuting with the Sox in July, and Ernie Banks would come along on the North Side in 1953 – but also (and more significantly) the very first indisputably "black" Cuban and "black" Latin American player to take his position on a big-league diamond. There were Cubans (Marsans, Almeida, Mike González), Puerto Ricans (Hi Bithorn, Luís Olmo Rodríguez), and Venezuelans (Alex Carrasquel) before him whose skin was dark enough to stir debate about violations of the gentlemen's agreement that cheapened the sport, but Miñoso was a pure black, like Martín Dihigo or José Méndez, and thus had only Jackie Robinson to thank for his "welcome" to the big leagues.

Yet it was nonetheless something of a misfortune that the Cuban Comet's debut in 1949 should have been with the Cleveland Indians, a team already featuring two headline-hogging blacks named Larry Doby and Satchel Paige. Doby earned the lion's share of notoriety as the first American-Leaguer to represent his race; and venerable Satchel Paige was a full-blown Negro-league legend who while far past his pitching prime, was as much a celebrity in Cleveland as he was everywhere else. Had Miñoso's debut been staged with any other junior-circuit club, it might have stirred far greater media and fan attention than it could have with Bill Veeck's already-integrated Cleveland Indians.

Miñoso's somewhat ill-timed debuts with the Indians and White Sox were only two disheartening foreshadowings of things to come. The Cuban sensation would parlay speed and daring on the base paths and in the outfield, along with power and clutch base hits at the plate, into a truly phenomenal rookie season. And yet it was a season doomed to be packed with little more than "second-best" accolades. At season's end, the colorful "colored" Chisox rookie would indeed be the league pacesetter in several lesser-noted categories such as stolen bases (31) and triples (14), but his brilliant batting mark of .326 (one of the highest ever for an "official" rookie) would fall second-best to Philadelphia's "Punch-and-Judy" hitting first sacker, Ferris Fain. His 112 runs scored also fell a single tally short of pacesetter Dom DiMaggio of the Boston Red Sox. But the biggest near-miss came at the ballot box. Although dubbed top rookie by the *Sporting News*, Miñoso would surprisingly finish only second in voting for a more prestigious baseball writers' rookie award. Winner Gil McDougald of the world champion New York Yankees had not only trailed Miñoso in all offensive categories save homers (where McDougald had a slim 14–10 edge) but finished a distant ninth in the same sportswriters' poll for league MVP. Miñoso placed only fourth for the latter award despite loud protests by all supporters of Chicago baseball.

It was the matter of pennant winning, however, that provided the epitome of Miñoso's career-long timing problems. His brief debut with the 1949 Indians came but a single spring after the rare Cleveland pennant-winning season of 1948. Moving on to Chicago in a blockbuster trade that opened the 1951 campaign, Miñoso would next be laboring in Chicago and not in Cleveland when the Indians soon charged to yet another league title flag three summers later. Then a second headline-grabbing trade between the 1957 and 1958 seasons would shuttle Miñoso back to Cleveland while ironically providing the Chicago White Sox with their own missing pennant ingredient in the form of Hall of Fame hurler Early "Gus" Wynn. Miñoso remained in a Cleveland uniform just long enough to miss the single Chicago pennant run in the final season of the decade. In a final bitter touch of irony from Miñoso's point of view, Cleveland GM Frank "Trader" Lane apparently engineered a deal that would have returned the Cuban outfielder to the Windy City in 1959 and just in time for the Comiskey Park pennant party. But Miñoso went on an ill-timed hitting tear the very week the deal was quietly being negotiated, and this sudden upswing in performance made even the trade-happy Lane fearful of a fan rebellion in Cleveland. The deal was postponed until the year-end league winter meetings and once again until after the opening of the new spring season.

The greatest irony of all surrounding Miñoso was that his "Go-Go" White Sox ballclub could transform the freewheeling base-running style brought orignally by Miñoso into a serious pennant challenge only after the inspired Cuban had been sent packing. Bill Veeck, Miñoso's original boss in Cleveland and new White Sox owner by 1959, worked to rectify the situation but was unable to reel Miñoso back to Chicago until after the American League pennant had been hoisted above Comiskey Park. Veeck would nonetheless charitably recognize Minnie's earlier contributions to the ballclub by presenting the newly reacquired Miñoso with an honorary (and well deserved) World Series ring. But it was little true consolation for the "Cuban Comet." While his former team, the Sox, had celebrated in the World Series of 1959, Minnie Miñoso was still an also-ran stuck back in the baseball wasteland of Cleveland.

Miñoso's full career (a career that stretched nearly 30 seasons in the majors, Cuba, and Mexico) would from beginning to end be marked by tantalizing near-miss brushes with the highest levels of diamond fame—painfully close encounters with achievement and celebrity far greater than what actually materialized. Here was the most colorful dark-skinned Cuban ballplayer of the post–Robinson integration years. Yet Miñoso's flashy style and dramatic flair translated into huge efforts at doing precisely what was needed to win ballgames for his team. He played with a reckless abandon aimed always at achieving nothing short of total victory; his was a flair with a clear work ethic. He stole bases with a game on the line, harassed pitchers with daring base-running ploys, took extra bases and made impossible wall-crashing catches. For this he was always appreciated by fans and teammates, yet never quite so celebrated as his equally flashy rival Vic Power of Puerto Rico.

The flamboyance of Vic Power was more tainted with staged showmanship, and usually a brand of showmanship that was more personal in performance and far less team oriented in impact. Thus Power drew a fanclub following from Kansas City to New York to Boston to Detroit, while Miñoso was far more quietly revered in the 1950s baseball wasteland that was Chicago. When today's middle-aged fans recall the 1950s of their youthful fandom, it is more likely to be Power who is first mentioned when the talk turns to early examples of unbridled Latin American big-league ballplaying enthusiasm.

In all this tendency to achieve much on the diamond yet always suffer the ultimate humiliation of never receiving true credit, Miñoso was seemingly only repeating a fate specially reserved for the earliest black-skinned ballplayers, those who poured from the Cuban cane fields and Puerto Rican barrios in the decades immediately before and after Jackie Robinson's debut with the Dodgers. Miñoso set the model that would motivate claims later voiced by Roberto Clemente: black Hispanic ballplayers never received their full due from managers, writers, teammates, fans, owners, or anyone else in the baseball establishment. Dihigo was the earliest prototype, robbed of a career in the big leagues by his skin color. Luís Tiant, Sr., Perucho Cepeda, and hundreds of others before Miñoso suffered equal ignominy. Miñoso would soon fully underscore the tradition, as would his friendly rival Vic Power (despite the latter's special cult-figure stature in the 1950s and early 1960s). And down the road, Clemente, Tony Oliva, and Orlando Cepeda would soon enough be equal victims under the heel of baseball's ongoing if now more subtle racism. Yet sometimes, as with Minnie Miñoso of the Go-Go Chicago White Sox, it all seemed just a matter of exceedingly poor timing.

One measure of the Latin ballplayer's often schizophrenic personality and ongoing identity crisis is the apparent frequency with which his North American fans forget, misapprehend or altogether butcher his proud family names. The greatest of Cuban players, Martín Dihigo, remained a name totally unknown to stateside fans for all the years of his brilliant career. Once Dihigo's name had been belatedly rescued from anonymity, it was just as likely to be mispronounced by uniformed stateside fans. The first name of this Hall-of-Famer is still more often than not pronounced with incorrect stress on the first syllable, as if it were English. The family name, on the other hand, likely proves unpronounceable on first encounter. This is not totally surprising when one of baseball's most glorified radio and television voices, Harry Caray, to this day makes humorous light of his frequent stumbles over Hispanic names like Vizcaino ("Vis-cane-oh" for Harry), Peña ("Pena"), Cedeño ("Cedeno"), Guillen (Caray never pronounces it the same way twice) and the like. No one, after all, ever had such difficulty with names like Yastrzemski, DiMaggio, Kluszewski, or even Lajoie.

While the name of Cuba's greatest preintegration diamond star seemed to have been altogether lost, two of the greats among the first post–Jackie Robinson black Latin big-leaguers suffered equal "name abuse" despite their newfound fame. Vic Power of Puerto Rico carried a false last name because his earliest pro-baseball contacts and local writers could not properly decipher (and thus pronounce) his mother's true name—Pellot. And Pedro Oliva of Cuba bore a false first name for equally ludicrous reasons—the need to substitute a brother's birth certificate when signing a first pro-baseball contract. Oliva had little wherewithal and less courage to correct the error in months that followed. For both Victor Pellot and Pedro Oliva, it was less trouble to assume a new name along with a new life in the big leagues than it was to insist that powerful strangers pay due respect to an old name and an old identity.

Minnie Miñoso, by sad contrast, carried with him neither a proper first nor last name when he arrived sensationally upon the big-league scene in the early 1950s. Born with the imposing title of Saturnino Orestes Arrieta Armas, Miñoso would much later volunteer in his entertaining autobiography (*Extra Innings: My Life in Baseball*, 1983) the true story behind his designation as Miñoso and not as Nino Armas. It was all a matter of mistaken identity back in Cuba. The young ballplayer's half brothers from his mother's first marriage were also his older teammates in earliest sandlot days, and it was they who were named Miñoso. Once the youngest member of the ballplaying family began attracting attention around his hometown Perico and throughout the wider province of Matanzas, he was naturally referred to by fans, scouts, and the press alike as Miñoso – an unavoidable confusion with his siblings. Once a reputation was earned, it was foolish indeed to spurn it, and thus by the time he hooked up with a semipro factory team in Havana, the name had stuck like glue. The budding young star quickly realized that to abandon his false name was also to abandon his small but vital ballplaying reputation and his diamond identity. Once the name was affixed in Cuba and among the big-league scouts, the young and insecure prospect was not about to torpedo his chances by abandoning it.

But what about the strange moniker "Minnie"? Here the surviving story seems to be altogether muddled. Even Miñoso cannot give an adequate accounting. First there is the story attributing the handle to Joe Gordon, the veteran Indian second sacker who reputedly hung the designation on his rookie teammate in the 1949 Cleveland spring-training camp. Others (though not Boudreau) contend that Lou Boudreau, Cleveland manager, first used the alliterative nickname with his young Cuban third baseman. Some have suggested that it was used in the Cleveland camp as a shorter and easier form of Miñoso; others that it referred to a smallish ballplayer who was under six feet. Then there is Miñoso's shadowy story of a visit to a Chicago dentist's office. Miñoso suggests (in *Extra Innings*) that he heard his dentist calling to someone named Minnie, and thought he was being addressed when it was the doctor's receptionist who was being hailed. This would in no way account for how the colorful name quickly spread among Chicago fans and Miñoso watchers around the league. As with the best of baseball legends, all parties seemed early on to have adopted a tacit conspiracy of silence on the matter. Whatever the truth, the fictions and fantasies seemed better still.

Whatever they called him, American League fans were soon in love with Saturnino Orestes Armas Arrieta "Minnie" Miñoso. Larry Doby, the American League's first black pioneer, possessed a stable temperament that made him far more like Jackie Robinson's teammate Roy Campanella – a quiet revolutionary determined to lead by strong silent slugging and soft-spoken clubhouse diplomacy. Miñoso – Doby's teammate for a brief spell in 1949 and the first black to grace the roster of the Chicago White Sox when traded there two seasons later – burned instead with Robinson's dignified fire. The "Cuban Comet" also burned up the American League base paths with three consecutive stolen-base titles (1951–1953) in an age when base speed was of little premium and rarely an offensive strategy of preference. The flashy style he brought to the game was guaranteed to cement Miñoso's reputation with fair-minded fans, just as it would further fan the

Minnie Miñoso's Latin American and Winter-League Batting Record

Mexican League (Summer)

	Club	G	AB	R	H	2B	3B	HR	RBI	B.A.
1965	Jalisco	134	469	*106*	169	*35*	10	14	82	.360
1966	Jalisco	107	376	70	131	18	1	6	45	.348
1967	Orizaba	36	100	20	35	7	3	5	19	.350
	Jalisco	13	37	5	9	1	2	0	3	.243
1968	Puerto Mexico	56	145	30	53	17	2	4	23	.366
	Jalisco	22	54	9	16	5	1	2	13	.296
1969	Puerto Mexico	74	193	33	58	10	2	2	32	.301
	Jalisco	36	103	18	33	3	1	2	14	.320
1970	Gómez Palacio	40	47	6	22	6	0	2	17	.468
1971	Gómez Palacio	112	336	37	106	15	2	6	57	.315
1972	Gómez Palacio	181	425	48	121	24	1	12	63	.285
1973	Gómez Palacio	120	407	50	108	15	1	12	83	.265
Totals	9 Seasons	931	2,692	432	861	156	26	67	451	.320

Italics = League Leader

Cuban League (Winter)

	Club	G	AB	R	H	2B	3B	HR	RBI	B.A.
1945-46	Marianao*	37	143	14	42	7	2	0	13	.294
1946-47	Marianao	64	253	36	63	9	5	0	20	.249
1947-48	Marianao	70	270	43	77	15	13**	1	36	.285
1948-49	Marianao	69	260	42	69	8	5	4	27	.265
1949-50	Did Not Play	----	----	----	----	----	----	----	----	----
1950-51	Marianao	66	252	54	81	12	6	4	41	.321
1951-52	Marianao	42	144	19	39	6	1	2	10	.271
1952-53	Marianao	71	266	67**	87	9	5	13	42	.327
1953-54	Marianao	47	176	25	52	9	3	9	36	.295
1954-55	Did Not Play	----	----	----	----	----	----	----	----	----
1955-56	Marianao	64	252	47	69	10	3	8	35	.274
1956-57	Marianao	50	218	40	68	13	3	7	38	.312
1957-58	Marianao	58	238	37	60	9	1	8	34	.252
1958-59	Marianao	55	223	33	60	8	1	5	25	.269
1959-60	Marianao	45	169	25	39	3	2	4	23	.231
1960-61	Marianao	35	128	12	32	7	1	1	12	.250
Totals	14 Seasons	773	2,992	494	838	125	51	66	392	.280

* = Rookie of the Year
** = Cuban League record

flames of hatred among those spectators and opponents who could not stand to see such a flashy black man upstaging everyone else on the field.

Shortened by the color barrier, which robbed him of perhaps five productive early-career seasons, Miñoso's 17-year big-league numbers today fall slightly short of Cooperstown standards in most eyes. He won stolen-base titles but never copped a hitting crown; he fell short of 2,000 base hits (though only by a handful); his career batting average in the end was also a hair's breadth under the magic .300 level. Yet Minnie might stand as one of the greatest stars of all time if his total statistics in organized baseball were summed into a single listing. That is in part because Miñoso's seemingly endless career continued in the Mexican League for nearly 10 more summers (well beyond the age of 50) after his regular big-league tenure had ended in 1964. The records earned in Mexico and on the winter circuit are rarely seen by today's students of big-league history but are enough to nail down a certain measure of immortality.

Refusing to admit the encroachment of natural aging, Miñoso appeared back in the big time once more in 1976 and again in 1980 for cameo appearances with the White Sox, making him the second-oldest big-leaguer ever (Satchel Paige was probably 59 when he took the mound for three innings with Kansas City in 1965) and only the second player (Nick Altrock was the first) to don a major league uniform in five decades. In the second of his three 1976 game appearances Miñoso would collect his final base hit—a big-league record at the age of 54.

Some belittle these late-career cameos as shameless publicity stunts. Even the ballplayers of the 1993 American League champion Chicago White Sox reportedly balked when rumors were circulated that the ageless Cuban would achieve six-decade status with a late-season pinch-hitting appearance at 71. Several White Sox players commented to an eager press corps that any such appearance by the grandfatherly Miñoso would certainly weaken the game's integrity. In the spirit of team cooperation that always marked his every onfield and off-field move, Minnie Miñoso quickly informed club officials that he had no intention of tarnishing the image of the game he so loved.

However, if Minnie Miñoso's recent baseball decades have been filled with joyous enthusiasm and marked with an infectious spirit of internationl goodwill, his early lot in the majors was every bit as rough as that known by Robinson, Doby, Campanella, and numerous other black pioneers. Miñoso was an immediate favorite with hometown fans during debut seasons in Cleveland and Chicago, but he was nonetheless taunted mercilessly by opposing rooters and rival dugouts. It has been widely reported (by Miñoso and by former teammates) that opposing manager Jimmy Dykes of Philadelphia regularly indulged a favored pastime of releasing a black dog on the dugout steps every time the dark-skinned Miñoso appeared

Minnie Miñoso's Composite Professional Batting Numbers

		G	AB	R	H	2B	3B	HR	RBI	B.A.
Majors	17 Seasons	1,830	6,589	1,136	1,962	336	83	186	1,023	.299
Minors	3 Seasons	369	1,349	265	429	77	18	47	217	.318
Mexico	9 Seasons	931	2,692	432	861	156	26	67	451	.320
Cuba	14 Seasons	773	2,992	494	838	125	51	66	392	.280
Totals	43 Seasons	3,903	13,622	2,327	4,090	694	178	366	2,083	.300

in the visiting team on-deck circle. And the vicious racial epithets that flew constantly had to be endured with the same bravery as a life-threatening Bob Feller and Early Wynn fastball.

If Miñoso was often overlooked, overshadowed, and just plain underappreciated throughout his lengthy baseball career, he certainly left a mark that was difficult to deny for long. In a career that seemed to stretch on and on without pause on both sides of the Caribbean, Miñoso finally overwhelmed his critics and naysayers with mere longevity and the weight of amassed ballplaying numbers. Combine his big-league career with those in Cuba and Mexico, and few ever played so long or so well.

But it is for his sensational rookie year that Miñoso is best remembered. Throughout a sensational first full-time summer, the nearly middle-aged rookie tore up the American League, inspired a climb in the standings for the longtime doormat White Sox, and single-handedly put Cuban baseball on the big-league map. By season's end, he had defined a new age of hit-and-run daredevil baseball in the Windy City and revived a long-slumbering baseball franchise in the process. The Chicago White Sox were a sixth-place ballclub in 1950, as they had been in 1949 and 1947 (they finished dead last in 1948). After Miñoso came on the scene with his rookie explosion of 1951, the same club climbed to fourth (their first time in the first division in a full decade), then nestled into a comfortable position as a pennant contender with five-straight third-place finishes. If Minnie Miñoso was not there to finish the pennant drive in 1959, he was clearly the one who more than any other launched the once-hapless ballclub to full recovery after four decades of debilitating "Black Sox" swoon.

Miñoso is most recognizable in our memories for his hustling style of play. None ever hustled more in a big-league uniform – not even Pepper Martin or Pete Rose. And none played with more dedication to the twin tasks of winning ballgames and entertaining the fans. Minnie's motto always seemed to be "hit or get hit," and he crowded the batter's box determined never to give the slightest quarter. A pitch from Detroit's Frank Lary once cracked his jaw and loosened all his teeth, yet Miñoso characteristically demanded to finish out the inning as a lively base runner. For a half-dozen years from 1956 through 1961 it was Miñoso who would regularly pace the junior circuit in the number of times hit by a pitch. If this was his most inglorious big-league record, it was also a record that most accurately reflected the hell-bent and fearless style with which he always played every game.

But the flair of his style and the energy of his play today seem buried under an avalanche of press clippings concerning yet another aspect of Miñoso's storied career—his exceptional longevity. For if Miñoso was aptly dubbed "The Cuban Comet," a daring meteor flashing across the base paths, he was hardly a momentary heavenly body for the continuing glow of his endless diamond career. Here is baseball's unique five-decade ballplayer. If Miñoso played in only slightly more than 15 big-league campaigns it must be remembered that Cuban and Negro-league tours plus two full years in the Pacific Coast League preceded his debut and that a decade of Mexican League play stretched out after his last full big-league summer. Count winter-league seasons as well, and Miñoso took the field for an amazing total of 43 baseball campaigns. Never has a baseball player proved more durable.

Yet this longevity somehow tarnishes Miñoso in many fans' eyes. Were not these final appearances, after all, little more than outrageous Bill Veeck–engineered promotional gimmicks? Did not the aging athlete, a mere shell of his dashing earlier self, take the field merely to pack grandstands with his popularity and shamelessly sell tickets for a struggling franchise in trouble at the ticket counter? It is unfortunate, to say the least, that this circuslike aspect of his later career has cast such long shadows over the brilliance of Miñoso's tireless performance in the first decade of his big-league sojourn.

Miñoso remains one of baseball's most beloved figures and best goodwill ambassadors, especially in the dual-league city of Chicago. For years he has been a familiar face almost everywhere on the Chicago baseball scene. If Miñoso once sold White Sox ducats with his flashy base running and thunderous slugging, then later promoted the ballclub in leaner days with the magnetism of his ageless presence, he now provides much-needed public relations with his infectious smile, endless baseball stories, and irrepressible love for the game of his youth and his middle age. Annually he makes the rounds for the Chicago ballclub, entertaining youth groups, senior citizens, and civic and business groups throughout the Chicago area. Never was baseball more in need of such an ambassador than in this present epoch, an era when big-league players have been so distanced from rooters by astronomical salaries, the impersonal nature of televised baseball, and the inevitable commercialism that has descended on America's national pastime. Minnie Miñoso never won a pennant for Chicago; yet like Ernie

Banks on the city's North Side, he continues to bring more priceless prizes to the city's baseball-loving youth—love for the game and for those who perform its magic.

In the end, Miñoso has never seemed to receive the full notice he deserved. In this tragic sense, the meteoric ballplaying career of one of Cuba's greatest major-leaguers is somehow reduced to little more than a bright comet flashing through the star-filled baseball heavens. In this sense, then, one of baseball's most colorful nicknames remains doubly appropriate. Chicago fans often bemoan the absence of Nellie Fox from Cooperstown as a grave injustice. But Miñoso arguably deserves to be there even more. The career numbers would certainly argue this way, especially when the 16 full seasons of Fox are compared with Miñoso's 11 campaigns. And when it comes to ground-breaking achievement and pioneering influence, Miñoso is head and shoulders above his teammate Fox.

It is indeed ironic, yet not surprising, that Minnie Miñoso receives so little Hall of Fame support from his Chicago fans while teammate Nellie Fox draws so many cries of "injustice" each season when passed over by Cooperstown's Veterans Committee. While an excellent clutch player and standby of the Go-Go Sox during the Paul Richards and Al Lopez era, Fox was hardly more a fan favorite at the time, nor did he provide the inspiration and hell-bent style responsible for the team's lasting go-go reputation. Fox and Miñoso also boast career statistics (offensive and defensive) roughly comparable. But this is only the final injustice. None loved the game more than the Cuban who was Latin America's first black star on the big-league scene. None gave the game more of himself. And none could have been less concerned about the slights that have been aimed his way. ("I never look for anything," Miñoso today recounts. "I only do my duty and offer my friendship to everyone.") Yet none got back so little of what he deserved. None was a more infectious and more ceaselessly joyful ambassador of the game. If there were a hall of fame for selfless champions of the game, Miñoso would have owned the first pedestal, smack in the entryway.

There is a special fascination with the truly versatile ballplayer. Baseball is not a game for specialists; the true diamond hero hits with power or at least precision, possesses a glue-filled glove and a riflelike throwing arm, runs the base paths with abandon. It is for this reason more than all others that traditionalists among today's fans abhor the designated hitter. Ballplayers who can perform efficiently at multiple positions often capture fans' hearts and managers' eternal gratitude.

No truly versatile ballplayers have been more plentiful and noteworthy than the Latin big-leaguers. Only two men have ever played all nine positions in a single "official" big-league game, and both were Latins. First, Bert

Campaneris turned the trick (September 9, 1965) in one of Charlie Finley's notorious publicity stunts with the Kansas City Athletics; later, César Tóvar of the Minnesota Twins would imitate Campaneris (September 22, 1968) with his own inning-by-inning whirlwind around the diamond. Admittedly, these were both publicity stunts designed to entertain fans of also-ran ballclubs. Yet Tóvar was truly versatile and played regularly at four positions (outfield, third, second, and short) while leading the junior circuit in 1967 game appearances. (Tóvar was also a clutch batsman who broke up more no-hitters, five, than any other batter in baseball history.) Campaneris was equally comfortable at any of the infield slots (exclusive of first base) and occasionally saw outfield duty in a pinch. The nine-position single-game feats of these two Latin utilitymen may have been more showmanship than anything else, yet no other ballplayers in history have ever been up to the task.

There is another Latin ballplayer, however, who stands in a class by himself for defensive versatility. Imagine a ballplayer who played all positions (all but one) not as a once-in-a-lifetime stunt but an everyday occurrence. And imagine such a ballplayer being praised by famous rivals and teammates alike for his unparalleled mastery at each position. Imagine such a ballplayer and you have Martín Dihigo, baseball's greatest all-around Negro-leaguer and in the eyes of many old-timers the best ballplayer ever. Little wonder that Cubans long called him "The Immortal" and far and wide – in the Dominican Republic, Mexico, Puerto Rico, Venezuela, and on the Negro-league diamonds of Chicago, New York, Pittsburgh, and Kansas City – he was known simply as "The Maestro" in tribute to his on-field grace, star quality, and unrivaled technical knowledge of the game.

It is reported that Dihigo (pronounced "*Dee*-go") often showed off his all-around skill by taking a turn at all nine positions in numerous Negro-league contests. In a career that stretched to a quarter century in Cuba and included at least a dozen Mexican winter seasons and 14 Negro-league campaigns (1923–1936) the black Cuban giant was most dominant as a pitcher. His mound credentials would eventually include no-hitters in three countries (Mexico, Venezuela, and Puerto Rico), a documented 119-57 Mexican League record (18-2, 0.90 ERA in 1938), a 93-48 record over his last dozen Cuban seasons (1935–1946), a 218-106 (.673) winter-league and Negro-league ledger in games officially documented, and perhaps dozens of more victories lost to history through shoddy record keeping that marked the barnstorming circuits. As a hitter he was equally devastating on the opposition: a .317 lifetime average in Mexico, where he paced the circuit at .387 in 1938 (the same season as his 0.90 ERA upon the mound); 9 seasons of documented .300 hitting in his native Cuba; more than 130 career homers, with more than 11 seasons for which his home-run numbers are entirely missing. While the numbers of hits and pitching victories were never very well recorded for Martín Dihigo the anecdotal evidence for his greatness is often overwhelming. Stories abound of the Cuban's flaming fastball, his deadly throwing arm, his fence-rattling lumber, and his rare grace at virtually every position except catcher.

Such documented testimonies to Dihigo's versatility and greatness are legion and make impressive reading. Negro-league great Buck Leonard leads the parade of those who spoke reverently (when interviewed by John Holway, *Blackball Stars*, 244) of Dihigo as the game's greatest all-around talent. Leonard was unequivocal: "He was the greatest all-around player I know. I'd say he was the best ballplayer of all time, black or white. . . . If he's not the greatest I don't know who is. You take your Ruths, Cobbs, and DiMaggios. Give me Dihigo. I bet I would beat you almost every time." And Leonard's blackball sidekicks agreed almost to a man. When surviving former Negro-leaguers were polled in the early 1980s regarding an all-time Negro-league lineup, it was Dihigo who wound up as the second baseman of choice. His selection was all the more remarkable, however, when one considers that numerous ballots were cast for The Maestro at two other positions—outfield and third base.

Dihigo did not begin as a player of such remarkable skill, but raw talent was observed from the outset. He learned the game as an eager teenager when taken under the wing of black barnstorming greats (especially Oscar Charleston and John Henry Lloyd) visiting Cuba at the close of the World War I era. As a 17-year-old rookie of little polish with the powerhouse Havana Reds, the tall skinny kid from Matanzas (a two-hour cart ride from Havana) would bat an anemic .179 and hold his roster spot only by gaudy displays of defensive potential. A first trip northward with Alex Pompez's Cuban Stars in 1923 dramatically demonstrated two things about the lanky youngster to all who saw him play at second and short. You simply could not hit a ball by him in the infield and it was easy to throw almost any curveball right past the overanxious youngster when he was in the batter's box. His speed and range around second base drew highest praise from most sportswriters on the blackball circuit, and despite weak hitting he was quickly hailed as the best Cuban import since José Méndez.

At first his impact as a Negro-leaguer was minimal due to befuddlement in the face of the teasing curveball. But the slow start did not last long for a player of such natural talent, dedication, and willingness to correct his defects. In a few years Dihigo was one of the true greats of Negro-league play. Diligently practicing his timing against the curveball delivery of batting-practice hurlers, Dihigo was soon pushing his batting average skyward. In two years he would hit .301, and in two more his mark would climb to .331 (along with a league-best 18 homers) in the Negro-league circuit.

Yet Dihigo did not restrict his baseball challenges to North American

Negro-league play nor merely to hitting and fielding the baseball for a living. Soon he was tearing up Mexican league clubs. And he was doing so as a dominating moundsman and airtight infield defender and part-time outfielder with a throwing arm that veteran Negro-leaguer Ted Page would later call even better than Clemente's. It was in Mexico that Dihigo would first prove his special prowess as a pitching wonder, hurling the league's first recorded no-hitter (in 1937) and establishing its all-time standards for single-season ERA and lifetime winning percentage. Yet the conversion to pitching meant no slacking off in other aspects of his balanced game. The late 1920s and early 1930s saw Dihigo's winter-league batting averages in his native Cuba soar from .300 to .344 to .415 to .450. In one remarkable individual performance the black Cuban giant would nip out teammate Willie Wells for a Cuban-league batting title by registering a five-for-five outing on the season's final day, a shade better than Wells's four-for-four in the same ballgame.

Despite a fastball that was often compared with that of Satchel Paige, it was as a hitter that Dihigo was always the greatest threat. Blackball historian John Holway has reasonably ranked Dihigo among the greatest of all blackball sluggers, season after season. And some of Dihigo's hitting feats border on the legendary. Holway cites one former blackball ace reporting a Dihigo line drive that nearly decapitated a paralyzed shortstop and scorched against the outfield fence before the amazed defender could raise his hands in defense. The skinny kid who arrived with the Cuban Stars looking like Marty Marion soon filled out and developed wrists seen since only on Ernie Banks and Hank Aaron. He regularly led the Cuban circuit in roundtrippers in ballparks where the outfield fences were a long pony ride from home plate. While ballpark size and a short league schedule might today diminish the impact of Dihigo's raw hitting numbers, Holway's reconstructed blackball record for the Cuban great makes impressive reading by almost any standard.

When playing days finally faded for the ageless Cuban, Dihigo had other baseball challenges to conquer and other immense contributions to make. As a player-manager, he piloted teams to league championships in Cuba (1936, 1937), Venezuela (1953), and Mexico (1942), and managed the 1953 Venezuelan entry in Caribbean World Series play. A cheery personality and considerable facility with English made Dihigo equally popular with Negro-leaguers, native Hispanics, and big-leaguers seeking winter-league experience. It has been claimed that it was Dihigo's immense popularity (as well as the pure fun of playing for the easygoing bench boss) that attracted the large number of blackball stars who made their winter diamond homes in Cuba during the 1930s and 1940s. Each time a new Negro-league great inherited his rightful spot as "greatest ever" at a new slot on the diamond – say, Satchel Paige on the mound, Oscar Charleston in the

Dihigo's Lost Blackball Statistics
(estimated by John Holway)

Year	Club	G	AB	H	2B	3B	HR	BA	W-L	ERA
1922	Cuba	NA	28	5	NA	NA	NA	.179	NA	NA
1923	NY Cubans (NL)	12	48	11	NA	NA	NA	.230	1-1	NA
----	Cuba	1	2	0	0	0	0	.000	2-3	NA
1924	NY Cubans (NL)	32	132	31	1	0	0	.235	1-1	NA
----	Cuba	27	50	15	5	3	3	.300	2-3	NA
1925	NY Cubans (NL)	28	96	28	3	1	2	.292	4-7	NA
----	Cuba	9	32	11	3	2	1	.334	0-0	NA
1926	NY Cubans (NL)	40	169	55	8	3	*11*	.325	NA	NA
----	Cuba	27	95	40	4	1	3	.421	3-0	NA
1927	NY Cubans (NL)	61	246	77	3	1	*12*	.313	1-0	NA
----	Cuba	33	130	54	12	3	2	.415	4-2	NA
1928	Homestead (NL)	5	20	4	1	0	0	.200	0-1	NA
----	Cuba	NA	152	46	NA	NA	NA	.303	2-1	NA
1929	Philadelphia (NL)	23	79	24	2	0	5	.304	4-2	NA
----	Cuba	NA	180	51	NA	NA	NA	.282	1-2	NA
1930	Philadelphia (NL)	14	60	26	1	2	6	.434	--	--
1931	Philadelphia (NL)	65	245	65	2	3	5	.265	1-1	NA
----	Cuba	NA	49	16	2	0	0	.327	--	--
1933	Venezuela	--	--	--	--	--	--	--	6-0	0.15
1935	NY Cubans (NL)	46	161	52	11	4	*9*	.323	6-2	NA
----	Cuba	47	176	63	NA	NA	NA	.358	11-2	NA
1936	NY Cubans (NL)	28	92	36	9	1	11	*.391*	5-3	NA
----	Cuba	69	229	74	NA	NA	NA	.323	14-10	NA
1937	Mexico	7	28	10	1	2	1	.357	4-0	0.93
----	Dominican Rep.	25	97	34	6	2	4	.351	--	--
----	Cuba	52	165	50	NA	NA	NA	.303	11-5	NA
1938	Mexico	42	142	55	8	2	6	*.387*	18-2	*0.90*
----	Cuba	NA	145	37	NA	NA	NA	.255	14-2	NA
1939	Mexico	51	187	63	11	3	5	.336	15-8	2.87
----	Cuba	NA	79	23	NA	NA	NA	.291	6-4	NA
1940	Mexico	78	302	110	17	6	9	.364	8-6	3.54
----	Cuba	NA	110	20	NA	NA	NA	.182	8-3	NA
1941	Mexico	92	329	102	25	4	12	.310	9-10	4.01
----	Cuba	NA	123	28	6	0	1	.228	8-3	NA
1942	Mexico	85	279	89	12	4	8	.319	22-7	*2.53*
----	Cuba	NA	135	36	NA	NA	NA	.267	4-8	NA
1943	Mexico	75	238	66	14	3	7	.277	16-8	3.10
----	Cuba	NA	87	22	NA	NA	NA	.253	8-1	2.23
1944	Mexico	60	189	47	10	2	4	.249	12-10	3.14

Dihigo's Lost Blackball Statistics, *cont.*

Year	Club	G	AB	H	2B	3B	HR	BA	W-L	ERA
----	Cuba	NA	110	20	NA	NA	NA	.182	3-3	3.84
1945	NY Cubans (NL)	17	54	11	0	0	3	.204	1-2	NA
----	Cuba	34	71	16	3	0	0	.225	5-4	NA
1946	Mexico	66	177	56	9	2	3	.316	11-4	2.83
----	Cuba	15	10	1	0	0	0	.100	1-3	10.80
1947	Mexico	20	46	9	3	1	0	.196	4-2	4.37
Totals	24 Years	NA	5,374	1,689	192	55	133	.304	256-136	NA

NA = not available.
Italics = league leader.
(NL) = Negro leagues.

outfield, Judy Johnson at third, or Buck Leonard at first—it was common practice to note that the new immortal had no parallel at his chosen position except the immortal Dihigo.

For a while he even tried his hand successfully at umpiring in his native Cuba. And in the final years of his life there is evidence that his activities as Castro's first official minister of sports helped establish a rich and still-thriving baseball tradition throughout the now-isolated Cuban nation. Dihigo's statue as a national hero in Cuba was so elevated by the time Castro seized power that El Maestro was the natural choice to lead the communist dictator's newly organized socialistic sports program despite the fact that Dihigo had earlier been a personal favorite of ousted strongman Fulgencio Batista.

Of course, all this was never enough to bring Dihigo into the baseball limelight of the North American big leagues. He was born with the wrong skin color and raised in the wrong decade for such a dream. If there was an ironic appropriateness to Miñoso's moniker ("The Comet," whose fame burned bright yet all too briefly), there is an equal irony in the nickname "The Maestro." Ultimately, Dihigo's contributions would receive only tardy recognition with his enshrinement in Cooperstown as a onetime Negro-league great. Long before Cooperstown recognition, the Cuban legend had been "officially" sanctioned as a Hall-of-Famer in his homeland and Mexico. He thus remains baseball's only three-nation hall-of-fame hero. Yet The Maestro would never have a chance to work his artistry on the grandest stages of all, the American League or National League ballparks. He played a rich diamond music that fell upon the deaf ears of a white-oriented sports press. His concert halls always lay far off the beaten baseball paths.

Thus the true tragedy of Dihigo's exclusion from the white major leagues is impossible not to recognize—legendary status and belated hall-of-fame enshrinements aside. Beyond all else there was the loss for two generations of white fans of seeing him play. There was the absence of a Dihigo on the major league mound in legendary combat with Bob Feller or Dizzy Dean; or perhaps Dihigo roaming the same outfield with a young DiMaggio or plugging the same infield with Marty Marion, Luke Appling, or Billy Herman. Dihigo would never know the sweet taste of glory that might have been his in a big-league arena. And for a game so soaked in historical records and fed by statistical documentation, the unarguable numbers by which each hero is measured are in this case simply not there for our latter-day perusal. Attempts have been made by blackball historians like John Holway and Cuban historians like Angel Torres to set the record straight with reconstructed statistical data. Yet the incompleteness and inconsistencies of their efforts only raise further doubts and arguments where they should document the glory of a true immortal. A brief comparison of Holway's career numbers for Dihigo (above) with those of Torres (below) dramatically underscores this point.

Minnie Miñoso's childhood baseball idol, not surprisingly, was Cuban Negro-leaguer Martín Dihigo. Both hailed from the Matanzas province, and both would travel a similar pathway through racial harassment to eventual baseball stardom. Miñoso has often recorded his debt to the idol of all who knew the heyday of Cuban baseball: "Dihigo once let me carry his shoes and glove and that's how I got into the ball park down there when I was a kid. He was a big man, all muscle with not an ounce of fat on him. He helped me by teaching me how to play properly. When I played a few years in the Negro leagues, with the New York Cubans, Dihigo was past his prime and just a manager then, so I never really competed against him as a player. But it is difficult to explain what a great hero he was in Cuba. Everywhere he went he was recognized and mobbed for autographs. I'd have to say he was most responsible for me getting to the major leagues. He was a big man, but he was big in all ways, as a player, as a manager, as a teacher, as a man."

In Miñoso's own eloquent words, it is virtually impossible, especially in today's world crammed with instant celebrities but void of lasting heroes, to understand just how large a national treasure Dihigo was in the small baseball-crazed nation of Cuba. Here was a disadvantaged youth from Miñoso's cane-field background of poverty who had somehow ignored all disadvantage to achieve ultimate hero status. The reasons for Miñoso's choice of hero are therefore quite obvious. The irony, perhaps quite unapparent to Miñoso in his youth or even at his career's end, was just how alike their parallel careers were.

Conditions of his birth cast a cruel fate for the baseball-loving Martín Dihigo. Miñoso was the ironic recipient of seemingly better timing. Yet the

Dihigo's Incomplete Cuban Statistics

(compiled by Angel Torres)

Cuban Batting Record (Incomplete as shown)

Year	Club	G	AB	R	H	2B	3B	HR	RBI	B.A.
1922-23	Havana	NA	28	3	5	NA	NA	NA	NA	.179
1923-24	Almendares	1	2	0	0	0	0	0	0	.000
1924-25	Havana	27	50	12	15	3	3	1	NA	.300
1925-26	Havana	9	32	11	11	3	2	1	NA	.344
1926-27	Havana	22	75	20	31	4	1	3	NA	.413
----------	Marianao	5	20	8	9	NA	NA	NA	NA	.450
1927-28	Havana	33	130	32	54	12	3	2	NA	.415
1928-29	Havana	NA	152	29	46	NA	NA	NA	NA	.303
1929-30	Almendares	NA	180	23	51	NA	NA	NA	NA	.282
1930-31	Did Not Play									
1931-32	Almendarista	NA	39	5	13	NA	NA	NA	NA	.333
----------	Almendares	3	10	2	3	2	0	0	0	.300
1932-33	Did Not Play									
1933-34	Season Cancelled									
1934-35	Did Not Play									
1935-36	Santa Clara	47	176	42	63	NA	NA	NA	38	.358
1936-37	Marianao	69	229	38	74	NA	NA	NA	34	.323
1937-38	Marianao	52	165	21	50	NA	NA	NA	28	.303
1938-39	Havana	NA	145	24	37	NA	NA	NA	12	.255
1939-40	Cienfuegos	NA	79	10	23	NA	NA	NA	17	.291
1940-41	Havana	NA	110	16	20	NA	NA	NA	5	.182
1941-42	Havana	NA	123	19	28	6	0	1	7	.228
1942-43	Havana	NA	135	14	36	NA	NA	NA	17	.267
1943-44	Havana	NA	87	11	22	NA	NA	NA	17	.253
1944-45	Havana	NA	29	3	6	NA	NA	NA	3	.207
1945-46	Cienfuegos	34	71	9	16	3	0	0	8	.225
1946-47	Cienfuegos	15	10	0	1	0	0	0	2	.100
Totals	21 Seasons	317	2,077	352	614	33	9	8	188	.296

NA = not available.

Cuban Pitching Record (Incomplete as shown)

Year	Club	G	CG	W	L	Pct.	IP	SO	BB	ERA
1923-24	Almendares	20	1	2	3	.400	NA	NA	NA	NA
1924-25	Havana	20	1	2	3	.400	NA	NA	NA	NA
1925-26	Havana	1	0	0	0	.000	NA	NA	NA	NA
1926-27	Havana	2	1	2	0	1.000	NA	3	0	NA

Year	Club	G	CG	W	L	Pct.	IP	SO	BB	ERA
----------	Marianao	1	0	1	0	1.000	NA	NA	NA	NA
1927-28	Havana	6	5	4	2	.667	NA	NA	NA	NA
1928-29	Havana	5	2	2	1	.667	NA	NA	NA	NA
1929-30	Almendares	3	2	1	2	.333	NA	NA	NA	NA
1930-31	Did Not Play									
1931-32	Almendarista	2	2	2	0	1.000	NA	NA	NA	NA
----------	Almendares	Played only as infielder								
1932-33	Did Not Play									
1933-34	Season Cancelled									
1934-35	Did Not Play									
1935-36	Santa Clara	18	13	11	2	.846	NA	NA	NA	NA
1936-37	Marianao	30	22	14	10	.583	NA	NA	NA	NA
1937-38	Marianao	20	12	11	5	.688	NA	NA	NA	NA
1938-39	Havana	21	14	14	2	.875	NA	NA	NA	NA
1939-40	Cienfuegos	19	9	6	4	.600	NA	NA	NA	NA
1940-41	Havana	13	10	8	3	.727	NA	NA	NA	NA
1941-42	Havana	17	11	8	3	.727	NA	NA	NA	NA
1942-43	Havana	14	7	4	8	.333	NA	NA	NA	NA
1943-44	Havana	15	4	8	1	.889	72.2	29	30	2.23
1944-45	Havana	13	2	3	3	.500	61	18	30	3.84
1945-46	Cienfuegos	17	4	5	4	.556	NA	31	46	NA
1946-47	Cienfuegos	8	0	1	3	.250	16.2	13	16	10.80
Totals	20 Seasons	265	122	109	59	.649	NA	NA	NA	NA

NA = not available.

Angel Torres, *La Historia del Béisbol Cubano*, "The Story of Cuban Baseball" (Los Angeles, California [self-published volume], 1976), 119.

---

question may well be raised which of the two suffered more severely in the face of contrasting circumstances. Dihigo was barred from the big-league fields with their promise of limitless fame and fortune. Yet he enjoyed the lengthy status of national baseball idol in Cuba and played for decades in relaxing sunshine and high-spirited integrated leagues throughout the Caribbean basin. He knew little of racial prejudice firsthand and suffered far less mistreatment outside big-league ballparks. For Miñoso, the doors had swung open to big-league forutne, yet it must have seemed at times as though he had been thrown from the frying pan into the blistering fire.

Nearly a decade after Jackie Robinson had reputedly silenced baseball's bigotry, Minnie Miñoso would continue to suffer painful harassment and endless taunting as he attempted to play the game he loved. It would take an extraordinary man, one like the legendary Robinson himself, to bear up under such pressures and withstand such vitriol from his fellow athletes. For several seasons beyond his Chicago rookie campaign Miñoso would be condemned to ignore as well as he could the merciless taunts of Jimmy Dykes and other managers and rival ballplayers. Jimmy Dykes had once been a ballplaying hero himself in Chicago (Dykes managed the White Sox during the lean Depression and World War II seasons) and valued his Windy City reputation enough to mute his attacks against the popular Miñoso on those occasions when the Philadelphia A's visited Comiskey Park. Ballplayers and fans in rival cities like Philadelphia, St. Louis, Baltimore, and Boston were not so averse to such ruthless intolerance.

Dykes was a special thorn, and even the otherwise placid Miñoso has eventually spoken out in recent years about the vicious treatment he received at the hands of the Philadelphia Athletics skipper. It was treatment paralleling that meted out in the City of Brotherly Love against Robinson by Phillies skipper Ben Chapman only a handful of seasons earlier. In one disgraceful incident tensions were apparently especially high after Dykes revealed publicly that he had ordered pitcher Mario Fricano to fire the baseball directly at Miñoso's head (more precisely, the manager's order was to "hit that black so-and-so squarely in the head"). Finding caution the better part of valor, Chisox skipper Paul Richards promptly offered his Cuban star a full day off for a doubleheader engagement at Shibe Park. Richards simply did not want to risk the safety of his club leader in light of Dykes's unpredictable behavior and irrational threats. A fearless Miñoso was resolute, however, in his desire to stay in the lineup. "If you take me out now," Miñoso pleaded, "next time they will actually try to kill me." Nothing would get the best of Miñoso's manly Cuban pride. Nothing would get in the way of a team victory either, especially not the fear of physical intimidation.

Raised in more racially open Cuba, Miñoso was at first shocked by what he saw during Negro-league and minor league seasons in North America. He and three black teammates (Connie Johnson, Bob Boyd, and Sam Hairston) were banned from one spring-training exhibition contest at Memphis (in March 1953) by local laws prohibiting integrated athletics anywhere in public facilities. On his arrival at a first minor league stop in Dayton, Ohio, the Cuban Comet batted above .500 during a brief appearance at season's end only to have some of the local fans cancel their season tickets as a direct result of his presence. It was Silvio García, the Cuban legend bypassed by Branch Rickey in 1946 and with whom Minnie roomed when playing for the New York Cubans, upon whom Miñoso leaned most heavily for his early support and to whom he turned for his early education in baseball and racial tolerance. But most of all it was Minnie's total involvement in the game he passionately loved that allowed him to ignore these painful distractions and concentrate on entertaining ballpark patrons.

And there was the ever-cheerful personality that allowed the popular ballplayer always to see the brightest side of human nature, even when facing the rudest intolerance of his fellow man. In his 1983 autobiography, Miñoso (unlike Cepeda or Oliva, or other wounded athletes) meticulously avoids any opportunity to speak out about his mistreatment during his earliest playing days. Miñoso's book has no room for invective but is filled with tales of wonderful treatment he received at the hands of Chicago's enthusiastic fans. And when a negative incident is reported, it is only to underscore the humorous side of the Miñoso experience, such as eating in a favorite Chinese restaurant in Boston (with a number of other Latin ballplayers who were also aficionados of oriental cuisine) and observing waiters huddled in a corner watching him intently and whispering about their dark-skinned guests. It turns out that they were simply amazed to see a black man (Miñoso) handle chopsticks with such dexterity. The irrepressible Miñoso found nothing but humor in the incident.

Mindless prejudice against Miñoso, Tony Taylor, Orlando Cepeda, Tony Oliva, and other black Latins of the 1950s and 1960s can be easily documented in numerous published interviews with the often stoic victims. Such stories are today quite surprising to contemporary fans who have grown up with the black ballplayer and Latin ballplayer as a major presence in the modern sport. For early waves of Latin big-leaguers, however, it required discipline and concentration to cast such insults aside and focus on the ballplaying tasks at hand. Cuban infielder Tony Taylor, one of the earliest blacks to star for the Philadelphia Phillies throughout the entire decade of the 1960s, has spoken of his incredulous dismay at first encountering back-of-the-bus treatment of blacks across southern and northern cities during his earliest minor league years at the tail end of the 1950s. Taylor would later recount (during a 1989 NBC-TV documentary on Latin ballplayers) that at his first exposure to such injustices it was only the absence of an $86 one-way air fare to Havana that prevented him from leaving immediately for his Cuban homeland. It seems that Taylor was a minor-leaguer in Texas with but $84 in his pocket at the time he finally reached the frustration point and inquired about a plane ticket home. Taylor would joke, perhaps with a touch of bitterness, that it was this lack of $2 that had saved his life and kept him from abandoning a promising baseball carer. Possessed of the $2, Taylor would have met a far worse fate in his native Cuba, a prospect he now shudders to consider.

For blacks like Miñoso and Taylor, it was hard to understand the treatment of black ballplayers and citizens they soon witnessed in an affluent land. In their integrated homelands such problems had never existed to any noticeable extent. Blacks and whites lived and worked side by side; they intermarried and shared families as well as schoolrooms and baseball dugouts. And they played baseball side by side without discord or disharmony.

If Jackie Robinson had his Ben Chapman and Minnie Miñoso had his Jimmy Dykes, Orlando Cepeda would have his Alvin Dark to test his resolve as a man and measure his mettle as a dedicated big-league ballplayer. No tale of racial intolerance and prejudice is more blatant than that which surrounds the career of Orlando Cepeda and his half-dozen Latin American teammates of the San Francisco Giants in the early 1960s under manager Alvin Dark. Dark was a man with little tolerance for black-skinned and Hispanic ballplayers and (as Dark saw it) their fun-loving attitudes and childlike enthusiasms. And he was more than mildly outspoken in his views. Although the worst of Dark's public attacks on his Spanish-speaking players may have been somewhat exaggerated by misquotations in the press (see Chapter 4 for details), it is fair to say that Dark's treatment of his Hispanic stars on the San Francisco team was barely tolerant.

Al Dark's unfortunate remarks and attitude toward some of his players had severe consequences for the Giants ballclub and Dark himself. It was the infamous quotation of Dark's off-color remarks (Chapter 4) about Latins published by a Long Island newspaper that would eventually destroy clubhouse harmony on the team and cost the outspoken Dark his job in the process. But no one suffered more by the incidents than men like Cepeda, Alou, Pagán, and star pitcher Juan Marichal. Cepeda's baseball reputation was seemingly tarnished permanently to a large degree by Dark's racist remarks, and so to a lesser degree was Marichal's. Both men would later speak candidly of their experience. Cepeda (in his 1983 book *High and Inside*, p. 33) was later free to call Dark the most hateful man he ever knew ("When I first met him I thought Alvin Dark was an angel. He came on like a saint and fooled everybody. But it did not take long for me to find out that he was the most vicious man I would ever meet in baseball. Without mincing words, I can easily and honestly say that Alvin Dark was a liar and a bigot"). And Marichal's memories of Dark were hardly complimentary. For much of three seasons at the height of his career (1961–1963) Juan Marichal would struggle continuously over ambivalent feelings about pitching for a manager who had frequently gone public with comments that his ace pitcher was a quitter and a man with little pride or courage.

Cepeda especially was plagued in his early big-league career by his Hispanic background and language difficulties in ways that went far beyond his unsettling experiences with manager Dark. Speaking candidly during the filming of a 1989 NBC-TV documentary, "Baseball with a Latin Beat," Cepeda would humorously report his experiences during his earliest minor league visit to the States. It seems that Cepeda was released from his team in southern Virginia only days after the death of his father back in Puerto Rico. The devastated rookie had already resigned himself to a one-way return trip to his native Puerto Rico when he received news that came as a mixed blessing. Another minor league club in the New York Giants organization had lost both third basemen to injury and needed emergency reinforcement. His baseball career was temporarily salvaged since Cepeda was being shipped to Kokomo, Indiana, on a temporary 10-day contract. With imperfect English and absolutely no knowledge of where Indiana might be, the confused youngster next found himself on a two-day train ride to Kokomo, where club officials would supposedly meet him at the train station. The frightened Puerto Rican never slept a wink for two days, petrified that he might miss the call for Kokomo and end up hopelessly stranded somewhere in the forbidding American heartland.

Later in his career similar misunderstandings would persist. If Pete Rose charged an opponent on the base paths or crashed into a catcher defending home plate, he would be praised by fans as Charlie Hustle and glorified as a never-say-die winner. But should Cepeda play with the same fire-in-the-eye enthusiasm, he could count on being labeled a hot dog or a showboat. Cepeda's two excellent autobiographies are filled with accounts of this phenomenon. And one most unfortunate event of postballplaying days (his bust for marijuana smuggling) helped this not altogether positive image gain further hold on the public consciousness. Today Cepeda waits outside the gates of Cooperstown attempting to prepare himself for pain and rejection.

As the first important Dominican big-leaguer and a teammate of Cepeda's under Alvin Dark, Felipe Alou would soon be suffering a similar burden of intolerance and underappreciation. Alou reports that in spring training of 1961 there were 11 Latins on the Giants roster (half the starters at the time were Latin), yet Spanish was totally banned in the clubhouse. This was a special blow for Felipe Alou, who was thus effectively banned from speaking with his own brother Matty by Dark's directive.

Alou has captured those years of frustration in speaking of the incident involving his teammate and countryman Juan Marichal and the latter's 1965 confrontation with Dodger catcher John Roseboro. For Alou, it is understandable if not excusable that Marichal lashed out with his bat against Roseboro or any other enemy ballplayer in the big leagues. Alou explains that as a young Dominican he (like Marichal and others of his countrymen) grew up with an intimidating impression of his North American rivals. North Americans for Alou were all perceived as "supermen," as comic-book superheroes who would knock out 10 opponents with a single blow or enter a foreign land and perform feats requiring 10,000 men of another race. It was indeed a fanciful stereotype. Yet Alou today speaks poignantly of how he and other Latins often felt helpless and overwhelmed by the seeming invincibility of rivals like Al Dark, John Roseboro, or Sandy Koufax.

A tiny handful of the early black Latins of the 1950s were the first to integrate their teams, and with such brave roles inevitably came the even larger burdens of being exiled strangers in a hostile big-league world. Nino

Escalera, a Puerto Rican outfielder-infielder, played the part in Cincinnati, yet stirred little excitement with his landmark achievement. Unfortunately for Escalera, a black North American teammate would crack the lineup the same day. Ironically, many accounts of Cincinnati baseball history have assigned the integration credit to the man who batted in the lineup immediately behind Escalera on the day in 1954 when racial barriers tumbled in the oldest National League city. Chuck Harmon is often cited as the first black Cincinnati Red, being a North American of African descent, while Escalera is more often than not thought of as a "foreigner" who briefly intruded upon the Queen City baseball scene.

Another Latin black who received even less credit for his pioneering role than Escalera was Cuban shortstop Humberto "Chico" Fernández. Fernández first appeared in the majors with little fanfare in Brooklyn, a place where black players were already commonplace by the time he debuted in 1956. With little hope of unseating Hall-of-Famer Pee Wee Reese from the shortstop slot in Ebbets Field, the rookie had little future with Walter Alston's Dodgers. He was a hot enough prospect, however, for the Phillies to peddle five players to obtain his services for the 1957 season. Upon moving to the Phillies, Fernández would miss through a misunderstanding similar to the one in Cincinnati on the chance to earn a spot in the history books as the first black player for the Philadelphia team. The distinction wrongfully went to another shortstop named John Kennedy, who was purchased that same spring from the Kansas City Monarchs and thus became the last player to jump directly from the Negro leagues to the majors. Yet fate was in the end on the side of Chico Fernández. Kennedy would injure his shoulder after but two at-bats and never again appear in a major league uniform. Before the month was out, it was Fernández who took over as the first black regular in the Phillies lineup, and he would retain the club's shortstop position until he slumped badly at the plate midway through the 1959 season. Kennedy is usually cited as the first black Phillie for his April 22 appearance, yet Fernández had cracked the line-up six days earlier, on Opening Night of the season.

It was on to Detroit for Fernández, just in time for another near-miss, this time as the first black ballplayer in the Motor City. While the Phillies were the last National League ballclub across the integration border, the Tigers edged in only ahead of the Boston Red Sox among American League franchises. It was the Dominican-born and New York–raised Ossie Virgil who would integrate the Tigers in 1958 as the club's first "official" black. But Virgil's Detroit stopover would be limited to 49 games in 1959 and 62 in 1960, mostly as a utility player and late-inning defensive fill-in. Fernández, by contrast, would be handed the starting shortstop slot by Detroit for the 1960 campaign, becoming the first black regular for a second ballclub. The sojourn would again last but a couple of seasons and would include a

First Blacks and Latins with Original Sixteen Major League Clubs

	First Black Ballplayer *(Latins in Italics)*	First Latin Ballplayer *(Blacks in Italics)*
Brooklyn Dodgers	Jackie Robinson (April 15, 1947)	Adolfo Luque (1930)
Cleveland Indians	Larry Doby (July 5, 1947)	*Minnie Miñoso* (1949)
St. Louis Browns	Hank Thompson (July 17, 1947)	Oscar Estrada (1929)
New York Giants	Hank Thompson (July 8, 1949)	Emilio Palmero (1915)
Boston Braves	Sam Jethroe (April 18, 1950)	Mike González (1912)
Chicago White Sox	*Minnie Miñoso* (May 1, 1951)	Chico Carrasquel (1950)
Philadelphia Athletics	Bob Trice (September 13, 1953)	Luís Castro (1902)
Chicago Cubs	Ernie Banks (September 17, 1953)	Hiram Bithorn (1942)
Pittsburgh Pirates	Curt Roberts (April 13, 1954)	Mosquito Ordeñana (1943)
St. Louis Cardinals	Tom Alston (April 13, 1954)	Oscar Tuero (1918)
Cincinnati Reds	*Nino Escalera* (April 17, 1954)	Armando Marsans (1911)
Washington Senators	*Carlos Paula* (September 6, 1954)	Mérito Acosta (1913)
New York Yankees	Elston Howard (April 14, 1955)	Angel Aragón (1914)
Philadelphia Phillies	*Chico Fernández* (April 16, 1957)	Chili Gómez (1935)
Detroit Tigers	*Ossie Virgil* (June 6, 1958)	*Ossie Virgil* (1958)
Boston Red Sox	Pumpsie Green (July 21, 1959)	Eusebio González (1918)

surprise power display with 20 homers during the 1962 pennant chase. But all record of the role of Chico Fernández as a pioneering black ballplayer has been conveniently expunged from the short memories of Motor City fans, just as it has been lost to a generation of Phillies fanatics.

Tony Oliva was another Cuban pioneer who experienced especially hard times in the wintry climates of a North American big-league city – this time Minneapolis. For Oliva, who was released from his first minor league tryout camp just months after the failed Bay of Pigs invasion, a return to Cuba after 1960 was unthinkable. Given a second chance to remain on U.S. soil, the talented youngster quickly delivered, posting a .410 average with Wytheville of the Appalachian League, a feat that brought him a silver Louisville Slugger as the top hitter in professional baseball for 1961 and a guaranteed spot in the Minnesota Twins organization. Yet at times the world of big-league baseball must have appeared as complex and frightening as the politics of Oliva's unsettled and revolution-wracked Cuban homeland. Oliva today speaks eloquently of the loneliness and pain of his earliest big-league days. Knowing little English and frightened by an unfamiliar and often hostile environment, Oliva would walk the dozen miles each day from his apartment to the Bloomington ballpark where the Twins played. The fearless ballplayer who held his own against wicked enemy fastballs was nonetheless fearful of a bus ride on which he might become hopelessly lost without any English to aid him. And he was also simply too poorly paid as a 1962 rookie to afford the daily cab fare. One of the hottest prospects of the American League would walk almost everywhere he went, undoubtedly strengthening his powerful legs in the process. It was just one more case of how the irrepressible Oliva always managed to extract a positive value from the most negative of his early baseball experiences.

And even three decades later the struggle continues for the often misunderstood and mishandled Latin ballplayer. Dominican superstar George Bell, for example, is one island ballplayer whose long road from the poverty of his homeland to the wealth and celebrity of big-league stardom has been paved with many rocky turns and frustrating setbacks. If Bell is often portrayed in the media as sullen, uncooperative, and selfish, this stilted portrait only masks the true story of Bell's pockmarked professional career.

Bell's mistreatment as a rookie minor-leaguer has played a central role in his later and much publicized run-ins with the North American press. A first minor league season in Montana (with Helena in the Pioneer League) brought bitter lessons about the fate awaiting an untutored Latin youngster adrift thousands of miles from his family and his native culture. Bell has talked freely on only a few occasions of what he perceives as the stark contrast between the way Latin ballplayers have long assisted North American winter-league visitors and the way impressible youngsters from the Caribbean are mishandled when they cross north of the borders of their island homelands. Bell assesses the problem as one of North American coldness: "We Latin players are so naive that we help the American players when they come to our countries for winterball – take them to restaurants, show them what to order and eat, help them get around. But when we get here there is nobody willing to help us." Bell's year in Helena contained some very bitter lessons: "The white players all had good apartments, but we Latins were living in a witch house. We had money like the others but we couldn't rent anything, couldn't buy a car, nothing." And there was the matter of wounded pride: "When you finally make it to the majors no one knows about the pain you had in the minors. It hurts when no one respects that you have pride, when you are smart and no one thinks you are intelligent because you don't speak their language." Such discrepancies and injustices have left their lasting mark on the sensitive George Bell. And no million-dollar big-league contract has quite erased their memory.

With George Bell, then, it is not hard to understand why an established star might often appear withdrawn from a public that has often treated him so callously, or short-tempered with a press that has so often backed him into a corner. The Latin superstar's role is often even more of an impossible balancing act than the burden of a raw Latin rookie minor-leaguer faced with uneatable food, an unintelligible language, and confusing cultural perspectives. Bell has found, like Miñoso and Clemente before him, that the Latin ballplayer is doomed when ushered before the American press. North American reporters want ballplayers who are easily quotable and always colorful, and with the Latin player, that often translates into a ready-made excuse for the reigning stereotypes of broken English and humorous naivete. For a proud Latin athlete like Roberto Clemente or George Bell, this was especially galling. Their words are turned into slapstick comedy when they speak freely. When they are silent in self-defense, they are quickly branded as haughty and inconsiderate. There is no safe middle ground.

For the young and eager prospect from the Dominican Republic, Puerto Rico, Venezuela, or elsewhere in the Caribbean basin, the major league and minor league ballfields of the United States no longer house such breeding grounds of racial hatred and unacceptance. Yet the problems of cultural and linguistic adjustment still provide almost insurmountable barriers, just as they did a few decades ago for Miñoso, Clemente, Alou, and so many others. For the glove-toting Latin teenager set adrift in a strange land far from his island home—a forbidding land of skyscrapers and bustle where the language is unintelligible, the food unpalatable, the music unsettling, and the ways of fans and teammates unfathomable—ballplaying skills are the least intimidating obstacles they face. This is why the few who make it to major league stardom display such grace and poise under fire. This is why they play with such burning desire and flaunt such irrepressible confidence while on the field. It is certainly why their triumphs consist of far more than dollars, base hits, and adulation. It is why they have always been the idols of their countrymen and the standard-bearers of national pride.

Suggested Readings

Cepeda, Orlando (with Charles Einstein). *My Ups and Downs in Baseball.* New York: Putnam, 1968.

________ (with Bob Markus). *High and Inside: Orlando Cepeda's Story.* South Bend, Indiana: Icarus Press, 1984.

Holway, John B. *Blackball Stars: Negro League Pioneers.* New York: Carroll and Graf, 1992; Westport, Connecticut: Meckler, 1988, 236–247.

Lindberg, Richard C. "Miñoso by Any Other Name." *The International Pastime: A Review of Baseball History* (Society for American Baseball Research) 12 (1992): 55–57. Edited by Peter C. Bjarkman.

Miñoso, Orestes Minnie (with Fernando Fernández and Robert Kleinfelder). *Extra Innings: My Life in Baseball.* Chicago: Regnery Gateway, 1983.

Oliva, Tony. *Tony O! The Trials and Triumphs of Tony Oliva.* New York: Hawthorn, 1973.

Young, A. S. "Doc." *Great Negro Baseball Stars and How They Made the Major Leagues.* New York: A. S. Barnes, 1953.

CHAPTER 9

Pan-America's Diamond Mine: Birthrights of the Caribbean National Game

> There is a tradition here, a rich history that speaks of ancient heroes and sleeping giants. —ED LINN

Professor Linn had in mind the narrow rivalry of two teams playing in the American League and featuring giants named DiMaggio and Williams, Lefty Grove and Lefty Gomez, Boggs and Mattingly, Phil Rizzuto and Bobby Doerr. Yet there is many a resident of Caracas, Havana, or San Juan who dreams of equally ancient rivalries pitting heroes named José Méndez and Adolfo Luque, Chico Carrasquel and José "Carrao" Bracho, Davalillo and Aparicio. Baseball has long reigned as a "Pan"-American national pastime, and its frontiers thus lie deep along the Orinoco River and the far edges of the Amazon rain forest, not merely in the westernmost of big-league cities.

We North Americans, of course, are unduly protective about the homespun birthrights of our native games and sporting rituals. It was such overblown concern, after all, that fostered for so many decades the outrageous Abner Doubleday baseball creation myth. This is the preposterous myth of an instantaneous baseball immaculate conception taking place on the outskirts of Cooperstown, New York, in 1839. In reality, baseball's lineage is anything but entirely red, white, and blue. And as essayist and evolutionist Stephen Jay Gould has so often cautioned us, baseball's sources, like those of the rest of our social and biological inheritance, are the slow products of evolutionary process and not the instantaneous gifts of creative genius. Yet as Professor Gould also observes, we Americans are destined to prefer our creation myths to our evolutionary reality.

With other American institutions as well, this paradox exists. What game could be more North American, for example, than the winter sport of basketball, a modern pastime whose uncomplicated lineage we can trace to the exact moment of conception. Basketball was indeed *invented*, after all, and its nativity is thoroughly documented. But even here the pure bloodlines are tainted. Basketball's inventor, Dr. James Naismith, was a native son of Canada and not an American of U.S. parentage. Let it also be remembered that basketball's showcase league, the National Basketball Association, was born in the years immediately following World War II out of the narrow economic interests of Canadian and U.S. hockey promoters. Basketball was a way to fill up an idle arena on nights when the NHL or Eastern Hockey League teams were not scheduled. In this sense, then, the latest American national game is but a stepchild of the older Canadian national game. It is a long forgotten fact that the infant NBA (known in 1946 as the Basketball Association of America) played its first league game on Canadian soil, the New York Knickerbockers challenging the Toronto Huskies in Toronto's Maple Leaf Gardens. More relevant still is the reality that the modern hoop sport arrived in full prominence at the end of the twentieth century only when it became a truly international game played as enthusiastically in Italy, Spain, or Brazil as in the playgrounds and gymnasiums of New York and Chicago.

Baseball now boasts a rich international flavor as well, for all its longstanding residence in the United States. Today's important diamond talent fonts look across the Caribbean and stretch into such distant outposts as New Zealand and Australia. The nineteenth-century game's greatest original promoter and popularizer, Henry Chadwick, was by birth a Britisher. Many of baseball's most exciting stars are no longer U.S.-born and bred. And for a full century, usually unnoticed north of Texas and Florida ports of entry, baseball has flowered as a national pastime in five other nations that share with Uncle Sam the Western Hemisphere.

An overview of baseball's origins throughout the Western Hemisphere indicates that ballplaying on American soil (that is, the mainland United States) was never all that far ahead of the game's evolution in other nations of the region. Canada and Cuba seem to share almost equally in the game's earliest history and prehistory. A pastoral bat-and-ball contest much like modern baseball was first played in Beechville, Ontario, a full year before the reputed Doubleday game transpired in Cooperstown and eight long summers before the documented founding of the "New York Game" by Alexander Cartwright in Hoboken, New Jersey. The Beechville game was a strange version of baseball (featuring five bases or posts and the large playing rosters of English rounders and "town ball"), but it was a first cousin of baseball. And while Cuba imported its baseball from the United States in the late 1860s and early 1870s, its first professional league followed the granddaddy of U.S. leagues, the National League, by only two seasons. It was Cuba far more than the United States that was ultimately responsible for the rapid spreading of baseball throughout the rest of the hemisphere, especially to the island neighbors of Puerto Rico and the Dominican Republic. Cubans, then, were the sport's first true and highly effective international apostles.

The following chronologies (on pp. 237–238) indicate in capsule form the evolution of baseball throughout the Western Hemisphere. Such an outline not only establishes the true international flavor of the baseball movement but documents the long-standing roots of baseball play throughout the major Caribbean nations. These chronologies demonstrate baseball's legitimate claim as a genuine Pan-American national pastime.

The pages that follow outline a capsule history of baseball as it has evolved in five nations (including the U.S. protectorate Puerto Rico) that share the game with the United States. The story focuses on those countries with a legitimate and continuing baseball tradition stretching to the dawn of the twentieth century and even before – Cuba, the Dominican Republic, Puerto Rico, Mexico, and Venezuela. It is a rich and evolving story, one that can be painted here only in briefest capsule form.

Cuba, Proud Apostle of the Caribbean Game

> Success has many fathers; failure none. —John Thorn

Mystery has always been the byword of Cuban baseball history. The origins of the game in this "cradle of the Caribbean" are shrouded in hopeless confusion and enmeshed in a tangled web of contradictory accounts. The most recent decades of Cuban baseball, on the other hand, provide an equal mist of speculation and misinformation. Furthermore, rich historical connections with the North American black leagues in the decades between the two world wars constitute winter baseball's most tragically lost story. And even during the brief period of exposure to North American eyes during the fifties and sixties, the Cuban big-league heroes like Camilo Pascual, Orestes Miñoso, Pete Ramos, Tony Oliva, and Tony Pérez were often misvalued, mislabeled, and misunderstood.

But there can be little doubt that Cuba was in the vanguard of baseball's earliest twentieth-century Caribbean explosion. From the time of the American Civil War, baseball was already being played on the Cuban island, and in the third quarter of the past century the Cubans were the energetic disciples and apostles of the new sport, spreading it almost everywhere throughout the rest of the Caribbean basin. Of course, the first emissaries of Cuban baseball were U.S.-trained schoolboys who learned the new game on their trips to the United States (often for university education

Baseball's Origins in the Western Hemisphere

Country	First Recorded Baseball Play (Amateur and Professional)
United States	1839, Abner Doubleday "invents" baseball in Cooperstown (unsubstantiated)
	1846, Alexander Cartwright codifies "New York" rules and holds contest between members of Knickerbocker Club on Elysian Fields in Hoboken (June 19, 1846)
Canada	1838, first reported baseball-like game in Beechville, Ontario (June 4, 1838)
	1859, "New York Game" first introduced to Canada
Cuba	1866, Nemesio Guillot introduces first baseball equipment to island of Cuba
	1874, first recorded game (Havana vs. Matanzas), organized by Esteban Bellán
Mexico	1877, U.S. sailors demonstrate game of baseball at port of Guaymas
	1877, U.S. railroad construction chief John Tayson holds games in Nuevo Laredo
	1890s, Cuban settlers introduce baseball contests in Yucatán Peninsula
Dominican Republic	1880s, Cuban settlers reportedly introduce game to sugarcane field workers
	1916–1917, U.S. Consul Arthur McLean promotes baseball throughout the island
Nicaragua	1889, U.S. businessman Albert Adlesbury introduces game in town of Bluefields (Adlesbury wished to counter ongoing British promotions of cricket)
Venezuela	1895, Cuban Emilio Cramer introduces and demonstrates baseball
Puerto Rico	1897, first newspaper account of baseball amateur contest
	1898, first organized game with spectators attending (January 9, 1898)
Panama	1903–1914, Canal construction workers import baseball play to Canal Zone
	1912, Panama amateur league officially functions

Professional/Organized Baseball in the Western Hemisphere

Country	Introduction of Professional/Organized Baseball
United States	1869, Cincinnati Red Stockings tour as first all-professional baseball club
	1871, National Association formed as first professional league
	1876, National League founded

Professional/Organized Baseball in the Western Hemisphere, *cont.*

Country	Introduction of Professional/Organized Baseball
Canada	1860s, amateur play (club teams) popular across Ontario and other provinces
	1873, Guelph Maple Leafs play against touring Boston Red Stockings
	1876, Canadian Association of Ballplayers, first pro league (London Tecumsehs, Guelph Maple Leafs, plus Toronto, Hamilton, and Kingston ballclubs)
Cuba	1878, Cuban Professional League play (Havana, Matanzas and Almendares)
Mexico	1887, "Mexico Club" team organized in Mexico City
	1925, Mexican Professional League (Summer league) organized
	1940s, Mexican League stabilized and popularized under Jorge Pasquel
	1945, Mexican Pacific Coast League (Winter league) organized
Nicaragua	1889, two organized ballclubs compete (Club Southern and White Rose)
	1892, competition between Managua and Granada club teams
	1935, Nicaraguan national team tours Panama (wins 18 of 19 games)
	1939, Nicaragua first enters World Amateur Championships
	1956–1966, Nicaraguan Winter League functions
Dominican Republic	1930s, Negro league barnstormers tour country each winter
	1937, Dictator Trujillo's "Grand Tournament" (featuring Negro league players)
	1942, Dominican national team first enters World Amateur Championships
	1951–1954, Dominican Summer League play launched (Licey, Escogido, Aguilas Cibaenas and Estrellas Orientales)
	1955, Dominican Winter League begins play
Panama	1935, Panama national team first enters Central American and Caribbean Games
	1936, Panama Olympic team trained by Negro leaguer Bill Yancey
	1946, Panama Professional League inaugurated
Puerto Rico	1938, Puerto Rican Winter League inaugurated (San Juan, Mayaguez, Guayama, Ponce, Caguas and Humacao)
Venezuela	1940, Venezuela first enters World Amateur Championships
	1946, Venezuelan Winter League established (Venezuela, Magallanes, Cervecería Caracas, Vargas)

and usually in New York), then brought it back to their homeland. The first among these enthusiastic Cuban "baseball importers" history has recorded is Nemesio Guillot, a Havana-born student who introduced equipment and play to his friends on the island as early as 1866.

Two names, however, vie for the mythical title of Father of Cuban Baseball, and each has a legitimate claim. The baseball-playing career of each begins (as with Nemesio Guillot) in the United States. A fellow student of Guillot's was Esteban Enrique Bellán, Latin America's first representative to organized baseball. Dark-skinned Steve Bellán was the most accomplished player of the dozen or more original Cuban converts who received both their schoolbook and ballplaying education deep in Yankee territory. Bellán, however, was destined to become the first Latin American big-leaguer, signing with the National Association's Troy Haymakers fresh off the campus of Fordham University in 1871 and later playing a handful of games with the New York Mutuals. His professional career was hardly distinguished: parts of three seasons, 59 games with 288 official at-bats, 68 hits, a lame dead-ball batting average of .236. Little is known of Bellán's life beyond the fact that he was born in Havana (in 1850) and died there on August 8, 1932. But Cuban fanáticos remember him for a more significant pioneering role as organizer of the first formal game between his own hastily assembled Havana club and a team from Matanzas late in 1874. Bellán earned additional distinction as the first player to connect for three home runs in a single Cuban game when he accomplished this rare dead-ball feat in that first one-sided contest (Havana was victorious, 51–9) on December 27, 1874. As one historian puts it, if Guillot introduced the sport to island culture, Bellán performed the marriage between baseball and the Cuban people.

Bellán's rival in the early years of Cuban baseball was fellow Habanero Emilio Sabourín. Like Bellán, Sabourín contributed as a player yet made his greater mark on history as a league organizer and club manager in the pioneering years of Cuban organized ball. It was Emilio Sabourín (Ruck calls him the A. G. Spalding of Cuban baseball) who led establishment of the Liga de Béisbol Profesional Cubana and a first league tournament in 1878, which was launching pad for eight decades of pre–Castro Cuban professional baseball. Sabourín also took the field for the first historic game in Havana in December 1874. (It should be noted that this pioneering game can be fixed as occurring in 1874, not in 1868 as Rob Ruck erroneously reports in *Total Baseball*. Several credible sources agree on the later date.) Bellán caught, reportedly hitting his three homers and scoring seven runs for the winners. Sabourín played in the outfield for Havana and scored eight markers. Emilio Sabourín would then go on to manage, in the same manner as Bellán, once professional play began in Cuba a mere four years later. Again like Bellán (who managed the Havana club to championships during the first three seasons of league play), Sabourín claimed three titles as the bench leader for the same Havana ballclub (1889, 1890, 1892).

Bellán's ballplaying and managerial rival was also a colorful character whose life away from the baseball diamond was immersed deeply in Cuban politics and the ongoing independence struggle with Spain. A 10-year war for independence waged against the Spanish brought continued chaos to Cuba between 1868 and 1878 and ceased temporarily in the winter when Emilio Sabourín launched his first professional-league tournament. Evidence that baseball and politics were already as inseparable in Cuba in the late nineteenth century as they have remained in the late twentieth century is found in the fact that revenues from this tourney were apparently surreptitiously funneled directly into the hands of those carrying on guerrilla rebellions against Spanish overseers.

Eventually this mixture of baseball with anti-Spanish politics led to Sabourín's arrest in 1895 and sentence to a Moroccan prison, where the erstwhile baseball manager died of pneumonia only two years later. In the end, Sabourín's contributions of baseball revenues to the anti-Spanish independence movement of José Martí not only cost the ballplaying patriot his personal freedom but resulted in a short-lived Spanish ban of the game across much of the island colony. Throughout three final decades (1870s through 1890s) of foreign control in Cuba, Spanish colonial authorities had always deeply distrusted rebellious Cuban students and likely assumed that bats and balls used in the popular pastime of *pelota americana* were merely cleverly disguised implements of rebel warfare. Sabourín was easy enough to eliminate with imprisonment, but the new sporting passion of the masses proved far more difficult to eradicate.

Sabourín's claim to the parentage of Cuban baseball may lie to a great extent in his adjunct status as Cuban revolutionary hero, especially during fervent patriotic days that followed Castro's ascension to power. Although a documented player and manager in his country, Sabourín never played in any professional or amateur league in the United States and was thus more a popularizer than an importer of the popular pastime. Sabourín's position as baseball inventor is hardly as tenuous as that of Abner Doubleday, but if Bellán is more rightfully the Cuban version of Alexander Cartwright, Sabourín may be more justly set down as a Cuban Henry Chadwick.

The first half century of Cuban professional play (1880s–1930s) was especially noted for its great pitching legends. First there was Adolfo Luján, who led the Cuban pro circuit in pitching victories the first three seasons that such records were kept (1887–1889) and the Dominican import Enrique Hernández (known in his homeland as "Indio Bravo"), who possessed an unhittable curveball and soon shared domination of the hill with José Pastoriza (twice league leader in victories and three times in complete games during the 1890s). Next came Carlos Royer at the turn of the century. Royer was the Cuban league's first 20-game winner in 1903 (21-12), and his single-season victory mark was not matched until Raymond Brown compiled 21 victories in 1937. When the Cuban professional league would finally close its doors in the shadow of Castro's revolution, it would still be Royer, incredibly, who held the records for consecutive wins in a season (17), consecutive victories over two campaigns (20 during 1902 and 1903), consecutive complete games (69 between 1901 and 1904), and consecutive complete games in a season (33 in 1903).

It was the fate of these marvelous early Cuban pitchers to labor in almost complete island obscurity. José de la Caridad Méndez changed all that with his performance against touring big-leaguers, especially his first two startling shutouts against the visiting Cincinnati Reds during the 1908 winter season (Chapter 6). Méndez also proved beyond any shadow of a doubt that he was more than a mere flash when he continued domination of Cuban-league play of the period with a record five seasons (between 1908 and 1914) as the circuit's winningest moundsman. Finally came Dolf Luque with his starring role (Chapter 1) in the North American big leagues and his stellar performances (he led the circuit four times in victories between 1916 and 1929) over almost three decades of Cuban winter play. There were others of legendary status, like José Acosta (who tied Méndez's record as five-time champion pitcher between 1915 and 1925) and Oscar Tuero, owner of three solid post–World War I seasons with the National League St. Louis Cardinals. Oscar Tuero, it should be underscored, was a true native son of Havana and not Canada, as erroneously reported in Thorn and Palmer's *Total Baseball* (1993 edition).

The 1940s would also boast its great diamond stars, again led primarily by the pitchers. Foremost in rank were Ramón Bragaña, a true star mainly in the blackball leagues of North America, and diminutive right-hander Agapito Mayor. While Mayor would pace the Cuban circuit several times in victories during World War II, his lasting legend would like Bragaña's be earned outside Cuban borders. Mayor brought the island one of its greatest triumphs on the international scene with his 1949 stellar performance in the week-long inaugural Caribbean World Series, the first formal showdown of Caribbean winter-league champions. His gutty performance of three victories in a single Caribbean Series has never been equaled in 35 seasons of CWS contests. Bragaña, by contrast, garnered much of his fame in Mexico, setting a long string of Mexican summer-league hurling records between 1938 and the mid–1950s. None of the "Professor's" Mexican marks were more noteworthy than his 211 career victories, 222 complete games, and 3,375 total innings pitched. Ramón Bragaña would register a dozen winning seasons in Mexico and post a 2.58 ERA during the 1940 season.

But none was more legendary both inside and outside the tiny island nation than "Lefty" Luís Tiant, master of the tantalizing "fadeaway" or screwball pitch. Tiant's only flaw as a moundsman was that like so many of his countrymen, he was black and thus not available for big-league service. While he twirled magic in the North American Negro leagues (starring for Alex Pompez's New York Cuban Giants and Cuban Stars), Tiant was also a year-after-year stalwart of winter-league baseball in his homeland. Five times between 1931 and 1941 Tiant paced the Cuban circuit in shutouts, reaching a high-water mark of 12 in 1936-37. Tiant's shutout skein stands as a record never surpassed in Cuban professional play. This lefty's screwball magic was clearly as effective in winterball play of the tropics as it long was in the shadows of the recently rediscovered Negro leagues.

While pitchers were usually the hallmark of Cuban baseball, there was a legacy of fence-busting hitters as well, names like Regino García, Armando Marsans, Alejandro Oms, Cristóbal Torriente, and the ubiquitous Martín Dihigo. But none, save all-around performer Dihigo, was quite as great for quite so long as the equally versatile Silvio García. From 1931 through 1954, García worked his magic in the Cuban league as a hitter, defensive stalwart, and pitcher. He would hold the Cuban record for lifetime base hits (891) and win two batting titles a decade apart, in 1942 and 1951. His reputation as an all-around star who could shift positions almost as freely as Dihigo surpassed the mere numbers he recorded. It is little wonder that when Branch Rickey's postwar search for a black ballplayer to integrate the majors turned to the talent font of Cuba, it was Silvio García (unfortunately well past his prime by this time) who was first recommended to the Mahatma by a host of veteran Cuban baseball watchers.

The legacy of pre–Castro Cuban baseball was thus indeed a rich one, perhaps the richest in Latin America, and the brightest stars of the 75 years of play between Bellán and Castro have fittingly found their way into the original Cuban Baseball Hall of Fame. It is a fitting testimony to the lengthy history of Cuban baseball that the Cuban Hall of Fame was founded in 1936, the same year as its counterpart in Cooperstown (which did not open formally until three years after the Cuban hall). Notables enshrined in Havana include a veritable who's who of Cuban winter-league stars as well as three U.S. big-leaguers (Almeida, Marsans, Jack Calvo) who distinguished themselves with brief spells of big-league play. Notable by his absence is the great Adolfo Luque, whose all-star play in his homeland (he won but one pitching title, in 1928-29) never quite matched the glories of his North American big-league career.

In addition to their enshrinement in Havana, several great Cuban stars rest in the Mexican Baseball Hall of Fame, a fitting honor for their outstanding play in the Mexican League of the late 1930s and early 1940s. The great Dihigo served nine seasons in Mexico (the first in 1937, the last in 1950) and hurled the first no-hitter (1937) on Mexican soil. As a batsman, Dihigo, who played for the Veracruz team, distinguished himself with the first six-for-six single-game batting performance and set career pitching records for winning percentage (119-57, .676) and ERA (2.81) while recording a lifetime .317 batting average. Roberto Ortiz was a powerful slugging outfielder of the 1940s and 1950s while playing in Mexico City, Nuevo Laredo, and

Yucatán. Ortiz authored a 35-game hitting streak in 1948 and was first to lead the Mexican circuit in homers four straight seasons. Ramón Bragaña won 30 games for Veracruz in 1944 and thus became the only league hurler to top the 30-victory mark. As a fleet-footed left fielder throughout the 1940s, Agustín Bejerano still reigns as the all-time Mexican stolen-base champion with 313 total steals and an unsurpassed four consecutive league base-stealing titles. The last Cuban immortal enshrined in Mexico was Lazaro Sálazar, who established a superior pitching ledger (113-77) and a .333 career batting average but earned his greatest plaudits as the winningest Mexican League manager of all time. Sálazar was the first to pilot seven championship teams (with Veracruz, Córdoba, and Monterrey) during a Mexican League managerial career.

Cuba first rocketed into our North American consciousness at the time of the first tours of the island by big-league teams. While the first grand ballplaying tours were those that encountered embarrassment at the hands of phenoms José Méndez and Eustaquio Pedroso during the winter seasons of 1908 and 1909, other such tours would follow, and each would create legends of its own. With each new visit to the "gem of the Caribbean," an eloquent John McGraw or Frankie Frisch or some other big-league manager would return home with praise for the talented black Cuban baseballers he lusted after for his own roster but could not hope to sign in a league still cursed by a "gentleman's agreement" to shun blacks.

Much later, Cuba would also receive further headline-grabbing attention as spring-training base for the 1947 Brooklyn Dodgers featuring Jackie Robinson. It was ironic that while Cuban stars perhaps suffered more than any group under the exclusionary "gentleman's agreement" during the century's first half (for no place were there more blacks clearly capable of immediate stardom in the big time circuit), it would be the nation of Cuba that would eventually provide the ideal stage for the prologue and opening act of Branch Rickey and Jackie Robinson's bold integration drama during the 1946 and 1947 seasons. Robinson was first sheltered in Montreal during the 1946 minor league campaign since Canada provided a largely color-blind city likely to accept the pioneering Negro on ballplaying talent alone. If Montreal was largely free from the bigotry of big-league cities, Havana was an even more ideal location for Robinson's final spring tuneup previous to the precedent-shattering 1947 campaign. Cuba was a winter diamond paradise that had been showcasing black and white ballplayers on the same field throughout the first half of the century. And Cuba meant a distant escape from the New York media glare that would have been unavoidable stateside in the usual spring-training venues of Florida or Arizona.

In the decade following the Second World War, North American baseball would become a more regular visitor to Fulgencio Batista's Cuba, suddenly offering far more than spring-training tuneups or occasional barn-

Cuban Baseball Hall of Fame (Players Enshrined Before 1975)

Italics = U.S. major leaguers

Martín Dihigo
Luís Bustamente
José de la Caridad Méndez
Antonio Márquez García
Gervasio González
Rafael Almeida
Cristóbal Torriente
Adolfo Luján
Carlos Royer
Alfredo Arcaño
Regino García
Emilio Sabourín
Agustín Molina
Alfredo Cabrera
Armando Marsans
Heliodoro Hidalgo
Julián Castillo
Luís Padrón
Carlos Maciá
Alejandro Oms
Juan Pastoriza
Carlos Morán
Bernardo Baro
José Muñoz
Valentín Dreke
Wenceslao Gálvez
Rogelio Valdés
Francisco Poto
Ricardo Caballero
Arturo Valdés
Juan Antiga
Antonio Mesa
Tomás Romañach
Jacinto ("Jack") Calvo
Valentín González
Rafael Hernández
Nemesio Guillot
Aquiles Martínez
Ramón Calzadilla
Leopoldo de Sola (president of the first Cuban League)

Cubans in Mexican Baseball Hall of Fame

Martín Dihigo ("El Maestro"), elected in 1954
Ramón Bragaña ("El Professor"), elected in 1954
Lazaro Sálazar ("El Principe de Belen"), elected in 1954
Roberto Ortiz ("El Guajiro"), elected in 1972
Agustín Bejerano ("Pijini"), elected in 1972

---

storming tours by big-league outfits. For in 1954 the North American minor leagues arrived on the scene. A final chapter of the Cuban baseball saga is that surrounding the minor league Havana Sugar Kings (1954–1960) and International League play during the years immediately preceding the outbreak of Fidel Castro's revolution. Havana businessman Bobby Maduro (later an assistant to Commissioner Bowie Kuhn and the inspiration for a stadium of the same name now located in Miami) owned the new Havana franchise and hoped this entry into organized baseball would be a first step toward landing a major league franchise for baseball-crazy Havana. Unfortunately, however, the most famous incident surrounding the short-lived Havana International League ballclub is now forever linked with the costly Castro revolution, which all but ended the Cuban baseball story.

Castro took great pride in the presence of the Havana Sugar Kings in International League play. Always a rabid fan of the game, which he himself had played in college, the new dictator saw professional baseball as an important boost to public morale at home and public relations abroad. But the political realities of the revolution he had created would stack the cards against Castro's hopes for maintaining a minor league or major league presence for Havana. Castro nonetheless became a regular spectator at Sugar Kings games in the months following his rise to power. The University of Havana hurler now turned guerrilla warlord would early and often use the public arena of the ballpark as his personal propaganda stage. Such was the case when the fastballing dictator took the mound at Estadio Latinoamericano on July 24, 1959, for an exhibition contest staged to show off his reported pitching talents. Castro hurled two scoreless innings to lead his Cuban army "Barbudos" (Bearded Ones) to victory over a local Military Police ballclub during the tuneup before an official International League matchup between the league-leading Sugar Kings and the Rochester Red Wings. An action photo of the celebrity right-hander warming up—replete with sunglasses, the familiar foot-long beard, and a uniform emblazoned with *Barbudos*—was featured in the next day's edition of the Rochester (New York) *Democrat and Chronicle*. The attached story covering Castro's famous mound appearance (with a bold headline, "Castro Scores Smash Hit as Baseball Player") was also featured, set in prominent center-page position above the smaller account of that night's Red Wings–Sugar Kings league contest.

It was to be a final hurrah before disaster struck Castro's baseball fantasy a single night later. On the evening of July 25, 1959, gunfire (reportedly the aimless discharge of rifles outside the stadium from a band of loyalists celebrating revolutionary fervor on the anniversary of Castro's takeover) disrupted play as stray pellets struck both Red Wings third-base coach Frank Verdi (nicking his batting helmet) and Sugar Kings shortstop Leo Cárdenas (tearing his uniform sleeve) in the infield. The night's play was immediately suspended with the game tied 4–4 in the twelfth frame, and both ballclubs hastily took the next day's plane out of the country. Havana's team was forced by league officials to play out the remainder of the midseason series in Rochester and much of the remainder of the league schedule on the road, a fact that did not block the powerful Cuban team from claiming the International League pennant that summer.

While play did return to Havana in time for the fall's "Little World Series" in which the Havana club defeated the American Association champion Minneapolis Millers, the days of professional baseball in Cuba were now severely numbered. Before the middle of the next season (July 8, 1960) the International League board of governors (perhaps under some political pressure from Washington officials, who sought every available avenue to embarrass Castro) voted to relocate the Cuban Sugar Kings franchise to Jersey City, New Jersey. With the overnight departure of Havana's minor league franchise, the curtain was rung down on nearly three-quarters of a century of Cuban baseball glory.

Baseball did not die in Cuba after the doors to the island were closed by Castro and his Washington rivals. It may better be said that the sport underwent a strange and (for the outside world) silent rebirth in an unprecedented level of amateur play. On the international level of competition, Cuba has won 12 of the 15 world amateur baseball tournaments since 1969, thus establishing the same grip on international amateur competition that the island once exerted on Caribbean World Series professional play. The talented Cuban national team would lose only one of 73 games it played against international competition in the five-year span that separated the 1987 Pan American Games in Indianapolis from the 1992 Barcelona Olympics. Most prominent among the members of the powerhouse Cuban team of this era were pitcher Rene Arocha (the first Cuban player to defect during the Castro era and now a regular with the St. Louis Cardinals) and third baseman Omar Linares, a 25-year-old who in 1993 was considered by most a can't-miss major-leaguer and the best amateur ballplayer in the world.

Behind an iron wall of secrecy the pace of Cuban amateur play has continued unabated on the home front. From November through February, 450 ballplayers with an average age of 23–24 compete on 18 teams in a 48-game national tournament designed to select eastern and western representatives to meet in a final national round-robin national championship. Each of the ballclubs in this competitive amateur league represents a Cuban province, and thus regional pride and socialist ideals of sportsmanship have replaced professional salaries as the driving force of league play. When the regular-season playoffs close down, a second league and schedule of games fill the void. The 63-game Selective League is a formalized tryout period that runs from February through late summer. The circuit is composed of eight ballclubs (again representing provinces, with several provinces often collapsing into a single ballclub) and features 225 of the island's best young athletes. The prize is not so much a team championship but a spot for the two dozen best players on the nation's crack national team, which will compete in Pan-American, World Tournament, and Olympic play.

Cuban ballplayers are today again very much in the North American limelight with the recent defections of pitcher Rene Arocha and others from the Cuban national team. Arocha's departure from the Cuban team in Miami two years ago served to send a single Cuban athlete dreaming of fame and fortune offered by U.S. professional sports. When Arocha's defection passed without dangerous consequences for members of his family in Cuba, a handful of less talented Cuban ballplayers from the nation's second- and third-level touring teams also defected during visits of Cuban teams to Venezuela and Buffalo (site of the 1993 World University Games). Rumors of more widespread defections now plague the Cuban national team as the dream of big-league stardom grows more enticing in a desperate Cuban economy. Arocha's 1991 defection also sent ripples through major league front offices as team and league officials struggled to assess and regulate the possible Cuban talent flood. A special draft procedure has already been instituted to distribute Cuban talent to big-league takers. The Cardinals earned the rights to Arocha through such a lottery, and more recent defectors—first baseman Luís Alvarez Estrada and outfielder Alexis Cabreja (defectors in Venezuela in October 1992) and pitcher Ivan Alvarez (who defected in Mérida, Mexico, in 1992)—have subsequently been allocated to the Texas Rangers and San Francisco Giants minor league systems.

If Cuba has lapsed as a wellspring of big-league talent in recent decades, the island that produced Steve Bellán, Dolf Luque, and Minnie Miñoso will always boast the fountainhead from which the Pan-American pastime poured into the Caribbean basin in the final decades of the nineteenth century. And it was Cuba that single-handedly launched the Latin invasion of major league stadiums over the half century preceding Rickey and Robinson. On July 4, 1911, the first two Cuban imports took the field for Cincinnati at Chicago's West Side Park, and no season has passed in the 80 years since without at least one Cuban in big-league uniform. The influx of Cuban players into the United States would peak during the 1967 season with 30 Cubans on American and National League rosters. And a quarter century later the long drought of Cuban talent may at last be over with Castro's social experiment crumbling and a flurry of recent defections signaling a new tidal wave of Cuban talent around the corner.

Yet the future of Cuban baseball raises numerous questions that do not admit to easy answers. Are the recent defections of Cuban ballplayers a true signal of a ground swell of new talent or a mere temporary aberration? Will Castro's government cave in to economic necessities and begin peddling the front-line Cuban players as his most valuable natural export? Are the top Cuban players truly of major league caliber, and if they are, how many are future Miñosos, Pascuals, Luques, or Olivas? Will the current crop of Cuban stars prove to be less than promising big-league prospects due to the lack of first-rate competition in their amateur league back home? How will big-league teams divide the Cuban talent (will the present lottery system prevent secret signings and other skullduggery), and how will the new flock of Cuban ballplayers affect recruiting from the other Caribbean

Honor Roll of Cuba's Greatest Players

Cuban Major League Stars:

Adolfo Luque—27 victories for Cincinnati Reds in 1923 and 194 lifetime big league wins
Minnie Miñoso—Most exciting Latin major leaguer of 1950s (before Roberto Clemente)
Camilo Pascual—Retired in 1971 as second winningest big league Latin American moundsman
Pedro Ramos—Retired in 1970 with most big league losses (160) by a Latin American hurler
Mike Cuellar—First Latin American pitcher ever to win the Cy Young Award (1969)
Pedro "Tony" Oliva—Only player ever to win batting titles in his first two major league seasons
Tony Pérez—All-time big league home run leader (with Orlando Cepeda) among Latin Americans

Cuban Winter League and Blackball Stars:

Martín Dihigo—Blackball star and Hall of Famer in U.S., Cuba, Mexico and Venezuela
Ramón Bragaña—Blackball and Mexican League mound legend of the 1940s (30 wins in 1944)
Luís "Lefty" Tiant, Sr.—Unhittable master of the screwball in Negro league play of the 1930s
Cristóbal Torriente—Blackball slugging star with the 1920s Chicago American Giants
José Méndez—Blackball pitching phenom who shut down visiting big leaguers from 1908 to 1911
Silvio García—Hitting and pitching star of 1930s and 1940s in Cuban Winter leagues
Agapito Mayor—Star of first Caribbean Series (1949) and only three-game winner in single CWS

---

nations? And what will happen to baseball in Cuba once the island's best players again have access to major league careers? Only time holds the answers to what may be the most exciting baseball questions of the final decade of the twentieth century.

Dominican Republic, Cradle of Shortstops

Fernando Valenzuela was the indelible morning star who glittered most brightly at the dawn of the previous decade. And if the 1980s Latin baseball story was launched with Mexico's Valenzuela, the 1990s seemed to rocket off the booming bats of Puerto Rico's Juan González and Venezuela's Andrés Galarraga. Not since Cepeda and Pérez were Latin sluggers so prominent in the consciousness of North American fans.

Yet if there was one dominant story regarding the Latin invasion of North American ballparks during the 1980s, it was indisputably the one featuring the Dominican connection and a newfound baseball mecca, San Pedro de Macoris. Merely 10 years ago the man-in-the-street fan knew little more about Caribbean baseball heritage than the flashy feats of Roberto Clemente and the overblown infamy of the hot-blooded Latino star. The prototype foisted by an ignorant press on Marichal and Cepeda had been kept alive and well by the 1985 World Series tantrums of Joaquín Andújar. The past few seasons, by contrast, have witnessed few hotter items in the literature of the national pastime than debates and speculations about the inexplicable phenomenon provided by the shortstop-spawning town of San Pedro.

As a storehouse of big-league talent, the Dominican Republic long stood a distant third (behind Cuba and Puerto Rico), a situation destined to change only with the most recent seasons. Cubans hit the big leagues in full force in the wake of Jackie Robinson, and Mexico (Bobby Avila, 1954) and Puerto Rico (Clemente, 1961) could both boast major league batting champions before the demise of eight-team leagues and baseball's first expansion of 1961. Venezuela's Aparicio and Cuba's Miñoso were already redefining big-league base running by the time the first Dominicans (Ossie Virgil, 1956, and Felipe Alou, 1958) appeared on the scene. In the 1960s and 1970s, however, the Dominican imports matched those of Puerto Rico body for body, and the 1980s and 1990s have welcomed 104 Dominican big-leaguers (through 1992) compared with only 67 Puerto Ricans, 38 Venezuelans, and 21 Mexicans.

Full-scale recruitment throughout the Dominican hinterland, launched in the wake of Marichal and the Alou brothers, has now resulted in a tidal wave of ballplayers that has propelled the Dominicans into a narrow lead in the Latin talent race (see Appendix C). And the gap between Trujillo's former playground and the rapidly diminishing Venezuelan and Puerto Rican baseball pipelines is certain to widen dramatically in coming summers. For the Dominican Republic seems to possess a natural resource not found in other Latin nations—the fecund baseball city of San Pedro de Macoris. By the outset of the 1991 campaign, 36 major-leaguers had seen their first daylight and hit their first fastball (usually a pop-bottle top stroked with a gnarled sugarcane pole) on the dusty streets and byways of San Pedro. This sprawling seaport town (100,000 population in a nation of 6 million) with its unparalleled baseball heritage is best known for its current fleet of glue-fingered shortstops (Tony Fernández, Mariano Duncan, Manny Lee, José Offerman, Rafael Ramírez among others), yet San Pedro has produced a bundle of fence-rattling sluggers (Rico Carty, Pedro Guerrero, George Bell, Julio Franco, Sammy Sosa, Juan Samuel) and at least one dominating pitcher (Joaquín Andújar).

This unprecedented Dominican phenomenon has generated considerable popular press and media attention and thus contributed heavily to the shifting of popular focus to issues of Latin baseball and Latin ballplayers. Casual fans and stuffy SABR historians alike now puzzle over hidden explanations for the disproportionate Dominican impact on the North American national pastime. One of baseball literature's voguish topics (along with Bill Jamesian sabermetrics, astronomical player salaries, and unbridled nostalgia about lost eras of real-grass baseball in the 1940s and 1950s) has become the saga of those rare diamond urchins springing full grown from the sugar-mill towns of the Dominican Republic.

Recent literary seasons have welcomed three important books exploring this topic from similar socio-cultural-economic perspectives. Alan Klein (*Sugarball: The American Game, the Dominican Dream*, 1991) focuses on how Dominican winter-season baseball fosters national pride and inspires fierce competition with a mistrusted North American neighbor. Klein's thesis is that the Dominican national sport is far from anti–Yankee in spirit, promoting tenuous acceptance of the North American presence felt everywhere throughout the island country. Canadian journalist Gare Joyce (*The Only Ticket Off the Island*, 1990) relies more heavily on personalized player portraits (George Bell, Rico Carty, Dámaso García among others) and finely etched Dominican ballpark atmosphere to craft a detailed, lively, and moving picture of the recent Dominican baseball experience. And most recently Rob Ruck (*The Tropic of Baseball: Baseball in the Dominican Republic*, 1991) provides the most detailed and introspective look at an ingrained Dominican baseball heritage, one that suggests why Abner Doubleday's imported game has become this nation's principal art form in the twentieth century. Ruck's chapter on Juan Marichal (reprinted in 1990 as "Juan Marichal: Baseball in the Dominican Republic") is perhaps the most balanced and intimate personal portrait of a Latin American player delivered to the North American baseball reading audience.

Ruck also comes closest to cracking the riddle of why a single tiny nation can provide such an abundance of baseball talent from such a parched soil of economic stagnation. The answer is partly historical and partly socioeconomic (as Ruck cleverly demonstrates in his chapter "Three Kings Day in Consuelo"). Like blacks in the ghettos of North America who bounce basketballs endlessly on playground pavements once occupied by inner-city heroes Isiah Thomas, Moses Malone, or Clyde Drexler, hosts of Dominican youngsters without shoes or schoolbooks know from their earliest years that sure-handed infield play and fearless skill when facing a big-league fastball are the only tickets out of a life of poverty and obscurity. The visible images of the baseball dream annually appear when Tony Peña, Pedro Guerrero, Juan Samuel, Alfredo Griffin, and a fleet of other diamond stars return to their roots each winter to bask in unimagined luxury and the glow of a nation's limitless adulation. The Latin baseball story might be read on one level, then, as the last and most dramatic chapter of a century-long saga. It is a tale of baseball's role as the wide-eyed immigrant's most instantaneous key (if he can run like the wind and hit a breaking ball with grace) to unlocking the riches of the American dream.

The story of our national pastime in the Dominican Republic, as Rob Ruck has documented more thoroughly than any other scholar, stretches back through the present century. And if there is a recurrent theme, it is the integral role in baseball's growth of the dominant Dominican sugarcane industry. From the outset, sugarcane and baseball have been inseparable in molding the island's exciting baseball saga. And it is Dominican sugar that enigmatically holds the key to the often-asked question about true sources for today's Dominican baseball dominance.

The story of Dominican baseball begins with the story of Dominican cricket. And it begins equally with the saga of Cuban sugarcane production. The game of "bats and balls" was inherited in its most primitive form from the island's British rather than Hispanic ancestors and is thus not strictly a product imported directly from Cuban sources alone. Yet the Cubans did play a major role in transporting the American form of the game to Hispaniola and Puerto Rico and numerous other Caribbean ports of call. But first the Cubans brought their sugarcane industry, one that truly revolutionized life on Hispaniola.

Escaping a destructive 10-year independence war with the Spaniards back home, several thousand Cubans settled in Dominican coastal towns and villages in the early years of the 1870s. That war of independence had already succeeded in largely obliterating Cuba's thriving sugar production at the very time sugar had emerged as an item of highest demand and a new working-class addiction in Europe and most of the Western Hemisphere. Settling on the coastal plains surrounding San Pedro de Macoris and La Romana, the exiled Cubans were soon busily constructing the steam-powered mills that would almost overnight turn the Dominican Republic into a major player in the world sugar market.

In addition to these remnants of a booming Cuban sugar trade, these expatriate settlers brought the game of baseball, which they were soon teaching to Hispaniola's coastal inhabitants. And once the sugar mills were up and operating, there was an immediate need for a substantial labor force to carry out the tasks of cutting and processing on which the new industry heavily depended. The small population of the Dominican island itself (less than a quarter million in the 1870s) had easy access to abundant land and thus little incentive to tackle the slavelike conditions in the sugar mills and cane fields. The labor had to be imported from overpopulated neighboring Caribbean islands, especially the British Virgin Islands and Dutch Antilles, romantic places with names like Tortula, St. Kitts, Barbados, Jamaica,

Trinidad, and Antigua. And with this batch came a new breed of ballplayers, those raised on the British game of cricket, which reigned as the supreme pastime of Jamaica, Trinidad, and Barbados. By the dawn of the twentieth century, two new sporting traditions coexisted in the sugar-mill towns of the Dominican Republic. British Virgin Islanders were as dedicated to their ancient native game of cricket as the Cuban descendants were to their far younger North American version of rounders.

The labor backbone of the Dominican sugar industry in the last three decades of the nineteenth century was the Cocolos, dark-skinned English-speaking Tortolans who first migrated in seasonal waves to the Dominican sugar fields and eventually stayed on as permanent settlers in the region of San Pedro and La Romana. While not all of these settlers were from British outposts and many hailed from French, Danish, and Dutch colonies, the Cocolos soon dropped their separate identities and began referring to themselves simply as "the English." This separate cultural identity, their black skin (associated with Haitian slave populations), higher levels of education, English language, and Protestant religion all conspired to make the new laboring class the focus of considerable antagonisms from the native Dominican population.

The prosperous Dominican sugar industry had overnight become a multinational affair. The operating capital was North American; the technical expertise was Cuban; only the land was Dominican. And the labor was a strange mix of British (language and culture) and African since Cocolos were direct descendants of those African slaves brought into the region by British and Dutch merchants throughout much of the seventeenth and eighteenth centuries. The most visible symbol of the rare mixture was the Sunday-afternoon cricket matchups that in the early decades of the present century became a San Pedro tradition.

But British games and all things culturally English were doomed in a Spanish sphere constantly becoming more ethnocentric. While the Cocolos proudly sustained their emotional links with the past by maintaining their cricket matches throughout the immediate pre–World War I era, their sons were soon turning their attentions to the more native Cuban game. Barnstorming Negro-league ballclubs, crack visiting Cuban teams, and an occasional contingent of touring big-leaguers also fueled interest in the North American game. But as the new Dominican fascination with baseball grew in the decades between the two world wars, it was the descendants of the Cocolo crickets who would emerge as the new ballplaying stars of the San Pedro coastal region.

It was Rob Ruck (*Tropic of Baseball*, Chapter 7) who first underscored the fact that while not all of today's Dominican big-leaguers are of English descent, it is inescapable that the greatest concentrations of Dominican baseball talent are found on those sugar-mill estates of the San Pedro region that once boasted the most English populations and consequently the best cricket. The names are a dead giveaway: Griffin (Alfredo), Bell (George), Offerman (José), Duncan (Mariano), Norman (Nelson), Lee (Manuel), Samuel (Juan), Carty (Rico). These future big-leaguers had inherited from their cricket-playing fathers the key elements of a British sporting tradition that translated easily into eventual baseball success: rigid family discipline, an uncompromising approach to sport, a penchant for organization and structure, and the genetic transfer of outstanding batting and hurling skills.

Once baseball had been established on Hispaniola as a thriving amateur sport, the professional game would not lag far behind. The Dominican professional version of the game was soon up and running. Organized winter-league competition as we know it today did not commence in its earliest forms until the early 1950s, however, when Dictator Trujillo sanctioned a four-team summer circuit composed of the long-standing Dominican amateur teams—Escogido, Licey, Estrellas Orientales (San Pedro de Macoris), and Aguilas Cibaeñas (Santiago). This first league would last four seasons (two titles for Licey and one each for the Estrellas and the Aguilas) yet would face an immediate and debilitating shortcoming resulting from its summertime schedule. Since the circuit operated head-to-head with major league baseball, the loss of any outstanding talent to the big leagues would deplete the quality of local play. Under such an arrangement, the Dominicans—unlike the Cubans, Puerto Ricans, Venezuelans, or Mexicans—could not root for the local heroes both at home and abroad during the same year. The disadvantages were obvious, and the Dominican League was forced to reconstitute after only a brief trial at summer play.

But the most fabled teams of the new professional league, Licey and Escogido, could already boast a history stretching back four decades and more before the advent of a 1951 pro circuit on the island. The story of Dominican organized baseball really begins with the founding of the Licey baseball club, then closely parallels the growth and fortunes of that national baseball institution. What transpired between the earliest Cuban baseball invasions and the modern winter leagues was the great period from the turn of the century to the late 1930s, today known to islanders as the "romantic epoch" of Dominican baseball history.

Organized as a popular Santo Domingo club team in 1907 and sporting their blue-and-white-striped flannels from the earliest years, the Licey baseball club (Los Azules) fanned the sporting passions of the Dominican capital city in the years immediately preceding World War I. Island championship tournaments were soon held, and the Nuevo club captured the first in 1912. The Ponce team from Puerto Rico would make the first barnstorming visit by a foreign ballclub four years later, and by 1921, Escogido (Los Rojos) was organized to challenge the Licey team's island baseball superiority. The new team was actually a merger of three teams from the capital city

(San Carlos, Delco-Light, and Los Muchachos). Five games were played between the new rivals that first year, with Licey taking a narrow 3–2 edge behind Puerto Rican slugging star Pedro Miguel Caratini and the first great Dominican moundsman, Enrique Hernández ("Indio Bravo"). Another pioneering Dominican player was Juan "Tetelo" Vargas, an established visiting star in the Cuban league and later a Puerto Rican Hall-of-Famer who would earn batting and base-stealing championships on the latter island in the late 1930s and early 1940s as he approached 40. The fleet-footed Dominican infielder would once smash seven consecutive homers in a two-game span during 1931 Negro-league play, later hit .404 in Puerto Rico in 1943-44, and star with the barnstorming Havana Red Sox, New York Cubans, and New York Cuban Stars.

By the late 1920s it had become fashionable to important high-priced Cuban baseball mercenaries for the Dominican annual championship tournaments, and the rosters of Licey and Escogido were soon jammed with Cuban fixtures like batting champion Alejandro Oms, versatile hurler and hitter Martín Dihigo, pitchers Ramón Bragaña and Cocaína García, and outstanding infielders Pedro Arango and Pelayo Chacón. This escalation of talent and stakes reached its climax with the great summer championship of 1937 in which newly established strongman Rafael "Papa" Trujillo found his power riding on the prestige of his personally chosen Los Dragones ballclub (Chapter 6). Having renamed Santo Domingo in his own image as Ciudad Trujillo, "El Jefe" combined the rosters of ancient rivals Licey and Escogido to do battle under his personal banner against the rural Aguilas Cibaeñas and Estrellas Orientales ballclubs. Trujillo unleashed a torrent of under-the-table pesos to recruit his superteam of stellar Cubans and marquee blackballers like Josh Gibson and Satchel Paige. With an army of well-paid imports, Trujillo would narrowly win his cherished championship during the most famous island round-robin matchup of the "amateur" baseball years. Yet even that summer's memorable tournament remains only slightly more than a footnote played against the backdrop of several decades of fierce Licey and Escogido rivalry.

The great rivalries of the Dominican championship series have taken on a new luster in the years since 1951, Licey and Escogido combining for 26 titles in 38 subsequent seasons of league play. After 1937, Dominican baseball had gone into hibernation for more than a decade. But by 1951, with Licey's first professional island championship, the game came roaring back in full glory. And after the short experiment in summer baseball, the Dominican winter circuit kicked in for the 1955-56 season with even greater hopes for grabbing its full share of winterball headlines.

The new circuit was indeed one-sided for a while. Escogido (which had not won a title in four years of summer play) took the first three winter pennants and five of the first six. Big-leaguers were now invited onto the

Dominican rosters, and the league thus displayed a wealth of talent comparable to competing winter circuits. It was not surprising that Escogido dominated for the remainder of the 1950s since Trujillo's favored ballclub was owned by the dictator's brother and was thus assured of special clout for stockpiling the best of local and imported talent. Many Escogido stars of that first decade are names familiar to every big-league fan: Matty, Felipe, and Jesús Alou, Juan Marichal, Ossie Virgil, Frank Howard, Stan Williams, Bill White, Willie Kirkland, Andre Rogers, Willie McCovey. If the Escogido roster seemed to boast a disproportionate number of New York and San Francisco Giants, this was not an accident. Giants scout Alex Pompez (once owner of the New York Cubans Negro-league ballclub) had already signed the first two Dominican big-league imports—Felipe Alou and Juan Marichal—and 40 years of connections with the Latin baseball scenes had earned Pompez special standing with Trujillo's hand-picked agent for Dominican ballplayers, the dictator's son Ramfis.

Modern Dominican League action has spawned its handful of heroes largely ignored outside the island. Every Latin nation has its closet baseball legend or two, remembered and even cherished epic feats hidden from North American fans and the sporting press but of true mythic status on the homefront. In Cuba, such status, at least in the pre-Castro epoch, was long reserved for José Méndez and Cristóbal Torriente as well as screwball master Luís Tiant the elder. In Mexico, there will always be Héctor Espino, the Latin Babe Ruth. In Venezuela, hero worship surrounds the elder Luís Aparicio as much as his major league son and the pioneering moundsman Alejandro Carrasquel as much as the unrelated big-league shortstop with the same surname. In Puerto Rico, barroom tales still feature Perucho Cepeda and Poncho Coimbre, occasionally Canena Márquez or Luís Olmo. And in the Dominican Republic, the name that demands such reverence is Guayubin Olivo, the ageless Dominican left-handed pitcher of the 1950s and 1960s who debuted unnoticed as a 41-year-old major leaguer in Pittsburgh while an entire nation proudly watched back home.

Like Tony (Pedro) Oliva in Cuba and Vic Power (Pollet) of Puerto Rico, this Dominican hero came to the big leagues under another name, one somewhat different from the popular moniker he wore back home. He was born as Diómedes Antonio Olivo in the tiny village of Guayubin nestled in the province of Montecristi on the northwest side of the island. During his debut seasons of the early 1940s with a semipro club from Puerto Plata, Olivo was endlessly referred to by fans and press alike simply as "the great pitcher from Guayubin," and the designation stuck, as such colorful handles so often do in the world of sport. Oblivious to the tradition, however, U.S. media and fans knew him simply by the name Diómedes Olivo. That is, if they paid him any attention.

Once he had arrived in "the show," his most productive early years lost to the big-league color barrier, Olivo made only a tiny impression on the collective baseball memory banks. It was a rather considerable impression at the moment of its occurrence, however, especially if one hailed from Pittsburgh or Hispaniola. Olivo was hardly a major factor in his first Pittsburgh relief appearance on the afternoon of September 5, 1960, but over the final three weeks of the tense 1960 pennant chase the Dominican would enjoy four crucial mop-up assignments. He handled them brilliantly, recording a 10-inning 2.70 ERA and fanning 10 enemy batters in the process. While it would be something of an exaggeration to claim that Olivo actually saved a pennant in Pittsburgh that fall, it would not be amiss to suggest that he helped. And for Dominican baseball watchers, it was all sweet justification for the man who had been the greatest lefty of Dominican baseball throughout the 1950s and perhaps all time.

Guayubin Olivo merits a small niche in baseball history if only for his distinction as baseball's oldest-ever rookie (this distinction depending on Satchel Paige's true birthdate). Yet his contribution, minimal as it was on the major league scene, consists of more than trivia. During what actually constituted an "official" rookie season in 1962 (at 43, and in a minimun number of appearances to qualify for full rookie status), Olivo took the National League by storm, baffling the league's hitters with a 5-1 record, 2.77 ERA, and 7 important saves across 62 appearances. It was a last proud hurrah for a fading veteran with a spent fastball, however, and Olivo lost all five of his 1963 decisions with the St. Louis Cardinals.

For Dominican fans, it hardly matters that Guayubin Olivo had only a brief moment in the North American sunshine. Important records and feats in Dominican League history are a heritage of every Dominican fanático, just as the epic events of the major leagues are for the North American fan. And many of those feats involved Guayubin Olivo. As early as 1944, Olivo had starred on his country's team in the amateur world series staged in Caracas. Two seasons later, he did the same during Pan American Games competition in Barranquilla, Colombia. An outstanding batsman as well as fearsome moundsman, Guayubin played regularly in the outfield when not serving on the mound. And in September 1947 he hurled a memorable no-hitter for Licey against ancient rival Escogido in the Dominican capital city. Once organized professional play returned to the island in 1951, Olivo paced the same Licey club with league-best totals in wins (10), strikeouts (65), and ERA (1.90) during the maiden season. While again leading the circuit in ERA in both 1952 and 1954, Guayubin also continued to make history with his bat, once breaking up a memorable scoreless duel (and no-hitter) between big-leaguer Ewell Blackwell and Negro-leaguer Johnny Wright with a clutch pinch-hit ninth-inning single. A week after his memorable pinch hitting Diómedes Olivo would hurl his second Dominican no-hitter, again versus the rival Escogido ballclub.

Lost Pitching Records of Diomedes "Guayubin" Olivo

Olivo's Dominican Winter-League Record

Year	Team	League	W-L	Pct.	G	IP	ERA	SO	Hits
1951	Licey	Dominican (Summer)	10-5	.667	16	107	1.90	65	107
1952	Licey	Dominican (Summer)	10-5	.667	19	115.1	1.33	79	93
1953	Licey	Dominican (Summer)	6-2	.750	19	96	2.34	57	104
1954	Licey	Dominican (Summer)	8-2	.800	13	87	1.86	33	75
55-56	Licey	Dominican (Winter)	8-3	.728	16	105.2	1.53	37	103
56-57	Licey	Dominican (Winter)	10-4	.714	16	107.2	1.84	45	89
57-58	Licey	Dominican (Winter)	4-8	.333	18	82.2	4.79	65	98
58-59	Licey	Dominican (Winter)	4-2	.667	21	17.2	2.13	66	65
59-60	Licey	Dominican (Winter)	7-6	.538	22	116	2.33	98	98
60-61	Licey	Dominican (Winter)	10-6	.625	20	142	1.58	160	95
63-64	Licey	Dominican (Winter)	9-3	.750	18	114	2.37	37	115
Totals			86-46	.652	198	1,088.9	2.11	742	1,042

Olivo's "Foreign" Career Record

Year	Team	League	W-L	Pct.	G	IP	ERA	SO	Hits
1955	Havana	Cuban (Winter)	0-1	.000	7	13	5.54	4	21
1955	Mexico City	Mexican	8-6	.571	28	141	4.91	120	151
1956	Mexico City	Mexican	15-8	.652	32	197	2.65	115	197
1957	Mexico City	Mexican	3-1	.750	5	36	2.00	29	27
1958	Mexico City	Mexican	8-6	.571	28	151	3.81	122	160
1959	Poza Rica	Mexican	21-8	.724	35	247	3.02	233	219
1960	Pittsburgh	National	0-0	.000	4	10	2.70	10	8
1961	Columbus	International	11-7	.611	66	130	2.01	118	100
1962	Pittsburgh	National	5-1	.833	62	84	2.79	66	88
1963	St. Louis	National	0-5	.000	19	13.1	5.40	9	16
Major League Totals			**5-6**	**.455**	**85**	**107.1**	**3.10**	**85**	**112**
Overall "Foreign" Totals			71-43	.623	286	1,022.1	NA	826	987

When the curtain finally dropped on his lengthy career, this greatest of Dominican southpaws had left a truly impressive legacy. Included were lifetime league bests in ERA (2.11), winning percentage (86-46, .652), victories (86), and total strikeouts (742). A third career no-hitter was added to his portfolio during the 1961 International League season, tossed by a 44-year-old. The career ledger of Diomedes Olivo is as impressive as it is almost unknown to fans who thought of him only as a mere "one-year-wonder" with the Clemente-led Pirates of the Bill Mazeroski and Bob Friend era.

In the end, the Dominican League's greatest boasting point is its role as a major league farm system stocked with a seemingly endless supply of fresh arms and potent bats. The trickle started with Olivo and Marichal and Alou. Ossie Virgil was technically the first of his countrymen to reach the promised land when he donned a New York Giants uniform in 1956, but Virgil was raised in the environs of New York City and qualifies as a Dominican ballplayer by birth certificate alone. It was on the playgrounds of the Bronx, not the sugar fields of Santo Domingo or San Pedro, where Ossie Virgil learned to hit, run, and field ground balls. In the 1970s and 1980s the floodgates opened full force; Dominicans dotted almost every big-league roster. By the early 1990s, the Dominican Republic had passed Cuba and Canada in the race to supply the most foreign-grown U.S. baseball talent. By 1993, Canadians could slap one another on the back in celebration of two World Series triumphs by their beloved Toronto Blue Jays and point with pride to the fact that their Dominicans had finally beaten the Yankee Dominicans.

And another point of pride is a Dominican domination of sorts during the second phase of Latin baseball's winter showcase, the Caribbean World Series. The Dominicans first entered the series in the year of its revival, 1970. They were a substitute, along with Mexico, for the Cubans and Panamanians, the cream and the chaff of the first decade of play. Dominican performance in the second phase of CWS competition has been a proper reflection of the general upgrade of the Dominican winter circuit and the quantum leap in the nation's big-league talent parade during the same quarter century. In 23 winters of renewed play the Dominican entrants have captured the most games (74 through 1992), won the most tournament titles (8, compared with 6 for Puerto Rico in the same period), and established the highest overall winning percentage (barely a nose above Puerto Rico and Venezuela, who have each won a total of 70 ballgames). Slowly but steadily, the Dominican League teams have built their trophy stash, beginning with a first CWS title in 1971 and culminating in two victories during the 1990 and 1991 Miami-based experiments. Despite missing out on the first 11 years of competition the Dominican-Leaguers now trail only Puerto Rico (with 11 titles) in total tournament championships, having finally overhauled the Cubans, who dominated the first decade of Caribbean playoffs.

Yet despite the effusive attention from media and fans, Dominican baseball is still surrounded with numerous misconceptions. The foremost misunderstanding is a notion that the Dominican Republic is exclusively a proving ground for shortstops and other weak-sticking infielders of the Pepe Frías and Mario Mendoza type. None would dispute that Dominican shortstops have earned a chunk of the island's fame in the popular imagination. All true baseball fanatics can recite the litany of at least a handful—Fernández, Griffin, Manuel Lee, Mariano Duncan, and Julio César Franco. To date, several dozen have reached the big leagues. But shortstops alone have not cornered the market on Dominican imports. The greatest island big-leaguer, indeed the small nation's most noted sporting emissary, was a pitcher from the tiny village of Laguna Verde. Next in stature to the Dominican Dandy are the three Alou brothers, all outfielders by trade. And perhaps the greatest recent stars have been outfielder César Cedeño and shortstop-turned-second-sacker Julio Franco.

If the exclusivity of shortstops is something of a misconception in compartmentalizing the Dominican talent pool, so is the prominence of San Pedro de Macoris. The all-time roster of big-leaguers born in San Pedro de Macoris recently totaled 38 (through the 1992 season), certainly a considerable number for any city. Not on the San Pedro list, however, are the three greatest Dominican players of all time—Marichal, Felipe Alou, and Manny Mota. And it can be noted that while San Pedro holds an indelible reputation as the birthplace of shortstops, only a dozen Macoricanos have actually made it to the majors at this position. The best of the lot, Julio César Franco, hails from the neighboring sugar-mill village of Hato Mayor but was raised a native son of San Pedro. It can be said of Franco, however, that while he broke into organized baseball as a shortstop, his big-league tenure has branded him a second baseman and (after injuries) a designated hitter. Also, catcher Tony Peña was raised in San Pedro and learned his baseball there (thus hiking the number of big-league native sons to 39), although Peña's birthplace is technically the nearby village of Montecristi.

Certainly the Dominican island has produced its fair portion of slugging and hurling heroes and its complement of vacuum-cleaner glue-fingered middle infielders, as the earlier chapters of this book have demonstrated. The numbers suggest far more great sluggers and hurlers than infield wizards. And among the true greats, Marichal, Mota, the eldest Alou, Carty, George Bell (and perhaps even Pedro Guerrero with his 215 career homers and .300 lifetime average) overshadow all others, especially current standard-bearing infielders Franco and Fernández.

Yet these great stars of the past aside, the future of Dominican baseball seems to stand at a dangerous crossroads. The player pipeline shows no immediate signs of running dry, and even the opening of Cuba does not suggest any immediate replacement for Dominican talent. But the winter-league season that has been the heart and soul of the island sport is facing a wrenching economic crisis. Politics seems to disrupt each winter's play on the Dominican homefront with an endless series of electric shutdowns that dim stadium lights and marketplace collapses that strip the pockets of potential fans. Plans for a replacement wintertime Arizona league sponsored

San Pedro de Macoris Major League Roster

(Grouped by field position and ordered by date of major league debut)

Player	Position	Birthdate	Big-League Debut Date (Team)
Amado Samuel	Shortstop	12-6-1938	4-10-1962 (Milwaukee Braves)
Rafael Robles	Shortstop	10-20-1947	4-8-1969 (San Diego Padres)
Pepe Frías	Shortstop	7-14-1948	4-6-1973 (Montreal Expos)
Nelson Norman	Shortstop	5-23-1959	5-20-1978 (Texas Rangers)
Rafael Ramírez	Shortstop	2-18-1958	8-4-1980 (Atlanta Braves)
Tony Fernández	Shortstop	8-6-1962	9-2-1983 (Toronto Blue Jays)
Mariano Duncan	Shortstop	3-13-1963	4-9-1985 (Los Angeles Dodgers)
Manuel "Manny" Lee	Shortstop	6-17-1965	4-10-1985 (Toronto Blue Jays)
Juan "Tito" Bell	Shortstop	3-29-1968	9-6-1989 (Baltimore Orioles)
José Offerman	Shortstop	11-8-1968	8-19-1990 (Los Angeles Dodgers)
Andres Santana	Shortstop	2-5-1968	9-16-1990 (San Francisco Giants)
Manny Alexander	Shortstop	3-20-1971	9-18-1992 (Baltimore Orioles)
Pedro González	Infield	12-12-1937	4-11-1963 (New York Yankees)
Rick Joseph	Infield/Outfield	8-24-1939	6-18-1964 (Kansas City Athletics)
Rafael Batista	First Base	10-20-1947	6-17-1973 (Houston Astros)
Juan Bernhardt	Infield	8-31-1953	7-10-1976 (New York Yankees)
Art DeFreitas	First Base	4-26-1953	9-7-1978 (Cincinnati Reds)
Pedro Guerrero	Infield/Outfield	6-29-1956	9-22-1978 (Los Angeles Dodgers)
Julio Franco	Second Base	8-23-1958	4-23-1982 (Philadelphia Phillies)
Juan Samuel	Infield/Outfield	12-9-1960	8-24-1983 (Philadelphia Phillies)
Juan Castillo	Infield	1-25-1962	4-12-1986 (Milwaukee Brewers)
Manny Jiménez	Outfield	11-19-1938	4-11-1962 (Kansas City Athletics)
Rico Carty	Outfield	9-1-1939	9-15-1963 (Milwaukee Braves)
Elvio Jiménez	Outfield	1-6-1940	10-4-1964 (New York Yankees)
Al Javier	Outfield	2-4-1954	9-9-1976 (Houston Astros)
George (Jorge) Bell	Outfield	10-21-1959	4-9-1981 (Toronto Blue Jays)
Carmen Castillo	Outfield	6-8-1958	7-17-1982 (Cleveland Indians)
Alejandro Sánchez	Outfield	2-14-1959	9-6-1982 (Philadelphia Phillies)
Sammy Sosa	Outfield	11-10-1968	6-16-1989 (Texas Rangers)
Luís Mercedes	Outfield	2-15-1968	9-8-1991 (Baltimore Orioles)
Santiago Guzmán	Pitcher	7-25-1949	9-30-1969 (St. Louis Cardinals)
Joaquín Andújar	Pitcher	11-12-1952	4-8-1976 (Houston Astros)
Santo Alcala	Pitcher	12-23-1952	4-10-1976 (Cincinnati Reds)
Ramón Romero	Pitcher	1-8-1959	9-18-1984 (Cleveland Indians)
Balvino Galvez	Pitcher	3-31-1964	5-7-1986 (Los Angeles Dodgers)
Ravelo Manzanillo	Pitcher	10-17-1963	9-25-1988 (Chicago White Sox)
Josias Manzanillo	Pitcher	10-16-1967	10-5-1991 (Boston Red Sox)
Ben Rivera	Pitcher	1-11-1969	4-9-1992 (Atlanta Braves)

Honor Roll of the Dominican Republic's Greatest Players

Pitcher	Juan Marichal (major leagues, 1960–1975; elected to Cooperstown, 1983)
Pitcher	Joaquín Andújar (major leagues, 1976–1988)
Pitcher	Diomedes "Guayubin" Olivo (winter leagues and major leagues, 1960–1962)
Infielder	Tony Fernández (major leagues, 1983–1993)
Infielder	Julio Franco (major leagues, 1982–1993; American League batting champion)
Outfielder	Juan "Tetelo" Vargas (winter league and blackball star, 1930s and 1940s)
Outfielder	Felipe Alou (major leagues, 1958–1974)
Outfielder	Matty Alou (major leagues, 1960–1974; National League batting champion)
Outfielder	George Bell (major leagues, 1981–1993; American League MVP)
Outfielder	Rico Carty (major leagues, 1963–1979)
Outfielder	Manny Mota (major leagues, 1962–1982)

by major league baseball can only spell further long-range trouble. Will the player talent spew forth as it has once the island is robbed of its showcase display of highly competitive winter-league action during coming decades? Will sugar-mill youth still worship and emulate the nation's great ballplayer heroes once those heroes are no more than dusty legends of the past rather than contemporary flesh-and-blood inspirations? The jury is still out, and likely to remain so for some time.

Puerto Rico, Big-League Launching Pad

If Puerto Rico seems to trail its Caribbean rivals Cuba and the Dominican Republic in historical tradition and big-league impact, this is in many ways an illusion. Puerto Rico's rosy winter-league tradition is second to none despite setbacks of late in playing conditions and showcase talent. Its major league native sons will measure up to those of Cuba and the Dominican Republic, especially in the decades of the sixties and seventies, as well as in the current epoch. And it is this half country and half state alone that can boast as its native son the greatest Latin American baseball hero of them all. Yet in some respects the island nation caught between statehood and political sovereignty has always been forced to play second fiddle to its baseball-proud neighbors.

Perhaps poverty has as much to do with this as anything. Like youngsters raised on the U.S. mainland, Puerto Rican youth of the most recent decades have had other options to pursue as their means of livelihood and a pathway to fame and fortune. Unlike the Third World island Hispaniola, Puerto Rico has bolted almost overnight from a sleepy agricultural society to a teeming extension of Miami and Nueva York. Baseball has never been an exclusive ticket to the Yankee dream of wealth and stardom; the youth of San Juan are not as bound by hopeless poverty as those living in the shadows of the sugar factories that rim the outskirts of San Pedro de Macoris.

And if the level of talent and sheer numbers of Puerto Rican ballplayers have been tailing off of late, it is also true that the winterball of the island has fallen on equally hard times. Longtime Puerto Rican baseball official Luís Rodríguez Mayoral has traced the malaise of the island's winter season to the sharp drop in big-name talent that was already noticeable by the late 1970s. While native stars like Tony Peña, Tony Fernández, and Alfredo Griffin still make at least token appearances in their hometown leagues during off-season months, the same is no longer true of Puerto Rico. Whereas Roberto Clemente, Juan Pizarro, Orlando Cepeda, and Vic Power could once be counted on to draw out the fans of San Juan and Mayaguez in record numbers during December and January, today's high-salaried native sons have little need to suit up after a tough major league grind has finally wound down in October. A mid–1950s outfield of the Santurce Crabbers once boasted the likes of Clemente, Willie Mays, and Bob Thurman. The same ballclub in 1990 boasted a triple-A outfield featuring names like Albert Hall, Mark Ryal, and Osvaldo Sánchez.

But the island nation nonetheless still boasts a glorious half century of professional baseball tradition. The amateur foundations of Puerto Rican ballplaying rest in the same final decade of the nineteenth century that brought baseball's discovery to almost all of Cuba's Caribbean neighbors. The first newspaper reports of an amateur contest on the island dated from 1897 (the year of Puerto Rico's independence from Spain), and first accounts of an organized game complete with spectators appeared in January of the following year. This landmark contest, played upon San Juan's grassy bicycle course with patrons paying a 40-cent admission charge, was between a club called Borinquen (local Indian name for the island) and another christened Almendares after an already-popular Cuban ballclub. True baseball tradition fittingly intervened from the very first moment with a rainout after three innings; thus the pioneering contest was not actually completed until three weeks later, and then only after a second attempt at play was washed out by the uncooperative elements.

Professional play arrived in Puerto Rico in 1938 with the founding of the island nation's winter circuit, a league that has featured essentially the same franchises (Caguas, Ponce, Mayaguez, San Juan, Santurce, Bayamón, Guayama) throughout the circuit's entire 55-year history. Los Brujos

(Witches) of Guayama would reign victorious in the first two league tournaments of 1938-39 and 1939-40. Ponce dominated play in the early and mid–1940s, taking five league titles in the six seasons between 1942 and 1947. It was the decade of the 1950s, however, that witnessed the league's "golden age" with such native stars as Power, Clemente, Pizarro, Orlando Cepeda, Luís Arroyo, and Rubén Gómez carving out memorable performances alongside such illustrious imports as Mays, Bob Thurman, Willard Brown, Luke Easter, Sam Jones, Bobo Holloman, Earl Wilson, Wes Covington, George Crowe, Hank Aaron, Bob Cerv, and Bob Boyd. The strength of the Puerto Rican winter circuit during this epoch was fittingly measured not only by its illustrious lineups of front-line major-leaguers but by its four championships earned during the first seven years of Caribbean World Series competition.

Memorable stars of the lost eras of Puerto Rican league play were not limited to household-name big-leaguers but included many island heroes and Negro-league standouts. Most notable were Puerto Rico's two chief ballplaying idols from those earliest years before Roberto Clemente charged onto the scene. By the late 1920s and throughout the 1930s, Pedro "Perucho" Cepeda, father of the future big-leaguer, carved out his special niche with barnstorming ballclubs throughout Puerto Rico and the Dominican Republic. In the first season of Puerto Rican professional play it was Cepeda who led all batsmen with a remarkable .465 average, and in 1939-40 Cepeda reigned as batting champion with an equally lofty .383 mark. In four more seasons with Guayama the following decade the remarkable outfielder compiled a composite .394 average (293 for 743) while posting a single-season hits record (81) that stood for the first full decade of island play. Francisco "Pancho" Coimbre matched Cepeda feat for feat and hit for hit throughout much of the pre–World War II period and captured league hitting titles in 1942-43 and 1944-45. Not to be outdone by his rival, Coimbre nearly matched Cepeda's 1939 campaign with a .425 average during the 1945 winter season. Only U.S. import Willard Brown (.347) would eventually hold a higher lifetime batting mark in the second-oldest Caribbean winter circuit than the .337 career number posted by the talented Poncho Coimbre.

Others carved out their considerable reputations as well. Saturnino Escalera would one day be the first black player to wear a Cincinnati Reds uniform, but first the Santurce native would earn a solid winterball following with a credible .275 career hitting mark and more than 1,000 lifetime base hits. Nino Escalera still ranks third all time in Puerto Rican–league base hits and career runs scored, trailing only Luís "Canena" Márquez and Carlos Bernier in both categories. Canena Márquez was a dark-skinned outfielder who barely sneaked into the big leagues for a journeyman's "cup of coffee" in the shadow of Jackie Robinson (recording 99 games and less than 150 at-bats with the Braves and Cubs in 1951 and 1954), yet the brilliant "Canena" built a two-decade winter career that brought him 3,457 hits and a .306 lifetime hitting ledger. The diminutive Juan "Felo" Guilbe, on the other hand, is the name still revered by old-timers as the island's greatest outfielder, a flychaser on a par with Mays or the immortal Clemente. A star with Negro-league clubs like the New York Cuban Stars and Indianapolis Clowns, Guilbe was a regular attraction on ballfields throughout Venezuela, the Dominican Republic, Colombia, the United States, and Canada across most of three decades. Big-league star Juan Pizarro also paced the island circuit in strikeouts a remarkable five-straight seasons as the 1950s merged with the 1960s. José Guillermo "Pantalones" Santiago was a pitcher whose brief major league credentials (3-2 in three short seasons with Cleveland and Kansas City) do not do even partial justice to a never-to-be-forgotten island legend. And Carlos Bernier, cup-of-coffee outfielder and Clemente's teammate with the Pittsburgh Pirates, is another stateside journeyman who stood far taller, threw harder, ran faster, and swung a meatier bat during the winter months.

Throughout the fifties the Puerto Rican winter league earned a reputation as something of a launching pad for major league stardom. Bob Clemente, of course, first earned his wings on hometown turf in the uniform of the Santurce Crabbers. Luís Olmo would emerge from an illustrious Puerto Rican winter career that spanned 15 seasons to earn unique distinction as the first Puerto Rican to stroke a home run in World Series play. Olmo earned his piece of Puerto Rican baseball history by connecting for Brooklyn in game three of the 1949 classic. And Luís Arroyo would learn the craft on his native island that would eventually make him one of the most feared relievers of the 1960s with the Yankees. Arroyo, who led the island circuit in strikeouts with 145 in 1956-57, would eventually post a league-best 29 saves for a powerhouse 1961 New York club forever immortalized by the record home-run onslaughts of Roger Maris and Mickey Mantle. The list of other big-leaguers who cut their teeth during winter-league action in San Juan, Ponce, and Mayaguez reads like a who's-who of 1950s and 1960s big-league stars: North Americans Roy Campanella, Johnny Logan, Bob Buhl, Jim Rivera, Brooks Lawrence, Lew Burdette, Bill Skowron, Billy Hunter, Henry Aaron, Bob Turley, Frank Robinson, Don Zimmer, Sandy Koufax and Maury Wills; Puerto Ricans Clemente, Rubén Gómez, Juan Pizarro, Orlando Cepeda, and Vic Power; Cubans Tony Oliva, Luís Tiant, Jr., and Tony Pérez; Dominicans Manny Mota, Ossie Virgil, Sr., and Julian Javier.

And the league remained an exceptional training ground for budding North American stars in later years. Future Hall-of-Famer Mike Schmidt would eventually credit his adjustments to major league pitching to a 1973-74 trip around the Puerto Rican winter circuit. The touted Phillies rookie had batted only .196 in his 1973 rookie campaign but jumped nearly 100 points and paced the National league in roundtrippers the very next season. And Rickey Henderson would hone his base-running skills on the island in the mid–1970s. Henderson smashed all earlier base-running records for island winter play when he pilfered 44 bases during 1980-81 (a 60-game season) while enjoying his second December–January visit with the Ponce Lions.

Many of the greatest feats of Puerto Rican league play were performed by outsiders, often Negro-leaguers like Willard "Ese Hombre" Brown, Bob Thurman, and Luke Easter. It was Brown during the late 1940s and early 1950s who became the largest star in the Puerto Rican winter-baseball firmament with two triple crowns, a record career .347 batting mark, and a season-record 27 roundtrippers (1947-48). An aging Luke Easter blasted winter pitching for years and captured a home-run crown (1955-56) two years after his big-league career had collapsed with the Cleveland Indians. And strapping black outfielder Bob Thurman enjoyed several seasons on a par with those registered during the same decade by Willard Brown. Thurman would eventually overhaul Brown's career home-run record (finishing with 120) yet would capture only one individual long ball title (shared with Brown in 1948-49). Bob Thurman's big-league career would remain a disappointment, generating only 35 roundtrippers during five journeyman seasons in Cincinnati. Thurman's Puerto Rican stature was so elevated, however, that many island veterans still argue passionately that the 1954-55 Santurce outfield of Thurman, Clemente, and Willie Mays was the best ever seen upon any diamond in any country in any year and by any standard, offensive or defensive.

The instabilities of government and currency that have threatened winter play in the Dominican Republic of late are not factors in the equal downturn plaguing Puerto Rican winterball. Absence of high-visibility North American or Dominican stars and high-salaried native heroes (like Carlos Baerga, Rubén Sierra, or Juan González) are exclusively the culprits here, along with a severe assist from bad weather in two of the past three seasons. Only approximately 450 patrons were on hand in 17,000-seat Hiram Bithorn Stadium to witness each of the league's final games between the Mayaguez Indians and San Juan Metros in January 1992. Such a drought for Puerto Rican baseball, however, only seems to magnify the glories of the league's true heyday several decades back. Nonetheless, there is legitimate concern these days that the league may not be able to survive too many more winters of such spotty attendance. And it is not the apathetic fans or greedy and lazy ballplayers alone who are to blame for this sad state of affairs. Longtime Puerto Rican club official Luís Rodríquez Mayoral holds league and team managements largely responsible. Mayoral notes that stadium promotions are almost nonexistent, corporate sponsor-

Puerto Rican Baseball Hall of Fame Inductees (Players)

First Induction in Ponce, October 1991:

Luís Angel "Canena" Márquez—1954 winter-league batting champion and big-leaguer (1951–1954)

Francisco "Poncho" Coimbre—Highest lifetime winter-league average (.337) by a Puerto Rican

Pedro "Perucho" Cepeda—Winter-league and blackball barnstorming star of 1930s and 1940s

Roberto Clemente—Puerto Rico's greatest star and first Latin American inducted in Cooperstown

Robert "El Mucaro" Thurman (USA)—Winter-league slugging and pitching star of the 1940s and 1950s

Willard "Ese Hombre" Brown (USA)—Highest lifetime winter-league batting average (.347)

Orlando "Peruchin" Cepeda—First Latin American big-league home-run and RBI champion (1961)

Victor Pollet Power—Big league star of the 1950s known for fancy fielding at first base

Rubén Gómez—Relief ace with the New York Giants who started first West Coast big-league game

Juan "Terin" Pizarro—Eighth-winningest Latin American in major leagues with 131 victories

Second Induction in Ponce, November 1992:

Luís "Tite" Arroyo—Eight-year big-leaguer in 1950s (1955–1963) with 40-32 record

Carlos Bernier—Winter-league star and major-leaguer with Pittsburgh Pirates (1953)

Pedro Miguel Caratini—Slugging winter-league outfielder of the 1920s with Ponce Lions

Saturnino "Nino" Escalera—Winter-leaguer and first black player with Cincinnati Reds (1954)

José "El Olimpico" Figueroa—Winter-leaguer and Negro league star pitcher of the 1940s

Juan Guilbe—Winter-leaguer and Negro league pitcher and outfielder of the 1940s

Emilio "Millito" Navarro—Winter-league infielder and outfielder, 1922–1942

Rafael "Rafaelito" Ortiz—Star winter-league pitcher (1938–1948) with career 85-61 record

Luís Rodriguez Olmo—Winter-league star and major leaguer, 1943–1951

Jorge "Griffin" Tirado—Winter-league star, 1938–1951

Juan Esteban "Tetelo" Vargas (Dominican Republic)—Winter-league star, 1939–1946 ships are equally unknown, and league officials did next to nothing to counter movement of the 1990 and 1991 Caribbean World Series tournaments onto U.S. soil in Miami.

If baseball in Puerto Rico has now fallen on hard economic times and suffers waning interest, love for the long-standing traditions of the game seems largely untarnished. Nowhere have Puerto Rican fanáticos better displayed their passion for the game and its island history than with the recent institution in the city of Ponce of a Puerto Rican Baseball Hall of Fame meant to rival those of Havana, Mexico City, and Cooperstown. The roster of celebrated players during two initial induction banquets of 1991 and 1992 reads like a Puerto Rican baseball who's-who culled from five decades of exciting winter play. Two North Americans and one Dominican take their places in the hall of honor alongside 18 native islanders. The pantheon, now located in Ponce, is one Latin American baseball shrine not dominated by upstart Dominicans or Cubans who so long reigned as apostles of the Caribbean national pastime.

Honor Roll of Puerto Rico's Greatest Players

Pitcher	Juan Pizarro (major leagues, 1957–1974)
Catcher	Benito Santiago (major leagues, 1986–1993; National League Rookie of the Year)
Infielder	Perucho Cepeda (winter leagues and blackball star of 1930s and 1940s)
Infielder	Orlando Cepeda (major leagues, 1958–1974; National League home-run champion)
Infielder	Carlos Baerga (major leagues, 1990–1993)
Infielder	Sandy Alomar, Sr. (major leagues, 1964–1978)
Infielder	Roberto Alomar (major leagues, 1988–1993)
Infielder	Francisco "Poncho" Coimbre (winter leagues, 1930s and 1940s)
Outfielder	Roberto Clemente (major leagues, 1955–1972; elected to Cooperstown, 1973)
Outfielder	José Cruz (major leagues, 1970–1988)

When today's fan assesses the big-league scene, it is impossible not to observe a handful of young superstars who now carry the tradition of proud Roberto Clemente. Argument can be made that despite their lesser numbers (when compared to Dominican and Cuban products), the current handful of Puerto Rican stars surpass those of any other nation. Juan González may well be the game's future power-slugging great and seems destined to challenge the 50— and even the 60—home-run barrier. Rubén Sierra (despite a dip in production after a trade from Texas to Oakland) is still the closest thing in two decades to Clemente. Ivan Rodríguez and Benito Santiago are the two best Latin catchers ever to strap on the tools of ignorance, despite the defensive flair of Tony Peña and the clutch hitting of the late Venezuelan Bo Díaz. No infielder anywhere is better than Roberto Alomar day in and day out, wielding a bat or knocking down enemy base hits. And switch-hitting Carlos Baerga in three short seasons has given plenty of notice of a possible Hall of Fame career. Whatever clouds may now hang over Puerto Rico's winterball seasons, the island pipeline now open between San Juan and big-league camps has never been filled with a richer flow of quality talent.

Venezuela, Stepchild of Latin American Baseball

Venezuelan baseball gets none of its deserved respect. Neighbors located on the northern side of the Caribbean basin always somehow draw all the headlines. This is especially true when it comes to the Latin Americans serving in the big leagues. Cuba's Miñoso was the sensation of the 1950s; Clemente of Puerto Rico and Marichal of the Dominican grabbed headlines in the 1960s; Pérez and Cepeda kept the Cuban and Puerto Rican connections alive and well in the 1970s; Valenzuela was the media darling of the early 1980s; the past decade has fallen in love with the fairy-tale saga of Dominican shortstops from San Pedro de Macoris. Between Aparicio in the fifties and the sudden superstar status of Andrés Galarraga in 1993, Venezuela has clearly sunk to the back pages of Latin baseball history.

But Venezuela touts lustrous and well-documented diamond traditions and has spawned its own batch of big-league heroes on a par with those of its Caribbean neighbors. Only Cuba (1871) and Mexico (1933) preceded Venezuela (Alex Carrasquel in 1939) in cracking the big-league player roster. Puerto Rico (1952) and the Dominican Republic (1956) lagged far behind in first denting the big-league scene. A half-century-old Venezuelan winter league boasts a tradition second to none. And while the collection of Venezuelan big-leaguers may be somewhat overshadowed by the Dominican, Cuban, and Puerto Rican forces in mere numbers, when it comes to quality, the issue is open for debate.

It is the coastal plain of Venezuela and not the Dominican island that is the true home of shortstops. Here is the birthplace of Chico Carrasquel, the first big-league shortstop of distinction and the first Latin to appear in U.S. baseball's midsummer All-Star classic. Aparicio is not only arguably the best Latin shortstop ever to pull on spikes and glove but one of the tiny enclave of players at that position ever to earn Hall of Fame status. Davy Concepción and Ozzie Guillén are unmatched among Latin middle infielders of the 1970s and 1980s, respectively, and while Concepción may well be Latin America's next Cooperstown inductee, Guillén is rivaled only by Tony Fernández for pure glove work among Caribbean shortstops of the recent era. Venezuela's tally is thus two Hall-of-Famers (with the assumption that Concepción will soon be there) and two unmatched defensive greats (Carrasquel and Guillén). Carrasquel and Aparicio launched the popular image of the perfect Latin shortstop, an image that has long been at the heart of the Latin baseball story.

And there have been sluggers and hurlers launched out of Caracas and the oil-rich Venezuelan coastal plains. Tony Armas, long ranked as the best home-run producer of the region behind Pérez and Cepeda (he now also trails George Bell with 251 circuit blasts at the time of his retirement). Armas was the first Latin swinger to win two home-run titles (1981 with Oakland and 1984 with Boston), and while the first of these was tinged with illegitimacy by the strike-shortened 1981 season, the second came via a respectable 43 roundtrippers that outdistanced all American League rivals. Armas was also an RBI champion in the junior circuit in 1984 and narrowly missed home-run titles in 1980 (fourth with 35) and 1983 (second to Jim Rice with 36).

Yet it is Davy Concepción who now closely rivals Aparicio as the most noteworthy of Venezuelan big-leaguers. In the end, Concepción may be one of the most overlooked of all Latin American superstars. Here is an unflashy player by Latin standards who quickly amassed Cooperstown numbers while blessed with playing on baseball's most powerful teams of the early and mid-1970s. Wearing the unlucky uniform number 13 and showcasing consistent gold-glove performances across almost two decades, Davy Concepción became one of baseball's greatest shortstops of the expansion era. A mainstay of the Big Red Machine teams in Cincinnati, Concepción was elected team captain (1973) just in time to lead the powerhouse Reds to a string of postseason successes between 1973 and 1976, culminating in back-to-back world championships. He would play more than 100 games at the shortstop position for a dozen straight seasons and in 14 of 15 years (1971–1985); he would retire only 44 games shy of Larry Bowa's National League record for games played at the position. Only five Latin Americans now stand ahead of him in career base hits, and only four Latins (Aparicio, Pérez, Clemente, and Carew) enjoyed more big-league at-bats. It now seems only a matter of time until Davy Concepción is the next Latin welcomed through the portals of Cooperstown.

There have been other Venezuelan greats. Wilson Alvarez is rapidly developing as one of the best Latin hurlers of the mid-1990s and years beyond. Few left-handers in baseball are as dominating as the classy left-hander, with one of the smoothest deliveries and most accurate fastballs of the current epoch. Alvarez also holds the distinction of tossing a rare no-hitter in his first legitimate big-league start (with the Chicago White Sox in August 1991 versus Baltimore). The Alvarez no-hitter remains the only masterpiece tossed by a Venezuelan in big-league action. Two fine pitchers and a host of exceptional middle infielders have added to the increasingly lustrous Venezuelan diamond saga. Luís Leal was often erratic in his hot-and-cold career with Toronto's Blue Jays, once giving up a record five-straight hits at the opening of a ballgame and on another occasion allowing a team-record single-game 10 earned runs. By the time of his 1985 release, however, Leal trailed only Jim Clancy and Dave Stieb as Toronto's career leader in starts, innings, wins, losses, walks, and strikeouts. Ramón Monzant was a curveballing reliever for the New York Giants of the 1950s whose career exhibited erratic swings yet who started 16 games, hurled 150 innings, and won 8 contests during the Giants' maiden season of West Coast play. The best of the middle infielders include César Tóvar, César Gutiérrez, Alvaro Espinosa, and Fred Manrique. Tóvar and Gutiérrez will always be memorable to trivia buffs for unique single-game feats. Tóvar once played nine positions in a Minnesota Twins contest; Gutiérrez once belied his good-field-no-hit image with a miraculous six singles and one double during seven at-bats of game two (12 innings) during a June 1970 doubleheader. Alvaro Espinosa and Fred Manrique were players contributing quietly and steadily during the 1990s, Espinosa holding down regular shortstop positions for brief terms in New York and Cleveland and Manrique forming a slick White Sox doubleplay combination in 1987-88 with countryman Ozzie Guillén, squarely in the mold of those once anchored by Carrasquel and Aparicio.

It is a fact worth mentioning that Venezuelan baseball history is a most fertile ground for Latin baseball enthusiasts due in large part to a fine collection of materials that have found their way into print. The local writers of Caribbean winter-baseball history have been more active in Venezuela than anywhere else, and while all of these books are in Spanish, they are not very difficult to locate in the now considerable used-baseball-book marketplace. Thus a number of fine books are available to document the Venezuelan baseball saga across 47 seasons of winter-league play and 54 summers of Venezuelan big-league contributions. Among the best is a richly illustrated work, *Momentos Inolvidables del Béisbol Profesional Venezolano, 1946–1984* (Unforgettable Moments of Venezuelan Pro Baseball), which traces the greatest moments of Venezuelan baseball history. This tome by author Alexis Salas is a rare treat for any who can read their baseball history in Spanish. Hundreds of rare black-and-white action photos and player portraits supplement game-by-game accounts (replete with relevant box scores) of more than 150 incidents that have defined the classic rivalries and heroic feats of this ballplaying nation. Many of the reported events are those involving U.S. big-leaguers like Willie Mays, Bob Gibson, and Pete Rose, and a host of Dominican and Cuban stars receive extensive coverage. Smaller in scale than the Salas history yet equally valuable to all those interested in Venezuelan big-leaguers is a small paperback volume by Daniel F. Gutiérrez (*50 Años de Big Leaguers Venezolanos*, 1990) packed full of portraits and anecdotes concerning every native son who (through 1989 at least) has enjoyed even the briefest cup of coffee in a big-league ballpark.

Venezuelan baseball, like that of its Caribbean neighbors, stretches back before the turn of the century, and the nation's first exposure to the game can again be traced to Cuban sources. The true apostles of Latin baseball arrived on Venezuelan shores only a few short years after they brought their favorite sport to the cities and towns of Caribbean islands to the north, west, and east. Less than a decade after Cuban adventurers offered demonstration matches in the Mexican Yucatan and Cuban sugar-mill works began competitions in the Dominican Republic, a Cuban baseball apostle was at work in Venezuela. In 1895, Emilio Cramer first demonstrated the game there.

Yet if baseball came early to Venezuela, it developed more slowly here. It was 1940 when the country first tested the waters of international competition with an entry in the world amateur tournament played that year in distant Hawaii. While the Venezuelans were barely competitive the first time around with a respectable fifth-place finish, their showing indicated that a half century of amateur play at home had developed a fair mastery of the game. The world of amateur baseball was hardly prepared, however, for the surprise performance of the 1941 world-tourney entrant from Venezuela, which upset heavily favored Cuba and walked away with championship laurels in their second international competition. To prove that their sudden arrival on the amateur scene was no fluke, the Venezuelan team captured the 1944 and 1945 wartime world amateur championships.

True baseball respectability comes only with the professional game, however, and it was these amateur triumphs that lit the hunger for professional league play on the Venezuelan homefront. A professional winter circuit modeled after those of Cuba and Mexico was founded in 1946 with four ballclubs filling their rosters with local and imported Cuban and U.S. talent. Inaugural teams represented Cervecería Caracas (sponsored by a leading brewery in the nation's capital), Vargas, Magallanes, and Club Venezuela. Two of these clubs had already been longtime national rivals whose matchups fueled the emotions of the local fandom. Venezuelan professional play was thus launched with a respectable tradition of local competition already well established.

The first two winters of Venezuelan winter play brought much excitement and were already the substance of lasting legend. The very first batter of the first league game in 1946 was local hero Luís Aparicio, Sr., a crack shortstop for Magallanes whose son would be the greatest star the nation would ever produce. The elder Aparicio never saw big-league action, but one of his teammates already had. The pitcher in the opening game was the first Venezuelan big-leaguer of note, Alex Carrasquel. Carrasquel braved racial taunts for a number of years around the American League in the decade before Jackie Robinson. And in the opening game he hurled Magallanes to victory over Club Venezuela. While Carrasquel never became a big-league household name, his nephew soon would, for also playing in the first Venezuelan professional season was a shortstop on the roster of Cervecería Caracas named Alfonso Carrasquel, soon better known to North American fans as "Chico" Carrasquel. The younger Carrasquel debuted dramatically in Caracas only five days after the opening league match. Chico would blast a game-winning seventh-inning homer in his first pro contest, which launched him to immediate idol status among the nation's passionate fans.

The first true notice of Venezuelan baseball for the fans and observers of the major league game would come a year later in the second season of Venezuelan winter competition. During the spring-training season of 1947 (at the time Jackie Robinson was preparing in Havana for his dramatic big-league debut) the New York Yankees paid a barnstorming visit for a four-game tour of the country. With stars like Berra, DiMaggio, Rizzuto, Henrich, and Allie Reynolds, the Yankees would use the 1947 season as a springboard to a two-decade domination of American League and World Series play. That spring the New Yorkers won three of their four exhibition contests with the Venezuelan League teams but lost the opener on a ninth-inning homer by Vargas player Lloyd Davenport, a U.S. import. While it was obvious that such exhibitions held little stake for the touring big-leaguers and that the Venezuelans clubs (filled with imports) only nominally represented the Latin country or its brand of native play, the victory over the 1947 American League champion Yankees went far to boost the home-front and stateside reputations of the new Venezuelan professional circuit.

The most southern of the winter-baseball circuits continued to enjoy a steady if not always spectacular growth once regular Venezuelan migration to the big leagues began in the 1950s. Cervecería Caracas renamed its sponsored club the Caracas Lions once it was determined that visible outward sponsorship of the team was hurting sales of its beer among fans of the other league ballclubs. By the mid-fifties, the circuit had expanded by six teams and split into eastern and western divisions. Renewal of a second phase of competition in the season-ending Caribbean World Series by 1970 brought the Venezuelan League back into direct postseason competition with its rival circuits, and the first phase two CWS tourney, staged appropriately in Caracas, also brought the league its first CWS title triumph when Magallanes under Cuban manager Carlos Pascual swept aside the competition behind the slugging of native son César Tóvar and the pitching of imported Cubans Orlando Peña and Aurelio Monteagudo. Venezuela's CWS representatives would soon claim four additional championship flags, in 1979, 1982, 1984, and 1989. Able to escape the brutal acts of nature (floods and tropical storms) that eventually plagued Puerto Rican winter play of the late 1980s and the worsening political instability that has recently threatened Dominican action, the Venezuelan winter league has emerged as the most solid circuit of all entering the increasingly lean winter-league years of the 1990s.

Honor Roll of Venezuela's Greatest Players

Pitcher	Alejandro Carrasquel (major leagues, 1939–1949)
Catcher	Bo Díaz (major leagues, 1977–1989)
Infielder	Luís Aparicio (major leagues, 1956–1973; elected to Cooperstown, 1984)
Infielder	Alfonso "Chico" Carrasquel (major leagues, 1950–1959)
Infielder	Davy Concepción (major leagues, 1970–1988)
Infielder	Ozzie Guillén (major leagues, 1985–1993; American League Rookie of the Year)
Outfielder	Tony Armas (major leagues, 1976–1989; American League home-run champion)
Outfielder	Andrés Galarraga (major leagues, 1985–1993; National League batting champion)
Outfielder	Vic Davalillo (major leagues, 1963–1980)

Venezuelans, like other Latins, are most proud of the home-grown big-league talent that Venezuelan winter baseball has provided through the years. Forty years of Venezuelan winter-league play have brought many a hero, and not an insignificant number have been home-grown sons who have eventually found their way into big league ballparks. For years the major league career of Tony Armas, for example, was followed with an intensity rivaling national affairs of state. There was a particularly strong love affair during the 1993 season with native son Andrés Galarraga. As the Big Cat chased a batting title with the expansion Colorado Rockies and even flirted with hitting .400 for more than two-thirds of a season, the local Venezuelan press trumpeted his every at-bat along the way.

Venezuelan fans followed Galarraga's every game throughout the 1993 summer campaign with a national passion that awoke echoes of earlier fanaticism surrounding the careers of such potent native sons as Carrasquel, Aparicio, and Armas. While their saga has not been as widely acclaimed in the North American press, Venezuelan partisans have remained as dedicated to their national pastime as fans anywhere in the Caribbean baseball-loving world.

Mexico, Escaping Minor League Shadows

Mexican baseball history is dominated by three towering figures. Jorge Pasquel failed grandly in his noble project to bring major league status to a nation battling a debilitating two-century inferiority complex. Héctor Espino built a legend in obscurity, slugging home runs on a par with Sadaharu Oh and Babe Ruth yet remaining virtually unknown outside his nation's borders. And Fernando Valenzuela captured imaginations both north and south of the border as he single-handedly launched the Latin American big-league invasion of the 1980s. Each of these three baseball giants, however, has contributed mightily to an image of Mexican baseball as irrepressibly "minor league" in stature and accomplishment. Mexico continues to play out its baseball pageant in relative obscurity, always remaining the poor cousin of the Caribbean baseball family.

The popular account of Jorge Pasquel's brazen postwar raid on big-league rosters is one of the most familiar pieces of Latin baseball fact and folklore. The facts, to be sure, are familiar enough to the game's casual historian. It is the true motives and eventual strategies of the Mexican promoter that still generate considerable controversy a half century later.

Did Jorge Pasquel in 1946 and 1947 raid the U.S. majors in a selfish and ambitious attempt to put Mexican professional baseball squarely on the map alongside the Cuban and North American circuits? Or was the entire episode merely an ostentatious display of personal power and an effort at base self-aggrandizement? Or is there some truth to the reports that Pasquel's grabbing of U.S. ballplayers was connected with an underhanded effort to buy an upcoming presidential election for Miguel Aleman, a personal friend and benefactor of the powerful Pasquel family? Pasquel's deepest motives undoubtedly perished with him in the March 1955 plane crash that snuffed out his life. A reasonable explanation of events might suggest that national and personal pride motivated the "Mexican baseball wars" far more than any economic or political profit for Pasquel and his allies. But in the end one thing is certain: the whole sorry business doomed the immediate and long-range future of Mexican baseball.

Jorge Pasquel was a wealthy Veracruz entrepreneur who along with his brothers rode herd over an expanding business empire built originally from his father's profitable cigar factory and customs brokerage firm. By the mid–1940s, it is estimated Pasquel's family fortune numbered in the tens of millions of dollars and that much of this exploding fortune had been earned through Jorge's astute (and often illegal) business dealings. And by this time Pasquel and his brothers had bought controlling interest in the Mexican League Veracruz Blues and held at least partial interest in a number of the other league ballclubs. Pasquel's control over Mexican League affairs crystallized when he was named president of the eight-team circuit (including Veracruz, Mexico City, Monterrey, Tampico, Torreón, Puebla, San Luís Potosi, Nuevo Laredo) in time for the 1946-47 season. Pasquel's interest in Mexican baseball certainly seemed genuine; he had been a sandlot player as a youth and loved to take batting practice with the Veracruz club he controlled. Like George Steinbrenner and dozens of modern big-league owners, Pasquel was living out the fantasy of ballclub ownership enjoyed by a wealthy businessman possessed of the ultimate adult toy chest.

The new Mexican League president of 1946 was also a man driven by nationalistic fervor and perhaps a smoldering hatred of the Yanqui interests, fueled in large part by U.S. Marine bombardments of Veracruz during his childhood years. His personal frontal attack on Yanqui imperialism would come in a plan to build the newly prosperous Mexican League into a full-fledged rival of the major league circuits operating to the north. Drawing upon some of the best of black Cuban and American talent banned from organized baseball, Mexican baseball had begun to thrive during the World War II years at the very hour when the majors suffered a severe wartime talent drought. Pasquel's power brokering was first apparent in 1943 when he arranged U.S. draft deferments for Negro-league stars Theolic Smith and Quincy Trouppe, freeing them for Mexican League play. The Mexican tycoon arranged the deferments by promising the loan of 80,000 Mexican laborers to assist the overburdened U.S. war-industry effort.

Further respectability came to Mexican baseball in 1944 and 1945 when Hall-of-Famer Rogers Hornsby was lured away as a manager and several Latin big-leaguers (catcher Chico Hernández of the Chicago Cubs and pitcher Tomás de la Cruz of the Cincinnati Reds among others also) took their modest ballplaying talents south. Encouraged by this small reverse migration of Latin talent, Pasquel spent $285,000 to tour big-league and U.S. minor league facilities for a firsthand look in 1944. It was this closer exposure that apparently hatched a scheme for throwing plenty of dollars (which the Pasquel family certainly had) at ballplaying talent north of the border in a full-blown attempt to turn the Mexican circuit into a rival third major league.

In 1946 Pasquel decided to launch a full-scale raid on the majors. Among the players tempted to abandon big-league status for truckloads of Mexican pesos were Cardinals pitcher Max Lanier, Giants hurler Sal Maglie and infielder George Hausmann, Brooklyn catcher Mickey Owen, much-traveled slugger Lou Klein, Cuban outfielder Roberto Ortiz of the Washington Senators, and several dozen less talented but seasoned major-leaguers. New baseball commissioner Albert "Happy" Chandler was quick to respond to the outrageous Mexican inroads by announcing lifetime bans against all ballplayers who departed for Pasquel's Mexican circuit, a ban that several dozen underpaid big-leaguers were apparently prepared to accept. One who was not, however, was future Hall-of-Famer Stan Musial of the 1944 world champion St. Louis Cardinals. Pasquel's agents are rumored to have laid $50,000 in cold cash on Musial's spring-training hotel bed in Florida, but whatever the true amount, it was not sufficient to lure Stan the Man from his $13,000-a-year perch in the St. Louis outfield.

The motive for Pasquel's raid on U.S. talent may have been in part an upcoming presidential campaign by his business partner and childhood pal Miguel Aleman. Aleman's election promised a windfall of preferential treatment for Pasquel business interests, and any bolstering of big-time baseball by the Aleman-Pasquel camp could not fail to impress the baseball-crazy Mexican electorate. Max Lanier would later complain that such politicking was squarely behind the scheme and that once Aleman had won the 1946 election, Pasquel began reneging on his contracts, salaries of imported players being cut by as much as half. The true fact of the matter may have been that Pasquel, for all his wealth, had largely overcommited himself and was running out of pocket money to throw at baseball. No capital upgrade in stadiums had accompanied the high-priced player talent; the Mexican population, for all its reported fervor, was not large enough to support a big-time circuit; and gate revenues simply did not offset the bloated payrolls. In short, within a year after the arrival of Lanier, Owen, Hausmann, and company, the Mexican League began to self-destruct.

In the end, the U.S. talent flow was small, short-lived, and completely ineffectual in launching major league status. Losses for the league were reported to be close to $400,000 for the 1947 and 1948 campaigns; league management was in disarray; the eight-team circuit crumbled to four franchises by July 1948, and all games were scheduled for Mexico City, which possessed the only sufficient fan pool; players (North Americans and Cubans) left in droves; and by September 1948, the league collapsed totally. Embarrassed big-leaguers like Lanier, Maglie, and Owen returned to the States to find that the threatened lifetime ban had more bark than bite. Lanier served a one-year suspension and returned to the St. Louis Cardinals in 1949, though his career was largely behind him. Maglie was back in the Polo Grounds in 1950 in time to lead the National League in winning percentage. Mickey Owen was back in uniform with the Chicago Cubs in 1949 and played in the big leagues for another half-dozen seasons.

With the collapse of Pasquel's ambitious scheme faded any grand dream of a Mexican baseball tradition on a par with the baseball of Cuba and the United States. That lofty dream would never materialize despite total reorganization of the Mexican League in 1949 (with entirely new management, although Pasquel did retain his interests in the Veracruz club until his 1955 death). Ironically, it was only months after Pasquel's passing that the Mexican League was fully accepted into the family of organized baseball as a sanctioned minor league circuit. Yet Mexican baseball would continue to be largely provincial, its stars and its events barely known beyond the borders of the country. This would remain the case despite the sudden and complete demise of Cuban professional baseball only a few years later and the eventual big-league presence of Latin talents like Clemente, Marichal, Cepeda, and Pérez, who soon put Caribbean island nations squarely on the baseball map for hordes of North American major league fans.

But if Mexican baseball became more isolated after the early 1950s, it still managed to produce two great heroes whose ballplaying feats became truly legendary inside and outside the land of tortillas and Pancho Villa. One burst on the scene overnight after electing to head north and seek his fortune in big-league ballparks. Screwballing Fernando Valenzuela carried the Mexican banner so proudly in the early 1980s that he overshadowed all others from the Latin arena for a brief span of seasons. The other great Mexican star decided to remain sequestered at home and shun the limelight of the majors. His exploits are consequently not nearly so universally celebrated as those of Valenzuela. Yet for fans of Tijuana, Monterrey, or Mexico City, the name of Héctor Espino is perhaps the most magical Mexican baseball name of all.

Héctor Espino may have been one of the game's greatest hitters. The talented muscleman slugged home runs and posted batting averages across a 23-year career (1962–1984) that suggest he should have been a major league star of grandest proportions. But no one ever knew much about Espino beyond the borders of Monterrey and Tijuana. Because he did not opt to appear in the majors when the opportunity arose, his legend will always remain generally suspect, and his achievements will always be overlooked and excused as somewhat illegitimate. When Espino began slugging homers at a record clip in 1961 (the very season when Roger Maris undermined Babe Ruth), he was doing so in tiny Mexican ballparks against inconsistent Mexican League pitching that was AAA caliber at best. And he was doing so without the headlines that cement legends in the U.S. sporting press. The fate of Espino is thus largely parallel to that of Japan's Sadaharu Oh, or to the fate of great Negro-leaguers of a previous generation who never played in the big time and thus never earned legitimacy in the public record.

Héctor Espino's story is quite different from that of Dihigo, Torriente, or Luís Tiant, Sr. No onerous and immoral rules of onfield and off-field segregation slammed the doors of big-league stardom on Espino. Rather, it was a matter of personal pride and an issue of the proud man himself. Yet Espino's decision to stay at home when big-league opportunity knocked was not that different in motive from those of many of his countrymen equally distinguished by a proud Latino dignity. The difference is that other rebels, like Clemente and Cepeda and George Bell, carried out their battles for dignity on the big-league stage. Espino chose to play by an entirely different set of rules.

In the early 1960s Héctor Espino was a most valued big-league commodity. If North American fans knew nothing of his earliest exploits, the same could not be said for big-league bird dogs. He was scouted first by the Dodgers, signed by former Havana Sugar Kings owner Bobby Maduro, and even had a cup of coffee in the minor leagues. Espino played 32 games with the 1964 Jacksonville Suns of the International League and posted a respectable short-term average of exactly .300, banging 3 roundtrippers in 100 at-bats. But the prized Mexican recruit was not at all happy with the life of a U.S. minor-leaguer and had little motive to return after his late-season debut in Jacksonville. Maduro would later report that it was largely an issue of homesickness and clashes of culture. In Maduro's assessment, Espino "couldn't adjust to things here, the food, the manner of living, anything" (quoted in a 1985 *Sport* magazine article by Leo Banks). Other sources suggest that the real issue was the slugger's horror at the incidents of racial discrimination he encountered during his month-long sojourn in northern Florida. The whole incident seems to foreshadow the equally inhospitable minor league road traveled by George Bell in Montana a decade later.

Simply put, Espino could not adjust, and he seemed to look for any excuse not to continue. That excuse came almost immediately when his contract was sold to the St. Louis Cardinals. He was thus subject to the same conditions as other Mexican League prospects plucked by U.S. teams. Espino would receive a regular contract from the Cardinals, but his signing bonus (several thousand dollars) went directly to the Monterrey club owner. This was the long-standing agreement established between the U.S. and Mexican baseball establishments once the Pasquel "player wars" had ended and a reconstituted Mexican League (AAA) had joined the ranks of organized baseball in the mid–1950s. Espino saw it as ruthless exploitation. He demanded 10 percent of the signing bonus from Monterrey boss Anuar Canavati, and when Canavati denied the request, Espino flatly refused to report for his Cardinal minor league reassignment. He would play for the hated Canavati in Monterrey rather than endure minor league bus rides in a hostile foreign land. Later he would repeatedly claim that he would have gone back to the U.S. had he been fairly compensated. But it seems that Espino's real desire was to be a larger-than-life baseball hero in his native homeland rather than a wealthy mercenary abroad.

And a hero he certainly was. Over the next two decades, Héctor Espino reached new heights each summer in the Mexican League, playing eventually with teams in Tampico, San Luís Potosi, and Monterrey. Then he tore up the winterball Mexican Pacific League each December and January. Espino would claim four Mexican League batting titles (1964, 1966–1968) and four home-run crowns (1964, 1968–1969, 1972). Like Aaron's, his homers mounted up over a quarter century due to consistency and longevity, and the total eventually reached 763 for combined summer- and winter-league play; the total of 453 Mexican summer-league roundtrippers stands as the minor league career record, and his 46 homers in 1964 remained a league record for 22 seasons. Espino thus left a legacy comparable to that

Profile of Héctor Espino, "The Mexican Babe Ruth"

Leagues: Mexican League (Summer); Mexican Pacific League (Winter)
Teams: Monterrey Sultanes (ML); Tampico (ML); San Luís Potosi Tuneros (ML); Hermosillo Naranjeros (MPL)
Seasons: 23 (1962–1984)
Career Home Runs (Total): 763 (Sadaharu Oh, 868; Hank Aaron, 755, Babe Ruth, 714)
Career Home Runs (Mexican League): 453
Career Home Runs (Mexican Pacific League): 310
Career Batting Average: .333
Career Runs Batted In: 2,693
Hall of Fame: Mexican Baseball Hall of Fame

Espino's Ten Greatest Career Moments:

1962: Named Mexican League Rookie of the Year winner
1964 (May 10): Hits four homers and a double for Monterrey in contest versus Poza Rica
1964: Sets Mexican League record of 46 home runs in a single season
1969 (April 27): Receives four intentional walks in doubleheader opener against Mexico City
1969 (April 27): Also collects career base hit number 1,000 in game two of same doubleheader
1969 (May 15–19): Smashes a record eight homers in six-game period for Monterrey
1972: Wins a record fourth Mexican League home-run crown
1976: Leads Hermosillo team to Mexico's first Caribbean World Series title in Santo Domingo
1982: Appears in fifth and final Caribbean World Series at Hermosillo's Héctor Espino Stadium
1984: Retires as all-time home-run champion (with 453) of Mexican League history

---

of Ruth, Aaron, and Mays in the big leagues or Sadaharu Oh, professional baseball's all-time home-run champion, in the Japanese leagues. And he lived the comfort of a hometown hero with a more than modest income and the lasting adulation of his nation's fans, even if he had sacrificed the potential glitter of big-time international baseball stardom.

Valenzuela's status as Mexican national hero is almost as large as Espino's. But somehow Valenzuela was always something more of a sideshow for Mexican baseball and big-league baseball alike. His heroics were carried on far from the view of his hometown countrymen, a flickering image on the television set or a newspaper headline but never a crowd-pleasing spectacle in the local ballpark. An instant hero in Los Angeles in 1981, Fernando became more of a rallying point for North American chicanos than for native Mexican fanáticos. And his fame as a big-league star was short-lived when compared to that of Clemente, Marichal, Cepeda, or even Luís Aparicio.

Fernando Valenzuela was one of the best young pitchers of the early 1980s without dispute, and his 1981 triple-crown feat of combining Cy Young, MVP, and Rookie-of-the-Year honors in a single season earned the roly-poly Mexican a lasting niche in baseball's all-time annals. But Fernando was hardly a Hall-of-Famer like Marichal or even a long-lasting force like Cubans Dolf Luque and Luís Tiant, Jr. And the biggest downside of Valenzuela's flaming comet was the fact that it implanted a notion, for big-league fans at any rate, that there has been only one truly great Mexican ballplayer worth remembering and celebrating.

In the end it is hard to say which was the more notable story—his unprecedented rookie-season sensation or his equally sudden lapse into almost total mediocrity. Few pitchers have ever turned as rapidly from being spitting-image apparitions of Dizzy Dean or Cy Young into disappointing approximations of Mike Moore or Bill Monbouquette. Part of the issue, of course, was the fact that Valenzuela's remarkable debut was in some senses a matter of excessive hype by big-league scribes and much premature celebration by proud Hispanic supporters. His first two or three seasons were meritorious enough (a better than .600 winning percentage) and he would claim league bests in victories (21) and complete games (20) as late as 1986. But his overall record was not that miraculous—an average of just 14 wins per season over the full decade and one 20-victory campaign. It must also be remembered that a rookie sweep of pitching honors (gained on a 13-7 ledger with 180 strikeouts in 192 innings) was aided by a bizarre and disruptive strike-plagued season. What started out looking like Hall of Fame numbers, then, ended in the middle of the pack among career Latin American pitching leaders. A decade and a half later, Valenzuela is still traveling the circuit, now the American League circuit, far more as a forgotten role-player than as celebrated star. He rebounded from premature career death with an adequate and even surprising 1993 campaign in Baltimore. But it is now clear that he will never threaten Marichal, Tiant, or even Dennis Martínez among all-time Latin aces.

Other Mexican stars in the major leagues have been few when compared to those of neighboring countries around the Caribbean basin. Three adequate infielders and two steady if unspectacular pitchers seem about all that stand out. Aurelio López (dubbed "Señor Smoke" for his lively fastball) made a modest mark as a relief artist of minor stature, mostly by laboring for the 1980s Detroit Tigers as a seasoned veteran well into his thirties.

Much of López's best stuff was left behind in Mexico, however, where he labored a dozen seasons and earned MVP honors in 1977 with a sterling 19-8 (2.01 ERA) record. Jorge Orta and Aurelio Rodríguez were solid big-league infielders of the same decade. Orta was son to slugging winter-leaguer Pedro Orta (known in some circles as the "Babe Ruth of Cuban winter play") and made his mark with his bat, first by finishing second to Rod Carew in the AL batting race of 1974 and later by stroking a record-tying six base hits in a single game for Cleveland at the end of the decade. Rodríguez was, by contrast, strictly a defensive standout. For much of the 1970s with Detroit he remained a friendly rival to Baltimore's Brooks Robinson as the junior circuit's slickest hot-corner glove man. But of this small pack of "others," it is Bobby Avila of the 1954 AL champion Cleveland Indians ballclub who earned the largest chunk of lasting fame. Avila's fame, ironically, would come as much from controversy as anything else.

If Mexican baseball and its heroes have most often been overshadowed, nowhere is this more true than with the strange case of Roberto Avila. Bobby Avila will long be remembered by most "cranks" as the first Latin American native to earn a big-league batting crown. Others will always contend that Avila did not "earn" the coveted title but swiped it from its rightful owner by virtue of a bothersome technicality. For despite his great season in 1954, it was Avila's fate to own a title tinged with ongoing controversy. Avila spent the long summer season locked in a heated hitting duel with Boston's Ted Williams, with Williams eventually besting the Mexican infielder by a mere four percentage points. Williams had registered only 386 official at-bats, however, an insufficient number to claim the title under rules then applicable to a league batting race. Controversy was spawned largely by the fact that the Boston slugger's low at-bats total had resulted largely from the league-leading 136 free passes awarded to the "Splendid Splinter" by wary pitchers. It was this very dispute that soon brought about a revision in the standards of batting leadership qualification. A substitution of "plate appearances" for "official at-bats" was almost immediately in the offing.

Although only a technicality crowned Avila in the end, it should be noted for the record that Latin America's first hitting champion bravely played more than half the season with a broken thumb, a painful injury that would have slowed almost any other hitter and knocked out many. Some baseball encyclopedias adept at revisionist history (such as Thorn and Palmer's *Total Baseball*) list Ted Williams as the 1954 batting champion despite the contemporary realities of the era. But Bobby Avila had gained another prize that season that neither Williams nor the historians could expunge from the record books. He had earned the rare opportunity (rare indeed for one playing in Cleveland) to perform on a championship ballclub and thus to appear in major league baseball's World Series.

The legitimacy of Bobby Avila as batting champion and baseball hero was never questioned in the adept second sacker's native Mexico. Avila reigned as a national hero throughout his career. Baseball fame would also propel him to a lengthy career in the public eye once baseball days closed for the Veracruz native. The handsome, dapper, personable baseballer would return to Mexico at the end of his playing days in 1960 to enter the political arena, first serving as mayor of his home city and later enjoying a term as Mexican League president.

Beyond these limited stories of big-league success, Mexican baseball has remained largely second class. Its professional summer league has long held minor league status yet is nonetheless almost unknown to dedicated followers of stateside AAA minor league play. Its winter circuit receives little press when stacked against the Dominican, Venezuelan and Puerto Rican circuits and thus draws the tiniest portion of the small collection of big-leaguers still traveling the winter circuit. Past legends of Mexican baseball today have their own pantheon in the Mexican Baseball Hall of Fame, yet this small-scale shrine located on the grounds of a brewery in Monterrey enjoys neither the pastoral setting nor lush tourist trade of its Cooperstown model. Mexico's hall was inaugurated with a newspaper poll selecting Mexican greats back in 1939—all in honor of Cooperstown's grand opening that summer—but a brick-and-mortar home for the archives was not actually constructed until 1973. Mexico's Salon de Fama shares several Negro-league greats with its Cooperstown counterpart—Roy Campanella, Josh Gibson, Martín Dihigo, Monte Irvin, and Ray Dandridge. And one can wander its halls and discover that black American Al Pinkston hit .372 during the late 1950s in Mexico to record the highest career average in Mexican history and that a decade earlier another American black, Burnis "Wild Bill" Wright, carved his special niche as the "black DiMaggio" of Mexican fame.

Mexico's professional baseball league (as well as the semipro leagues and barnstorming circuits that preceded it) has enjoyed a few grand moments in the sun since its debut 1937 season. Here was the baseball birthplace of Fernando Valenzuela, Melo Almada (Mexico's first big-leaguer in 1933), Teddy Higuera, and Aurelio López. Héctor Espino created long-ball lore here, and James "Cool Papa" Bell stopped long enough to burn up the base paths for several summers of the late 1930s and early 1940s; pitching legends have been carved out here by such illustrious winterball and Negro-league stars as Martín Dihigo, Ramón Araño Bravo, Ramón Bragaña, Adrian Zabala, and Vidal López.

But in the end Mexico has always been the place that fading ballplayers go to die, figuratively and literally. Dihigo languished here at the tail end of a lost blackball career. The ageless Miñoso eventually disappeared into Mexico for a decade of washed-up play as a 50-year-old journeyman who was more sideshow than main attraction. There was also the ill-fated exodus

Honor Roll of Mexico's Greatest Players

Pitcher	Fernando Valenzuela (major leagues, 1981–1993; Cy Young Award-winner)
Pitcher	Ramón Araño Bravo (Mexican League, 1959–1986)
Pitcher	Aurelio López (major leagues, 1974–1987)
Infielder	Roberto Avila (major leagues, 1949–1959; American League batting champion)
Infielder	Aurelio Rodríguez (major leagues, 1967–1983)
Infielder	Jorge Orta (major leagues, 1972–1987)
Outfielder	Héctor Espino (Mexican League, 1962–1984)

of that handful of mercenary ballplayers attracted by Pasquel's unrealistic expansion plans and the lure of loose pesos. And there were Hi Bithorn, shot to death on New Year's Day of 1952 while attempting a futile comeback in Mexico City, and Dolf Luque still laboring as a minor league manager in the 1940s and tutoring Sal Maglie in the art of the brushback pitch that Luque had once used so effectively on terrorized hitters from New York to Havana. There was Francisco Barrios, as well, dying in his homeland of a drug overdose at the age of 29 and in the ghostly shadow of a failed big-league career. And there were Luke Easter and Tommy de la Cruz and Jerry Hairston – all chasing an elusive baseball dream from Tampico to Monterrey to Hermosillo long after their fragile talents had left them forever. All found Mexico as a final refuge, and all vanished forever once they quietly slipped below the border.

Suggested Readings

Banks, Leo. "Babe Ruth of Mexico (Héctor Espino)." *Sport Magazine* 80 (February 1958): 70.

Bjarkman, Peter C. "Forgotten Americans and the National Pastime: Literature on Baseball's Ethnic, Racial and Religious Diversity" (Part I). *MultiCultural Review* 1:2 (April 1992): 46–48.

________. "Forgotten Americans and the National Pastime: Literature on Baseball's Ethnic, Racial and Religious Diversity" (Part II). *MultiCultural Review* 1:3 (July 1992): 34–39.

________. "Forgotten Americans and the National Pastime: Literature on Baseball's Ethnic, Racial and Religious Diversity" (Part III: Bibliography). *MultiCultural Review* 1:4 (October 1992): 40–47, 55.

García, Carlos J. *Baseball Forever.* Mexico City, Mexico (self-published volume), 1980.

Gould, Stephen Jay. "The Creation Myths of Cooperstown." *Natural History* (November 1989): 14–24.

Joyce, Gare. *The Only Ticket Off the Island.* Toronto, Ontario: Lester and Orpen Dennys, 1990.

Klein, Alan M. *Sugarball: The American Game, the Dominican Dream.* New Haven, Connecticut: Yale University Press, 1991.

Littlefield, Bill. "A Real World Series at Last?" *World Monitor* (*Christian Science Monitor* Monthly) 1:(2) (November 1988): 84–86.

Mijares, Rubén. *Béisbol por Dentro* (Native Baseball, Venezuelan Baseball History). Mérida, Venezuela: Editorial Alfa, 1989.

Piña Campora, Tony. *Los Grandes Finales* (The Great Finals, Dominican Baseball Playoffs). Santo Domingo, Dominican Republic: Editora Colegial, 1981.

________. *Presencia Dominicana* (Dominican Presence in the Big Leagues). Santo Domingo, Dominican Republic (self-published edition), 1990.

Ruck, Rob. "Baseball in the Caribbean." In *Total Baseball,* first edition, edited by John Thorn and Pete Palmer. New York: Warner, 1989, 605–611.

________. "Baseball in the Caribbean." In *Total Baseball,* third edition, edited by John Thorn and Pete Palmer. New York: HarperCollins, 1993, 533–539.

________. "Chicos and Gringos of Béisbol Venezolana." *Baseball Research Journal* (Society for American Baseball Research) 15 (1986): 75–78.

________. "The Crisis in Winter Baseball: Can It Survive?" *Baseball America* (February 25–March 9, 1990): 8–10.

________. "Dominican Real Fan and Talent Hotbed." *Baseball Research Journal* 13 (1984): 3–6.

________. "Juan Marichal: Baseball in the Dominican Republic." In *Baseball History 3: An Annual of Original Baseball Research.* Westport, Connecticut: Meckler, 1990, 49–70.

________. *The Tropic of Baseball: Baseball in the Dominican Republic.* New York: Carroll and Graf, 1993; Westport, Connecticut: Meckler, 1991.

Salas, Alexis. *Momentos Inolvidables del Béisbol Profesional Venezolano, 1946–1984.* Caracas, Venezuela: Miguel Angel García, 1985.

Vaughn, Gerald F. "George Hausmann Recalls the Mexican League of 1946-47." *Baseball Research Journal* 19 (1990): 59–63.

________. "Jorge Pasquel and the Evolution of the Mexican League." *The Inter-National Pastime: A Review of Baseball History* (Society for American Baseball Research) 12 (1992): 9–13.

CHAPTER 10

No Dragons, Only Shortstops: Sagas of Caribbean Winterball

> Summer afternoon—summer afternoon. To me those have always been the two most beautiful words in the English language.
>
> —HENRY JAMES

Almost any red-blooded North American youngster raised anywhere from the crowded suburbs of Boston to the spacious farming plains of Salinas, Kansas, would be quick to provide a hearty cheer and a slight twist of focus for those immortal words of novelist Henry James. While our staid middle-aged and expatriate author (himself not a fan of "ball-games") perhaps pined for quietly sociable afternoon teas and leisurely contemplative walks through shaded English gardens, thousands upon thousands of bat-and-glove-toting youths would conjure more robust images of towering outfield flies and the dangerous drama of dashes around the base paths.

Of course, baseball has long been played in Spanish-language settings as well as English-language environs, and across the blue crystal of the Caribbean the calendar peels its leaves backward and the clock ticks in a more southerly direction. Each crisp autumn season at the conclusion of televised prime-time World Series excitement, baseball does not, contrary to popular opinion, roll up its battered base paths, pack away its barren bullpens, and silently disappear into hiberation for the long winter months. Unbeknownst to most casual observers, the national pastime merely migrates south of the border for several more weeks of exciting big-league-caliber winterball competition.

Winter baseball has reigned for decades as the revered national sport in such tropical paradise settings as Cuba, Puerto Rico, and the Dominican Republic. And it is a safe bet that General Abner Doubleday's quaint and marvelous pastoral game enjoys equal popularity throughout Mexico,

Nicaragua, and Panama. It is one of the triumphs of the past decade that few stateside fans remain uninformed about the big-league impact of such slick Latino infielders as Tony Fernández, Manny Lee, or Roberto Alomar, or the slugging heroics of present and past Hispanic stars like George Bell and Orlando Cepeda. Equally true, however, is the unaccountable fact that fewer still are aware of the thriving tropical baseball world that flowers during each Caribbean winter season.

While stateside fans are left during winter's harsher months with only hot-stove scuttlebutt about the hometown nine or perhaps a steady diet of financial bulletins concerning baseball's exploding list of instant millionaires that today replaces more standard debate about fresh outfield phenoms or long-of-tooth and lame-armed mound veterans, island natives seize their moment to thrill to the crack of ashwood on horsehide and the infectious daily cry of "Plei bol!" or "jonrón!" spread across two delightful months of *béisbol* celebration Caribbean-style.

The bread and butter of this hidden Caribbean season remains the four winter-league pennant races that now operate in the Dominican Republic, Puerto Rico, Venezuela, and Mexico—the latter nation also serving as home to the AAA Mexican League for traditional summer play. The crown jewel, however, remains the exciting week-long championship playoff series—the *Serie del Caribe,* as it is known to Latin fanáticos—an intense 12-game round-robin battle between the four winter-league champions each February as the culmination of the 10-week Caribbean season. Far more than a mere tourist attraction designed to boost the local economy of participating host countries, this four-nation winter-league season, along with the Caribbean Series with which it concludes, has also been the spawning ground for numerous big-league stars over the past four or more decades.

Retired 1980s home-run king Mike Schmidt, the game's greatest-ever third baseman, publicly traces his sudden sophomore successes of 1974 to a long-forgotten (by the media, perhaps, but not Schmidt) 1973 winter-league education in Puerto Rico. Two decades before Schmidt's Puerto Rican trial by fire, there were other future big-league stars like Sandy Koufax, Orlando Cepeda, Roberto Clemente, Charlie Neal, Rubén Gómez, Hank Aaron, Luke Easter, Vic Power, and Bob Buhl—Spanish- and English-speaking prospects alike—honing their skills in hotly contested ballgames spread across the face of Puerto Rico. Winterball has thus long been the familiar off-season stomping grounds for dozens of travel-weary big-league scouts and player personnel directors seeking the elusive untouted prospect or supervising extra work details for scores of sore-armed rehabilitating pitchers, overanxious youthful batsmen with landing-strip strike zones, and shaky journeyman infielders struggling to perfect a big-league double-play pivot.

This is not to suggest that Caribbean winterball is mere diamond meat market or boot camp for untutored minor-leaguers. Winterball, with all its salsa music, fiestalike trappings, and unbridled nationalistic fervor, is also an incomparable baseball culture. Here one uncovers a rich universe of Latino-flavored *mano a mano* play that looms larger and more important—at least for thousands of fanáticos spread throughout a half-dozen Caribbean basin countries—than major league play. And let us not forget in making this claim that these same Caribbean fans who show such enthusiasm for winterball each December and January know their big-league history as well as any of their stateside counterparts. Local sports pages follow the daily exploits of Latino big-leaguers religiously throughout the summer months (every 1993 at-bat of Andrés Galarraga was replayed as front-page news in Caracas). Radio accounts of major league contests were beamed to Cuba regularly in the days before Castro's revolution, and Roberto Clemente remains perhaps the greatest national hero (both inside and outside the sporting world) Puerto Rico has produced.

The 1992 Mexican-based Caribbean Series, contested in Hermosillo's plush stadium, marked the thirty-fourth renewal of this colorful winter-baseball ritual, a joyous baseball festival that has witnessed a checkered but often lively past history. The first phase (*primera etapa*), launched in the Gran Stadium of Havana in the spring of 1949, lasted through 1960 and was dominated in the final years by the strong Cuban entrants who won 7 of the 12 round-robins and finished as runner-up on three occasions. Only Venezuela failed to capture a single tourney in the first 12 years of play, a period that saw Puerto Rico take four crowns and Panama eke out a single title in 1950. The *primera etapa* was the scene for such legendary Latin diamond events as Agapito Mayor's unmatched three mound victories for host Cuba in 1949, American Tommy Fine's unique no-hitter (the only one in Caribbean Series play to date) of 1952, and Willie Mays' dramatic game-winning circuit clout during the 1955 final round.

A full decade of suspended play followed, brought about by economic difficulties in the region and the disappearance of reigning powerhouse Cuba from winter-league play. Caribbean baseball, like larger Caribbean economic life, had suffered an inevitable fallout of cold war mentality in the wake of damaged relations between Washington and Castro's rebellious Cuba. The series was thankfully renewed in 1970 (*segunda etapa*) and has been played each year since (except for a second brief suspension in 1981), the Dominican Republic and Puerto Rico (13 titles between them) continuing to dominate championship play. Venezuela has subsequently won four Caribbean titles, and Mexico (Panama's replacement in the second phase) has captured two, while Cuba's stand-in, the talent-rich Dominican Republic, has hoisted eight championship banners during the renewed phase of the competition.

Phase two of this 35-year baseball extravaganza has provided its own special unmatched treasure trove of records, statistics, legends, lore, and memorable baseball feats (many summarized throughout the latter portions of this chapter).* Unfortunately, however, there is little printed record of the fabulous Caribbean Series and its most notable baseball moments in our English-language culture, although several fine Spanish chronicles (especially the two books by José Antero Nuñez) have been recently published about winterball and Caribbean Series play.

For all its glory, Latin America's Caribbean Series remains the forgotten lore of American baseball. Today the true triumphs and glories of play south of the border remain an even more desperately lost segment of our baseball past than the blackball world of Negro-league play. Satchel Paige and Josh Gibson have long been household names for literate fans, but Martín Dihigo, Napoleón Reyes, Agapito Mayor, Héctor Espino, and Willard Brown remain lost in the shadows.

A ballpark is a place of pure and unrivalled magic, like so many commonplace sites first discovered in childhood. The ballpark is at the same time one of the truly rare locations at which such magic persists into the cynical age of adulthood. This is an axiom as well known to the Caribbean patron as to hardened fans anywhere in U.S. towns and cities. By the same token, winter-league play, and especially the February Caribbean Series, boasts an appearance entirely unique to the Latin American baseball world. This is no mere Grapefruit League or Cactus League campaign transported to quaint island ballparks of a sunnier clime. Each game is a small but joyous festival and a true celebration of national pride and spirit. No matter what happens on the field, no one sits on his or her hands in the grandstands of Hermosillo, Caracas, Caguas, or Santo Domingo.

Mariachi bands blare from the grandstand, and inebriated fans dance throughout nine innings in a constant fandango of excitement. Strange aromatic feasts, foreign to North American taste buds, are served throughout the teeming bleachers. Onfield play is often wild, woolly, and totally

**A major change in the makeup of teams representing the four competing nations occurred between the phase-one (1949–1960) and phase-two (1970–present) versions of the otherwise consistent Caribbean World Series. The earliest version of competition featured championship teams (with their regular winter-league rosters) from the four Caribbean circuits (Cuba, Puerto Rico, Panama, Venezuela). With the 1970 revival of play (minus Cuba and Panama but with the addition of Mexico and the Dominican Republic), the format was slightly altered. Winning ballclubs from the four winter-league postseason tournaments are still the Caribbean Series entrants, but these clubs are now allowed to reinforce their rosters with a select number of stars (including North Americans) from other league teams. Caribbean World Series play now more closely resembles a playoff among league all-star squads than between true league champions.*

unparalleled on most big-league diamonds, reminiscent at times of the old slapstick St. Louis Brownies or 1930s Daffiness Dodgers before the former escaped east of the Mississippi to staid Baltimore and the latter exchanged Babe Herman for Duke Snider and Wilbert Robinson for Jackie Robinson. Sometimes young children race into the outfield for autographs between pitches. Local beauty queens, resplendent in their roles as team mascots, often sit stoically in the home-team dugout. Sports scribes and television crews scour the benches for cherished interviews between innings and sometimes while the ball is still in play. Thus an ongoing collage of color and action makes even the informalities of spring training (pitchers running wind sprints in the outfield or sea gulls alighting upon the infield) seem structured and staid by comparison.

But legendary baseball feats have been accomplished down through the years in ballparks from Santiago to Santurce to Tijuana to Mexicali. What dedicated Dominican or Mexican or Venezuelan fanático could forget Jesús "Chiquitín" Cabrera's .619 batting average, which stunned fans at the 1951 Caracas series? (Chiquitín Cabrera's heroic single-series batting exploits took place in Caracas and still inspire the same enthusiasm around that Venezuelan capital city as those of Williams or Doerr might evoke among 1950s fans anywhere in New England.)

What longtime fan of the Caribbean pastime does not also recall Texan Tommy Fine's delicate no-hitter (twirled for Cuba) at Panama City in 1952, still the only perfect pitching masterpiece recorded in Caribbean Series play? Or the legendary home-run feats compiled down through the years by Latin big-leaguers Tony Armas (Venezuela) and Rico Carty (Dominican Republic), Mexican-Leaguer Héctor Espino, and North America's journeyman minor league hero Phil Stephenson? Or perhaps Barry Jones's record five homers struck in the misshapen Orange Bowl during a more recent campaign when the 1990 series inaugurated a brief two-year residence for Caribbean Series play on U.S. soil?

Famed big-league names (Willie Mays, Bob Clemente, the three Alou brothers, Tony Armas, Camilo Pascual, Monte Irvin, Don Baylor, Luís Aparicio, and Chico Carrasquel, to list but a handful) have left their lasting marks on local play and in the process emblazoned indelible legends into the rich baseball traditions of Venezuela, Mexico, Panama, Puerto Rico, and the Dominican Republic. So have obscure minor league toilers like Tommy Fine, Chuck "Rifleman" Connors, and Dan Bankhead (major league baseball's first Afro-American pitcher); Negro-league immortals like Satchel Paige, Wilmer Fields and Luke Easter; and local Latin heroes like Héctor Espino (Mexico), Héctor Rodríguez (Cuba), and José "Carrao" Bracho (Venezuela). Fabled winter-league exploits on the order of Juan Pizarro's 17 strikeouts in a single 1958 contest and Rico Carty's five towering homers during four consecutive games of the 1977 Caribbean Series stand among the game's great moments in Spanish-speaking lands, remaining entirely lost to summertime fans north of the border.

There is space here to review only a handful of the most glorious moments from the annals of more than three decades of Caribbean Series play, and there is no better place to begin than Havana, Cuba, in 1949 with the inaugural year of series competition. The dozen years that composed the first stage of Caribbean Series action were the scene of a lopsided domination by Cuban teams featuring not only dark-skinned Cuban stars but a stellar assortment of black and white North American big-leaguers. Never was this more true than in the very first tourney when the Almendares club, representing the host country and managed by native son and Philadelphia Athletics catcher Fermín "Mike" Guerra, swept through its entire six games undefeated while hardly breaking a sweat.

Starring for the locals were outfielders Al Gionfriddo (famed for his 1947 World Series catch in Yankee Stadium), Monte Irvin (longtime Negro-leaguer and star of the New York Giants), and Boston Braves rookie sensation Sam Jethroe. Philadelphia Phillies second sacker Granny Hamner (soon to earn fame as one of the 1950 Phillies Whiz Kids) anchored the infield, along with Brooklyn first baseman Chuck "Rifleman" Connors (also a talented professional basketballer and later television celebrity) and sure-handed Cuban third-base defender Héctor Rodríguez. Washington Senators moundsman Connie Marrero was a pitching victor in the opening game for Almendares, and another Almendares pitcher, Eddie Wright, hurled the first shutout of inaugural Caribbean Series play.

Without question, the biggest story of the opening Caribbean Series, however, was Cuban hurler Agapito Mayor. In his three outings, the slender right-hander proved largely unhittable as he cruised to three consecutive victories (one as a starter and two in relief). Mayor thus established a mark of three series victories that would still stand 45 seasons later despite subsequent challenges by talented Caribbean Series pitchers like Camilo Pascual, Juan Pizarro, and Pedro Borbón, all of whom dominated later individual tournaments. Mayor had already firmly established a solid Caribbean reputation by the late 1940s (he twice led the Cuban winter league in victories during that decade, 1941-42 and 1946-47) but would nonetheless never find his way onto a big-league diamond.

Three additional years of early series play would also provide immense thrills and memories as well as stellar individual feats of landmark proportion. Cuba's Jesús Lorenzo Cabrera, black first baseman for the Havana Reds, would post his sensational .619 batting mark during the 1951 round robin by socking 13 base hits in 21 trips to the plate. It was a sweet performance for the often overshadowed Cabrera, who had only recently recorded three seasons of excellent batting marks (.322 in 1949, .330 in 1950, .342 in 1951) in Cuban winter-league play, only to lose out narrowly for the batting title (to Alejandro Crespo, Pedro Formental, and Silvio García) all three winters.

A season later, Tommy Fine would provide the only no-hitter of Caribbean Series competition. In 1954, pitching mastery took a backseat to record-breaking long-ball slugging as North American Willard "Ese Hombre" Brown hammered a record four roundtrippers while leading Santurce to the first repeat title in tournament history. And in 1955 big-league star Willie Mays (fresh off a National League batting title the previous fall) would clinch yet another flag for Santurce by stroking perhaps the most dramatic home run ever blasted in championship-level Latin American competition. Mays's circuit blast (with Roberto Clemente on base) came in the bottom of the eleventh frame of a tense 2–2 game between Puerto Rico and Venezuela (Magallanes). The dramatic hit was ironically registered against Mays's summertime Giants teammate Ray Monzant and put a resounding end to Willie's 0-for-12 slump. With Mays registering 14 hits over his final 19 trips to the plate (.469 for series), the Santurce Crabbers ballclub waltzed to a fourth Puerto Rican championship in the first seven years of CWS play.

But even the memorable Mays homer does not enjoy quite the legendary status of Tommy Fine's unique 1952 no-hit effort. Fine would twirl his masterpiece for the title-winning Havana ballclub of manager Mike González and against the Venezuelan entry, Cervecería Caracas. Another North American, knuckleballer Al Papai, would be the losing hurler, allowing a single run and but four hits across seven stellar innings of work. It would be future Brooklyn World Series hero Sandy Amoros who would single home pitcher Tommy Fine with the game's only tally in the sixth inning. Fine struck out four and walked three during his masterpiece, two additional Caracas baserunners reaching on errors. Defensive gems by third baseman Vern Benson (later Atlanta Braves manager) and center fielder Pedro Formental robbed opposing hitters of two base hits.

Papai would enjoy only a brief and undistinguished big-league career (9-14 lifetime mark) with the Cardinals, Browns, Red Sox, and White Sox. Fine was even less distinguished as a major-leaguer, appearing in but 23 games over two seasons with the Red Sox and St. Louis Browns and gaining a single major league victory. Yet on February 21, 1952, the two diminutive right-handers teamed up to provide a display of championship moundsmanship that will long be fondly remembered by those for whom the winter season is depository for the largest storehouse in hometown ballpark thrills.

Sometimes the Caribbean Series has been seemingly owned by one man, and that was clearly the case during 1958 in San Juan, Puerto Rico. Hometown hero Juan Pizarro, soon to earn his full measure of big-league fame with the Milwaukee Braves and Chicago White Sox, would that year put on a one-day display never seen before or since in the countless dramatic clashes of winterball legend. The tenth annual CWS was crammed full of outstanding individual performances: Pedro Ramos won two games on the mound for the Cuban champions (Marianao); Panama's first big-leaguer, Humberto Robinson (Pizarro's teammate in Milwaukee), also won two contests and even blanked the victorious Cubans; Victor Pollet Power batted .458 for Puerto Rico; Chicago White Sox ace Bob Shaw hurled a title-clinching shutout for the Cubans. Yet none escaped the shadow of Pizarro. A big-league 131-game winner, the Puerto Rican lefty was never better than on February 8, 1958, when his dominant fastball struck out 17 batters in the Panama (Carta Vieja) lineup. Pizarro allowed but two harmless safeties (a single and double) and walked a mere three in one of the most dominant CWS pitching performances ever witnessed. An additional 25 CWS competitions have yet to bring a serious challenge to Pizarro's long-standing one-game strikeout record.

Two years after Pizarro, it was time for still another hurler of established big-league credentials to etch his name permanently into Caribbean winterball legend. Cuba's Camilo Pascual would win two games in a single series playdown for the third time in 1960, establishing an all-time-best career series record of six victories without a single defeat. Pascual's 1956 CWS performance brought two complete games, one a shutout. His two 1960 victories were also earned via complete games, with one again coming via the shutout route. Over three tourneys Pascual would fail to complete only one of his six outings, allowing two or fewer runs four times and posting an overall ERA of 1.90. All this came on the eve of a dramatic upswing in Camilo Pascual's big-league career with a franchise shift of his big-league club from Washington to Minnesota and a sudden emergence of the Cuban as the most dominant American League right-hander of the early 1960s.

When the series resumed after its long hiatus (1961–1969) and new legends were built during the 1970s, it would be the Dominicans and Puerto Ricans who would vie for total domination of a competition once owned by the powerhouse teams from pre–Castro Cuba. Nowhere was Dominican power more in evidence than in Caracas in 1977 when 14-year big-league veteran Rico Carty pounded out five roundtrippers to pace the Licey ballclub to their third CWS title in seven years. It was not all Dominican firepower, however, as U.S. import Mitchell Page (author of 21 rookie homers with Oakland's Athletics in 1977) unleashed firepower of his own during the 1979 series. Behind a ninth-inning game-winning roundtripper by Page in San Juan's Hiram Bithorn Stadium, the Venezuelan ballclub (Magallanes) earned only the second title for that country in three decades of Caribbean Series play.

When it came to home-run firepower, however, no account of Caribbean Series highlights down through the years could overlook the display

Caribbean World Series Pitching Record of Camilo Pascual

Year	Opponents	Game Scores	IP	Hits	Runs	Earned Runs	BB	SO
1956	Panama	13–5 (W)	9	6	5	4	3	6
1956	Venezuela	7–0 (W)	9	4	0	0	0	7
1959	Panama	4–1 (W)	9	6	1	1	2	7
1959	Venezuela	8–2 (W)	9	4	2	2	0	9
1960	Venezuela	8–5 (W)	7.1	11	5	4	4	8
1960	Puerto Rico	4–0 (W)	9	1	0	0	1	7
Totals		6W	52.1	32	13	11	10	44

by a contingent of Puerto Rican bombers in 1987 at the Héctor Espino Stadium in Hermosillo, Mexico. Team Caguas would establish a lofty standard that year by smacking eight homers in a single contest. The roundtrippers came off the bats of six batters in the power-packed Caguas lineup—Hedi Vargas (two), Carmelo Martínez (two), Germán Rivera, Candy Maldonado, Bobby Bonilla, and Henry Cotto. Yet somehow the eventual champions would nonetheless lose that fan-pleasing contest to the Dominicans (Cibao Aguilas), falling by a 14–13 count in the memorable slugfest.

Despite so rich a past, all has not gone well for winterball in recent epochs. First there is the matter of media and fan exposure. For literate baseball fans the world over, a spate of recent articles and books (especially Robert Whiting's best-selling *You Gotta Have Wa*, published in 1989) have successfully spread the word far and wide about Japanese professional baseball, and recent televised tours by big-league all-stars to the new Tokyo Dome and other Japanese pro ballparks have increased interest tenfold in the distant Japanese league. By contrast, Latin American professional play has remained largely relegated to the world of trivia and obscurity, buried deep in the back pages of *Baseball America* or *USA Today Baseball Weekly* and thus reserved for only a select (and thus miniscule) baseball readership and viewership.

This is irrevocably true despite obvious long-standing big-league ties for winter-league competition over the past four or more decades as well as the increasingly undeniable impact of Caribbean-born players on major league games being played stateside. Almost any U.S. fan can tell you everything about the diamond talent font for shortstops that has sprung forth in tiny San Pedro de Macoris, though few if any can name a single winter-league club based in the Dominican Republic or tell you what league champion copped last winter's Caribbean Series title.

It is not entirely surprising, then, that when winter-league play was first launched on North American soil in February 1990, the landmark event went largely unnoticed by the nation's baseball press and the nation's hard-core fandom. North American fans, faced with an impending spring-training lockout and likely suspension of major league play in April, were for the first time being offered a rare glimpse at the showcase of Caribbean winterball. A set of most discouraging economic circumstances had suddenly meant that for the first time the sponsors of Latin baseball's prime showcase would have to court U.S. television and advertising money. The Caribbean Series, facing severe economic problems of its own on the island circuit, was now transporting the thirty-third renewal of its annual spectacle lock, stock, and barrel into Miami's Orange Bowl for a pioneering one-week engagement aimed at attracting a North American audience with much larger supplies of expendable income. Amid sparse advanced publicity, however, and surrounded by even less apparent interest than the moribund Senior Professional Baseball League, which had played its own final winter of discontent to empty stadiums and indifferent fans throughout the Florida State League ballparks only weeks earlier, the first North American version of the Caribbean Series would quickly prove a mammoth public-relations boondoggle, to say nothing of an unparalleled show-business disaster.

The baseball action that unfolded in front of empty grandstands in the hastily revamped Orange Bowl Stadium on February 5 to 11 lived up to every onfield expectation of the devoted winter-league fan. Overambitious promoters, hoping to grab North American exposure, perhaps secure a lucrative television package, and thus rescue the financially troubled winter-league circuit, had suffered a rude setback at the hands of inexcusably bad planning. They had also fallen victim to an apparently naive notion that Hispanic-flavored Miami (southern Florida with its huge Spanish-speaking population) would bring an inevitable and automatic rush of fans to glimpse firsthand Caribbean baseball's best-kept wintertime secret.

The Caribbean Series was admittedly embarking on treacherous new ground with its first North American visit in 1990. While North American appeal for such an event was both unmeasured and untapped, enthusiastic crowds had always filled Mexican and Dominican stadiums to overflowing. The week-long Caribbean Series, furthermore, was an established national tradition throughout the winter-league nations. Yet the move seemed to have indisputable economic logic. Major league stars on the order of Willie Mays, Roberto Clemente, or Steve Garvey had long since abandoned the Caribbean circuit for the North American hot stove banquet circuit; today's lofty player salaries rule out the need for extra games, and guaranteed contracts preclude exhibition appearances that might result in career-threatening injury. Absence of celebrity big-league ballplayers had drained attendance dramatically during recent 10-week regular-season winter-league schedules; political haggling in the Dominican Republic had literally short-circuited electric power to ballparks in Santo Domingo and Santiago during late 1989; hurricane damage had killed attendance that same fall in the Puerto Rican venues. And the low ticket prices (an unavoidable economic reality in Latin countries with starvation wages) and lack of corporate sponsorsip had conspired to make Caribbean Series play a losing proposition in recent years despite packed stadiums and leather-lunged crowds of fanatic patrons.

Once under way, the unprecedented yet underpublicized 1990 Miami series provided a stirring week-long baseball festival marked with its full share of controversy and contention. Hoping to draw large throngs from the local Hispanic (especially Cuban American) population, a hastily formed partnership between local Miami sports promoters and the Venezuelan firm ProEventos Deportivos had just as hastily selected the 55,000-seat Orange Bowl as temporary home for the first American-based series. There had been surprisingly little uproar on the Caribbean sporting scene when it was first announced that the series would leave its traditional home for Florida dates in 1990 and 1991. (Mexico was again penciled in for 1992, and it was hoped that a planned return to Miami in 1993 would at last provide a permanent home for the struggling event.) Promotions mogul Juan Morales, president of ProEventos Deportivos, had invested $1.5 million to acquire rights to the languishing series and move it lock, stock, and batting cages from its Caribbean homeland into the lucrative stateside venue. It was assumed that four teams of (mostly) Latin ballplayers and a huge supply of seats were all it would take to bring Caribbean baseball fervor to Miami.

But it was not a happy marriage of North and South from the very outset. Playing conditions in Miami's Orange Bowl, which had not housed baseball since 52,000 turned out to witness a 1956 Miami Marlins exhibition game featuring the legendary Negro-leaguer Satchel Paige, seemed to demonstrate that North American promoters (led by Senior League president Rick Horrow) did not take seriously the tradition of first-class ballpark conditions regularly found throughout island winter-league play. Flustered by reported criticism of the site selection, especially by Dominican and Venezuelan team delegations, the baseball-naive Horrow responded with all the tact of an ugly gringo. Quoted in published reports by *USA Today*, Horrow snapped angrily that Caribbean ballplayers ought to be happy with the Orange Bowl facilities since they all played on "rock piles" and "cow pastures" back home in Venezuela and the Dominican Republic.

Horrow's ill-conceived remarks almost sent the Dominican and Venezuelan delegations packing at the end of two days of rough competition. Once the dust and controversy had settled and fastballs began to fly, however, the landmark series proved one of the most dramatic and hotly contested in years. Records fell, and good baseball abounded as the Dominican team (Leones de Escogido, paced by the bats of big-leaguers Junior Felix, Nelson Liriano, and Geronimo Berroa and hot prospect Moises Alou) triumphed for the second time in three years. Highlights were plentiful. Atlanta farmhand Barry Jones slugged his way to a record-tying five homers (matching Rico Carty's 1977 output) and kept an undermanned Puerto Rican team in contention until the final day of the tourney. Two marvelous pitching performances under the adverse conditions of a bad-hop infield and Orange Bowl "Chinese Wall" were crafted by minor-leaguer hurlers Doug Linton (Toronto Blue Jays) and Bob Patterson (Pittsburgh Pirates). Several fan-pleasing slugfests featured a cloudburst of homers and ground-rule doubles as well as astronomical scores of 20–8 and 10–8 in the first days of play. A memorable old-timers game featured past Caribbean immortals Tony Oliva (author of a gigantic 350-foot homer in his first at-bat), Juan Marichal, José Tartabull, Camilo Pascual, and Bobby Avila (Latin America's first big-league batting champion). It was the old-timers matchup that best reminded Orange Bowl patrons of the unique blend of past and present that is the lifeblood of Caribbean baseball and drew the largest paying crowds of the otherwise sparsely attended week-long event.

Perhaps more than anything else, the inaugural Caribbean Series on North American soil fell victim to atrociously bad timing. The 1990 spring season was hardly a fortuitous one for the national pastime, with a big-league players union labor action looming on the horizon. Spring training would be delayed by an ownership lockout of the ballplayers. Caribbean Series play in Miami was unfortunately surrounded with every bit as much bad planning, off-field bickering and contentiousness, and generalized confusion as the aborted 1990 Grapefruit and Cactus seasons only a month later.

Promoter Horrow's off-the-cuff comments about Caribbean playing conditions piqued the ire of all four visiting delegations and required a hasty press conference and formal public apology from Horrow to soothe the proud Latin visitors. Most memorable about this inaugural Miami Series had to be the playing locale itself. Miami's antique Orange Bowl Stadium (home to the University of Miami footballers and earlier the NFL Miami Dolphins) had an eerie resemblance to the legendary Los Angeles Coliseum that had greeted Walter O'Malley's renegade Dodgers in 1958. The strange configuration carved out of a football oval featured a 200-feet-deep and 60-feet-high wire left-field fence exactly like the one that three decades earlier found Gil Hodges, Charlie Neal, and Carl Furillo (as well as every visiting right-handed slugger) salivating in Los Angeles. Miami's newfangled "Orange Monster" even necessitated a unique set of ground rules: balls hit over the wall were counted only as doubles unless reaching the second tier of grandstand seats, in which case they were allowed as homers. The right-field fence was only 315 feet from home plate, yet hitters reported pacing off the distances to both left-field and right-field barriers and finding them closer to 180 feet and 300 feet than the reported distances. Infield conditions were more troublesome still – a sea of dips, rocks, and soft spots – thus the hastily constructed diamond was hardly up to big-league or even minor league or collegiate standards by any conceivable measures.

Yet questionable stadium conditions as usual seemed no real match for skilled pitching performances as Venezuela's top U.S. import, Doug Linton of the Toronto Blue Jays, hurled a masterful five-hit shutout (featuring 11 strikeouts) at Puerto Rico's San Juan team during game eight and Pittsburgh Pirate lefty Bob Patterson (with relief aid from Ramón Peña) shut down Caracas 2–1 with another masterful piece of moundsmanship in game three. It was not quality baseball that was missing from the 1990 Orange Bowl competition but the anticipated throngs of enthusiastic Latino fans. High ticket prices and poor promotion of the event, as well as the reputation of a crime-ridden neighborhood surrounding the ramshackle Orange Bowl, had conspired to keep crowds in the neighborhood of 2,000 per game. To the dismay of the games' promoters, it was also quickly discovered that Puerto Rican, Venezuelan, or Dominican south Florida expatriates might show up in modest numbers to watch their national representative in one game of an evening doubleheader but would quickly depart as soon as their countrymen were not on the field.

The first stateside Caribbean Series departed Miami after a week of exciting if sparsely attended baseball with many questions still hanging tenuously in the balance. What would be the venue for this proud series when the following winter season rolled around? Would it return to Miami despite the lack of 1990 success at the ticket gate and the drawing board? And if so, in what ballpark would a second Miami tournament be held? Could the current promoters (Harrow and ProEventos Deportivos) be foolish enough to risk injury to budding major league prospects and unleash the anger of traditional ballfans by staging their event in the makeshift confines of a creaky and misshapen Orange Bowl? Would quaint Bobby Maduro Stadium, longtime spring-training home to the Baltimore Orioles, provide a more attractive setting despite its similar location in a reputedly unsafe low-income Hispanic neighborhood?

And what about the sagging status of the economically depressed winter leagues themselves? No one has captured the issues surrounding a depressed winter-league scene more succinctly than noted Latin baseball historian Rob Ruck, writing in his excellent recent assessment of Caribbean baseball economics (February 25, 1990, issue of *Baseball America*). Can winter-league season play survive the economic disasters created by such taxing local conditions as Hurricane Hugo (which flooded Puerto Rican ballparks and severely damaged Dominican electrical hookups in 1989) and the continued absence of yesteryear's superstar big-league players (now too wealthy to covet off-season employment), who in past campaigns filled the local stadiums with enthusiastic fanáticos panting to see the legendary North American ballplayers? Given the current economics of big-league baseball, Ruck assumes that any strong revival of a healthy and star-filled Dominican, Venezuelan, or Puerto Rican winter league seems a bleak prospect at best. And new plans by major league baseball for its Arizona Fall League player-development circuit (implemented in 1992) now seem even further to doom a long-standing Caribbean baseball tradition.

Fortunately for the series and its backers, the worst fears generated by the disappointing 1990 CWS were not realized during a second season of stateside play. Luckily, the Orange Bowl had been abandoned, and although attendance was still sparse in 1991, the venue of Bobby Maduro Stadium provided the familiar spectacle of real baseball. New corporate sponsorship also meant a healthier financial result, even if the corporate decision to rename the tournament Winterball I could not have set well with tradition-minded fans throughout the Caribbean winter-league countries. Bobby Maduro had been spiced up for the 1991 renewal of CWS play with a display of outfield billboard commercials (Coors Light Beer, Diet Pepsi, American Airlines, and several Hispanic magazines), and infield conditions, outfield dimensions, sound system, and electronic scoreboard all now reflected major league conditions. Perhaps the biggest blow to traditionalists, however, was not a new corporate name for the event but a novel playoff structure for the thirty-third renewal of play. Now a six-game round-robin was designed to eliminate two countries, followed by a best-of-three matchup between the two survivors. Little embarrassment resulted from the revised format, fortunately, as for the second straight year in Miami the Dominican entrant proved clearly dominant. This time it was Licey that captured all three of its first-round games, then slaughtered Venezuela 13–4 and 13–1 in two championship contests.

If a clearly better tournament occurred in Miami in 1991, buoyed by a new stadium venue and a new sense of pride and organization, the real revival came only when CWS play returned to its rightful home on Latin soil a year later. Fans once again flocked to Héctor Espino Stadium in Hermosillo, Mexico, this time to the tune of 15,000 and more per contest. It was better than a threefold attendance upswing from the Miami years, suggesting that low ticket prices and baseball-hungry Caribbean fans are the true touchstone of ongoing CWS success. And the Mexican throngs who turned out at Hermosillo were fittingly rewarded with one of the best series ever contested. The double-round-robin format now in effect left two clubs, Mayaguez of Puerto Rico and Zuila of Venezuela, with identical 4-2 records. For one of the rare times in CWS history, the final contest of the final night was played for all the marbles and saw Mayaguez crush Zuila 8–0 behind the three-hit shutout pitching of Roberto Hernández and two relievers and the home-run slugging of Cleveland Indians star Carlos Baerga. A special footnote to the 1992 playdown was the dramatic story of catcher Chad Kreuter, who had entered winter-league play without a 1992 big-league contract and subsequently earned a Detroit Tigers roster spot with his outstanding Puerto Rican and CWS MVP performances.

When all is said and done, a bleak future seems to hang over the Caribbean winter championship playoffs. The future is uncertain regarding both the economically unstable Caribbean winter leagues and the constantly evolving tournament that still follows them. With an Arizona Fall League now in place and being televised on cable networks, more talent is now being siphoned from the player-thin Caribbean winter circuits. And without topflight ballplayers, the Caribbean fans simply will not come to the now less popular winter-league games. Latin crowds, after all, have been spoiled by a half century of baseball at the highest professional levels. Their parks seem to offer only double-A prospects while television now brings the real big-league games from Chicago, New York, and Los Angeles straight into their homes. These most fanatical of America's fans are used to cheering for stars, not unheralded rookie prospects.

Whatever the resolutions to these mounting problems, colorful winter-league baseball will likely continue its frenetic excitement for at least several more seasons during the otherwise dormant hot-stove months of December and January. And for at least a few more Februaries a handful of true fanáticos who count themselves among the privileged, alongside an army of professional scouts and journalists, will again cast their glance southward to witness professional baseball's best-kept-secret celebration of the impending rites of spring.

Capsule History of the Caribbean World Series

1949, Havana—Series 1

Champion: Alacranes de Almendares (Cuba), managed by Fermín Guerra. **Highlights:** Cuban ace Agapito Mayor provides a stellar performance and leads his Almendares club to victory in the first Caribbean Series, becoming the only pitcher to win three games in a single tourney. Two victories come in short relief stints and the third in an 11–4 romp over Puerto Rico in which the Cuban starter hurls seven successful frames. **Outstanding Players:** Brooklyn's 1947 World Series hero Al Gionfriddo paces all batters with his .533 average (8 for 15), but Negro-leaguer and winter-league legend Wilmer Fields (Puerto Rico) turns in an even more outstanding all-around performance, finishing third in hitting (.450), first in runs scored (8), third in hits (9), second in doubles and homers, and third in RBIs (6), also pitching one game. **Team Standings (Managers):** Alemendares (Cuba, Fermín Guerra) 6-0; Cervecería Caracas (Venezuela, José Casanova) 3-3; Spur Cola (Panama, Leon Treadway) 2-4; Mayaguez (Puerto Rico, Artie Wilson) 1-5.

1950, San Juan — Series 2

Champion: Carta Vieja (Panama), managed by Wayne Blackburn. **Highlights:** Panama's Carta Vieja club wins that country's only CWS title and the only championship triumph of the *primera etapa* not registered by Cuba or Puerto Rico. Fine relief work by Negro-leaguer Chet Brewer leads Carta Vieja to a title-clinching 9–3 win over Puerto Rico, the Panamaneans pounding two top Caguas pitchers (Dan Bankhead and Rubén Gómez) in the process. **Outstanding Players:** Dan Bankhead (first big-league black pitcher) and Washington Senators Cuban ace Conrado Marrero (Almendares) hook up in an outstanding duel, finally won by Bankhead 1–0 on a five-hitter. Dan Bankhead (Brooklyn) thus authors the second series shutout, the first having come a year earlier in form of an eight-hitter thrown by Eddie Wright of Cuba versus Panama. **Team Standings (Managers):** Carta Vieja (Panama, Wayne Blackburn) 5-2; Caguas (Puerto Rico, Luís Rodríguez Olmo) 4-3; Almendares (Cuba, Fermín Guerra) 3-3; Magallanes (Venezuela, Vidal López) 1-5.

1951, Caracas — Series 3

Champion: Cangrejeros de Santurce (Puerto Rico), managed by George Scales. **Highlights:** Puerto Rico registers its first championship victory, setting the tone early with an opening 13–1 spanking of Cuba. Luís Olmo slugs two homers for the Puerto Rican team, and José "Pantalones" Santiago proves to be the staff ace by winning two games on the hill. Cuba, behind the stellar pitching of Hoyt Wilhelm, hands Santurce its only defeat 2–1. **Outstanding Player:** Stellar Cuban first baseman Jesús Lorenzo "Chiquitín" Cabrera of the Havana Reds establishes a long-lasting (and perhaps unchallengeable) hitting mark by batting a stratospheric .619 on 13 safeties in 21 official at-bats. **Team Standings (Managers):** Santurce (Puerto Rico, George Scales) 5-1; Havana (Cuba, Mike González) 4-2; Magallanes (Venezuela, Lazaro Sálazar) 2-4; Spur Cola (Panama, Leon Kellman) 1-5.

1952, Panama City — Series 4

Champion: Leones de la Habana (Cuba), managed by Mike González. **Highlights:** Cuba becomes the first repeat champion under the direction of

Latin America's first big-league manager, Mike González. A tie with Puerto Rico, however, prevents González's team from becoming the second club to record an unblemished tournament record. Future major league World Series hero Edmundo "Sandy" Amoros (Brooklyn) is the year's batting star (.450) for the Cubans. **Outstanding Player:** Texas-born hurler Tommy Fine (a lifetime 1-3 major-leaguer) pitches for Havana and hurls the first and only no-hit, no-run game in series history, a 1–0 blanking of Cervecería Caracas. The veteran right-hander walks three and strikes out four along the way to his rare and unexpected once-in-a-lifetime masterpiece. **Team Standings (Managers):** Havana (Cuba, Mike González) 5-0-1; Cervecería Caracas (Venezuela, José Casanova) 3-3; Carta Vieja (Panama, Al Leap) 3-3; San Juan (Puerto Rico, Freddie Thon) 0-5-1.

1953, Havana—Series 5

Champion: Cangrejeros de Santurce (Puerto Rico), managed by Buster Clarkson. **Highlights:** The Santurce Crabbers become the first club to repeat as champions, also allowing Puerto Rico to become the second country to garner multiple team titles. Santurce is also only the second team to post an unblemished six-game record. Bobo Holloman (on the eve of his one major league season with the St. Louis Browns) wins two games on the hill for the talented Santurce team. **Outstanding Players:** Willard "Ese Hombre" Brown establishes a record with four homers. Cuban center fielder Pedro Formental bats .560, a level surpassed only twice in 30-plus years (Jesús Lorenzo Cabrera in 1951 and Manny Mota in 1971). **Team Standings (Managers):** Santurce (Puerto Rico, Buster Clarkson) 6-0; Havana (Cuba, Mike González) 3-3; Chesterfield (Panama, Graham Stanford) 2-4; Caracas (Venezuela, Martín Dihigo) 1-5.

1954, San Juan—Series 6

Champion: Criollos de Caguas (Puerto Rico), managed by Mickey Owen. **Highlights:** Puerto Rico becomes the first three-time champion as Caguas repeats Santurce's two earlier triumphs. Mickey Owen, a goat of the 1941 World Series in Brooklyn but an astute baseball man nonetheless, is the successful Puerto Rican skipper. "Jungle Jim" Rivera of the Chicago White Sox (.450) paces the Puerto Ricans at the plate. **Outstanding Players:** Ray Orteig (Cuba) becomes only the third player to slug two homers in a single game, accomplishing the feat (which gave him the home-run title) against Panama. Russian-born pitcher Victor Strizka (raised in Panama) leads the pitchers with a perfect 2-0 mark. **Team Standings (Managers):** Caguas (Puerto Rico, Mickey Owen) 4-2; Almendares (Cuba, Bob Bragan) 3-3; Carta Vieja (Panama, Joseph Tuminelli) 3-3; Pastora (Venezuela, Napoleón Reyes) 2-4.

1955, Caracas – Series 7

Champion: Cangrejeros de Santurce (Puerto Rico), managed by Herman Franks. **Highlights:** Willie Mays, fresh from his 1954 National League batting title and memorable World Series catch against Vic Wertz, strokes an eleventh-inning home run off Giants teammate Ramón Monzant (pitching for Magallanes of Venezuela). Mays's smash, with Roberto Clemente on base, earns an important 4–2 victory for Santurce (Puerto Rico), the eventual 1955 champion. Mays's gigantic home run also breaks up a nagging 0-for-12 slump for the future Hall-of-Famer and remains one of the most dramatic clouts of Caribbean Series history. Puerto Rico reigns as champion for the third straight year. **Outstanding Players:** Never known as a power hitter, diminutive shortstop and future big-league manager Don Zimmer (Brooklyn) becomes the third player in series history to smack three roundtrippers in a single tournament. More muscular slugger Rocky Nelson (also Brooklyn) takes the batting title with a .471 average. **Team Standings (Managers):** Santurce (Puerto Rico, Herman Franks) 5-1; Magallanes (Venezuela, Lazaro Sálazar) 4-2; Almendares (Cuba, Bob Bragan) 2-4; Carta Vieja (Panama, Al Kubski) 1-5.

1956, Panama City – Series 8

Champion: Elefantes de Cienfuegos (Cuba), managed by Oscar Rodríguez. **Highlights:** Cuba claims its third title and launches a new string of victories that will stretch over five winters and reach throughout the remainder of phase-one tournament play. Cienfuegos will eventually capture two of those five titles, as will Marianao. Dick Farrell of Venezuela (Philadelphia Phillies) narrowly misses repeating Tommy Fine's no-hit masterpiece of 1952 but loses his no-hitter and shutout on Ramón Maldonado's late-inning roundtripper for Puerto Rico. **Outstanding Players:** Camilo Pascual records the first of his three 2-0 marks over the next five-year period. Pascual (Cuba), in his first CWS appearance, establishes himself as the most effective pitcher (at least in wins and losses) in series history. Catcher Rafael "Ray" Noble (Cuba, New York Giants) becomes the fourth batsman to hit .500 (10 for 20) for the week-long tournament. **Team Standings (Managers):** Cienfuegos (Cuba, Oscar Rodríguez) 5-1; Chesterfield (Panama, Graham Stanford) 3-3; Caguas (Puerto Rico, Ben Gerahty) 3-3; Valencia (Venezuela, Regino Otero) 1-5.

1957, Havana – Series 9

Champion: Tigres de Marianao (Cuba), managed by Napoleón Reyes. **Highlights:** Marianao captures its first of two straight titles under manager Napoleón Reyes. While native Cuban Minnie Miñoso is a prominent batting star for the victorious Marianao club, big-league import Jim Bunning (Detroit Tigers) is the mound standout with a 2-0 record. Cuba's only loss comes in a 6–0 whitewashing at the hands of Puerto Rico and former Cleveland Indians hurler José "Pantalones" Santiago. **Outstanding Players:** Big-league outfielder Sammy Drake (Chicago Cubs) hits .500 (10 for 20) for Cuba, the fifth player to reach the magic .500 level. José Santiago (Mayaguez over Marianao), George Brunet (Balboa over Mayaguez), and Winston Brown (Balboa over Caracas) all throw complete-game shutouts. **Team Standings (Managers):** Marianao (Cuba, Napoleón Reyes) 5-1; Club Balboa (Panama, Leon Kellman) 3-3; Mayaguez (Puerto Rico, Mickey Owen) 2-4; Caracas (Venezuela, Clay Bryant) 2-4.

1958, San Juan—Series 10

Champion: Tigres de Marianao (Cuba), managed by Napoleón Reyes. **Highlights:** Marianao completes its two-year domination under manager Napoleón Reyes, this time barely edging out Panama and Puerto Rico by a single game. Marianao clinches the title with a clutch 2–0 three-hit shutout of Puerto Rico thrown by right-hander Bob Shaw of the Chicago White Sox. **Outstanding Player:** Striking out at least one batter in every inning, lefty big-league star Juan Pizarro (Puerto Rico) fans an incredible 17 hitters against the Carta Vieja club of Panama City, a record that stands today. Pizarro allows but two scratch hits and walks only three batters in an 8–0 Puerto Rican victory. **Team Standings (Managers):** Marianao (Cuba, Napoleón Reyes) 4-2; Carta Vieja (Panama, Wilmer Schantz) 3-3; Caguas (Puerto Rico, Ted Norbert) 3-3; Valencia (Venezuela, Regino Otero) 2-4.

1959, Caracas—Series 11

Champion: Alacranes de Almendares (Cuba), managed by Clemente Carreras. **Highlights:** Cuba threatens to turn the annual series into a full-blown sham with a fourth straight triumph. This year the team is new, however, as Almendares returns to the scene under rookie skipper Clemente Carreras. While Cuba is the best team, Venezuela dominates the individual statistics, at least those for hitting. Jesús Mora of Oriente wins the batting title (.417), and Oriente's Norm Cash (Chicago White Sox, later Detroit Tigers) blasts out the most homers with two and knocks in the most runs with eight. **Outstanding Players:** Camilo Pascual (Cuba) wins two games without a defeat for the second time. Orlando Peña provides marvelous hurling for Cuba's Almendares, hooking up in two great mound duels against the Puerto Rican ballclub. Peña is defeated by National League rival Rubén Gómez in a first contest but blanks Santurce 1–0 in a rematch. **Team Standings (Managers):** Almendares (Cuba, Clemente Carreras) 5-1; Oriente

(Venezuela, Kerby Farrell) 4-2; Santurce (Puerto Rico, Moses Concepción) 3-3; Cocle (Panama, Lester Peden) 0-6.

1960, Panama City—Series 12

Champion: Elefantes de Cienfuegos (Cuba), managed by Antonio Castaños. **Highlights:** Cuba makes it five in a row, this time leaving no suspense from the outset by sweeping all six of its contests. Stan Palys (Panama) sets an RBI record of 12, which still stands 33 years later. Two other prominent major-leaguers also enjoy a fine tournament as Tommy Davis (Dodgers) wins the batting title for Puerto Rico and infielder Héctor López (Yankees) slams three home runs for his native Panama. **Outstanding Player:** Veteran major-leaguer Camilo Pascual (Cuba) wins two games in a single series for a record third time, establishing an all-time career series record of six victories without a single defeat. **Team Standings (Managers):** Cienfuegos (Cuba, Antonio Castanos) 6-0; Marlboro (Panama, Wilmer Schantz) 3-3; Caguas (Puerto Rico, Vic Pollet "Power") 2-4; Rapiños (Venezuela, Les Moss) 1-5.

1970, Caracas—Series 13

Champion: Navegantes de Magallanes (Venezuela), managed by Carlos Pascual. **Highlights:** The only country not to win a title in the first phase of CWS play, Venezuela celebrates the tournament's renewal with its initial championship banner. Ponce (Puerto Rico) and Licey (Dominican Republic) are the only invited opposition, yet it is a handful of Cuban expatriates who remind all in attendance of previous Cuban domination in CWS contests. In a crucial early game, Cuban hurler Orlando Peña (Venezuela) outduels fellow Cuban Mike Cuellar (Puerto Rico) 3–1. Peña and another Cuban moundsman, Aurelio Monteagudo, hurl two victories each for title-bound Magallanes. **Outstanding Players:** Catcher Ray Fosse, outfielders César Tóvar, and Gonzalo Márquez (the batting champion at .478), and pitchers Larry Jaster (1-0) and Jay Ritchie (1-0) all contribute heavily to a first Venezuelan team title. **Team Standings (Managers):** Magallanes (Venezuela, Carlos Pascual) 7-1; Ponce (Puerto Rico, Jim Fregosi) 4-4; Licey (Dominican Republic, Manny Mota) 1-7; no Mexican entry.

1971, San Juan—Series 14

Champion: Tigres de Licey (Dominican Republic), managed by Manny Mota. **Highlights:** A powerful Dominican team becomes the fourth undefeated and untied squad and the first in second-phase play. All three opponents finish with identical marks of 2-4 and never challenge Manny Mota's juggernaut. Chris Zachery wins two games on the hill for Licey, retiring 11 straight batters at one point during his first outing. **Outstanding Players:** Manny Mota not only manages Licey to an undefeated sweep of tourney play but leads all hitters with a stratospheric .579 average (11 for 19), the second-highest BA of series history. Manny Mota's amazing hitting even overshadows the power display of Mexico's Celerino Sánchez, who paces the tournament in both homers (3) and RBIs (9). **Team Standings (Managers):** Licey (Dominican Republic, Manny Mota) 6-0; Hermosillo (Mexico, Maurice "Maury" Wills) 2-4; Santurce (Puerto Rico, Frank Robinson) 2-4; La Guaira (Venezuela, Graciano Ravelo) 2-4.

1972, Santo Domingo – Series 15

Champion: Leones de Ponce (Puerto Rico), managed by Frank Verdi. **Highlights:** Venezuelan champion Aragua features a double-play combination of future Hall-of-Famers (playing manager Rod Carew at second base and Davy Concepción at shortstop), but it is not enough to prevent Puerto Rico from running away from the pack with five-straight opening victories. This is the first CWS tournament hosted by the Dominican Republic, and enthusiastic Dominican fanáticos cheer their Cibao team on toward a respectable second-place finish. **Outstanding Players:** Big-leaguers Sandy Alomar, Don Baylor, Pat Corrales, Bernie Carbo, and Carlos May provide the heavy hitting for Ponce, while the Puerto Rican team also features a rare native-son brother trio of major league reserve outfielders – José, Tommy, and Héctor Cruz. **Team Standings (Managers):** Ponce (Puerto Rico, Frank Verdi) 5-1; Cibao (Dominican Republic, Osvaldo "Ossie" Virgil) 3-3; Aragua (Venezuela, Rod Carew) 3-3; Guasave (Mexico, Vinicio García) 1-5.

1973, Caracas – Series 16

Champion: Tigres de Licey (Dominican Republic), managed by Tommy Lasorda. **Highlights:** Future longtime Los Angeles Dodgers manager Tom Lasorda provides leadership in Licey's runaway championship campaign. Caracas gets two shutouts from its pitchers (Milt Wilcox and Diego Seguí) in its first three games but then falters and drops three straight. Lasorda's team already sports a Dodgers flavor with Steve Garvey at first base and Manny Mota at third, and features Bobby Valentine (ex-Dodger) at shortstop and Jesús Alou (Houston Astros) in the outfield. **Outstanding Players:** Pedro Borbón wins two starts for Licey, the second and third victories of his eventual 5-0 lifetime won-lost mark. Jesús Alou also joins the select circle of six (at that time) batsman hitting .500 or better for a single CWS. **Team Standings (Managers):** Licey (Dominican Republic, Tommy Lasorda)

5-1; Caracas (Venezuela, Osvaldo "Ossie" Virgil) 3-3; Santurce (Puerto Rico, Frank Robinson) 3-3; Obregón (Mexico, Dave García) 1-5.

1974, Hermosillo – Series 17

Champion: Criollos de Caguas (Puerto Rico), managed by Bobby Wine. **Highlights:** Puerto Rico proves a penchant for winning on new ground by copping the first tournament held in Mexico (the Puerto Ricans also having won the inaugural CWS on Dominican soil two seasons earlier). A players' strike keeps the Venezuelan entry at home, and host Mexico therefore provides two entrants – Obregón (1973 Mexican League winner) and Mazatlán (1974 Mexican champion). **Outstanding Players:** Two likely Cooperstown Hall-of-Famers pace Caguas to the title – Mike Schmidt at third base and Gary Carter catching. Mexican legend Héctor Espino (Obregón) wins the batting title (.429), however, in his first hometown performance of CWS play. **Team Standings (Managers):** Caguas (Puerto Rico, Bobby Wine) 4-2; Licey (Dominican Republic, Tommy Lasorda) 3-3; Obregón* (Mexico, Mike Alejandro) 3-3; Mazatlán* (Mexico, Ramón Camacho) 2-4; *Two Mexican teams and no Venezuelan entry.

1975, San Juan – Series 18

Champion: Vaqueros de Bayamón (Puerto Rico), managed by José Pagán. **Highlights:** Puerto Rico (this time the Bayamón team) garners the first back-to-back championships of phase two as play returns to San Juan for the first time since 1971 and the fifth time overall. While Ken Griffey paces the batters, first baseman Willie Montañez provides much of the Puerto Rican firepower by blasting home 10 crucial runs, two short of the CWS RBI record (12 in 1960) by Stan Palys. **Outstanding Players:** Ken Griffey becomes the eighth player to bat .500 (12 for 24) or better during CWS play (there have been six others since Griffey). Héctor Espino (Mexico) slugs two of his eventual six CWS homers, both coming in a single contest versus Aragua of Venezuela. **Team Standings (Managers):** Bayamón (Puerto Rico, José Pagán) 5-1; Hermosillo (Mexico, Benjamin Reyes) 3-3; Cibao (Dominican Republic, Al Widmar) 3-3; Aragua (Venezuela, Ossie Virgil) 1-5.

1976, Santo Domingo – Series 19

Champion: Naranjeros de Hermosillo (Mexico), managed by Benjamin Reyes. **Highlights:** Hermosillo drops its opener to a Cibao team playing in its own ballpark, then rallies for five straight victories and the first-ever Mexican title. Veteran hurler George Brunet tosses the clinching victory for the Mexicans, and slugging star Héctor Espino provides the batting power with his fourth lifetime CWS homer and a year's-best seven RBIs. **Outstanding Player:** Juan Pizarro (Puerto Rico) hurls his second CWS shutout (his first recorded in 1958) and thus becomes only the second hurler (Camilo Pascual was first) to author two shutouts in lifetime series play. **Team Standings (Managers):** Hermosillo (Mexico, Benjamin Reyes) 5-1; Aragua (Venezuela, Osvaldo "Ossie" Virgil) 3-3; Bayamón (Puerto Rico, José Pagán) 2-4; Cibao (Dominican Republic, Tim Murtaugh) 2-4.

1977, Caracas – Series 20

Champion: Tigres de Licey (Dominican Republic), managed by Bob Rodgers. **Highlights:** Licey sweeps all six games and posts a 45–7 scoring margin over its opponents in the most one-sided tourney yet. Licey thus becomes the second undefeated team in phase two and the fifth in CWS history. Pedro Borbón (Cincinnati Reds) posts a shutout for the champions and thus increases his overall series record to 5-0, second only to Camilo Pascual's 6-0 as the best lifetime pitching mark. **Outstanding Player:** Rico Carty (Licey) pounds out five roundtrippers to lead his Dominican countrymen to their third title in seven years, also establishing the new milepost for home runs in a single CWS tournament. Carty also knocks in 10 runs and posts a batting average of .476 and a slugging mark of 1.333, perhaps the greatest all-around batting performance of any winter-league finale. **Team Standings (Managers):** Licey (Dominican Republic, Bob Rodgers) 6-0; Magallanes (Venezuela, Don Leppert) 3-3; Mazatlán (Mexico, Alfredo Ortiz) 2-4; Caguas (Puerto Rico, Doc Edwards) 1-5.

1978, Mazatlán – Series 21

Champion: Indios de Mayaguez (Puerto Rico), managed by Rene Lachemann. **Highlights:** Mexico returns to the role of host, and Puerto Rico (also a winner in Mexico in 1974) returns to the role of champion. Mayaguez opens with five quick victories and is never headed, although Cibao and Caracas manage three wins apiece. Puerto Rico's José Morales is the batting champion (.421) while Venezuela's Leon Roberts (Seattle Mariners) leads in homers (2) and paces the tourney in RBIs (6). **Outstanding Player:** Nicaraguan hurler Tony Chávez (Caracas) strikes out six straight batters to establish a new CWS record. In still another remarkable mound performance, 42-year-old former big-leaguer George Brunet returns to CWS play and loses twice for Culiacán. Brunet, who pitched for Panama in the 1950s, thus finishes his lengthy career with a 3-4 CWS record. **Team Standings (Managers):** Mayaguez (Puerto Rico, Rene Lachemann) 5-1; Cibao (Dominican Republic, Johnny Lipon) 3-3; Caracas (Venezuela, Felipe Alou) 3-3; Culiacán (Mexico, Raúl Cano) 1-5.

1979, San Juan – Series 22

Champion: Navegantes de Magallanes (Venezuela), managed by Willie Horton. **Highlights:** Big-league outfielder Mitchell Page (Oakland Athletics) smashes a hefty 450-foot home run in the penultimate series game to clinch the team championship for Magallanes, only the second championship title earned by a Venezuelan ballclub in three decades of Caribbean Series play. The Magallanes triumph ends a nine-year drought for Venezuela and thus gives the Magallanes ballclub bookend CWS titles at the two corners of the 1970s. **Outstanding Player:** Magallanes is sparked by several outstanding individual performances. Mike Norris hurls a one-hitter (11–0) against Caguas; outfielder Jerry White paces all hitters at .522; first baseman Mitchell Page hits .417 and leads with two homers. Mexican shortstop Mario Mendoza bats a lofty .286 in his fifth and final CWS yet still finishes with a career CWS average of .159, far south of his famous "Mendoza Line" standard (.200 BA) for offensive futility. **Team Standings (Managers):** Magallanes (Venezuela, Willie Horton) 5-1; Cibao (Dominican Republic, Johnny Lipon) 4-2; Caguas (Puerto Rico, Félix Millán) 2-4; Navojoa (Mexico, Chuck Coggins) 1-5.

1980, Santo Domingo – Series 23

Champion: Tigres de Licey (Dominican Republic), managed by Del Crandall. **Highlights:** Licey's fourth CWS crown comes on home turf as the Dominicans win their first four contests, then watch as Mexico eliminates Caracas from title contention on the final day. Licey pitchers toss two shutouts (Gerald Hannahs and Dennis Lewallyn), and Joaquín Andújar also twirls a 3–1 masterpiece over runner-up Venezuela. Lewallyn's 10-inning blanking of Bayamón is the first extra-inning shutout in series history. **Outstanding Player:** CWS home-run king Tony Armas powers a grand slam (the tenth in tourney history) to provide all the runs in a 4–2 Caracas defeat of Licey, postponing by one day the Dominicans' eventual tournament title clincher. **Team Standings (Managers):** Licey (Dominican Republic, Del Crandall) 5-1; Caracas (Venezuela, Felipe Alou) 3-3; Bayamón (Puerto Rico, Art Howe) 2-4; Hermosillo (Mexico, Benjamin Reyes) 2-4.

1982, Hermosillo – Series 24

Champion: Leones de Caracas (Venezuela), managed by Alfonso Carrasquel. **Highlights:** Play resumes after a players' strike forces cancellation of 1981 CWS action. Under manager Chico Carrasquel, Caracas cruises to victory on the strength of productive hitting, paced by two Bo Díaz homers (.400 BA) and six well-timed Tony Armas RBIs (and .375 BA). Fernando

Valenzuela makes his only CWS appearance, earning one of two victories registered by host team Hermosillo. **Outstanding Player:** Mexican hitting legend Héctor Espino plays his fifth and final CWS with Hermosillo, extending his career totals to 46 hits, 6 homers, and a .297 BA. Fittingly, this year's tourney is played in renamed Héctor Espino Stadium. **Team Standings (Managers):** Caracas (Venezuela, Alfonso "Chico" Carrasquel) 5-1; Ponce (Puerto Rico, Edward Nottle) 3-3; Hermosillo (Mexico, Tom Harmon) 2-4; Escogido (Dominican Republic, Felipe Alou) 2-4.

1983, Caracas—Series 25

Champion: Lobos de Arecibo (Puerto Rico), managed by Ron Clark. **Highlights:** Arecibo is crushed 17–2 by Licey in their opener, yet the Lobos rebound immediately to win five straight on their way to a ninth pennant for Puerto Rico. Hometown Venezuela (La Guaira) features a power-packed lineup spotted with big-league stars like Dave Concepción at shortstop, Tony Armas and Luís Salazar in the outfield, and catcher Bo Díaz, who extends his record CWS consecutive appearances streak to 30 games. Mexico's Culiacán "Tomato Pickers" become the first ballclub to lose all their games since Panama did so in 1959. **Outstanding Players:** Venezuela's Tony Armas launches his 1980s CWS home-run onslaught with three roundtrippers, the first of his two 3-HR CWS performances. Minor-leaguer Rick Anderson (New York Mets) pitches a five-hit shutout for La Guaira versus punchless Culiacán. **Team Standings (Managers):** Arecibo (Puerto Rico, Ron Clark) 5-1; La Guaira (Venezuela, Ossie Virgil) 4-2; Licey (Dominican Republic, Manny Mota) 3-3; Culiacán (Mexico, Francisco Estrada) 0-6.

1984, San Juan—Series 26

Champion: Aguilas de Zulia (Venezuela), managed by Rubén Amaro. **Highlights:** Poor attendance does little to inspire the host Mayaguez team, which manages only one win and one tie for a last-place deadlock with the Dominicans. Big-league star third sacker Aurelio Rodríguez makes his final CWS appearance and inspires Los Mochis to a fast second-place finish at 4-2. Zulia takes the title with top performances from catcher Bobby Ramos, third baseman Luís Salazar, and batting leader (.529) Leo Carrión. **Outstanding Players:** Toronto Blue Jays slugger George Bell does most of the heavy hitting with three homers and six RBIs. Dominican Luís Leal and Nicaraguan Porfi Altamirano (Los Mochis) turn in the top pitching performances. **Team Standings (Managers):** Zulia (Venezuela, Rubén Amaro) 5-1; Los Mochis (Mexico, Vinicio García) 4-2; Mayaguez (Puerto Rico, Frank Verdi) 1-4-1; Licey (Dominican Republic, Manny Mota) 1-4-1.

1985, Mazatlán – Series 27

Champion: Tigres de Licey (Dominican Republic), managed by Terry Collins. **Highlights:** Licey grabs its fifth CWS team crown and thus cements itself as all-time club champion. Four solo homers (including two by import Glenn Davis and one by native George Bell) spark an opening 4–2 victory over La Guaira. After a tight second-game loss against Mexico, the Dominicans take four straight (including a combined shutout by Mike Torrez and José Rijo) to lock up the title. **Outstanding Player:** Glenn Davis wins the home-run title, becoming only the eleventh player to sock three or more homers in a single CWS tournament, the twelfth to blast two in one game. **Team Standings (Managers):** Licey (Dominican Republic, Terry Collins) 5-1; Culiacán (Mexico, Francisco Estrada) 3-3; San Juan (Puerto Rico, Mako Olivares) 2-4; La Guaira (Venezuela, Aurelio Monteagudo) 2-4.

1986, Maracaibo – Series 28

Champion: Aguilas de Mexicali (Mexico), managed by Benjamin Reyes. **Highlights:** Ten years after their first triumph, Mexico wins its only other CWS flag, again under veteran skipper Benjamin Reyes. Mexico is actually shut out twice (11–0, 6–0) in its first three games, but after four contests all four teams are tied at 2-2 for the first time ever. Mexicali finishes strong and backs into the title when host Venezuela is stopped by Cibao in the final contest. Mexicali's 14–0 triumph over La Guaira is the second-most lopsided single-game affair in tourney history. **Outstanding Players:** Manager Benjamin Reyes joins Cuban skipper Napoleón Reyes as the only bench bosses to win two CWS titles. Luís DeLeón of Mayaguez hurls a two-hit complete-game shutout (6–0) against the eventual champions. **Team Standings (Managers):** Mexicali (Mexico, Benjamin Reyes) 4-2; Cibao (Dominican Republic, Winston Llenas) 3-3; La Guaira (Venezuela, José Martínez) 3-3; Mayaguez (Puerto Rico, Nick Leyva) 2-4.

1987, Hermosillo – Series 29

Champion: Criollos de Caguas (Puerto Rico), managed by Ramón Aviles. **Highlights:** Caguas (the eventual champion) establishes a lofty team standard by smacking eight home runs in a single contest against the outmanned Dominicans; nevertheless, Puerto Rico falls in this strange game by a close 14–13 score. Puerto Rico falls victim to another unique event as well when manager Tim Foli is removed from his post after three contests (1-2), thus becoming the only manager ever fired in the midst of CWS play. **Outstanding Player:** Journeyman big-league outfielder Carmelo Martínez (Puerto Rico) blasts three homers (his third multiple-homer series) to secure second spot on the all-time CWS roundtripper list with eight. Martínez also captures this year's batting title with .556. **Team Standings (Managers):** Caguas (Puerto Rico, Tim Foli, Ramón Aviles) 5-2; Cibao (Dominican Republic, Winston Llenas) 4-3; Mazatlán (Mexico, Carlos Paz) 2-4; Caracas (Venezuela, Bill Plummer) 2-4.

1988, Santo Domingo – Series 30

Champion: Leones de Escogido (Dominican Republic), managed by Phil Regan. **Highlights:** Host club Escogido rides to victory on the arms of its strong pitching staff (José DeLeón, José Núñez, Luís Encarnación) and clinches the 1988 flag in its fifth contest with a 2–1 victory over Caracas. This is the sixth Dominican title, but the first won by a team other than Licey. Phil Regan (former Cubs and Dodgers relief ace) skippers the Escogido Lions in his first pro managerial assignment. **Outstanding Players:** Former "cup of coffee" big-leaguer and Dominican legend Rufino Linares enjoys another fine winter as the series MVP, batting .389 and knocking in five runs. Cardinals catching prospect Tom Pagnozzi (Puerto Rico) is the leading hitter (.474) in the tournament. DeLeón and Encarnación, along with Ramón de los Santos, pace the standout Dominican staff to a combined 1.80 ERA. But the final hour of glory belongs to Tony Armas (Venezuela), who cements his career series home-run lead (11) with two final CWS roundtrippers. **Team Standings (Managers):** Escogido (Dominican Republic, Phil Regan) 4-2; Mayaguez (Puerto Rico, Jim Riggleman) 3-3; Tijuana (Mexico, George Ficht) 3-3; Caracas (Venezuela, Bill Robinson) 2-4.

1989, Mazatlán – Series 31

Champion: Aguilas de Zulia (Venezuela), managed by Pete McKannin. **Highlights:** A surprise entry that had finished second in the Venezuelan winter league, Zulia comes on strong at tournament time with four opening wins plus a 13-inning 8–7 fifth-game victory over Escogido in the clincher. An earlier 16-inning match between the same two teams lasts a record 5 hours and 23 minutes. **Outstanding Players:** Career minor league first baseman Phil Stephenson (Chicago Cubs) narrowly misses a Venezuelan-league triple crown, then continues his hot hitting with a Caribbean Series MVP performance (3 HRs, 7 RBIs, .385 BA). Dale Polley (Braves) and Leonard Damian (Cubs) also lead a Zulia pitching corps, which registers a sizzling 1.68 staff ERA over the first five contests of the six-game series. Zulia is later blown out 11–1 by Mayaguez in a meaningless final game. **Team Standings (Managers):** Zulia (Venezuela, Pete McKannin) 5-1; Mayaguez (Puerto Rico, Tomás Gomboa) 4-2; Mexicali (Mexico, David Machemmer) 2-4; Escogido (Dominican Republic, Phil Regan) 1-5.

1990, Miami—Series 32

Champion: Leones de Escogido (Dominican Republic), managed by Felipe Alou. **Highlights:** Series play takes place on "foreign" soil for the first time in the tourney's 32-year history, and the results are a baseball travesty and a public-relations disaster. Makeshift conditions in Miami's Orange Bowl result in poor infield play, a bevy of cheap homers, plus high-scoring contests and almost nonexistent fan support. **Outstanding Players:** Muscular Atlanta Braves outfield prospect Barry Jones ties Rico Carty's single-series home-run mark with five long circuit blows for the San Juan Metros. A lefty pull hitter, Jones thus achieves his record without an assist from the controversial shortened left-field fence (188 feet) required by the patchwork Orange Bowl diamond. **Team Standings (Managers):** Escogido (Dominican Republic, Felipe Alou) 5-1; San Juan (Puerto Rico, Mako Oliveras) 3-3; Caracas (Venezuela, Phil Regan) 3-3; Hermosillo (Mexico, Tim Johnson) 1-5.

1991, Miami—Series 33

Champion: Tigres de Licey (Dominican Republic), managed by John Roseboro. **Highlights:** Licey's Tigers prove dominant by outscoring the opposition 50–8 over five games and slaughtering Lara of Venezuela 13–4 and 13–1 in the best-of-three final round. This second U.S.-based tourney enjoys a new short-lived corporate name (Winterball I) and a new baseball-friendly home (Bobby Maduro Stadium), and attendance thus increases moderately over 1990 (6 of 11 games draw 5,000-plus fans). **Outstanding Players:** Two Licey sluggers, both owned by the Los Angeles Dodgers, share MVP honors: first sacker Henry Rodríguez hits .458 with six RBIs to cop preliminary-round MVP honors; outfielder James Brooks bats .473 and records six RBIs in the opening championship game, earning final-round MVP status. **Team Standings (Managers):** Licey (Dominican Republic, John Roseboro) 5-0; Lara (Venezuela, Domingo Carrasquel) 3-4; Tijuana (Mexico, Joel Serna) 1-3; Santurce (Puerto Rico, Mako Oliveras) 1-3.

1992, Hermosillo—Series 34

Champion: Indios de Mayaguez (Puerto Rico), managed by Patrick Kelly. **Highlights:** Mayaguez and Zulia complete the double-round elimination portion of the schedule with identical records, forcing a single head-to-head playoff contest. Paced by Carlos Baerga's (Cleveland Indians) two-run homer and the strong pitching of Roberto Hernández (Chicago White Sox), Puerto Rico breezes in the playoff game 8–0, capturing the island's first Caribbean title since 1987. Crowds of 15,000 and up jam Héctor Espino

Stadium throughout the six-day tournament. **Outstanding Players:** Detroit Tigers catcher Chad Kreuter (Puerto Rico) climaxes a hot winter season with three homers, four RBIs, and a .391 average to grab MVP honors in Hermosillo. Wilson Alvarez (Chicago White Sox) wins his only series decision and is tabbed winter-league Player of the Year on the strength of his brilliant 13-0 (including playoffs) Venezuelan-league record. **Team Standings (Managers):** Mayaguez (Puerto Rico, Patrick Kelly) 5-2; Zulia (Venezuela, Rubén Amaro) 4-3; Hermosillo (Mexico, Tim Johnson) 3-3; Escogido (Dominican Republic, Felipe Alou) 1-5.

Caribbean Series Championship Summaries

First Phase (*Primera Etapa*), 1949–1960

Year	Location	Championship Team (Country)	Winning Manager
1949	Havana, Cuba	Alacranes de Almendares (Cuba)	Fermín Guerra
1950	San Juan, Puerto Rico	Carta Vieja (Panama)	Wayne Blackburn
1951	Caracas, Venezuela	Cangrejeros de Santurce (Puerto Rico)	George Scales
1952	Panama City, Panama	Leones de La Habana (Cuba)	Mike González
1953	Havana, Cuba	Cangrejeros de Santurce (Puerto Rico)	Buster Clarkson
1954	San Juan, Puerto Rico	Criollos de Caguas (Puerto Rico)	Mickey Owen
1955	Caracas, Venezuela	Cangrejeros de Santurce (Puerto Rico)	Herman Franks
1956	Panama City, Panama	Elefantes de Cienfuegos (Cuba)	Oscar Rodríguez
1957	Havana, Cuba	Tigres de Marianao (Cuba)	Napoleón Reyes
1958	San Juan, Puerto Rico	Tigres de Marianao (Cuba)	Napoleón Reyes
1959	Caracas, Venezuela	Alacranes de Almendares (Cuba)	Clemente Carreras
1960	Panama City, Panama	Elefantes de Cienfuegos (Cuba)	Antonio Castaños

Composite Standings in First Phase (1949–1960)

Team (Country)	Games Played	Wins	Losses	Ties	Percentage	Championships
Cuba**	72	51	20	1	.708	7
Puerto Rico	73	38	34	1	.521	4
Panama*	73	29	44	0	.397	1
Venezuela	72	26	46	0	.361	0

**Cuba replaced by Dominican Republic in second phase.

*Panama replaced by Mexico in second phase.

Second Phase (*Segunda Etapa*), 1970–1992

Year	Location	Championship Team (Country)	Winning Manager
1970	Caracas, Venezuela	Navegantes de Magallanes (Venezuela)	Carlos Pascual
1971	San Juan, Puerto Rico	Tigres de Licey (Dominican)	Manny Mota
1972	Santo Domingo, DR	Leones de Ponce (Puerto Rico)	Frank Verdi
1973	Caracas, Venezuela	Tigres de Licey (Dominican)	Tommy Lasorda
1974	Hermosillo, Mexico	Criollos de Caguas (Puerto Rico)	Bobby Wine
1975	San Juan, Puerto Rico	Vaqueros de Bayamón (Puerto Rico)	José Pagán
1976	Santo Domingo, DR	Naranjeros de Hermosillo (Mexico)	Benjamin Reyes
1977	Caracas, Venezuela	Tigres de Licey (Dominican)	Bob Rodgers
1978	Mazatlán, Mexico	Indios de Mayaguez (Puerto Rico)	Rene Lachemann
1979	San Juan, Puerto Rico	Navegantes de Magallanes (Venezuela)	Willie Horton
1980	Santo Domingo, DR	Tigres de Licey (Dominican)	Del Crandall
1981	Series Cancelled		
1982	Hermosillo, Mexico	Leones de Caracas (Venezuela)	Alfonso Carrasquel
1983	Caracas, Venezuela	Lobos de Arecibo (Puerto Rico)	Ron Clark
1984	San Juan, Puerto Rico	Aguilas de Zulia (Venezuela)	Rubén Amaro
1985	Mazatlán, Mexico	Tigres de Licey (Dominican)	Terry Collins
1986	Maracaibo, Venezuela	Aguilas de Mexicali (Mexico)	Benjamin Reyes
1987	Hermosillo, Mexico	Criollos de Caguas (Puerto Rico)	Ramón Aviles
1988	Santo Domingo, DR	Leones de Escogido (Dominican)	Phil Regan
1989	Mazatlán, Mexico	Aguilas de Zulia (Venezuela)	Pete McKannin
1990	Miami, USA	Leones de Escogido (Dominican)	Felipe Alou
1991	Miami, USA	Tigres de Licey (Dominican)	John Roseboro
1992	Hermosillo, Mexico	Indios de Mayaguez (Puerto Rico)	Patrick Kelly

Composite Standings in Second Phase (1970–1992)

Team (Country)	Games Played	Wins	Losses	Ties	Percentage	Championships
Dominican Republic**	134	74	59	1	.552	8
Venezuela	129	70	59	0	.543	5
Puerto Rico	134	70	63	1	.522	7
Mexico*	126	46	80	0	.365	2

**Dominican Republic replaced Cuba in second phase.
*Mexico replaced Panama in second phase.

All-Time Composite Standings in Caribbean Series (1949–1960; 1970–1992)

Team (Country)	Games Played	Wins	Losses	Ties	Percentage	Championships
Cuba*	72	51	20	1	.708	7
Dominican Republic**	134	74	59	1	.552	8

Team (Country)	Games Played	Wins	Losses	Ties	Percentage	Championships
Puerto Rico	207	108	97	2	.522	11
Venezuela	201	96	105	0	.478	5
Panama*	73	29	44	0	.397	1
Mexico**	126	46	80	0	.365	2

*Cuba and Panama participated in first phase only.
**Dominican Republic and Mexico participated in second phase only.
Note: Venezuela did not enter in 1974; Mexico did not enter in 1970 (entered two teams in 1974).

Composite Championships in Caribbean Series (1949–1960; 1970–1992)

Team (Country)	Host#	First Phase Titles	Second Phase Titles	Titles
Puerto Rico	7	4 (51; 53–55)	7 (72, 74–75, 78, 83, 87, 92)	11
Dominican Republic	4	–	8 (71, 73, 77, 80, 85, 88, 90–91)	8
Cuba**	3	7 (49, 52, 56–60)	–	7
Venezuela	8	0	5 (70, 79, 82, 84, 89)	5
Mexico	7	–	2 (76, 86)	2
Panama*	3	1 (50)	–	1

#Two Caribbean Series played on neutral territory in Miami, Florida.
**Cuba replaced by Dominican Republic in second phase (1970–1992).
*Panama replaced by Mexico in second phase (1970–1992).

Milestone Events of Caribbean Series History (1949–1992)

All-Time Series Career Home-Run Leader:
Tony Armas (Venezuela), 11

Most Home Runs for a Single Series:
Rico Carty (Dominican Republic), 5 (1977)
Barry Jones (Puerto Rico), 5 (1990)

Highest Batting Average for a Single Series:
Lorenzo Cabrera (Cuba, 1951), .619 (13 hits, 21 at-bats)

Most Base Hits for a Single Series:
Pedro Formental (Cuba, 1953), 14 (25 at-bats, .560 BA)

Most Runs Batted In for a Single Series:
Stan Palys (Panama, 1960), 12

Most Lifetime Pitching Victories:
Camilo Pascual (Cuba, 1956, 1959, 1960), 6 (6-0, 1.000)

Rubén Gómez (Puerto Rico, 1950, 1951, 1953, 1954, 1955, 1959, 1971), 6 (6-2, .750)

José "Carracho" Bracho (Venezuela, 1949, 1951, 1952, 1953, 1955, 1958), 6* (6-4, .600)

*Also series record for most pitching decisions.

Best Career Pitching Record in Four or More Series:

Pedro Borbón (Dominican Republic, 1971, 1973, 1974, 1977, 1984), 5 wins-0 losses

Orlando Peña (Cuba, Venezuela, 1959, 1960, 1970, 1971), 5 wins-1 loss

Best Lifetime Earned Run Average:

Francisco Oliveras (Puerto Rico), 1.00 (36 innings pitched)

Odell Jones (Dominican Republic and Venezuela), 1.38 (52 innings pitched)

Camilo Pascual (Cuba), 1.90 (52.1 innings pitched)

All-Time Strikeout Leader (Pitchers):

Juan Pizarro (Puerto Rico), 61

Best Lifetime Strikeout Ratio (Pitchers):

José Rijo (Dominican Republic), 1.45 strikeouts per inning (26.2 innings pitched with 38 total strikeouts), based on minimum 24 innings pitched

Best Managerial Lifetime Record:

James "Buster" Clarkson (Puerto Rico, Santurce, 1953), 6 wins-0 losses

Antonio Castaños (Cuba, Cienfuegos, 1960), 6 wins-0 losses

Bob Rodgers (Dominican Republic, Licey, 1977), 6 wins-0 losses

Most Managerial Victories Lifetime:

Benjamin Reyes (Mexico, 1975, 1976, 1980, 1986), 14 (14-10, .583)

Ossie Virgil (Dominican Republic, 1972–73, 1975–76, 1983), 14 (14-16, .467)

Team Championship Leader:

Tigres de Licey (Dominican Republic), 6 (1971, 1973, 1977, 1980, 1985, 1991)

Series-by-Series Individual Leaders (1949–1992)

Year	Batting Champion	Home-Run Leader	Pitching Champion
1949	Al Gionfriddo (Cuba) .533	Monte Irvin (Cuba) 2	Agapito Mayor (Cuba) 3-0
1950	Héctor Rodríguez (Cuba) .474	Joe Tuminelli (Pan) 2	Bobo Hooper (Cuba) 2-0
1951	Lorenzo Cabrera (Cuba) .619	Luís Olmo (PR) 3	José Santiago (PR) 2-0
1952	Sandy Amoros (Cuba) .450	Wilmer Fields (Ven) 2	Thomas Fine (Cuba) 2-0
1953	Pedro Formental (Cuba) .560	Willard Brown (PR) 4	Bobo Holloman (PR) 2-0
1954	Jim Rivera (PR) .450	Ray Orteig (Cuba) 2	Vic Strizka (Pan) 2-0
1955	Rocky Nelson (Cuba) .471	Don Zimmer (PR) 3	Bill Greason (PR) 2-0
1956	Rafael Noble (Cuba) .500	Elias Osorio (Pan) 3	Camilo Pascual (Cuba) 2-0
1957	Sammy Drake (Cuba) .500	Luís Márquez (PR) 2	Jim Bunning (Cuba) 2-0
1958	Bob Wilson (Ven) .400	Lou Limmer (Ven) 2	Bert Robinson (Pan) 2-0

Year	Batting Champion	Home-Run Leader	Pitching Champion
1959	Jesús Mora (Ven) .417	Norm Cash (Ven) 2	Camilo Pascual (Cuba) 2-0
1960	Tommy Davis (PR) .409	Héctor López (Panama) 3	Camilo Pascual (Cuba) 2-0
	No Caribbean Series		
1970	Gonzalo Márquez (Ven) .478	Six Tied with 1 each	Three Tied at 1-0
1971	Manny Mota (Dom) .579	Celerino Sánchez (Mex) 3	Chris Zachery (Dom) 2-0
1972	Carlos May (PR) .455	Four Tied with 1 each	Gaby Jones (PR) 2-0
1973	Jesús Alou (Dom) .500	Fourteen Tied with 1 each	Pedro Borbón (Dom) 2-0
1974	Héctor Espino (Mex) .429	Darrel Thomas (Mex) 2	Two Tied at 1-0
1975	Ken Griffey (PR) .500	Four Tied with 2 each	Charlie Hough (Dom) 2-0
1976	Enos Cabell (Ven) .400	Seven Tied with 1 each	Mark Wiley (Ven) 2-0
1977	Félix Rodríguez (Ven) .522	Rico Carty (Dom) 5	Three Tied at 2-0
1978	José Morales (PR) .421	Leon Roberts (Ven) 2	Three Tied at 2-0
1979	Jerry White (Ven) .522	Mitchell Page (Ven) 2	Mike Norris (Ven) 2-0
1980	Jaime Rosario (PR) .417	Five Tied with 1 each	Dave Smith (PR) 2-0
1981	Series Cancelled		
1982	Baudilio Díaz (Ven) .412	Baudilio Díaz (Ven) 2	Luís Leal (Ven) 2-0
1983	Darrel Thomas (Ven) .476	Tony Armas (Ven) 3	Eleven Tied at 1-0
1984	Leonel Carrión (Ven) .529	George Bell (Dom) 3	Eight Tied at 1-0
1985	Juan Navarrete (Mex) .533	Glenn Davis (Dom) 3	Tom Brennan (Dom) 2-0
1986	Randy Ready (PR) .467	Andrés Galarraga (Ven) 2	Jaime Orozco (Mex) 2-0
1987	Carmelo Martínez (PR) .556	Candy Maldonado (PR) 4	Francis Oliveras (PR) 2-0
1988	Tom Pagnozzi (PR) .474	Tony Armas (Ven) 2	Ten Tied at 1-0
1989	Matias Carrillo (Mex) .500	Phil Stephenson (Ven) 3	Dale Polley (Ven) 2-0
1990	Cornelio García (Mex) .520	Barry Jones (PR) 5	Mel Rojas (Dom) 2-0
1991	Edwin Alicea (PR) .500	Seven Tied with 1 each	Melido Pérez (Dom) 2-0
1992	Chad Kreuter (PR) .450	Chad Kreuter (PR) 3	Six Tied at 1-0

Suggested Readings

Antero Nuñez, José. *Serie del Caribe 1988* (Tomo II). Caracas, Venezuela: Impresos Urbina, 1988.

________. *Serie del Caribe 1989* (Tomo III). Caracas, Venezuela: Impresos Urbina, 1989.

Gammons, Peter. "Plei Bol! – Four Teams Did That at the Caribbean Series." *Sports Illustrated* 70(8) (February 20, 1989): 16–21.

Littlefield, Bill. "A Real World Series at Last?" *World Monitor* (*Christian Science Monitor* monthly) 1:(2) (November 1988): 84–86.

Piña Campora, Tony. *Los Grandes Finales.* Santo Domingo, Dominican Republic: Editora Colegial, 1981.

Ruck, Rob. "Baseball in the Caribbean." In *Total Baseball*, edited by John Thorn and Pete Palmer. New York: Warner, 1989, 605–611.

________. "Baseball in the Caribbean." In *Total Baseball*, third edition, edited by John Thorn and Pete Palmer. New York: Harper Collins, 1993, 533–541.

________."The Crisis in Winter Baseball: Can It Survive?" *Baseball America* (February 25–March 9, 1990): 8–10.

Salas, Alexis. *Momentos Inolvidables del Béisbol Profesional Venezolano, 1946–1984.* Caracas, Venezuela: Miguel Angel García, 1985.

Van Hyning, Thomas E. "Hall of Famers Shine in Puerto Rico." Edited by Peter C. Bjarkman. *The International Pastime: A Review of Baseball History* (Society for American Baseball Research) 12 (1992): 14–16.

PART III

Appendices

Those who analyze baseball by the numbers may, sometimes, hear the music of the spheres.

—JOHN THORN AND PETE PALMER

APPENDIX A

Latin American Baseball Chronology — Greatest Moments in Latin American Baseball History

Baseball stood as a national pastime throughout Caribbean nations as early as the same decade (the 1860s) that witnessed the game's first burst of popularity upon North American diamonds. For more than a century and a quarter baseball heroics have been regularly performed on dusty Latin American diamonds in Cuba, Puerto Rico, Venezuela, Mexico, and the Dominican Republic. And since the birth of professional baseball's live-ball era during the 1920s, Latin ballplayers have been performing big-league feats of note, and with an ever-increasing frequency. Jackie Robinson's smashing of baseball's racial barriers in 1947 would soon spill forth a floodtide of dark-skinned Latin talent upon big-league diamonds across the era of Minnie Miñoso, Vic Power, and Roberto Clemente.

Some of the most sterling and memorable moments of Latin American baseball history unfortunately remain as buried relics of a lost blackball era or the haphazard barnstorming era of winter-league play, totally unfamiliar to almost all stateside diamond enthusiasts. Other such moments stand as familiar milestones from the past three decades of big-league action. A synopsis of Latin baseball's finest and most fateful moments is recorded in the pages that follow.

June 1866 Caribbean baseball is apparently born when sailors from an American naval ship, anchored at port in Matanzas Bay, demonstrate diamond play for a crowd of Cuban dockhands employed to load sugarcane on a North American vessel. The Cubans were later reported to joke that their American instructors seemed largely motivated by a desire to sell baseball equipment to these raw diamond recruits. One competing account of baseball's Cuban origins suggests that it was actually Nemesio Guillot, an upper-class youth educated in the United States, who first brought equipment and demonstrations of the Yankee sport with him upon his 1866 return to his native Havana.

April 1871 Cuban Esteban "Steve" Bellán mans third base for the Troy Haymakers during an inaugural season for the National Association, baseball's first recognized big-league circuit. Bellán, who learned his baseball while a student at Fordham University in New York and later hit .236 in 59 games over a three-year professional career, thus becomes the first official Latin American big-league ballplayer.

December 1874 A mere eight years after the game's introduction in Matanzas, the city known as the "Athens of Cuba" hosts Havana in the first recorded organized ballgame between native Cuban teams. Playing for the Havana club were two early giants of Cuban baseball, former big-leaguer Steve Bellán and Emilio Sabourín, organizing genius behind Cuba's first professional league. Bellán played third base, and Sabourín scored eight runs for the Havana club during its 51–9 rout of the talent-thin Matanzas nine.

December 29, 1878 The Professional Baseball League of Cuba begins play in Havana, making the Cuban league the world's second-oldest professional baseball organization, trailing North America's National League by only two seasons. The new Cuban circuit first consists of only three clubs—Havana, Matanzas, and Almendares—and the Havana ballclub, behind founder and manager Emilio Sabourín, soon dominates the new circuit, claiming nine pennants over 14 campaigns between 1878 and 1892. Sabourín's role in organizing the new league and the champion Havana ballclub fixes his claim as the true patriarch of Cuban baseball.

January 21, 1882 An apparent single-game world record 60 errors are committed in a Cuban semipro contest between Club Caridad (39 miscues) and Club Ultimatum (21). It seems safe to assume that ballplayers at this sloppy Havana spectacle wore no gloves during their crude ragtag match.

February 13, 1887 The first professional league no-hitter is pitched in Cuba by Carlos Maciá as Almendares defeats Carmelita by a 38–0 margin. This may also have been the first no-hit, no-run game pitched anywhere in Latin America, although historical records remain cloudy on this matter.

July 14, 1889 A second professional no-hit, no-run game is pitched in Cuba by Eugenio de Rosas, hurler for Club Progreso, during an 8–0 victory over Team Cárdenas. This game's highly unusual line score shows Cárdenas with no runs or hits but an astronomical total of 14 errors. This would be the final Cuban no-hitter for 47 seasons and only four more such flawless masterpieces would be tossed by Cuban hurlers during the six pre–Castro decades of twentieth-century Cuban play.

November 1908 Matanzas-born black Cuban hurler José Méndez, later immortalized by New York Giants manager John McGraw as "Cuba's Black Diamond," posts a string of impressive performances against the touring Cincinnati Reds. First the wiry 20-year-old phenom would post a 1–0 one-hit victory over the National-Leaguers; two weeks later he followed up with 7 innings of shutout relief work plus a second 9-inning scoreless performance—a total of

25 scoreless innings against the befuddled big-league visitors. Competing against U.S. Negro-league stars during a North American tour the following autumn, Méndez would soon distinguish himself with an outstanding 44-2 mound record.

July 1911 Outfielders Armando Marsans and Rafael Almeida debut with the Cincinnati Reds, becoming the first twentieth-century Cubans and modern Latin Americans to appear in major league action. Complaints about the dark skin color of both ballplayers are met by an official club press release that these are "two of the purest bars of Castilian soap ever floated to these shores."

October 3, 1919 Cuban Adolfo Luque becomes the first Latin American major-leaguer to appear in a World Series game, pitching one inning of relief for the Cincinnati Reds in game three against Charlie Comiskey's infamous Black Sox team in Chicago. Luque, who would later win 27 games during the 1923 season for Cincinnati, also pitched four relief innings in game seven, at Redlands Field on October 8.

October 1923 At season's end, Cincinnati Reds hurler Adolfo "Dolf" Luque of Cuba has a major-league-leading won-lost record of 27-8 and an ERA mark of 1.93, still the best single-season performance posted by a Latin American big-league pitcher.

January 1, 1929 Outfielder James ("Cool Papa") Bell, a North American Negro-leaguer playing for Cienfuegos, becomes the first slugger to connect for three homers in a single game during Cuban league play. Bell's feat occurs at Aida Park in a 15–11 slugfest victory over Havana. Bell's three homers are struck against Oscar Levis, "Campanita" Bell, and Hall-of-Famer Martín Dihigo, although Bell would later erroneously claim all three came off blackballer Johnny Allen.

October 7, 1933 Dolf Luque provides 4.1 innings of stellar relief to gain the championship-clinching victory in game five of the 1933 World Series. In notching the fall classic title for the New York Giants against the Washington Senators, Luque becomes the first Latin American to post a World Series pitching victory.

November 7, 1936 Raymond "Jabao" Brown of Santa Clara hurls the first twentieth-century no-hitter in Cuba, a 7–0 victory over Team Havana.

September 16, 1937 Black Cuban Hall-of-Famer Martín Dihigo (the only player enshrined in the baseball hall of immortals in four different countries – the United States, Mexico, Cuba, and Venezuela) pitches the first professional no-hit, no-run game on Mexican soil, a 4–0 victory against Nogales in Veracruz.

June 5, 1938 In one of the most incredible pitching duels of organized baseball history, semipro Venezuelan hurlers Andres Julio Baez (Club Pastora) and Lázaro Sálazar (Gavilanes) battle for 20 innings in a game played at Maracaibo. With the game lasting an incredible 6 hours and 30 minutes, Pastora emerges victorious by a 1–0 count, Baez facing 65 batters and Sálazar 67.

September 18, 1938 Cuban star Martín Dihigo, author of the first Mexican League no-hitter, also becomes the first Mexican League hitter to register six hits in six at-bats while playing for Veracruz against Agrario.

September 14, 1940 The United States, Hawaii Territory (not yet a state), Cuba, Mexico, Puerto Rico, Nicaragua, and Venezuela meet in the third annual World Amateur Baseball Championship tournament, the first championship series to feature more than three participants and the second held on Latin American soil. Cuba, the host country, is the easy victor for the second consecutive year. The initial tourney had been held in England in 1939 and was won by the host country, Great Britain.

December 11, 1943 Manuel "Cocaína" García of Club Havana pitches the fourth no-hit, no-run game in Cuban-league history, besting Club Marianao 5–0.

September 6, 1944 Tommy de la Cruz, Cuban-born right-hander, pitches the first one-hitter by a Latin American pitcher in big-league annals. Ironically, Cruz pitches just this single wartime season for the Cincinnati Reds, recording a 9-9 won-lost record and a 3.25 ERA. Tommy de la Cruz was exceedingly dark-skinned, a fact which may have hastened his departure from the Cincinnati ballclub immediately after the 1944 wartime campaign.

January 3, 1945 Cuban baseball witnesses its fifth no-hit, no-run game, pitched by former big-leaguer Tommy de la Cruz of Almendares against the rival Havana Club, 7–0.

January 7, 1945 In the most violent incident in Cuban baseball history, outfielder Roberto Ortiz of Almendares attacks umpire Bernardino Rodríguez in a dispute at home plate and knocks the umpire unconscious.

May 6, 1945 Monterrey establishes a new Mexican League record for lopsided victories, pounding Puebla 21–0 and erasing the 19–0 standard set by Mexico City versus Carta Blanca on August 31, 1941.

December 8, 1945 Rafael Gallis Tello connects for the first home run ever hit in the Estadio Olímpico of Maracaibo. The fifth-inning blow propels Team Gavilanes to a 5–2 victory over semipro rival Pastora before 10,000 spectators in the inaugural game at one of Venezuela's most famous and tradition-bound ballparks.

January 12, 1946 The first professional game is played in Venezuela between Team Venezuela and Magallanes, launching the newly constituted four-team Liga be Béisbol Profesional de Venezuela. The game, played in Cervecería Caracas Stadium, is won by Magallanes 5–2, with Luís Aparicio, Sr. ("El Grande"), father of future Hall-of-Famer Luís Aparicio, Jr. ("Junior"), starting at shortstop for the victors.

January 13, 1946 The second professional game occurs in Venezuela, with Vargas routing Cervecería Caracas 12–1 behind the stellar play of North American Negro-league stars Roy Welmaker (the winning pitcher), outfielder

Sam Jethroe (later of the Boston Braves), and future Brooklyn Dodger catching great Roy Campanella.

January 17, 1946 Venezuelan great Alfonso "Chico" Carrasquel, future star of the Chicago White Sox, makes his professional baseball debut at age 17 in a Venezuelan-league game between Team Venezuela and Cervecería Caracas. Carrasquel, later considered the all-time most popular player by Venezuelan fans (edging Hall-of-Famer Luís Aparicio, Jr., for the honor), achieves lasting fame by hitting the first home run registered in Venezuelan-league play, providing the game-winning run in the top of the seventh inning for Cervecería Caracas.

January 20, 1946 Venezuelan pitching great Alejandro Carrasquel (10-year major leaguer with the 1940s Senators and White Sox) and Negro-league star Roy Welmaker face off in a sensational pitching duel still considered the greatest of Venezuelan professional baseball history. Carrasquel of Magallanes defeats Welmaker 3–2 during a 17-inning contest that sees both hurlers go the full distance.

March 7, 1946 Negro-league star second baseman Marvin Williams, playing for Vargas against Magallanes, enjoys his finest career day, setting a still-existing Venezuelan league single-game batting record. Williams registers eight RBIs with two homers and two singles in leading his team to a 16–9 triumph at Caracas.

April 1946 Millionaire Mexican businessman Jorge Pasquel creates the first serious competition against big-league monopoly since the long-defunct Federal League, causing a small defection of major league players south of the border with his offer of huge salaries for Mexican League contracts. A total of 26 players (17 National-Leaguers and 9 American-Leaguers) defect, including Dodger catcher Mickey Owen, Giant pitcher Sal Maglie and outfielder Danny Gardella, Cardinal pitcher Max Lanier, and St. Louis Browns infielder Vern "Junior" Stephens. Commissioner Happy Chandler announces a lifetime suspension for defecting players, later reduced to five years.

October 9, 1946 A team of National League all-stars begins a seven-game exhibition schedule against the Cuban national all-star team in Havana. The National League team, featuring Buddy Kerr and Sid Gordon of the Giants and Brooklyn Dodgers Eddie Stanky and Ralph Branca, wins the opening game of the tour 3–2.

October 26, 1946 A record 31,000 fans (estimated) attend the inaugural game of the new Stadium del Cerro in Havana, watching Almendares defeat Cienfuegos 9–1. At the time, this was the largest crowd ever to see a professional baseball game in Cuba.

October 16, 1947 Don Newcombe, first star black major league pitcher of the early 1950s, makes a sensational winter-league debut with a 4–0 complete-game victory for Club Vargas against Team Venezuela at Caracas. Newcombe, who soon enjoys his big-league debut with Brooklyn in 1949, dominates the

1947-48 Venezuelan-league season capturing the triple crown of pitching with league-leading figures in victories (10), ERA (2.13), and strikeouts (94).

November 30, 1947 Guillermo Vento, left fielder with Cervecería Caracas, establishes a yet-unbroken Venezuelan league record, recording six hits (five singles and a double) in six at-bats during a 12–6 rout of Magallanes in the Cervecería Stadium at Caracas.

December 26, 1947 Luís "Mono" Zuloaga, Venezuelan pitching immortal, hurls the finest single game in Venezuelan-league history, a one-hit 5–0 masterpiece for Cervecería Caracas against Team Venezuela during which he registers 10 strikeouts and permits no runner to reach second base.

January 4, 1948 One of the most bizarre moments in professional baseball history occurs during a Venezuelan-league game in Caracas when Team Venezuela pitcher "Tuerto" Arrieta yields an eleventh-inning base on balls to Cervecería Caracas batter Benítez Redondo with the bases filled, yet no run scores. The unprecedented set of circumstances is set in motion when third-base runner Luís Romero Petit delays coming home on the fourth ball, seeing that batter Benítez has not started toward first. When Romero finally approaches the plate, he is tagged by catcher Humberto Leal, who completes his clever decoy by shouting, "You're out!" The enraged and confused Romero then commits baseball's greatest bonehead play, grabbing the ball from the catcher's mitt and heaving it toward the backstop. Umpire Henry Tatler immediately rules Romero out on perhaps the rarest interference play of all time.

June 5, 1948 Venezuelan teams Gavilanes and Pastora begin an unprecedented string of five consecutive games extending into extra innings, a record perhaps never duplicated by any other two teams anywhere in organized baseball. The final game of this rare string is won 5–4 by Pastora in 11 innings at Maracaibo on June 26.

July 10, 1948 In still another among the most bizarre events in the annals of organized baseball, first-base umpire Robinson Pirale is arrested by police during a 30-minute suspension of play that features an ugly rock-throwing incident between the panicked arbiter and unruly spectators. The event occurs during an emotional 5–3 victory by Pastora over Gavilanes at Maracaibo, Venezuela, and the incarcerated umpire is eventually released by authorities later that evening after signing an agreement to engage in no further public rock throwing.

July 25, 1948 Luís "El Grande" Aparicio (father of the major-leaguer) achieves the rare feat of hitting three triples in a single game for Gavilanes versus Pastora in Venezuelan play. While such a feat is rare for modern major league play, it will be repeated several times in subsequent years in the Venezuelan league.

August 21, 1948 Representatives of Cuba, Panama, Puerto Rico, and Venezuela, meeting in Havana, agree to stage a four-country round-robin 12-game tournament to be known as the Serie del Caribe (Caribbean Series) to be launched in Cuba during February 1949. This series, the highlight of winter-league play, will continue uninterrupted through 1960 (series 12), then be reinstituted in 1970 and continue to the present. In addition to the four founding countries, the Dominican Republic (replacing Cuba) and Mexico (replacing Panama) will later participate on a regular basis.

February 25, 1949 Agapito Mayor wins his third game of the first annual Caribbean Series, pitching for Almendares (Cuba) against Spur Cola (Panama), thus becoming the first and only pitcher to win three games in a single year during the 35 seasons of Caribbean Series play.

Al Gionfriddo, 1947 Brooklyn Dodgers World Series hero with a miraculous catch of Joe DiMaggio's near home run in game six, completes a three-game 8-for-15 batting rampage that makes him the first Caribbean Series batting champion sporting a .533 average. Gionfriddo plays for Almendares (Cuba) in the first Serie del Caribe, staged in Estadio del Cerro, Havana.

November 17, 1949 Luís "Camaleón" García, third baseman for Magallanes of the Venezuelan league, begins a record 518 consecutive-game playing streak that does not end until October 26, 1960. This record for longevity has yet to be surpassed in winter-league play.

February 6, 1950 The sixth no-hitter in the history of Cuban baseball is pitched by Rogelio "Limonar" Martínez as he leads Marianao to victory 3–0 over Almendares.

December 6, 1950 Cuban catcher Carlos Colás provides one of the greatest single-game batting displays ever witnessed in winter-league play. Colás registers five hits in five at-bats for Team Venezuela during a 10–9 loss to Venezuelan rival Vargas. In this game Colás also performs the truly rare feat of three triples in a single contest.

January 14, 1951 Incomparable Venezuelan pitching star José de la Trinidad "Carrao" Bracho enjoys his finest single game, a 10–0 one-hitter for Cervecería Caracas against Team Venezuela. During his illustrious career, Bracho leads all Venezuelan pitchers in victories four times, compiles the most single-season wins (15 in 1961-62), the most lifetime victories (110), the most games started (192), years pitched (23), games completed (93), and innings pitched (1,758).

July 10, 1951 At Briggs Stadium in Detroit, the eighteenth annual All-Star Game is held, the Nationals victorious 8–3. History is made when Venezuelan shortstop Alfonso "Chico" Carrasquel of the Chicago White Sox becomes the first Latin American player to appear in a midsummer classic.

September 15, 1951 The first game of the first Dominican World Series (Los Grandes Finales) is played between Licey and Escogido in Santiago. Behind the hitting of Alonzo Perry (.400 series average) and the pitching of Marion "Sugar" Caine, Licey wins the opener 8–0 and goes on to take the series 4–1 and become the first champion of Dominican professional baseball.

November 18, 1951 Venezuelan-league champion Cervecería Caracas sets a winter-league record that still stands, winning its seventeenth consecutive game, a 4–3 triumph in Caracas against Vargas. This incredible streak consisted of 18 straight games without a loss, one contest having ended in a suspended-game tie.

January 31, 1952 What is believed to be the shortest game in winter-league history transpires in Venezuelan play at Caracas. Team Venezuela edges Cervecería Caracas 2–1 in night-game action that lasts only 1 hour and 15 minutes.

February 7, 1952 North American pitcher Bill Samson achieves an undistinguished winter-league record by walking 14 Vargas batters in six innings pitching for Cervecería Caracas of the Venezuelan league. This negative feat matches a big-league record set in 1906 by Henry Mathewson (Christy's brother) of the New York Giants, who needed nine full innings for an equal display of wildness.

February 14, 1952 The longest game in winter-league history is played in Venezuela as Magallanes and Cervecería Caracas battle to a 3–3 18-inning tie that lasts 3 hours and 10 minutes. Two notable feats occur during this game: Johnny Hetki pitches all 18 innings for Magallanes; teammate Jesús "Chucho" Ramos handles a record 21 putouts at first base without a miscue.

February 21, 1952 Tommy Fine, North American right-hander who posted only four major league decisions with the Boston Red Sox and St. Louis Browns, achieves immortality by pitching the only no-hit, no-run game in the three-decade history of the Caribbean Series. Fine hurls for Club Havana (Cuba) against Cervecería Caracas (Venezuela), striking out three and walking three in the 1–0 victory during the fourth Serie del Caribe at Panama City.

September 2, 1952 Mike Fornieles, Cuban-born right-hander with the Washington Senators, makes his sensational major league debut by tossing a one-hitter, becoming the first Latin-born pitcher and second American-Leaguer to toss a one-hitter in his first big-league outing. The only American League pitcher preceding Fornieles with this feat was Addie Joss, with Cleveland in 1902, and the achievement has been duplicated only once since, by William Rohr with Boston in 1967. The only National League hurlers to duplicate Fornieles' debut were also Latin American pitchers—Juan Marichal with the Giants in 1960 and Silvio Martínez of the St. Louis Cardinals in 1978.

October 19, 1952 North American John Mackinson makes his Venezuelan-league debut one of the most spectacular in baseball history, pitching 10.2 innings of no-hit, no-run ball before allowing three singles in the twelfth and thirteenth innings. Mackinson's Magallanes team defeats Caracas 10–1, with nine runs scored in the top of the thirteenth.

October 21, 1952 Pedro "Pajita" Rodríguez of Vargas makes Venezuelan history by stealing three bases in a single inning against Team Caracas in Ciudad Universitaria Stadium.

October 23, 1952 Henry Schenz, veteran of six years of major league play with the Cubs and Pirates, begins a batting onslaught that will eclipse the Venezuelan hitting-streak record held by Sam Hairston. Playing for Team Venezuela, Schenz launches his own streak on October 23 against Caracas with two hits, and the hitting string continues through December 19, reaching 27 consecutive games.

January 8, 1953 Negro-leaguer Quincy Trouppe, catcher for Magallanes of the Venezuelan league, records the most improbable feat of six bases on balls in six at-bats during a game against Caracas in Ciudad Universitaria Stadium. Trouppe thus scores three runs without a single official plate appearance.

October 14, 1953 Club Magallanes establishes a winter-league record with six home runs in a single contest against Pastora in the Olympic Stadium at Maracaibo. Major-leaguers Foster Castleman and Billy Gardner record two of the roundtrippers in the 8–3 Magallanes victory.

November 18, 1953 Future Hall-of-Famer Luís Aparicio, Jr., makes his Venezuelan professional baseball debut for Gavilanes versus Pastora at the Olympic Stadium in his hometown, Maracaibo. The following night the 19-year-old shortstop records his first winter-league base hit against major league hurler Ralph Beard.

May 5, 1954 Edrick Kellman, playing for Laredo against Mexico City, becomes the first batter in Mexican League history to connect for two grand slams in a single game, a record later tied by Arnoldo Castro of the Mexico City Tigers on June 18, 1967.

September 30, 1954 Roberto "Beto" Avila, second baseman for the Cleveland Indians, becomes the first Mexican and first Latin-born player to win a major league batting championship, leading the American League with .341. This was Avila's only season to bat over .304, and he finished his 11-year major league career with a lifetime .281 average.

Cuban Sandy Consuegra of the Chicago White Sox becomes the second Latin American pitcher to lead his league in winning percentage, completing the year with a sparkling 16-3 mark (.842). Cuban Dolf Luque, 27-8 with the Cincinnati Reds in 1923, was the first south-of-the-border pitcher to gain such a memorable distinction.

October 1, 1954 Puerto Rico's Rubén Gómez becomes the second Latin American pitcher to win a World Series contest, gaining a 6–2 victory over the Indians in game three at Cleveland's Municipal Stadium. Four seasons later Gómez would become the first pitcher to win a West Coast game when baseball expansion by the Dodgers and Giants brought a first summer of coast-to-coast play to the majors.

February 11, 1955 Perhaps the most emotional and memorable game in the history of the Caribbean Series is played in the University Stadium, Caracas. Emilio Cueche, legendary Venezuelan pitcher, throws a brilliant two-hitter for

Magallanes (Venezuela) yet loses 1–0 to Club Almendares (Cuba). A near riot in the grandstand, in dispute of a close call on the base paths, delays the game for over 45 minutes as spectators throw objects onto the field. Major-leaguers Vern Rapp, Roman Mejías, Rocky Nelson, Gus Triandos, and Willie Miranda are featured in the Cuban starting lineup during this famous game.

February 12, 1955 In a second consecutive memorable night of Caribbean Series play in Venezuela, Willie Mays and Roberto Clemente belt crucial home runs to lead Santurce (Puerto Rico) over Magallanes (Venezuela) 4–2 in 11 innings, the second heartbreaking loss for the host Venezuelans in as many nights. Mays's eleventh-inning homer is still celebrated as the most dramatic homer in Venezuelan baseball history.

October 4, 1955 Brooklyn defeats the New York Yankees 2–0 in game seven to capture the Dodgers' first world championship. Cuban journeyman outfielder Sandy Amoros is the ultimate Dodger hero with a miraculous left-field catch of a Yogi Berra line drive, a one-handed grab at the fence that launches the game-saving double play.

October 30, 1955 North American Ron Mronzinski completes the most sensational winter-league pitching debut on record, hurling his third consecutive shutout in Venezuelan play for Team Valencia. Mronzinski establishes a string of 27 consecutive shutout innings with victories on October 14 (against Caracas), 22 (Magallanes), and 30 (Pampero).

December 8, 1955 Hurling for Team Caracas, journeyman Leonard Yochim pitches the first no-hit, no-run game in the history of the nine-year-old Venezuelan league, defeating Magallanes 3–0 at Caracas.

December 15, 1955 Stanley Jok, playing for Caracas against Pampero, achieves winter-league immortality by becoming the first player in Venezuelan-league history to sock three home runs in a single game. Jok earlier appeared in only 12 major league games with the Philadelphia Phillies and Chicago White Sox.

January 8, 1956 Stanley Jok's single-game Venezuelan record of three home runs is shattered by Russell Rac, who hits four roundtrippers for Pastora against Cabimas. At the time, Rac was only the eighth player in professional baseball history to achieve the feat of four homers during a single game.

January 16, 1956 Clarence "Buddy" Hicks, shortstop for Pampero of the Venezuelan league, matches the July 25, 1948, achievement of Luís Aparicio and the December 1950 feat of Cuban slugger Carlos Colás, socking three triples in a single game.

July 17, 1956 One of baseball's most memorable beanball incidents (perhaps second in infamy only to the Marichal-Roseboro incident of 1965) occurs in Milwaukee when Puerto Rican pitcher Rubén Gómez of the Giants reinforces a familiar stereotype about hot-blooded Latin players. Having hit Braves slugger Joe Adcock on the wrist with an errant pitch, Gómez fires the ball at Adcock a second time as the angered Milwaukee batsman approaches the mound. A panic-stricken Gómez then flees to the Giants dugout with an enraged Adcock in hot pursuit. Gómez races all the way to the Giants clubhouse where he obtains a lethal ice pick and attempts to return to the field to do battle with a willing Adcock. Gómez is restrained by his teammates and ejected from the contest.

October 1956 Venezuelan Luís Aparicio, Jr., having replaced countryman Chico Carrasquel as Chicago White Sox shortstop and champion base stealer, becomes the first Latin American player to win Rookie of the Year, named recipient of the American League honor. Aparicio would eventually be inducted into the Hall of Fame at Cooperstown in 1984.

April 15, 1958 The historic opening game of major league baseball on the West Coast has a decidedly Latin American flavor. While the San Francisco Giants are defeating the Los Angeles Dodgers 8–0 before 23,449 in Seals Stadium, veteran Puerto Rican hurler Rubén Gómez pitches a six-hit shutout for the Giants, and rookie Puerto Rican slugger Orlando Cepeda leads the hitting attack with his first major league homer. The first big-league pitcher to record a West Coast victory is thus a Latin American pitcher, but Cepeda loses this honor in the home-run department, his four-bagger following Daryl Spencer's earlier historic blast for the Giants.

August 14, 1958 Flamboyant Puerto Rican Vic Power scores the winning run with a steal of home in the tenth inning as the Indians defeat Detroit 10–9 in Cleveland. Power had also stolen home in the eighth inning, thus becoming the ninth player in major league history, but the first since 1927, to steal home twice in a single game. Power was also the first Latin-born player to accomplish this feat.

November 10, 1958 Giants slugger Orlando Cepeda is named National League Rookie of the Year after leading the senior circuit in doubles with 38 and blasting 25 roundtrippers. The Puerto Rican first baseman thus becomes the first Latin American to capture this distinction as a National-Leaguer.

July 25, 1959 Fidel Castro supporters, enjoying a raucous July 26 celebration in El Cerro Stadium in downtown Havana, bring to a halt the International League contest between the Rochester Red Wings and Havana Sugar Kings with several random gunshots from the grandstand. Rochester third-base coach Frank Verdi and Havana shortstop Leo Cárdenas suffer minor flesh wounds during this infamous incident, which causes Red Wings manager Cot Deal to pull his team from the field and retreat to their nearby hotel. International League officials promptly cancel the remainder of the Havana team's current homestand, eventually relocating the franchise to Newark for the 1960 season. The little-reported event would also effectively signal the end of Cuba's participation in professional baseball.

July 19, 1960 Dominican Dandy Juan Marichal, arguably the greatest Latin American hurler in major league history, enjoys an incredible big-league debut, becoming the second Latin pitcher and first National-Leaguer ever to toss a one-hitter in his initial game. Defeating the Phillies 2–0 at Candlestick Park, Marichal retires the first 19 batters, striking out 12, and finally gives up a pinch-hit two-out single to Clay Dalrymple in the seventh. Latin pitchers Mike Fornieles of the Washington Senators (September 2, 1952) and Silvio Martínez of the St. Louis Cardinals (May 30, 1978) also hurled one-hit ballgames in their first major league starts.

January 6, 1961 In one of the legendary pitching performances of winter-league play, Gary Peters of Rapinos and Julián Ladera of Valencia duel for 17 innings in a Venezuelan-league game in Maracaibo, Peters emerging as the victor 2–1.

September 25, 1961 Puerto Rican first sacker Orlando Cepeda has four RBIs in a 10–2 Giant rout of Philadelphia, raising his season's total to 140 and establishing himself as the greatest slugging Latin American major-leaguer to that time. Cepeda's 142-RBI season breaks a Giant record for first basemen of 138 set by Hall-of-Famer Johnny Mize in 1947. Cepeda thus becomes the first Latin American to lead the league in RBI totals and the first Latin home-run champion (with 46).

September 30, 1961 Roberto Clemente of the Pirates closes the season with a .351 batting average, becoming the first Latin American player to win a senior-circuit batting title. Orlando Cepeda of the Giants concludes the year with 46 roundtrippers, becoming the first Latin-born major-leaguer to win a home-run crown.

January 25, 1962 Venezuelan immortal José "Carrao" Bracho establishes a still-standing Venezuelan-league record for single-season victories at 15 with a 7–1 victory for Club Oriente over Pampero. In his previous start four nights earlier, Bracho barely missed what would have been his only career no-hitter, allowing two ninth-inning singles.

July 10, 1962 Dominican Juan Marichal becomes the first Latin American pitcher to win a major league All-Star Game, the victorious hurler in a 3–1 National League victory during 1962's first All-Star Game at District of Columbia Stadium in Washington. Senators Cuban ace Camilo Pascual is the game's loser, becoming the first Latin-born pitcher to lose an All-Star Game.

August 13, 1962 Cuban native Bert Campaneris pitches two relief innings for Daytona of the Florida State League against Ft. Lauderdale, throwing as a right-hander and a left-hander and allowing only one run during this stunt while striking out four batters. Normally an infielder, Campaneris was later to make big-league history in September 1965 by appearing at all nine positions for the Kansas City Athletics in a single nine-inning game.

May 19, 1963 Scoring in every inning, the Monterrey Sultanes equal their own Mexican League record with a 21–0 conquest of Reynosa. The previous standard for lopsided victories had been established by Monterrey against Puebla on May 6, 1945.

June 15, 1963 Juan Marichal becomes the first Latin American hurler to toss a major league no-hitter with a brilliant 1–0 victory at San Francisco over the Houston Colt .45s. This season, perhaps his finest, sees Marichal record 25 victories, strike out 248 batters while walking only 61, and lead the majors with 321 innings pitched – the best single-season pitching performance ever recorded by a Latin American big-leaguer.

September 3, 1963 Dominican Juan Marichal defeats the Chicago Cubs 16–3 to become the first Latin American pitcher to win 20 games in a single major league season since Dolf Luque became the first Latin American 20-game winner with 27 victories for Cincinnati in 1923.

September 10, 1963 For the first time in major league history, three brothers appear in a starting lineup. In a game at the Polo Grounds, won by the Giants over the Mets 4–2, San Francisco features an improbable outfield of three Dominican brothers – Jesús, Matty, and Felipe Alou. This Giants tandem does not last long, however, as Felipe Alou departs to the Milwaukee Braves in time for the 1964 season opener.

November 18, 1963 Mel Nelson, laboring for Orientales against Caracas, pitches the second no-hitter in Venezuelan-league history. Nelson was to win only four games in an undistinguished major leauge career spanning parts of six seasons.

January 6, 1964 José de la Trinidad "Carrao" Bracho becomes the first pitcher in Venezuelan-league history to record 100 career victories. Bracho achieves the feat with a 5–0 three-hit shutout for Orientales versus La Guaira in Caracas.

May 2, 1964 Cuban rookie sensation Tony Oliva of the Minnesota Twins blasts the first of a big-league record-tying four consecutive Twins homers in the eleventh inning, pacing a 7–4 victory at Kansas City. Following Oliva with roundtrippers were Bob Allison, Jimmie Hall, and Harmon Killebrew, equaling a feat performed by Milwaukee in 1961 and repeated by Cleveland in 1963. Oliva goes on that season, his first full campaign in the big leagues, to lead the junior circuit in hitting with a sparkling .332 average, becoming the first freshman to gain an American League batting title.

May 3, 1964 Monterrey batter Saul Villegas slugs his second grand slam in as many days against Team Pericos in Puebla, becoming the first and only player in Mexican League history to accomplish such a feat.

May 10, 1964 Monterrey's Héctor Espino makes Mexican League history by belting four home runs (two in each game) and producing 10 RBIs as the Sultanes post doubleheader victories over Poza Rica 5–4 and 8–5. Espino also homers twice more in the next two outings, achieving an incredible six roundtrippers in three days.

May 20, 1964 Cuban pitcher José Ramón López of Monterrey records 16 strikeouts, 9 in succession, in a 5–2 victory over the Diablos Rojos team, thus tying a short-lived Mexican League record set in 1959 by Dominican Diomedes "Guayubín" Olivo with Poza Rica.

July 7, 1964 Giants ace Juan Marichal is the pitcher of record in the National League's 7–4 All-Star Game victory at New York's Shea Stadium, becoming the first and only Latin American pitcher to record two All-Star Game victories.

July 23, 1964 Cuban rookie Bert Campaneris of the Kansas City Athletics becomes the second man in baseball history to hit two homers in his inaugural big-league appearance, the first roundtripper coming on the initial pitch served by Twins hurler Jim Kaat. Bob Nieman of the St. Louis Browns earlier homered on his first two big-league at-bats in 1951; Campaneris accomplishes this feat with his first and fourth trips to the plate.

October 1964 Minnesota Twins slugger Tony Oliva becomes the first black ballplayer to garner a batting title and Rookie-of-the-Year honors in the same season. By pacing the American League with a .323 average, the Cuban standout becomes only the third Latino to win a league batting championship.

January 25, 1965 All-time major league hit leader Pete Rose enjoys his greatest day of winter-league play, going five-for-six for Team Caracas against Magallanes (Venezuelan league), with five runs scored, one home run, two doubles, and four RBIs.

August 22, 1965 In what is now referred to as Bloody Sunday at Candlestick and lives forever among baseball's most infamous incidents, temperamental Giants pitcher Juan Marichal strikes Dodgers catcher John Roseboro on the head with his bat in a violent dispute over a toss Marichal thought was aimed at his head. The event causes a brawl that takes 14 minutes to calm and results in a nine-day suspension and a then-huge $1,750 fine for the flamboyant Dominican pitcher. This outrageous display of poor sportsmanship is also believed to have delayed Marichal's eventual (1983) election into the Cooperstown Hall of Fame.

September 8, 1965 Infielder Bert Campaneris of the Kansas City Athletics becomes the first player in major league history to play all nine positions in a single contest. The versatile Cuban plays one position per inning against the Los Angeles Angels, recording a single error (in right field), allowing one run and two hits while on the mound, and catching the final inning during which he is injured in a home-plate collision with Ed Kirkpatrick and forced to leave the game. Campaneris would later be the first batter to face Venezuelan utility man César Tóvar during the first inning of a September 22, 1968, game in which Tóvar would duplicate Campaneris's strange feat.

October 1965 Cuban infielder Zoilo Versalles of the American League champion Minnesota Twins blazes new trails as he becomes the first Latin American ballplayer to earn MVP honors, named as the junior circuit's most valued performer.

November 3, 1965 Kansas City Athletics right-hander Lew Krausse enjoys one of the finest pitching performances in winter-league history throwing a one-hitter for Caracas against Lara and establishing the following still unsurpassed marks: most strikeouts in a nine-inning game (21), most consecutive strikeouts (10), most strikeouts in two consecutive games (33).

January 21, 1966 Dominican slugger and 1970 National League batting champion Rico Carty sets a single-season Venezuelan-league home-run record of 13 roundtrippers in 32 games. Playing for Aragua, Carty blasts two homers against Magallanes on January 12 and two more against La Guaira on January 21 to obtain the record.

August 13, 1966 Cuban strikeout king José Ramón López establishes an all-time standard of 309 strikeouts for a single season, reaching 309 in a game against Reynosa. It is a small irony of this day that López, while striking out a dozen batters, loses the contest 2–0.

October 25, 1966 Luís "Camaleón" García, third baseman for Magallanes, becomes the first player in Venezuelan-league history to achieve the plateau of 1,000 career base hits. Hitting two singles against Cardenales, García reaches the 1,000-hit total in 864 games and 3,304 official at-bats.

January 22, 1967 Eugene Brabender, regularly of the Baltimore Orioles, achieves a rare distinction of winter-league play. Hurling for La Guaira against Caracas, Brabender wins both ends of a doubleheader, achieving two victories on a single day. Brabender's first-game victory comes in a starting role against big-league rival Luís Tiant; his second is earned in three innings of relief.

May 26, 1967 Juan Marichal defeats the Dodgers 4–1 in Candlestick Park, upping his career record against Los Angeles to 14-0 at Candlestick, but more important, surpassing Whitey Ford's major league record winning percentage of .690 for pitchers with over 100 victories. Marichal, whose record was 138-61 (.693) at the time, would finish his career at 243-132 (.631), considerably below Ford's still-standing mark.

July 11, 1967 Cincinnati Reds third baseman Tony Pérez hits a dramatic fifteenth-inning home run off Jim "Catfish" Hunter to give the Nationals a 2–1 victory in the midsummer classic at Anaheim. The hitting heroics of the Cuban slugger not only ended the longest contest in All-Star Game history but capped one of the most ironic games of the long series: third basemen accounted for all three runs in this contest, Dick Allen of the Phillies and Brooks Robinson of the Orioles also homering for the game's only other tallies.

October 4, 1967 Puerto Rican hurler José Santiago of the Boston Red Sox becomes the only pitcher in World Series history to lose a game (2–1 to the Cardinals) in which he also hit a home run. Santiago homered off St. Louis ace Bob Gibson in his first World Series at-bat.

September 20, 1968 Dominican Juan Marichal records his twenty-sixth victory (against eight defeats) in a 9–1 San Francisco win over Atlanta, thus recording the most single-season victories in Giants history since Carl Hubbell's 26 in 1936 and Christy Mathewson's 27 in 1910. This is also the second-most victories in a single campaign recorded by a Latin American major league hurler, surpassed only by Dolf Luque's 27 victories for Cincinnati in 1923.

September 22, 1968 Venezuelan utility player César "Pepe" Tóvar of the Minnesota Twins writes his name forever in the baseball trivia books by becoming the second man to play all nine positions, in a 2–1 victory over the Oakland A's. Tóvar starts with a one-inning stint on the mound, striking out Reggie Jackson, then rotates through the other positions, one per inning. Ironically, the first and only other player to attempt such a stunt was a fellow Latin American, Kansas City's Bert Campaneris (the first batter Tóvar would face during his one-inning mound stint) on September 8, 1965.

October 14, 1968 Dominican outfielder Manny Mota is selected by the Montreal Expos off the roster of the Pittsburgh Pirates, the first player taken in the 1968 National League expansion draft. Mota thus becomes the first official player on the roster of a Canadian major league team. It is ironically fitting that the majors' first non–U.S. team should select as its first player a non–U.S. athlete.

October 24, 1968 Howie Reed, journeyman pitcher with four major league clubs, hurls the third no-hitter in Venezuelan-league history, a 5–0 masterpiece for Caracas against Magallanes. Reed faces only one batter over the minimum by allowing but a single base on balls.

April 8, 1969 Dominican outfielder Jesús Alou, a member of the Houston Astros, is the first hitter in the grand opening of San Diego's Jack Murphy Stadium, completing a miraculous family coincidence of stadium-opening lead-off appearances. Brother Matty, with the Pittsburgh Pirates, had been the first batter to the plate on April 12, 1966, in the inaugural game at Fulton County Stadium in Atlanta. Brother Felipe, of the Atlanta Braves, performed the same honor a month later for the opening of the St. Louis Busch Memorial Stadium on May 12, 1966.

April 27, 1969 Monterrey slugger Héctor Espino enjoys the rare experience of receiving four consecutive intentional walks during a Mexican League game against Mexico City. At the time of this incident, Espino had already connected for four home runs in his previous six times to the plate over a two-day period. In the second game of this memorable doubleheader, Espino also homers for hit number 1,000 of his illustrious Mexican League career.

May 19, 1969 Incomparable Mexican League slugging star Héctor Espino of Monterrey belts two homers against Aguila, his seventh and eighth over six consecutive games. This establishes a new Mexican League record, surpassing the mark of six homers in six games set by Cuban Witty Quintana during the 1961 campaign.

June 16, 1969 Panamanian Rod Carew of the Minnesota Twins ties an American League season record with six successful steals of home, a mark held jointly by Ty Cobb and Bobby "Braggo" Roth and standing for 52 seasons. Carew's steal occurs in Minnesota and comes against right-hander Tom Murphy of the California Angels.

July 16, 1969 In the first game of a doubleheader in Bloomington, Minnesota, versus the Chicago White Sox, Panamanian-born Rod Carew establishes a major league record with his seventh steal of home, eclipsing the single-season American League mark held by Ty Cobb and Bobby Roth and tying the major league standard set in 1946 by Pete Reiser. The record steal comes off Sox rookie right-hander Gerry Nyman, occurs in the seventy-fourth game of Carew's third major league season, and completes a string of home-base steals begun on April 9 in Kansas City. Carew's string of seven steals came on only seven attempts, and an injury that sidelined him for over a month in the late part of the season may have prevented Carew from ultimately breaking Pete Reiser's still-standing mark.

October 2, 1969 Puerto Rican relief pitcher Miguel Fuentes closes his brief one-year major league career by pitching the final inning of the final game for the Seattle Pilots (versus the Oakland A's), bringing to a conclusion the shortest franchise history in modern major league play.

Rod Carew of the Minnesota Twins wins the American League batting title with a .332 average, his first of seven batting championships over the next 10 seasons. Although born in the U.S. territory of the Panama Canal Zone, Carew is widely recognized over the next decade as the greatest Latin American hitter ever to perform in the big leagues.

November 11, 1969 Completing a streak which began on October 13, La Guaira hurler Mike Hedlund establishes a Venezuelan-league record of 38 consecutive scoreless innings pitched. Hedlund's unprecedented streak extends over five games and comes to a sudden end in a game against Caracas on November 11, a game in which Hedlund is knocked out of the box with a three-run ninth-inning rally by the home team.

Cuba's Mike Cuellar is the first Latin American winner of the coveted Cy Young Award, leading a powerhouse Baltimore Orioles staff (2.83 team ERA, 20 staff shutouts) with an outstanding 23-11 record and 2.38 ERA.

June 21, 1970 Diminutive 5'8", 150-pound Venezuelan infielder César Gutiérrez, playing for the Tigers at Cleveland's Municipal Stadium, goes seven-for-seven at the plate to become the first of over 10,000 major league players between 1892 and 1970 to duplicate the performance 78 years earlier of Wilbert Robinson, a catcher with the Baltimore Orioles in the premodern era. Gutiérrez's heroics occur in the 12-inning second game of a Sunday doubleheader when the sparsely used utility player records six singles and a double, a feat that boosts his batting average 38 points to .249 and earns him the starting shortstop position for the remainder of the season. Another Latin player, Rennie Stennett, would later become the first player ever to go seven-for-seven in a nine-inning game on September 16, 1975.

August 22, 23, 1970 Roberto Clemente, Hall-of-Fame outfielder with Pittsburgh's Pirates, and perhaps the greatest right fielder in baseball history, enjoys the finest two-day performance by any modern player, rapping out 10 hits in two consecutive games versus the Los Angeles Dodgers. Clemente's onslaught, at age 36, is all the more remarkable for the fact that his August 22 5-hit day occurs in a marathon 15-inning 2–1 Pirate triumph that does not end until 1:00 A.M. Although he might have been rested the following day, an injury to Willie Stargell necessitates keeping Clemente's bat in the lineup, and Roberto responds with a second 5-hit outing, climaxed by an eighth-inning homer off Dodger rookie Charlie Hough in an 11–0 Pittsburgh victory.

August 28, 1970 Juan Marichal, battling back from a slow start in the 1970 season due to negative reactions to penicillin injections, defeats the Pirates 5–1 for his 200th career victory, thus becoming the first post-World War II pitcher to reach the 200-victory plateau in as few as 11 seasons. Marichal also thus becomes the first Latin American 200-game winner.

October 1, 1970 Dominican slugger Rico Carty of the Atlanta Braves wins the National League batting race with an outstanding .366 average, a feat all the more remarkable because Carty missed the entire 1968 season due to a life-threatening battle with tuberculosis.

April 8, 1971 Three pitchers for Mexico City's Tigers – Enrique Icedo, José Lyva, and Nicolas García – combine for the first multiple-pitcher no-hit, no-run game in Mexican League history. This feat is accomplished during a 3–0 seven-inning victory over Mexico City.

September 30, 1972 Roberto Clemente climaxes the 1972 season with his 3,000th hit, making him only the third active player (along with Hank Aaron and Willie Mays) to reach this exalted level of hitting performance. Clemente's milestone hit, a double to center field off New York Mets southpaw Jon Matlack in a 5–0 Pirate victory at Three Rivers Stadium, is surrounded with cruel irony since it also proves to be the final career hit for Puerto Rico's greatest star. Clemente would be tragically killed in an off-season plane crash only three months later.

November 4, 1972 Antonio "Tony" Armas, Venezuelan-born slugger who will later become the second Latin player (1981) to lead the American League in homers, slugs his first winter-league roundtripper in his native Venezuela. Armas connects for his first four-bagger against big-league hurler Ken Forsch while playing for Caracas against La Guaira.

November 22, 1972 Dámaso Blanco, shortstop for the Magallanes club of the Venezuelan league, achieves a rare distinction in winter-league play by performing an unassisted triple play, the first in the history of Venezuelan professional baseball.

December 31, 1972 Roberto Clemente, perhaps the greatest Latin American player ever to appear in the major leagues, is killed at age 38 in his native Puerto Rico. An overloaded plane carrying Clemente, tons of supplies, and two other volunteers on a mercy mission to aid thousands left homeless by a devastating earthquake in Nicaragua, goes down off the coast of San Juan, killing all aboard.

January 6, 1973 Urbano Lugo, pitching for Caracas against La Guaira, becomes the first native Venezuelan to pitch a no-hit, no-run game in Venezuelan-league play, the fourth such game in the history of the winter circuit. Lugo gives up only one walk and allows but one outfield fly ball during his 6–0 masterpiece.

August 6, 1973 Roberto Clemente, in the wake of his tragic premature death, is voted into the Baseball Hall of Fame with a special dispensation that waives the normal five-year waiting period. Clemente thus becomes the first Latin-born player to achieve enshrinement at Cooperstown.

November 27, 1973 Teolindo Acosta, nicknamed "Inventor del Hit" and one of Venezuela's greatest hitting stars, becomes the second player to achieve 1,000 career hits in Venezuelan-league play. Acosta, an outfielder for Aragua, achieves the distinction over 18 seasons in 3,254 career at-bats.

December 5, 1974 Victor Davalillo, Caracas first baseman who also played 17 seasons in the big leagues, becomes the third player in Venezuelan-league history to record 1,000 hits, achieving the cherished plateau over 17 seasons, 792 games, and 2,906 at-bats.

September 16, 1975 With four singles, two doubles, and a triple in seven at-bats, Panamanian infielder Rennie Stennett of the Pittsburgh Pirates becomes the first and only player in major league history to collect seven hits in a nine-inning game. The Pirates' 22–0 rout of the Chicago Cubs that day is also the most lopsided shutout in big-league history. Stennett collects three hits the following night to become the only player to register 10 hits in two consecutive nine-inning games. Stennett's feat is further highlighted by the tying of a second major league record, his two hits in each of two separate innings in the same game.

January 4, 1976 Executives of the International Amateur Baseball Association (IABA) meet in Mexico City to end a long-standing feud between delegations, creating a new organization named the Asociación Internacional de Béisbol Amateur (AINBA). With the United States returning to the IABA fold for these meetings after a several-year absence, the first AINBA World Championship is scheduled for Cartagena, Colombia, and Cuban Manuel González Guerra is named first AINBA president.

July 28, 1976 Mexican journeyman pitcher Francisco Barrios of the Chicago White Sox combines with John "Blue Moon" Odom to become the first Latin American pitcher to hurl part of a multipitcher no-hitter in the major leagues. The rare feat is accomplished in a 2–1 victory versus the Oakland Athletics.

September 12, 1976 Orestes "Minnie" Miñoso becomes the oldest player to record a hit in major league play, singling off of Sid Monge in the first game of a doubleheader against the California Angels. Seeing limited duty as a designated hitter, the Cuban star gets his only hit during eight 1976 plate appearances. Miñoso is nine months past his fifty-third birthday at the time, thus eclipsing a mark set in 1929 by Nick Altrock, who collected his final hit for the Washington Senators only days after turning 53.

November 13, 1976 César Tóvar, Minnesota Twins infielder-outfielder playing with Aragua, becomes the fourth man in Venezuelan-league play to achieve the 1,000-hit plateau. Tóvar reaches the milestone during his eighteenth season of winter-league play.

November 26, 1976 Adrian Garrett, an eight-year major-leaguer, hits safely in his twenty-eighth consecutive game with Caracas, breaking the long-standing Venezuelan mark owned by Henry Schenz and established in 1952.

June 27, 1977 Héctor Torres, a Mexican-born outfielder with the Toronto Blue Jays, homers with the bases full against the Yankees in Toronto's Exhibition Stadium, the first grand-slam home run on Canadian soil in American League history.

August 8, 1977 Black Cuban star Martín Dihigo, considered by most the greatest all-around performer in the history of the Negro leagues, is voted into Cooperstown by the BWAA Veterans Committee. Dihigo becomes the second Latin player to make the Hall of Fame and the first player to be enshrined in three national baseball halls of fame—Cuba, Mexico, and the United States. Martín Dihigo was a top pitcher and a standout at every position on the diamond, was a batting and home-run champion several times in Negro-league play, and is also credited with pitching the first no-hitter in the history of Mexican League play.

December 26, 1978 Designated hitter Angel Bravo of La Guaira connects for a fifth-inning single against Club Zulia and thus becomes the fifth player in Venezuelan league history to register 1,000 hits. Bravo earlier appeared in three brief seasons of major league play with the Chicago White Sox and Cincinnati Reds, playing in the 1970 World Series with Cincinnati.

August 14, 1979 Leonardo Valenzuela of Monterrey establishes an all-time Mexican League mark by connecting for his nineteenth triple of the season against Team Tampico.

January 12, 1980 Baudilio "Bo" Díaz, major league catcher with the Phillies and Reds, becomes the first Venezuelan-league slugger to register 20 home runs in a single winter campaign, breaking Bobby Darwin's mark of 19 and earning the lasting title in Venezuela of "Rey del Jonrón."

January 13, 1980 Victor Davalillo of Club Aragua establishes a new all-time single-season mark for hits in the Venezuelan League, stroking his 100th of the 1979-80 campaign. On January 9, Davalillo had surpassed the old mark of 95 set by former Cleveland Indian and Baltimore Oriole Dave Pope in 1953-

54. Davalillo is also the only hitter to bat .400 for a complete season in Venezuela, posting that mark during the 1962-63 winter campaign.

October 4, 1980 After nearly four seasons as a coach and public-relations executive, Cuban Orestes "Minnie" Miñoso makes a token pinch-hitting appearance for the Chicago White Sox. Miñoso thus becomes the second player in big-league history to appear in official league play during five decades. The popular Miñoso enjoyed four earlier stints with the White Sox: 1951–1957, 1960–1961, 1964, and 1976. He was 57 at the time of his final pinch-hitting appearance, a promotional stunt orchestrated by Sox owner and ultimate baseball showman Bill Veeck.

Panama's Ben Oglivie posts 41 roundtrippers for the Milwaukee Brewers at season's end to become the first Latin American junior-circuit home-run titlist.

October 1981 Sensational Mexican rookie hurler Fernando Valenzuela completes a dazzling first big-league campaign and a summer of fever-pitch "Fernandomania" throughout Los Angeles and southern California by capturing both the Cy Young trophy and Rookie-of-the-Year accolades in baseball's senior circuit. Valenzuela thus becomes the first Latino winner of Cy Young honors in the National League.

November 10, 1981 Major league hurler Eric Rasmussen throws the sixth no-hit, no-run game in Venezuelan-league history, a 3–0 victory for Lara over La Guaira. Two runners reach base for La Guaira on errors by Lara shortstop Fred Manrique, later a defensive stalwart for the Montreal Expos and Chicago White Sox.

January 16, 1983 Future Houston Astros slugger Kevin Bass establishes a winter-league mark in Venezuelan-league play, accounting for eight RBIs during a single game for Caracas against the Lara ballclub. Bass slugs two homers and a single in five at-bats, including a culminating mammoth grand-slam homer in the eighth inning.

July 31, 1983 Juan Marichal becomes the first and only pitcher of Latin birthright to be elected into baseball's Hall of Fame in Cooperstown. Marichal was actually the first Latin American player elected to Cooperstown by the regular voting procedure, Clemente having received an exemption to the normal election process and Negro-leaguer Martín Dihigo having been selected by the Veterans Committee. The infamous Roseboro incident of 1965, however, remained for many balloters a substantial blemish on Marichal's otherwise fine career and likely delayed by several years his Cooperstown enshrinement.

January 7, 1984 Future major-leaguer Jeff Stone (a Philadelphia Phillies rookie in 1984), playing for the Zulia Eagles, pilfers three bases against Magallanes to establish a new Venezuelan single-season mark of 43 steals.

August 12, 1984 Venezuelan Luís "Little Looie" Aparicio, considered by many the finest defensive shortstop in the history of the game, becomes only the second Latin American player to be voted into baseball's ultimate shrine at Cooperstown via the regular voting procedures. Aparicio enjoyed a marvelous

18-year major league career with Chicago's White Sox (twice), Baltimore, and Boston—all of the American League.

October 2, 1984 Venezuelan Tony Armas becomes the second Latin to win an American League home-run title outright, slugging 43 homers for the Boston Red Sox. Armas had also earlier shared the junior-circuit title with Dwight Evans (Boston), Bobby Grich (California), and Eddie Murray (Baltimore) during the strike-shortened 1981 campaign, each connecting for 22 roundtrippers.

May 14, 1985 Derek Bryant of Tamaulipas becomes the first player in Mexican League history to connect for four homers in a nine-inning game. Bryant goes on a memorable home-run streak, hitting a record five roundtrippers in three consecutive games a week earlier (May 9, 11, 12).

October 3, 1987 San Diego Padres catcher Benito Santiago closes out the season with a 34-game hitting streak. The string is the longest ever by a rookie, a catcher, or a Latin American player in the big leagues and earns the 22-year-old Puerto Rican backstop National League Rookie-of-the-Year honors.

George Bell wins American League MVP honors for his hefty slugging (47 homers, 134 RBIs, .308 BA) despite slumping badly in the season's final week as the Toronto Blue Jays blow a seemingly certain Eastern Division title.

Juan Samuel (Dominican Republic infielder) of the Philadelphia Phillies becomes the first player in major league history to reach double figures in doubles, triples, homers, and stolen bases for four consecutive seasons.

February 9, 1988 Tony Armas, California Angels slugger, homers off Jesse Orosco of Tijuana (Mexico) playing for Caracas (Venezuela) in the thirtieth Caribbean Series, his eleventh career homer in the winter-league classic. Armas becomes the only player to hit more than 10 homers in Caribbean Series play, followed on the all-time list by Carmelo Martínez with 8 and Rico Carty with 7.

Club Escogido (Dominican Republic) loses 5–1 to Mayaguez (Puerto Rico) in the final game of the thirtieth Serie del Caribe (Caribbean Series) in Santo Domingo. The final-game loss, however, does not prevent the host team from reigning as champion of the 1988 Caribbean Series, emerging in first place with a 4-2 record over the five-day four-country round-robin tournament. Mexico and Puerto Rico tie for second (3-3), and Venezuela finishes last (2-4).

April 4, 1988 Dominican slugger George Bell of Toronto's Blue Jays becomes the first player in major league annals to connect for three homers on opening day, stroking three roundtrippers versus the Kansas City ballclub at Royals Stadium.

September 24, 1988 Dominican hurler Pascual Pérez of the Montreal Expos pitches a rain-shortened no-hitter in a 1–0 victory over the Phillies. This is the first abbreviated no-hitter by a Latin American pitcher in major league history, and also the first no-hitter in the history of Philadelphia's 17-year-old Veterans Stadium.

February 1990 The Escogido Lions (Dominican Republic) ride the slugging of Moises Alou (7 RBI), the pitching of Mel Rojas (2-0, 1.69 ERA), and the managing skills of Felipe Alou to post a 5-1 record and capture the 1990 Caribbean Series title. San Juan's Metros (Puerto Rico) and the Caracas Lions (Venezuela) tie for second place with identical 3-3 records before sparse crowds at Miami's Orange Bowl Stadium during the first Caribbean Series staged on North American soil.

June 30, 1990 In a final glory moment with the Dodgers, Fernando Valenzuela pitches the seventh no-hitter in club history. Valenzuela's no-hitter is against the St. Louis Cardinals (6–0) at Dodgers Stadium on the same night as one pitched by Oakland's Dave Stewart in Toronto and the day before a losing no-hit effort by Yankee Andy Hawkins in Chicago.

July 28, 1991 Dennis Martínez pitches a perfect game for the Montreal Expos at Dodgers Stadium (2–0), becoming the first Latin American hurler to author a big-league perfect game.

August 1991 Rod Carew of the Panama Canal Zone is inducted into the National Baseball Hall of Fame in Cooperstown, becoming only the fifth Latin American Hall-of-Famer and only the fourth Latin big-leaguer to be so honored.

August 11, 1991 Venezuelan rookie Wilson Alvarez, making his hurling debut for the Chicago White Sox against the Orioles in Baltimore's Memorial Stadium, becomes the eighth-youngest pitcher in major league history to hurl a no-hit, no-run game. Alvarez is 21 years and 4 months old at the time of his masterpiece; he also becomes both the first Venezuelan and the first White Sox left-hander to pitch a hitless and scoreless game.

September 11, 1991 Dominican relief pitcher Alejandro Peña of the Atlanta Braves teams with starter Kent Mercker and fellow reliever Mark Wohlers for a rare combined no-hit, no-run game against the San Diego Padres in Atlanta. Peña also registers 14 saves over the course of the season for the pennant-winning Atlanta team.

October 1991 Julio Franco (Dominican Republic) of the Texas Rangers captures an American League batting title by hitting .341. The right-handed-hitting second baseman thus becomes the first Latino batting champion since Rod Carew's final title in 1978, 13 seasons earlier.

Franco's Texas Rangers teammate, strapping rookie outfielder Juan González of Puerto Rico, knocks in 102 runs while belting 27 homers and stroking 34 doubles, thus establishing himself as one of the true slugging stars in the major leagues.

October 22, 1991 The newly formed Hall of Fame of Puerto Rican Professional Baseball holds its inaugural induction ceremonies at the Interamerican University in Ponce. A first class of inductees features Negro-league and winter-league stars Luís Angel "Canena" Márquez, Francisco "Pancho" Coimbre, Pedro "Perucho" Cepeda, Robert "El Múcaro" Thurman, and Willard "Ese

Hombre" Brown. Also honored in the induction ceremonies are big-leaguers Roberto Clemente, Orlando Cepeda, Victor Pellot Power, Rubén Gómez, and Juan "Terín" Pizarro.

December 10, 1991 Benjamin "Cananea" Reyes, the winningest manager in Mexican baseball history, dies at age 54 after an extended bout with cancer. In addition to winning 14 Mexican League titles, Reyes piloted the Hermosillo and Mexicali clubs to Caribbean Series championships in 1976 and 1986, the only two Caribbean titles claimed by the Mexicans.

July 1992 Felipe Alou takes over the managerial reins of the Montreal Expos, thus becoming the first Dominican big-league manager. Added flavor is given to Alou's debut managerial summer by the fact that his son Moises is one of the star Expos players, creating the first Latin father-son manager-ballplayer combo.

August 31, 1992 The Texas Rangers and Oakland Athletics swap Latin American sluggers José Canseco and Rubén Sierra in the most sensational trade to involve Hispanic superstars. Canseco joins Texas in exchange for the switch-hitting Sierra, relief ace Jeff Russell, and starting hurler Bobby Witt. With Canseco now in the same lineup alongside junior-circuit home-run leader Juan González, potent Rafael Palmeiro, and former batting champ Julio Franco, the Texas Rangers would subsequently boast the most potent Latin slugging knockout punch ever assembled.

October 1992 Juan González clinches an American League home-run title with 43 circuit blasts in his second full-time season. Puerto Rico's González also sets a Texas Rangers team standard for roundtrippers and becomes the third-youngest (at 21 years, 11 months, 19 days) to hit 40-plus homers during a big-league season. Only Mel Ott and Eddie Mathews (twice) previously reached the 40-homer level at an earlier age than González.

Dominican utilityman Francisco Cabrera becomes a household name by striking a pennant-winning hit for Atlanta's Braves in the crucial seventh game of NLCS play. Cabrera's dramatic pinch-hit blow came with two outs in the bottom of the ninth to snatch a comeback 3–2 victory and a National League pennant from the Eastern Division champion Pittsburgh Pirates. A crucial ninth-inning error by Pittsburgh's gold-glove second baseman José "Chico" Lind (Puerto Rico) is significant in opening the door for the dramatic Atlanta pennant-winning rally.

November 8, 1992 Puerto Rico's Professional Baseball Hall of Fame conducts its second formal induction ceremonies at the Interamerican University in Ponce. Second-year inductees include former major-leaguers Luis Arroyo, Carlos Bernier, Luís Rodríguez Olmo, and Saturnino "Nino" Escalera. Also inducted are Negro-leaguers Juan Esteban "Tetelo" Vargas, José Antonio Figueroa, Rafael "Rafaelito" Ortiz and local island stars and nonplayers Jorge "Griffin" Tirado, Pedro Miguel Caratini, Ceferino Conde y Faria, Juan Guilbe, Rafael Ponte Flores, Pedro "Pedrin" Zorrilla, Pedro Vázquez, and Emilio "Millito" Navarro.

April 1993 Tony Pérez debuts as manager of the Cincinnati Reds, but the debut is anything but successful as Pérez is fired only 44 games into the 1993 season. Hopes were high in Cincinnati for a Reds pennant challenge, and when the local ballclub floundered early in the season (20-24 on May 24, the date of Pérez's firing), even the stature of Pérez as a revered star of the 1970s Big Red Machine was not enough to save his slow-starting managerial career.

April 8, 1993 Carlos Baerga, switch-hitting Puerto Rican second baseman with the Cleveland Indians, achieves the rarest of feats when he becomes the first player in major league history to homer from both sides of the plate during the same inning. Baerga's two circuit blasts come in the opening frame of a 15–5 rout over the New York Yankees at Cleveland's Municipal Stadium.

April 9, 1993 José Canseco (Cuba) of the Texas Rangers becomes the first player since Ted Williams (1947) and the seventeenth in baseball history to reach the 750 career RBI plateau in 1,000 games or less. Canseco's milestone RBI comes in a game (his 999th career contest) against the Royals in Kansas City.

June 17, 1993 Carlos Baerga becomes the twelfth Latin American slugger to pound three homers in a single contest. Previous batsmen achieving the feat include Bobby Avila (1951), Héctor López (1958), Manny Jiménez (1964), Tony Oliva (1973), Ben Oglivie (1979, 1982, 1983), Otto Velez (1980), Juan Beníquez (1986), George Bell (1988), José Canseco (1988), Danny Tartabull (1991), and Juan González (1992).

June 18, 1993 Montreal Expos ace right-hander Dennis Martínez wins his 200th career game (200-161), becoming the ninety-second hurler overall but only the third Latin American to reach this coveted milestone for career victories. With his fifth-straight win of the young season, by a 2–1 count over the Atlanta Braves, the Nicaraguan pitcher joins Juan Marichal (243) and Luís Tiant (229) as the only Latin Americans to reach the charmed 200-victory plateau.

June 20, 1993 Dominican slugger George Bell hits his tenth career grand-slam homer for the Chicago White Sox in a game against the California Angels at Anaheim Stadium. This roundtripper moved Bell into the all-time lead for bases-loaded homers among Latin American batsmen, surpassing Orlando Cepeda and Danny Tartabull, who had each previously stroked nine. Bell's 13 homers during the 1993 season would also move him into third place on the all-time Latin list with 265.

July 1993 Launching one of the great personal comebacks in recent baseball history, first baseman Andrés Galarraga smacks the ball at a torrid .400-plus pace for almost the entire first half of the 1993 season, maintaining a .401 BA for the expansion Colorado Rockies as late as the season's halfway point of July 6, date of the club's eighty-second game. Galarraga had hit only .256, .219, and .243 over the previous three campaigns, causing first the Montreal Expos and later the St. Louis Cardinals to give up on this Venezuelan slugger's sagging career. Galarraga battles injuries throughout the season but maintains his torrid hitting pace to become the National League's Comeback Player of the Year.

October 3, 1993 The Texas Rangers play their final game in Arlington Stadium, losing to the Kansas City Royals. Puerto Rican slugger Juan González is the last batter in stadium history as he flies out to left field. Ironically, another Latin player, California Angels second baseman Sandy Alomar, also a Puerto Rican native, was the first official batter in stadium history on April 21, 1972.

The Milwaukee Brewers add Angel Miranda and Rafael Novoa to the club's starting rotation in late season, marking the first time that four Latin hurlers (all Puerto Ricans) had composed the starting rotation of a big-league ballclub. Jaime Navarro and Ricky Bones were also members of the Milwaukee Brewer starting staff during the final month of the season.

Andrés Galarraga reaches the minimum qualification number in official plate appearances during the season's final week and thus becomes the first expansion-team player to win a major league batting crown, pacing the National League with a .370 average.

Juan González of the Texas Rangers powers past the 40-homer plateau for the second consecutive campaign, becoming the first Latin slugger ever to post back-to-back 40-homer seasons in the big leagues. At season's end González leads the American League in roundtrippers with 46, his second consecutive home-run title. González thus also becomes the third Latin batsman (after Tony Armas in 1981 and 1984 and José Canseco in 1988 and 1991) to garner two home-run crowns and the first to accomplish the feat in consecutive seasons.

The Texas Rangers announce an All-Time Rangers All-Star Team covering the first twenty-two (1972–1993) seasons of ballclub history (and corresponding with the closing of the original Arlington Stadium). This mythical team includes five Latin American players: Rafael Palmeiro, first base; Julio Franco, second base; Juan González and Rubén Sierra, outfielders; and Iván Rodríguez, catcher. González (84 percent of ballots) was the second-highest votegetter, surpassed only by pitcher Nolan Ryan (94 percent). Palmeiro (68 percent) ranked fourth in highest percentage of votes earned.

APPENDIX B

Complete Roster of Latin American Major League Players, by Nationality

The following roster contains the names and statistical data for all 613 Latin-born players who have appeared in the major leagues (including recognized nineteenth-century big league circuits like the National Association and American Association) through the end of the 1992 season. Names in boldface are the names by which players are most commonly known. U.S.-born players of Hispanic surname (such as John Candelaria or Bobby Bonilla) are not considered Latin American ballplayers and are thus not included here. Two U.S.-born Latin players (Moises Alou and Dickie Thon) are included, however, since their Latin American parents were temporarily residing in the States at the time of their births.

Several members of SABR's Latin America Committee and Biographical Committee have been of considerable assistance in compiling portions of this present list and should be singled out for mention. While the format and statistical details here are the work of the present author, a half-dozen SABR researchers have contributed variously to the working roster of Latin players. Acknowledged here for their assistance are SABR researchers Rich Topp, Bill Carle, Robert F. Schulz, Luís Rodríguez-Mayoral, José de Jesús Jiménez, and Rob Ruck.

Dominican Republic

(First Dominican major-leaguer: Ossie Virgil [September 23, 1956]; 166 players)

Alba y Rosando, Gibson Alberto (**Gibson Alba**) (b. 1-18-1960, Santiago) Debut: 5-3-1988 (1988) Team: St. Louis (N) Position: Pitcher (BL TL) Stats: 0 W, 0 L, 3.1 IP, 2.70 ERA, 3 SO, 2 BB, 0 SV, 3 G

Alcala (Anibal y Alcala), Santo (**Santo Alcala**) (b. 12-23-1952, San Pedro de Macoris) Debut: 4-10-1976 (1976-1977) Teams: Cincinnati (N), Montreal (N) Position: Pitcher (BR TR) Stats: 14 W, 11 L, 249.1 IP, 4.76 ERA, 140 SO, 121 BB, 2 SV, 68 G

Dominican Republic, *cont.*

Alexander, Manuel de Jesús (**Manny Alexander**) (b. 3-20-1971, San Pedro de Macoris) Debut: 9-18-1992 (1992) Team: Baltimore (A) Position: Shortstop (BR TR) Stats: 4 G, 5 AB, 1 H, 1 R, 0 HR, 0 RBI, .200 BA

Alou (Rojas y Alou), Felipe (**Felipe Alou**) (b. 5-12-1935, Santo Domingo) Debut: 6-8-1958 (1958–1974) Teams: San Francisco (N), Milwaukee (N), Atlanta (N), Oakland (A), New York (A), Montreal (N), Milwaukee (A) Position: Outfield (BR TR) Stats: 2082 G, 7339 AB, 2101 H, 985 R, 206 HR, 852 RBI, .286 BA (Brother of Jesús Alou and Matty Alou; Father of Moises Alou)

Alou (Rojas y Alou), Jesús Maria (**Jesús Alou**) (b. 3-24-1942, Haina) Debut: 9-10-1963 (1963–1975) Teams: San Francisco (N), Houston (N), Oakland (A), New York (N), Houston (N) Position: Outfield (BR TR) Stats: 1380 G, 4345 AB, 1216 H, 448 R, 32 HR, 377 RBI, .280 BA (Brother of Felipe Alou and Matty Alou)

Alou (Rojas y Alou), Mateo (**Matty Alou**) (b. 12-22-1938, Haina) Debut: 9-26-1960 (1960–1974) Teams: San Francisco (N), Pittsburgh (N), St. Louis (N), Oakland (A), New York (A), San Diego (N) Position: Outfield (BL TL) Stats: 1667 G, 5789 AB, 1777 H, 780 R, 31 HR, 427 RBI, .307 BA (Brother of Felipe Alou and Jesús Alou)

Alou, Moises (**Moises Alou**) (b. 7-3-1966, Atlanta, Georgia, USA) Debut: 1990 (1990) Teams: Pittsburgh (N), Montreal (N) Position: Outfield (BR TR) Stats: 131 G, 361 AB, 100 H, 57 R, 9 HR, 56 RBI, .277 BA (Son of Felipe Alou)

Andújar, Joaquín (**Joaquín Andújar**) (b. 12-12-1952, San Pedro de Macoris) Debut: 4-8-1976 (1976–1988) Teams: Houston (N), St. Louis (N), Oakland (A), Houston (N) Position: Pitcher (BR TR) Stats: 127 W, 118 L, 2153.1 IP, 3.58 ERA, 1032 SO, 731 BB, 9 SV, 405 G

Astacio, Pedro Julio (**Pedro Astacio**) (b. 11-28-1969, Hato Mayor) Debut: 7-3-1992 (1992) Team: Los Angeles (N) Position: Pitcher (BR TR) Stats: 5 W, 5 L, 82 IP, 1.98 ERA, 43 SO, 20 BB, 0 SV, 11 G

Báez (Mota y Báez), José Antonio (**José Báez**) (b. 12-31-1953, San Cristobal) Debut: 4-6-1977 (1977–1978) Team: Seattle (A) Positions: Second Base, DH (BR TR) Stats: 114 G, 355 AB, 87 H, 47 R, 1 HR, 19 RBI, .245 BA

Batista y Decartes, Miguel Jerez (**Miguel Batista**) (b. 12-19-1971, Santo Domingo) Debut: 4-11-1992 (1992) Team: Pittsburgh (N) Position: Pitcher (BR TR) Stats: 0 W, 0 L, 2 IP, 9.00 ERA, 1 SO, 3 BB, 0 SV, 1 G

Batista y Sánchez, Rafael (**Rafael Batista**) (b. 10-20-1947, San Pedro de Macoris) Debut: 6-17-1973 (1973, 1975) Team: Houston (N) Position: First Base (BL TL) Stats: 22 G, 25 AB, 7 H, 2 R, 0 HR, 2 RBI, .280 BA

Bautista y Arias, José Joaquín (**José Bautista**) (b. 7-25-1964, Bani) Debut: 4-9-1988 (1988–1992) Teams: Baltimore (A), Chicago (N) Position: Pitcher (BR TR) Stats: 10 W, 20 L, 281.2 IP, 4.79 ERA, 124 SO, 72 BB, 0 SV, 75 G

Bell y Mathey, Jorge Antonio (**George "Jorge" Bell**) (b. 10-21-1959, San Pedro de Macoris) Debut: 4-9-1981 (1981–1992) Teams: Toronto (A), Chicago (N), Chicago (A) Positions: Outfield, DH (BR TR) Stats: 1485 G, 5713 AB, 1613 H, 778 R, 252 HR, 938 RBI, .282 BA (Brother of Juan Bell)

Bell y Mathey, Juan (**Juan "Tito" Bell**) (b. 3-29-1968, San Pedro de Macoris) Debut: 9-6-1989 (1989–1992) Teams: Baltimore (A), Philadelphia (N), Milwaukee (A) Position: Shortstop (BR TR) Stats: 159 G, 362 AB, 66 H, 41 R, 2 HR, 23 RBI, .182 BA (Brother of George Bell)

Belliard y Matias, Rafael Leonidas (**Rafael Belliard**) (b. 10-24-1961, Puerto Nuevo Mao) Debut: 9-6-1982 (1982–1992) Teams: Pittsburgh (N), Atlanta (N) Position: Shortstop (BR TR) Stats: 777 G, 1689 AB, 377 H, 171 R, 1 HR, 113 RBI, .223 BA

Beltre, Esteban (**Esteban Beltre**) (b. 12-26-1967, Ingenio Quisfella) Debut: 9-3-1991 (1991–1992) Team: Chicago (A) Position: Shortstop (BR TR) Stats: 57 G, 116 AB, 22 H, 21 R, 1 HR, 10 RBI, .190 BA

Bernhardt y Coradin, Juan Ramón (**Juan Bernhardt**) (b. 8-31-1953, San Pedro de Macoris) Debut: 7-10-1976 (1976–1979) Teams: New York (A), Seattle (A) Positions: Infield, DH (BR TR) Stats: 154 G, 492 AB, 117 H, 46 R, 9 HR, 43 RBI, .238 BA

Berróa (Letta y Berróa), Gerónimo Emiliano (**German Berróa**) (b. 3-18-1965, Santo Domingo) Debut: 4-5-1989 (1989–1990, 1992) Teams: Atlanta (N), Cincinnati (N) Position: Outfield (BR TR) Stats: 101 G, 155 AB, 40 H, 9 R, 2 HR, 9 RBI, .258 BA

Borbón, Pedro Félix (**Pedro Borbón, Jr.**) (b. 11-15-1967, Mao) Debut: 10-2-1992 (1992) Team: Atlanta (N) Position: Pitcher (BR TL) Stats: 0 W, 1 L, 1.1 IP, 6.75 ERA, 1 SO, 1 BB, 0 SV, 2 G (Son of Pedro Borbón, Sr.)

Borbón y Rodríguez, Pedro (**Pedro Borbón, Sr.**) (b. 12-2-1946, Valverde do Mao) Debut: 4-9-1969 (1969–1980) Teams: California (A), Cincinnati (N), San Francisco (N), St. Louis (N) Position: Pitcher (BR TR) Stats: 69 W, 39 L, 1026 IP, 3.52 ERA, 409 SO, 251 BB, 80 SV, 593 G (Father of Pedro Borbón, Jr.)

Bournigal, Rafael Antonio (**Rafael Bournigal**) (b. 5-12-1966, Azusa) Debut: 9-1-1992 (1992) Team: Los Angeles (N) Position: Infield (BR TR) Stats: 10 G, 20 AB, 3 H, 1 R, 0 HR, 0 RBI, .150 BA

Brito, Bernardo (**Bernardo Brito**) (b. 12-4-1963, San Cristobal) Debut: 9-15-1992 (1992) Team: Minnesota (A) Positions: Outfield, DH (BR TR) Stats: 8 G, 14 AB, 2 H, 1 R, 0 HR, 2 RBI, .143 BA

Cabrera y Paulino, Francisco (**Francisco Cabrera**) (b. 10-10-1966, Santo Domingo) Debut: 7-24-1989 (1989–1992) Teams: Toronto (A), Atlanta (N) Positions: Catcher, First Base, DH (BR TR) Stats: 126 G, 268 AB, 69 H, 24 R, 13 HR, 51 RBI, .257 BA

Campusano y Díaz, Silvestre (**Sil Campusano**) (b. 12-31-1965, Santo Domingo) Debut: 4-4-1988 (1988, 1990–1991) Teams: Toronto (A), Philadelphia (N) Positions: Outfield, DH (BR TR) Stats: 154 G, 262 AB, 53 H, 26 R, 5 HR, 23 RBI, .202 BA

Cano y Soriano, Joselito (**José Cano**) (b. 3-7-1962, Boca de Soco) Debut: 8-28-1989 (1989) Team: Houston (N) Position: Pitcher (BR TR) Stats: 1 W, 1 L, 23 IP, 5.09 ERA, 8 SO, 7 BB, 0 SV, 6 G

Carty (Jacobo y Carty), Ricardo Adolfo (**Rico Carty**) (b. 9-1-1939, San Pedro de Macoris) Debut: 9-15-1963 (1963–1979) Teams: Milwaukee (N), Atlanta (N), Texas (A), Chicago (N), Oakland (A), Cleveland (A), Toronto (A) Positions: Outfield, DH (BR TR) Stats: 1651 G, 5606 AB, 1677 H, 712 R, 204 HR, 890 RBI, .299 BA

Castillo, Braulio (**Braulio Castillo**) (b. 5-13-1968, Elias Piña) Debut: 8-18-1991 (1991–1992) Team: Philadelphia (N) Position: Outfield (BR TR) Stats: 56 G, 128 AB, 24 H, 15 R, 2 HR, 9 RBI, .188 BA

Castillo, Monte Carmelo (**Carmen Castillo**) (b. 6-8-1958, San Pedro de Macoris) Debut: 7-17-1982 (1982–1991) Teams: Cleveland (A), Minnesota (A) Positions: Outfield, DH (BR TR) Stats: 631 G, 1519 AB, 383 H, 190 R, 55 HR, 197 RBI, .252 BA

Castillo y Bryas, Juan (**Juan Castillo**) (b. 1-25-1962, San Pedro de Macoris) Debut: 4-12-1986 (1986–1989) Team: Milwaukee (A) Positions: Shortstop, Outfield, DH (BB TR) Stats: 199 G, 469 AB, 101 H, 60 R, 3 HR, 38 RBI, .215 BA

Castillo y Cabrera, Esteban Manuel Antonio (**Manny Castillo**) (b. 4-1-1957, Santo Domingo) Debut: 9-1-1980 (1980–1983) Teams: Kansas City (A), Seattle (A) Position: Third Base (BB TR) Stats: 236 G, 719 AB, 174 H, 63 R, 3 HR, 73 RBI, .242 BA

Castro y Checo, William Radhames (**Bill Castro**) (b. 12-13-1953, Santiago) Debut: 8-20-1974 (1974–1983) Teams: Milwaukee (A), New York (A), Kansas City (A) Position: Pitcher (BR TR) Stats: 31 W, 26 L, 545.1 IP, 3.33 ERA, 203 SO, 145 BB, 45 SV, 303 G

Cedeño y Domastorg, Andújar (**Andújar Cedeño**) (b. 8-21-1969, La Romana) Debut: 9-2-1990 (1990–1992) Team: Houston (N) Position: Shortstop (BR TR) Stats: 145 G, 479 AB, 99 H, 42 R, 11 HR, 49 RBI, .207 BA (Son of César Cedeño)

Cedeño y Encarnación, César (**César Cedeño**) (b. 2-25-1951, Santo Domingo) Debut: 6-20-1970 (1970–1986) Teams: Houston (N), Cincinnati (N), St. Louis (N), Los Angeles (N) Position: Outfield (BR TR) Stats: 2006 G, 7310 AB, 2087 H, 1084 R, 199 HR, 976 RBI, .285 BA (Father of Andújar Cedeño)

DeFreitas y Simon, Arturo Marcelino (**Art DeFreitas**) (b. 4-26-1953, San Pedro de Macoris) Debut: 9-7-1978 (1978–1979) Team: Cincinnati (N) Position: First Base (BR TR) Stats: 32 G, 53 AB, 11 H, 3 R, 1 HR, 6 RBI, .208 BA

de la Cruz y Gil, Victor Manuel (**Victor Cruz**) (b. 12-24-1957, Rancho Viejo La Vega) Debut: 6-24-1978 (1978–1983) Teams: Toronto (A), Cleveland (A), Pittsburgh (N), Texas (A) Position: Pitcher (BR TR) Stats: 18 W, 23 L, 271.1 IP, 3.08 ERA, 248 SO, 132 BB, 37 SV, 187 G

de la Rosa, Jesús (**Jesús de la Rosa**) (b. 7-28-1953, Santo Domingo) Debut: 8-2-1975 (1975) Team: Houston (N) Position: Pinch Hitter (BR TR) Stats: 3 G, 3 AB, 1 H, 1 R, 0 HR, 0 RBI, .333 BA

Dominican Republic, *cont.*

de la Rosa y Jiménez, Francisco (**Francisco de le Rosa**) (b. 3-3-1966, La Romana) Debut: 9-7-1991 (1991) Team: Baltimore (A) Position: Pitcher (BB TR) Stats: 0 W, 0 L, 4 IP, 4.50 ERA, 1 SO, 2 BB, 0 SV, 2 G

DeLeón y Chestaro, José (**José DeLeón**) (b. 12-20-1960, Le Vega) Debut: 7-23-1983 (1983–1992) Teams: Philadelphia (N), Pittsburgh (N), Chicago (A), St. Louis (N), Philadelphia (N) Position: Pitcher (BR TR) Stats: 75 W, 113 L, 1697 IP, 3.73 ERA, 1422 SO, 745 BB, 4 SV, 293 G

de los Santos y Genero, Ramón (**Ramón de los Santos**) (b. 1-19-1949, Santo Domingo) Debut: 8-21-1974 (1974) Team: Houston (N) Position: Pitcher (BL TL) Stats: 1 W, 1 L, 12 IP, 2.25 ERA, 7 SO, 9 BB, 0 SV, 12 G

de los Santos y Martínez, Luís Manuel (**Luís de los Santos**) (b. 12-29-1966, San Cristobal) Debut: 9-7-1988 (1988–1989, 1991) Teams: Kansas City (A), Detroit (A) Positions: First Base, DH, Outfield (BR TR) Stats: 55 G, 139 AB, 29 H, 8 R, 0 HR, 7 RBI, .209 BA

Diloné y Reyes, Miguel Angel (**Miguel Diloné**) (b. 11-1-1954, Santiago) Debut: 9-2-1974 (1974–1985) Teams: Pittsburgh (N), Oakland (A), Chicago (N), Cleveland (A), Chicago (A), Montreal (N), San Diego (N) Position: Outfield (BB TR) Stats: 800 G, 2000 AB, 530 H, 314 R, 6 HR, 129 RBI, .265 BA

Duncan y Nalasco, Mariano (**Mariano Duncan**) (b. 3-13-1963, San Pedro de Macoris) Debut: 4-9-1985 (1985–1992) Teams: Los Angeles (N), Cincinnati (N), Philadelphia (N) Position: Infield (BB TR) Stats: 788 G, 2830 AB, 722 H, 368 R, 53 HR, 253 RBI, .255 BA

Encarnación (Lora y Encarnación), Luís Martín (**Luís Encarnación**) (b. 10-20-1963, Santo Domingo) Debut: 7-27-1990 (1990) Team: Kansas City (A) Position: Pitcher (BR TR) Stats: 0 W, 0 L, 10 IP, 7.84 ERA, 8 SO, 4 BB, 0 SV, 4 G

Espino y Reyes, Juan (**Juan Espino**) (b. 3-16-1956, Bonao) Debut: 6-25-1982 (1982–1986) Team: New York (A) Position: Catcher (BR TR) Stats: 49 G, 73 AB, 16 H, 2 R, 1 HR, 8 RBI, .219 BA

Espinosa (Acevedo y Espinosa), Arnulfo (**Nino Espinosa**) (b. 8-15-1953, Villa Altagracia) Debut: 9-13-1974 (1974–1981) Teams: New York (N), Philadelphia (N), Toronto (A) Position: Pitcher (BR TR) Stats: 44 W, 55 L, 821 IP, 4.17 ERA, 338 SO, 252 BB, 0 SV, 140 G

Eusebio (Bare y Eusebio), Raul Antonio (**Tony Eusebio**) (b. 4-27-1967, San José de los Llamos) Debut: 8-8-1991 (1991) Team: Houston (N) Position: Catcher (BR TR) Stats: 10 G, 19 AB, 2 H, 4 R, 0 HR, 0 RBI, .105 BA

Félix y Sánchez, Junior Francisco (**Junior Félix**) (b. 10-3-1967, Laguna Sabada) Debut: 5-3-1989 (1989–1992) Teams: Toronto (A), California (A), Florida (N) Position: Outfield (BB TR) Stats: 442 G, 1617 AB, 419 H, 230 R, 35 HR, 209 RBI, .259 BA

Fermín y Minaya, Félix José (**Félix Fermín**) (b. 10-9-1963, Mao Valverde) Debut: 7-8-1987 (1987–1992) Teams: Pittsburgh (N), Cleveland (A) Position: Shortstop (BR TR) Stats: 578 G, 1692 AB, 431 H, 169 R, 1 HR, 111 RBI, .255 BA

Fernández y Castro, Octavio Antonio (**Tony Fernández**) (b. 8-6-1962, San Pedro de Macoris) Debut: 9-2-1983 (1983–1992) Teams: Toronto (A), San Diego (N), New York (N), Toronto (A) Position: Shortstop (BB TR) Stats: 1328 G, 5132 AB, 1465 H, 675 R, 48 HR, 479 RBI, .285 BA

Figueroa, Bienvenido (**Bien Figueroa**) (b. 2-7-1964, Santo Domingo) Debut: 5-17-1992 (1992) Team: St. Louis (N) Position: Infield (BR TR) Stats: 12 G, 11 AB, 2 H, 1 R, 0 HR, 4 RBI, .182 BA

Figueroa y Figueroa, Jesús Maria (**Jesús Figueroa**) (b. 2-20-1957, Santo Domingo) Debut: 4-22-1980 (1980) Team: Chicago (N) Position: Outfield (BL TL) Stats: 115 G, 198 AB, 50 H, 20 R, 1 HR, 11 RBI, .253 BA

Franco (Robles y Franco), Julio César (**Julio Franco**) (b. 8-23-1958, San Pedro de Macoris) Debut: 4-23-1982 (1982–1992) Teams: Philadelphia (N), Cleveland (A), Texas (A) Position: Second Base (BR TR) Stats: 1402 G, 5416 AB, 1630 H, 807 R, 86 HR, 679 RBI, .301 BA

Frías y Andújar, Jesús Maria (**Pepe Frías**) (b. 7-14-1948, San Pedro de Macoris) Debut: 4-6-1973 (1973–1981) Teams: Montreal (N), Atlanta (N), Texas (A), Los Angeles (N) Positions: Shortstop, Second Base (BR TR) Stats: 723 G, 1346 AB, 323 H, 132 R, 1 HR, 108 RBI, .240 BA

Galvez y Jerez, Balvino (**Balvino Galvez**) (b. 3-31-1964, San Pedro de Macoris) Debut:

5-7-1986 (1986) Team: Los Angeles (N) Position: Pitcher (BR TR) Stats: 0 W, 1 L, 20.2 IP, 3.92 ERA, 11 SO, 12 BB, 0 SV, 10 G

García y Peralta, Leonardo Antonio (**Leo García**) (b. 11-6-1962, Santiago) Debut: 4-6-1987 (1987–1988) Team: Cincinnati (N) Position: Outfield (BL TL) Stats: 54 G, 58 AB, 10 H, 10 R, 1 HR, 2 RBI, .172 BA

García y Sánchez, Dámaso Domingo (**Dámaso García**) (b. 2-7-1955, Moca) Debut: 6-24-1978 (1978–1989) Teams: New York (A), Toronto (A), Atlanta (N), Montreal (N) Positions: Second Base, DH (BR TR) Stats: 1032 G, 3914 AB, 1108 H, 490 R, 36 HR, 323 RBI, .283 BA

Gerónimo y Zorrilla, César Francisco (**César Gerónimo**) (b. 3-11-1948, El Seibo) Debut: 4-16-1969 (1969–1983) Teams: Houston (N), Cincinnati (N), Kansas City (A) Position: Outfield (BL TL) Stats: 1522 G, 3780 AB, 977 H, 460 R, 51 HR, 392 RBI, .258 BA

González y Gutiérrez, José Rafael (**José González**) (b. 11-23-1964, Puerta Plata) Debut: 9-2-1985 (1985–1992) Teams: Los Angeles (N), Pittsburgh (N), Cleveland (A), California (A) Position: Outfield (BR TR) Stats: 461 G, 676 AB, 144 H, 95 R, 9 HR, 42 RBI, .213 BA

González y Manzueta, Denio Mariano (**Denny González**) (b. 7-22-1963, Sabana Grande Boya) Debut: 8-6-1984 (1984–1989) Teams: Pittsburgh (N), Cleveland (A) Position: Infield (BR TR) Stats: 98 G, 262 AB, 54 H, 29 R, 4 HR, 18 RBI, .206 BA

González y Olivares, Pedro (**Pedro González**) (b. 12-12-1937, San Pedro de Macoris) Debut: 4-11-1963 (1963–1967) Teams: New York (A), Cleveland (A) Position: Infield (BR TR) Stats: 407 G, 1084 AB, 264 H, 99 R, 8 HR, 70 RBI, .244 BA

Griffin (Baptist y Griffin), Alfredo Claudino (**Alfredo Griffin**) (b. 10-6-1957, Santo Domingo) Debut: 9-4-1976 (1976–1992) Teams: Cleveland (A), Toronto (A), Oakland (A), Los Angeles (N), Toronto (A) Position: Shortstop (BB TR) Stats: 1916 G, 6685 AB, 1668 H, 744 R, 24 HR, 524 RBI, .250 BA

Guante y Magallane, Cecilio (**Cecilio Guante**) (b. 2-1-1960, Villa Mella) Debut: 5-1-1982 (1982–1990) Teams: Pittsburgh (N), New York (A), Texas (A), Cleveland (A) Position: Pitcher (BR TR) Stats: 29 W, 34 L, 595 IP, 3.48 ERA, 503 SO, 236 BB, 35 SV, 363 G

Guerrero, Juan Antonio (**Juan Guerrero**) (b. 2-1-1967, Los Llanos) Debut: 4-9-1992 (1992) Team: Houston (N) Positions: Shortstop, Outfield (BR TR) Stats: 79 G, 125 AB, 25 H, 8 R, 1 HR, 14 RBI, .200 BA

Guerrero, Pedro (**Pedro Guerrero**) (b. 6-29-1956, San Pedro de Macoris) Debut: 9-22-1978 (1978–1992) Teams: Los Angeles (N), St. Louis (N) Positions: Outfield, Third Base, First Base (BR TR) Stats: 1536 G, 5392 AB, 1618 H, 730 R, 215 HR, 898 RBI, .300 BA

Guerrero y Abud, Mario Miguel (**Mario Guerrero**) (b. 9-28-1949, Santo Domingo) Debut: 4-8-1973 (1973–1980) Teams: Boston (A), St. Louis (N), California (A), Oakland (A) Position: Shortstop (BR TR) Stats: 697 G, 2251 AB, 578 H, 166 R, 7 HR, 170 RBI, .257 BA

Guzmán (Donovan y Guzmán), Santiago (**Santiago Guzmán**) (b. 7-25-1949, San Pedro de Macoris) Debut: 9-30-1969 (1969–1972) Team: St. Louis (N) Position: Pitcher (BR TR) Stats: 1 W, 2 L, 32 IP, 4.50 ERA, 29 SO, 18 BB, 0 SV, 12 G

Guzmán y Correa, Juan Andres (**Juan Guzmán**) (b. 10-28-1966, Santo Domingo) Debut: 6-7-1990 (1991–1992) Team: Toronto (A) Position: Pitcher (BR TR) Stats: 26 W, 8 L, 319.1 IP, 2.79 ERA, 288 SO, 138 BB, 0 SV, 51 G

Guzmán y Estrella, Ramón Dionny (**Johnny Guzmán**) (b. 1-21-1971, Hatillo Palma) Debut: 6-8-1991 (1991) Team: Oakland (A) Position: Pitcher (BR TL) Stats: 1 W, 0 L, 8 IP, 10.13 ERA, 3 SO, 2 BB, 0 SV, 7 G

Hernández (Montas y Hernández), Pedro Julio Montas (**Pedro Hernández**) (b. 4-4-1959, La Romana) Debut: 9-8-1979 (1979, 1982) Team: Toronto (A) Positions: Third Base, Outfield, DH (BR TR) Stats: 11 G, 9 AB, 0 H, 2 R, 0 HR, 0 RBI, .000 BA

Hernández y Fuentes, Rudolph Albert (**Rudy Hernández**) (b. 12-10-1931, Santiago) Debut: 7-3-1960 (1960–1961) Team: Washington (A) Position: Pitcher (BR TR) Stats: 4 W, 2 L, 43.2 IP, 4.12 ERA, 26 SO, 24 BB, 0 SV, 28 G

Hernández y Montas, Manuel Antonio (**Manny Hernández**) (b. 5-7-1961, La Romana) Debut: 6-5-1986 (1986–1987, 1989) Teams: Houston (N), New York (N) Position: Pitcher (BR TR) Stats: 2 W, 7 L, 50.1 IP, 4.47 ERA, 22 SO, 17 BB, 0 SV, 16 G

Hernández y Pérez, Cásar Dario (**César Hernández**) (b. 9-28-1966, Yamasa) Debut: 7-19-1992 (1992) Team: Cincinnati (N) Position: Outfield (BR TR) Stats: 34 G, 51 AB, 14 H, 6 R, 0 HR, 4 RBI, .275 BA

Dominican Republic, *cont.*

Javier (Wilkes y Javier), Ignacio Alfredo (**Al Javier**) (b. 2-4-1954, San Pedro de Macoris) Debut: 9-9-1976 (1976) Team: Houston (N) Position: Outfield (BR TR) Stats: 8 G, 24 AB, 5 H, 1 R, 0 HR, 0 RBI, .208 BA

Javier y DeJavier, Stanley Julián Antonio (**Stan Javier**) (b. 1-9-1964, San Francisco de Macoris) Debut: 4-15-1984 (1984, 1986–1992) Teams: New York (A), Oakland (A), Los Angeles (N), Philadelphia (N) Positions: Outfield, DH (BB TR) Stats: 758 G, 1798 AB, 442 H, 250 R, 10 HR, 147 RBI, .246 BA (Son of Julián Javier)

Javier y Liranzo, Manuel Julián (**Julián Javier**) (b. 8-9-1936, San Francisco de Macoris) Debut: 5-28-1960 (1960–1972) Teams: St. Louis (N), Cincinnati (N) Position: Second Base (BR TR) Stats: 1622 G, 5722 AB, 1469 H, 722 R, 78 HR, 506 RBI, .257 BA (Father of Stan Javier)

Jiménez y Martes, Juan Antonio (**Juan Jiménez**) (b. 3-8-1949, La Torre) Debut: 9-9-1974 (1974) Team: Pittsburgh (N) Position: Pitcher (BR TR) Stats: 0 W, 0 L, 4 IP, 6.75 ERA, 2 SO, 2 BB, 0 SV, 4 G

Jiménez y Rivera, Félix Elvio (**Elvio Jiménez**) (b. 1-6-1940, San Pedro de Macoris) Debut: 10-4-1964 (1964) Team: New York (A) Position: Outfield (BR TR) Stats: 1 G, 6 AB, 2 H, 0 R, 0 HR, 0 RBI, .333 BA (Brother of Manny Jiménez)

Jiménez y Rivera, Manuel Emilio (**Manny Jiménez**) (b. 11-19-1938, San Pedro de Macoris) Debut: 4-11-1962 (1962–1969) Teams: Kansas City (A), Pittsburgh (N), Chicago (N) Position: Outfield (BL TR) Stats: 429 G, 1003 AB, 273 H, 90 R, 26 HR, 144 RBI, .272 BA (Brother of Elvio Jiménez)

José, Domingo Félix Andújar (**Félix José**) (b. 5-2-1965, Santo Domingo) Debut: 9-2-1988 (1988–1992) Teams: Oakland (A), St. Louis (N) Positions: Outfield, DH (BB TR) Stats: 439 G, 1566 AB, 449 H, 190 R, 33 HR, 210 RBI, .287 BA

Joseph y Harrigan, Ricardo Emelindo (**Rick Joseph**) (b. 8-24-1939, San Pedro de Macoris; d. 9-8-1979, Santiago) Debut: 6-18-1964 (1964, 1967–1970) Teams: Kansas City (A), Philadelphia (N) Positions: First Base, Third Base, Outfield (BR TR) Stats: 270 G, 633 AB, 154 H, 69 R, 13 HR, 65 RBI, .243 BA

Landestoy y Santana, Rafael Silvaldo (**Rafael Landestoy**) (b. 5-28-1953, Bani) Debut: 8-27-1977 (1977–1984) Teams: Los Angeles (N), Houston (N), Cincinnati (N), Los Angeles (N) Position: Infield (BB TR) Stats: 596 G, 1230 AB, 291 H, 134 R, 4 HR, 83 RBI, .237 BA

Lee, Manuel Lora (**Manuel "Manny" Lee**) (b. 6-17-1965, San Pedro de Macoris) Debut: 4-10-1985 (1985–1992) Teams: Toronto (A), Texas (A) Position: Infield (BB TR) Stats: 753 G, 2152 AB, 547 H, 231 R, 16 HR, 199 RBI, .254 BA

Linares (de la Cruz y Linares), Rufino (**Rufino Linares**) (b. 2-28-1951, Ingerio Quiqueya) Debut: 4-10-1981 (1981–1985) Teams: Atlanta (N), California (A) Positions: Outfield, DH (BR TR) Stats: 207 G, 545 AB, 147 H, 66 R, 11 HR, 63 RBI, .270 BA

Liriano y Bonilla, Nelson Arturo (**Nelson Liriano**) (b. 6-3-1964, Santo Domingo) Debut: 8-25-1987 (1987–1991, 1993) Teams: Toronto (A), Minnesota (A), Kansas City (A), Colorado (N) Position: Second Base (BB TR) Stats: 381 G, 1229 AB, 313 H, 167 R, 11 HR, 115 RBI, .255 BA

Llenas y Davilla, Winston Enriquillo (**Winston Llenas**) (b. 9-23-1943, Santiago) Debut: 8-15-1968 (1968–1969, 1972–1975) Team: California (A) Positions: Infield, Outfield, DH (BR TR) Stats: 300 G, 531 AB, 122 H, 50 R. 3 HR, 61 RBI, .230 BA

Lois (Louis y Pie), Alberto Louis (**Alberto Lois**) (b. 5-6-1956, Hato Major) Debut: 9-8-1978 (1978–1979) Team: Pittsburgh (N) Position: Outfield (BR TR) Stats: 14 G, 4 AB, 1 H, 6 R, 0 HR, 0 RBI, .250 BA

Manon y Reyes, Ramón (**Ramón Manon**) (b. 1-20-1968, Santo Domingo) Debut: 4-19-1990 (1990) Team: Texas (A) Position: Pitcher (BR TR) Stats: 0 W, 0 L, 2 IP, 13.50 ERA, 0 SO, 3 BB, 0 SV, 1 G

Manzanillo y Adams, Josias (**Josias Manzanillo**) (b. 10-16-1967, San Pedro de Macoris) Debut: 10-5-1991 (1991) Team: Boston (A) Position: Pitcher (BR TR) Stats: 0 W, 0 L, 1 IP, 18.00 ERA, 1 SO, 3 BB, 0 SV, 1 G (Brother of Ravelo Manzanillo)

Manzanillo y Adams, Ravelo (**Ravelo Manzanillo**) (b. 10-17-1963, San Pedro de Macoris) Debut: 9-25-1988 (1988) Team: Chicago (A) Position: Pitcher (BR TR) Stats: 0 W, 1 L, 9.1 IP, 5.79 ERA, 10 SO, 12 BB, 0 SV, 2 G (Brother of Josias Manzanillo)

Marichal y Sánchez, Juan Antonio (**Juan Marichal**) (b. 10-20-1937, Laguna Verde) Debut: 7-19-1960 (1960–1975) Teams: San Francisco (N), Boston (A), Los Angeles (N) Position: Pitcher (BR TR) Stats: 243 W, 142 L, 3509.1 IP, 2.89 ERA, 2303 SO, 709 BB, 2 SV, 471 G (**Hall of Fame, 1983**)

Martínez, Domingo Emelio (**Domingo Martínez**) (b. 8-4-1967, Santo Domingo) Debut: 9-11-1992 (1992) Team: Toronto (A) Position: First Base (BR TR) Stats: 7 G, 8 AB, 5 H, 2 R, 1 HR, 3 RBI, .625 BA

Martínez (Jaime y Martínez), Pedro (**Pedro Martínez**) (b. 7-25-1971, Manoguayabo) Debut: 9-24-1992 (1992) Team: Los Angeles (N) Position: Pitcher (BR TR) Stats: 0 W, 1 L, 8 IP, 2.25 ERA, 8 SO, 1 BB, 0 SV, 2 G (Brother of Ramón Martínez)

Martínez (Jaime y Martínez), Ramón (**Ramón Martínez**) (b. 3-22-1968, Santo Domingo) Debut: 8-13-1988 (1988–1992) Team: Los Angeles (N) Position: Pitcher (BR TR) Stats: 52 W, 37 L, 739.2 IP, 3.32 ERA, 586 SO, 268 BB, 0 SV, 115 G (Brother of Pedro Martínez)

Martínez y Cabrera, Silvio Ramón (**Silvio Martínez**) (b. 8-19-1955, Santiago) Debut: 4-9-1977 (1977–1981) Teams: Chicago (A), St. Louis (N) Position: Pitcher (BR TR) Stats: 31 W, 32 L, 582.2 IP, 3.88 ERA, 230 SO, 237 BB, 1 SV, 107 G

Martínez y Encarnción, Teodoro Noel (**Teddy Martínez**) (b. 12-10-1947, Central Barahona) Debut: 7-18-1970 (1970–1979) Teams: New York (N), St. Louis (N), Oakland (A), Los Angeles (N) Position: Infield (BR TR) Stats: 657 G, 1480 AB, 355 H, 165 R, 7 HR, 108 RBI, .240 BA

Mata y Abreu, Victor José (**Vic Mata**) (b. 6-17-1961, Santiago) Debut: 7-22-1984 (1984–1985) Team: New York (A) Position: Outfield (BR TR) Stats: 36 G, 77 AB, 24 H, 9 R, 1 HR, 6 RBI, .312 BA

Mejías, Samuel Ellis (**Sam Mejías**) (b. 5-9-1952, Santiago) Debut: 9-6-1976 (1976–1981) Teams: St. Louis (N), Montreal (N), Chicago (N), Cincinnati (N) Position: Outfield (BR TR) Stats: 334 G, 348 AB, 86 H, 51 R, 4 HR, 31 RBI, .247 BA

Mercedes y Pérez, Henry Félipe (**Henry Mercedes**) (b. 7-23-1969, Santo Domingo) Debut: 4-22-1992 (1992) Team: Oakland (A) Position: Catcher (BR TR) Stats: 9 G, 5 AB, 4 H, 1 R, 0 HR, 1 RBI, .800 BA

Mercedes y Santana, Luís Roberto (**Luís Mercedes**) (b. 2-15-1968, San Pedro de Macoris) Debut: 9-8-1991 (1991–1992) Team: Baltimore (A) Positions: Outfield, DH (BR TR) Stats: 42 G, 104 AB, 18 H, 17 R, 0 HR, 6 RBI, .173 BA

Mesa, José Ramón (**José Mesa**) (b. 5-22-1966, Pueblo Viejo) Debut: 9-10-1987 (1987, 1990–1992) Teams: Baltimore (A), Cleveland (A) Position: Pitcher (BR TR) Stats: 17 W, 28 L, 362.1 IP, 5.09 ERA, 167 SO, 174 BB, 0 SV, 64 G

Moreno (Mauricio y Moreno), José de los Santos Mauricio (**José Moreno**) (b. 11-1-1957, Santo Domingo) Debut: 5-24-1980 (1980–1982) Teams: New York (N), San Diego (N), California (A) Positions: Outfield, Infield, DH (BB TR) Stats: 82 G, 97 AB, 20 H, 14 R, 2 HR, 15 RBI, .206 BA

Mota y Gerónimo, Manuel Rafael (**Manny Mota**) (b. 2-18-1938, Santo Domingo) Debut: 4-16-1962 (1962–1982) Teams: San Francisco (N), Pittsburgh (N), Montreal (N), Los Angeles (N) Positions: Outfield, Infield, Pinch Hitter (BR TR) Stats: 1536 G, 3779 AB, 1149 H, 496 R, 31 HR, 438 RBI, .304 BA (Father of Andy Mota and José Mota)

Mota y Matos, Andres Alberto (**Andy Mota**) (b. 3-4-1966, Santo Domingo) Debut: 8-31-1991 (1991) Team: Houston (N) Position: Second Base (BR TR) Stats: 27 G, 90 AB, 17 H, 4 R, 1 HR, 6 RBI, .189 BA (Son of Manny Mota; Brother of José Mota)

Mota y Matos, José Manuel (**José Mota**) (b. 3-16-1965, Santo Domingo) Debut: 5-25-1991 (1991) Team: San Diego (N) Position: Infield (BB TR) Stats: 17 G, 36 AB, 8 H, 4 R, 0 HR, 2 RBI, .222 BA (Son of Manny Mota; Brother of Andy Mota)

Noboa y Díaz, Milciades Arturo (**Junior Noboa**) (b. 11-10-1964, Azua) Debut: 8-22-1984 (1984, 1987–1992) Teams: Cleveland (A), California (A), Montreal (N), New York (N) Positions: Infield, DH (BR TR) Stats: 298 G, 451 AB, 105 H, 44 R, 1 HR, 27 RBI, .233 BA

Norman, Nelson Augusto (**Nelson Norman**) (b. 5-23-1958, San Pedro de Macoris) Debut: 5-20-1978 (1978–1982, 1987) Teams: Texas (A), Pittsburgh (N), Montreal (N) Position: Shortstop (BB TR) Stats: 198 G, 429 AB, 95 H, 42 R, 0 HR, 25 RBI, .221 BA

Núñez y Jiménez, José (**José Núñez**) (b. 1-13-1964, Jarabacoa) Debut: 4-9-1987 (1987–1990) Teams: Toronto (A), Chicago (N) Position: Pitcher (BR TR) Stats: 9 W, 10 L, 197.2 IP, 5.05 ERA, 171 SO, 111 BB, 0 SV, 77 G

Dominican Republic, *cont.*

Offerman y Doño, José Antonio (**José Offerman**) (b. 11-8-1968, San Pedro de Macoris) Debut: 8-19-1990 (1990–1992) Team: Los Angeles (N) Position: Shortstop (BB TR) Stats: 230 G, 705 AB, 170 H, 84 R, 2 HR, 40 RBI, .241 BA

Olivo y Maldonado, Diomedes Antonio (**Diomedes "Guayubín" Olivo**) (b. 1-22-1919, Guayubín; d. 2-15-1977, Santo Domingo) Debut: 9-5-1960 (1960, 1962–1963) Teams: Pittsburgh (N), St. Louis (N) Position: Pitcher (BL TL) Stats: 5 W, 6 L, 107.1 IP, 3.10 ERA, 85 SO, 39 BB, 7 SV, 85 G (Brother of Chi Chi Olivo)

Olivo y Maldonado, Federico Emilio (**Chi Chi Olivo**) (b. 3-18-1928, Guayubin; d. 2-3-1977, Guayubín) Debut: 6-5-1961 (1961, 1964–1966) Teams: Milwaukee (N), Atlanta (N) Position: Pitcher (BR TR) Stats: 7 W, 6 L, 141 IP, 3.96 ERA, 98 SO, 50 BB, 12 SV, 96 G (Brother of Diomedes "Guayubín" Olivo)

Peguero, Julio César (**Julio Peguero**) (b. 9-7-1968, San Isidro) Debut: 4-8-1992 (1992) Team: Philadelphia (N) Position: Outfield (BB TR) Stats: 14 G, 9 AB, 2 H, 3 R, 0 HR, 0 RBI, .222 BA

Peña (Zapata y Peña), Roberto César (**Roberto "Baby" Peña**) (b. 4-17-1937, Santo Domingo; d. 7-23-1982, Santiago) Debut: 4-12-1965 (1965–1971) Teams: Chicago (N), Philadelphia (N), San Diego (N), Oakland (A), Milwaukee (A) Position: Infield (BR TR) Stats: 587 G, 1907 AB, 467 H, 174 R, 13 HR, 154 RBI, .245 BA

Peña y Concepción, Hipólito (**Hipólito Peña**) (b. 1-30-1964, Fantino) Debut: 9-1-1986 (1986–1988) Teams: Pittsburgh (N), New York (A) Position: Pitcher (BL TL) Stats: 1 W, 7 L, 48.1 IP, 4.84 ERA, 32 SO, 38 BB, 2 SV, 42 G

Peña y Martinez, Gerónimo (**Gerónimo Peña**) (b. 3-29-1967, Districto Nacional) Debut: 9-5-1990 (1990–1992) Team: St. Louis (N) Positions: Second Base, Outfield (BB TR) Stats: 184 G, 433 AB, 118 H, 74 R, 12 HR, 50 RBI, .273 BA

Peña y Padilla, Antonio Francisco (**Tony Peña**) (b. 6-4-1957, Monte Cristi) Debut: 9-1-1980 (1980–1992) Teams: Pittsburgh (N), St. Louis (N), Boston (A) Position: Catcher (BR TR) Stats: 1624 G, 5550 AB, 1481 H, 584 R, 95 HR, 614 RBI, .267 BA (Brother of Ramón Peña)

Peña y Padilla, Ramón Arturo (**Ramón Peña**) (b. 5-5-1962, Santiago) Debut: 4-27-1989 (1989) Team: Detroit (A) Position: Pitcher (BR TR) Stats: 0 W, 0 L, 18 IP, 6.00 ERA, 12 SO, 8 BB, 0 SV, 8 G (Brother of Tony Peña)

Peña y Vásquez, Alejandro (**Alejandro Peña**) (b. 6-25-1959, Cambiaso Puerta Plata) Debut: 9-14-1981 (1981–1992) Teams: Los Angeles (N), New York (N), Atlanta (N) Position: Pitcher (BR TR) Stats: 50 W, 48 L, 969.2 IP, 2.95 ERA, 743 SO, 310 BB, 67 SV, 433 G

Pérez (Gross y Pérez), Melido Turpin (**Melido Pérez**) (b. 2-15-1966, San Cristobal) Debut: 9-4-1987 (1987–1992) Teams: Kansas City (A), Chicago (A), New York (A) Position: Pitcher (BR TR) Stats: 58 W, 62 L, 971 IP, 3.90 ERA, 791 SO, 398 BB, 1 SV, 183 G (Brother of Pascual Pérez)

Pérez (Gross y Pérez), Pascual (**Pascual Pérez**) (b. 5-17-1957, San Cristobal) Debut: 5-7-1980 (1980–1991, 1993) Teams: Pittsburgh (N), Atlanta (N), Montreal (N), New York (A) Position: Pitcher (BR TR) Stats: 67 W, 68 L, 1244.1 IP, 3.44 ERA, 822 SO, 344 BB, 0 SV, 207 G (Brother of Melido Pérez)

Pérez, Yorkis Miguel (**Yorkis Pérez**) (b. 9-3-1967, Bajos de Haina) Debut: 9-30-1991 (1991) Team: Chicago (N) Position: Pitcher (BL TL) Stats: 1 W, 0 L, 4.1 IP, 2.08 ERA, 3 SO, 2 BB, 0 SV, 3 G

Pichardo, Hipólito (**Hipólito Pichardo**) (b. 8-22-1969, Jicome Esperanza) Debut: 4-21-1992 (1992) Team: Kansas City (A) Position: Pitcher (BR TR) Stats: 9 W, 6 L, 143.2 IP, 3.95 ERA, 59 SO, 49 BB, 0 SV, 31 G

Polonia y Almonte, Luís Andrew (**Luís Polonia**) (b. 10-12-1964, Santiago) Debut: 4-24-1987 (1987–1992) Teams: Oakland (A), New York (A), California (A) Position: Outfield (BB TL) Stats: 753 G, 2740 AB, 818 H, 426 R, 13 HR, 242 RBI, .299 BA

Pujols y Toribio, Luís Bienvenido (**Luís Pujols**) (b. 11-18-1955, Santiago) Debut: 9-22-1977 (1977–1985) Teams: Houston (N), Kansas City (A), Texas (A) Position: Catcher (BR TR) Stats: 316 G, 850 AB, 164 H, 50 R, 6 HR, 81 RBI, .193 BA

Ramírez y Peguero, Rafael Emilio (**Rafael Ramírez**) (b. 2-18-1958, San Pedro de Macoris) Debut: 8-4-1980 (1980–1992) Teams: Atlanta (N), Houston (N) Position: Shortstop (BR TR) Stats: 1539 G, 5494 AB, 1432 H, 562 R, 53 HR, 484 RBI, .261 BA

Ramos y DeRamos, Domingo Antonio (**Domingo Ramos**) (b. 3-29-1958, Santiago) Debut: 9-8-1978 (1978, 1980–1990) Teams: New York (A), Toronto (A), Seattle (A), Cleveland (A), California (A), Chicago (N) Position: Infield (BR TR) Stats: 507 G, 1086 AB, 261 H, 109 R, 8 HR, 85 RBI, .240 BA

Reyes y Polanco, Gilberto Rolando (**Gilberto Reyes**) (b. 12-10-1963, Santo Domingo) Debut: 6-11-1983 (1983–1985, 1987–1991) Teams: Los Angeles (N), Montreal (N) Position: Catcher (BR TR) Stats: 122 G, 258 AB, 52 H, 13 R, 0 HR, 14 RBI, .202 BA

Ríjo y Abreu, José Antonio (**José Ríjo**) (b. 5-13-1965, San Cristobal) Debut: 4-5-1984 (1984–1992) Teams: New York (A), Oakland (A), Cincinnati (N) Position: Pitcher (BR TR) Stats: 83 W, 68 L, 1287.1 IP, 3.26 ERA, 1096 SO, 498 BB, 3 SV, 256 G

Rivera, Bienvenido Santana (**Ben Rivera**) (b. 1-11-1969, San Pedro de Macoris) Debut: 4-9-1992 (1992) Teams: Atlanta (N), Philadelphia (N) Position: Pitcher (BR TR) Stats: 7 W, 4 L, 117.1 IP, 3.07 ERA, 77 SO, 45 BB, 0 SV, 28 G

Robles y Natera, Rafael Orlando (**Rafael Robles**) (b. 10-20-1947, San Pedro de Macoris) Debut: 4-8-1969 (1969–1970, 1972) Team: San Diego (N) Position: Shortstop (BR TR) Stats: 47 G, 133 AB, 25 H, 7 R, 0 HR, 3 RBI, .188 BA

Rodríguez y Lorenzo, Henry Anderson (**Henry Rodríguez**) (b. 11-8-1967, Santo Domingo) Debut: 7-5-1992 (1992) Team: Los Angeles (N) Positions: Outfield, First Base (BL TL) Stats: 53 G, 146 AB, 32 H, 11 R, 3 HR, 14 RBI, .219 BA

Rodríguez y Martínez, Rubén Dario (**Rubén Rodríguez**) (b. 8-4-1964, Cabrera) Debut: 9-15-1986 (1986, 1988) Team: Pittsburgh (N) Position: Catcher (BR TR) Stats: 4G, 8 AB, 1 H, 1 R, 0 HR, 1 RBI, .125 BA

Rojas y Medrano, Melquiades (**Mel Rojas**) (b. 12-10-1966, Haina) Debut: 8-1-1990 (1990–1992) Team: Montreal (N) Position: Pitcher (BR TR) Stats: 13 W, 5 L, 188.2 IP, 2.48 ERA, 133 SO, 71 BB, 17 SV, 128 G

Román y Sarita, José Rafael (**José Román**) (b. 5-21-1963, Puerto Plata) Debut: 9-5-1984 (1984–1986) Team: Cleveland (A) Position: Pitcher (BR TR) Stats: 1 W, 8 L, 44.1 IP, 8.12 ERA, 24 SO, 42 BB, 0 SV, 14 G

Romero y de los Santos, Ramón (**Ramón Romero**) (b. 1-8-1959, San Pedro de Macoris) Debut: 9-18-1984 (1984–1985) Team: Cleveland (A) Position: Pitcher (BL TL) Stats: 2 W, 3 L, 67.1 IP, 6.28 ERA, 41 SO, 38 BB, 0 SV, 20 G

Rosario y Rivera, Victor Manuel (**Vic Rosario**) (b. 8-28-1966, Hato Major del Rey) Debut: 9-6-1990 (1990) Team: Atlanta (N) Position: Shortstop, Second Base (BR TR) Stats: 9 G, 7 AB, 1 H, 3 R, 0 HR, 0 RBI, .143 BA

Samuel, Amado Ruperto (**Amado Samuel**) (b. 12-6-1938, San Pedro de Macoris) Debut: 4-10-1962 (1962–1964) Teams: Milwaukee (N), New York (N) Position: Infield (BR TR) Stats: 144 G, 368 AB, 79 H, 23 R, 3 HR, 25 RBI, .215 BA

Samuel, Juan Milton (**Juan Samuel**) (b. 12-9-1960, San Pedro de Macoris) Debut: 8-24-1983 (1983–1992) Teams: Philadelphia (N), New York (N), Los Angeles (N), Kansas City (A), Cincinnati (N) Positions: Infield, Outfield (BR TR) Stats: 1310 G, 5146 AB, 1338 H, 718 R, 128 HR, 574 RBI, .260 BA

Sánchez y Pimentel, Alejandro (**Alejandro Sánchez**) (b. 2-14-1959, San Pedro de Macoris) Debut: 9-6-1982 (1982–1987) Teams: Philadelphia (N), San Francisco (N), Detroit (A), Minnesota (A), Oakland (A) Positions: Outfield, DH (BR TR) Stats: 109 G, 214 AB, 49 H, 28 R, 8 HR, 21 RBI, .229 BA

Santana y Belonis, Andres Confesor (**Andres Santana**) (b. 2-5-1968, San Pedro de Macoris) Debut: 9-16-1990 (1990) Team: San Francisco (N) Position: Shortstop (BB TR) Stats: 6 G, 2 AB, 0 H, 0 R, 0 HR, 1 RBI, .000 BA

Santana y de la Cruz, Rafael Francisco (**Rafael Santana**) (b. 1-31-1958, La Romana) Debut: 4-5-1983 (1983–1990) Teams: St. Louis (N), New York (N), New York (A), Cleveland (A) Position: Shortstop (BR TR) Stats: 668 G, 2021 AB, 497 H, 188 R, 13 HR, 156 RBI, .246 BA

Segura y Mota, José Altagracia (**José Segura**) (b. 1-26-1963, Fundación) Debut: 4-10-1988 (1988–1989, 1991) Teams: Chicago (A), San Francisco (N) Position: Pitcher (BR TR) Stats: 0 W, 2 L, 31 IP, 9.00 ERA, 16 SO, 16 BB, 0 SV, 22 G

Silverio y Delmonte, Luís Pascual (**Luís Silverio**) (b. 10-23-1956, Villa González) Debut: 9-9-1978 (1978) Team: Kansas City (A) Positions: Outfield, DH (BR TR) Stats: 8 G, 11 AB, 6 H, 7 R, 0 HR, 3 RBI, .545 BA

Dominican Republic, *cont.*

Silverio y Veloz, Tomás Roberto (**Tom Silverio**) (b. 10-14-1945, Santiago) Debut: 4-30-1970 (1970–1972) Team: California (A) Position: Outfield (BL TL) Stats: 31 G, 30 AB, 3 H, 2 R, 0 HR, 0 RBI, .100 BA

Solano (Mercado y Solano), Julio César (**Julio Solano**) (b. 1-8-1960, Aqua Blanca) Debut: 4-5-1983 (1983–1989) Teams: Houston (N), Seattle (A) Position: Pitcher (BR TR) Stats: 6 W, 8 L, 174 IP, 4.55 ERA, 102 SO, 82 BB, 3 SV, 106 G

Sosa (Ynocencio y Sosa), José (**José Sosa**) (b. 12-28-1952, Santo Domingo) Debut: 7-22-1975 (1975–1976) Team: Houston (N) Position: Pitcher (BR TR) Stats: 1 W, 3 L, 58.2 IP, 4.60 ERA, 36 SO, 29 BB, 1 SV, 34 G

Sosa, Samuel Peralta (**Sammy Sosa**) (b. 11-10-1968, San Pedro de Macoris) Debut: 6-16-1989 (1989–1992) Teams: Texas (A), Chicago (A), Chicago (N) Positions: Outfield, DH (BR TR) Stats: 394 G, 1293 AB, 303 H, 179 R, 37 HR, 141 RBI, .234 BA

Sosa y Martínez, Elias (**Elias Sosa**) (b. 6-10-1950, La Vega) Debut: 9-8-1972 (1972–1983) Teams: San Francisco (N), Atlanta (N), Los Angeles (N), Oakland (A), Montreal (N), Detroit (A), San Diego (N) Position: Pitcher (BR TR) Stats: 59 W, 51 L, 918 IP, 3.32 ERA, 538 SO, 334 BB, 83 SV, 601 G

Soto, Mario Melvin (**Mario Soto**) (b. 7-12-1956, Bani) Debut: 7-21-1977 (1977–1988) Team: Cincinnati (N) Position: Pitcher (BR TR) Stats: 100 W, 92 L, 1730.1 IP, 3.47 ERA, 1449 SO, 657 BB, 4 SV, 297 G

Suero, Williams Urban (**William Suero**) (b. 11-7-1965, Santo Domingo) Debut: 4-9-1992 (1992) Team: Milwaukee (A) Positions: Infield, DH (BR TR) Stats: 18 G, 16 AB, 3 H, 4 R, 0 HR, 0 RBI, .188 BA

Taveras y Betances, Alejandro Antonio (**Alex Taveras**) (b. 10-9-1955, Santiago) Debut: 9-9-1976 (1976, 1982–1983) Teams: Houston (N), Los Angeles (N) Position: Infield (BR TR) Stats: 35 G, 53 AB, 11 H, 4 R, 0 HR, 4 RBI, .208 BA

Taveras y Fabian, Franklin Cristostomo (**Frank Taveras**) (b. 12-24-1949, Las Matas de Santa Cruz) Debut: 9-25-1971 (1971–1982) Teams: Pittsburgh (N), New York (N), Montreal (N) Position: Shortstop (BR TR) Stats: 1150 G, 4043 AB, 1029 H, 503 R, 2 HR, 214 RBI, .255 BA

Tejada y Andújar, Wilfredo Aristides (**Wil Tejada**) (b. 11-12-1962, Santo Domingo) Debut: 9-9-1986 (1986, 1988) Team: Montreal (N) Position: Catcher (BR TR) Stats: 18 G, 40 AB, 10 H, 2 R, 0 HR, 4 RBI, .250 BA

Thomas (Pérez y Thomas), Andres (**Andres Thomas**) (b. 11-10-1963, Boca Chica) Debut: 9-3-1985 (1985–1990) Team: Atlanta (N) Position: Shortstop (BR TR) Stats: 577 G, 2103 AB, 493 H, 182 R, 42 HR, 228 RBI, .234 BA

Torres y Ruíz, Angel Rafael (**Angel Torres**) (b. 10-24-1952, Las Ciengas Azua) Debut: 9-12-1977 (1977) Team: Cincinnati (N) Position: Pitcher (BL TL) Stats: 0 W, 0 L, 8.1 IP, 2.16 ERA, 8 SO, 8 BB, 0 SV, 5 G

Uribe (González y Uribe), José Altagarcia (**José Uribe**) (b. 1-21-1959, San Cristobal) Debut: 9-13-1984 (1984–1992) Teams: St. Louis (N), San Francisco (N), Houston (N) Position: Shortstop (BB TR) Stats: 993 G, 3011 AB, 725 H, 303 R, 19 HR, 216 RBI, .241 BA

Valdez, Efrain Antonio (**Efrain Valdez**) (b. 7-11-1966, Nizao de Bani) Debut: 8-13-1990 (1990–1992) Team: Cleveland (A) Position: Pitcher (BL TL) Stats: 1 W, 1 L, 29.2 IP, 2.73 ERA, 14 SO, 17 BB, 0 SV, 20 G

Valdez (Castillo y Valdez), Julio Julián (**Julio Valdez**) (b. 6-3-1956, San Cristobal) Debut: 9-2-1980 (1980–1983) Team: Boston (A) Positions: Shortstop, Second Base (BB TR) Stats: 65 G, 87 AB, 18 H, 11 R, 1 HR, 8 RBI, .207 BA

Valdez (Sanchez y Valdez), Sergio (**Sergio Valdez**) (b. 9-7-1964, Elias Pina) Debut: 9-10-1986 (1986–1992) Teams: Montreal (N), Atlanta (N), Cleveland (N), Montreal (N) Position: Pitcher (BR TR) Stats: 8 W, 14 L, 219 IP, 4.89 ERA, 155 SO, 83 BB, 0 SV, 87 G

Valdez y Díaz, Rafael Emilio (**Rafael Valdez**) (b. 12-17-1967, Nizao de Bani) Debut: 4-18-1990 (1990) Team: San Diego (N) Position: Pitcher (BR TR) Stats: 0 W, 1 L, 5 IP, 11.12 ERA, 3 SO, 2 BB, 0 SV, 3 G

Vásquez y Santiago, Rafael (**Rafael Vásquez**) (b. 6-28-1958, La Romana) Debut: 4-6-1979 (1979) Team: Seattle (A) Position: Pitcher (BR TR) Stats: 1 W, 0 L, 16 IP, 5.06 ERA, 9 SO, 6 BB, 0 SV, 9 G

Velazquez y Velasquez, Federico Antonio (**Freddie Velazquez**) (b. 12-6-1937, Santo Domingo) Debut: 4-20-1969 (1969, 1973) Teams: Seattle (A), Atlanta (N) Position: Catcher (BR TR) Stats: 21 G, 39 AB, 10 H, 3 R, 0 HR, 5 RBI, .256 BA

Vidal y Nicholas, José (**José "Papito" Vidal**) (b. 4-3-1940, Batey Lechugas) Debut: 9-5-1966 (1966–1969) Teams: Cleveland (A), Seattle (A) Positions: Outfield, First Base (BR TR) Stats: 88 G, 146 AB, 24 H, 20 R, 3 HR, 10 RBI, .164 BA

Virgil y Pichardo, Osvaldo José (**Ossie Virgil**) (b. 5-17-1933, Montecristi) Debut: 9-23-1956 (1956–1969) Teams: New York (N), Detroit (A), Kansas City (A), Baltimore (A), Pittsburgh (N), San Francisco (N) Positions: Infield, Outfield, Catcher (BR TR) Stats: 324 G, 753 AB, 174 H, 75 R, 14 HR, 73 RBI, .231 BA (Father of Ozzie Virgil, listed under Puerto Rico)

Vizcaíno y Pimental, José Luís (**José Viscaíno**) (b. 3-26-1968, San Cristobal) Debut: 9-10-1989 (1989–1992) Teams: Los Angeles (N), Chicago (N) Position: Infield (BB TR) Stats: 233 G, 491 AB, 118 H, 37 R, 1 HR, 29 RBI, .240 BA

Wagner, Héctor Raul Guerrero (**Héctor Wagner**) (b. 11-26-1968, San Juan) Debut: 9-10-1990 (1990) Team: Kansas City (A) Position: Pitcher (BR TR) Stats: 1 W, 3 L, 33.1 IP, 7.83 ERA, 19 SO, 14 BB, 0 SV, 7 G

Puerto Rico

(First Puerto Rican major-leaguer: Hiram Bithorn [April 15, 1942]; 147 players)

Agosto y González, Juan Roberto (**Juan Agosto**) (b. 2-23-1958, Rio Piedras) Debut: 9-7-1981 (1981–1992) Teams: Chicago (A), Minnesota (A), Houston (N), St. Louis (N), Seattle (A) Position: Pitcher (BL TL) Stats: 40 W, 33 L, 620.1 IP, 3.99 ERA, 304 SO, 248 BB, 29 SV, 537 G

Aguayo y Muriel, Luís (**Luís Aguayo**) (b. 3-13-1959, Vega Baja) Debut: 4-19-1980 (1980–1989) Teams: Philadelphia (N), New York (A), Cleveland (A) Position: Infield (BR TR) Stats: 568 G, 1104 AB, 260 H, 142 R, 37 HR, 109 RBI, .236 BA

Alcaraz y Acosta, Angel Luís (**Angel "Luís" Alcaraz**) (b. 6-20-1941, Humacao) Debut: 9-13-1967 (1967–1970) Teams: Los Angeles (N), Kansas City (A) Position: Infield (BR TR) Stats: 115 G, 365 AB, 70 H, 30 R, 4 HR, 29 RBI, .192 BA

Alicea y de Jesús, Luís Rene (**Luís Alicea**) (b. 7-29-1965, Santurce) Debut: 4-23-1988 (1988, 1991–1992) Team: St. Louis (N) Position: Infield (BB TR) Stats: 234 G, 630 AB, 141 H, 51 R, 3 HR, 56 RBI, .224 BA

Alomar y Conde, Santos (**Sandy Alomar, Sr.**) (b. 10-19-1943, Salinas) Debut: 9-15-1964 (1964–1978) Teams: Milwaukee (N), Atlanta (N), New York (N), Chicago (A), California (A), New York (A), Texas (A) Position: Infield (BB TR) Stats: 1481 G, 4760 AB, 1168 H, 558 R, 13 HR, 282 RBI, .245 BA (Father of Sandy Alomar, Jr. and Roberto Alomar)

Alomar y Velazquez, Roberto (**Roberto Alomar**) (b. 2-5-1968, Ponce) Debut: 4-22-1988 (1988–1992) Teams: San Diego (N), Toronto (A) Position: Second Base (BB TR) Stats: 761 G, 2962 AB, 862 H, 439 R, 39 HR, 302 RBI, .291 BA (Brother of Sandy Alomar, Jr.; Son of Sandy Alomar, Sr.)

Alomar y Velazquez, Santos (**Sandy Alomar, Jr.**) (b. 6-18-1966, Salinas) Debut: 9-30-1988 (1988–1992) Teams: San Diego (N), Cleveland (A) Position: Catcher (BR TR) Stats: 280 G, 948 AB, 248 H, 93 R, 12 HR, 105 RBI, .262 BA (Brother of Roberto Alomar; Son of Sandy Alomar, Sr.)

Alvarado y Martínez, Luís César (**Luís Alvarado**) (b. 1-15-1949, La Jas) Debut: 9-13-1968 (1968–1977) Teams: Boston (A), Chicago (A), St. Louis (N), Cleveland (A), New York (N), Detroit (A) Position: Infield (BR TR) Stats: 463 G, 1160 AB, 248 H, 116 R, 5 HR, 84 RBI, .214 BA

Alvarez y Monge, Jesús Manuel Orlando (**Jesús "Orlando" Alvarez**) (b. 2-28-1952, Rio Grande) Debut: 9-1-1973 (1973–1976) Teams: Los Angeles (N), California (A) Positions: Outfield, DH (BR TR) Stats: 25 G, 51 AB, 8 H, 4 R, 2 HR, 8 RBI, .157 BA

Aquino y Colon, Luís Antonio (**Luís Aquino**) (b. 5-19-1964, Santurce) Debut: 8-8-1986 (1986,

Puerto Rico, *cont.*

1988–1992) Teams: Toronto (A), Kansas City (A) Position: Pitcher (BR TR) Stats: 23 W, 20 L, 474.2 IP, 3.60 ERA, 203 SO, 149 BB, 3 SV, 121 G

Arroyo, Luís Enrique (**Luís Arroyo**) (b. 2-18-1927, Penuelas) Debut: 4-20-1955 (1955–1963) Teams: St. Louis (N), Pittsburgh (N), Cincinnati (N), New York (A) Position: Pitcher (BL TL) Stats: 40 W, 32 L, 531.1 IP, 3.93 ERA, 336 SO, 208 BB, 44 SV, 244 G

Aviles y Mirando, Ramón Antonio (**Ramón Aviles**) (b. 1-22-1952, Manati) Debut: 7-10-1977 (1977, 1979–1981) Teams: Boston (A), Philadelphia (N) Position: Infield (BR TR) Stats: 117 G, 190 AB, 51 H, 21 R, 2 HR, 24 RBI, .268 BA

Ayala y Félix, Benigno (**Benny Ayala**) (b. 2-7-1951, Yauco) Debut: 8-27-1974 (1974–1985) Teams: New York (N), St. Louis (N), Baltimore (A), Cleveland (A) Positions: Outfield, DH (BR TR) Stats: 425 G, 865 AB, 217 H, 114 R, 38 HR, 145 RBI, .251 BA

Baerga y Ortiz, Carlos Obed (**Carlos Baerga**) (b. 11-4-1968, Santurce) Debut: 4-14-1990 (1990–1992) Team: Cleveland (A) Position: Infield (BB TR) Stats: 427 G, 1562 AB, 457 H, 218 R, 38 HR, 221 RBI, .293 BA

Beníquez y Torres, Juan José (**Juan Beníquez**) (b. 5-13-1950, San Sebastian) Debut: 9-4-1971 (1971–1988) Teams: Boston (A), Texas (A), New York (A), Seattle (A), California (A), Baltimore (A), Kansas City (A), Toronto (A) Positions: Outfield, Infield, DH (BR TR) Stats: 1500 G, 4651 AB, 1274 H, 610 R, 79 HR, 476 RBI, .274 BA

Bernazard y García, Antonio (**Tony Bernazard**) (b. 8-24-1956, Caguas) Debut: 7-13-1979 (1979–1991) Teams: Montreal (N), Chicago (A), Seattle (A), Cleveland (A), Oakland (A), Detroit (A) Positions: Infield, DH (BB TR) Stats: 1071 G, 3700 AB, 970 H, 523 R, 75 HR, 391 RBI, .262 BA

Bernier y Rodriguez, Carlos (**Carlos Bernier**) (b. 1-28-1929, Juana Díaz; d. 4-6-1989, Juana Díaz) Debut: 4-22-1953 (1953) Team: Pittsburgh (N) Position: Outfield (BR TR) Stats: 105 G, 310 AB, 66 H, 48 R, 3 HR, 31 RBI, .213 BA

Bithorn y Sosa, Hiram Gabriel (**Hiram Bithorn**) (b. 3-18-1916, Santurce; d. 1-1-1952, El Mante, Mexico) Debut: 4-15-1942 (1942–1943, 1946–1947) Teams: Chicago (N), Chicago (A) Position: Pitcher (BR TR) Stats: 34 W, 31 L, 509.2 IP, 3.16 ERA, 185 SO, 171 BB, 5 SV, 105 G

Bones, Ricardo Ricky (**Ricky Bones**) (b. 4-7-1969, Salinas) Debut: 8-11-1991 (1991–1992) Teams: San Diego (N), Milwaukee (A) Position: Pitcher (BR TR) Stats: 13 W, 16 L, 217.1 IP, 4.64 ERA, 96 SO, 66 BB, 0 SV, 42 G

Bonilla y Urania, Juan Guillermo (**Juan Bonilla**) (b. 2-12-1955, Santurce) Debut: 4-9-1981 (1981–1983, 1985–1987) Teams: San Diego (N), New York (A), Baltimore (A), New York (A) Positions: Infield, DH (BR TR) Stats: 429 G, 1462 AB, 375 H, 145 R, 7 HR, 101 RBI, .256 BA

Calderón y Pérez, Iván (**Iván Calderón**) (b. 3-19-1962, Fajardo) Debut: 8-10-1984 (1984–1992) Teams: Seattle (A), Chicago (A), Montreal (N), Boston (A) Positions: Outfield, DH (BR TR) Stats: 842 G, 3073 AB, 851 H, 444 R, 103 HR, 422 RBI, .277 BA

Cepeda y Penne, Orlando Manuel (**Orlando Cepeda**) (b. 9-17-1937, Ponce) Debut: 4-15-1958 (1958–1974) Teams: San Francisco (N), St. Louis (N), Atlanta (N), Oakland (A), Boston (A), Kansas City (A) Positions: First Base, Outfield, DH (BR TR) Stats: 2124 G, 7927 AB, 2351 H, 1131 R, 379 HR, 1365 RBI, .297 BA

Clemente y Walker, Roberto (**Roberto Clemente**) (b. 8-18-1934, Carolina; d. 12-31-1972, San Juan) Debut: 4-17-1955 (1989–1991) Team: Pittsburgh (N) Position: Outfield (BR TR) Stats: 2433 G, 9454 AB, 3000 H, 1416 R, 240 HR, 1305 RBI, .317 BA (**Hall of Fame, 1972**)

Cocanower y Geiser, James Stanley (**Jamie Coconower**) (b. 2-14-1957, San Juan) Debut: 9-7-1983 (1983–1986) Team: Milwaukee (A) Position: Pitcher (BR TR) Stats: 16 W, 25 L, 365.2 IP, 3.99 ERA, 139 SO, 201 BB, 0 SV, 79 G

Concepción y Cardona, Onix Cardona (**Onix Concepción**) (b. 10-5-1957, Dorado) Debut: 8-30-1980 (1980–1985, 1987) Teams: Kansas City (A), Pittsburgh (N) Position: Infield (BR TR) Stats: 390 G, 1041 AB, 249 H, 108 R, 3 HR, 80 RBI, .239 BA

Conde y Ramón, Ramón Luís (**Ramón Conde**) (b. 12-29-1934, Juana Díaz) Debut: 7-17-1962 (1962) Team: Chicago (A) Position: Third Base (BR TR) Stats: 14 G, 16 AB, 0 H, 0 R, 0 HR, 1 RBI, .000 BA

Cora y Amaro, José Manuel (**Joey Cora**) (b. 5-14-1965, Caguas) Debut: 4-6-1987 (1987, 1989–

1992) Teams: San Diego (N), Chicago (A) Position: Second Base (BB TR) Stats: 308 G, 710 AB, 175 H, 104 R, 0 HR, 43 RBI, .246 BA

Cordero, Wilfredo (**Wil Cordero**) (b. 10-3-1971, Mayaguez) Debut: 7-24-1992 (1992) Team: Montreal (N) Position: Infield (BR TR) Stats: 45 G, 126 AB, 38 H, 17 R, 2 HR, 8 RBI, .302 BA

Correa y Andino, Edwin Josue (**Ed Correa**) (b. 4-29-1966, Hato Rey) Debut: 9-18-1985 (1985–1987) Teams: Chicago (A), Texas (A) Position: Pitcher (BR TR) Stats: 16 W, 19 L, 282.2 IP, 5.16 ERA, 260 SO, 189 BB, 0 SV, 52 G

Cruz y Dilan, Cirilo (**Tommy Cruz**) (b. 2-15-1951, Arroyo) Debut: 9-4-1973 (1973, 1977) Teams: St. Louis (N), Chicago (A) Position: Outfield (BL TL) Stats: 7 G, 2 AB, 0 H, 2 R, 0 HR, 0 RBI, .000 BA (Brother of José Cruz and Héctor Cruz)

Cruz y Dilan, Héctor Louis (**Héctor "Heity" Cruz**) (b. 4-3-1953, Arroyo) Debut: 8-11-1973 (1973, 1975–1982) Teams: St. Louis (N), Chicago (N), San Francisco (N), Cincinnati (N), Chicago (N) Positions: Outfield, Third Base (BR TR) Stats: 624 G, 1607 AB, 361 H, 186 R, 39 HR, 200 RBI, .225 BA (Brother of José Cruz and Tommy Cruz)

Cruz y Dilan, José (**José Cruz**) (b. 8-8-1947, Arroyo) Debut: 9-19-1970 (1970–1988) Teams: St. Louis (N), Houston (N), New York (A) Position: Outfield (BL TL) Stats: 2353 G, 7917 AB, 2251 H, 1036 R, 165 HR, 1077 RBI, .284 BA (Brother of Héctor Cruz and Tommy Cruz)

DeJesús y Alvarez, Iván (**Iván DeJesús**) (b. 1-9-1953, Santurce) Debut: 9-13-1974 (1974–1988) Teams: Los Angeles (N), Chicago (N), Philadelphia (N), St. Louis (N), New York (A), San Francisco (N), Detroit (A) Position: Shortstop (BR TR) Stats: 1371 G, 4602 AB, 1167 H, 595 R, 21 HR, 324 RBI, .254 BA

DeLeón y Tricoche, Luís Antonio (**Luís DeLeón**) (b. 8-19-1958, Ponce) Debut: 9-6-1981 (1981–1985, 1987, 1989) Teams: St. Louis (N), San Diego (N), Baltimore (A), Seattle (A) Position: Pitcher (BR TR) Stats: 17 W, 19 L, 334.1 IP, 3.12 ERA, 248 SO, 77 BB, 32 SV, 207 G

Delgado y Robles, Luís Felipe (**Luís "Puchy" Delgado**) (b. 2-2-1954, Hatillo) Debut: 9-6-1977 (1977) Team: Seattle (A) Position: Outfield (BB TL) Stats: 13 G, 22 AB, 4 H, 4 R, 0 HR, 2 RBI, .182 BA

Díaz y Serrano, Edgar (**Edgar Díaz**) (b. 2-8-1964, Santurce) Debut: 9-16-1986 (1986, 1989) Team: Milwaukee (A) Positions: Infield, DH (BR TR) Stats: 91 G, 231 AB, 62 H, 27 R, 0 HR, 14 RBI, .268 BA

Díaz y Torres, Mario Rafael (**Mario Díaz**) (b. 1-10-1962, Humacao) Debut: 9-12-1987 (1987–1992) Teams: Seattle (A), New York (N), Texas (A) Position: Infield (BR TR) Stats: 222 G, 404 AB, 97 H, 45 R, 2 HR, 43 RBI, .240 BA

Escalera, Saturnino Cuadrado (**Nino Escalera**) (b. 12-1-1929, Santurce) Debut: 4-17-1954 (1954) Team: Cincinnati (N) Position: Outfield (BL TR) Stats: 73 G, 69 AB, 11 H, 15 R, 0 HR, 3 RBI, .159 BA

Ferrer y Marrero, Sergio (**Sergio Ferrer**) (b. 1-29-1951, Santurce) Debut: 4-5-1974 (1974–1975, 1978–1979) Teams: Minnesota (A), New York (N) Position: Infield (BB TR) Stats: 125 G, 178 AB, 43 H, 41 R, 0 HR, 3 RBI, .242 BA

Figueroa y Padilla, Eduardo (**Ed Figueroa**) (b. 10-14-1948, Ciales) Debut: 4-9-1974 (1974–1981) Teams: California (A), New York (A), Texas (A), Oakland (A) Position: Pitcher (BR TR) Stats: 80 W, 67 L, 1309.2 IP, 3.51 ERA, 571 SO, 443 BB, 1 SV, 200 G

Flores y Garcia, Gilberto (**Gil Flores**) (b. 10-27-1952, Ponce) Debut: 5-8-1977 (1977–1979) Teams: California (A), New York (N) Positions: Outfield, DH (BR TR) Stats: 185 G, 464 AB, 121 H, 58 R, 2 HR, 37 RBI, .261 BA

Fuentes y Pinet, Miguel (**Miguel Fuentes**) (b. 5-10-1946, Loiza) Debut: 9-1-1969 (1969) Team: Seattle (A) Position: Pitcher (BR TR) Stats: 1 W, 3 L, 26 IP, 5.18 ERA, 14 SO, 16 BB, 0 SV, 8 G

García y Delfi, Pedro Modesto (**Pedro García**) (b. 4-17-1950, Guayama) Debut: 4-6-1973 (1973–1977) Teams: Milwaukee (A), Detroit (A), Toronto (A) Positions: Second Base, DH (BR TR) Stats: 558 G, 1797 AB, 395 H, 196 R, 37 HR, 184 RBI, .220 BA

Gómez y Colon, Rubén (**Rubén Gómez**) (b. 7-13-1927, Arroyo) Debut: 4-17-1953 (1953–1962, 1967) Teams: New York (N), San Francisco (N), Philadelphia (N), Cleveland (A), Minnesota (A), Philadelphia (N) Position: Pitcher (BR TR) Stats: 76 W, 86 L, 1454 IP, 4.09 ERA, 677 SO, 574 BB, 5 SV, 289 G

Puerto Rico, *cont.*

Gómez y Velez, Leonardo (**Leo Gómez**) (b. 3-2-1966, Canovanas) Debut: 9-17-1990 (1990–1992) Team: Baltimore (A) Positions: Third Base, DH (BR TR) Stats: 267 G, 898 AB, 224 H, 105 R, 33 HR, 110 RBI, .249 BA

González y Hernández, Julio César (**Julio González**) (b. 12-25-1952, Caguas) Debut: 4-8-1977 (1977–1983) Teams: Houston (N), St. Louis (N), Detroit (A) Position: Infield (BR TR) Stats: 370 G, 969 AB, 228 H, 90 R, 4 HR, 66 RBI, .235 BA

González y Quinones, José Fernando (**Fernando "José" González**) (b. 6-19-1950, Arecibo) Debut: 9-15-1972 (1972–1974, 1977–1979) Teams: Pittsburgh (N), Kansas City (A), New York (A), Pittsburgh (N), San Diego (N) Position: Infield (BR TR) Stats: 404 G, 1038 AB, 244 H, 85 R, 17 HR, 104 RBI, .235 BA

González y Vázquez, Juan Alberto (**Juan González**) (b. 10-20-1969, Arecibo) Debut: 9-1-1989 (1989–1992) Team: Texas (A) Positions: Outfield, DH (BR TR) Stats: 346 G, 1279 AB, 331 H, 172 R, 75 HR, 230 RBI, .259 BA

Gotay y Sánchez, Julio Enrique (**Julio Gotay**) (b. 6-9-1939, Fajardo) Debut: 8-6-1960 (1960–1969) Teams: St. Louis (N), Pittsburgh (N), California (A), Houston (N) Position: Infield (BR TR) Stats: 389 G, 988 AB, 257 H, 106 R, 6 HR, 70 RBI, .260 BA

Guzmán y Mirabel, José Alberto (**José Guzmán**) (b. 4-9-1963, Santa Isabel) Debut: 9-10-1985 (1985–1992) Teams: Texas (A), Chicago (N) Position: Pitcher (BR TR) Stats: 66 W, 62 L, 1013.2 IP, 3.90 ERA, 715 SO, 395 BB, 0 SV, 159 G

Hernaiz y Rodríguez, Jesús Rafael (**Jesús Hernaiz**) (b. 1-8-1945, Santurce) Debut: 6-14-1974 (1974) Team: Philadelphia (N) Position: Pitcher (BR TR) Stats: 2 W, 3 L, 41.1 IP, 5.88 ERA, 16 SO, 25 BB, 1 SV, 27 G

Hernández y Figueroa, José Antonio (**José Hernández**) (b. 7-14-1969, Rio Piedras) Debut: 8-9-1991 (1991–1992) Teams: Texas (A), Cleveland (A) Positions: Shortstop, Third Base (BR TR) Stats: 48 G, 102 AB, 18 H, 8 R, 0 HR, 4 RBI, .176 BA

Hernández y González, Ramón (**Ramón Hernández**) (b. 8-31-1940, Carolina) Debut: 4-11-1967 (1967–1968, 1971–1977) Teams: Atlanta (N), Chicago (N), Pittsburgh (N), Chicago (N), Boston (A) Position: Pitcher (BB TL) Stats: 23 W, 15 L, 430.1 IP, 3.03 ERA, 255 SO, 135 BB, 46 SV, 337 G

Hernández y González, Roberto Manuel (**Roberto Hernández**) (b. 11-11-1964, Santurce) Debut: 9-2-1991 (1991–1992) Team: Chicago (A) Position: Pitcher (BR TR) Stats: 8 W, 3 L, 86 IP, 2.72 ERA, 74 SO, 27 BB, 12 SV, 52 G

Hernández y Villanueva, Guillermo (**Guillermo "Willie" Hernández**) (b. 11-14-1954, Aguada) Debut: 4-9-1977 (1977–1989) Teams: Chicago (N), Philadelphia (N), Detroit (A) Position: Pitcher (BL TL) Stats: 70 W, 63 L, 1044.2 IP, 3.38 ERA, 788 SO, 349 BB, 147 SV, 744 G

Isales Y Pizarro, Orlando (**Orlando Isales**) (b. 12-22-1959, Santurce) Debut: 9-11-1980 (1980) Team: Philadelphia (N) Position: Outfield (BR TR) Stats: 3 G, 5 AB, 2 H, 1 R, 0 HR, 3 RBI, .400 BA

Laboy, José Alberto (**Coco Laboy**) (b. 7-3-1939, Ponce) Debut: 4-8-1969 (1969–1973) Team: Montreal (N) Position: Infield (BR TR) Stats: 420 G, 1247 AB, 291 H, 108 R, 28 HR, 166 RBI, .233 BA

Lezcano y Curras, Sixto Joaquín (**Sixto Lezcano**) (b. 11-28-1953, Arecibo) Debut: 9-10-1974 (1974–1985) Teams: Milwaukee (A), St. Louis (N), San Diego (N), Philadelphia (N), Pittsburgh (N) Position: Outfield (BR TR) Stats: 1291 G, 4134 AB, 1122 H, 560 R, 148 HR, 591 RBI, .271 BA (Brother of Carlos Lezcano)

Lezcano y Rubio, Carlos Manuel (**Carlos Lezcano**) (b. 9-30-1955, Arecibo) Debut: 4-10-1980 (1980–1981) Team: Chicago (N) Position: Outfield (BR TR) Stats: 49 G, 102 AB, 19 H, 16 R, 3 HR, 14 RBI, .186 BA (Brother of Sixto Lezcano)

Librán y Rosas, Francisco (**Francisco "Frankie" Librán**) (b. 5-6-1948, Mayaguez) Debut: 9-3-1969 (1969) Team: San Diego (N) Position: Shortstop (BR TR) Stats: 10 G, 10 AB, 1 H, 1 R, 0 HR, 1 RBI, .100 BA

Lind y Salgado, José (**José Lind**) (b. 5-1-1964, Toabaja) Debut: 8-28-1987 (1987–1992) Teams: Pittsburgh (N), Kansas City (A) Position: Second Base (BR TR) Stats: 779 G, 2816 AB, 717 H, 292 R, 8 HR, 249 RBI, .255 BA

López, Javier Torres (**Javier "Javy" López**) (b. 11-5-1970, Ponce) Debut: 9-18-1992 (1992) Team:

Atlanta (N) Position: Catcher (BR TR) Stats: 9 G, 16 AB, 6 H, 3 R, 0 HR, 2 RBI, .375 BA

López y Rodríguez, Arturo (**Arturo "Art" López**) (b. 6-8-1937, Mayaguez) Debut: 4-12-1965 (1965) Team: New York (A) Position: Outfield (BL TL) Stats: 38 G, 49 AB, 7 H, 5 R, 0 HR, 0 RBI, .143 BA

Maldonado y Guadarrama, Candido (**Candy Maldonado**) (b. 9-5-1960, Humacao) Debut: 9-7-1981 (1981–1992) Teams: Los Angeles (N), San Francisco (N), Cleveland (A), Milwaukee (A), Toronto (A), Chicago (N) Positions: Outfield, DH (BR TR) Stats: 1196 G, 3603 AB, 928 H, 437 R, 124 HR, 541 RBI, .258 BA

Mangual y Guilbe, Angel Luís (**Angel Mangual**) (b. 3-19-1947, Juana Díaz) Debut: 9-15-1969 (1969, 1971–1976) Teams: Pittsburgh (N), Oakland (A) Position: Outfield (BR TR) Stats: 450 G, 1241 AB, 304 H, 122 R, 22 HR, 125 RBI, .245 BA (Brother of Pepe Mangual)

Mangual y Guilbe, José Manual (**Pepe Mangual**) (b. 5-23-1952, Ponce) Debut: 9-6-1972 (1972–1977) Teams: Montreal (N), New York (N) Position: Outfield (BR TR) Stats: 319 G, 972 AB, 235 H, 155 R, 16 HR, 83 RBI, .242 BA (Brother of Angel Mangual)

Mantilla y Lamela, Félix (**Félix Mantilla**) (b. 7-29-1934, Isabela) Debut: 6-21-1956 (1956–1966) Teams: Milwaukee (N), Boston (A), Houston (N) Positions: Infield, Outfield (BR TR) Stats: 969 G, 2707 AB, 707 H, 360 R, 89 HR, 330 RBI, .261 BA

Márquez y Sánchez, Luís Angel (**Luís Márquez**) (b. 10-28-1925, Aguadilla; d. 3-1-1988, Aguadilla) Debut: 4-18-1951 (1951, 1954) Teams: Boston (N), Chicago (N), Pittsburgh (N) Position: Outfield (BR TR) Stats: 99 G, 143 AB, 26 H, 24 R, 0 HR, 11 RBI, .182 BA

Martínez y Salgado, Carmelo (**Carmelo Martínez**) (b. 7-28-1960, Dorado) Debut: 8-22-1983 (1983–1991) Teams: Chicago (N), San Diego (N), Philadelphia (N), Pittsburgh (N), Kansas City (A), Cincinnati (N) Position: Outfield (BR TR) Stats: 1003 G, 2906 AB, 713 H, 350 R, 108 HR, 424 RBI, .245 BA

Melendez y García, José Luís (**José Melendez**) (b. 9-2-1965, Naguabo) Debut: 9-11-1990 (1990–1992) Teams: Seattle (A), San Diego (N) Position: Pitcher (BR TR) Stats: 14 W, 12 L, 188.1 IP, 3.35 ERA, 149 SO, 47 BB, 3 SV, 90 G

Melendez y Santana, Luís Antonio (**Luís Melendez**) (b. 8-11-1949, Albonito) Debut: 9-7-1970 (1970–1977) Teams: St. Louis (N), San Diego (N) Position: Outfield (BR TR) Stats: 641 G, 1477 AB, 366 H, 167 R, 9 HR, 122 RBI, .248 BA

Melendez y Villegas, Francisco Javier (**Francisco Melendez**) (b. 1-25-1964, Rio Piedras) Debut: 8-26-1984 (1984, 1986–1989) Teams: Philadelphia (N), San Francisco (N), Baltimore (A) Positions: First Base, Outfield, Shortstop (BL TL) Stats: 74 G, 84 AB, 18 H, 4 R, 1 HR, 9 RBI, .214 BA

Mercado y Rodríguez, Orlando (**Orlando Mercado**) (b. 11-7-1961, Arecibo) Debut: 9-13-1982 (1982–1984, 1986–1990) Teams: Seattle (A), Texas (A), Detroit (A), Los Angeles (N), Oakland (A), Minnesota (A), New York (N), Montreal (N) Position: Catcher (BR TR) Stats: 253 G, 562 AB, 112 H, 40 R, 7 HR, 45 RBI, .199 BA

Merced y Villanueva, Orlando Luís (**Orlando Merced**) (b. 11-2-1966, Hato Rey) Debut: 6-27-1990 (1990–1992) Team: Pittsburgh (N) Positions: First Base, Outfield (BB TR) Stats: 279 G, 840 AB, 218 H, 136 R, 16 HR, 110 RBI, .260 BA

Millán y Martínez, Félix Bernardo (**Félix Millán**) (b. 8-21-1943, Yabucoa) Debut: 6-2-1966 (1966–1977) Teams: Atlanta (N), New York (N) Position: Second Base (BR TR) Stats: 1480 G, 5791 AB, 1617 H, 699 R, 22 HR, 403 RBI, .279 BA

Montalvo y Torres, Rafael Edgardo (**Rafael Montalvo**) (b. 3-31-1964, Rio Piedras) Debut: 4-13-1986 (1986) Team: Houston (N) Position: Pitcher (BR TR) Stats: 0 W, 0 L, 1 IP, 9.00 ERA, 0 SO, 2 BB, 0 SV, 1 G

Montañez y Naranjo, Guillermo (**Willie Montañez**) (b. 4-1-1948, Catano) Debut: 4-12-1966 (1966, 1970–1982) Teams: California (A), Philadelphia (N), San Francisco (N), Atlanta (N), New York (N), Texas (A), San Diego (N), Montreal (N), Pittsburgh (N), Philadelphia (N) Positions: First Base, Outfield (BL TL) Stats: 1632 G, 5843 AB, 1604 H, 645 R, 139 HR, 802 RBI, .275 BA

Morales y Torres, Julio Rubén (**Jerry Morales**) (b. 2-18-1949, Yabucao) Debut: 9-5-1969 (1969–1983) Teams: San Diego (N), Chicago (N), St. Louis (N), Detroit (A), New York (N), Chicago (N) Position: Outfield (BR TR) Stats: 1441 G, 4528 AB, 1173 H, 516 R, 95 HR, 570 RBI, .259 BA

Moret y Torres, Rogelio (**Rogelio Moret**) (b. 9-16-1949, Guayama) Debut: 9-13-1970 (1970–

Puerto Rico, *cont.*

1978) Teams: Boston (A), Atlanta (N), Texas (A) Position: Pitcher (BB TL) Stats: 47 W, 27 L, 723.1 IP, 3.66 ERA, 408 SO, 339 BB, 12 SV, 168 G

Múñiz y Rodríguez, Manuel (**Manny Múñiz**) (b. 12-31-1947, Caguas) Debut: 9-3-1971 (1971) Team: Philadelphia (N) Position: Pitcher (BR TR) Stats: 0 W, 1 L, 10.1 IP, 6.97 ERA, 6 SO, 8 BB, 0 SV, 5 G

Múñoz y González, Pedro Javier (**Pedro Múñoz**) (b. 9-19-1968, Ponce) Debut: 9-1-1990 (1990–1992) Team: Minnesota (A) Positions: Outfield, DH (BR TR) Stats: 200 G, 641 AB, 175 H, 72 R, 19 HR, 102 RBI, .273 BA

Navarro y Cintrón, Jamie (**Jamie Navarro**) (b. 3-27-1967, Bayamón) Debut: 6-20-1989 (1989–1992) Team: Milwaukee (A) Position: Pitcher (BR TR) Stats: 47 W, 38 L, 739 IP, 3.71 ERA, 345 SO, 210 BB, 1 SV, 119 G (Son of Julio Navarro)

Navarro y Ventura, Julio (**Julio Navarro**) (b. 1-9-1936, Vieques) Debut: 9-3-1962 (1962–1966, 1970) Teams: Los Angeles (A), Detroit (A), Atlanta (N) Position: Pitcher (BR TR) Stats: 7 W, 9 L, 212.1 IP, 3.65 ERA, 151 SO, 70 BB, 17 SV, 130 G (Father of Jaime Navarro)

Nieves, Melvin Ramos (**Mel Nieves**) (b. 12-28-1971, San Juan) Debut: 9-1-1992 (1992) Team: Atlanta (N) Position: Outfield (BR TR) Stats: 12 G, 19 AB, 4 H, 0 R, 0 HR, 1 RBI, .211 BA

Nieves y Cruz, Juan Manuel (**Juan Nieves**) (b. 1-5-1965, Las Lomas) Debut: 4-10-1986 (1986–1988) Team: Milwaukee (A) Position: Pitcher (BL TL) Stats: 32 W, 25 L, 490.2 IP, 4.71 ERA, 352 SO, 227 BB, 1 SV, 94 G

Novoa, Rafael Angel (**Rafael Novoa**) (b. 10-26-1967, New York, USA) Debut: 7-31-1990 (1990) Teams: San Francisco (N) Position: Pitcher (BL TL) Stats: 0 W, 1 L, 18.2 IP, 6.75 ERA, 14 SO, 13 BB, 1 SV, 7 G (Raised in Puerto Rico)

Núñez y Martínez, Edwin (**Edwin Núñez**) (b. 5-27-1963, Humacao) Debut: 4-7-1982 (1982–1992) Teams: Seattle (A), New York (N), Detroit (A), Milwaukee (A), Texas (A) Position: Pitcher (BR TR) Stats: 25 W, 30 L, 561.2 IP, 4.04 ERA, 435 SO, 241 BB, 53 SV, 356 G

Olivares y Balzac, Edward (**Ed Olivares**) (b. 11-5-1938, Mayaguez) Debut: 9-16-1960 (1960–1961) Team: St. Louis (N) Positions: Third Base, Outfield (BR TR) Stats: 24 G, 35 AB, 5 H, 2 R, 0 HR, 1 RBI, .143 BA (Father of Omar Olivares)

Oliveras y Noa, Francisco Javier (**Francisco Oliveras**) (b. 1-31-1963, Santurce) Debut: 5-3-1989 (1989–1992) Teams: Minnesota (A), San Francisco (N) Position: Pitcher (BR TR) Stats: 11 W, 15 L, 235 IP, 3.71 ERA, 130 SO, 68 BB, 5 SV, 116 G

Oliveras y Palqu, Omar (**Omar Olivares**) (b. 7-6-1967, Mayaguez) Debut: 8-18-1990 (1990–1992) Team: St. Louis (N) Position: Pitcher (BR TR) Stats: 21 W, 17 L, 413.2 IP, 3.68 ERA, 235 SO, 141 BB, 1 SV, 69 G (Son of Ed Olivares)

Olmo (Rodríguez y Olmo), Luís Francisco (**Luís Olmo**) (b. 8-11-1919, Arecibo) Debut: 7-23-1943 (1943–1945, 1949–1951) Teams: Brooklyn (N), Boston (N) Positions: Outfield, Infield (BR TR) Stats: 462 G, 1629 AB, 458 H, 208 R, 29 HR, 272 RBI, .281 BA

Oquendo y Contreras, José Manuel (**José Oquendo**) (b. 7-4-1963, Rio Piedras) Debut: 5-2-1983 (1983–1992) Teams: New York (N), St. Louis (N) Positions: Infield, Outfield (BB TR) Stats: 1001 G, 2780 AB, 726 H, 288 R, 12 HR, 224 RBI, .261 BA

Ortiz y Colon, Adalberto (**Junior Ortiz**) (b. 10-24-1959, Humacao) Debut: 9-20-1982 (1982–1992) Teams: Pittsburgh (N), New York (N), Pittsburgh (N), Minnesota (A), Cleveland (A) Position: Catcher (BR TR) Stats: 625 G, 1569 AB, 408 H, 120 R, 5 HR, 157 RBI, .260 BA

Ortiz y Irizarry, José Luís (**José Ortiz**) (b. 6-25-1947, Ponce) Debut: 9-4-1969 (1969–1971) Teams: Chicago (A), Chicago (N) Positions: Outfield, Infield (BR TR) Stats: 67 G, 123 AB, 37 H, 14 R, 0 HR, 6 RBI, .301 BA

Pagán y Rodríguez, José Antonio (**José Pagán**) (b. 5-5-1935, Barceloneta) Debut: 8-4-1959 (1959–1973) Teams: San Francisco (N), Pittsburgh (N), Philadelphia (N) Positions: Infield, Outfield (BR TR) Stats: 1326 G, 3689 AB, 922 H, 387 R, 52 HR, 372 RBI, .250 BA

Parrilla, Samuel (**Samuel Parrilla**) (b. 6-12-1943, Santurce) Debut: 4-11-1970 (1970) Team: Philadelphia (N) Position: Outfield (BR TR) Stats: 11 G, 16 AB, 2 H, 0 R, 0 HR, 0 RBI, .125 BA

Peña y Rivera, Adalberto (**Bert Peña**) (b. 7-11-1959, Santurce) Debut: 9-14-1981 (1981, 1983–1987) Team: Houston (N) Position: Infield (BR TR) Stats: 88 G, 153 AB, 31 H, 18 R, 1 HR, 10 RBI, .203 BA

Peraza y Ríos, Luís (**Luís Peraza**) (b. 6-7-1942, Rio Piedras) Debut: 4-9-1969 (1969) Team:

Philadelphia (N) Position: Pitcher (BR TR) Stats: 0 W, 0 L, 9 IP, 6.00 ERA, 7 SO, 2 BB, 0 SV, 8 G

Pérez y Ortega, Michael Irvin (**Mike Pérez**) (b. 10-19-1964, Yauco) Debut: 9-5-1990 (1990–1992) Team: St. Louis (N) Position: Pitcher (BR TR) Stats: 10 W, 5 L, 123.2 IP, 2.62 ERA, 58 SO, 42 BB, 1 SV, 104 G

Pizarro y Cordova, Juan Ramón (**Juan Pizarro**) (b. 2-7-1937, Santurce) Debut: 5-4-1957 (1957–1974) Teams: Milwaukee (N), Chicago (A), Pittsburgh (N), Boston (A), Cleveland (A), Oakland (A), Chicago (N), Houston (N), Pittsburgh (N) Position: Pitcher (BL TL) Stats: 131 W, 105 L, 2034.1 IP, 3.43 ERA, 1522 SO, 888 BB, 28 SV, 488 G

Ponce y Díaz, Carlos Antonio (**Carlos Ponce**) (b. 2-7-1959, Río Piedras) Debut: 8-14-1985 (1985) Team: Milwaukee (N) Positions: Outfield, DH, Pinch Hitter (BR TR) Stats: 21 G, 62 AB, 10 H, 4 R, 1 HR, 5 RBI, .161 BA

Power (Pellot y Power), Victor Pellot (**Vic Power**) (b. 11-1-1931, Arecibo) Debut: 4-13-1954 (1954–1965) Teams: Philadelphia (A), Kansas City (A), Cleveland (A), Minnesota (A), Los Angeles (A), Philadelphia (N), California (A) Positions: First Base, Infield (BR TR) Stats: 1627 G, 6046 AB, 1716 H, 765 R, 126 HR, 658 RBI, .284 BA

Quinones y Santiago, Rey Francisco (**Rey Quinones**) (b. 11-11-1963, Río Piedras) Debut: 5-17-1986 (1986–1989) Teams: Boston (A), Seattle (A), Pittsburgh (N) Position: Shortstop (BR TR) Stats: 451 G, 1533 AB, 373 H, 173 R, 29 HR, 159 RBI, .243 BA

Quinones y Torruellas, Luís Raul (**Luís Quinones**) (b. 4-28-1962, Ponce) Debut: 5-27-1983 (1983, 1986–1992) Teams: Oakland (A), San Francisco (N), Chicago (N), Cincinnati (N), Minnesota (A) Position: Infield (BB TR) Stats: 442 G, 1003 AB, 227 H, 102 R, 19 HR, 106 RBI, .226 BA

Quintana y Santos, Luís Joaquín (**Luís Quintana**) (b. 12-25-1951, Vega Baja) Debut: 7-9-1974 (1974–1975) Team: California (A) Position: Pitcher (BL TL) Stats: 2 W, 3 L, 19.2 IP, 5.03 ERA, 16 SO, 20 BB, 0 SV, 22 G

Ramírez y Barboza, Milton (**Milton Ramírez**) (b. 4-2-1950, Mayaguez) Debut: 4-11-1970 (1970–1971, 1979) Teams: St. Louis (N), Oakland (A) Position: Infield (BR TR) Stats: 94 G, 152 AB, 28 H, 14 R, 0 HR, 6 RBI, .184 BA

Ramírez y Torres, Mario (**Mario Ramírez**) (b. 9-12-1957, Yauco) Debut: 4-25-1980 (1980–1985) Teams: New York (N), San Diego (N) Position: Infield (BR TR) Stats: 184 G, 286 AB, 55 H, 33 R, 4 HR, 28 RBI, .192 BA

Ríos (Velez y Ríos), Juan Onofre (**Juan Ríos**) (b. 6-14-1942, Mayaguez) Debut: 4-9-1969 (1969) Team: Kansas City (A) Position: Infield (BR TR) Stats: 87 G, 196 AB, 44 H, 20 R, 1 HR, 5 RBI, .224 BA

Rivera y Díaz, Germán (**Germán Rivera**) (b. 7-6-1960, Santurce) Debut: 9-2-1983 (1983–1985) Teams: Los Angeles (N), Houston (N) Position: Third Base (BR TR) Stats: 120 G, 280 AB, 72 H, 24 R, 2 HR, 19 RBI, .257 BA

Rivera y Pedraza, Luís Antonio (**Luís Rivera**) (b. 1-3-1964, Cidra) Debut: 8-3-1986 (1986–1992) Teams: Montreal (N), Boston (A) Position: Shortstop (BR TR) Stats: 638 G, 1940 AB, 452 H, 209 R, 24 HR, 187 RBI, .233 BA

Rivera y Torres, Jesús Manuel (**Jesús "Bombo" Rivera**) (b. 8-2-1952, Ponce) Debut: 4-17-1975 (1975–1976, 1978–1980, 1982) Teams: Montreal (N), Minnesota (A), Kansas City (A) Positions: Outfield, DH (BR TR) Stats: 335 G, 831 AB, 220 H, 109 R, 10 HR, 83 RBI, .265 BA

Rodríguez y Delgado, Eliseo (**Ellie Rodríguez**) (b. 5-24-1946, Fajardo) Debut: 5-26-1968 (1968–1976) Teams: New York (A), Kansas City (A), Milwaukee (A), California (A), Los Angeles (N) Positions: Catcher, DH (BR TR) Stats: 775 G, 2173 AB, 533 H, 220 R, 16 HR, 203 RBI, .245 BA

Rodríguez y Morales, Edwin (**Edwin Rodríguez**) (b. 8-14-1960, Ponce) Debut: 9-28-1982 (1982–1983, 1985) Teams: New York (A), San Diego (N) Position: Infield (BR TR) Stats: 11 G, 22 AB, 5 H, 3 R, 0 HR, 1 RBI, .227 BA

Rodríguez y Reyes, Eduardo (**Eduardo Rodríguez**) (b. 3-6-1952, Barceloneta) Debut: 6-20-1973 (1973–1979) Teams: Milwaukee (A), Kansas City (A) Position: Pitcher (BR TR) Stats: 42 W, 36 L, 734 IP, 3.89 ERA, 430 SO, 323 BB, 32 SV, 264 G

Rodríguez y Torres, Iván (**Iván "Pudge" Rodríguez**) (b. 11-27-1971, Manati) Debut: 6-20-1991 (1991–1992) Team: Texas (A) Position: Catcher (BR TR) Stats: 211 G, 700 AB, 183 H, 63 R, 11 HR, 64 RBI, .261 BA

Puerto Rico, *cont.*

Romero y Rivera, Edgardo Ralph (**Ed Romero**) (b. 12-9-1957, Santurce) Debut: 7-16-1977 (1977, 1980–1990) Teams: Milwaukee (A), Boston (A), Atlanta (N), Milwaukee (A), Detroit (A) Positions: Infield, Outfield, DH (BR TR) Stats: 730 G, 1912 AB, 473 H, 218 R, 8 HR, 155 RBI, .247 BA

Roque y Vargas, Jorge (**Jorge Roque**) (b. 4-28-1950, Ponce) Debut: 9-4-1970 (1970–1973) Teams: St. Louis (N), Montreal (N) Position: Outfield (BR TR) Stats: 65 G, 139 AB, 19 H, 14 R, 2 HR, 12 RBI, .137 BA

Rosado y Robles, Luís (**Luís Rosado**) (b. 12-6-1955, Santurce) Debut: 9-8-1977 (1977, 1980) Team: New York (N) Positions: First Base, Catcher (BR TR) Stats: 11 G, 28 AB, 5 H, 1 R, 0 HR, 3 RBI, .179 BA

Rosario, Santiago (**Santiago Rosario**) (b. 7-25-1939, Guayanilla) Debut: 6-23-1965 (1965) Team: Kansas City (A) Position: Outfield (BL TL) Stats: 81 G, 85 AB, 20 H, 8 R, 2 HR, 8 RBI, .235 BA

Rosario y Ferrer, Angel Ramón (**Jimmy Rosario**) (b. 5-5-1945, Bayamón) Debut: 4-8-1971 (1971–1972, 1976) Teams: San Francisco (N), Milwaukee (A) Positions: Outfield, DH (BB TR) Stats: 114 G, 231 AB, 50 H, 31 R, 1 HR, 18 RBI, .216 BA

Rosello y Rodríguez, David (**David Rosello**) (b. 6-26-1950, Mayaguez) Debut: 9-10-1972 (1972–1981) Teams: Chicago (N), Cleveland (A) Positions: Infield, DH (BR TR) Stats: 422 G, 873 AB, 206 H, 114 R, 10 HR, 76 RBI, .236 BA

Rossy y Ramos, Elam José (**Rico Rossy**) (b. 2-16-1964, San Juan) Debut: 9-11-1991 (1991–1992) Teams: Atlanta (N), Kansas City (A) Position: Infield (BR TR) Stats: 64 G, 150 AB, 32 H, 21 R, 1 HR, 12 RBI, .213 BA

Ruiz y Cruz, Manuel (**Chico Ruiz**) (b. 11-1-1951, Santurce) Debut: 7-29-1978 (1978, 1980) Team: Atlanta (N) Position: Infield (BR TR) Stats: 43 G, 72 AB, 21 H, 6 R, 0 HR, 4 RBI, .292 BA

Sánchez y Guadalupe, Rey Francisco (**Rey Sánchez**) (b. 10-5-1967, Río Piedras) Debut: 9-8-1991 (1991–1992) Team: Chicago (N) Positions: Shortstop, Second Base (BR TR) Stats: 87 G, 278 AB, 70 H, 25 R, 1 HR, 21 RBI, .252 BA

Sánchez y Marquez, Orlando (**Orlando Sánchez**) (b. 9-7-1956, Canovanas) Debut: 5-6-1981 (1981–1984) Teams: St. Louis (N), Kansas City (A), Baltimore (A) Position: Catcher (BL TR) Stats: 73 G, 110 AB, 24 H, 11 R, 0 HR, 12 RBI, .218 BA

Santiago y Alfonso, José Rafael (**José Santiago**) (b. 8-15-1940, Juana Díaz) Debut: 9-9-1963 (1963–1970) Teams: Kansas City (A), Boston (A) Position: Pitcher (BR TR) Stats: 34 W, 29 L, 556 IP, 3.74 ERA, 404 SO, 200 BB, 8 SV, 163 G

Santiago y Guzmán, José Guillermo (**José "Pantalones" Santiago**) (b. 9-4-1928, Coamo) Debut: 4-17-1954 (1954–1956) Teams: Cleveland (A), Kansas City (A) Position: Pitcher (BR TR) Stats: 3 W, 2 L, 56 IP, 4.66 ERA, 29 SO, 33 BB, 0 SV, 27 G

Santiago y Rivera, Benito (**Benito Santiago**) (b. 3-9-1965, Ponce) Debut: 9-14-1986 (1986–1992) Teams: San Diego (N), Florida (N) Position: Catcher (BR TR) Stats: 789 G, 2872 AB, 758 H, 312 R, 85 HR, 375 RBI, .264 BA

Santo Domingo y Molina, Rafael (**Rafael Santo Domingo**) (b. 11-24-1955, Orocovis) Debut: 9-7-1979 (1979) Team: Cincinnati (N) Positions: Outfield, Infield (BB TR) Stats: 7 G, 6 AB, 1 H, 0 R, 0 HR, 0 RBI, .167 BA

Sierra y García, Rubén Angel (**Rubén Sierra**) (b. 10-6-1965, Rio Piedras) Debut: 6-1-1986 (1986–1992) Teams: Texas (A), Oakland (A) Positions: Outfield, DH (BB TR) Stats: 1060 G, 4144 AB, 1160 H, 588 R, 156 HR, 673 RBI, .280 BA

Sierra y Pizarro, Ulises (**Candy Sierra**) (b. 3-27-1967, Rio Piedras) Debut: 4-6-1988 (1988) Teams: San Diego (N), Cincinnati (N) Position: Pitcher (BR TR) Stats: 0 W, 1 L, 27.2 IP, 5.53 ERA, 24 SO, 12 BB, 0 SV, 16 G

Tartabull y Mora, Danilo (**Danny Tartabull**) (b. 10-30-1962, San Juan) Debut: 9-7-1984 (1984–1992) Teams: Seattle (A), Kansas City (A), New York (A) Positions: Outfield, DH (BR TR) Stats: 946 G, 3340 AB, 950 H, 507 R, 177 HR, 620 RBI, .284 BA (Son of José Tartabull, listed under Cuba)

Thomas, Valmy (**Valmy Thomas**) (b. 10-21-1928, Santurce) Debut: 4-16-1957 (1957–1961) Teams: New York (N), San Francisco (N), Philadelphia (N), Baltimore (A), Cleveland (A) Position: Catcher (BR TR) Stats: 252 G, 626 AB, 144 H, 56 R, 12 HR, 60 RBI, .230 BA

Thon, Richard William (**Dickie Thon**) (b. 6-20-1958, South Bend, Indiana USA) Debut: 5-22-1979 (1979–1992) Teams: California (A), Houston (N), San Diego (N), Philadelphia (N), Texas (A) Positions: Shortstop, Infield (BR TR) Stats: 1302 G, 4204 AB, 1110 H, 473 R, 70 HR, 402 RBI, .264 BA (Born of Puerto Rican parents and raised in Puerto Rico)

Torres y Hernández, Rosendo (**Rusty Torres**) (b. 9-30-1948, Aguadilla) Debut: 9-20-1971 (1971–1974, 1976–1980) Teams: New York (A), Cleveland (A), California (A), Chicago (A), Kansas City (A) Positions: Outfield, DH (BB TR) Stats: 654 G, 1314 AB, 279 H, 159 R, 35 HR, 126 RBI, .212 BA

Torres y Sánchez, Felix (**Felix Torres**) (b. 5-1-1932, Ponce) Debut: 4-10-1962 (1962–1964) Team: Los Angeles (A) Positions: Third Base, First Base (BR TR) Stats: 365 G, 1191 AB, 302 H, 109 R, 27 HR, 153 RBI, .254 BA

Valentín, José Antonio (**José Valentín**) (b. 10-12-1969, Manati) Debut: 9-17-1992 (1992) Team: Milwaukee (A) Position: Infield (BB TR) Stats: 4 G, 3 AB, 0 H, 1 R, 0 HR, 1 RBI, .000 BA

Valera y Torres, Julio Enrique (**Julio Valera**) (b. 10-13-1968, Aguadilla) Debut: 9-1-1990 (1990–1992) Teams: New York (N), California (A) Position: Pitcher (BR TR) Stats: 9 W, 12 L, 203 IP, 3.90 ERA, 120 SO, 75 BB, 0 SV, 35 G

Valle, Héctor José (**Héctor Valle**) (b. 10-27-1940, Vega Baja) Debut: 6-6-1965 (1965) Team: Los Angeles (N) Position: Catcher (BR TR) Stats: 9 G, 13 AB, 4 H, 1 R, 0 HR, 2 RBI, .308 BA

Vargas, Roberto Enrique (**Roberto Vargas**) (b. 5-29-1929, Santurce) Debut: 4-17-1955 (1955) Team: Milwaukee (N) Position: Pitcher (BL TL) Stats: 0 W, 0 L, 24.2 IP, 8.76 ERA, 13 SO, 14 BB, 2 SV, 25 G

Vargas y Rodriguez, Hediberto (**Hedi "Eddie" Vargas**) (b. 2-23-1959, Guanica) Debut: 9-8-1982 (1982, 1984) Team: Pittsburgh (N) Position: First Base (BR TR) Stats: 26 G, 39 AB, 10 H, 4 R, 0 HR, 5 RBI, .256 BA

Vega y Morales, Jesús Anthony (**Jesús Vega**) (b. 10-14-1955, Bayamón) Debut: 9-5-1979 (1979, 1980–1982) Team: Minnesota (A) Positions: DH, Outfield (BR TR) Stats: 87 G, 236 AB, 58 H, 26 R, 5 HR, 33 RBI, .246 BA

Velazquez y Quinones, Carlos (**Carlos Velazquez**) (b. 3-22-1948, Loiza) Debut: 7-20-1973 (1973) Team: Milwaukee (A) Position: Pitcher (BR TR) Stats: 2 W, 2 L, 38.1 IP, 2.58 ERA, 12 SO, 10 BB, 2 SV, 18 G

Velez y Franceschi, Otoniel (**Otto Velez**) (b. 11-29-1950, Ponce) Debut: 9-4-1973 (1973–1983) Teams: New York (A), Toronto (A), Cleveland (A) Positions: Outfield, DH, First Base (BR TR) Stats: 637 G, 1802 AB, 452 H, 244 R, 78 HR, 272 RBI, .251 BA

Villanueva y Balasquide, Héctor (**Héctor Villanueva**) (b. 10-2-1964, Río Piedras) Debut: 6-1-1990 (1990–1992) Teams: Chicago (N), St. Louis (N) Position: Catcher (BR TR) Stats: 174 G, 418 AB, 101 H, 46 R, 22 HR, 63 RBI, .242 BA

Virgil y López, Osvaldo José (**Ozzie Virgil**) (b. 12-7-1956, Mayaguez) Debut: 10-5-1980 (1980–1990) Teams: Philadelphia (N), Atlanta (N), Toronto (A) Position: Catcher (BR TR) Stats: 739 G, 2258 AB, 549 H, 258 R, 98 HR, 307 RBI, .243 BA (Son of Ossie Virgil, listed under Dominican Republic)

Williams y Figueroa, Bernabe (**Bernie Williams**) (b. 9-13-1968, San Juan) Debut: 7-7-1991 (1991–1992) Team: New York (A) Position: Outfield (BB TR) Stats: 147 G, 581 AB, 149 H, 82 R, 8 HR, 60 RBI, .256 BA

Cuba

(First Cuban major-leaguer: Esteban ["Steve"] Enrique Bellán [May 9, 1871]; 129 players)

Acosta y Fernández, Baldomero Pedro (**Mérito Acosta**) (b. 5-19-1896, Bauta; d. 11-17-1963, Miami USA) Debut: 6-15-1913 (1913–1916, 1918) Teams: Washington (A), Philadelphia (A) Position: Outfield (BL TL) Stats: 180 G, 436 AB, 111 H, 56 R, 0 HR, 37 RBI, .255 BA (Brother of José Acosta)

Acosta y Fernández, José "Acostica" (**José Acosta**) (b. 3-4-1891, Havana; d. 11-16-1977, Havana) Debut: 7-28-1920 (1920–1922) Teams: Washington (A), Chicago (A) Position:

Cuba, *cont.*

Pitcher (BR TR) Stats: 10 W, 10 L, 213.1 IP, 4.51 ERA, 45 SO, 68 BB, 4 SV, 55 G (Brother of Merito Acosta)

Almeida, Rafael D. (**Rafael "Mike" Almeida**) (b. 7-30-1887, Havana; d. 3-14-1968, Havana) Debut: 7-4-1911 (1911–1913) Team: Cincinnati (N) Positions: Outfield, Infield (BR TR) Stats: 102 G, 285 AB, 77 H, 32 R, 3 HR, 46 RBI, .270 BA

Aloma y Barba, Luís (**Luís "Witto" Aloma**) (b. 7-23-1923, Havana) Debut: 4-19-1950 (1950–1953) Team: Chicago (A) Position: Pitcher (BR TR) Stats: 18 W, 3 L, 235.1 IP, 3.44 ERA, 115 SO, 111 BB, 15 SV, 116 G

Alvarez y González, Oswaldo (**Ossie Alvarez**) (b. 10-19-1933, Matanzas) Debut: 4-19-1958 (1958–1959) Teams: Washington (A), Detroit (A) Position: Infield (BR TR) Stats: 95 G, 198 AB, 42 H, 20 R, 0 HR, 5 RBI, .212 BA

Alvarez y Hernández, Rogelio (**Rogelio "Borrego" Alvarez**) (b. 4-18-1938, Pinar del Río) Debut: 9-18-1960 (1960, 1962) Team: Cincinnati (N) Position: First Base (BR TR) Stats: 17 G, 37 AB, 7 H, 2 R, 0 HR, 2 RBI, .189 BA

Amor y Alvarez, Vicente (**Vicente Amor**) (b. 8-8-1932, Havana) Debut: 4-16-1955 (1955, 1957) Teams: Chicago (N), Cincinnati (N) Position: Pitcher (BR TR) Stats: 1 W, 3 L, 33.1 IP, 5.67 ERA, 12 SO, 13 BB, 0 SV, 13 G

Amoros y Isasi, Edmundo (**Sandy Amoros**) (b. 1-30-1930, Havana; d. 6-27-1992, Tampa, Florida USA) Debut: 8-22-1952 (1952, 1954–1957, 1959–1960) Teams: Brooklyn (N), Los Angeles (N), Detroit (A) Position: Outfield (BL TL) Stats: 517 G, 1311 AB, 334 H, 215 R, 43 HR, 180 RBI, .255 BA

Aragón y Reyes, Angel Valdes (**Jack Aragón**) (b. 11-20-1915, Havana; d. 4-4-1988, Clearwater, Florida USA) Debut: 8-13-1941 (1941) Team: New York (N) Position: Pinch Runner (BR TR) Stats: 1 G, 0 AB, 0 H, 0 R, 0 HR, 0 RBI, .000 BA (Son of Angel Aragón)

Aragón y Valdes, Angel (**Angel "Pete" Aragón**) (b. 8-2-1890, Havana; d. 1-24-1952, New York USA) Debut: 8-20-1914 (1914, 1916–1917) Team: New York (A) Positions: Third Base, Shortstop, Outfield (BR TR) Stats: 32 G, 76 AB, 9 H, 4 R, 0 HR, 5 RBI, .118 BA (Father of Jack Aragón)

Arcia y Orta, José Raimundo (**José Arcia**) (b. 8-22-1943, Havana) Debut: 4-10-1968 (1968–1970) Teams: Chicago (N), San Diego (N) Positions: Infield, Outfield (BR TR) Stats: 293 G, 615 AB, 132 H, 78 R, 1 HR, 35 RBI, .215 BA

Arias y Martínez, Rodolfo (**Rudy Arias**) (b. 6-6-1931, Las Villas) Debut: 4-10-1959 (1959) Team: Chicago (A) Position: Pitcher (BL TL) Stats: 2 W, 0 L, 44 IP, 4.09 ERA, 28 SO, 20 BB, 2 SV, 34 G

Azcue y López, José Joaquín (**Joe Azcue**) (b. 8-18-1939, Cienfuegos) Debut: 8-3-1960 (1960, 1962–1970, 1972) Teams: Cincinnati (N), Kansas City (A), Cleveland (A), Boston (A), California (A), Milwaukee (A) Positions: Catcher, Infield (BR TR) Stats: 909 G, 2828 AB, 712 H, 201 R, 50 HR, 304 RBI, .252 BA

Bauta y Galvez, Eduardo (**Ed Bauta**) (b. 1-6-1935, Florida Camaguey) Debut: 7-6-1960 (1960–1964) Teams: St. Louis (N), New York (N) Position: Pitcher (BR TR) Stats: 6 W, 6 L, 149 IP, 4.35 ERA, 89 SO, 70 BB, 11 SV, 97 G

Becquer y Villagas, Julio (**Julio Becquer**) (b. 12-20-1931, Havana) Debut: 9-13-1955 (1955, 1957–1961, 1963) Teams: Washington (A), Los Angeles (A), Minnesota (A) Positions: First Base, Outfield, Pitcher (BL TL) Hitting Stats: 488 G, 974 AB, 238 H, 100 R, 12 HR, 114 RBI, .244 BA; Pitching Stats: 0 W, 0 L, 2.1 IP, 15.43 ERA, 0 SO, 1 BB, 0 SV, 2 G

Bellán, Esteban Enrique (**Esteban "Steve" Bellán**) (b. 1850, Havana; d. 8-8-1932, Havana) Debut: 5-9-1871 (1871–1873) Teams: Troy (NA), New York (NA) Positions: Infield, Outfield (BR TR) Stats: 60 G, 278 AB, 69 H, 52 R, 0 HR, 42 RBI, .248 BA

Calvo y González, Jacinto (**Jack Calvo**) (b. 6-11-1894, Havana; d. 6-15-1965, Miami USA) Debut: 9-5-1913 (1913, 1920) Team: Washington (A) Position: Outfield (BL TL) Stats: 34 G, 56 AB, 9 H, 10 R, 1 HR, 4 RBI, .161 BA

Campaneris (Campaneria) y Blanco, Dagoberto (**Bert "Campy" Campaneris**) (b. 3-9-1942, Pueblo Nuevo) Debut: 7-23-1964 (1964–1983) Teams: Kansas City (A), Oakland (A), Texas (A), California (A), New York (A) Position: Shortstop (BR TR) Stats: 2328 G, 8684 AB, 2249 H, 1181 R, 79 HR, 646 RBI, .259 BA

Campos y López, Francisco José (**Frank "Cisco" Campos**) (b. 5-11-1924, Havana) Debut: 9-11-1951 (1951–1953) Team: Washington (A) Positions: Outfield (BL TL) Stats: 71 G, 147 AB, 41 H, 13 R, 0 HR, 13 RBI, .279 BA

Canseco y Capas, José (**José Canseco**) (b. 7-2-1964, Havana) Debut: 9-2-1985 (1985–1992) Teams: Oakland (A), Texas (A) Positions: Outfield, DH (BR TR) Stats: 972 G, 3655 AB, 974 H, 614 R, 235 HR, 734 RBI, .266 BA (Brother of Ozzie Canseco)

Canseco y Capas, Osvaldo (**Ozzie Canseco**) (b. 7-2-1964, Havana) Debut: 7-18-1990 (1990, 1992) Teams: Oakland (A), St. Louis (N) Position: Outfield (BR TR) Stats: 18 G, 48 AB, 10 H, 8 R, 0 HR, 4 RBI, .208 BA (Brother of José Canseco)

Cardenal (Domec y Cardenal), José Rosario (**José Cardenal**) (b. 10-7-1943, Matanzas) Debut: 4-14-1963 (1963–1980) Teams: San Francisco (N), California (A), Cleveland (A), St. Louis (N), Milwaukee (A), Chicago (N), Philadelphia (N), New York (N), Kansas City (A) Position: Outfield (BR TR) Stats: 2017 G, 6964 AB, 1913 H, 936 R, 138 HR, 775 RBI, .275 BA

Cárdenas y Alfonso, Leonardo Lazaro (**Leo Cárdenas**) (b. 12-17-1938, Matanzas) Debut: 7-25-1960 (1960–1975) Teams: Cincinnati (N), Minnesota (A), California (A), Cleveland (A), Texas (A) Position: Shortstop (BR TR) Stats: 1941 G, 6707 AB, 1725 H, 662 R, 118 HR, 689 RBI, .257 BA

Casanova y Ortiz, Paulino (**Paul Casanova**) (b. 12-21-1941, Matanzas) Debut: 9-18-1965 (1965–1974) Teams: Washington (A), Atlanta (N) Position: Catcher (BR TR) Stats: 859 G, 2786 AB, 627 H, 214 R, 50 HR, 252 RBI, .225 BA

Comellas y Pous, Jorge (**Jorge "Poncho" Comellas**) (b. 12-7-1916, Havana) Debut: 4-19-1945 (1945) Team: Chicago (N) Position: Pitcher (BR TR) Stats: 0 W, 2 L, 12 IP, 4.50 ERA, 6 SO, 6 BB, 0 SV, 7 G

Consuegra y Castello, Sandalio Simeon (**Sandy Consuegra**) (b. 9-3-1920, Potrerillos) Debut: 6-10-1950 (1950–1957) Teams: Washington (A), Chicago (A), Baltimore (A), New York (N) Position: Pitcher (BR TR) Stats: 51 W, 32 L, 809.1 IP, 3.37 ERA, 193 SO, 246 BB, 26 SV, 248 G

Cuellar y Santana, Miguel Angel (**Mike Cuellar**) (b. 5-8-1937, Las Villas) Debut: 4-18-1959 (1959, 1964–1977) Teams: Cincinnati (N), St. Louis (N), Houston (N), Baltimore (A), California (A) Position: Pitcher (BL TL) Stats: 185 W, 130 L, 2808 IP, 3.14 ERA, 1632 SO, 822 BB, 11 SV, 453 G

Cueto y Concepción, Dagoberto (**Bert Cueto**) (b. 8-14-1937, San Luís Pinar) Debut: 6-18-1961 (1961) Team: Minnesota (A) Position: Pitcher (BR TR) Stats: 1 W, 3 L, 21.1 IP, 7.17 ERA, 5 SO, 10 BB, 0 SV, 7 G

Cueto y Melo, Manuel (**Manolo Cueto**) (b. 2-8-1892, Guanajay; d. 6-29-1942, Regla Havana) Debut: 6-25-1914 (1914, 1917–1919) Teams: St. Louis (F), Cincinnati (N) Positions: Outfield, Infield (BR TR) Stats: 151 G, 379 AB, 86 H, 36 R, 1 HR, 31 RBI, .227 BA

de la Cruz y Rivero, Tomás (**Tommy de la Cruz**) (b. 9-18-1911, Marianao; d. 9-6-1958, Havana) Debut: 4-20-1944 (1944) Team: Cincinnati (N) Position: Pitcher (BR TR) Stats: 9 W, 9 L, 191.1 IP, 3.25 ERA, 65 SO, 45 BB, 1 SV, 34 G

de la Hoz y Piloto, Miguel Angel (**Mike de la Hoz**) (b. 10-2-1938, Havana) Debut: 7-22-1960 (1960–1967, 1969) Teams: Cleveland (A), Milwaukee (N), Atlanta (N), Cincinnati (N) Position: Infield (BR TR) Stats: 494 G, 1114 AB, 280 H, 116 R, 25 HR, 115 RBI, .251 BA

Delis, Juan Francisco (**Juan Delis**) (b. 2-27-1928, Santiago) Debut: 4-16-1955 (1955) Team: Washington (A) Positions: Outfield, Infield, Shortstop (BR TR) Stats: 54 G, 132 AB, 25 H, 12 R, 0 HR, 11 RBI, .189 BA

Destrade y Cucuas, Orestes (**Orestes Destrade**) (b. 5-8-1962, Santiago) Debut: 9-11-1987 (1987–1988, 1993) Teams: New York (A), Pittsburgh (N), Florida (N) Position: First Base (BB TR) Stats: 45 G, 66 AB, 12 H, 7 R, 1 HR, 4 RBI, .182 BA

Dibut y Villafana, Pedro (**Pedro Dibut**) (b. 11-18-1892, Cienfuegos; d. 12-4-1979, Hialeah, Florida USA) Debut: 5-1-1924 (1924–1925) Team: Cincinnati (N) Position: Pitcher (BR TR) Stats: 3 W, 0 L, 36.2 IP, 2.70 ERA, 15 SO, 12 BB, 0 SV, 8 G

Donoso y Galeta, Lino (**Lino Donoso**) (b. 9-23-1922, Havana; d. 10-13-1990, Vera Cruz, Mexico) Debut: 6-18-1955 (1955–1956) Team: Pittsburgh (N) Position: Pitcher (BL TL) Stats: 4 W, 6 L, 96.2 IP, 5.21 ERA, 39 SO, 36 BB, 1 SV, 28 G

Estalella y Ventoza, Roberto (**Roberto "Bobby" Estalella**) (b. 4-25-1911, Cárdenas; d. 1-6-1991, Hialeah, Florida USA) Debut: 9-7-1935 (1935–1936, 1939, 1941–1945, 1949) Teams: Wash-

Cuba, *cont.*

ington (A), St. Louis (A), Washington (A), Philadelphia (A) Position: Outfield (BR TR) Stats: 680 G, 2196 AB, 620 H, 279 R, 44 HR, 308 RBI, .282 BA

Estrada, Oscar (**Oscar Estrada**) (b. 2-15-1904, Havana; d. 1-2-1978, Havana) Debut: 4-21-1929 (1929) Team: St. Louis (A) Position: Pitcher (BL TL) Stats: 0 W, 0 L, 1 IP, 0.00 ERA, 0 SO, 1 BB, 0 SV, 1 G

Fernández y Mosquera, Lorenzo Marto (**Chico Fernández**) (b. 4-23-1939, Havana) Debut: 4-20-1968 (1968) Team: Baltimore (A) Positions: Infield, Shortstop (BR TR) Stats: 24 G, 18 AB, 2 H, 0 R, 0 HR, 0 RBI, .111 BA

Fernández y Pérez, Humberto (**Chico Fernández**) (b. 3-2-1932, Havana) Debut: 7-14-1956 (1956–1963) Teams: Brooklyn (N), Philadelphia (N), Detroit (A), New York (N) Position: Shortstop (BR TR) Stats: 856 G, 2778 AB, 666 H, 270 R, 40 HR, 259 RBI, .240 BA

Fleitas y Husta, Angel Félix (**Angel Fleitas**) (b. 11-10-1914, Los Abreus) Debut: 7-5-1948 (1948) Team: Washington (A) Position: Shortstop (BR TR) Stats: 15 G, 13 AB, 1 H, 1 R, 0 HR, 1 RBI, .077 BA

Fornieles y Torres, José Miguel (**Mike Fornieles**) (b. 1-18-1932, Havana) Debut: 9-2-1952 (1952–1963) Teams: Washington (A), Chicago (A), Baltimore (A), Boston (A), Minnesota (A) Position: Pitcher (BR TR) Stats: 63 W, 64 L, 1156.2 IP, 3.96 ERA, 576 SO, 421 BB, 55 SV, 432 G

Fossas y Morejon, Emilio Antonio (**Tony Fossas**) (b. 9-23-1957, Havana) Debut: 5-15-1988 (1988–1992) Teams: Texas (A), Milwaukee (A), Boston (A) Position: Pitcher (BL TL) Stats: 8 W, 9 L, 182.2 IP, 3.84 ERA, 114 SO, 76 BB, 4 SV, 212 G

Fuentes y Peat, Rigoberto (**Tito Fuentes**) (b. 1-4-1944, Havana) Debut: 8-18-1965 (1965–1967, 1969–1978) Teams: San Francisco (N), San Diego (N), Detroit (A), Oakland (A) Positions: Second Base, Infield (BB TR) Stats: 1499 G, 5566 AB, 1491 H, 610 R, 45 HR, 438 RBI, .268 BA

Garbey y Garbey, Bárbaro (**Bárbaro Garbey**) (b. 12-4-1956, Santiago) Debut: 4-3-1984 (1984–1985, 1988) Teams: Detroit (A), Texas (A) Positions: Outfield, Third Base, DH (BR TR) Stats: 226 G, 626 AB, 167 H, 76 R, 11 HR, 86 RBI, .267 BA

García y García, Ramón (**Moín García**) (b. 3-5-1924, La Esperanza) Debut: 4-19-1948 (1948) Team: Washington (A) Position: Pitcher (BR TR) Stats: 0 W, 0 L, 3.2 IP, 17.18 ERA, 2 SO, 4 BB, 0 SV, 4 G

Gómez y Martínez, Pedro (**Preston "Pedro" Gómez**) (b. 4-20-1923, Preston) Debut: 5-5-1944 (1944) Team: Washington (A) Positions: Second Base, Shortstop (BR TR) Stats: 8 G, 7 AB, 2 H, 2 R, 0 HR, 2 RBI, .286 BA

González, Orlando Eugene (**Orlando González**) (b. 11-15-1951, Havana) Debut: 6-7-1976 (1976, 1978, 1980) Teams: Cleveland (A), Philadelphia (N), Oakland (A) Positions: Outfield, DH, First Base (BL TL) Stats: 79 G, 164 AB, 39 H, 16 R, 0 HR, 5 RBI, .238 BA

González y Cordero, Miguel Angel (**Mike González**) (b. 9-24-1890, Havana; d. 2-19-1977, Havana) Debut: 9-28-1912 (1912, 1914–1929, 1931–1932) Teams: Boston (N), Cincinnati (N), St. Louis (N), New York (N), St. Louis (N), Chicago (N), St. Louis (N) Positions: Catcher, First Base (BR TR) Stats: 1042 G, 2829 AB, 717 H, 283 R, 13 HR, 263 RBI, .253 BA

González y González, Andres Antonio (**Tony González**) (b. 8-28-1936, Central Cunagua) Debut: 4-12-1960 (1960–1971) Teams: Cincinnati (N), Philadelphia (N), San Diego (N), Atlanta (N), California (A) Position: Outfield (BL TR) Stats: 1559 G, 5195 AB, 1485 H, 690 R, 103 HR, 615 RBI, .286 BA

González y Herrera, Julio Enrique (**Enrique "Julio" González**) (b. 12-20-1920, Banes) Debut: 8-9-1949 (1949) Team: Washington (A) Position: Pitcher (BR TR) Stats: 0 W, 0 L, 34.1 IP, 4.72 ERA, 5 SO, 27 BB, 0 SV, 13 G

González y López, Eusebio Miguel (**Eusebio González**) (b. 7-13-1892, Havana; d. 2-4-1976, Havana) Debut: 7-26-1918 (1918) Team: Boston (A) Positions: Shortstop, Third Base (BR TR) Stats: 3 G, 5 AB, 2 H, 2 R, 0 HR, 0 RBI, .400 BA

González y O'Reilly, Wenceslao (**Vince González**) (b. 9-28-1925, Quivican; d. 3-11-1981, Ciudad del Carmen Campache, Mexico) Debut: 4-13-1955 (1955) Team: Washington (A) Position: Pitcher (BL TL) Stats: 0 W, 0 L, 2 IP, 27.00 ERA, 1 SO, 3 BB, 0 SV, 2 G

Guerra y Romero, Fermín (**Mike Guerra**) (b. 10-11-1912, Havana) Debut: 9-19-1937 (1937,

1944–1951) Teams: Washington (A), Philadelphia (A), Boston (A), Washington (A) Position: Catcher (BR TR) Stats: 565 G, 1581 AB, 382 H, 168 R, 9 HR, 168 RBI, .242 BA

Hernández y López, Gregorio Evelio (**Evelio Hernández**) (b. 12-24-1930, Guanabacoa) Debut: 9-12-1956 (1956–1957) Team: Washington (A) Position: Pitcher (BR TR) Stats: 1 W, 1 L, 58.2 IP, 4.45 ERA, 24 SO, 28 BB, 0 SV, 18 G

Hernández y Ramos, Salvador José (**Sal "Chico" Hernández**) (b. 1-3-1916, Havana; d. 1-3-1986, Havana) Debut: 4-16-1942 (1942–1943) Team: Chicago (N) Position: Catcher (BR TR) Stats: 90 G, 244 AB, 61 H, 16 R, 0 HR, 16 RBI, .250 BA

Hernández y Zulueta, Jacinto (**Jackie Hernández**) (b. 9-11-1940, Central Tinguaro) Debut: 9-14-1965 (1965–1973) Teams: California (A), Minnesota (A), Kansas City (A), Pittsburgh (N) Positions: Shortstop, Third Base (BR TR) Stats: 618 G, 1480 AB, 308 H, 153 R, 12 HR, 121 RBI, .208 BA

Herrera, Ramón (**Mike Herrera**) (b. 12-19-1897, Havana; d. 2-3-1978, Havana) Debut: 9-22-1925 (1925–1926) Team: Boston (A) Position: Infield (BR TR) Stats: 84 G, 276 AB, 76 H, 22 R, 0 HR, 27 RBI, .275 BA

Herrera y Willavicencio, Juan Francisco (**Pancho Herrera**) (b. 6-16-1934, Santiago) Debut: 4-15-1958 (1958, 1960–1961) Team: Philadelphia (N) Positions: First Base, Infield (BR TR) Stats: 300 G, 975 AB, 264 H, 122 R, 31 HR, 128 RBI, .271 BA

Izquierdo y Valdes, Enrique Roberto (**Hank Izquierdo**) (b. 3-20-1931, Matanzas) Debut: 8-9-1967 (1967) Team: Minnesota (A) Positions: Catcher, Pinch Hitter (BR TR) Stats: 16 G, 26 AB, 7 H, 4 R, 0 HR, 2 RBI, .269 BA

Lauzerique, George Albert (**Jorge Lauzerique**) (b. 7-22-1947, Havana) Debut: 9-17-1967 (1967–1970) Teams: Kansas City (A), Oakland (A), Milwaukee (A) Position: Pitcher (BR TR) Stats: 4 W, 8 L, 113.1 IP, 5.00 ERA, 73 SO, 48 BB, 0 SV, 34 G

León y Becerra, Isidoro (**Sid "Izzy" León**) (b. 1-4-1911, Cruces, Las Villas) Debut: 6-21-1945 (1945) Team: Philadelphia (N) Position: Pitcher (BR TR) Stats: 0 W, 4 L, 38.2 IP, 5.35 ERA, 11 SO, 19 BB, 0 SV, 14 G

López, Marcelino Pons (**Marcelino López**) (b. 9-23-1943, Havana) Debut: 4-14-1963 (1963, 1965–1967, 1969–1972) Teams: Philadelphia (N), California (A), Baltimore (A), Milwaukee (A), Cleveland (A) Position: Pitcher (BR TL) Stats: 31 W, 40 L, 653 IP, 3.62 ERA, 426 SO, 317 BB, 2 SV, 171 G

López y Hevia, José Ramón (**Ramón López**) (b. 5-26-1933, Las Villas; d. 9-4-1982, Miami, Florida USA) Debut: 8-21-1966 (1966) Team: California (A) Position: Pitcher (BR TR) Stats: 0 W, 1 L, 7 IP, 5.14 ERA, 2 SO, 4 BB, 0 SV, 4 G

Luque, Adolfo Domingo de Guzmán (**Dolf Luque**) (b. 8-4-1890, Havana; d. 7-3-1957, Havana) Debut: 5-20-1914 (1914–1915, 1918–1935) Teams: Boston (N), Cincinnati (N), Brooklyn (N), New York (N) Position: Pitcher (BR TR) Stats: 194 W, 179 L, 3220.1 IP, 3.24 ERA, 1130 SO, 918 BB, 28 SV, 550 G

McFarlane y Quesada, Orlando DeJesús (**Orlando McFarlane**) (b. 6-28-1938, Oriente) Debut: 4-23-1962 (1962, 1964, 1966–1968) Teams: Pittsburgh (N), Detroit (A), California (A) Positions: Catcher, Outfield (BR TR) Stats: 124 G, 292 AB, 70 H, 22 R, 5 HR, 20 RBI, .240 BA

Maestri y García, Héctor Anibal (**Héctor Maestri**) (b. 4-19-1935, Havana) Debut: 9-24-1960 (1960–1961) Team: Washington (A) Position: Pitcher (BR TR) Stats: 0 W, 1 L, 8 IP, 1.13 ERA, 3 SO, 3 BB, 0 SV, 2 G

Marrero y Ramos, Conrado Eugenio (**Connie Marrero**) (b. 4-25-1911, Las Villas) Debut: 4-21-1950 (1950–1954) Team: Washington (A) Position: Pitcher (BR TR) Stats: 39 W, 40 L, 735.1 IP, 3.67 ERA, 297 SO, 249 BB, 3 SV, 118 G

Marsans, Armando (**Armando Marsans**) (b. 10-3-1887, Matanzas; d. 9-3-1960, Havana) Debut: 7-4-1911 (1911–1918) Teams: Cincinnati (N), St. Louis (F), St. Louis (A), New York (A) Positions: Outfield, Infield (BR TR) Stats: 655 G, 2273 AB, 612 H, 267 R, 2 HR, 221 RBI, .269 BA

Martínez y Azcuiz, José (**José Martínez**) (b. 7-26-1941, Cárdenas) Debut: 6-18-1969 (1969–1970) Team: Pittsburgh (N) Positions: Infield, Outfield (BR TR) Stats: 96 G, 188 AB, 46 H, 21 R, 1 HR, 16 RBI, .245 BA

Martínez y Díaz, Gabriel Antonio (**Tony Martínez**) (b. 3-18-1940, Perico; d. 8-24-1991, Miami, Florida USA) Debut: 4-9-1963 (1963–1966) Team: Cleveland (A) Positions: Shortstop, Second Base (BR TR) Stats: 73 G, 175 AB, 30 H, 13 R, 0 HR, 10 RBI, .171 BA

Cuba, *cont.*

Martínez y Oliva, Orlando (**Marty Martínez**) (b. 8-23-1941, Havana) Debut: 5-2-1962 (1962, 1967–1972) Teams: Minnesota (A), Atlanta (N), Houston (N), St. Louis (N), Oakland (A), Texas (A) Positions: Infield, Catcher, Outfield (BB TR) Stats: 436 G, 945 AB, 230 H, 97 R, 0 HR, 57 RBI, .243 BA

Martínez y Santos, Rodolfo Héctor (**Héctor Martínez**) (b. 5-11-1939, Las Villas) Debut: 9-30-1962 (1962–1963) Team: Kansas City (A) Position: Outfield (BR TR) Stats: 7 G, 15 AB, 4 H, 2 R, 1 HR, 3 RBI, .267 BA

Martínez y Ulloa, Rogelio (**Limonar Martínez**) (b. 11-5-1918, Cidra) Debut: 7-13-1950 (1950) Team: Washington (A) Position: Pitcher (BR TR) Stats: 0 W, 1 L, 1.1 IP, 27.00 ERA, 0 SO, 2 BB, 0 SV, 2 G

Mejias y Gómez, Roman (**Roman Mejías**) (b. 8-9-1930, Abreus, Las Villas) Debut: 4-13-1955 (1955, 1957–1964) Teams: Pittsburgh (N), Houston (N), Boston (A) Position: Outfield (BR TR) Stats: 627 G, 1768 AB, 449 H, 212 R, 54 HR, 202 RBI, .254 BA

Mendoza y Carreras, Cristóbal Rigoberto (**Minnie Mendoza**) (b. 11-16-1933, Ceiba del Agua) Debut: 4-9-1970 (1970) Team: Minnesota (A) Position: Infield (BR TR) Stats: 16 G, 16 AB, 3 H, 2 R, 0 HR, 2 RBI, .188 BA

Menendez, Tony (**Tony Menendez**) (b. 2-20-1965, Havana) Debut: 6-22-1992 (1992) Team: Cincinnati (N) Position: Pitcher (BR TR) Stats: 1 W, 0 L, 4.2 IP, 1.93 ERA, 5 SO, 0 BB, 0 SV, 3 G

Miñoso (Arrieta), Saturnino Orestes Armas (**Minnie Miñoso**) (b. 11-29-1922, Havana) Debut: 4-19-1949 (1949, 1951–1964, 1976, 1980) Teams: Cleveland (A), Chicago (A), Cleveland (A), Chicago (A), St. Louis (N), Washington (A), Chicago (A) Positions: Outfield, Third Base (BR TR) Stats: 1835 G, 6579 AB, 1963 H, 1136 R, 186 HR, 1023 RBI, .298 BA

Miranda y Pérez, Guillermo (**Willie Miranda**) (b. 5-24-1926, Velasco) Debut: 5-6-1951 (1951–1959) Teams: Washington (A), Chicago (A), St. Louis (A), Chicago (A), St. Louis (A), New York (A), Baltimore (A) Positions: Shortstop, Infield (BB TR) Stats: 824 G, 1914 AB, 423 H, 176 R, 6 HR, 132 RBI, .221 BA

Monteagudo y Cintra, Aurelio Faustino (**Aurelio Monteagudo**) (b. 11-19-1943, Caibarien; d. 11-10-1990, Saltillo, Mexico) Debut: 9-1-1963 (1963–1967, 1970, 1973) Teams: Kansas City (A), Houston (N), Chicago (A), Kansas City (A), California (A) Position: Pitcher (BR TR) Stats: 3 W, 7 L, 132 IP, 5.05 ERA, 58 SO, 62 BB, 4 SV, 72 G (Son of Rene Monteagudo)

Monteagudo y Miranda, Rene (**Rene Monteagudo**) (b. 3-12-1916, Havana; d. 9-14-1973, Hialeah, Florida USA) Debut: 9-6-1939 (1938, 1940, 1945) Team: Washington (A), Philadelphia (N) Position: Pitcher (BL TL) Stats: 3 W, 7 L, 168.1 IP, 6.42 ERA, 93 SO, 95 BB, 2 SV, 46 G (Father of Aurelio Monteagudo)

Montejo y Bofill, Manuel (**Manuel "Manny" Montejo**) (b. 10-16-1935, Caibarien) Debut: 7-25-1961 (1961) Team: Detroit (A) Position: Pitcher (BR TR) Stats: 0 W, 0 L, 16.1 IP, 3.86 ERA, 15 SO, 6 BB, 0 SV, 12 G

Morejón y Torres, Daniel (**Dan Morejón**) (b. 7-21-1930, Havana) Debut: 7-11-1958 (1958) Team: Cincinnati (N) Position: Outfield (BR TR) Stats: 12 G, 26 AB, 5 H, 4 R, 0 HR, 1 RBI, .192 BA

Moreno y González, Julio (**Julio Moreno**) (b. 1-28-1921, Guines; d. 1-2-1987, Miami, Florida USA) Debut: 9-8-1950 (1950–1953) Team: Washington (A) Position: Pitcher (BR TR) Stats: 18 W, 22 L, 336.2 IP, 4.25 ERA, 119 SO, 157 BB, 2 SV, 73 G

Naranjo, Lazaro Ramón Gonzalo (**Gonzalo "Cholly" Naranjo**) (b. 11-25-1934, Havana) Debut: 7-8-1956 (1956) Team: Pittsburgh (N) Position: Pitcher (BL TR) Stats: 1 W, 2 L, 34.1 IP, 4.46 ERA, 26 SO, 17 BB, 0 SV, 17 G

Noble y Magee, Rafael Miguel (**Ray Noble**) (b. 3-15-1919, Central Hatillo) Debut: 4-18-1951 (1951–1953) Team: New York (N) Position: Catcher (BR TR) Stats: 107 G, 243 AB, 53 H, 31 R, 9 HR, 40 RBI, .218 BA

Oliva y López, Pedro (**Tony Oliva**) (b. 7-20-1940, Pinar del Río) Debut: 9-9-1962 (1962–1976) Team: Minnesota (A) Positions: Outfield, DH (BL TR) Stats: 1676 G, 6301 AB, 1917 H, 870 R, 220 HR, 947 RBI, .304 BA

Ordenana y Rodríguez, Antonio (**Mosquito Ordenana**) (b. 10-30-1918, Guanabacoa; d. 9-29-1988, Miami, Florida USA) Debut: 10-3-1943 (1943) Team: Pittsburgh (N) Position: Shortstop (BR TR) Stats: 1 G, 4 AB, 2 H, 0 R, 0 HR, 3 RBI, .500 BA

Ortiz y Núñez, Oliverio (**"Baby" Ortiz**) (b. 12-5-1919, Camaguey; d. 3-27-1984, Central Senado) Debut: 9-23-1944 (1944) Team: Washington (A) Position: Pitcher (BR TR) Stats: 0 W, 2 L, 13 IP, 6.23 ERA, 4 SO, 6 BB, 0 SV, 2 G (Brother of Roberto Ortiz)

Ortiz y Núñez, Roberto Gonzalo (**Roberto Ortiz**) (b. 6-30-1915, Camaguey; d. 9-15-1971, Miami, Florida USA) Debut: 9-6-1941 (1941–1944, 1949–1950) Teams: Washington (A), Philadelphia (A) Position: Outfield (BR TR) Stats: 213 G, 659 AB, 168 H, 67 R, 8 HR, 78 RBI, .255 BA (Brother of "Baby" Ortiz)

Otero y Gómez, Regino José (**Reggie Otero**) (b. 9-7-1915, Havana; d. 10-21-1988, Hialeah, Florida USA) Debut: 9-2-1945 (1945) Team: Chicago (N) Position: First Base (BL TR) Stats: 14 G, 23 AB, 9 H, 1 R, 0 HR, 5 RBI, .391 BA

Palmeiro y Corrales, Rafael (**Rafael Palmeiro**) (b. 9-24-1964, Havana) Debut: 9-8-1986 (1986–1992) Teams: Chicago (N), Texas (A) Positions: First Base, Outfield, DH (BL TL) Stats: 886 G, 3270 AB, 968 H, 463 R, 95 HR, 421 RBI, .296 BA

Palmero, Emilio Antonio (**Emilio "Pal" Palmero**) (b. 6-13-1895, Guanabacoa; d. 7-15-1970, Toledo, Ohio USA) Debut: 9-21-1915 (1915–1916, 1921, 1926, 1928) Teams: New York (N), St. Louis (A), Washington (A), Boston (A) Position: Pitcher (BR TR) Stats: 6 W, 15 L, 141 IP, 5.17 ERA, 48 SO, 83 BB, 0 SV, 41 G

Pascual y Lus, Camilo (**Camilo Pascual**) (b. 1-20-1934, Havana) Debut: 4-15-1954 (1954–1971) Teams: Washington (A); Minnesota (A); Los Angeles (N); Cleveland (A) Position: Pitcher (BR TR) Stats: 174 W, 170 L, 2930.2 IP, 3.63 ERA, 2167 SO, 1069 BB, 10 SV, 529 G (Brother of Carlos Pascual)

Pascual y Lus, Carlos Alberto (**Carlos Pascual**) (b. 3-13-1931, Havana) Debut: 9-24-1950 (1950) Team: Washington (A) Position: Pitcher (BR TR) Stats: 1 W, 1 L, 17 IP, 2.12 ERA, 3 SO, 8 BB, 0 SV, 2 G (Brother of Camilo Pascual)

Paula y Conill, Carlos (**Carlos Paula**) (b. 11-28-1927, Havana; d. 4-25-1983, Miami USA) Debut: 9-6-1954 (1954–1956) Team: Washington (A) Position: Outfield (BR TR) Stats: 157 G, 457 AB, 124 H, 44 R, 9 HR, 60 RBI, .271 BA

Peña y Quevara, Orlando Gregorio (**Orlando Peña**) (b. 11-17-1933, Victoria de Las Tunas) Debut: 8-24-1958 (1958–1975) Teams: Cincinnati (N), Kansas City (A), Detroit (A), Cleveland (A), Pittsburgh (N), Baltimore (A), St. Louis (N), California (A) Position: Pitcher (BR TR) Stats: 56 W, 77 L, 1202 IP, 3.71 ERA, 818 SO, 352 BB, 40 SV, 427 G

Pérez y Rigal, Atanasio (**Tony Pérez**) (b. 5-14-1942, Camaguey) Debut: 76-26-1964 (1964–1986) Teams: Cincinnati (N), Montreal (N), Boston (A), Philadelphia (N), Cincinnati (N) Positions: First Base, Third Base, DH (BR TR) Stats: 2777 G, 9778 AB, 2732 H, 1272 R, 379 HR, 1652 RBI, .279 BA

Posada y Hernández, Leopoldo Jesús (**Leo Posada**) (b. 4-15-1936, Havana) Debut: 9-21-1960 (1960–1962) Team: Kansas City (A) Position: Outfield (BR TR) Stats: 155 G, 426 AB, 109 H, 51 R, 8 HR, 58 RBI, .256 BA

Ramos, Roberto (**Bobby Ramos**) (b. 11-5-1955, Havana) Debut: 9-26-1978 (1978, 1980–1984) Teams: Montreal (N), New York (A), Montreal (N) Position: Catcher (BR TR) Stats: 103 G, 232 AB, 44 H, 20 R, 4 HR, 17 RBI, .190 BA

Ramos y Guerra, Pedro (**Pedro "Pete" Ramos**) (b. 4-28-1935, Pinar del Rio) Debut: 4-11-1955 (1955–1970) Teams: Washington (A), Minnesota (A), Cleveland (A), New York (A), Philadelphia (N), Pittsburgh (N), Cincinnati (N), Washington (A) Position: Pitcher (BB TR) Stats: 117 W, 160 L, 2355.2 IP, 4.08 ERA, 1305 SO, 724 BB, 55 SV, 582 G

Reyes y Aguilera, Napoleón (**Napoleón "Nap" Reyes**) (b. 11-24-1919, Santiago) Debut: 5-19-1943 (1943–1945, 1950) Team: New York (N) Positions: First Base, Third Base, Outfield (BR TR) Stats: 279 G, 931 AB, 264 H, 90 R, 13 HR, 110 RBI, .284 BA

Roche y Báez, Armando (**Armando Roche**) (b. 12-7-1926, Havana) Debut: 5-10-1945 (1945) Team: Washington (A) Position: Pitcher (BR TR) Stats: 0 W, 0 L, 6 IP, 6.00 ERA, 0 SO, 2 BB, 0 SV, 2 G

Rodríguez, José (**Joseito Rodríguez**) (b. 2-23-1894, Havana; d. 1-21-1953, Havana) Debut: 10-5-1916 (1916–1918) Team: New York (N) Position: Infield (BR TR) Stats: 58 G, 145 AB, 24 H, 17 R, 0 HR, 17 RBI, .166 BA

Rodríguez y Borrego, Fernando Pedro (**Freddie Rodríguez**) (b. 4-29-1924, Havana) Debut: 4-18-1958 (1958–1959) Teams: Chicago (N), Philadelphia (N) Position: Pitcher (BR TR) Stats: 0 W, 0 L, 9.1 IP, 8.68 ERA, 6 SO, 5 BB, 2 SV, 8 G

Cuba, *cont.*

Rodríguez y Ordenana, Héctor Antonio (**Héctor Rodríguez**) (b. 6-13-1920, Alquizar) Debut: 4-15-1952 (1952) Team: Chicago (A) Position: Third Base (BR TR) Stats: 124 G, 407 AB, 108 H, 55 R, 1 HR, 40 RBI, .265 BA

Rojas y Landin, Minervino Alejandro (**Minnie Rojas**) (b. 11-26-19, Remidios) Debut: 5-30-1966 (1966–1968) Team: California (A) Position: Pitcher (BR TR) Stats: 23 W, 16 L, 261 IP, 3.00 ERA, 153 SO, 68 BB, 43 SV, 157 G

Rojas y Rivas, Octavio Victor (**Cookie Rojas**) (b. 3-6-1939, Havana) Debut: 4-10-1962 (1962–1977) Teams: Cincinnati (N), Philadelphia (N), St. Louis (N), Kansas City (A) Position: Infield (BR TR) Stats: 1822 G, 6309 AB, 1660 H, 714 R, 54 HR, 593 RBI, .263 BA

Ruiz y Sablon, Hiraldo (**Chico Ruiz**) (b. 12-5-1938, Santo Domingo; d. 2-9-1972, San Diego USA) Debut: 4-13-1964 (1964–1971) Teams: Cincinnati (N), California (A) Position: Infield (BB TR) Stats: 565 G, 1150 AB, 276 H, 133 R, 2 HR, 69 RBI, .240 BA

Sánchez y Matos, Israel (**Israel Sánchez**) (b. 8-20-1963, Falcón Lasvias) Debut: 7-7-1988 (1988, 1990) Team: Kansas City (A) Position: Pitcher (BL TL) Stats: 3 W, 2 L, 45.1 IP, 5.36 ERA, 19 SO, 21 BB, 1 SV, 30 G

Sánchez y Rodríguez, Raul Guadalupe (**Raul Sánchez**) (b. 12-12-1930, Marianao) Debut: 4-17-1952 (1952, 1957, 1960) Teams: Washington (A), Cincinnati (N) Position: Pitcher (BR TR) Stats: 5 W, 3 L, 89.2 IP, 4.62 ERA, 48 SO, 43 BB, 5 SV, 49 G

Santovenia y Mayol, Nelson Gil (**Nelson Santovenia**) (b. 7-27-1961, Pinar del Rio) Debut: 9-16-1987 (1987–1992) Teams: Montreal (N), Chicago (A) Position: Catcher (BR TR) Stats: 293 G, 876 AB, 205 H, 77 R, 22 HR, 116 RBI, .234 BA

Seguí y González, Diego Pablo (**Diego Seguí**) (b. 8-17-1937, Holguin) Debut: 4-12-1962 (1962–1977) Teams: Kansas City (A), Washington (A), Kansas City (A), Oakland (A), Seattle (A), Oakland (A), St. Louis (N), Boston (A), Seattle (A) Position: Pitcher (BR TR) Stats: 92 W, 111 L, 1807.2 IP, 3.81 ERA, 1298 SO, 786 BB, 71 SV, 639 G (Father of David Seguí, born in U.S.)

Suarez, Luís Adelardo (**Luís Suarez**) (b. 8-24-1916, Alto Songo; d. 6-5-1991, Havana) Debut: 5-28-1944 (1944) Team: Washington (A) Position: Third Base (BR TR) Stats: 1 G, 2 AB, 0 H, 0 R, 0 HR, 0 RBI, .000 BA

Sutherland y Cantin, Leonardo (**Leo Sutherland**) (b. 4-6-1958, Santiago) Debut: 8-11-1980 (1980–1981) Team: Chicago (A) Positions: Outfield, Third Base (BL TL) Stats: 45 G, 101 AB, 25 H, 15 R, 0 HR, 5 RBI, .248 BA

Tartabull y Guzmán, José Milages (**José Tartabull**) (b. 11-27-1938, Cienfuegos) Debut: 4-10-1962 (1962–1970) Teams: Kansas City (A), Boston (A), Oakland (A) Position: Outfield (BL TL) Stats: 749 G, 1857 AB, 484 H, 247 R, 2 HR, 107 RBI, .261 BA (Father of Danny Tartabull, listed under Puerto Rico)

Taylor y Sánchez, Antonio Nemesio (**Tony Taylor**) (b. 12-19-1935, Central Alara) Debut: 4-15-1958 (1958–1976) Teams: Chicago (N), Philadelphia (N), Detroit (A), Philadelphia (N) Position: Infield (BR TR) Stats: 2195 G, 7680 AB, 2007 H, 1005 R, 75 HR, 598 RBI, .261 BA

Tiant y Vega, Luís Clemente (**Luís "Looie" Tiant, Jr.**) (b. 11-23-1940, Marianao) Debut: 7-19-1964 (1964–1982) Teams: Cleveland (A), Minnesota (A), Boston (A), New York (A), Pittsburgh (N), California (A) Position: Pitcher (BR TR) Stats: 229 W, 172 L, 3486.1 IP, 3.30 ERA, 2416 SO, 1104 BB, 15 SV, 573 G

Torres y Martínez, Ricardo Jiménez (**Ricardo Torres**) (b. 4-16-1891, Regla; d. 4-17-1960, Regla) Debut: 5-18-1920 (1920–1922) Team: Washington (A) Positions: Catcher, First Base (BR TR) Stats: 22 G, 37 AB, 11 H, 9 R, 0 HR, 3 RBI, .297 BA

Torres y Núñez, Don Gilberto (**Gil Torres**) (b. 8-23-1915, Regla; d. 1-10-1983, Regla) Debut: 4-25-1940 (1940, 1944–1946) Team: Washington (A) Positions: Infield, Shortstop, Pitcher (BR TR) Hitting Stats: 44 G, 61 AB, 16 H, 5 R, 0 HR, 2 RBI, .262 BA; Pitching Stats: 0 W, 0 L, 9.2 IP, 5.59 ERA, 3 SO, 3 BB, 1 SV, 5 G

Tuero y Monzón, Oscar (**Oscar Tuero**) (b. 12-17-1898, Havana; d. 10-21-1960, Houston) Debut: 5-30-1918 (1918–1920) Team: St. Louis (N) Position: Pitcher (BR TR) Stats: 6 W, 9 L, 199.2 IP, 2.88 ERA, 58 SO, 53 BB, 4 SV, 58 G

Ullrich y Castello, Carlos Santiago (**Santiago "Sandy" Ullrich**) (b. 7-25-1921, Havana) Debut: 5-3-1944 (1944–1945) Team: Washington (A) Position: Pitcher (BR TR) Stats: 3 W, 3 L, 91 IP, 5.04 ERA, 28 SO, 38 BB, 1 SV, 31 G

Valdes y Rojas, Rogelio Lazaro (**Roy Valdez**) (b. 2-20-1920, Havana) Debut: 5-3-1944 (1944) Team: Washington (A) Position: Pinch Hitter (BR TR) Stats: 1 G, 1 AB, 0 H, 0 R, 0 HR, 0 RBI, .000 BA

Valdespino y Borroto, Hilario (**Sandy Valdespino**) (b. 1-14-1939, San José de Las Lajas) Debut: 4-12-1965 (1965–1971) Teams: Minnesota (A), Atlanta (N), Houston (N), Seattle (A), Milwaukee (A), Kansas City (A) Position: Outfield (BL TL) Stats: 382 G, 765 AB, 176 H, 96 R, 7 HR, 67 RBI, .230 BA

Valdez (Gutiérrez y Valdez), Rene (**Rene Valdez**) (b. 6-2-1929, Guanabacoa) Debut: 4-21-1957 (1957) Team: Brooklyn (N) Position: Pitcher (BR TR) Stats: 1 W, 1 L, 13 IP, 5.54 ERA, 10 SO, 7 BB, 0 SV, 5 G

Valdivielso y López, José Martínez (**José Valdivielso**) (b. 5-22-1934, Matanzas) Debut: 6-21-1955 (1955–1956, 1959–1961) Teams: Washington (A), Minnesota (A) Position: Shortstop (BR TR) Stats: 401 G, 971 AB, 213 H, 89 R, 9 HR, 85 RBI, .219 BA

Versalles y Rodríguez, Zolio Casanova (**Zolio "Zorro" Versalles**) (b. 12-18-1939, Veldado) Debut: 8-1-1959 (1959–1971) Teams: Washington (A), Minnesota (A), Los Angeles (N), Cleveland (A), Washington (A), Atlanta (N) Position: Shortstop (BR TR) Stats: 1400 G, 5141 AB, 1246 H, 650 R, 95 HR, 471 RBI, .242 BA

Zabala y Rodríguez, Adrian (**Adrian Zabala**) (b. 8-26-1916, San Antonio de los Baños) Debut: 8-11-1945 (1945, 1949) Team: New York (N) Position: Pitcher (BL TL) Stats: 4 W, 7 L, 84.1 IP, 5.02 ERA, 27 SO, 30 BB, 1 SV, 26 G

Zamora y Sosa, Oscar José (**Oscar Zamora**) (b. 9-23-1944, Camaguey) Debut: 6-18-1974 (1974–1976, 1978) Teams: Chicago (N), Houston (N) Position: Pitcher (BR TR) Stats: 13 W, 14 L, 224.2 IP, 4.53 ERA, 99 SO, 58 BB, 23 SV, 158 G

Zardón y Sanchez, José Antonio (**José Zardón**) (b. 5-20-1923, Havana) Debut: 4-18-1945 (1945) Team: Washington (A) Positions: Outfield, Infield (BR TR) Stats: 54 G, 131 AB, 38 H, 13 R, 0 HR, 13 RBI, .290 BA

Venezuela

(First Venezuelan major-leaguer: Alex Carrasquel [April 23, 1939]; 64 players)

Alvarez y Fuenmayor, Wilson Eduardo (**Wilson Alvarez**) (b. 3-24-1970, Maracaibo) Debut: 7-24-1989 (1989, 1991–1992) Teams: Texas (A), Chicago (A) Position: Pitcher (BL TL) Stats: 8 W, 6 L, 156.2 IP, 4.77 ERA, 98 SO, 96 BB, 1 SV, 45 G

Aparicio y Montiel, Luís Ernesto (**Luís Aparicio**) (b. 4-29-1934, Maracaibo) Debut: 4-17-1956 (1956–1973) Teams: Chicago (A), Baltimore (A), Chicago (A), Boston (A) Position: Shortstop (BR TR) Stats: 2599 G, 10230 AB, 2677 H, 1335 R, 83 HR, 791 RBI, .262 BA (**Hall of Fame, 1984**)

Aponte y Yuripa, Luís Eduardo (**Luís Aponte**) (b. 6-14-1953, El Tigre) Debut: 9-4-1980 (1980–1984) Teams: Boston (A), Cleveland (A) Position: Pitcher (BR TR) Stats: 9 W, 6 L, 220 IP, 3.27 ERA, 113 SO, 68 BB, 7 SV, 110 G

Armas y Machado, Antonio Rafael (**Tony Armas**) (b. 7-2-1953, Anzoatequi) Debut: 9-6-1976 (1976–1989) Teams: Pittsburgh (N), Oakland (A), Boston (A), California (A) Positions: Outfield, DH (BR TR) Stats: 1432 G, 5164 AB, 1302 H, 614 R, 251 HR, 815 RBI, .252 BA

Azocar y Azocar, Oscar Gregorio (**Oscar Azocar**) (b. 2-21-1965, Soro) Debut: 7-17-1990 (1990–1992) Teams: New York (A), San Diego (N) Positions: Outfield, DH (BL TL) Stats: 202 G, 439 AB, 99 H, 38 R, 5 HR, 36 RBI, .226 BA

Blanco y Caripe, Dámaso (**Dámaso Blanco**) (b. 12-11-1941, Curiepe) Debut: 5-26-1972 (1972–1974) Team: San Francisco (N) Position: Infield (BR TR) Stats: 72 G, 33 AB, 7 H, 9 R, 0 HR, 2 RBI, .212 BA

Blanco y Díaz, Oswaldo Carlos (**Oswaldo "Ossie" Blanco**) (b. 9-8-1945) Debut: 5-26-1970 (1970, 1974) Teams: Chicago (A), Cleveland (A) Positions: First Base, DH (BR TR) Stats: 52 G, 102 AB, 20 H, 5 R, 0 HR, 10 RBI, .196 BA

Bravo y Urdaneta, Angel Alfonso (**Angel Bravo**) (b. 8-4-1942, Maracaibo) Debut: 6-6-1969

Venezuela, *cont.*

(1969–1971) Teams: Chicago (A), Cincinnati (N), San Diego (N) Position: Outfield (BL TL) Stats: 149 G, 218 AB, 54 H, 26 R, 1 HR, 12 RBI, .248 BA

Carrasquel y Aparicio, Alejandro Eloy (**Alex Carrasquel**) (b. 7-24-1912, Caracas; d. 8-19-1969, Caracas) Debut: 4-23-1939 (1939–1945, 1949) Teams: Washington (A), Chicago (A) Position: Pitcher (BR TR) Stats: 50 W, 39 L, 861 IP, 3.73 ERA, 252 SO, 347 BB, 16 SV, 258 G

Carrasquel y Colon, Alfonso (**Chico Carrasquel**) (b. 1-23-1928, Caracas) Debut: 4-18-1950 (1950–1959) Teams: Chicago (A), Cleveland (A), Kansas City (A), Baltimore (A) Position: Shortstop (BR TR) Stats: 1325 G, 4644 AB, 1199 H, 568 R, 55 HR, 474 RBI, .258 BA

Carreño y Adrian, Amalio Rafael (**Amalio Carreño**) (b. 4-11-1964, Chacachacare) Debut: 7-7-1991 (1991) Team: Philadelphia (N) Position: Pitcher (BR TR) Stats: 0 W, 0 L, 3.1 IP, 16.20 ERA, 2 SO, 3 BB, 0 SV, 3 G

Castillo y Jiménez, Antonio José (**Tony Castillo**) (b. 3-1-1963, Quibor) Debut: 8-14-1988 (1988–1991) Teams: Toronto (A), Atlanta (N), New York (N) Position: Pitcher (BL TL) Stats: 9 W, 4 L, 151 IP, 4.17 ERA, 111 SO, 47 BB, 2 SV, 112 G

Chacón y Rodríguez, Elio (**Elio Chacón**) (b. 10-26-1936, Caracas; d. 4-24-1992, Caracas) Debut: 4-20-1960 (1960–1962) Teams: Cincinnati (N), New York (N) Positions: Infield, Outfield (BR TR) Stats: 228 G, 616 AB, 143 H, 89 R, 4 HR, 39 RBI, .232 BA

Chávez y Silva, Nestor Isais (**Nestor Chávez**) (b. 7-6-1947, Chacao; d. 3-16-1969, Maracaibo) Debut: 9-9-1967 (1967) Team: San Francisco (N) Position: Pitcher (BR TR) Stats: 1 W, 0 L, 5 IP, 0.00 ERA, 3 SO, 3 BB, 0 SV, 2 G

Colon, Cristóbal (**Cristóbal "Cris" Colon**) (b. 1-3-1969, LaGuaira) Debut: 9-18-1992 (1992) Team: Texas (A) Position: Shortstop (BB TR) Stats: 14 G, 36 AB, 6 H, 5 R, 0 HR, 1 RBI, .167 BA

Concepción y Benitez, David Ismael (**Davy Concepción**) (b. 6-17-1948, Aragua) Debut: 4-6-1970 (1970–1987) Team: Cincinnati (N) Position: Shortstop (BR TR) Stats: 2488 G, 8723 AB, 2326 H, 993 R, 101 HR, 950 RBI, .267 BA

Davalillo y Romero, Pompeyo Antonio (**Pompeyo "Yo Yo" Davalillo**) (b. 6-30-1931, Caracas) Debut: 8-1-1953 (1953) Team: Washington (A) Position: Shortstop (BR TR) Stats: 19 G, 58 AB, 17 H, 10 R, 0 HR, 2 RBI, .293 BA (Brother of Vic Davalillo)

Davalillo y Romero, Victor José (**Vic Davalillo**) (b. 7-31-1936, Cabimas) Debut: 4-9-1963 (1963–1980) Teams: Cleveland (A), California (A), St. Louis (N), Pittsburgh (N), Oakland (A), Los Angeles (N) Position: Outfield (BL TL) Stats: 1458 G, 4017 AB, 1122 H, 509 R, 36 HR, 329 RBI, .279 BA (Brother of Pompeyo Davalillo)

Díaz y Seijas, Baudilio José (**Bo Díaz**) (b. 3-23-1953, Cua; d. 11-24-1990, Caracas) Debut: 9-6-1977 (1977–1989) Teams: Boston (A), Cleveland (A), Philadelphia (N), Cincinnati (N) Position: Catcher (BR TR) Stats: 993 G, 3274 AB, 834 H, 327 R, 87 HR, 452 RBI, .255 BA

Escobar y Rivas, Angel Rubenque (**Angel Escobar**) (b. 5-12-1965, LaSabana) Debut: 5-17-1988 (1988) Team: San Francisco (N) Position: Infield (BB TR) Stats: 3 G, 3 AB, 1 H, 1 R, 0 HR, 0 RBI, .333 BA

Escobar y Sánchez, José Elias (**José Escobar**) (b. 10-30-1960, Las Flores) Debut: 4-13-1991 (1991) Team: Cleveland (A) Position: Infield (BR TR) Stats: 10 G, 15 AB, 3 H, 0 R, 0 HR, 1 RBI, .200 BA

Espinoza y Ramírez, Alvaro Alberto (**Alvaro Espinoza**) (b. 2-19-1962, Valencia) Debut: 9-14-1984 (1984–1991, 1993) Teams: Minnesota (A), New York (A), Cleveland (A) Position: Shortstop (BR TR) Stats: 517 G, 1523 AB, 387 H, 142 R, 7 HR, 104 RBI, .254 BA

Galarraga (Padovani y Galarraga), Andrés José (**Andrés Galarraga**) (b. 6-18-1961, Caracas) Debut: 8-23-1985 (1985–1991) Teams: Montreal (N), St. Louis (N), Colorado (N) Position: First Base (BR TR) Stats: 942 G, 3407 AB, 909 H, 432 R, 116 HR, 472 RBI, .267 BA

Garces y Mendoza, Richard (**Rich Garces**) (b. 5-18-1971, Maracay) Debut: 9-18-1990 (1990) Team: Minnesota (A) Position: Pitcher (BR TR) Stats: 0 W, 0 L, 5.2 IP, 1.59 ERA, 1 SO, 4 BB, 2 SV, 5 G

Garcia y Fortunato, Ramón (**Ramón García**) (b. 12-9-1969, Guanare) Debut: 5-31-1991 (1991) Team: Chicago (A) Position: Pitcher (BR TR) Stats: 4 W, 4 L, 78.1 IP, 5.40 ERA, 40 SO, 31 BB, 0 SV, 16 G

García y Guerrero, Carlos Jesus (**Carlos García**) (b. 10-15-1967, Tachira) Debut: 9-20-1990

(1990–1992) Team: Pittsburgh (N) Positions: Infield, Pinch Hitter (BR TR) Stats: 38 G, 67 AB, 16 H, 7 R, 0 HR, 5 RBI, .239 BA

García y Sifontes, Miguel Angel (**Miguel García**) (b. 4-19-1966, Caracas) Debut: 4-30-1987 (1987–1989) Teams: California (A), Pittsburgh (N) Position: Pitcher (BL TL) Stats: 0 W, 2 L, 20.1 IP, 8.41 ERA, 11 SO, 12 BB, 0 SV, 14 G

Gil y Guillén, Tomás Gustavo (**Gus Gil**) (b. 4-19-1939, Caracas) Debut: 4-11-1967 (1967, 1969–1971) Teams: Cleveland (A), Seattle (A), Milwaukee (A) Position: Infield (BR TR) Stats: 221 G, 468 AB, 87 H, 46 R, 1 HR, 37 RBI, .186 BA

González y Caraballo, Germán José (**Germán González**) (b. 3-7-1962, Río Caribe) Debut: 8-5-1988 (1988–1989) Team: Minnesota (A) Position: Pitcher (BR TR) Stats: 3 W, 2 L, 50.1 IP, 4.11 ERA, 44 SO, 19 BB, 1 SV, 38 G

Guillén y Barrios, Oswaldo José (**Ozzie Guillén**) (b. 1-20-1964, Oculare del Tuy) Debut: 4-9-1985 (1985–1992) Team: Chicago (A) Position: Shortstop (BL TR) Stats: 1095 G, 3841 AB, 1021 H, 432 R, 10 HR, 338 RBI, .266 BA

Gutiérrez, César Dario (**César Gutiérrez**) (b. 1-26-1943, Coro) Debut: 4-16-1967 (1967, 1969–1971) Teams: San Francisco (N), Detroit (A) Position: Infield (BR TR) Stats: 223 G, 545 AB, 128 H, 61 R, 0 HR, 26 RBI, .235 BA

Heredia y Martínez, Ubaldo José (**Ubaldo Heredia**) (b. 5-4-1956, Ciudad Bolivar) Debut: 5-12-1987 (1987) Team: Montreal (N) Position: Pitcher (BR TR) Stats: 0 W, 1 L, 10 IP, 5.40 ERA, 6 SO, 3 BB, 0 SV, 2 G

Hermoso, Angel Remigio (**Angel "Remy" Hermoso**) (b. 10-1-1946, Carabobo) Debut: 9-14-1967 (1967, 1969, 1970, 1974) Teams: Atlanta (N), Montreal (N), Cleveland (A) Position: Infield (BR TR) Stats: 91 G, 223 AB, 47 H, 25 R, 0 HR, 8 RBI, .211 BA

Hernández, Enzo Octavio (**Enzo Hernández**) (b. 2-12-1949, Valle de Guanape) Debut: 4-17-1971 (1971–1978) Teams: San Diego (N), Los Angeles (N) Position: Shortstop (BR TR) Stats: 714 G, 2327 AB, 522 H, 241 R, 2 HR, 113 RBI, .224 BA

Hernández (Antiah y Hernández), Leonardo Jesús (**Leo Hernández**) (b. 11-6-1959, Santa Lucia) Debut: 9-19-1982 (1982–1983, 1985–1986) Teams: Baltimore (A), New York (A) Positions: Third Base, Outfield, DH (BR TR) Stats: 85 G, 248 AB, 56 H, 23 R, 7 HR, 30 RBI, .226 BA

Hernández y Almeida, Carlos Alberto (**Carlos Hernández**) (b. 5-24-1967, San Felix) Debut: 4-20-1990 (1990–1992) Team: Los Angeles (N) Position: Catcher (BR TR) Stats: 94 G, 207 AB, 52 H, 14 R, 3 HR, 19 RBI, .251 BA

Hernández y Alvarado, Rafael Tobias (**Toby Hernández**) (b. 11-30-1958, Calabozo) Debut: 6-22-1984 (1984) Team: Toronto (A) Position: Catcher (BR TR) Stats: 3 G, 2 AB, 1 H, 1 R, 0 HR, 0 RBI, .500 BA

Herrera y Ontiveros, José Concepción (**José Herrera**) (b. 4-8-1942, San Lorenzo) Debut: 6-3-1967 (1967–1970) Teams: Houston (N), Montreal (N) Positions: Outfield, Infield, DH (BR TR) Stats: 80 G, 231 AB, 61 H, 16 R, 2 HR, 20 RBI, .264 BA

Infante y Carpio, Fermín Alexis (**Alex Infante**) (b. 12-4-1961, Barquisimeto) Debut: 9-27-1987 (1987–1990) Teams: Toronto (A), Atlanta (N) Positions: Infield, DH (BR TR) Stats: 60 G, 55 AB, 6 H, 11 R, 0 HR, 0 RBI, .109 BA

Leal (Albarado y Leal), Luís Enrique (**Luís Leal**) (b. 3-21-1957, Barquisimeto) Debut: 5-25-1980 (1980–1985) Team: Toronto (A) Position: Pitcher (BR TR) Stats: 51 W, 58 L, 946 IP, 4.14 ERA, 491 SO, 320 BB, 1 SV, 165 G

León, Danilo Enrique (**Dan León**) (b. 4-3-1967, La Concepción) Debut: 6-6-1992 (1992) Team: Texas (A) Position: Pitcher (BR TR) Stats: 1 W, 1 L, 18.1 IP, 5.89 ERA, 15 SO, 10 BB, 0 SV, 15 G

Lugo y Colina, Rafael Urbano (**Urbano Lugo**) (8-12-1962, Punto Fijo) Debut: 4-28-1985 (1985–1990) Teams: California (A), Montreal (N), Detroit (A) Position: Pitcher (BR TR) Stats: 6 W, 7 L, 162.2 IP, 5.31 ERA, 91 SO, 67 BB, 0 SV, 50 G

Machado y Rondón, Julio Segundo (**Julio Machado**) (b. 12-1-1965, Zulia) Debut: 9-7-1989 (1989–1991) Teams: New York (N), Milwaukee (A) Position: Pitcher (BR TR) Stats: 7 W, 5 L, 147 IP, 3.12 ERA, 151 SO, 83 BB, 6 SV, 101 G

Manrique y Reyes, Fred Eloy (**Fred Manrique**) (b. 5-11-1961, Edo Bolivar) Debut: 8-23-1981 (1981, 1984–1990) Teams: Toronto (A), Montreal (N), St. Louis (N), Chicago (A), Texas (A), Minnesota (A), Oakland (A) Position: Infield (BR TR) Stats: 498 G, 1337 AB, 340 H, 151 R, 20 HR, 151 RBI, .254 BA

Venezuela, *cont.*

Márquez y Mora, Gonzalo Enrique (**Gonzalo Márquez**) (b. 3-31-1946, Carupano; d. 12-20-1984, Valencia) Debut: 8-11-1972 (1972–1974) Teams: Oakland (A), Chicago (N) Positions: First Base, Outfield, DH (BL TL) Stats: 76 G, 115 AB, 27 H, 9 R, 1 HR, 10 RBI, .235 BA

Martínez (Escobar y Martínez), Carlos Alberto (**Carlos Martínez**) (b. 8-11-1964, LaGuaira) Debut: 9-2-1988 (1988–1992) Teams: Chicago (A), Cleveland (A) Positions: Third Base, First Base, Outfield, DH (BR TR) Stats: 359 G, 1162 AB, 308 H, 112 R, 19 HR, 121 RBI, .265 BA

Monzant y Espina, Ramón Segundo (**Ray Monzant**) (b. 1-4-1933, Maracaibo) Debut: 7-2-1954 (1954–1985, 1960) Teams: New York (N), San Francisco (N) Position: Pitcher (BR TR) Stats: 16 W, 21 L, 316.2 IP, 4.38 ERA, 201 SO, 134 BB, 1 SV, 106 G

Paredes y Isambert, Johnny Alfanso (**Johnny Paredes**) (b. 9-2-1962) Debut: 4-29-1988 (1988, 1990–1991) Teams: Montreal (N), Detroit (A), Montreal (N), Detroit (A) Positions: Infield, Outfield (BR TR) Stats: 60 G, 123 AB, 26 H, 12 R, 1 HR, 11 RBI, .211 BA

Pedrique y García, Alfredo José (**Al Pedrique**) (b. 8-11-1960, Aragua) Debut: 4-14-1987 (1987–1989) Teams: New York (N), Pittsburgh (N), Detroit (A) Position: Infield (BR TR) Stats: 174 G, 449 AB, 111 H, 32 R, 1 HR, 36 RBI, .247 BA

Peraza, Oswaldo José (**Oswaldo Peraza**) (b. 10-19-1962, Puerto Cabello) Debut: 4-4-1988 (1988) Team: Baltimore (A) Position: Pitcher (BR TR) Stats: 5 W, 7 L, 86 IP, 5.55 ERA, 61 SO, 37 BB, 0 SV, 19 G

Polidor y González, Gustavo Adolfo (**Gus Polidor**) (b. 10-26-1961, Caracas) Debut: 9-7-1985 (1985–1990) Teams: California (A), Milwaukee (A) Position: Infield (BR TR) Stats: 222 G, 428 AB, 89 H, 33 R, 2 HR, 35 RBI, .208 BA

Quintana y Hernández, Carlos Narcis (**Carlos Quintana**) (b. 8-26-1965, Estado Miranda) Debut: 9-16-1988 (1988–1992) Teams: Boston (A) Positions: First Base, Outfield, DH (BR TR) Stats: 337 G, 1073 AB, 306 H, 132 R, 18 HR, 146 RBI, .285 BA

Ramos y García, Jesús Manuel (**Chucho Ramos**) (b. 4-12-1918, Maturin; d. 9-2-1977, Caracas) Debut: 5-7-1944 (1944) Team: Cincinnati (N) Position: Outfield (BR TL) Stats: 4 G, 10 AB, 5 H, 1 R, 0 HR, 0 RBI, .500 BA

Rodríguez y Múñoz, Roberto (**Bobby Rodríguez**) (b. 11-29-1941, Caracas) Debut: 5-13-1967 (1967, 1970) Teams: Kansas City (A), Oakland (A), San Diego (N), Chicago (N) Position: Pitcher (BR TR) Stats: 4 W, 3 L, 112.1 IP, 4.81 ERA, 91 SO, 37 BB, 7 SV, 57 G

Salazar y García, Luís Ernesto (**Luís Salazar**) (b. 5-19-1956, Barcelona) Debut: 8-15-1980 (1980–1992) Teams: San Diego (N), Chicago (A), San Diego (N), Detroit (A), San Diego (N), Chicago (N) Position: Infield (BR TR) Stats: 1302 G, 4101 AB, 1070 H, 438 R, 94 HR, 455 RBI, .261 BA

Salazar y Vepez, Argenis Antonio (**Angel Salazar**) (b. 11-4-1961, El Tigre) Debut: 8-10-1983 (1983–1984, 1986–1988) Teams: Montreal (N), Kansas City (A), Chicago (N) Position: Infield (BR TR) Stats: 383 G, 886 AB, 188 H, 69 R, 2 HR, 59 RBI, .212 BA

Sánchez (Escoba y Sánchez), Luís Mercedes Escoba (**Luís Sánchez**) (b. 8-24-1953, Cariaco) Debut: 4-10-1981 (1981–1985) Team: California (A) Position: Pitcher (BR TR) Stats: 28 W, 21 L, 369.2 IP, 3.75 ERA, 216 SO, 145 BB, 27 SV, 194 G

Sarmiento y Aponte, Manuel Eduardo (**Manny Sarmiento**) (b. 2-2-1956, Cagua) Debut: 7-30-1976 (1976–1980, 1982–1983) Teams: Cincinnati (N), Seattle (A), Pittsburgh (N) Position: Pitcher (BR TR) Stats: 26 W, 22 L, 513.2 IP, 3.49 ERA, 283 SO, 172 BB, 12 SV, 228 G

Sojo y Sojo, Luís Beltran (**Luís Sojo**) (b. 1-3-1966, Barquisimeto) Debut: 7-14-1990 (1990–1992) Teams: Toronto (A), California (A), Toronto (A) Position: Infield (BR TR) Stats: 252 G, 812 AB, 212 H, 89 R, 11 HR, 72 RBI, .261 BA

Straker y Bolnalda, Lester Paul (**Les Straker**) (b. 10-10-1959, Ciudad Bolivar) Debut: 4-11-1987 (1987–1988) Team: Minnesota (A) Position: Pitcher (BR TR) Stats: 10 W, 15 L, 237 IP, 4.22 ERA, 99 SO, 84 BB, 1 SV, 47 G

Torrealba y Torrealba, Pablo Arnoldo (**Pablo Torrealba**) (b. 4-28-1948, Barquisimeto) Debut: 4-9-1975 (1975–1979) Teams: Atlanta (N), Oakland (A), Chicago (A) Position: Pitcher (BL TL) Stats: 6 W, 13 L, 239.1 IP, 3.27 ERA, 113 SO, 104 BB, 5 SV, 111 G

Tóvar (Pérez y Tóvar), César Leonardo (**César Tóvar**) (b. 7-3-1940, Caracas) Debut: 4-12-1965 (1965–1976) Teams: Minnesota (A), Philadelphia (N), Texas (A), Oakland (A), New

York (A) Positions: Outfield, Infield (BR TR) Stats: 1488 G, 5569 AB, 1546 H, 834 R, 46 HR, 435 RBI, .278 BA

Trillo (Marcano y Trillo), Jesús Manuel (**Manny Trillo**) (b. 12-25-1950, Caripito) Debut: 6-28-1973 (1973–1989) Teams: Oakland (A), Chicago (N), Philadelphia (N), Cleveland (A), Montreal (N), San Francisco (N), Chicago (N) Position: Second Base (BR TR) Stats: 1780 G, 5950 AB, 1562 H, 598 R, 61 HR, 571 RBI, .263 BA

Visquel y González, Omar Enrique (**Omar Visquel**) (b. 5-15-1967, Caracas) Debut: 4-3-1989 (1989–1992) Team: Seattle (A) Position: Shortstop (BB TR) Stats: 502 G, 1551 AB, 388 H, 155 R, 4 HR, 100 RBI, .250 BA

Mexico

(First Mexican major-leaguer: Mel Almada [September 8, 1933]; 58 players)

Acosta y Miranda, Cecilio (**Cy Acosta**) (b. 11-22-1946, Sabino) Debut: 6-4-1972 (1972–1975) Teams: Chicago (A), Philadelphia (N) Position: Pitcher (BR TR) Stats: 13 W, 9 L, 186.2 IP, 2.66 ERA, 109 SO, 77 BB, 27 SV, 107 G

Almada, Baldomero Melo (**Mel Almada**) (b. 2-7-1913, Hwatabampo; d. 8-13-1988, Hermosillo) Debut: 9-8-1933 (1933–1939) Teams: Boston (A), Washington (A), St. Louis (A), Brooklyn (N) Position: Outfield (BL TL) Stats: 646 G, 2483 AB, 706 H, 363 R, 15 HR, 197 RBI, .284 BA

Amaro y Mora, Rubén (**Rubén Amaro**) (b. 1-6-1936, Veracruz) Debut: 6-29-1958 (1958, 1960–1969) Teams: St. Louis (N), Philadelphia (N), New York (A), California (A) Position: Infield (BR TR) Stats: 940 G, 2155 AB, 505 H, 211 R, 8 HR, 156 RBI, .234 BA

Avila y González, Roberto Francisco (**Bobby Avila**) (b. 4-2-1924, Veracruz) Debut: 4-30-1949 (1949–1959) Teams: Cleveland (A), Baltimore (A), Boston (A), Milwaukee (N) Position: Second Base (BR TR) Stats: 1300 G, 4620 AB, 1296 H, 725 R, 80 HR, 467 RBI, .281 BA

Barojas y Romero, Salomé (**Salomé Barojas**) (b. 6-16-1957, Cordoba) Debut: 4-11-1982 (1982–1985, 1988) Teams: Chicago (A), Seattle (A), Philadelphia (N) Position: Pitcher (BR TR) Stats: 18 W, 21 L, 389.2 IP, 3.95 ERA, 177 SO, 179 BB, 35 SV, 179 G

Barranca y Costales, Germán (**Germán Barranca**) (b. 10-19-1956, Veracruz) Debut: 9-2-1979 (1979–1982) Teams: Kansas City (A), Cincinnati (N) Position: Infield (BL TR) Stats: 67 G, 62 AB, 18 H, 19 R, 0 HR, 3 RBI, .290 BA

Barrios y Jiménez, Francisco Javier (**Francisco Barrios**) (b. 6-10-1953, Hermosillo; d. 4-9-1982, Hermosillo) Debut: 8-18-1974 (1974, 1976–1981) Team: Chicago (A) Position: Pitcher (BR TR) Stats: 38 W, 38 L, 717.2 IP, 4.15 ERA, 323 SO, 246 BB, 3 SV, 129 G

Carrillo, Matias García (**Matias Carrillo**) (b. 2-24-1963, Los Mochis) Debut: 5-23-1991 (1991) Team: Milwaukee (A) Position: Outfield (BL TL) Stats: 3 G, 0 AB, 0 H, 0 R, 0 HR, 0 RBI, .000 BA

Castilla y Soria, Vinicio (**Vinny Castilla**) (b. 7-4-1967, Oaxaca) Debut: 9-1-1991 (1991–1992) Teams: Atlanta (N), Colorado (N) Position: Infield (BR TR) Stats: 21 G, 21 AB, 5 H, 2 R, 0 HR, 1 RBI, .238 BA

Cecena y Lugo, José Isabel (**José Cecena**) (b. 8-20-1963, Ciudad Obregón) Debut: 4-6-1988 (1988) Team: Texas (A) Position: Pitcher (BR TR) Stats: 0 W, 0 L, 26.1 IP, 4.78 ERA, 27 SO, 23 BB, 1 SV, 22 G

Elvira y Delgado, Narciso Chicho (**Narciso Elvira**) (b. 10-29-1967, Vera Cruz) Debut: 9-9-1990 (1990) Team: Milwaukee (A) Position: Pitcher (BL TL) Stats: 0 W, 0 L, 5 IP, 5.40 ERA, 6 SO, 5 BB, 0 SV, 4 G

Escarrega y Acosta, Ernesto (**Ernesto "Chico" Escarrega**) (b. 12-27-1949, Los Mochis) Debut: 4-26-1982 (1982) Team: Chicago (A) Position: Pitcher (BR TR) Stats: 1 W, 3 L, 73.2 IP, 3.67 ERA, 33 SO, 16 BB, 1 SV, 38 G

Estrada y Soto, Francisco (**Frank Estrada**) (b. 2-12-1948, Navojoa) Debut: 9-14-1971 (1971) Team: New York (N) Position: Catcher (BR TR) Stats: 1 G, 2 AB, 1 H, 0 R, 0 HR, 0 RBI, .500 BA

Fajardo y Nabaratte, Héctor (**Héctor Fajardo**) (b. 11-16-1970, Sahuayo) Debut: 8-10-1991

Mexico, *cont.*

(1991) Teams: Pittsburgh (N), Texas (A) Position: Pitcher (BR TR) Stats: 0 W, 2 L, 25.1 IP, 6.75 ERA, 23 SO, 11 BB, 0 SV, 6 G

Flores y Sandoval, Jesse (**Jesse Flores**) (b. 11-2-1914, Guadalajara; d. 12-17-1991, Orange, California) Debut: 4-16-1942 (1942–1947, 1950) Teams: Chicago (N), Philadelphia (A), Cleveland (A) Position: Pitcher (BR TR) Stats: 44 W, 59 L, 973 IP, 3.18 ERA, 352 SO, 306 BB, 6 SV, 176 G

García, Vincio Uzcanga (**Chico García**) (b. 12-24-1924, Veracruz) Debut: 4-24-1954 (1954) Team: Baltimore (A) Position: Second Base (BR TR) Stats: 39 G, 62 AB, 7 H, 6 R, 0 HR, 5 RBI, .113 BA

Gómez y Rodríguez, José Luís (**Chile Gómez**) (b. 3-23-1909, Villa Union) Debut: 7-27-1935 (1935–1936, 1942) Teams: Philadelphia (N), Washington (A) Position: Infield (BR TR) Stats: 200 G, 627 AB, 142 H, 56 R, 0 HR, 50 RBI, .226 BA

Gómez y Sánchez, Luís (**Luís Gómez**) (b. 8-19-1951, Guadalajara) Debut: 4-28-1974 (1974–1981) Teams: Minnesota (A), Toronto (A), Atlanta (N) Positions: Infield, DH (BR TR) Stats: 609 G, 1251 AB, 263 H, 108 R, 0 HR, 90 RBI, .210 BA

Greenwood, Robert Chandler (**Robert "Bob" Greenwood**) (b. 3-13-1928, Cananea) Debut: 4-21-1954 (1954–1955) Team: Philadelphia (N) Position: Pitcher (BR TR) Stats: 1 W, 2 L, 39 IP, 3.92 ERA, 9 SO, 18 BB, 0 SV, 12 G

Hernández y Acosta, Rodolfo (**Rudy Hernández**) (b. 10-18-1951, Enpalme) Debut: 9-6-1972 (1972) Team: Chicago (A) Position: Shortstop (BR TR) Stats: 8 G, 21 AB, 4 H, 0 R, 0 HR, 1 RBI, .190 BA

Herrera (Rodríguez y Herrera), Procopio (**Bobby "Tito" Herrera**) (b. 7-26-1926, Nuevo Laredo) Debut: 4-19-1951 (1951) Team: St. Louis (A) Position: Pitcher (BR TR) Stats: 0 W, 0 L, 2.1 IP, 27.00 ERA, 1 SO, 4 BB, 0 SV, 3 G

Higuera y Valenzuela, Teodoro Valenzuela (**Teddy Higuera**) (b. 11-9-1958, Los Mochis) Debut: 4-23-1985 (1985–1991) Team: Milwaukee (A) Position: Pitcher (BB TL) Stats: 92 W, 56 L, 1291.1 IP, 3.37 ERA, 1019 SO, 391 BB, 0 SV, 188 G

Jiménez y Camarena, German (**German Jiménez**) (b. 12-5-1962, Santiago) Debut: 6-28-1988 (1988) Team: Atlanta (N) Position: Pitcher (BL TL) Stats: 1 W, 6 L, 55.2 IP, 5.01 ERA, 26 SO, 12 BB, 0 SV, 15 G

Jiménez y González, Alfonso (**Houston Jiménez**) (b. 10-30-1957, Navojoa) Debut: 6-13-1983 (1983–1984, 1987–1988) Teams: Minnesota (A), Pittsburgh (N), Cleveland (A) Position: Shortstop (BR TR) Stats: 158 G, 411 AB, 76 H, 34 R, 0 HR, 29 RBI, .185 BA

León y Molino, Maximino (**Max León**) (b. 2-4-1950, Pozo Hondo) Debut: 7-18-1973 (1973–1978) Team: Atlanta (N) Position: Pitcher (BR TR) Stats: 14 W, 18 L, 310.1 IP, 3.71 ERA, 170 SO, 100 BB, 13 SV, 162 G

López y Morales, Carlos Antonio (**Carlos López**) (b. 9-27-1950, Mazatlán) Debut: 9-17-1976 (1976–1978) Teams: California (A), Seattle (A), Baltimore (A) Position: Outfield (BR TR) Stats: 237 G, 500 AB, 130 H, 61 R, 12 HR, 54 RBI, .260 BA

López y Ríos, Aurelio Alejandro (**Aurelio López**) (b. 9-21-1948, Tecamachalco; d. 9-22-1992, Matehuala) Debut: 9-1-1974 (1974, 1978–1987) Teams: Kansas City (A), St. Louis (N), Detroit (A), Houston (N) Position: Pitcher (BR TR) Stats: 62 W, 36 L, 910.1 IP, 3.56 ERA, 635 SO, 367 BB, 93 SV, 459 G

Luna, Guillermo Romero (**Memo Luna**) (b. 6-25-1930, Tacubaya) Debut: 4-20-1954 (1954) Team: St. Louis (N) Position: Pitcher (BL TL) Stats: 0 W, 1 L, 0.2 IP, 27.00 ERA, 0 SO, 2 BB, 0 SV, 1 G

Magellanes y Espinoza, Everado (**Ever Magellanes**) (b. 11-6-1965, Chihuahua) Debut: 5-17-1991 (1991) Team: Cleveland (A) Position: Shortstop (BR TR) Stats: 3 G, 2 AB, 0 H, 0 R, 0 HR, 0 RBI, .000 BA

Mendoza y Aizpuru, Mario (**Mario Mendoza**) (b. 12-26-1950, Chihuahua) Debut: 4-26-1974 (1974–1982) Teams: Pittsburgh (N), Seattle (A), Texas (A) Position: Shortstop (BR TR) Stats: 686 G, 1337 AB, 287 H, 106 R, 4 HR, 101 RBI, .215 BA

Monge, Isidro Pedroza (**Sid Monge**) (b. 4-11-1951, Agua Preita) Debut: 9-12-1975 (1975–1984) Teams: California (A), Cleveland (A), Philadelphia (N), San Diego (N), Detroit (A) Position: Pitcher (BB TL) Stats: 49 W, 40 L, 764 IP, 3.53 ERA, 471 SO, 356 BB, 56 SV, 435 G

Montemayor, Félipe Angel (**Félipe "Monty" Montemayor**) (b. 2-7-1930, Monterrey) Debut: 4-14-1953 (1953, 1955) Team: Pittsburgh (N) Position: Outfield (BL TL) Stats: 64 G, 150 AB, 26 H, 15 R, 2 HR, 10 RBI, .173 BA

Mora y Ibara, Andres (**Andres Mora**) (b. 5-25-1955, Río Bravo) Debut: 4-13-1976 (1976–1978, 1980) Teams: Baltimore (A), Cleveland (A) Positions: Outfield, DH (BR TR) Stats: 235 G, 700 AB, 156 H, 71 R, 27 HR, 83 RBI, .223 BA

Moreno y Veneroso, Angel (**Angel Moreno**) (b. 6-6-1955, La Mendosa Soledád) Debut: 8-15-1981 (1981–1982) Team: California (A) Position: Pitcher (BL TL) Stats: 4 W, 10 L, 80.2 IP, 4.02 ERA, 34 SO, 37 BB, 1 SV, 21 G

Orta y Núñez, Jorge (**Jorge Orta**) (b. 11-26-1950, Mazatlán) Debut: 4-15-1972 (1972–1987) Teams: Chicago (A), Cleveland (A), Los Angeles (N), Toronto (A), Kansas City (A) Positions: Infield, Outfield, DH (BL TR) Stats: 1755 G, 5829 AB, 1619 H, 733 R, 130 HR, 745 RBI, .278 BA

Palacios y Díaz, Vicente (**Vicente Palacios**) (b. 7-19-1963, Veracruz) Debut: 9-4-1987 (1987–1992) Team: Pittsburgh (N) Position: Pitcher (BR TR) Stats: 12 W, 8 L, 203.1 IP, 4.03 ERA, 133 SO, 91 BB, 6 SV, 76 G

Peña y Gutiérrez, José (**José Peña**) (b. 12-3-1942, Ciudad Juarez) Debut: 6-1-1969 (1969–1972) Teams: Cincinnati (N), Los Angeles (N) Position: Pitcher (BR TR) Stats: 7 W, 4 L, 112.1 IP, 4.97 ERA, 82 SO, 58 BB, 5 SV, 61 G

Perezchica y Gonzáles, Antonio Llamas (**Tony Perezchica**) (b. 4-20-1966, Mexicali) Debut: 9-7-1988 (1988–1992) Teams: San Francisco (N), Cleveland (A) Position: Infield (BR TR) Stats: 69 G, 101 AB, 23 H, 10 R, 0 HR, 5 RBI, .228 BA

Piña y García, Horacio (**Horacio Piña**) (b. 3-12-1945, Coahuila) Debut: 8-14-1968 (1968–1974, 1978) Teams: Cleveland (A), Washington (A), Texas (A), Oakland (A), Chicago (N), California (A), Philadelphia (N) Position: Pitcher (BR TR) Stats: 23 W, 23 L, 432 IP, 3.25 ERA, 278 SO, 216 BB, 38 SV, 314 G

Puente y Aguilar, Miguel Antonio (**Miguel Puente**) (b. 5-8-1948, San Luís Potosi) Debut: 5-3-1970 (1970) Team: San Francisco (N) Position: Pitcher (BR TR) Stats: 1 W, 3 L, 18.2 IP, 8.20 ERA, 14 SO, 11 BB, 0 SV, 6 G

Pulido y Manzo, Alfonso (**Alfonso Pulido**) (b. 1-23-1957, Veracruz) Debut: 9-5-1983 (1983–1984, 1986) Teams: Pittsburgh (N), New York (A) Position: Pitcher (BL TL) Stats: 1 W, 1 L, 34.2 IP, 5.19 ERA, 16 SO, 11 BB, 1 SV, 12 G

Reynoso y Gutiérrez, Armando Martín (**Armando Reynoso**) (b. 5-1-1966, San Luís Potosi) Debut: 8-11-1991 (1991–1992) Teams: Atlanta (N), Colorado (N) Position: Pitcher (BR TR) Stats: 3 W, 1 L, 31 IP, 5.81 ERA, 12 SO, 12 BB, 1 SV, 9 G

Robles y Valenzuela, Sergio (**Sergio Robles**) (b. 4-16-1946, Magdalena) Debut: 8-27-1972 (1972–1973, 1976) Teams: Baltimore (A), Los Angeles (N) Position: Catcher (BR TR) Stats: 16 G, 21 AB, 2 H, 0 R, 0 HR, 0 RBI, .095 BA

Rodríguez y Echavarría, Rosario Isabel (**Rosario Rodríguez**) (b. 7-8-1969, Los Mochis) Debut: 9-1-1989 (1989–1991) Teams: Cincinnati (N), Pittsburgh (N) Position: Pitcher (BR TL) Stats: 2 W, 2 L, 30 IP, 4.80 ERA, 18 SO, 13 BB, 6 SV, 34 G

Rodríguez y Ituarte, Aurelio (**Aurelio Rodríguez**) (b. 12-28-1947, Cananea, Sonora) Debut: 9-1-1967 (1967–1983) Teams: California (A), Washington (A), Detroit (A), San Diego (N), New York (A), Chicago (A), Baltimore (A), Chicago (A) Position: Third Base (BR TR) Stats: 2017 G, 6611 AB, 1570 H, 612 R, 124 HR, 648 RBI, .237 BA

Rodríguez y Márquez, Carlos (**Carlos Rodríguez**) (b. 11-1-1967, Mexico City) Debut: 6-16-1991 (1991) Team: New York (A) Position: Shortstop (BB TR) Stats: 15 G, 37 AB, 7 H, 1 R, 0 HR, 2 RBI, .189 BA

Romo y Navarro, Enrique (**Enrique Romo**) (b. 7-15-1947, Santa Rosalia) Debut: 4-7-1977 (1977–1982) Teams: Seattle (A), Pittsburgh (N) Position: Pitcher (BR TR) Stats: 44 W, 33 L, 603 IP, 3.45 ERA, 436 SO, 203 BB, 52 SV, 350 G (Brother of Vicente Romo)

Romo y Navarro, Vincente (**Vicente Romo**) (b. 4-12-1943, Santa Rosalia) Debut: 4-11-1968 (1968–1974, 1982) Teams: Los Angeles (N), Cleveland (A), Boston (A), Chicago (A), San Diego (N), Los Angeles (N) Position: Pitcher (BR TR) Stats: 32 W, 33 L, 645.2 IP, 3.36 ERA, 416 SO, 280 BB, 52 SV, 335 G (Brother of Enrique Romo)

Rubio y Chávez, Jorge Jesús (**Jorge Rubio**) (b. 4-23-1945, Mexicali) Debut: 4-21-1966 (1966–1967) Team: California (A) Position: Pitcher (BR TR) Stats: 2 W, 3 L, 42.1 IP, 3.19 ERA, 31 SO, 25 BB, 0 SV, 10 G

Mexico, *cont.*

Sánchez y Pérez, Celerino (**Celerino Sánchez**) (b. 2-3-1944, Veracruz) Debut: 6-13-1972 (1972–1973) Team: New York (A) Positions: Infield, Outfield, DH (BR TR) Stats: 105 G, 314 AB, 76 H, 30 R, 1 HR, 31 RBI, .242 BA

Solis, Marcelino (**Marcelino Solis**) (b. 7-19-1930, San Luís Potosi) Debut: 7-16-1958 (1958) Team: Chicago (N) Position: Pitcher (BL TL) Stats: 3 W, 3 L, 52 IP, 6.06 ERA, 15 SO, 20 BB, 0 SV, 15 G

Tollentino y Franco, José (**José Tollentino**) (b. 6-3-1961, Mexico City) Debut: 7-28-1991 (1991) Team: Houston (N) Position: Outfield (BL TL) Stats: 44 G, 54 AB, 14 H, 6 R, 1 HR, 6 RBI, .259 BA

Torres y Marroquin, Héctor Epitacio (**Héctor Torres**) (b. 9-16-1945, Monterrey) Debut: 4-10-1968 (1968–1977) Teams: Houston (N), Chicago (N), Montreal (N), Houston (N), San Diego (N), Toronto (A) Position: Shortstop (BR TR) Stats: 622 G, 1738 AB, 375 H, 148 R, 18 HR, 115 RBI, .216 BA

Treviño y Castro, Alejandro (**Alex Treviño**) (b. 8-26-1957, Monterrey) Debut: 9-11-1978 (1978–1990) Teams: New York (N), Cincinnati (N), Atlanta (N), San Francisco (N), Los Angeles (N), Houston (N), New York (N), Cincinnati (N) Position: Catcher (BR TR) Stats: 939 G, 2430 AB, 604 H, 245 R, 23 HR, 244 RBI, .249 BA (Brother of Bobby Treviño)

Treviño y Castro, Carlos (**Bobby Treviño**) (b. 8-15-1943, Monterrey) Debut: 5-22-1968 (1968) Team: California (A) Position: Outfield (BR TR) Stats: 17 G, 40 AB, 9 H, 1 R, 0 HR, 1 RBI, .225 BA (Brother of Alex Treviño)

Valenzuela, Benjamin Beltran (**Benny Valenzuela**) (b. 6-2-1933, Los Mochis) Debut: 4-27-1958 (1958) Team: St. Louis (N) Position: Third Base (BR TR) Stats: 10 G, 14 AB, 3 H, 0 R, 0 HR, 0 RBI, .214 BA

Valenzuela y Anguamea, Fernando (**Fernando Valenzuela**) (b. 11-1-1960, Navajoa) Debut: 9-15-1980 (1980–1991) Teams: Los Angeles (N), California (A), Baltimore (A) Position: Pitcher (BL TL) Stats: 141 W, 118 L, 2355 IP, 3.34 ERA, 1764 SO, 918 BB, 2 SV, 333 G

Velasquez, Guillermo (**Guillermo Velasquez**) (b. 4-23-1968, Mexicali) Debut: 9-14-1992 (1992) Team: San Diego (N) Position: First Base (BL TL) Stats: 15 G, 23 AB, 7 H, 1 R, 1 HR, 5 RBI, .304 BA

Panama

(First Panamanian major-leaguer: Humberto Robinson [April 20, 1955]; 23 players)

Acosta y López, Eduardo Elixbet (**Eduardo Acosta**) (b. 3-9-1944, Boquete) Debut: 9-7-1970 (1970–1972) Teams: Pittsburgh (N), San Diego (N) Position: Pitcher (BB TR) Stats: 6 W, 9 L, 138 IP, 4.04 ERA, 70 SO, 39 BB, 1 SV, 57 G

Berenguer, Juan Bautista (**Juan Berenguer**) (b. 11-30-1954, Aguadulce) Debut: 8-17-1978 (1978–1992) Teams: New York (N), Kansas City (A), Toronto (A), Detroit (A), San Francisco (N), Minnesota (A), Atlanta (N), Kansas City (A) Position: Pitcher (BR TR) Stats: 67 W, 62 L, 1205 IP, 3.90 ERA, 975 SO, 604 BB, 32 SV, 490 G

Chavarría y Quijano, Osvaldo (**Ossie Chavarría**) (b. 8-5-1940, Colon) Debut: 4-14-1966 (1966–1967) Team: Kansas City (A) Position: Infield (BR TR) Stats: 124 G, 250 AB, 52 H, 28 R, 2 HR, 14 RBI, .208 BA

Clarke, Vibert Ernesto (**Webbo Clarke**) (b. 6-8-1928, Colon) Debut: 9-4-1955 (1955) Team: Washington (A) Position: Pitcher (BL TL) Stats: 0 W, 0 L, 21.1 IP, 4.64 ERA, 9 SO, 14 BB, 0 SV, 7 G

Garrido, Gil Gonzalo (**Gil Garrido**) (b. 6-26-1941, Panama City) Debut: 4-24-1964 (1964, 1968–1972) Teams: San Francisco (N), Atlanta (N) Position: Infield (BR TR) Stats: 334 G, 872 AB, 207 H, 81 R, 1 HR, 51 RBI, .237 BA

Haywood, William Kiernan (**Bill Haywood**) (b. 4-21-1937, Colon) Debut: 7-28-1968 (1968) Team: Washington (A) Position: Pitcher (BR TR) Stats: 0 W, 0 L, 23.1 IP, 4.63 ERA, 10 SO, 12 BB, 0 SV, 14 G

Kelly y Gray, Roberto Conrado (**Bobby Kelly**) (b. 10-1-1964, Panama City) Debut: 7-29-1987 (1987–1992) Teams: New York (A), Cincinnati (N) Position: Outfield (BR TR) Stats: 638 G, 2277 AB, 637 H, 320 R, 56 HR, 258 RBI, .280 BA

Lewis, Allan Sydney (**Al Lewis**) (b. 12-12-1941, Colon) Debut: 4-11-1967 (1967–1970, 1972–1973) Teams: Kansas City (A), Oakland (A) Position: Outfield (BB TR) Stats: 156 G, 29 AB, 6 H, 47 R, 1 HR, 3 RBI, .207 BA

López y Swainson, Héctor Headley (**Héctor López**) (b. 7-9-1929, Colon) Debut: 5-12-1955 (1955–1966) Teams: Kansas City (A), New York (A) Position: Infield (BR TR) Stats: 1451 G, 4644 AB, 1251 H, 623 R, 136 HR, 591 RBI, .269 BA

Maldonado y Delgado, Carlos César (**Carlos Maldonado**) (b. 10-18-1966, Chepo) Debut: 9-16-1990 (1990–1991) Teams: Kansas City (A), Milwaukee (A) Position: Pitcher (BR TR) Stats: 0 W, 0 L, 13 IP, 8.56 ERA, 10 SO, 13 BB, 0 SV, 9 G

Moreno y Quintero, Omar Renan (**Omar Moreno**) (b. 10-24-1952, Puerto Armuelles) Debut: 9-6-1975 (1975–1986) Teams: Pittsburgh (N), Houston (N), New York (A), Kansas City (A), Atlanta (N) Position: Outfield (BL TL) Stats: 1382 G, 4992 AB, 1257 H, 699 R, 37 HR, 386 RBI, .252 BA

Murrell y Peters, Iván Augustus (**Iván Murrell**) (b. 4-24-1945, Almirante) Debut: 9-28-1963 (1963–1964, 1967–1974) Teams: Houston (N), San Diego (N), Atlanta (N) Position: Outfield (BR TR) Stats: 564 G, 1306 AB, 308 H, 126 R, 33 HR, 123 RBI, .236 BA

Oglivie, Benjamin Ambrosio (**Ben Oglivie**) (b. 2-11-1949, Colon) Debut: 9-4-1971 (1971–1986) Teams: Boston (A), Detroit (A), Milwaukee (A) Positions: Outfield, DH (BL TL) Stats: 1754 G, 5913 AB, 1615 H, 784 R, 235 HR, 901 RBI, .273 BA

Phillips y Lopez, Aldolfo Emilio (**Adolfo Phillips**) (b. 12-16-1941, Bethania) Debut: 9-2-1964 (1964–1972) Teams: Philadelphia (N), Chicago (N), Montreal (N), Cleveland (A) Position: Outfield (BR TR) Stats: 649 G, 1875 AB, 463 H, 270 R, 59 HR, 173 RBI, .247 BA

Prescott, George Bertrand (**Bobby Prescott**) (b. 3-27-1931, Colon) Debut: 6-17-1961 (1961) Team: Kansas City (A) Position: Outfield (BR TR) Stats: 10 G, 12 AB, 1 H, 0 R, 0 HR, 0 RBI, .083 BA

Ramsey, Fernando (**Fernando Ramsey**) (b. 12-20-1965, Rainbow) Debut: 9-7-1992 (1992) Team: Chicago (N) Position: Outfield (BR TR) Stats: 18 G, 25 AB, 3 H, 0 R, 0 HR, 2 RBI, .120 BA

Roberts, David Leonard (**Dave Roberts**) (b. 6-30-1933, Panama City) Debut: 9-5-1962 (1962, 1964, 1966) Teams: Houston (N), Pittsburgh (N) Positions: Outfield, First Base (BL TL) Stats: 91 G, 194 AB, 38 H, 15 R, 2 HR, 17 RBI, .196 BA

Robinson, Humberto Valentino (**Humberto Robinson**) (b. 6-25-1930, Colon) Debut: 4-20-1955 (1955–1960) Teams: Milwaukee (N), Cleveland (A), Philadelphia (N) Position: Pitcher (BR TR) Stats: 8 W, 13 L, 213 IP, 3.25 ERA, 114 SO, 90 BB, 4 SV, 102 G

Salmon, Ruthford Eduardo (**Chico Salmon**) (b. 12-3-1951, Colon) Debut: 6-28-1964 (1964–1972) Teams: Cleveland (A), Baltimore (A) Positions: Outfield, Infield (BR TR) Stats: 658 G, 1667 AB, 415 H, 202 R, 31 HR, 149 RBI, .249 BA

Sanguillen y Magán, Manuel de Jesús (**Manny Sanguillen**) (b. 3-21-1944, Colon) Debut: 7-23-1967 (1967–1980) Teams: Pittsburgh (N), Oakland (A), Pittsburgh (N) Positions: Catcher, Outfield, First Base (BR TR) Stats: 1448 G, 5062 AB, 1500 H, 566 R, 65 HR, 585 RBI, .296 BA

Stennett y Porte, Renaldo Antonio (**Rennie Stennett**) (b. 4-5-1951, Colon) Debut: 7-10-1971 (1971–1981) Teams: Pittsburgh (N), San Francisco (N) Position: Infield (BR TR) Stats: 1237 G, 4521 AB, 1239 H, 500 R, 41 HR, 432 RBI, .274 BA

Toppin, Ruperto (**Rupe Toppin**) (b. 12-7-1941, Panama City) Debut: 7-28-1962 (1962) Team: Kansas City (A) Position: Pitcher (BR TR) Stats: 0 W, 0 L, 2 IP, 13.50 ERA, 1 SO, 5 BB, 0 SV, 2 G

Webster, Ramón Alberto (**Ramón Webster**) (b. 8-31-1942, Colon) Debut: 4-11-1967 (1967–1971) Teams: Kansas City (A), Oakland (A), San Diego (N), Chicago (N), Oakland (A) Position: First Base (BL TL) Stats: 380 G, 778 AB, 190 H, 76 R, 17 HR, 98 RBI, .244 BA

Canal Zone (Panama)

(First Canal Zone major-leaguer: Pat Scantlebury [April 19, 1956]; 4 players)

Carew y Scott, Rodney Cline (**Rod Carew**) (b. 10-1-1945, Gatun, Canal Zone) Debut: 4-11-1967 (1967–1985) Teams: Minnesota (A), California (A) Positions: Outfield, First Base (BL TR) Stats: 2469 G, 9315 AB, 3053 H, 1424 R, 92 HR, 1015 RBI, .328 BA (**Hall of Fame, 1991**)

Eden, Edward Michael (**Mike Eden**) (b. 5-22-1949, Fort Clayton, Canal Zone) Debut: 8-2-1976 (1976–1978) Teams: Atlanta (N), Chicago (A) Position: Infield (BB TR) Stats: 15 G, 25 AB, 2 H, 1 R, 0 HR, 1 RBI, .080 BA

Hughes, Thomas Edward (**Tom "Tommy" Hughes**) (b. 9-13-1934, Ancon, Canal Zone) Debut: 9-13-1959 (1959) Team: St. Louis (N) Position: Pitcher (BL TR) Stats: 0 W, 2 L, 4 IP, 15.75 ERA, 2 SO, 2 BB, 0 SV, 2 G

Scantlebury, Patricio Athelstan (**Pat Scantlebury**) (b. 11-11-1925, Gatun, Canal Zone; d. 5-23-1991, New York) Debut: 4-19-1956 (1956) Team: Cincinnati (N) Position: Pitcher (BL TL) Stats: 0 W, 1 L, 19 IP, 6.63 ERA, 10 SO, 5 BB, 0 SV, 6 G

Virgin Islands

(First Virgin Islands major-leaguer: Joe Christopher [May 26, 1959]; 8 players)

Browne, Jerome Austin (**Jerry Browne**) (b. 2-13-1966, Christiansted) Debut: 9-6-1986 (1986–1992) Teams: Texas (A), Cleveland (A), Oakland (A) Positions: Second Base, Outfield, DH (BB TR) Stats: 728 G, 2417 AB, 657 H, 341 R, 17 HR, 222 RBI, .272 BA

Christopher, Joe (**Joe Christopher**) (b. 12-13-1935, Frederiksted) Debut: 5-26-1959 (1959–1966) Teams: Pittsburgh (N), New York (N), Boston (A) Position: Outfield (BR TR) Stats: 638 G, 1667 AB, 434 H, 224 R, 29 HR, 173 RBI, .260 BA

Clarke, Horace Meredith (**Horace Clark**) (b. 6-2-1940, Fredericksted) Debut: 5-13-1965 (1965–1974) Teams: New York (A), San Diego (N) Position: Second Base (BB TR) Stats: 1272 G, 4813 AB, 1230 H, 548 R, 27 HR, 304 RBI, .256 BA

Cruz, Henry Acosta (**Henry Cruz**) (b. 2-27-1952, Christiansted) Debut: 4-18-1975 (1975–1978) Teams: Los Angeles (N), Chicago (N) Position: Outfield (BL TL) Stats: 171 G, 280 AB, 64 H, 32 R, 8 HR, 34 RBI, .229 BA

Hendricks, Elrod Jerome (**Elrod "Ellie" Hendricks**) (b. 12-22-1940, Charlotte Amalie) Debut: 4-13-1968 (1968–1979) Teams: Baltimore (A), Chicago (N), Baltimore (A), New York (A), Baltimore (A) Positions: Catcher, DH, Pinch Hitter (BL TR) Stats: 711 G, 1888 AB, 415 H, 205 R, 62 HR, 230 RBI, .220 BA

McBean, Alvin O'Neal (**Al McBean**) (b. 5-15-1938, Charlotte Amalie) Debut: 7-2-1961 (1961–1970) Teams: Pittsburgh (N), San Diego (N), Los Angeles (N), Pittsburgh (N) Position: Pitcher (BR TR) Stats: 67 W, 50 L, 1072.1 IP, 3.13 ERA, 575 SO, 365 BB, 63 SV, 409 G

Morales y Hernández, José Manuel (**José Morales**) (b. 12-30-1944, Fredericksted) Debut: 8-13-1973 (1973–1984) Teams: Oakland (A), Montreal (N), Minnesota (A), Baltimore (A), Los Angeles (N) Positions: First Base, Outfield, DH, Pinch Hitter (BR TR) Stats: 733 G, 1305 AB, 375 H, 126 R, 26 HR, 207 RBI, .287 BA

Plaskett, Elmo Alexander (**Elmo Plaskett**) (b. 6-27-1938, Fredericksted) Debut: 9-8-1962 (1962–1963) Team: Pittsburgh (N) Positions: Catcher, Third Base (BR TR) Stats: 17 G, 35 AB, 7 H, 3 R, 1 HR, 5 RBI, .200 BA

Nicaragua

(First Nicaraguan major-leaguer: Dennis Martínez [September 14, 1976]; 5 players)

Altamirano y Ramírez, Porfirio (**Porfi Altamirano**) (b. 5-17-1952, Darillo) Debut: 5-9-1982 (1982–1984) Teams: Philadelphia (N), Chicago (N) Position: Pitcher (BR TR) Stats: 7 W, 4 L, 91.2 IP, 4.03 ERA, 57 SO, 30 BB, 2 SV, 65 G

Aquilera y Chévez, Silvio Antonio (**Antonio "Tony" Chévez**) (b. 6-20-1954, Telica) Debut: 5-30-1977 (1977) Team: Baltimore (A) Position: Pitcher (BR TR) Stats: 0 W, 0 L, 8 IP, 12.38 ERA, 7 SO, 8 BB, 0 SV, 4 G

Green y Casaya, David Alejandro (**David Green**) (b. 12-4-1960, Managua) Debut: 9-4-1981 (1981–1987) Teams: St. Louis (N), San Francisco (N), St. Louis (N) Positions: Outfield, First Base, Infield, Pinch Hitter (BR TR) Stats: 489 G, 1398 AB, 374 H, 168 R, 31 HR, 180 RBI, .268 BA

Martínez y Emilia, José Dennis (**Dennis Martínez**) (b. 5-14-1955, Granada) Debut: 9-14-1976 (1976–1992) Teams: Baltimore (A), Montreal (N) Position: Pitcher (BR TR) Stats: 193 W, 156 L, 3160 IP, 3.62 ERA, 1693 SO, 926 BB, 5 SV, 523 G

Williams y DeSouza, Albert Hamilton (**Al Williams**) (b. 5-6-1954, Pearl Lagoon) Debut: 5-7-1980 (1980–1984) Team: Minnesota (A) Position: Pitcher (BR TR) Stats: 35 W, 38 L, 642.2 IP, 4.24 ERA, 262 SO, 227 BB, 2 SV, 120 G

Colombia

(First Colombian major-leaguer: Luís "Jud" Castro [April 23, 1902]; 3 players)

Castro, Luís Manuel (**Luís "Jud" Castro**) (b. circa 1877, Cartegena; d. Venezuela, no date known) Debut: 4-23-1902 (1902) Team: Philadelphia (A) Positions: Second Base, Outfield (BR TR) Stats: 42 G, 143 AB, 35 H, 18 R, 1 HR, 15 RBI, .245 BA

Gutiérrez y Hernández, Joaquín Fernando (**Jackie Gutiérrez**) (b. 6-27-1960, Cartagena) Debut: 9-6-1983 (1983–1988) Teams: Boston (A), Baltimore (A), Philadelphia (N) Position: Shortstop (BR TR) Stats: 356 G, 957 AB, 227 H, 106 R, 4 HR, 63 RBI, .237 BA

Ramírez y Leal, Orlando (**Orlando Ramírez**) (b. 12-18-1951, Cartagena) Debut: 7-6-1974 (1974–1979) Team: California (A) Position: Shortstop (BR TR) Stats: 143 G, 281 AB, 53 H, 24 R, 0 HR, 16 RBI, .189 BA

Spain

(First Spanish major-leaguer: Alfredo Cabrera [May 16, 1913]; 3 players)

Cabrera, Alfredo A. (**Alfredo Cabrera**) (b. 1883, Canary Islands; d. Havana, no date) Debut: 5-16-1913 (1913) Team: St. Louis (N) Position: Shortstop (BR TR) Stats: 1 G, 2 AB, 0 H, 0 R, 0 HR, 0 RBI, .000 BA

Oelkers, Brian Alois (**Brian Oelkers**) (b. 3-11-1961, Zaragoza) Debut: 4-9-1983 (1983, 1986) Teams: Minnesota (A), Cleveland (A) Position: Pitcher (BL TL) Stats: 3 W, 8 L, 103.1 IP, 6.01 ERA, 46 SO, 57 BB, 1 SV, 45 G

Pardo, Alberto Judas (**Al Pardo**) (b. 9-8-1962, Oviedo) Debut: 7-3-1985 (1985–1989) Teams: Baltimore (A), Philadelphia (N) Position: Catcher (BB TR) Stats: 53 G, 129 AB, 17 H, 6 R, 1 HR, 4 RBI, .132 BA

Honduras

(First Honduran major-leaguer: Gerald Young [July 8, 1987]; 1 player)

Young, Gerald Anthony (**Gerald Young**) (b. 10-22-1964, Tele) Debut: 7-8-1987 (1987–1992) Team: Houston (N) Position: Outfield (BR TR) Stats: 605 G, 1755 AB, 432 H, 249 R, 3 HR, 109 RBI, .246 BA

Curaçao (Netherlands Antilles)

(First Curaçao major-leaguer: Hensley Meulens [August 23, 1989]; 1 player)

Meulens, Hensley Filemón Acasio (**Hensley Meulens**) (b. 6-23-1967, Curaçao) Debut: 8-23-1989 (1989–1992) Team: New York (A) Positions: Outfield, DH (BR TR) Stats: 129 G, 404 AB, 92 H, 52 R, 10 HR, 41 RBI, .228 BA

Belize (British Honduras)

(First Belize major-leaguer: Chito Martínez [July 5, 1991]; 1 player)

Martínez, Reyenaldo Ignacio (**Chito Martínez**) (b. 12-19-1965, Belize City) Debut: 7-5-1991 (1991–1992) Team: Baltimore (A) Positions: Outfield, DH (BL TL) Stats: 150 G, 414 AB, 111 H, 58 R, 2 HR, 18 RBI, .268 BA

APPENDIX C

Chronological Listing of Latin American Major-Leaguers (1871–1992)

The roster of Latin Americans who have donned big-league uniforms over the past century and a quarter has continued to expand by leaps and bounds in recent seasons. The importation of Latin talent has reached floodtide proportions during the past decade; 613 players born in Latin countries had become big-leaguers through the end of the 1992 season. The Dominican Republic (166) has now overtaken Canada (154) as the reigning leader in production of foreign-born talent, and Puerto Rico (147, counting only island-born Puerto Ricans and not Americans of Puerto Rican descent) stands ready to move into second place. While several rosters of Hispanic players have recently been published, all contain errors and omissions. Following is an accurate list that may serve as a research guide for baseball scholars wishing to pursue the history of Latin American impact on big-league play. Players are listed in order by year of debut (including playing position and debut team). A special debt of gratitude is owed to SABR member Robert F. Schulz (of Fort Frances, Ontario, Canada) for his invaluable assistance in preparing this player list.

Latin American Player Debuts, by Decades

Country	1900s	1910s	1920s	1930s	1940s	1950s	1960s	1970s	1980s	1990s
Dominican Rep.	0	0	0	0	0	2	22	38	*64*	*40*
Puerto Rico	0	0	0	0	2	14	24	*40*	46	21
Cuba	1*	*12*	*5*	*3*	*22*	*36*	*36*	4	8	2
Venezuela	0	0	0	1	1	4	10	10	28	10
Mexico	0	0	0	2	2	8	7	18	12	9
Panama	0	0	0	0	0	5	13	6	1	2
Nicaragua	0	0	0	0	0	0	0	2	3	0
Virgin Islands	0	0	0	0	0	1	4	2	1	0
Colombia	1	0	0	0	0	0	0	1	1	0
Spain	0	1	0	0	0	0	0	0	2	0
Honduras	0	0	0	0	0	0	0	0	1	0

Latin American Player Debuts, by Decades, *cont.*

Country	1900s	1910s	1920s	1930s	1940s	1950s	1960s	1970s	1980s	1990s
Curaçao	0	0	0	0	0	0	0	0	0	1
Belize	0	0	0	0	0	0	0	0	0	1
Totals	2	13	5	6	27	70	116	121	*167*	86

*Enrique Esteban Bellán (Cuba) only nineteenth-century player (1871 debut in National Association).

Italics = decade leader

Dominican Republic (166 players)

Name	Debut		Debut Team
Ossie (Osvaldo) Virgil	1956	Infielder	New York Giants
Felipe Alou	1958	Outfielder	San Francisco Giants
Matty Alou	1960	Outfielder	San Francisco Giants
Julián Javier	1960	Infielder	St. Louis Cardinals
Juan Marichal	1960	Pitcher	San Francisco Giants
Rudy (Rudolph) Hernández	1960	Pitcher	Washington Senators
Diomedes (Guayubín) Olivo	1960	Pitcher	Pittsburgh Pirates
Chi Chi (Federico) Olivo	1961	Pitcher	Milwaukee Braves
Manny (Manuel) Jiménez	1962	Outfielder	Kansas City Athletics
Manny (Manuel) Mota	1962	Outfielder	San Francisco Giants
Amado Samuel	1962	Infielder	Milwaukee Braves
Jesús Alou	1963	Outfielder	San Francisco Giants
Pedro González	1963	Infielder	New York Yankees
Rico (Ricardo) Carty	1963	Outfielder	Milwaukee Braves
Elvio Jiménez	1964	Outfielder	New York Yankees
Rick (Ricardo) Joseph	1964	Third Base	Kansas City Athletics
Roberto Peña	1965	Infielder	Chicago Cubs
José Vidal	1966	Outfielder	Cleveland Indians
Winston Llenas	1968	Infielder	California Angels
Rafael Robles	1969	Shortstop	San Diego Padres
Freddie (Federico) Velázquez	1969	Catcher	Seattle Pilots
Pedro Borbón	1969	Pitcher	California Angels
Santiago Guzmán	1969	Pitcher	St. Louis Cardinals
César Gerónimo	1969	Outfielder	Houston Astros
César Cedeño	1970	Outfielder	Houston Astros
Teddy (Teodoro) Martínez	1970	Infielder	New York Mets
Tom (Tomás) Silverio	1970	Outfielder	California Angels
Frank (Franklin) Taveras	1971	Shortstop	Pittsburgh Pirates
Elias Sosa	1972	Pitcher	San Francisco Giants
Pepe (Jesús) Frías	1973	Infielder	Montreal Expos
Rafael Batista	1973	First Base	Houston Astros
Mario Guerrero	1973	Shortstop	Boston Red Sox
Bill (William) Castro	1974	Pitcher	Milwaukee Brewers
Ramón de los Santos	1974	Pitcher	Houston Astros
Nino (Arnulfo) Espinosa	1974	Pitcher	New York Mets
Juan Jiménez	1974	Pitcher	Pittsburgh Pirates
Miguel Diloné	1974	Outfielder	Pittsburgh Pirates
José Sosa	1975	Pitcher	Houston Astros
Jesús de la Rosa	1975	Pinch Hitter	Houston Astros
Alfredo Ignácio Javier	1976	Outfielder	Houston Astros
Sam (Samuel) Mejías	1976	Outfielder	St. Louis Cardinals

Name	Debut		Debut Team
Alex (Alejandro) Taveras	1976	Infielder	Houston Astros
Santo Alcalá	1976	Pitcher	Cincinnati Reds
Joaquín Andújar	1976	Pitcher	Houston Astros
Juan Bernhardt	1976	Infielder	New York Yankees
Alfredo Griffin	1976	Shortstop	Cleveland Indians
Mario Soto	1977	Pitcher	Cincinnati Reds
Rafael Landestoy	1977	Infielder	Los Angeles Dodgers
Luís Pujols	1977	Catcher	Houston Astros
Silvio Martínez	1977	Pitcher	Chicago White Sox
Angel Torres	1977	Pitcher	Cincinnati Reds
José Báez	1977	Second Base	Seattle Mariners
Pedro Guerrero	1978	Infielder	Los Angeles Dodgers
Nelson Norman	1978	Shortstop	Texas Rangers
Domingo Ramos	1978	Infielder	New York Yankees
Luís Silverio	1978	Outfielder	Kansas City Royals
Victor Cruz	1978	Pitcher	Toronto Blue Jays
Art (Arturo) DeFreites	1978	First Base	Cincinnati Reds
Dámaso García	1978	Second Base	New York Yankees
Alberto Lois	1978	Outfielder	Pittsburgh Pirates
Pedro Hernández	1979	Third Base	Toronto Blue Jays
Rafael Vásquez	1979	Pitcher	Seattle Mariners
Rafael Ramírez	1980	Shortstop	Atlanta Braves
José Moreno	1980	Outfielder	New York Mets
Tony (Antonio) Peña	1980	Catcher	Pittsburgh Pirates
Julio Valdez	1980	Second Base	Boston Red Sox
Pascual Pérez	1980	Pitcher	Pittsburgh Pirates
Manny (Esteban) Castillo	1980	Third Base	Kansas City Royals
Jesús Figueroa	1980	Outfielder	Chicago Cubs
George (Jorge) Bell	1981	Outfielder	Toronto Blue Jays
Rufino Linares	1981	Outfielder	Atlanta Braves
Alejandro Peña	1981	Pitcher	Los Angeles Dodgers
Alejandro Sánchez	1982	Outfielder	Philadelphia Phillies
Rafael Belliard	1982	Shortstop	Pittsburgh Pirates
Cecilio Guante	1982	Pitcher	Pittsburgh Pirates
Carmen (Carmelo) Castillo	1982	Outfielder	Cleveland Indians
Juan Espino	1982	Catcher	New York Yankees
Julio Franco	1982	Second Base	Philadelphia Phillies
Gilberto Reyes	1983	Catcher	Los Angeles Dodgers
Juan Samuel	1983	Infielder	Philadelphia Phillies
Rafael Santana	1983	Shortstop	St. Louis Cardinals
José DeLeón	1983	Pitcher	Philadelphia Phillies
Julio Solano	1983	Pitcher	Houston Astros
Tony (Octávio) Fernández	1983	Shortstop	Toronto Blue Jays
Stan (Stanley) Javier	1984	Outfielder	New York Yankees
Vic (Victor) Mata	1984	Outfielder	New York Yankees
Junior (Milciades) Noboa	1984	Infielder	Cleveland Indians
José Uribe (González)	1984	Shortstop	St. Louis Cardinals
José Rijo	1984	Pitcher	New York Yankees
José Román	1984	Pitcher	Cleveland Indians
Ramón Romero	1984	Pitcher	Cleveland Indians
Denny (Denio) González	1984	Infielder	Pittsburgh Pirates
Manny (Manuel) Lee	1985	Infielder	Toronto Blue Jays
José González	1985	Outfielder	Los Angeles Dodgers
Andres Pérez Thomas	1985	Shortstop	Atlanta Braves
Mariano Duncan	1985	Infielder	Los Angeles Dodgers
Rubén Rodríguez	1986	Catcher	Pittsburgh Pirates

Dominican Republic (166 players), *cont.*

Name	Debut		Debut Team
Wil (Wilfredo) Tejada	1986	Catcher	Montreal Expos
Balvino Galvez	1986	Pitcher	Los Angeles Dodgers
Manny (Manuel) Hernández	1986	Pitcher	Houston Astros
Hipólito Peña	1986	Pitcher	Pittsburgh Pirates
Sergio Valdez	1986	Pitcher	Montreal Expos
Juan Castillo	1986	Infielder	Milwaukee Brewers
Luís Polonia	1987	Outfielder	Oakland Athletics
Nelson Liriano	1987	Second Base	Toronto Blue Jays
José Mesa	1987	Pitcher	Baltimore Orioles
José Núñez	1987	Pitcher	Toronto Blue Jays
Melido Pérez	1987	Pitcher	Kansas City Royals
Félix Fermín	1987	Shortstop	Pittsburgh Pirates
Leo García	1987	Outfielder	Cincinnati Reds
Félix José	1988	Outfielder	Oakland Athletics
Gibson Alba	1988	Pitcher	St. Louis Cardinals
José Bautista	1988	Pitcher	Baltimore Orioles
Ravelo Manzanillo	1988	Pitcher	Chicago White Sox
Ramón Martínez	1988	Pitcher	Los Angeles Dodgers
José Segura	1988	Pitcher	Chicago White Sox
Sil (Silvestre) Campusano	1988	Outfielder	Toronto Blue Jays
Luís de los Santos	1988	First Base	Kansas City Royals
Juan Bell	1989	Infielder	Baltimore Orioles
Ramón Peña	1989	Pitcher	Detroit Tigers
Sammy (Samuel) Sosa	1989	Outfielder	Texas Rangers
José Vizcaíno	1989	Shortstop	Los Angeles Dodgers
José (Joselito) Cano	1989	Pitcher	Houston Astros
Germán (Gerónimo) Berróa	1989	Outfielder	Atlanta Braves
Francisco Cabrera	1989	Catcher	Toronto Blue Jays
Junior Félix	1989	Outfielder	Toronto Blue Jays
Adújar Cedeño	1990	Shortstop	Houston Astros
Moises Alou	1990	Outfielder	Pittsburgh Pirates
Luís Encarnación	1990	Pitcher	Kansas City Royals
Ramón Manon	1990	Pitcher	Texas Rangers
José Offerman	1990	Shortstop	Los Angeles Dodgers
Gerónimo Peña	1990	Second Base	St. Louis Cardinals
Mel (Melaquides) Rojas	1990	Pitcher	Montreal Expos
Vic (Victor) Rosario	1990	Shortstop	Atlanta Braves
Andres Santana	1990	Infielder	San Francisco Giants
Rafael Valdez	1990	Pitcher	San Diego Padres
Efrain Valdez	1990	Pitcher	Cleveland Indians
Héctor Wagner	1990	Pitcher	Kansas City Royals
Esteban Beltre	1991	Shortstop	Chicago White Sox
Braulio Castillo	1991	Outfielder	Philadelphia Phillies
Francisco de la Rosa	1991	Pitcher	Baltimore Orioles
Tony (Antonio) Eusebio	1991	Catcher	Houston Astros
Juan Guzmán	1991	Pitcher	Toronto Blue Jays
Johnny Guzmán	1991	Pitcher	Oakland Athletics
Josias Manzanillo	1991	Pitcher	Boston Red Sox
Luís Mercedes	1991	Outfielder	Baltimore Orioles
Andy Mota	1991	Infielder	Houston Astros
José Mota	1991	Infielder	San Diego Padres
Yorkis Pérez	1991	Pitcher	Chicago Cubs
Manny Alexander	1992	Shortstop	Baltimore Orioles
Pedro Astacio	1992	Pitcher	Los Angeles Dodgers

Name	Debut		Debut Team
Miguel Batista	1992	Pitcher	Pittsburgh Pirates
Pedro Borbón, Jr.	1992	Pitcher	Atlanta Braves
Rafael Bournigal	1992	Infielder	Los Angeles Dodgers
Bernardo Brito	1992	Outfielder	Minnesota Twins
Bien Figueroa	1992	Infielder	St. Louis Cardinals
Juan Guerrero	1992	Infielder	Houston Astros
César Hernández	1992	Outfielder	Cincinnati Reds
Domingo Martínez	1992	Infielder	Toronto Blue Jays
Pedro Martínez	1992	Pitcher	Los Angeles Dodgers
Henry Mercedes	1992	Catcher	Oakland Athletics
Julio Peguero	1992	Outfielder	Philadelphia Phillies
Hipólito Pichardo	1992	Pitcher	Kansas City Royals
Ben Rivera	1992	Pitcher	Atlanta Braves
Henry Rodríguez	1992	Outfielder	Los Angeles Dodgers
William Suero	1992	Infielder	Milwaukee Brewers

Puerto Rico (147 players; native-born Puerto Ricans only and not second-generation U.S.-born Puerto Ricans)

Name	Debut		Debut Team
Hiram Bithorn	1942	Pitcher	Chicago Cubs
Luís Rodríguez Olmo	1943	Outfielder	Brooklyn Dodgers
Luís Márquez	1951	Outfielder	Boston Braves
Rubén Gómez	1953	Pitcher	New York Giants
Carlos Bernier	1953	Outfielder	Pittsburgh Pirates
Victor Pellot (Vic Power)	1954	First Base	Philadelphia Athletics
Nino (Saturnino) Escalera	1954	Outfielder	Cincinnati Reds
José "Pantalones" Santiago	1954	Pitcher	Cleveland Indians
Luís Arroyo	1955	Pitcher	St. Louis Cardinals
Roberto Clemente	1955	Outfielder	Pittsburgh Pirates
Roberto Vargas	1955	Pitcher	Milwaukee Braves
Félix Mantilla	1956	Shortstop	Milwaukee Braves
Juan Pizarro	1957	Pitcher	Milwaukee Braves
Valmy Thomas	1957	Catcher	New York Giants
Orlando Cepeda	1958	First Base	San Francisco Giants
José Pagán	1959	Shortstop	San Francisco Giants
Julio Gotay	1960	Infielder	St. Louis Cardinals
Ed Olivares	1960	Outfielder	St. Louis Cardinals
Ramón Conde	1962	Third Base	Chicago White Sox
Félix Torres	1962	Third Base	Los Angeles Angels
Julio Navarro	1962	Pitcher	Los Angeles Angels
José Palillo Santiago	1963	Pitcher	Kansas City Athletics
Sandy (Santos) Alomar	1964	Second Base	Milwaukee Braves
Santiago Rosario	1965	First Base	Kansas City Athletics
Arturo Lopez	1965	Outfielder	New York Yankees
Héctor Valle	1965	Catcher	Los Angeles Dodgers
Félix Milan	1966	Shortstop	Atlanta Braves
Willie (Guillermo) Montañez	1966	First Base	California Angels
Angel Luis Alcaraz	1967	Infielder	Los Angeles Dodgers
Ramón Hernández	1967	Pitcher	Atlanta Braves
Luís Alvarado	1968	Infielder	Boston Red Sox
Ellie (Eliseo) Rodriguez	1968	Catcher	New York Yankees
Mickey (Miguel) Fuentes	1969	Pitcher	Seattle Pilots
José "Coco" Laboy	1969	Infielder	Montreal Expos

Puerto Rico (147 players), *cont.*

Name	Debut		Debut Team
Francisco Librán	1969	Shortstop	San Diego Padres
Angel Mangual	1969	Outfielder	Pittsburgh Pirates
Jerry (Julio) Morales	1969	Outfielder	San Diego Padres
José Ortiz	1969	Outfielder	Chicago White Sox
Luís Peraza	1969	Pitcher	Philadelphia Phillies
Juan Ríos	1969	Infielder	Kansas City Royals
José Cruz	1970	Outfielder	St. Louis Cardinals
Rogelio Moret	1970	Pitcher	Boston Red Sox
Luís Melendez	1970	Outfielder	St. Louis Cardinals
Samuel Parrilla	1970	Outfielder	Philadelphia Phillies
Milton Ramirez	1970	Infielder	St. Louis Cardinals
Jorge Roque	1970	Outfielder	St. Louis Cardinals
Juan Beníquez	1971	Outfielder	Boston Red Sox
Manny Muñíz	1971	Pitcher	Philadelphia Phillies
Jimmy (Angel) Rosario	1971	Outfielder	San Francisco Giants
Rusty (Rosendo) Torrez	1971	Outfielder	New York Yankees
José Fernando González	1972	Infielder	Pittsburgh Pirates
Pepe (José) Mangual	1972	Infielder	Montreal Expos
David Rosello	1972	Infielder	Chicago Cubs
Jesús Orlando Alvarez	1973	Outfielder	Los Angeles Dodgers
Héctor Cruz	1973	Outfielder	St. Louis Cardinals
Tommy (Cirilo) Cruz	1973	Outfielder	St. Louis Cardinals
Eduardo Rodríguez	1973	Pitcher	Milwaukee Brewers
Otto Velez	1973	Outfielder	New York Yankees
Carlos Velásquez	1973	Pitcher	Milwaukee Brewers
Benny (Benigno) Ayala	1974	Outfielder	New York Mets
Iván de Jesús	1974	Shortstop	Los Angeles Dodgers
Sergio Ferrer	1974	Shortstop	Minnesota Twins
Ed (Eduardo) Figueroa	1974	Pitcher	California Angels
Jesús Hernaiz	1974	Pitcher	Philadelphia Phillies
Sixto Lezcano	1974	Outfielder	Milwaukee Brewers
Luís Joaquín Quintana	1974	Pitcher	California Angels
Jesús ("Bombo") Rivera	1975	Outfielder	Montreal Expos
Ramón Avilés	1977	Infielder	Boston Red Sox
Luís Delgado	1977	Outfielder	Seattle Mariners
Gil (Gilberto) Flores	1977	Outfielder	California Angels
Julio González	1977	Infielder	Houston Astros
Pedro García	1977	Second Base	Milwaukee Brewers
Willie (Guillermo) Hernández	1977	Pitcher	Chicago Cubs
Ed (Edgar) Romero	1977	Infielder	Milwaukee Brewers
Luís Rosado	1977	First Base	New York Mets
Chico (Manual) Ruiz	1978	Infielder	Atlanta Braves
Tony (Antonio) Bernazard	1979	Second Base	Montreal Expos
Rafael Santo Domingo	1979	Pinch Hitter	Cincinnati Reds
Dickie Thon	1979	Shortstop	California Angels
Jesús Vega	1979	First Base	Minnesota Twins
Luís Aguayo	1980	Infielder	Philadelphia Phillies
Onix Concepción	1980	Infielder	Kansas City Royals
Orlando Isales	1980	Outfielder	Philadelphia Phillies
Carlos Lezcano	1980	Outfielder	Chicago Cubs
Mario Ramirez	1980	Shortstop	New York Mets
Ozzie Virgil	1980	Catcher	Philadelphia Phillies
Juan Agosto	1981	Pitcher	Chicago White Sox
Juan Bonilla	1981	Second Base	San Diego Padres

Name	Debut		Debut Team
Luís DeLeón	1981	Pitcher	St. Louis Cardinals
Candy (Candido) Maldonado	1981	Outfielder	Los Angeles Dodgers
Bert (Adalberto) Peña	1981	Infielder	Houston Astros
Orlando Sánchez	1981	Catcher	St. Louis Cardinals
Orlando Mercado	1982	Catcher	Seattle Mariners
Junior (Adalberto) Ortiz	1982	Catcher	Pittsburgh Pirates
Edwin Rodríguez	1982	Infielder	New York Yankees
Hedi (Heriberto) Vargas	1982	First Base	Pittsburgh Pirates
Edwin Núñez	1982	Pitcher	Seattle Mariners
James (Jaime) Cocanower	1983	Pitcher	Milwaukee Brewers
Carmelo Martínez	1983	Outfielder	Chicago Cubs
José Oquendo	1983	Infielder	St. Louis Cardinals
Germán Rivera	1983	Infielder	Los Angeles Dodgers
Iván Calderón	1984	Outfielder	Seattle Mariners
Francisco Melendez	1984	First Base	Philadelphia Phillies
Danny (Danilo) Tartabull	1984	Outfielder	Seattle Mariners
Edwin Correa	1985	Pitcher	Chicago White Sox
José Guzmán	1985	Pitcher	Texas Rangers
Carlos Ponce	1985	First Base	Milwaukee Brewers
Juan Nieves	1986	Pitcher	Milwaukee Brewers
Luís Aquino	1986	Pitcher	Toronto Blue Jays
Rafael Montalvo	1986	Pitcher	Houston Astros
Edgar Díaz	1986	Shortstop	Milwaukee Brewers
Luís Quiñones	1986	Infielder	Oakland Athletics
Rey Quiñones	1986	Shortstop	Boston Red Sox
Luís Rivera	1986	Infielder	Montreal Expos
Benito Santiago	1986	Catcher	San Diego Padres
Rubén Sierra	1986	Outfielder	Texas Rangers
Joey Cora	1987	Second Base	San Diego Padres
Mario Díaz	1987	Shortstop	Seattle Mariners
José Lind	1987	Shortstop	Pittsburgh Pirates
Candy (Ulises) Sierra	1988	Pitcher	San Diego Padres
Sandy Alomar, Jr.	1988	Catcher	San Diego Padres
Luís Alicea	1988	Second Base	St. Louis Cardinals
Roberto Alomar	1988	Second Base	San Diego Padres
Juan González	1989	Outfielder	Texas Rangers
Jaime Navarro	1989	Pitcher	Milwaukee Brewers
Francisco Javier Oliveras	1989	Pitcher	Minnesota Twins
Carlos Baerga	1990	Infielder	Cleveland Indians
Rafael Novoa	1990	Pitcher	San Francisco Giants
Leo Gómez	1990	Third Base	Baltimore Orioles
José Melendez	1990	Pitcher	Seattle Mariners
Orlando Merced	1990	First Base	Pittsburgh Pirates
Pedro Muñoz	1990	Catcher	Minnesota Twins
Omar Olivares	1990	Pitcher	St. Louis Cardinals
Mike Pérez	1990	Pitcher	St. Louis Cardinals
Julio Valera	1990	Pitcher	New York Mets
Héctor Villanueva	1990	Catcher	Chicago Cubs
Ricky Bones	1991	Pitcher	San Diego Padres
José Hernández	1991	Infielder	Texas Rangers
Roberto Hernández	1991	Pitcher	Chicago White Sox
Iván Rodríguez	1991	Catcher	Texas Rangers
Rico Rossy	1991	Infielder	Atlanta Braves
Rey Sánchez	1991	Infielder	Chicago Cubs
Bernie Williams	1991	Outfielder	New York Yankees
Wifredo Cordero	1992	Shortstop	Montreal Expos

Puerto Rico (147 players), *cont.*

Name	Debut		Debut Team
Javier López	1992	Catcher	Atlanta Braves
Melvin Nieves	1992	Outfielder	Atlanta Braves
José Valentín	1992	Infielder	Milwaukee Brewers

Cuba (129 players)

Name	Debut		Debut Team
Enrique Esteban Bellán	1871	Infielder	Troy Haymakers (National Association)
Armando Marsans	1911	Outfielder	Cincinnati Reds
Rafael Almeida	1911	Outfielder	Cincinnati Reds
Mike (Miguel) González	1912	Catcher	Boston Braves
Merito (Baldomero) Acosta	1913	Outfielder	Washington Senators
Jack (Jacinto) Calvo	1913	Outfielder	Washington Senators
Angel Aragón	1914	Infielder	New York Yankees
Adolfo Luque	1914	Pitcher	Boston Braves
Emilio Palmero	1915	Pitcher	New York Giants
Joseito Rodríguez	1916	Infielder	New York Giants
Manolo (Manuel) Cueto	1917	Outfielder	Cincinnati Reds
Eusebio González	1918	Shortstop	Boston Red Sox
Oscar Tuero	1918	Pitcher	St. Louis Cardinals
José Acosta	1920	Pitcher	Washington Senators
Ricardo Torres	1920	Catcher	Washington Senators
Pedro Dibut	1924	Pitcher	Cincinnati Reds
Pafto "Mike" (Ramón) Herrera	1925	Infielder	Boston Red Sox
Oscar Estrada	1929	Pitcher	St. Louis Browns
Roberto Estalella	1935	Outfielder	Washington Senators
Mike (Fermín) Guerra	1937	Catcher	Washington Senators
Rene Monteagudo	1938	Pitcher	Washington Senators
Gilberto Torres	1940	Infielder	Washington Senators
Jack (Angel) Aragón	1941	Pinch Runner	New York Giants
Roberto Ortíz	1941	Outfielder	Washington Senators
Sal (Salvador) Hernández	1942	Catcher	Chicago Cubs
Mosquito (Antonio) Ordeñana	1943	Shortstop	Pittsburgh Pirates
Nap (Napoleón) Reyes	1943	Infielder	New York Giants
Tommy (Tomás) de la Cruz	1944	Pitcher	Cincinnati Reds
Preston (Pedro) Gómez	1944	Infielder	Washington Senators
Baby (Oliverio) Ortíz	1944	Pitcher	Washington Senators
Luís Suarez	1944	Third Base	Washington Senators
Santiago (Carlos) Ullrich	1944	Pitcher	Washington Senators
Roy (Rogelio) Valdés	1944	Pinch Hitter	Washington Senators
Jorge Comellas	1945	Pitcher	Chicago Cubs
Sid (Isidoro) León	1945	Pitcher	Philadelphia Phillies
Armando Roche	1945	Pitcher	Washington Senators
Adrián Zabala	1945	Pitcher	New York Giants
José Zardón	1945	Outfielder	Washington Senators
Reggie (Regino) Otero	1945	First Base	Chicago Cubs
Angel Fleitas	1948	Shortstop	Washington Senators
Moín (Ramon) García	1948	Pitcher	Washington Senators
Enrique (Julio) González	1949	Pitcher	Washington Senators
Minnie (Orestes) Miñoso	1949	Outfielder	Cleveland Indians
Witto (Luís) Aloma	1950	Pitcher	Chicago White Sox

Name	Debut		Debut Team
Sandy (Sandalio) Consuegra	1950	Pitcher	Washington Senators
Connie (Conrado) Marrero	1950	Pitcher	Washington Senators
Limonar (Rogelio) Martínez	1950	Pitcher	Washington Senators
Julio Moreno	1950	Pitcher	Washington Senators
Carlos Pascual	1950	Pitcher	Washington Senators
Cisco (Francisco) Campos	1951	Outfielder	Washington Senators
Willie (Guillermo) Miranda	1951	Shortstop	Washington Senators
Ray (Rafael) Noble	1951	Catcher	New York Giants
Sandy (Edmundo) Amoros	1952	Outfielder	Brooklyn Dodgers
Mike (Miguel) Fornieles	1952	Pitcher	Washington Senators
Héctor Rodríguez	1952	Third Base	Chicago White Sox
Raul Sánchez	1952	Pitcher	Washington Senators
Carlos Paula	1954	Outfielder	Washington Senators
Camilo Pascual	1954	Pitcher	Washington Senators
Vicente Amor	1955	Pitcher	Chicago Cubs
Julio Becquer	1955	First Base	Washington Senators
Juan Delís	1955	Third Base	Washington Senators
Lino Donoso	1955	Pitcher	Pittsburgh Pirates
Vince (Wenceslao) González	1955	Pitcher	Washington Senators
Roman Mejías	1955	Outfielder	Pittsburgh Pirates
Pedro Ramos	1955	Pitcher	Washington Senators
José (Joe) Valdivielso	1955	Shortstop	Washington Senators
Chico (Humberto) Fernández	1956	Shortstop	Brooklyn Dodgers
Evelio (Gregorio) Hernández	1956	Pitcher	Washington Senators
Cholly (Lazaro) Naranjo	1956	Pitcher	Pittsburgh Pirates
Rene Valdez	1957	Pitcher	Brooklyn Dodgers
Ossie (Oswaldo) Alvarez	1958	Infielder	Washington Senators
Pancho (Juan) Herrera	1958	First Base	Philadelphia Phillies
Dan (Daniel) Morejón	1958	Outfielder	Cincinnati Reds
Orlando Peña	1958	Pitcher	Cincinnati Reds
Freddy (Fernando) Rodríguez	1958	Pitcher	Chicago Cubs
Tony (Antonio) Taylor	1958	Infielder	Chicago Cubs
Rudy (Rodolfo) Arias	1958	Pitcher	Chicago White Sox
Mike (Miguel) Cuellar	1959	Pitcher	Cincinnati Reds
Zoilo Versalles	1959	Shortstop	Washington Senators
Borrego (Rogelio) Alvarez	1960	First Base	Cincinnati Reds
Joe (Joaquín) Azcue	1960	Infielder	Cincinnati Reds
Ed (Eduardo) Bauta	1960	Pitcher	St. Louis Cardinals
Leo (Leonardo) Cárdenas	1960	Infielder	Cincinnati Reds
Mike (Miguel) de la Hoz	1960	Infielder	Cleveland Indians
Tony (Antonio) González	1960	Infielder	Cincinnati Reds
Héctor Maestri	1960	Pitcher	Washington Senators
Leo (Leopoldo) Posada	1960	Outfielder	Kansas City Athletics
Berto (Dagoberto) Cueto	1961	Pitcher	Minnesota Twins
Manny (Manuel) Montejo	1961	Pitcher	Detroit Tigers
Héctor (Rodolfo) Martínez	1962	Outfielder	Kansas City Athletics
Marty (Orlando) Martínez	1962	Infielder	Minnesota Twins
Orlando McFarlane	1962	Catcher	Pittsburgh Pirates
Tony (Pedro) Oliva	1962	Outfielder	Minnesota Twins
Cookie (Octavio) Rojas	1962	Infielder	Cincinnati Reds
Diego Seguí	1962	Pitcher	Kansas City Athletics
José Tartabull	1962	Outfielder	Kansas City Athletics
José Cardenal	1963	Infielder	San Francisco Giants
Marcelino López	1963	Pitcher	Philadelphia Phillies
Tony (Gabriel) Martínez	1963	Infielder	Cleveland Indians
Aurelio Monteagudo	1963	Pitcher	Kansas City Athletics

Cuba (129 players), *cont.*

Name	Debut		Debut Team
Bert (Dagoberto) Campaneris	1964	Shortstop	Kansas City Athletics
Tony (Atanasio) Pérez	1964	Infielder	Cincinnati Reds
Chico Ruiz	1964	Infielder	Cincinnati Reds
Luís Tiant	1964	Pitcher	Cleveland Indians
Paul (Paulino) Casanova	1965	Catcher	Washington Senators
Tito (Rigoberto) Fuentes	1965	Outfielder	San Francisco Giants
Jackie (Jacinto) Hernández	1965	Shortstop	California Angels
Sandy (Hilario) Valdespino	1965	Outfielder	Minnesota Twins
José Ramón López	1966	Pitcher	California Angels
Minnie (Minervino) Rojas	1966	Pitcher	California Angels
Hank (Enrique) Izquierdo	1967	Catcher	Minnesota Twins
George (Jorge) Lauzerique	1967	Pitcher	Kansas City Athletics
José Arcia	1968	Infielder	Chicago Cubs
Chico (Lorenzo) Fernández	1968	Infielder	Baltimore Orioles
José Martínez	1969	Infielder	Pittsburgh Pirates
Minnie (Rigoberto) Mendoza	1970	Infielder	Minnesota Twins
Oscar Zamora	1974	Pitcher	Chicago Cubs
Orlando González	1976	First Base	Cleveland Indians
Bobby (Roberto) Ramos	1978	Catcher	Montreal Expos
Leo (Leonard) Sutherland	1980	Outfielder	Chicago White Sox
Bárbaro Garbey	1984	Outfielder	Detroit Tigers
José Canseco	1985	Outfielder	Oakland Athletics
Rafael Palmeiro	1986	First Base	Chicago Cubs
Orestes Destrade	1987	First Base	New York Yankees
Nelson Santovenia	1988	Catcher	Montreal Expos
Israel Sánchez	1988	Pitcher	Kansas City Royals
Tony (Emilio) Fossas	1988	Pitcher	Texas Rangers
Ozzie Canseco	1990	Outfielder	Oakland Athletics
Tony Menéndez	1992	Pitcher	Cincinnati Reds

Venezuela (64 players)

Name	Debut		Debut Team
Alejandro (Alex) Carrasquel	1939	Pitcher	Washington Senators
Chucho (Jesús) Ramos	1944	Outfielder	Cincinnati Reds
Alfonso "Chico" Carrasquel	1950	Shortstop	Chicago White Sox
Pompeyo Davalillo	1953	Shortstop	Washington Senators
Ramón Monzant	1954	Pitcher	New York Giants
Luís Aparicio	1956	Shortstop	Chicago White Sox
Elio Chacón	1960	Infielder	Cincinnati Reds
Victor Davalillo	1963	Outfielder	Cleveland Indians
César Tóvar	1965	Infielder	Minnesota Twins
Nestor (Isaías) Chávez	1967	Pitcher	San Francisco Giants
César Gutiérrez	1967	Shortstop	San Francisco Giants
Bobby Rodríguez (Muñoz)	1967	Pitcher	Kansas City Athletics
José Herrera	1967	Outfielder	Houston Astros
Gustavo Gil	1967	Infielder	Cleveland Indians
Angel Remigio Hermoso	1967	Infielder	Atlanta Braves
Angel Bravo	1969	Outfielder	Chicago White Sox
Ossie (Osvaldo) Blanco	1970	First Base	Chicago White Sox
Davy Concepción	1970	Shortstop	Cincinnati Reds
Enzo Hernández	1971	Shortstop	San Diego Padres

Name	Debut		Debut Team
Dámaso Blanco	1972	Infielder	San Francisco Giants
Gonzalo Márquez	1972	First Base	Oakland Athletics
Manny Trillo	1973	Infielder	Oakland Athletics
Pablo Torrealba	1975	Pitcher	Atlanta Braves
Manny Sarmiento	1976	Pitcher	Cincinnati Reds
Tony (Antonio) Armas	1976	Outfielder	Pittsburgh Pirates
Bo (Baudilio) Díaz	1977	Catcher	Boston Red Sox
Luís Aponte	1980	Pitcher	Boston Red Sox
Luís Leal	1980	Pitcher	Toronto Blue Jays
Luís Salazar	1980	Third Base	San Diego Padres
Fred Manrique	1981	Infielder	Toronto Blue Jays
Luís Mercedes Sánchez	1981	Pitcher	California Angels
Leonardo Hernández	1982	Third Base	Baltimore Orioles
Angel (Argenis) Salazar	1983	Shortstop	Montreal Expos
Alvaro Espinoza	1984	Shortstop	Minnesota Twins
Toby (Tobias) Hernández	1984	Catcher	Toronto Blue Jays
Andrés Galarraga	1985	First Base	Montreal Expos
Ozzie (Osvaldo) Guillén	1985	Shortstop	Chicago White Sox
Gus (Gustavo) Polidor	1985	Infielder	California Angels
Urbano Lugo	1985	Pitcher	California Angels
Alexis Infante	1987	Shortstop	Toronto Blue Jays
Al (Alfredo) Pedrique	1987	Infielder	New York Mets
Miguel Angel García	1987	Pitcher	California Angels
Ubaldo Heredia	1987	Pitcher	Montreal Expos
Les (Lester) Straker	1987	Pitcher	Minnesota Twins
Carlos Quintana	1988	First Base	Boston Red Sox
Tony (Antonio) Castillo	1988	Pitcher	Toronto Blue Jays
Germán González	1988	Pitcher	Minnesota Twins
Osvaldo Peraza	1988	Pitcher	Baltimore Orioles
Angel Escobar	1988	Infielder	San Francisco Giants
Carlos Martínez	1988	First Base	Chicago White Sox
Johnny Paredes	1988	Infielder	Montreal Expos
Omar Visquel	1989	Shortstop	Seattle Mariners
Wilson Alvarez	1989	Pitcher	Texas Rangers
Julio Machado	1989	Pitcher	New York Mets
Oscar Azocar	1990	Outfielder	New York Yankees
Rich Garces	1990	Pitcher	Minnesota Twins
Carlos García	1990	Outfielder	Pittsburgh Pirates
Carlos Hernández	1990	Catcher	Los Angeles Dodgers
Luís Sojo	1990	Infielder	Toronto Blue Jays
José Escobar	1991	Infielder	Cleveland Indians
Amalio Carreño	1991	Pitcher	Philadelphia Phillies
Ramón García	1991	Pitcher	Chicago White Sox
Cristobal Colón	1992	Shortstop	Texas Rangers
Danilo León	1992	Pitcher	Texas Rangers

Mexico (58 players)

Name	Debut		Debut Team
Mel Almada	1933	Outfielder	Boston Red Sox
Chili (José) Gómez	1935	Infielder	Philadelphia Phillies
Jesse Flores	1942	Pitcher	Chicago Cubs
Beto (Roberto) Avila	1949	Second Base	Cleveland Indians
Tito Herrera	1951	Pitcher	St. Louis Browns

Mexico (58 players), *cont.*

Name	Debut		Debut Team
Felipe Montemayor	1953	Outfielder	Pittsburgh Pirates
Chico (Vincio) García	1954	Second Base	Baltimore Orioles
Bob (Robert) Greenwood	1954	Pitcher	Philadelphia Phillies
Memo (Guillermo) Luna	1954	Pitcher	St. Louis Cardinals
Rubén Amaro	1958	Infielder	St. Louis Cardinals
Marcelino Solis	1958	Pitcher	Chicago Cubs
Benny (Benjamin) Valenzuela	1958	Third Base	St. Louis Cardinals
Jorge Rubio	1966	Pitcher	California Angels
Aurelio Rodríguez	1967	Third Base	California Angels
Horacio Piña	1968	Pitcher	Cleveland Indians
Vicente Romo	1968	Pitcher	Los Angeles Dodgers
Bobby (Carlos) Treviño	1968	Outfielder	California Angels
Héctor Torres	1968	Infielder	Houston Astros
José Peña	1969	Pitcher	Cincinnati Reds
Miguel Puente	1970	Pitcher	San Francisco Giants
Francisco Estrada	1971	Catcher	New York Mets
Rudy (Rodolfo) Hernández	1972	Shortstop	Chicago White Sox
Jorge Orta	1972	Second Base	Chicago White Sox
Sergio Robles	1972	Catcher	Baltimore Orioles
Celerino Sánchez	1972	Infielder	New York Yankees
Cy (Cecilio) Acosta	1972	Pitcher	Chicago White Sox
Max (Máximo) León	1973	Pitcher	Atlanta Braves
Luís Gómez	1974	Shortstop	Minnesota Twins
Francisco Barrios	1974	Pitcher	Chicago White Sox
Aurelio López	1974	Pitcher	Kansas City Royals
Mario Mendoza	1974	Shortstop	Pittsburgh Pirates
Sid (Isidro) Monge	1975	Pitcher	California Angels
Carlos López	1976	Outfielder	California Angels
Andres Mora	1976	Outfielder	Baltimore Orioles
Enrique Romo	1977	Pitcher	Seattle Mariners
Alex Treviño	1978	Catcher	New York Mets
Germán Barranca	1979	Infielder	Kansas City Royals
Fernando Valenzuela	1980	Pitcher	Los Angeles Dodgers
Angel Moreno	1981	Pitcher	California Angels
Ernesto Escarrega	1982	Pitcher	Chicago White Sox
Salomé Barojas	1982	Pitcher	Chicago White Sox
Houston Jiménez	1983	Shortstop	Minnesota Twins
Alfonso Pulido	1983	Pitcher	Pittsburgh Pirates
Teddy (Teodoro) Higuera	1985	Pitcher	Milwaukee Brewers
Vicente Palacios	1987	Pitcher	Pittsburgh Pirates
José Cecena	1988	Pitcher	Texas Rangers
German Jiménez	1988	Pitcher	Atlanta Braves
Tony Perezchica	1988	Second Base	San Francisco Giants
Rosario Rodríguez	1989	Pitcher	Cincinnati Reds
Narciso Elvira	1990	Pitcher	Milwaukee Brewers
Matias Carrillo	1991	Outfielder	Milwaukee Brewers
Vinny Castilla	1991	Infielder	Atlanta Braves
Héctor Fajardo	1991	Pitcher	Pittsburgh Pirates
Everado Magellanes	1991	Infielder	Cleveland Indians
Armando Reynoso	1991	Pitcher	Atlanta Braves
Carlos Rodríguez	1991	Shortstop	New York Yankees
José Tollentino	1991	Outfielder	Houston Astros
Guillermo Velásquez	1992	First Base	San Diego Padres

Panama (27 players, including *Panama Canal Zone)

Name	Debut		Debut Team
Humberto Robinson	1955	Pitcher	Milwaukee Braves
Héctor López	1955	Infielder	Kansas City Athletics
Webbo (Vibert) Clarke	1955	Pitcher	Washington Senators
Pat Scantlebury*	1956	Pitcher	Cincinnati Reds
Tom (Thomas) Hughes*	1959	Pitcher	St. Louis Cardinals
Bobby (George) Prescott	1961	Outfielder	Kansas City Athletics
Dave Roberts	1962	First Base	Houston Colt .45s
Rupe (Ruperto) Toppin	1962	Pitcher	Kansas City Athletics
Ivan Murrell	1963	Outfielder	Houston Colt .45s
Gil Garrido	1964	Infielder	San Francisco Giants
Adolfo Phillips	1964	Outfielder	Philadelphia Phillies
Chico (Ruthford) Salmón	1964	Infielder	Cleveland Indians
Ossie (Osvaldo) Chavarría	1966	Infielder	Kansas City Athletics
Rod Carew*	1967	Infielder	Minnesota Twins
Manny (Manuel) Sanguillen	1967	Catcher	Pittsburgh Pirates
Al (Allan) Lewis	1967	Outfielder	Kansas City Athletics
Ramon Webster	1967	First Base	Kansas City Athletics
Bill (William) Heywood	1968	Pitcher	Washington Senators
Eduardo Acosta	1970	Pitcher	Pittsburgh Pirates
Ben (Benjamin) Oglivie	1971	Outfielder	Boston Red Sox
Rennie (Renaldo) Stennett	1971	Second Base	Pittsburgh Pirates
Omar Moreno	1975	Outfielder	Pittsburgh Pirates
Mike (Edward) Eden*	1976	Infielder	Atlanta Braves
Juan Berenguer	1978	Pitcher	New York Mets
Roberto Kelly	1987	Outfielder	New York Yankees
Carlos Maldonado	1990	Pitcher	Kansas City Royals
Fernando Ramsey	1992	Outfielder	Chicago Cubs

Virgin Islands (8 players)

Name	Debut		Debut Team
Joe Christopher	1959	Outfielder	Pittsburgh Pirates
Al McBean	1961	Pitcher	Pittsburgh Pirates
Elmo Plaskett	1962	Catcher	Pittsburgh Pirates
Horace Clarke	1965	Infielder	New York Yankees
Ellie (Elrod) Hendricks	1968	Catcher	Baltimore Orioles
José Morales	1973	First Base	Oakland Athletics
Henry Cruz	1975	Outfielder	Los Angeles Dodgers
Jerry Browne	1986	Second Base	Texas Rangers

Nicaragua (5 players)

Name	Debut		Debut Team
Dennis Martínez	1976	Pitcher	Baltimore Orioles
Tony (Silvio) Chévez	1977	Pitcher	Baltimore Orioles
Al (Albert) Williams	1980	Pitcher	Minnesota Twins
David Green	1981	Outfielder	St. Louis Cardinals
Porfirio Altamirano	1982	Pitcher	Philadelphia Phillies

Colombia (3 players)

Name	Debut		Debut Team
Luís Castro	1902	Infielder	Philadelphia Athletics
Orlando Ramírez	1974	Shortstop	California Angels
Jackie Gutiérrez	1983	Shortstop	Boston Red Sox

Spain (3 players)

Name	Debut		Debut Team
Alfredo Cabrera	1913	Shortstop	St. Louis Cardinals
Bryan Oelkers	1983	Pitcher	Minnesota Twins
Alberto Pardo	1985	Catcher	Baltimore Orioles

Honduras (1 player)

Name	Debut		Debut Team
Gerald Young	1987	Outfielder	Houston Astros

Curaçao, Netherlands Antilles (1 player)

Name	Debut		Debut Team
Hensley Meulens	1989	Outfielder	New York Yankees

Belize (1 player)

Name	Debut		Debut Team
Chito Martínez	1991	Outfielder	Baltimore Orioles

First Latin American Player for Each Major League Franchise
(Chronological Listing by Debut Year)

Ballclub	Player (Year)	Country
Philadelphia (Kansas City/Oakland) Athletics	Luís Castro (1902)	Colombia
Cincinnati Reds	Armando Marsans (1911)	Cuba
	Rafael Almeida (1911)	Cuba
Boston (Milwaukee/Atlanta) Braves	Mike González (1912)	Cuba
Washington Senators (Minnesota Twins)	Merito Acosta (1913)	Cuba
New York Yankees	Angel Aragón (1914)	Cuba
New York (San Francisco) Giants	Emilio Palmero (1915)	Cuba
Boston Red Sox	Eusebio González (1918)	Cuba
St. Louis Cardinals	Oscar Tuero (1918)	Cuba
St. Louis Browns (Baltimore Orioles)	Oscar Estrada (1929)	Cuba
Brooklyn (Los Angeles) Dodgers	Adolfo Luque (1930)	Cuba
Philadelphia Phillies	Chili (José) Gómez (1935)	Mexico
Pittsburgh Pirates	Mosquito Ordeñana (1943)	Cuba
Chicago Cubs	Hiram Bithorn (1942)	Puerto Rico
Cleveland Indians	Minnie Miñoso (1949)	Cuba
	Roberto Avila (1949)	Mexico
Chicago White Sox	José Acosta (1922)	Cuba

Ballclub	Player (Year)	Country
Detroit Tigers	Ossie Virgil (1958)	Dominican Rep.
New York Mets	Elio Chacon (1962)	Venezuela
	Felix Mantilla (1962)	Puerto Rico
Houston Astros	Roman Mejías (1962)	Cuba
Washington Senators (Texas Rangers)	Minnie Miñoso (1963)	Cuba
California Angels	Vic Power (1964)	Puerto Rico
Montreal Expos	Manny Mota (1969)	Dominican Rep.
San Diego Padres	Rafael Robles (1969)	Dominican Rep.
Kansas City Royals	Jackie Hernández (1969)	Cuba
Seattle Pilots (Milwaukee Brewers)	Gustavo Gil (1969)	Venezuela
	Diego Seguí (1969)	Cuba
Toronto Blue Jays	Otto Velez (1977)	Puerto Rico
	Rico Carty (1977)	Dominican Rep.
Seattle Mariners	Diego Seguí (1977)	Cuba
Colorado Rockies	Andrés Galarraga (1993)	Venezuela
Florida Marlins	Junior Félix (1993)	Dominican Rep.

APPENDIX D

All-Time Latin American Big-League Leaders and Record Holders

Top All-Time Latin American Batsmen
(minimum of 1,000 games played through 1993)

Batter	Years	BA	G	AB	H	HR	RBI
Rod Carew (Panama)	1967–85	.328	2,469	9,315	3,053	92	1,015
Roberto Clemente (Puerto Rico)	1955–72	.317	2,433	9,454	3,000	240	1,305
Matty Alou (Dominican)	1960–74	.307	1,667	5,789	1,777	31	427
Tony Oliva (Cuba)	1962–76	.304	1,676	6,301	1,917	220	947
Manny Mota (Dominican)	1962–82	.304	1,536	3,779	1,149	31	438
Julio Franco (Dominican)	1982–93	.300	1,546	5,948	1,784	100	763
Pedro Guerrero (Dominican)	1982–92	.300	1,536	5,392	1,618	215	898
Rico Carty (Dominican)	1963–79	.299	1,651	5,606	1,677	204	890
Minnie Miñoso (Cuba)	1949–80	.298	1,841	6,579	1,963	186	1,023
Orlando Cepeda (Puerto Rico)	1958–74	.297	2,124	7,927	2,351	379	1,365
Manny Sanguillen (Panama)	1967–80	.296	1,448	5,062	1,500	65	585
Rafael Palmeiro (Cuba)	1986–93	.296	1,046	3,867	1,144	132	526
Luís Polonia (Dominican)	1987–93	.294	905	3,316	974	14	274

Top All-Time Latin American Hurlers
(ranked by total games won in majors through 1993)

Pitcher	Years	W	L	Pct.	ERA	IP	SO
Juan Marichal (Dominican)	1960–74	243	142	.631	2.89	3,509	2,303
Luís Tiant Jr. (Cuba)	1964–82	229	172	.571	3.30	3,486	2,416
Dennis Martínez (Nicaragua)	1976–93	207	164	.558	3.64	3,369	1,821
Dolf Luque (Cuba)	1914–35	194	179	.519	3.24	3,220	1,130
Mike Cuellar (Cuba)	1959–77	185	130	.587	3.14	2,808	1,632
Camilo Pascual (Cuba)	1954–71	174	170	.506	3.63	2,930	2,167
Fernando Valenzuela (Mexico)	1980–93	149	128	.538	3.45	2,535	1,842
Juan Pizarro (Puerto Rico)	1957–74	131	105	.555	3.43	2,034	1,522
Joaquín Andújar (Dominican)	1976–88	127	118	.518	3.58	2,154	1,032
Pedro Ramos (Cuba)	1955–70	117	160	.422	4.08	2,355	1,305
Mario Soto (Dominican)	1977–88	100	92	.521	3.47	1,731	1,449
José Rijo (Dominican)	1985–93	96	71	.574	3.14	1,520	1,096
Teddy Higuera (Mexico)	1985–91	92	56	.622	3.37	1,291	1,019

All-Time Hispanic Dream Team

Position	Name (Career Years)	Country
First base	Orlando Cepeda (1958–1974)	Puerto Rico
Second base	Tony Taylor (1958–1976)	Cuba
Shortstop	Luís Aparicio (1956–1973)	Venezuela
Third base	Tony Pérez (1964–1986)	Cuba
Outfielder	Minnie Miñoso (1949–1980)	Cuba
Outfielder	Roberto Clemente (1955–1972)	Puerto Rico
Outfielder	Tony Oliva (1962–1976)	Cuba
Catcher	Manny Sanguillen (1967–1980)	Panama
Designated hitter	Rod Carew (1967–1985)	Panama
Utility	Manny Mota (1962–1982)	Dominican Rep.
Right-handed starter	Juan Marichal (1960–1974)	Dominican Rep.
Left-handed starter	Mike Cuellar (1959–1976)	Cuba
Right-handed relief	Pedro Borbón (1969–1980)	Dominican Rep.
Left-handed relief	Willie Hernández (1977–1989)	Puerto Rico
Manager	Preston Gómez (1969–1980)	Cuba

Honorable Mention Second Team

Position	Name (Career Years)	Country
First base	Vic Power (1954–1965)	Puerto Rico
Second base	Roberto Alomar (1988–1993*)	Puerto Rico
Shortstop	Tony Fernández (1983–1993*)	Dominican Rep.
Third base	Aurelio Rodríguez (1967–1983)	Mexico
Outfielder	Felipe Alou (1958–1974)	Dominican Rep.
Outfielder	José Canseco (1985–1993*)	Cuba
Outfielder	George Bell (1981–1993*)	Dominican Rep.
Catcher	Benito Santiago (1986–1993*)	Puerto Rico
Designated hitter	Matty Alou (1960–1974)	Dominican Rep.
Utility	César Cedeño (1970–1986)	Dominican Rep.
Right-handed starter	Adolfo Luque (1914–1935)	Cuba
Left-handed starter	Juan Pizarro (1957–1974)	Puerto Rico
Right-handed relief	Elias Sosa (1972–1983)	Dominican Rep.
Left-handed relief	Luís Arroyo (1955–1963)	Puerto Rico
Manager	Felipe Alou (1992–1993)	Dominican Rep.

* = Active player during 1993 season.

Latin Dream Team of the 1940s–1950s

Position	Name (Career Years)	Country
First base	Vic Power (1954–1965)	Puerto Rico
Second base	Roberto Avila (1949–1959)	Mexico
Shortstop	Chico Carrasquel (1950–1959)	Venezuela
Third base	Hector López (1955–1966)	Panama
Outfielder	Minnie Miñoso (1949–1980)	Cuba
Outfielder	Sandy Amoros (1952–1960)	Cuba
Outfielder	Luís Olmo (1943–1951)	Puerto Rico
Catcher	Ozzie Virgil (1956–1969)	Dominican Rep.
Right-handed starter	Camilo Pascual (1954–1971)	Cuba
Left-handed starter	Juan Pizarro (1957–1974)	Puerto Rico
Relief	Luís Arroyo (1955–1963)	Puerto Rico

Latin Dream Team of the 1960s–1970s

Position	Name (Career Years)	Country
First base	Orlando Cepeda (1958–1974)	Puerto Rico
Second base	Tony Taylor (1958–1976)	Cuba
Shortstop	Luís Aparicio (1956–1973)	Venezuela
Third base	Tony Pérez (1964–1986)	Cuba
Outfielder	Tony Oliva (1962–1976)	Cuba
Outfielder	Felipe Alou (1958–1974)	Dominican Rep.
Outfielder	Roberto Clemente (1955–1972)	Puerto Rico
Catcher	Manny Sanguillen (1967–1980)	Panama
Designated hitter	Rod Carew (1967–1985)	Panama
Right-handed starter	Juan Marichal (1960–1974)	Dominican Rep.
Left-handed starter	Mike Cuellar (1959–1976)	Cuba
Relief	Pedro Borbón (1969–1980)	Dominican Rep.

Latin Dream Team of the 1980s–1990s

Position	Name (Career Years)	Country
First base	Pedro Guerrero (1978–1992)	Dominican Rep.
Second base	Roberto Alomar (1988–1993)	Puerto Rico
Shortstop	Tony Fernández (1983–1993)	Dominican Rep.
Third base	Aurelio Rodríguez (1967–1983)	Mexico
Outfielder	George Bell (1981–1993)	Dominican Rep.
Outfielder	José Canseco (1985–1993)	Cuba
Outfielder	Tony Armas (1976–1989)	Venezuela
Catcher	Benito Santiago (1986–1993)	Puerto Rico
Designated hitter	César Cedeño (1970–1986)	Dominican Rep.
Right-handed starter	Dennis Martínez (1976–1993)	Nicaragua
Left-handed starter	Fernando Valenzuela (1981–1993)	Mexico
Relief	Guillermo Hernández (1977–1989)	Puerto Rico

Latin American Hall-of-Famers (Cooperstown)

Player	Country	Induction	Ballclub(s)
Roberto Clemente	Puerto Rico	1972	Pittsburgh Pirates
Martín Dihigo	Cuba	1977	Negro Leagues
Juan Marichal	Dominican Rep.	1983	Giants, Red Sox
Luís Aparicio	Venezuela	1984	White Sox, Orioles
Rod Carew	Panama (Canal Zone)	1991	Twins, Angels

Latin American Million-Dollar Players (1992 salaries)

Player	Country	Team	1992 Salary
Danny Tartabull	Puerto Rico	New York Yankees	$5,300,000
Rubén Sierra	Puerto Rico	Texas Rangers	$5,000,000
Roberto Alomar	Puerto Rico	Toronto Blue Jays	$4,600,000
José Canseco	Cuba	Texas Rangers	$4,300,000
Rafael Palmeiro	Cuba	Texas Rangers	$3,850,000
George Bell	Dominican Rep.	Chicago White Sox	$3,600,000
Teddy Higuera	Mexico	Milwaukee Brewers	$3,500,000
Dennis Martínez	Nicaragua	Montreal Expos	$3,333,000
Benito Santiago	Puerto Rico	San Diego Padres	$3,300,000

Player	Country	Team	1992 Salary
José Rijo	Dominican Rep.	Cincinnati Reds	$3,083,000
Tony Peña	Dominican Rep.	Boston Red Sox	$2,650,000
Iván Calderón	Puerto Rico	Montreal Expos	$2,600,000
José DeLeón	Dominican Rep.	St. Louis Cardinals	$2,466,000
Pedro Guerrero	Dominican Rep.	St. Louis Cardinals	$2,425,000
Alejandro Peña	Dominican Rep.	Atlanta Braves	$2,400,000
Julio Franco	Dominican Rep.	Texas Rangers	$2,387,000
Andrés Galarraga	Venezuela	St. Louis Cardinals	$2,366,000
Juan Samuel	Dominican Rep.	Los Angeles Dodgers	$2,325,000
Roberto Kelly	Panama	New York Yankees	$2,150,000
Tony Fernández	Dominican Rep.	San Diego Padres	$2,100,000
José Oquendo	Puerto Rico	St. Louis Cardinals	$2,050,000
Mariano Duncan	Dominican Rep.	Philadelphia Phillies	$2,000,000
José Lind	Puerto Rico	Pittsburgh Pirates	$2,000,000
Ozzie Guillén	Venezuela	Chicago White Sox	$1,900,000
Juan Agosto	Puerto Rico	St. Louis Cardinals	$1,668,000
José Uribe	Dominican Rep.	San Francisco Giants	$1,553,000
José Guzmán	Puerto Rico	Texas Rangers	$1,345,000
Candy Maldonado	Puerto Rico	Toronto Blue Jays	$1,250,000
Juan Berenguer	Panama	Atlanta Braves	$1,200,000
Melido Pérez	Dominican Rep.	New York Yankees	$1,165,000
Edwin Núñez	Puerto Rico	Milwaukee Brewers	$1,075,000
Luís Rivera	Puerto Rico	Boston Red Sox	$1,075,000
Manuel Lee	Dominican Rep.	Toronto Blue Jays	$1,000,000

Retired Uniform Numbers of Latin American Major Leaguers

National League:

Pittsburgh Pirates	Roberto Clemente	Puerto Rico	21
San Francisco Giants	Juan Marichal	Dominican Republic	27

American League:

California Angels	Rod Carew	Panama	29
Minnesota Twins	Rod Carew	Panama	29
Chicago White Sox	Minnie Miñoso	Cuba	9
Chicago White Sox	Luís Aparicio	Venezuela	11

All-Time Latin American Career Pitching Leaders (through 1993)

Victories:	
Juan Marichal	243 (243-142, .631)
Luís Tiant	229 (229-172, .571)
Dennis Martínez	207 (207-164, .558)
Adolfo Luque	194 (194-179, .519)
Mike Cuellar	185 (185-130, .587)
Camilo Pascual	174 (174-170, .506)

Losses:	
Adolfo Luque	179
Luís Tiant	172
Camilo Pascual	170
Dennis Martínez	164
Pedro Ramos	160
Juan Marichal	142

All-Time Latin American Career Pitching Leaders, *cont.*

Games Pitched:

Guillermo Hernández	744
Diego Seguí	639
Elias Sosa	601
Pedro Borbón	593
Pedro Ramos	582
Luís Tiant	573
Dennis Martínez	556
Adolfo Luque	550
Juan Agosto	537

Complete Games:

Juan Marichal	244
Adolfo Luque	206
Luís Tiant	187
Mike Cuellar	172
Camilo Pascual	132
Fernando Valenzuela	112
Dennis Martínez	110

Strikeouts:

Luís Tiant	2,416
Juan Marichal	2,303
Camilo Pascual	2,167
Fernando Valenzuela	1,842
Dennis Martínez	1,821

Shutouts:

Juan Marichal	52
Luís Tiant	49
Camilo Pascual	36 (tie)
Mike Cuellar	36 (tie)
Fernando Valenzuela	29

Earned Run Average (900 innings)

Juan Marichal	2.89 (3,506 innings)
Alejandro Peña	2.95 (969 innings)
Mike Cuellar	3.14 (2,808 innings)
José Rijo	3.14 (1,520 innings)
Adolfo Luque	3.24 (3,221 innings)

Relief Victories:

Diego Seguí	92
Guillermo Hernández	70
Pedro Borbón	69
Elias Sosa	59
Aurelio López	58

Games Saved:

Guillermo Hernández	147
Aurelio López	93
Elias Sosa	83
Pedro Borbón	80
Diego Seguí	71

All-Time Latin American Career Batting Leaders (through 1993)

Batting Average:

Rod Carew	.328
Roberto Clemente	.317
Matty Alou	.307
Tony Oliva	.304
Manny Mota	.304

Hits:

Rod Carew	3,053
Roberto Clemente	3,000
Tony Pérez	2,732
Luís Aparicio	2,677
Orlando Cepeda	2,351

Doubles:

Tony Pérez	505
Rod Carew	445
Roberto Clemente	440
César Cedeño	436
Orlando Cepeda	417

Triples:

Roberto Clemente	166
Rod Carew	112
Luís Aparicio	94
José Cruz	94
Tony Taylor	86
Bert Campaneris	86

Total Bases:

Tony Pérez	4,532
Roberto Clemente	4,492
Rod Carew	4,198
Orlando Cepeda	3,959
Luís Aparicio	3,504

At-Bats:

Luís Aparicio	10,230
Tony Pérez	9,778
Roberto Clemente	9,454
Rod Carew	9,315
Davy Concepción	8,723

Games Played:

Tony Pérez	2,777
Luís Aparicio	2,599
Davy Concepción	2,488
Rod Carew	2,469
Roberto Clemente	2,433
José Cruz	2,353

Home Runs:

Orlando Cepeda	379 (tie)
Tony Pérez	379 (tie)
George Bell	265
Tony Armas	251
José Canseco	245
Roberto Clemente	240
Ben Oglivie	235
Tony Oliva	220
Pedro Guerrero	215

Runs Batted In:

Tony Pérez	1,652
Orlando Cepeda	1,365
Roberto Clemente	1,305
José Cruz	1,077
Minnie Miñoso	1,023
César Cedeño	976

Runs Scored:

Rod Carew	1,424
Roberto Clemente	1,416
Luís Aparicio	1,335
Tony Pérez	1,272
Bert Campaneris	1,181

Bases on Balls:

Rod Carew	1,018
Tony Pérez	925
José Cruz	898
Minnie Miñoso	814
Davy Concepción	736
Luís Aparicio	736
César Cedeño	664

Stolen Bases:

Bert Campaneris	649
César Cedeño	550
Luís Aparicio	506
Omar Moreno	487
Rod Carew	353

Pinch Hits:

Manny Mota	150
José Morales	123
Victor Davalillo	95
Jesús Alou	82

Latin American Big-League Leaders, Champions, Award Winners

Most Valuable Player:

Zoilo Versalles	1965	American League (Minnesota Twins)
Roberto Clemente	1966	National League (Pittsburgh Pirates)
Orlando Cepeda	1967	National League (St. Louis Cardinals)
Rod Carew	1977	American League (Minnesota Twins)
Guillermo Hernández	1984	American League (Detroit Tigers)
George Bell	1987	American League (Toronto Blue Jays)
José Canseco	1988	American League (Oakland Athletics)

Cy Young Award:

Mike Cuellar	1969	American League (Baltimore Orioles)
Fernando Valenzuela	1981	National League (Los Angeles Dodgers)
Guillermo Hernández	1984	American League (Detroit Tigers)

Relief Pitcher of the Year:

Mike Fornieles	1960	American League (Boston Red Sox)
Luís Arroyo	1961	American League (New York Yankees)
Minnie Rojas	1967	American League (California Angels)

Rookie of the Year:

Luís Aparicio	1956	American League (Chicago White Sox)
Orlando Cepeda	1958	National League (San Francisco Giants)
Tony Oliva	1964	American League (Minnesota Twins)

Latin American Big-League Leaders, *cont.*

Rookie of the Year, *cont.*

Rod Carew	1967	American League (Minnesota Twins)	
Alfredo Griffin	1979	American League (Toronto Blue Jays)	
Fernando Valenzuela	1981	National League (Los Angeles Dodgers)	
Ozzie Guillén	1985	American League (Chicago White Sox)	
José Canseco	1986	American League (Oakland Athletics)	
Benito Santiago	1987	National League (San Diego Padres)	
Sandy Alomar Jr.	1990	American League (Cleveland Indians)	

League Stolen-Base Champion:

Minnie Miñoso	1951	American League (Chicago White Sox)	31
Minnie Miñoso	1952	American League (Chicago White Sox)	22
Minnie Miñoso	1953	American League (Chicago White Sox)	25
Luís Aparicio	1956	American League (Chicago White Sox)	21
Luís Aparicio	1957	American League (Chicago White Sox)	28
Luís Aparicio	1958	American League (Chicago White Sox)	29
Luís Aparicio	1959	American League (Chicago White Sox)	56
Luís Aparicio	1960	American League (Chicago White Sox)	51
Luís Aparicio	1961	American League (Chicago White Sox)	53
Luís Aparicio	1962	American League (Chicago White Sox)	31
Luís Aparicio	1963	American League (Baltimore Orioles)	40
Luís Aparicio	1964	American League (Baltimore Orioles)	57
Bert Campaneris	1965	American League (Kansas City A's)	51
Bert Campaneris	1966	American League (Kansas City A's)	52
Bert Campaneris	1967	American League (Kansas City A's)	55
Bert Campaneris	1968	American League (Oakland Athletics)	62
Bert Campaneris	1970	American League (Oakland Athletics)	42
Bert Campaneris	1972	American League (Oakland Athletics)	52
Frank Taveras	1977	National League (Pittsburgh Pirates)	70
Omar Moreno	1978	National League (Pittsburgh Pirates)	71
Omar Moreno	1979	National League (Pittsburgh Pirates)	77

League Batting Champion:

Roberto Avila	1954	American League (Cleveland Indians)	.341
Roberto Clemente	1961	National League (Pittsburgh Pirates)	.351
Roberto Clemente	1964	National League (Pittsburgh Pirates)	.339
Tony Oliva	1964	American League (Minnesota Twins)	.323
Roberto Clemente	1965	National League (Pittsburgh Pirates)	.329
Tony Oliva	1965	American League (Minnesota Twins)	.321
Matty Alou	1966	National League (Pittsburgh Pirates)	.342
Roberto Clemente	1967	National League (Pittsburgh Pirates)	.357
Rod Carew	1969	American League (Minnesota Twins)	.332
Rico Carty	1970	National League (Atlanta Braves)	.366
Tony Oliva	1971	American League (Minnesota Twins)	.337
Rod Carew	1972	American League (Minnesota Twins)	.318
Rod Carew	1973	American League (Minnesota Twins)	.350
Rod Carew	1974	American League (Minnesota Twins)	.364
Rod Carew	1975	American League (Minnesota Twins)	.359
Rod Carew	1977	American League (Minnesota Twins)	.388
Rod Carew	1978	American League (Minnesota Twins)	.333
Julio Franco	1991	American League (Texas Rangers)	.341
Andrés Galarraga	1993	National League (Colorado Rockies)	.370

League RBI Champion:

Orlando Cepeda	1961	National League (San Francisco Giants)	142

Orlando Cepeda	1967	National League (St. Louis Cardinals)	111
Tony Armas	1984	American League (Boston Red Sox)	123
George Bell	1987	American League (Toronto Blue Jays)	134
José Canseco	1988	American League (Oakland Athletics)	124
Rubén Sierra	1989	American League (Texas Rangers)	119

League Home-Run Champion:

Orlando Cepeda	1961	National League (San Francisco Giants)	46
Ben Oglivie	1980	American League (Milwaukee Brewers)	41
Tony Armas	1981	American League (Oakland Athletics)	22
Tony Armas	1984	American League (Boston Red Sox)	43
José Canseco	1988	American League (Oakland Athletics)	42
José Canseco	1991	American League (Oakland Athletics)	44
Juan González	1992	American League (Texas Rangers)	43
Juan González	1993	American League (Texas Rangers)	46

League ERA Champion:

Adolfo Luque	1923	National League (Cincinnati Reds)	1.93
Adolfo Luque	1925	National League (Cincinnati Reds)	2.63
Luís Tiant	1968	American League (Cleveland Indians)	1.60
Juan Marichal	1969	National League (San Francisco Giants)	2.10
Diego Seguí	1970	American League (Oakland Athletics)	2.56
Luís Tiant	1972	American League (Boston Red Sox)	1.91
Alejandro Peña	1984	National League (Los Angeles Dodgers)	2.48
Teddy Higuera	1988	American League (Milwaukee Brewers)	2.45
Dennis Martínez	1991	National League (Montreal Expos)	2.39

Latin America's Milestone Hitters (through 1993 season)

.300 Lifetime BA

Rod Carew (.328)
Roberto Clemente (.317)
Matty Alou (.307)
Tony Oliva (.304)
Manny Mota (.304)
Julio Franco (.301)
Pedro Guerrero (.300)

2,200 Career Hits

Rod Carew (3,053)
Roberto Clemente (3,000)
Tony Pérez (2,732)
Luís Aparicio (2,677)
Orlando Cepeda (2,351)
Davy Concepción (2,326)
José Cruz (2,251)

1,000 Career RBI

Tony Pérez (1,652)
Orlando Cepeda (1,365)
Roberto Clemente (1,305)
José Cruz (1,077)
Minnie Miñoso (1,023)

3,000 Total Bases

Tony Pérez (4,532)
Roberto Clemente (4,492)
Rod Carew (4,198)
Orlando Cepeda (3,959)
Luís Aparicio (3,504)

200 Career Home Runs

Orlando Cepeda (379)
Tony Pérez (379)
George Bell (265)
Tony Armas (251)
José Canseco (245)
Roberto Clemente (240)
Ben Oglivie (235)
Tony Oliva (220)
Pedro Guerrero (215)

1,000 Lifetime Runs Scored

Rod Carew (1,424)
Roberto Clemente (1,416)
Luís Aparicio (1,335)
Tony Pérez (1,272)
Minnie Miñoso (1,136)
Orlando Cepeda (1,131)
César Cedeño (1,084)
José Cruz (1,036)
Tony Taylor (1,005)

Latin America's Milestone Pitchers (through 1993 season)

175 Lifetime Wins

Juan Marichal (243)
Luís Tiant (229)
Dennis Martínez (207)
Adolfo Luque (194)
Mike Cuellar (185)

1,500 Career Strikeouts

Luís Tiant (2,416)
Juan Marichal (2,303)
Camilo Pascual (2,167)
Fernando Valenzuela (1,842)
Dennis Martínez (1,821)

575 Games Pitched

Guillermo Hernández (744)
Diego Seguí (639)
Elias Sosa (601)
Pedro Borbón (593)
Pedro Ramos (582)

3,000 Innings Pitched

Juan Marichal (3,507)
Luís Tiant (3,486.1)
Dennis Martínez (3369.1)
Adolfo Luque (3220.1)
Camilo Pascual (2930.2)

55 Career Saves

Guillermo Hernández (147)
Aurelio López (93)
Elias Sosa (83)
Pedro Borbón (80)
Diego Seguí (71)
Alejandro Peña (67)
Mike Fornieles (55)
Pedro Ramos (55)

20 Career Shutouts

Juan Marichal (52)
Luís Tiant (49)
Camilo Pascual (36)
Mike Cuellar (36)
Fernando Valenzuela (29)
Adolfo Luque (26)
Dennis Martínez (23)
Joaquín Andújar (19)

Latin American Big-League No-Hitters

Juan Marichal (Dominican Republic)
June 15, 1963, San Francisco (Candlestick Park)
San Francisco Giants 1, Houston Colt .45s 0
First no-hitter by Latin American pitcher

Francisco Barrios (Mexico)
Combined no-hitter (with John "Blue Moon" Odom)
July 28, 1976, Oakland (Oakland-Alameda County Coliseum)
Chicago White Sox 2, Oakland Athletics 1
First American League no-hitter involving Latin American pitcher

Juan Nieves (Puerto Rico)
April 15, 1987, Baltimore (Memorial Stadium)
Milwaukee Brewers 7, Baltimore Orioles 0
First American League nine-inning no-hitter by Latin American pitcher

Pascual Pérez (Dominican Republic)
Rain-shortened no-hitter (6 innings)
September 24, 1988, Philadelphia (Veterans Stadium)
Montreal Expos 1, Philadelphia Phillies 0

Melido Pérez (Dominican Republic)
Rain-shortened no-hitter (6 innings)
July 12, 1990, New York (Yankee Stadium)
Chicago White Sox 8, New York Yankees 0

Fernando Valenzuela (Mexico)
June 29, 1990, Los Angeles (Dodger Stadium)
Los Angeles Dodgers 6, St. Louis Cardinals 0

Dennis Martínez (Nicaragua)
Perfect game (first perfect game by Latin American pitcher)
July 28, 1991, Los Angeles (Dodger Stadium)
Montreal Expos 2, Los Angeles Dodgers 0

Wilson Alvarez (Venezuela)
August 11, 1991, Baltimore (Memorial Stadium)
Chicago White Sox 7, Baltimore Orioles 0

Alejandro Peña (Dominican Republic)
Combined no-hitter (with Kent Mecker and Mark Wohlers)
September 11, 1991, Atlanta (Fulton County Stadium)
Atlanta Braves 1, San Diego Padres 0

APPENDIX E

Winter-League Records (Cuba, Dominican Republic, Puerto Rico, Venezuela, Mexico)

Year by Year in Cuban Professional Baseball (1878–1961)

(Primary Source: Gabino Delgado and Severo Nieto, *Béisbol Cubano, Records y Estadisticas, 1878–1955* [Havana, 1955])

Championship Results

(Managers in italics are also U.S. major-leaguers)

Key: # = Non-Cuban manager; NA = Incomplete information.

Year	Championship Team	Manager	Record (W-L-T, Pct.)
1878-79	Havana	*Esteban Bellán*	4-0-1, 1.000
1879-80	Havana	*Esteban Bellán*	5-2-0, .714
1880-81	No Official Season		
1881-82	Season not completed (dispute between Havana and Club Fé)		
1882-83	Havana	*Esteban Bellán*	5-1-0, .833
1883-84	No Official Season		
1884-85	Havana	Ricardo Mora	4-3-0, .571
1885-86	Havana	Francisco Saavedra	6-0-0, 1.000
1886-87	Havana	Francisco Saavedra	10-2-0, .833
1887-88	Club Fé	Antonio Utrera	12-3-0, .800
1888-89	Havana	Emilio Sabourín	16-4-1, .800
1889-90	Havana	Emilio Sabourín	14-3-0, .824
1890-91	Club Fé	Luís Almoina	12-6-0, .667
1891-92	Havana	Emilio Sabourín	13-7-0, .650
1892-93	Matanzas	Luís Almoina	14-9-0, .609
1893-94	Almendares	Ramón Gutiérrez	17-7-1, .708
1894-95	Season not completed (War of Independence)		
1895-96	Season canceled (War of Independence)		
1896-97	Season canceled (War of Independence)		
1897-98	Season not completed (War of Independence)		
1898-99	Havanista	Alberto Azoy	9-3-0, .750
1900	San Francisco	Patrocinio Silverio	17-10-2, .630
1901	Havana	Alberto Azoy	16-3-1, .842
1902	Havana	Alberto Azoy	17-0-2, 1.000
1903	Havana	Alberto Azoy	21-13-0, .618

Championship Results, *cont.*

Year	Championship Team	Manager	Record (W-L-T, Pct.)
1904	Havana	Alberto Azoy	16-4-0, .800
1905	Almendares	Abel Linares	19-11-2, .633
1906	Club Fé	Alberto Azoy	15-9-0, .625
1907	Almendares	Eugenio Santa Cruz	17-13-1, .567
1908	Almendares	Juan Sánchez	37-8-1, .822
1908-09	Havana	Luís Someillan	29-13-1, .690
1910	Almendares	Juan Sánchez	13-3-1, .812
1910-11	Almendares	Juan Sánchez	21-6-3, .714
1912	Havana	Eduardo Laborde	22-12-1, .647
1913	Club Fé	Agustín Molina	21-11-0, .656
1913-14	Almendares	Eugenio Santa Cruz	22-11-2, .667
1914-15	Havana	*Mike González*	23-11-0, .676
1915-16	Almendares	Alfredo Cabrera	30-12-3, .714
1917	Orientales	*Armando Marsans*	8-6-1, .571
1918-19	Havana	*Mike González*	29-19-0, .604
1919-20	Almendares	*Adolfo Luque*	22-5-2, .815
1920-21	Havana	*Mike González*	23-10-5, .676
1921	Havana	*Mike González*	4-1-0, .800
1922-23	Marianao	*Baldomero Acosta*	35-19-1, .648
1923-24	Santa Clara	Agustín Molina	36-11-1, .766
1924-25	Almendares	José Rodríguez	33-16-1, .660
1925-26	Almendares	José Rodríguez	34-13-2, .723
1926-27	Havana	*Mike González*	20-11-0, .645
1927-28	Havana	*Mike González*	24-13-0, .649
1928-29	Havana	*Mike González*	43-12-1, .782
1929-30	Cienfuegos	Pelayo Chacón	33-19-2, .635
1930-31	Season not completed		
1931-32	Almendares	José Rodríguez	21-9-4, .700
1932-33	Almendares (Tie)	*Adolfo Luque*	13-9-0, .591
	Havana (Tie)	*Mike González*	13-9-0, .591
1933-34	No Official Season		
1934-35	Almendares	*Adolfo Luque*	18-9-1, .667
1935-36	Santa Clara	Martín Dihigo	34-14-1, .708
1936-37	Marianao	Martín Dihigo	36-30-3, .545
1937-38	Santa Clara	Lazaro Sálazar	44-18-4, .710
1938-39	Santa Clara	Lazaro Sálazar	34-20-2, .630
1939-40	Almendares	*Adolfo Luque*	28-23-1, .549
1940-41	Havana	*Mike González*	30-19-5, .633
1941-42	Almendares	*Adolfo Luque*	28-20-3, .583
1942-43	Almendares	*Adolfo Luque*	25-19-4, .568
1943-44	Havana	*Mike González*	32-16-0, .667
1944-45	Almendares	Reinaldo Cordeiro	32-16-6, .667
1945-46	Cienfuegos	*Adolfo Luque*	38-23-4, .617
1946-47	Almendares	*Adolfo Luque*	42-24-4, .636
1947-48	Havana	*Mike González*	39-33-9, .542
1948-49	Almendares	*Fermín Guerra*	47-25-0, .553
1949-50	Almendares	*Fermín Guerra*	38-34-4, .528
1950-51	Havana	*Mike González*	40-32-1, .556
1951-52	Havana	*Mike González*	41-30-1, .577
1952-53	Havana	*Mike González*	43-29-1, .597
1953-54	Almendares	*Bobby Bragan#*	44-28-1, .611
1954-55	Almendares	*Bobby Bragan#*	44-25-2, .638
1955-56	Cienfuegos	NA	NA
1956-57	Marianao	NA	NA

Year	Championship Team	Manager	Record (W-L-T, Pct.)
1957-58	Marianao	NA	NA
1958-59	Almendares	NA	NA
1959-60	Cienfuegos	NA	NA
1960-61	Cienfuegos	NA	NA

Individual Batting Leaders

(Players in italics are also U.S. major-leaguers)

Key: # 1921 season was shortened.

Year	BA	Home Runs	Runs Scored
1878-79	NA	NA	NA
1879-80	NA	NA	NA
1880-81	NA	NA	NA
1881-82	NA	NA	NA
1882-83	NA	NA	NA
1883-84	NA	NA	NA
1884-85	Pablo Ronquilla (.350)	NA	NA
1885-86	Wenceslao Gálvez (.345)	NA	NA
1886-87	Ricardo Martínez (.439)	NA	NA
1887-88	Antonio García (.448)	NA	NA
1888-89	Francisco Salabarría (.305)	NA	NA
1889-90	Antonio García (.364)	NA	NA
1890-91	Alfredo Crespo (.375)	NA	NA
1891-92	Antonio García (.362)	NA	NA
1892-93	Antonio García (.385)	NA	NA
1893-94	Miguel Prats (.394)	NA	NA
1894-95	Alfredo Arcaño (.430)	NA	NA
1895-96	Season canceled (War of Independence)		
1896-97	Season canceled (War of Independence)		
1897-98	Valentín González (.394)	NA	NA
1898-99	Valentín González (.414)	NA	NA
1900	Esteban Prats (.333)	NA	NA
1901	Julian Castillo (.454)	NA	NA
1902	Luís Padrón (.463)	NA	NA
1903	Julian Castillo (.330)	NA	NA
1904	Regino García (.397)	NA	NA
1905	Regino García (.305)	NA	NA
1906	Regino García (.304)	NA	NA
1907	Regino García (.324)	NA	NA
1908	Emilio Palomino (.350)	NA	Preston Hill (53)
1908-09	Julian Castillo (.315)	NA	NA
1910	Julian Castillo (.408)	NA	Gervasio González (18)
1910-11	Preston Hill (.365)	NA	*Armando Marsans* (22)
1912	Emilio Palomino (.440)	NA	Carlos Morán (32)
1913	*Armando Marsans* (.400)	NA	Spotswood Poles (40)
1913-14	Manuel Villa (.351)	NA	*Armando Marsans* (28)
1914-15	Cristóbal Torriente (.387)	NA	Cristóbal Torriente (33)
1915-16	Eustaquio Pedroso (.413)	NA	Cristóbal Torriente (41)
1917	*Adolfo Luque* (.355)	NA	*Mike González* (9)
1918-19	*Manuel Cueto* (.344)	NA	*Baldomero Acosta* (30)
1919-20	Cristóbal Torriente (.360)	NA	Bernardo Baro (21)
1920-21	Pelayo Chacón (.344)	NA	Cristóbal Torriente (19)
1921#	Bienvenido Jiménez (.619)	Manuel Cueto (1)	Bienvenido Jiménez (7)
1922-23	Bernardo Baro (.401)	Cristóbal Torriente (4)	Cristóbal Torriente (37)
1923-24	Oliver Marcell (.393)	Bienvenido Jiménez (4)	Oscar Charleston (59)

Individual Batting Leaders, *cont.*

Year	BA	Home Runs	Runs Scored
1924-25	Alejandro Oms (.393)	Esteban Montalvo (5)	Valentín Dreke (45)
1925-26	Johnny Wilson (.430)	Jud Wilson (3)	Johnny Wilson (37)
1926-27	Manuel Cueto (.404)	José Hernández (4)	Ramón Herrera (24)
1927-28	Johnny Wilson (.424)	Oscar Charleston (5)	Johnny Wilson (36)
1928-29	Alejandro Oms (.432)	James "Papa" Bell (5)	James "Papa" Bell (44)
1929-30	Alejandro Oms (.380)	Mule Suttles (7)	James "Papa" Bell (52)
1930-31	Season not completed ----------	----------	----------
1931-32	Ramón Couto (.400)	Alejandro Oms (3)	Alejandro Oms (28)
1932-33	*Mike González* (.432)	*Bobby Estalella* (3)	José Abreu (17)
1933-34	No Official Season ----------	----------	----------
1934-35	Lazaro Sálazar (.407)	NA	Cando López (18)
1935-36	Martín Dihigo (.358)	Jacinto Roque (5)	Martín Dihigo (42)
1936-37	Harry Williams (.349)	*Bobby Estalella* (5)	Lazaro Sálazar (47)
1937-38	Sammy Bankhead (.366)	NA	Sammy Bankhead (47)
1938-39	Antonio Castaño (.371)	Josh Gibson (11)	Josh Gibson (50)
1939-40	Antonio Castaño (.340)	Mule Suttles (4)	Sammy Bankhead (41)
1940-41	Lazaro Sálazar (.316)	Alejandro Crespo (3)	Pedro Pagés (37)
1941-42	Silvio García (.351)	NA	Silvio García (24)
1942-43	Alejandro Crespo (.337)	*Roberto Ortiz* (2)	Antonio Rodríguez (31)
1943-44	*Roberto Ortiz* (.337)	Saguita Hernández (3)	*Roberto Ortiz* (41)
1944-45	Claro Duany (.340)	Claro Duany (3)	Four Tied (29)
1945-46	Lloyd Davenport (.333)	*Dick Sisler* (9)	Roland Gladú (41)
1946-47	*Lou Klein* (.330)	*Roberto Ortiz* (11)	Avelino Cañizares (47)
1947-48	Harry Kimbro (.346)	Jesús Díaz (7)	*Sam Jethroe* (53)
1948-49	Alejandro Crespo (.326)	*Monte Irvin* (10)	*Hank Thompson* (60)
1949-50	Pedro Formental (.336)	*Roberto Ortiz* (15)	Pedro Formental (51)
1950-51	Silvio García (.347)	Four Tied (8)	*Orestes Miñoso* (54)
1951-52	Bert Hass (.323)	Pedro Formental (9)	Pedro Formental (47)
1952-53	*Sandy Amoros* (.373)	*Lou Klein* (16)	*Orestes Miñoso* (67)
1953-54	*Rocky Nelson* (.352)	*Earl Rapp* (10)	*Forrest Jacobs* (58)
1954-55	Angel Scull (.370)	*Rocky Nelson* (13)	*Rocky Nelson* (60)
1955-56	*Forrest Jacobs* (.321)	Ultus Alvarez (10)	NA
1956-57	*Orestes Miñoso* (.312)	Archie Wilson (11)	NA
1957-58	Milton Smith (.320)	Four Tied (9)	NA
1958-59	*Tony Taylor* (.303)	Jim Baxes (9)	NA
1959-60	*Cookie Rojas* (.322)	NA	NA

Individual Pitching Leaders

(Players in italics are also U.S. major-leaguers)

Key: # 1921 season was shortened.

Year	Pitching Victories	Complete Games	Shutouts Leader
1878-79	NA	NA	NA
1879-80	NA	NA	NA
1880-81	NA	NA	NA
1881-82	NA	NA	NA
1882-83	NA	NA	NA
1883-84	NA	NA	NA
1884-85	NA	NA	NA
1885-86	NA	Adolfo Luján (5)	Enrique Soler (3)
1886-87	Adolfo Luján (5-0)	Carlos Maciá (9)	Evaristo Cachurro (6)
1887-88	Adolfo Luján (11-4)	Adolfo Luján (15)	Enrique Ovares (10)
1888-89	Adolfo Luján (10-3)	Enrique Rosas (18)	Enrique Rojas (14)

Year	Pitching Victories	Complete Games	Shutouts Leader
1889-90	Miguel Prats (11–2)	José Pastoriza (14)	Salvador Villegas (6)
1890-91	José Pastoriza (10–5)	José Pastoriza (12)	Alfredo Crespo (7)
1891-92	Enrique Hernández (4–1)	José Pastoriza (15)	José Pastoriza (10)
1892-93	Francisco Hernández (4–1)	Miguel Prats (8)	Miguel Prats (6)
1893-94	José Pastoriza (16–7)	José Pastoriza (18)	Francisco Llanes (8)
1894-95	Enrique García (12–4)	Enrique García (15)	José Pastoriza (6)
1895-96	Season Canceled (War of Independence)		
1896-97	Season Canceled (War of Independence)		
1897-98	Season not completed		
1898-99	José Romero (5–2)	José Romero (7)	Salvador Rosado (3)
1900	Luís Padrón (13–4)	Luís Padrón (17)	José Múñoz (7)
1901	Carlos Royer (12–3)	José Múñoz (14)	Angel D'Mesa (9)
1902	Carlos Royer (17–0)	Carlos Royer (17)	José Múñoz (7)
1903	Carlos Royer (21–12)	Carlos Royer (28)	Carlos Royer (10)
1904	Carlos Royer (13–3)	Carlos Royer (16)	Juan Viola (7)
1905	Angel D'Mesa (10–4)	Luís González (16)	José Múñoz (9)
1906	Luís González (10–5)	Rube Foster (15)	Pedro Olave (10)
1907	George Mack (4–2)	Julián Pérez (13)	Luís González (7)
1908	José Múñoz (13–1)	NA	Luís González (11)
1908-09	José Méndez (15–6)	José Méndez (18)	Pastor Parera (7)
1910	José Méndez (7–0)	Pastor Parera (8)	Juan Marlotica (6)
1910-11	José Méndez (11–2)	José Méndez (12)	Jorge Ball (8)
1912	Fred Wickware (10–3)	José Méndez (13)	Eustaquio Pedroso (10)
1913	Eustaquio Pedroso (11–4)	Eustaquio Pedroso (11)	Alfredo Lazaga (7)
1913-14	José Méndez (10–0)	Pastor Parera (12)	Pastor Parera (9)
1914-15	Eustaquio Pedroso (10–5)	Eustaquio Pedroso (12)	Pedro González (9)
1915-16	*Adolfo Luque* (12–5)	Eustaquio Pedroso (12)	Francisco Campos (8)
1917	*José Acosta* (2–1)	*Adolfo Luque* (6)	*Adolfo Luque* (4)
1918-19	*José Acosta* (16–10)	*José Acosta* (17)	*José Acosta* (10)
1919-20	*Adolfo Luque* (10–4)	*José Acosta* (11)	*Oscar Tuero* (5)
1920-21	José Hernández (4–1)	*Oscar Tuero* (8)	Red Redding (6)
1921#	Julio Leblanc (2–0)	*Oscar Tuero* (2)	Pilar Alonso (2)
1922-23	*Adolfo Luque* (11–9)	*Adolfo Luque* (12)	*Adolfo Luque* (9)
1923-24	Bill Holland (10–2)	Oscar Fuhr (9)	Lucas Boada (8)
1924-25	*José Acosta* (4–1)	Oscar Levis (12)	*Bill Holland* (8)
1925-26	César Alvarez (10–2)	César Alvarez (9)	*Jesse Winters* (6)
1926-27	Juan Olmo (3–0)	Raul Alvarez (7)	John McClure (8)
1927-28	Oscar Levis (7–2)	Rube Foster (8)	Rube Foster (8)
1928-29	*Adolfo Luque* (9–2)	William Bell (11)	Johnny Williams (8)
1929-30	Yoyo Díaz (13–3)	Yoyo Díaz (11)	*Adolfo Luque* (8)
1930-31	Season not completed		
1931-32	Juan Eckelson (5–1)	Rodolfo Fernández (9)	Luís Tiant (6)
1932-33	Jesús Lorenzo (3–0)	Jesús Miralles (6)	Jesús Miralles (5)
1933-34	No Official Season		
1934-35	Lazaro Sálazar (6–1)	*Tommy de la Cruz* (7)	Jesús Miralles (8)
1935-36	Martín Dihigo (11–2)	Martín Dihigo (13)	Luís Tiant (10)
1936-37	Raymond Brown (21–4)	Raymond Brown (23)	Luís Tiant (12)
1937-38	Raymond Brown (12–5)	Raymond Brown (14)	Basilio Rosell (12)
1938-39	Martín Dihigo (14–2)	Raymond Brown (16)	Theolic Smith (9)
1939-40	Barney Morris (13–8)	Barney Morris (15)	Luís Tiant (9)
1940-41	Vidal López (12–5)	Vidal López (16)	Luís Tiant (7)
1941-42	Agapito Mayor (6–2)	Ramón Bragaña (11)	Steve Rachunock (9)
1942-43	Manuel García (10–3)	Adrian Zabala (14)	*Gilberto Torres* (9)
1943-44	Manuel García (12–4)	*Tommy de la Cruz* (10)	Manuel Fortes (12)
1944-45	Oliverio Ortiz (10–4)	Terris McDuffie (9)	Daniel Ríos (9)
1945-46	Pedro Jiménez (13–8)	*Sal Maglie* (9)	*Julio Moreno* (10)

Individual Pitching Leaders, *cont.*

Year	Pitching Victories	Complete Games	Shutouts Leader
1946-47	Agapito Mayor (10-4)	Adrian Zabala (14)	*Sandy Consuegra* (11)
1947-48	*Connie Marrero* (12-2)	Alex Patterson (18)	Alex Patterson (9)
1948-49	Dave Barnhill (13-8)	Dave Barnhill (13)	Max Manning (12)
1949-50	*Thomas Fine* (16-6)	Al Gerheauser (11)	*Sandy Consuegra* (12)
1950-51	*Connie Marrero* (11-7)	*Hoyt Wilhelm* (10)	Bill Ayers (9)
1951-52	*Joe Black* (15-6)	*Red Barrett* (12)	*Thomas Fine* (11)
1952-53	Mario Picone (13-8)	*Al Gettel* (13)	*Ed Roebuck* (11)
1953-54	Cliff Fannin (13-4)	*Al Sima* (12)	James Davis (11)
1954-55	Joe Hatten (13-5)	*Ed Roebuck* (12)	Floyd Woodridge (12)
1955-56	*Pedro Ramos* (13-5)	NA	NA
1956-57	*Camilo Pascual* (15-5)	NA	NA
1957-58	*Billy O'Dell* (7-2)	NA	NA
1958-59	*Orlando Peña* (13-5)	NA	NA
1959-60	NA	NA	NA

Year by Year in Cuban Amateur Baseball, National Championships (1962–1970)

National Championship Season

(Primary Source: *Béisbol 70: Guía Oficial Cubana* [Havana: Instituto Cubano del Libro, 1971])

Year	Champions	Batting Leader	HR Leader	Pitching Leader (ERA)
1962	Occidentales	Erwin Walter (.367)	Rolando Valdés (3)	Antonio Rubio (1.39)
1963	Industriales	Raul González (.348)	Rolando Valdés (3)	Modesto Verdura (1.58)
1964	Industriales	Pedro Chávez (.333)	Jorge Trigoura (3) Miguel Cuevas (3)	Orlando Rubio (0.63)
1965	Industriales	Urbano González (.359)	Miguel Cuevas (5)	Max Reyes (1.57)
1966	Industriales	Miguel Cuevas (.325)	Lino Betancourt (9)	Alfredo Street (1.09)
1967	Orientales	Pedro Chávez (.318)	Erwin Walter (7)	Ihos Gallegos (0.80)
1968	Havana	José Pérez (.328)	Felipe Sarduy (13)	Braudilio Vinent (1.03)
1969	Azucareros	Wilfredo Sánchez (.354)	Agustín Marquetti (19)	Roberto Valdés (1.03)
1970	Henequeneros	Wilfredo Sánchez (.351)	Raul Reyes (10)	Rolando Castillo (0.60)

Cuban Professional Baseball Records and Milestones

Cuban Individual Batting Records

Single Season Batting Average	Bienvenido Jiménez, .619 (1921, Short Season)
Single Season Batting Average	Julian Castillo, .454 (1901, 100 or more At-Bats)
Most Batting Titles Won	Antonio García, 4 (1887–88, 1889–90, 1891–92, 1892–93) Julián Castillo, 4 (1901, 1903, 1908–09, 1910) Regino García, 4 (1904, 1905, 1906, 1907)
Most Consecutive BA Titles	Regino García, 4 (1904, 1905, 1906, 1907)
Most Seasons Batting .300	Manuel Cueto (11) and Alejandro Oms (11)
Consecutive .300 Seasons	Alejandro Oms, 8 (1922–23 thru 1929–30)
Most RBIs in a Season	Pedro Formental, 57 (1952–53) Rocky Nelson, 57 (1954–55)
Most RBIs in Single Game	Walt Moryn, 8 (October 14, 1952)
Most Career RBIs	Alejandro Crespo (362) and Pedro Formental (362)

Most Seasons as RBI Leader	Leonard Pearson, 3 (1946-47, 1948-49, 1949-50)
Most Runs Scored in a Season	Orestes Miñoso, 67 (1952-53)
Most Runs Scored in Game	Amado Ibáñez, 6 (January 10, 1954)
Most Career Runs Scored	Pedro Formental, 431 (1942-43 thru 1954-55)
Most Seasons as Runs Leader	Cristóbal Torriente, 4 (1915, 1916, 1921, 1923)
Most Base Hits in a Season	Harry Kimbro, 104 (1947-48)
Most Base Hits in Game	Alejandro Oms, 6 (December 30, 1928)
	Antonio Castaño, 6 (December 25, 1938)
	Lloyd Davenport, 6 (January 17, 1946)
	Amado Ibáñez, 6 (January 10, 1954)
Most Career Base Hits	Silvio García, 891 (1931-32 thru 1953-54)
Most Seasons as Hits Leader	Valentín González, 5 (1893, 1895, 1899, 1902, 1905)
Longest Hitting Streak	Alejandro Oms, 30 Games (October 31 to December 24, 1928)
Most Home Runs in Game	James "Papa" Bell, 3 (January 1, 1929)
	Dick Sisler, 3 (January 24, 1946)
Most Career Home Runs	Pedro Formental, 54 (Lefthanded), 1942-43 thru 1954-55
	Roberto Ortiz, 51 (Righthanded), 1939-40 thru 1954-55
Most Home Runs in a Season	Lou Klein, 16 (1952-53)

Cuban Individual Pitching Records

Seasons as Pitching Champion	José Méndez, 5 (1908, 1909, 1910, 1911, 1914)
	José Acosta, 5 (1915, 1916, 1917, 1919, 1925)
Most Games Won in Season	Carlos Royer, 21 (1903)
	Raymond Brown, 21 (1936-37)
Consecutive Wins in Season	Carlos Royer, 17 (1902)
Most Consecutive Wins	Carlos Royer, 20 (1902-1903)
Most Career Victories	Martín Dihigo, 105 (1922-23 thru 1946-47)
Consecutive Relief Wins	Thomas Fine, 9 (1949-50)
Most Career Complete Games	Martín Dihigo, 120 (1922-23 thru 1946-47)
Consecutive Complete Games	Carlos Royer, 69 (1901-1904) (*Career Record)
	Carlos Royer, 33 (1903) (**Season Record, with Playoffs)
Most Games Pitched (Career)	Adrian Zabala, 331 (1935-36 thru 1954-55)
Most Games Pitched (Season)	Joe Coleman, 44 (1953-54)
Most Shutouts (Career)	Adrian Zabala, 83 (1935-36 thru 1954-55)
Most Shutouts (Season)	Enrique Rosas, 14 (1888-89)
Most Seasons Shutout Leader	Luís Tiant, 5 (1932, 1936, 1937, 1940, 1941)
Most Strikeouts (Season)	Carlos Royer, 181 (1903, including playoffs)
Most Walks Allowed (Season)	Robert Darnell, 107 (1953-54)
Most Hits Allowed (Season)	Al Sima, 209 (1953-54)
Most Runs Allowed (Season)	Carlos Royer, 128 (1903)
Most Strikeouts (Game)	George McCullar, 21 (November 23, 1879)
Strikeouts (Modern Game)	Dave Barnhill, 15 (15 innings), January 10, 1948
Consecutive Strikeouts	Adolfo Luque, 7 (February 17, 1923)

Cuban Unassisted Triple Plays

Baldomero Acosta	December 2, 1918	Havana versus Almendares

Cuban No-Hit Games Pitched

Pitcher	Date	Score
Carlos Maciá	February 13, 1887	Almendares 38, Carmelita 0
Eugenio de Rosas	July 14, 1889	Progreso 8, Cardenas 0
Raymond Brown	November 7, 1936	Santa Clara 7, Havana 0

Cuban No-Hit Games Pitched, *cont.*

Manuel García	December 11, 1943	Havana 5, Marianao 0
Tomás de la Cruz	January 3, 1945	Almendares 7, Havana 0
Rogelio Martínez	February 6, 1950	Marianao 6, Almendares 0

Year by Year in Dominican Republic Summer and Winter League Professional Baseball (1951–1992)

(Primary Source: Tony Piña Campora, *Guía del Béisbol Profesional Dominicano* [Santo Domingo, 1989])

Championship Teams, Managers, and Individual Dominican Batting Leaders

Year	Champion	Manager	Home Runs	Batting
Summer League:				
1951	Licey	Félix Delgado	Pedro Formental (13)	Luís Villodas (.346)
1952	Aguilas	Rodolfo Fernández	Alonzo Perry (11)	Luís Olmo (.344)
1953	Licey	Oscar Rodríguez	Alonzo Perry (11)	Tetelo Vargas (.355)
1954	Orientales	Ramón Bragaña	Bob Thurman (11)	Alonzo Perry (.326)
Winter League:				
55-56	Escogido	Frank Genovese	Willie Kirkland (9)	Bob Wilson (.333)
56-57	Escogido	Red Davis	Danny Kravitz (4)	Ossie Virgil (.312)
57-58	Escogido	Salty Parker	Dick Stuart (14)	Alonzo Perry (.332)
58-59	Licey	Joe Schultz	Jim McDaniels (12)	Felipe Alou (.351)
59-60	Escogido	Pete Reiser	Frank Howard (9)	Felipe Alou (.359)
60-61	Escogido	Pepe Lucas	Five Tied (4)	Manny Mota (.344)
61-62	Season not completed			
62-63	League suspended			
63-64	Licey	Vern Benson	Orlando McFarlane (10)	Manny Mota (.379)
64-65	Aguilas	Al Widmar	Orlando McFarlane (8)	Manny Mota (.364)
65-66	League suspended			
66-67	Aguilas	Pete Peterson	Winston Llenas (10)	Matty Alou (.363)
67-68	Orientales	Tony Pacheco	Bob Robertson (9)	Rico Carty (.350)
68-69	Escogido	Andy Gilbert	Nate Colbert (8)	Matty Alou (.390)
69-70	Licey	Manny Mota	Winston Llenas (9)	Ralph Garr (.387)
70-71	Licey	Fred Hatfield	César Cedeño (8)	Ralph Garr (.457)
71-72	Aguilas	Ossie Virgil	Charlie Sands (10)	Ralph Garr (.388)
72-73	Licey	Tommy Lasorda	Adrian Garrett (9)	Von Joshua (.358)
73-74	Licey	Tommy Lasorda	Rico Carty (9)	Dave Parker (.345)
74-75	Aguilas	Al Widmar	Bobby Darwin (8)	Bruce Bochte (.352)
75-76	Aguilas	Tim Murtaugh	Seven Tied (4)	Wilbur Howard (.341)
76-77	Licey	Bob Rogers	Pedro Guerrero (6)	Mario Guerrero (.365)
77-78	Aguilas	Johnny Lipon	Dick Davis (8)	Omar Moreno (.345)
78-79	Aguilas	Johnny Lipon	Bob Beall (7)	Ted Cox (.319)
79-80	Licey	Del Crandall	Five Tied (3)	Tony Peña (.317)
80-81	Escogido	Felipe Alou	Tony Peña (7)	Ken Landreaux (.394)
81-82	Escogido	Felipe Alou	Dave Hostetler (9)	Pedro Hernández (.408)
82-83	Licey	Manny Mota	Howard Johnson (8)	César Geronimo (.341)
83-84	Licey	Manny Mota	Reggie Whittemore (12)	Miguel Diloné (.343)
84-85	Licey	Terry Collins	Ralph Bryant (9)	Junior Noboa (.327)
85-86	Aguilas	Winston Llenas	Tony Peña (9)	Tony Fernández (.364)
86-87	Aguilas	Winston Llenas	Ralph Bryant (13)	Stan Javier (.374)

Year	Champion	Manager	Home Runs	Batting
87-88	Escogido	Phil Regan	Mark Parent (10)	Stan Javier (.363)
88-89	Escogido	Phil Regan	Domingo Michel (9)	Julio Peguero (.326)
89-90	Escogido	Felipe Alou	Denny González (5)	Angel González (.434)
90-91	Licey	John Roseboro	Francisco Cabrera (8)	Hensley Meulens (.338)
91-92	Escogido	Rick Williams	Five Tied (4)	Luís Mercedes (.333)

Dominican Pitching Leaders

Year	Pitching Wins	ERA Leader	Strikeouts Leader
Summer League:			
1951	Guayubín Olivo (10)	Guayubín Olivo (1.90)	Guayubín Olivo (65)
1952	Terry McDuffie (14)	Guayubín Olivo (1.33)	Luís Arroyo (101)
1953	Emilio Cueche (13)	Santiago Ulrich (1.98)	Emilio Cueche (96)
1954	Carrao Bracho (8)	Guayubín Olivo (1.86)	Julián Ladera (40)
Winter League:			
1955-56	Fred Waters (11)	Art Murray (0.57)	Chuck Templeton (108)
1956-57	Pete Burnside (11)	Pete Burnside (1.71)	Pete Burnside (109)
1957-58	Fred Kipp (11)	Vic Rehm (1.53)	Stan Williams (96)
1958-59	Bennie Daniels (12)	Octavio Acosta (1.66)	Dom Zanny (86)
1959-60	Stan Williams (12)	Fred Kipp (1.32)	Stan Williams (105)
1960-61	Danilo Riva (13)	Juan Marichal (1.41)	Guayubín Olivo (160)
1961-62	Season not completed		
1962-63	League suspended		
1963-64	Steve Blass (9)	Juan Marichal (1.35)	Gaylord Perry (106)
1964-65	Dick LeMay (8)	Pete Richert (1.51)	Gary Kroll (90)
1965-66	League suspended		
1966-67	Dock Ellis (9)	Dave Hernández (1.67)	Steve Bailey (101)
1967-68	Silvano Quezada (11)	Chuck Taylor (1.69)	Danny Coombs (90)
1968-69	Jay Ritchie (9)	Leslie Scott (1.29)	Santiago Guzmán (71)
1969-70	Gene Rounsaville (8)	Sal Campisi (0.74)	Santiago Guzmán (69)
1970-71	Rollie Fingers (9)	Wade Blasingame (2.22)	Archie Reynolds (79)
1971-72	Gene Garber (9)	Pedro Borbón (1.68)	Dick Tidrow (75)
1972-73	Pedro Borbón (9)	Tom Dettore (2.30)	Doug Rau (72)
1973-74	Rick Waits (8)	Charlie Hough (1.29)	Charlie Hough (.345)
1974-75	J. R. Richard (8)	J. R. Richard (1.64)	J. R. Richard (103)
1975-76	Nino Espinosa (8)	Kent Tekulve (1.00)	J. R. Richard (88)
1976-77	Angel Torres (10)	Doug Bair (1.26)	Odell Jones (70)
1977-78	Three Tied (7)	Tom Hume (1.97)	Mickey Mahler (80)
1978-79	Mike Proly (9)	Bo McLaughlin (1.80)	Frank Riccelli (82)
1979-80	Jerry Hannahs (9)	Silvano Quezada (1.49)	Mario Soto (62)
1980-81	Mario Soto (7)	Steve Ratzer (1.24)	Mario Soto (54)
1981-82	Pascual Pérez (10)	Oscar Brito (1.85)	Mario Soto (54)
1982-83	Pascual Pérez (9)	Pascual Pérez (2.23)	Juan Berenguer (59)
1983-84	Orel Hershiser (8)	Orel Hershiser (1.51)	Robin Fuson (61)
1984-85	Tom Filer (8)	Martín Rivas (1.34)	Ken Howell (71)
1985-86	Mickey Mahler (8)	Andy Araujo (1.36)	Chris Green (69)
1986-87	Three Tied (5)	Gibson Alba (1.17)	José Núñez (62)
1987-88	José Bautista (8)	Dave Otto (1.27)	José Núñez (85)
1988-89	Melido Pérez (8)	Rick Reed (1.27)	Balvino Galvez (70)
1989-90	Four Tied (6)	Jeff Edwards (2.17)	Jeff Edwards (76)
1990-91	Francisco DelaRosa (7)	Carlos Maldonado (0.84)	Francisco DelaRosa (49)
1991-92	José Núñez (6)	Julián Heredia (1.20)	José Núñez (58)

Dominican Professional Baseball Records and Milestones

Individual Dominican Career Batting Records (1938–1992)

Batting Average	Manny Mota (.333); Matty Alou (.327)
Slugging Average	Alonzo Perry (.488)
Seasons Played	Manny Mota (20); Jesús Alou (20); Rafael Batista (20)
Games Played	Rafael Batista (946)
At-Bats	Rafael Batista (3,200); Winston Llenas (3,144)
Base Hits	Miguel Diloné (866); Jesús Alou (865)
Singles	Miguel Diloné (738); Jesús Alou (690)
Doubles	Rafael Batista (157); Jesús Alou (136); Winston Llenas (111)
Triples	Manny Mota (41); Miguel Diloné (40)
Home Runs	Rico Carty (59); Winston Llenas (50); Alonzo Perry (49)
RBIs	Rafael Batista (395); Winston Llenas (377); Jesús Alou (339)
Runs Scored	Miguel Diloné (489)
Total Bases	Rafael Batista (1,160); Jesús Alou (1,098); Miguel Diloné (1,048)
Strikeouts (Batter)	Rafael Batista (529)
Walks (Batter)	Rafael Batista (379); Miguel Diloné (329)
Stolen Bases	Miguel Diloné (395)

Individual Dominican Career Pitching Records (1938–1992)

Games Won	Diomedes "Guayubín" Olivo (86)
Winning Percentage	Mickey Mahler (.702, 40-17)
ERA	Juan Marichal (1.87, 57.1 Innings Pitched)
Seasons Pitched	Silvano Quezada (21)
Games Started	Ramón de los Santos (364); Silvano Quezada (358)
Games Completed	Diomedes "Guayubín" Olivo (70)
Innings Pitched	Chichi Olivo (1335.2); Silvano Quezada (1198.1)
Shutouts	Chichi Olivo (69)
Saves	Charlie Hough (47); Victor Cruz (40)
Strikeouts (Pitcher)	Diomedes "Guayubín" Olivo (742)
Walks (Pitcher)	Joaquín Andújar (382)

Year by Year in Puerto Rican Winter League (1938–1992)

(Primary Source: Rafael Costas, *Enciclopedia Béisbol: Ponce Leones, 1938–1987* [Santo Domingo, 1989])

Puerto Rican Championship Teams and Managers

Year	Playoff Champion (Manager)	Regular Season Champion (Record)
1938-39	Guayama (Fernando García)	Guayama (27-12, .692)
1939-40	Guayama (Fernando García)	Guayama (39-17, .696)
1940-41	Caguas (José Seda)	Caguas (27-15, .643)
1941-42	Ponce (George Scales)	Ponce (30-13, .698)
1942-43	Ponce (George Scales)	Ponce (19-16, .543)
1943-44	Ponce (George Scales)	Ponce (37-7, .841)
1944-45	Ponce (George Scales)	Ponce (28-11, .718)
1945-46	San Juan (Robert Clark)	Mayaguez (24-16, .600)
1946-47	Ponce (George Scales)	Ponce (38-22, .633)
1947-48	Caguas-Guayama (Quincy Trouppe)	Mayaguez (39-21, .650)
1948-49	Mayaguez (Artie Wilson)	Mayaguez (51-29, .638)
1949-50	Caguas-Guayama (Luís Olmo)	Caguas (47-31, .603)
1950-51	Santurce (George Scales)	Caguas (57-20, .740)

Year	Playoff Champion (Manager)	Regular Season Champion (Record)
1951-52	San Juan (Freddie Thon)	San Juan (43-29, .597)
1952-53	Santurce (Buster Clarkson)	San Juan (45-27, .625)
1953-54	Caguas-Guayama (Mickey Owen)	Caguas (46-34, .575)
1954-55	Santurce (Herman Franks)	Santurce (47-25, .653)
1955-56	Caguas-Guayama (Ben Geraghty)	Santurce (43-29, .597)
1956-57	Mayaguez (Mickey Owen)	Santurce (43-29, .597)
1957-58	Caguas-Guayama (Ted Norbert)	Santurce (36-28, .563)
1958-59	Santurce (Monchile Concepción)	San Juan (38-24, .594)
1959-60	Caguas-Guayama (Vic Pollet "Power")	San Juan (41-23, .641)
1960-61	San Juan (Lum Harris)	San Juan (39-25, .609)
1961-62	Santurce (Vern Benson)	Mayaguez (45-35, .563)
1962-63	Mayaguez (Carl Ermer)	Mayaguez (42-28, .600)
1963-64	San Juan (Less Moss)	Caguas (41-29, .586)
1964-65	Santurce (Preston Gómez)	Santurce (41-28, .594)
1965-66	Mayaguez (Wayne Blackburn)	Mayaguez (42-28, .600)
1966-67	Santurce (Earl Weaver)	Ponce (46-25, .648)
1967-68	Caguas-Guayama (Nino Escalera)	Santurce (47-22, .681)
1968-69	Ponce (Rocky Bridges)	Santurce (49-20, .710)
1969-70	Ponce (Jim Fregosi)	Ponce (44-25, .638)
1970-71	Santurce (Frank Robinson)	Caguas (41-29, .585)
1971-72	Ponce (Frank Verdi)	San Juan (39-30, .565)
1972-73	Santurce (Frank Robinson)	Santurce (45-25, .642)
1973-74	Caguas-Guayama (Bobby Wine)	Ponce (42-28, .600)
1974-75	Bayamon (José Pagán)	Caguas (43-27, .614)
1975-76	Bayamon (José Pagán)	Caguas (35-25, .583)
1976-77	Caguas (Doc Edwards)	Caguas (40-20, .667)
1977-78	Mayaguez (Rene Lachemann)	Caguas (37-23, .617)
1978-79	Caguas (Félix Millán)	Ponce (33-27, .550)
1979-80	Bayamon (Art Howe)	Santurce (36-24, .600)
1980-81	Caguas (Félix Millán)	Bayamon (39-21, .650)
1981-82	Ponce (Edward Nottle)	Caguas (37-23, .617)
1982-83	Arecibo (Ron Clarke)	Santurce (35-26, .574)
1983-84	Mayaguez (Frank Verdi)	Mayaguez (38-22, .633)
1984-85	San Juan (Mako Oliveras)	Mayaguez (38-22, .633)
1985-86	Mayaguez (Nick Leyva)	Caguas (33-21, .611)
1986-87	Caguas (Tim Foli)	Ponce (34-19, .642)
1987-88	Mayaguez (Jim Riggleman)	Santurce (31-21, .596)
1988-89	Mayaguez (Tom Gamboa)	San Juan (35-25, .583)
1989-90	San Juan (Mako Olivares)	Ponce (31-19, .620)
1990-91	San Juan (Brad Fischer)	San Juan (33-25, .569)
1991-92	Mayaguez (Pat Kelly)	San Juan (29-21, .580)

Puerto Rican Individual Batting Leaders

Year	Batting	Home Runs	Hits
1938-39	Perucho Cepeda (.465)	Edward Stone (9)	Perucho Cepeda (79)
1939-40	Perucho Cepeda (.383)	Josh Gibson (6)	Perucho Cepeda (81)
1940-41	Roy Partlow (.443)	Roy Campanella (8) Buck Leonard (8)	Perucho Cepeda (67)
1941-42	Josh Gibson (.480)	Josh Gibson (13)	Juan Sánchez (67)
1942-43	Francisco Coimbre (.342)	Luís Olmo (4)	Leonardo Chapman (49)
1943-44	Tetelo Vargas (.410)	Juan Guilbe (2)	Francisco Coimbre (60)
1944-45	Francisco Coimbre (.425)	Three Tied (3)	Juan Sánchez (61)
1945-46	Fernando Díaz Perozo (.368)	Monte Irvin (3)	Monte Irvin (56)

Puerto Rican Individual Batting Leaders, *cont.*

Year	Batting	Home Runs	Hits
1946-47	Willard Brown (.390)	Luís Márquez (14)	Willard Brown (99)
1947-48	Willard Brown (.432)	Willard Brown (27)	Artie Wilson (102) Bob Thurman (102)
1948-49	Luke Easter (.402)	Willard Brown (18) Bob Thurman (18)	Artie Wilson (126)
1949-50	Willard Brown (.354)	Willard Brown (16)	Willard Brown (117)
1950-51	George Crowe (.375)	Buster Clarkson (17)	Bob Thurman (112)
1951-52	Bob Boyd (.374)	Three Tied (9)	Bob Boyd (114)
1952-53	George Freese (.330)	Three Tied (9)	George Freese (94)
1953-54	Luís Márquez (.333)	Hank Aaron (9)	Luís Márquez (94)
1954-55	Willie Mays (.395)	Bob Cerv (19)	Roberto Clemente (94)
1955-56	Victor Pollet "Power" (.358)	Luke Easter (17)	Vic Pollet "Power" (87) Wes Covington (87)
1956-57	Roberto Clemente (.396)	Wes Covington (15)	José García (94)
1957-58	Billy Harrell (.317)	Vic Pollet "Power" (13) Orlando Cepeda (13)	Orlando Cepeda (72)
1958-59	Orlando Cepeda (.362)	Johnny Powers (17)	Elmo Plaskett (81)
1959-60	Victor Pollet "Power" (.347)	Jim McDaniels (10)	Ramón Conde (79)
1960-61	Elmo Plaskett (.328)	Elmo Plaskett (15)	Elmo Plaskett (69)
1961-62	Miguel de la Hoz (.354)	Orlando Cepeda (19)	J. C. Martin (91)
1962-63	Joe Gaines (.352)	John Herstein (14)	Cookie Rojas (95)
1963-64	Tony Oliva (.365)	José Cardenal (16)	Danny Cater (82)
1964-65	Lou Johnson (.345)	Fred Hopke (12)	Jim Northrup (89)
1965-66	Jim Northrup (.353)	Dick Simpson (10)	Jim Northrup (85)
1966-67	Tony Pérez (.333)	Dick Simpson (12)	Tony Pérez (87)
1967-68	Tony Taylor (.344)	Degold Francis (14)	Sandy Alomar (84)
1968-69	Félix Millán (.317)	George Scott (13)	Sandy Alomar (82)
1969-70	Félix Millán (.345)	Nate Colbert (16)	Sandy Alomar (88)
1970-71	Sandy Alomar (.343)	Reggie Jackson (20)	Sandy Alomar (86)
1971-72	Don Baylor (.324)	Willie Montañez (15)	Enrique Rivera (81)
1972-73	Richard Coggins (.352)	Richie Zisk (14)	Jerry Morales (80)
1973-74	George Hendrick (.363)	Benigno Ayala (14) Jerry Morales (14)	Mickey Rivers (90)
1974-75	Ken Griffey (.357)	Danny Walton (14)	Ken Griffey (84)
1975-76	Dan Driessen (.331)	Benigno Ayala (14)	José Morales (76)
1976-77	Sixto Lezcano (.366)	Roger Freed (16)	Orlando Alvarez (76)
1977-78	Ron LeFlore (.396)	Roger Freed (17)	José Moralez (78)
1978-79	José Cruz (.370)	Jim Dwyer (15)	José Cruz (78)
1979-80	Dennis Walling (.330)	Dave Revering (9)	Dennis Walling (70)
1980-81	Dickie Thon (.329)	Candy Maldonado (10)	Dickie Thon (82)
1981-82	Dickie Thon (.333)	José Cruz (12)	Dickie Thon (68)
1982-83	Brian Harper (.378)	Carmelo Martínez (17)	Brian Harper (87)
1983-84	Don Mattingly (.368)	Jerry Willard (18)	Steve Lubratick (68)
1984-85	Orlando Sánchez (.333)	Jerry Willard (9)	Milt Thompson (68)
1985-86	Wally Joyner (.356)	Wally Joyner (14)	Wally Joyner (67)
1986-87	Victor Rodríguez (.377)	Iván Calderón (10)	Tracy Woodson (63)
1987-88	Randy Milligan (.347)	Iván Calderón (8)	Roberto Alomar (60)
1988-89	Lonnie Smith (.366)	Rickey Jordan (14)	Doug Dascenzo (73)
1989-90	Edgar Martínez (.424)	Greg Vaughn (10)	Carlos Baerga (61)
1990-91	Héctor Villanueva (.347)	Héctor Villanueva (12)	Rod Brewer (71)
1991-92	Alonzo Powell (.339)	Mike Simms (9)	Alonzo Powell (58) Eric Fox (58)

Puerto Rican Individual Pitching Leaders

Year	Pitching Victories	ERA Leader	Strikeouts Leader
1938-39	Rafaelito Ortiz (11)	NA	José Figueroa (96)
1939-40	Satchel Paige (19)	Silvio García (1.32)	Satchel Paige (208)
1940-41	Billy Byrd (15)	Roy Partlow (1.49)	Dave Barnhill (193)
1941-42	Barney Brown (16)	Raymond Brown (1.82)	Leon Day (168)
1942-43	Ceferino Conde (10)	Rafaelito Ortiz (1.83)	Ceferino Conde (69)
1943-44	Rafaelito Ortiz (15)	Tomás Quinonez (1.69)	Juan Santaella (86)
1944-45	Tomás Quinonez (16)	Tomás Quinonez (2.52)	Luís Cabrera (81)
1945-46	Tomás Quinonez (10)	Johnny Davis (2.42)	Luís Cabrera (75)
1946-47	Barney Brown (16)	Barney Brown (1.24)	Dan Bankhead (179)
1947-48	Ford Smith (13)	Rafaelito Ortiz (2.97)	Johnny Davis (100)
1948-49	Royce Lynn (13)	Royce Lynn (2.38)	Gene Collins (157)
1949-50	Rubén Gómez (14)	Cecil Kaiser (1.68)	Dan Bankhead (131)
1950-51	Mike Clark (14)	Mike Clark (2.10)	Pete Wojie (116)
1951-52	Rubén Gómez (14)	Earl Harris (1.24)	Sam Jones (140)
1952-53	Bobo Holloman (15)	Coot Deal (1.85)	Rubén Gómez (123)
1953-54	Jack Harshman (15)	Natalio Irizarry (1.49)	Bob Turley (143)
1954-55	Sam "Toothpick" Jones (14)	Sam Jones (1.88)	Sam Jones (171)
1955-56	Steve Ridzik (14)	Pete Wojie (2.46)	Jim Owens (134)
1956-57	Marion Fricano (12) Corky Valentine (12)	Bob Smith (1.94)	Luís Arroyo (145)
1957-58	Juan Pizarro (14)	Juan Pizarro (1.32)	Juan Pizarro (183)
1958-59	Rubén Gómez (12)	Lloyd Merritt (1.63)	Juan Pizarro (139)
1959-60	Earl Wilson (15)	Bob Bruce (1.98)	Juan Pizarro (141)
1960-61	Phil Regan (11)	Luís Arroyo (1.64)	Juan Pizarro (122)
1961-62	Joe Horlen (13)	Gordon Seyfried (1.67)	Juan Pizarro (154)
1962-63	Bob Dustal (11)	Bob Dustal (1.76)	Bob Veale (104)
1963-64	Juan Pizarro (10)	Joe Hoerner (1.21)	John Boozer (132)
1964-65	Denny McLain (12) Mike Cuellar (12)	Fred Talbot (1.30)	Denny McLain (126)
1965-66	John Boozer (15)	Ferguson Jenkins (1.38)	John Boozer (121)
1966-67	Nelson Briles (12)	Dick Hughes (1.79)	Grant Jackson (104)
1967-68	Darrell Osteen (12)	Tom Timmerman (0.88)	Juan Pizarro (108)
1968-69	Bill Kelso (10)	Jerry Johnson (1.29)	Bill Kelso (82) Rick Gardner (82)
1969-70	Wayne Simpson (11)	Wayne Simpson (1.55)	Wayne Simpson (114)
1970-71	Mike Weneger (9)	Tom Kelly (2.04)	William Parsons (97)
1971-72	Rogelio Moret (14)	John Strohmayer (1.71)	Rogelio Moret (89)
1972-73	Juan Pizarro (10)	Bert Strom (1.65)	Lynn McGlothen (130)
1973-74	Ed Figueroa (10)	Ernie McAnnally (1.72)	Ken Wright (147)
1974-75	Ed Figueroa (10)	Richard Krueger (1.40)	Roy Thomas (61) Chris Zachary (61)
1975-76	Odell Jones (11)	Tom Bruno (1.23)	Odell Jones (77)
1976-77	Eduardo Rodríguez (9)	José Martínez (1.91)	Dave Lemanczyck (78)
1977-78	Three Tied (8)	Scott McGregor (2.18)	Bob Galasso (71)
1978-79	Steve McCatty (8) Sheldon Burnside (8)	Steve McCatty (1.71)	Johnny Morris (58)
1979-80	Dennis Kinney (9)	Darrell Jackson (1.33)	Frank LeCorte (56)
1980-81	Greg Harris (8)	Dennis Martínez (1.39)	Eric Show (62)
1981-82	Edwin Núñez (9)	Edwin Núñez (1.72)	Edwin Núñez (67)
1982-83	Ken Dayley (9)	Ed Figueroa (2.93)	Greg Harris (84)
1983-84	Rick Mahler (10)	Kevin Hagen (1.92)	Julián González (72)
1984-85	Francisco Olivares (8)	José Guzmán (1.62)	Randy Niemann (54)
1985-86	José Guzmán (7)	José Guzmán (1.65)	Tom Candiotti (53)
1986-87	Five Tied (6)	Charles Corbell (2.21)	Doug Jones (46)

Puerto Rican Individual Pitching Leaders, *cont.*

Year	Pitching Victories	ERA Leader	Strikeouts Leader
1987-88	Five Tied (6)	Miguel Alicía (0.93)	Mike Kinnunen (54)
1988-89	Aris Tirado (9)	Dave Rosario (1.32)	Aris Tirado (67)
1989-90	Ricky Bones (8)	Jeff Gray (1.24)	Rick Reed (53)
1990-91	Kip Gross (7)	Trevor Wilson (2.07)	Rod Nichols (54)
1991-92	Turk Wendell (7)	Gino Minutelli (0.90)	Denny Naegle (64)

Puerto Rican Professional Baseball Records and Milestones

Puerto Rican Batting Records (1938–1992)

Highest Season Batting Average	Josh Gibson, .480 (1941-1942)
Highest Career Batting Average	Willard Brown, .347
	Francisco "Poncho" Coimbre, .339
Individual .400 Averages	Josh Gibson, .480 (1941-42)
	Perucho Cepeda, .465 (1938-39)
	Roy Partlow, .443 (1940-41)
	Willard Brown, .432 (1947-48)
	Francisco Coimbre, .425 (1944-45)
	Edgar Martínez, .424 (1989-90)
	Tetelo Vargas, .410 (1943-44)
	Luke Easter, .402 (1948-49)
Most Batting Titles Won	Willard Brown, 3 (1946-47, 1947-48, 1949-50)
Batting Triple Crowns	Willard Brown, 1947-48 (.432, 27 HR, 86 RBI)
	Willard Brown, 1949-50 (.354, 16 HR, 97 RBI)
	Elmo Plaskett, 1960-61 (.328, 15 HR, 45 RBI)
	Wally Joyner, 1985-86 (.356, 14 HR, 48 RBI)
	Héctor Villanueva, 1990-91 (.347, 12 HR, 44 RBI)
Most Runs (Season)	Luke Easter, 81 (1948-49)
Most Hits (Season)	Artie Wilson, 126 (1948-49)
Most Doubles (Season)	Luís Márquez, 27 (1946-47)
	Luke Easter, 27 (1948-49)
Most Triples (Season)	Luís Olmo, 10 (1940-41)
	Quincy Trouppe, 10 (1941-42)
	Luís Márquez, 10 (1945-46)
	Luís Márquez, 10 (1949-50)
Most Home Runs (Season)	Willard Brown, 27 (1947-48)
Most Home Runs (Career)	Bob Thurman, 120
Most RBIs (Season)	Willard Brown, 97 (1949-50)
Most Stolen Bases (Season)	Rickey Henderson, 44 (1980-81)

Puerto Rican Pitching Records (1938–1992)

Most Games Won (Season)	Satchel Paige, 19 (1939-40)
Lowest ERA (Season)	Tom Timmerman, 0.88 (1967-1968)
Most Strikeouts (Season)	Satchel Paige, 208 (1939-40)
First Recorded No-Hit Game	Tomás Quinonez, December 3, 1944 (Ponce 8, Mayaguez 0)

Year by Year in Venezuelan League Baseball (1946–1992)

Venezuelan Championship Teams, Managers, and Outstanding Rookies

Year	Championship Team (Manager)	Rookie of the Year
1946	Vargas (Daniel Canonico)	Not Awarded
46-47	Vargas (Daniel Canonico)	Alfonso "Chico" Carrasquel (Cervecería Caracas)
47-48	Cervecería Caracas (José Casanova)	Not Awarded
48-49	Cervecería Caracas (José Casanova)	José Bracho (Cervecería Caracas)
49-50	Magallanes (Lazaro Sálazar)	Luís García (Magallanes)
50-51	Magallanes (Lazaro Sálazar)	Emilio Cueche (Cervecería Caracas)
51-52	Cervecería Caracas (José Casanova)	Not Awarded
52-53	Caracas (Martín Dihigo)	Pompeyo Davalillo (Caracas)
53-54	Pastora (Buster Mills)	Luís Aparicio (Gavilanes)
54-55	Magallanes (Lazaro Sálazar)	Dario Rubenstein (Magallanes)
55-56	Valencia (Regino Otero)	Elio Chacón (Valencia)
56-57	Caracas (Clay Bryant)	Tedoro Obregón (Valencia)
1957	Valencia (Regino Otero)	José Ocanto (Oriente)
58-59	Valencia (Regino Otero)	Medardo Nava (Pastora)
1959	Players' Strike (Season not completed)	César Tóvar (Caracas)
60-61	Valencia (Rudolfo Hernández)	Damasco Blanco (Pastora)
61-62	Caracas (Regino Otero)	Héctor Urbano (Caracas)
62-63	Valencia (Bobby Hoffman)	Nelson Castellano (Oriente)
63-64	Caracas (Regino Otero)	Juan Quintana (La Guaira)
64-65	LaGuaira (José Casanova)	Isaias Chávez (Magallanes)
65-66	LaGuaira (Tony Pacheco)	José Manuel Tóvar (Aragua)
66-67	Caracas (Regino Otero)	Gustavo Sposito (Magallanes)
67-68	Caracas (Regino Otero)	Carlos Santeliz (Lara)
68-69	LaGuaira (Wilfredo Calvino)	Roberto Romero (La Guaira)
69-70	Magallanes (Carlos Pascual)	Virgilio Mata (Aragua)
70-71	LaGuaira (Dave García)	Simon Barreto (Caracas)
71-72	Aragua (Vern Rapp and Rod Carew)	Jesús "Manny" Trillo (Caracas)
72-73	Caracas (Osvaldo "Ossie" Virgil)	Tony Armas (Caracas)
73-74	Players' Strike (Playoffs not held)	Romo Blanco (La Guaira)
74-75	Aragua (Osvaldo "Ossie" Virgil)	Félix Rodríguez (Magallanes)
75-76	Aragua (Osvaldo "Ossie" Virgil)	Oswaldo Olivares (Magallanes)
76-77	Magallanes (Don Leppert)	Antonio García (Zulia)
77-78	Caracas (Felipe Alou)	Alfredo Torres (Magallanes)
78-79	Magallanes (Cookie Rojas)	Williams Ereu (Lara)
79-80	Caracas (Felipe Alou)	César Suarez (Zulia)
80-81	Caracas (Jim Leyland)	Gustavo Polidor (La Guaira)
81-82	Caracas (Alfonso "Chico" Carrasquel)	Argenis Sálazar (La Guaira)
82-83	LaGuaira (Osvaldo "Ossie" Virgil)	Norman Garrasco (La Guaira)
83-84	Zulia (Rubén Amaro)	Johnny Paredes (Zulia)
84-85	LaGuaira (Gustavo Gil)	Omar Bencomo (Magallanes)
85-86	LaGuaira (José Martínez)	Jesús Méndez (Aragua)
86-87	Caracas (Bill Plummer)	Luís Sojo (Lara)
87-88	Caracas (Bill Robinson)	Benigno Placeres (Lara)
88-89	Zulia (Pete Mackanin)	Not Awarded
89-90	Caracas (Phil Regan)	Roberto Pérez (Lara)
90-91	Lara (Domingo Carrasquel)	Juan Castillo (Magallanes)
91-92	Zulia (Rubén Amaro)	Not Awarded

Venezuelan League Individual Batting and Pitching Leaders (1967–1992)

Year	Batting	Home Runs	Pitching Victories
1967-68	Vic Davalillo (.395)	Dave Roberts (10)	Two Tied (12)
1968-69	Cito Gaston (.383)	Brant Alyea (17)	George Lauzerique (12)
1969-70	Cito Gaston (.360)	John Bateman (9)	Mike Corkins (11)
1970-71	Vic Davalillo (.379)	Larry Howard (12)	Bart Johnson (12)
1971-72	Rod Carew (.355)	Brant Alyea (12)	Bill Kirkpatrick (10)
1972-73	Enos Cabell (.371)	Bobby Darwin (19)	Jim Rooker (13)
1973-74	Al Bumbry (.367)	Pete Koegel (18)	Jim Todd (10)
1974-75	Al Bumbry (.354)	Dave Parker (8)	Tom House (10)
1975-76	Duane Kuiper (.357)	Cliff Johnson (11)	Scott McGregor (8)
1976-77	Dave Parker (.401)	Mitchell Page (14)	Two Tied (9)
1977-78	J. J. Cannon (.381)	Clint Hurdle (18)	Jerry Cram (13)
1978-79	Orlando González (.355)	Tom Grieve (14)	Tom Brennan (10)
1979-80	Eddie Miller (.368)	Bo Díaz (20)	Odell Jones (11)
1980-81	Tim Corcoran (.374)	Three Tied (9)	Porfirio Altamirano (8)
1981-82	Lloyd Moseby (.362)	Bo Díaz (13)	Tom Dixon (9)
1982-83	Tito Landrum (.345)	Darryl Strawberry (12)	Luís Leal (9)
1983-84	Alvin Davis (.342)	Two Tied (8)	Derek Botelho (9)
1984-85	Ossie Olivares (.352)	Ron Shepherd (9)	Bill Landrum (8)
1985-86	Joe Orsulak (.331)	Andrés Galarraga (14)	Ubaldo Heredia (8)
1986-87	Terry Francona (.350)	Cecil Fielder (19)	Stan Clarke (8)
1987-88	Cecil Fielder (.389)	Leo Hernández (11)	Jose Villa (9)
1988-89	Carlos Martínez (.331)	Phil Stephenson (9)	Julio Strauss (8)
1989-90	Luís Sojo (.351)	Willie Magallanes (8)	Jim Neidlinger (8)
1990-91	Luís Sojo (.362)	Eddie Zambrano (11)	Joe Ausanio (8)
1991-92	Chad Curtis (.338)	Three Tied (5)	Wilson Alvarez (8)

Venezuelan League Career Batting and Pitching Leaders

Games Played	Vic Davalillo, 1249
	Teolindo Acosta, 1130
	César Tóvar, 1114
Base Hits	Vic Davalillo, 1505
	Teolindo Acosta, 1289
Runs Scored	Vic Davalillo, 668
	César Tóvar, 635
Home Runs	Tony Armas, 91
	Leonardo Hernández, 72
Runs Batted In	Luís García, 531
	Vic Davalillo, 477
Stolen Bases	José Leiva, 148
	César Tóvar, 122
Innings Pitched	Carrao Bracho, 1386
	Luís Penalver, 1317
Games Won	Carrao Bracho, 110
	Luís Penalver, 84
Games Saved	Luís Aponte, 73
	Roberto Múñoz, 59
Strikeouts	Aurelio Monteagudo, 894
	Carrao Bracho, 853

Modern Venezuelan Individual Batting and Pitching Records (1967–1992)

Batting Average (Season)	Dave Parker, .401 (1976–77)
Most Batting Titles	Vic Davalillo, 2 (1967–68 and 1970–71)
	Cito Gaston, 2 (1968–69 and 1969–70)
	Al Bumbry, 2 (1973–74 and 1974–75)
	Luís Sojo, 2 (1989–90 and 1990–91)
Home Runs (Season)	Bo Díaz, 20 (1979–80)
Pitching Victories (Season)	Jim Rooker, 13 (1972–73)
	Jerry Cram, 13 (1977–1978)
Lowest ERA (Season)	Mike Hedlund, 0.75 (1969–70)

Year by Year in Mexican League Baseball (AAA Summer League)

(Primary Source: *Quien es Quien en El Béisbol Liga Mexicana, 1989 edition* [Mexico City, 1989])

Championship Teams, Managers, and Individual Mexican Batting Leaders (1937–1992)

Year	Champion (Manager)	Batting	Home Runs
1937	Veracruz (Augustín Verde)	Alfonso Nieto (.476)	Carlos Galina (6)
1938	Veracruz (Augustín Verde)	Martín Dihigo (.387)	Angel Castro (9)
1939	Córdoba (Lazaro Sálazar)	Lazaro Sálazar (.374)	Angel Castro (9)
1940	Mexico City Veracruz (Jorge Pasquel)	James "Papa" Bell (.437)	James "Papa" Bell (12)
1941	Mexico City Veracruz (Lazaro Sálazar)	Burnis Wright (.390)	Josh Gibson (33)
1942	Torreón (Martín Dihigo)	Monte Irvin (.397)	Monte Irvin (20)
1943	Monterrey (Lazaro Sálazar)	Burnis Wright (.366)	Burnis Wright (13)
1944	Mexico City Veracruz (Ramón Bragaña)	Alberto Hernández (.395)	Salvador Hernández (13)
1945	Tampico (Armando Marsans)	Claro Duany (.375)	Roberto Ortiz (26)
1946	Tampico (Armando Marsans)	Claro Duany (.364)	Roberto Ortiz (25)
1947	Monterrey (Lazaro Sálazar)	Roberto Avila (.346)	Roberto Ortiz (22)
1948	Monterrey (Lazaro Sálazar)	Ray Dandridge (.373)	Roberto Ortiz (19)
1949	Monterrey (Lazaro Sálazar)	Adolfo Cabrera (.382)	Jesús Díaz (13)
1950	Torreón (Guillermo Garibay)	Lorenzo Cabrera (.355)	Jesús Díaz (10)
1951	Mexico City Veracruz (Jorge Pasquel)	Angel Castro (.354)	Angel Castro (22)
1952	Veracruz (Santos Amaro)	Rene González (.370)	Rene González (21)
1953	Nuevo Laredo (Adolfo Luque)	Rene González (.336)	Héctor Lara (13)
1954	Nuevo Laredo (Adolfo Luque)	Rene González (.359)	Rene González (21)
1955	Mexico City Tigers (George Genovese)	Leo Rodríguez (.385)	Mario Ariosa (22)
1956	Mexico City Reds (Lazaro Sálazar)	Alonso Perry (.392)	Alonso Perry (28)
1957	Merida (Oscar Rodríguez)	Aldo Salvent (.359)	Earl Taborn (27)
1958	Nuevo Laredo (Cheo Ramos)	Pablo Bernard (.371)	Edward Moore (32)
1959	Poza Rica (Luís García)	Alfred Pinkston (.369)	Aldo Salvent (29)
1960	Mexico City Tigers (Guillermo Garibay)	Alfred Pinkston (.397)	Aldo Salvent (36)
1961	Veracruz (Santos Amaro)	Alfred Pinkston (.374)	Witremundo Quintana (23)
1962	Monterrey (Clemente Carreras)	Alfred Pinkston (.381)	Rolando Camacho (25)
1963	Puebla (Antonio Castaño)	Vinicio García (.368)	Rolando Camacho (39)
1964	Mexico City Reds (Tomás Herrera)	Héctor Espino (.371)	Héctor Espino (46)
1965	Mexico City Tigers (Luís García)	Emilio Sosa (.368)	George Prescott (39)
1966	Mexico City Tigers (Ricardo Garza)	Héctor Espino (.369)	George Prescott (41)
1967	Guadalajara (Guillermo Garibay)	Héctor Espino (.379)	Elrod Hendricks (41)
1968	Mexico City Reds (Tomás Herrera)	Héctor Espino (.365)	Héctor Espino (27)
1969	Reynosa (Miguel Sotelo)	Teolindo Acosta (.354)	Héctor Espino (37)
1970	Veracruz (Enrique Izquierdo)	Francisco Campos (.358)	Rogelio Alvarez (33)

Championship Teams, Managers, and Leaders, *cont.*

Year	Champion (Manager)	Batting	Home Runs
1971	Guadalajara (Benjamin Reyes)	Teolindo Acosta (.392)	Humberto García (23)
1972	Córdoba (Mario Pelaez)	Donald Anderson (.362)	Héctor Espino (37)
1973	Mexico City Reds (Wilfredo Calvino)	Héctor Espino (.377)	Romel Canada (26)
1974	Mexico City Reds (Benjamin Reyes)	Teolindo Acosta (.366)	Byron Browne (32)
1975	Tampico (Benjamin Valenzuela)	Patrick Bourque (.372)	Andres Mora (35)
1976	Mexico City Reds (Benjamin Reyes)	Lawrence Fritz (.355)	Jack Pierce (36)
1977	Nuevo Laredo (Jorge Fitch Díaz)	Vic Davalillo (.384)	Ismael Oquendo (34)
1978	Aguascalientes (Jaime Fabela)	Romel Canada (.366)	Harold King (28)
1979	Puebla (Jorge Fitch Díaz)	James Collins (.438)	Luís Alcaraz (24)
1980	Saltillo (Gregorio Luque)	Roberto Rodríguez (.404)	Ivan Murrell (32)
1981	Mexico City Reds (Winston Llenas)	Willie Norwood (.365)	Andres Mora (23)
1982	Ciudad Juarez (José Guerrero)	Robert Smith (.357)	Andres Mora (25)
1983	Campeche (Francisco Estrada Soto)	Ricardo Durán (.377)	Carlos Soto (22)
1984	Merida (Carlos Paz)	James Collins (.412)	Derek Bryant (41)
1985	Mexico City Reds (Benjamin Reyes)	Oswaldo Olivares (.397)	Andres Mora (41)
1986	Puebla (Rodolfo Sandoval)	Willie Aikens (.454)	Jack Pierce (54)
1987	Mexico City Reds (Benjamin Reyes)	Orlando Sánchez (.415)	Nelson Barrera (42)
1988	Mexico City Reds (Benjamin Reyes)	Nick Castaneda (.374)	Leo Hernández (36)
1989	Los Dos Laredos (José Guerrero)	Willie Aikens (.395)	Leo Hernández (39)
1990	Los Dos Laredos (José Guerrero)	Nick Castaneda (.388)	Alex Sánchez (28)
1991	Monterrey (Aurelio Rodríguez)	Rich Renteria (.442)	Roy Johnson (37)
1992	Mexico City Tigers (Ossie Alvarez)	Raul Pérez Tóvar (.416)	Ty Gainey (47)

Individual Mexican Pitching Leaders (1937–1992)

Year	W-L	ERA Leader	Strikeouts Leader
1937	Alberto Chávez (8–0, 1.000)	Alberto Chávez (0.78)	Basilio Rosell (71)
1938	Martín Dihigo (18–2, .900)	Martín Dihigo (0.90)	Martín Dihigo (184)
1939	John Taylor (11–1, .917)	John Taylor (1.19)	Martín Dihigo (202)
1940	William Jefferson (22–9, .710)	Ramón Bragaña (2.58)	Edward Porter (232)
1941	Robert Cabal (9–1, .900)	Jesús Valenzuela (3.12)	Edward Porter (133)
1942	Martín Dihigo (22–7, .759)	Martín Dihigo (2.53)	Martín Dihigo (211)
1943	Manuel Fortes (18–6, .750)	Vidal López (2.08)	Martín Dihigo (134)
1944	Adrian Zabala (10–2, .833)	Adrian Zabala (2.74)	Ramón Bragaña (144)
1945	Juan Guerrero (11–1, .846)	Juan Guerrero (2.87)	Agapito Mayor (156)
1946	Martín Dihigo (11–4, .733)	Max Lanier (1.94)	Booker Daniels (171)
1947	Armando Torres (14–6, .700)	Santiago Ulrich (2.65)	Booker Daniels (127)
1948	Pedro Ramírez (9–2, .818)	Guillermo López (2.37)	Agapito Mayor (92)
1949	Vicente Torres (13–5, .722)	Alfonso Ramírez (2.35)	Wilfredo Salas (158)
1950	William Creason (10–1, .909)	Pedro Antuñez (1.87)	Barney Brown (157)
1951	James Lamarque (19–6, .760)	Lino Donoso (2.55)	Lino Donoso (197)
1952	Guadalupe Ortegón (8–3, .727)	Vicente Torres (2.43)	Lino Donoso (235)
1953	Jesús Moreno (18–3, .857)	Jesús Moreno (1.63)	Lino Donoso (162)
1954	Tomás Arroyo (15–1, .938)	Humberto García (2.29)	Raul Galata (118)
1955	Fred Waters (18–3, .857)	Fred Waters (2.09)	Fred Walters (126)
1956	Francisco Ramírez (20–3, .870)	Francisco Ramírez (2.25)	Francisco Ramírez (148)
1957	Lino Donoso (8–2, .800)	Edward Locke (3.20)	Julian Ladera (136)
1958	Romeo Cadena (7–1, .875)	Julio Moreno (2.70)	Juan Piedra (159)
1959	Roberto Vargas (13–3, .813)	Roberto Vargas (2.55)	Diomedes Olivo (233)
1960	Luís Tiant (17–7, .708)	Silvio Castellanos (3.24)	Silvio Castellanos (122)
1961	Ramón Araño Bravo (11–3, .786)	Julio Moreno (3.01)	Juan Piedra (171)
1962	Ramón Araño Bravo (17–6, .739)	Ramón Araño Bravo (2.60)	Mike Cuellar (124)
1963	Ramón Araño Bravo (13–4, .765)	Arturo Cacheux (2.69)	Miguel Sotelo (208)
1964	Andres Ayon (16–5, .762)	Alberto Osorio (2.56)	José Ramón López (213)
1965	Frank Barnes (13–5, .722)	Frank Barnes (1.58)	José Ramón López (201)
1966	Waldo Velo (17–4, .810)	Waldo Velo (2.01)	José Ramón López (309)

Year	W-L	ERA Leader	Strikeouts Leader
1967	Andres Ayon (25-6, .806)	Juan Suby (2.36)	Frank Maytorena (175)
1968	Celso Contreras (14-6, .700)	James Horsford (1.59)	James Horsford (212)
1969	Manuel Lugo (14-6, .700)	Salvador Sánchez (1.84)	James Horsford (199)
1970	Blas Mason (13-5, .722)	Alfredo Mariscal (1.85)	Felipe Leal (170)
1971	José Soto (10-3, .769)	Andres Ayon (1.22)	Felipe Leal (223)
1972	Andres Ayon (22-3, .880)	Alfredo Meza (1.83)	Alvin Martin (166)
1973	Silvano Quezada (22-2, .917)	Manuel Lugo (1.60)	José Peña (195)
1974	Aurelio Monteagudo (12-0, 1.000)	Juan Pizarro (1.57)	Antonio Pollorena (183)
1975	Miguel Pereyra (8-0, 1.000)	Ricardo Sandate (1.42)	José Peña (199)
1976	Enrique Romo (20-4, .833)	Gary Ryerson (1.52)	Enrique Romo (239)
1977	Roberto Verdugo (8-2, .800)	Horacio Piña (1.70)	Byron McLaughlin (221)
1978	Carlos Sosa (9-1, .900)	Michael Nagy (1.64)	Aurelio Monteagudo (222)
1979	Miguel Solis (25-5, .833)	Rafael García (1.69)	Rafael García (222)
1980	Pilar Rodríguez (9-0, 1.000)	Gilberto Rondón (1.44)	Luís Mercedez (155)
1981	Rafael García (20-5, .800)	Vicente Romo (1.40)	Rafael García (187)
1982	José Peña (10-1, .909)	Ernesto Cordova (1.58)	Santos Alcala (192)
1983	Maximino León (13-1, .929)	Arturo González (1.92)	Teddy Higuera (165)
1984	Miguel Solis (17-4, .810)	Salvador Colorado (2.20)	Jesús Ríos (194)
1985	Eleazar Beltran (18-3, .857)	Jesús Ríos (2.52)	Ramón Serna (200)
1986	Octavio Orozco (13-2, .867)	Barry Bass (2.03)	Rafael García (155)
1987	Luís Leal (15-2, .882)	Robin Fuson (2.67)	Jesús Ríos (200)
1988	Dave Walsh (14-1, .933)	Dave Walsh (1.73)	Jesús Ríos (195)
1989	Idelfonso Velazquez (20-6, .769)	Mercedes Esquer (1.98)	Adolfo Navarro (150)
1990	Armando Reynoso (20-3, .870)	Guy Normand (2.08)	Armando Reynoso (170)
1991	Juan Palafox (17 wins)	Odell Jones (2.67)	NA
1992	Julio Purata (20-9, .690)	Mercedes Esquer (2.24)	Jesús Ríos (186)

Mexican League Records and Milestones

Individual Mexican Batting Records (1937–1990)

Seasons Played	Héctor Espino, 24 (1962–1985)
Games Played (Career)	Héctor Espino, 2388 (1962–1985)
Games Played (Season)	Rolando Camarero, 161 (1969)
Consecutive Games Played	Rolando Camarero, 1166 (1968–1976)
Batting Average (Career)	Alfred Pinkston, .372 (1204 Hits)
Batting Average (Season)	Willie Mays Aikens, .454 (1986)
Lowest BA for Batting Champ	Rene González, .336 (1953)
Most Batting Titles Won	Héctor Espino, 5 (1964, 1966, 1967, 1968, 1973)
Most Seasons Batting .300	Héctor Espino, 14 (1962–1975)
Most At-Bats (Career)	Héctor Espino, 8205 (1962–1985)
Most At-Bats (Season)	Pedro Cardenal, 649 (1959)
Most Seasons as At-Bats Leader	Gonzalo Villalobos, 4 (1965, 1968, 1975, 1978)
Runs Scored (Career)	Héctor Espino, 1505
Runs Scored (Season)	Nicholas Castaneda, 141 (1986)
Runs Scored (Game, 9 innings)	Alfred Pinkston, 6 (May 8, 1960) Teolindo Acosta, 6 (April 15, 1970) Humberto García, 6 (April 3, 1973)
Most Seasons as Runs Leader	Héctor Espino, 4 (1962, 1964, 1969, 1972)
Base Hits (Career)	Héctor Espino, 2752
Base Hits (Season)	Miguel Suarez López, 227 (1977)
Most Seasons as Hits Leader	Ray Dandridge, 3 (1943, 1947, 1948) Alfred Pinkston, 3 (1959, 1960, 1962) Miguel Suarez, 3 (1971, 1976, 1977)
Consecutive Base Hits	Héctor Espino, 11 (1980) Danny García, 11 (1982)

Individual Mexican Batting Records, *cont.*

	Willie Mays Aikens, 11 (1986)
Hitting Streak (Games)	Roberto Ortiz, 35 (1948)
Doubles (Career)	Héctor Espino, 373
Doubles (Season)	Vinicio García, 49 (1961)
Triples (Career)	Gonzalo Villalobos, 132
Triples (Season)	Albino Díaz, 19 (1975)
	Leonardo Valenzuela, 19 (1979)
Home Runs (Career)	Héctor Espino, 453
Home Runs (Season, Right)	Héctor Espino, 46 (1964)
Home Runs (Season, Left)	Jack Pierce, 54 (1986)
Most Seasons as HR Leader	Angel Castro, 4 (1938, 1939, 1950, 1951)
	Roberto Ortiz, 4 (1945, 1946, 1947, 1948)
	Héctor Espino, 4 (1964, 1968, 1969, 1972)
	Andres Mora, 4 (1974, 1981, 1982, 1985)
Home Runs (Game, 9 innings)	Derek Bryant, 4 (May 14, 1985)
Runs Batted In (Career)	Héctor Espino, 1573
Runs Batted In (Season)	Willie Mays Aikens, 154 (1986)
Total Bases (Career)	Héctor Espino, 4574
Total Bases (Season)	Willie Mays Aikens, 384 (1986)
Total Bases (Game)	Derek Bryant, 19 (May 14, 1985, four HRs and triple)
Stolen Bases (Career)	Antonio Briones Luna, 490
Stolen Bases (Season)	Donald Carter, 95 (1986)
Stolen Bases (Game, 9 innings)	Antonio Briones Luna, 7 (June 2, 1980)
Strikeouts (Career)	Rolando Camacho Durán, 1236
Strikeouts (Season)	William Parlier, 131 (1970)
Walks (Career)	Rolando Camacho Durán, 1409
Intentional Walks (Career)	Héctor Espino, 355

Individual Mexican Pitching Records (1937–1990)

Games Won (Career)	Ramón Araño Bravo, 332 (1959–1986)
Games Won (Season)	Ramón Bragaña, 30 (1944)
Games Lost (Career)	Ramón Araño Bravo, 262 (1959–1986)
Games Lost (Season)	Ramón Ramos, 21 (1957)
ERA (Career)	Vicente Romo, 1.49 (2535.2 innings)
ERA (Season)	Martín Dihigo, 0.90 (167 innings, in 1938)
Winning Percentage (Career)	Martín Dihigo, .676 (119–57)
Winning Percentage (Season)	Aurelio Monteagudo, 1.000 (12–0, in 1974)
Games Pitched (Career)	Ramón Araño Bravo, 840 (1959–1986)
Games Pitched (Season)	Aurelio López, 73 (1977)
Complete Games (Career)	Ramón Araño Bravo, 296 (1959–1986)
Complete Games (Season)	James Horsford, 30 (1969)
Games Started (Career)	Ramón Araño Bravo, 670 (1959–1986)
Games Started (Season)	Edward Locke, 35 (1959)
	Francisco Ramírez, 35 (1959)
	Ramón Araño Bravo, 35 (1970)
	Luís Mere, 35 (1978)
Saves (Career)	Aurelio López, 119 (1968–1977)
Saves (Season)	Aurelio López, 30 (1977)
Shutouts (Career)	Ramón Araño Bravo, 56 (1959–1986)
Shutouts (Season)	Gary Ryerson, 10 (1976)
	Luís Mere, 10 (1977)
	Vicente Romo, 10 (1979)
Consecutive Scoreless Innings	James Horsford, 51 (July 12, 1968 thru August 7, 1968)
Innings Pitched (Career)	Ramón Araño Bravo, 4745 (1959–1986)

Innings Pitched (Season)	Ramón Bragaña, 325 (1944)
Strikeouts (Career)	Ramón Araño Bravo, 2370 (1959–1986)
Strikeouts (Season)	José Ramón López, 309 (1966)
Strikeouts (Season, Relief)	Aurelio López, 165 (1977)
Strikeouts (Game)	Martín Dihigo, 22 (June 4, 1938, in 13 innings)
Strikeouts (Game, 9 innings)	Martín Dihigo, 18 (August 5, 1939)
	Lefty Glover, 18 (June 30, 1940)
	Lino Dinoso, 18 (March 21, 1951)
	Ricardo Sandate, 18 (May 6, 1974)
Bases on Balls (Career)	Daniel Ríos, 1439
Bases on Balls (Season)	Booker McDaniels, 176 (1946)
Bases on Balls (Game, 9 innings)	Carlos Hidalgo, 16 (June 27, 1982, in 5.2 innings)
Balks Committed (Career)	Ernesto Carlos Kuk Lee, 21
Balks Committed (Season)	Peter Bonfils, 6 (1978)
Wild Pitches (Career)	Ramón Araño Bravo, 144
Wild Pitches (Season)	Guillermo Gutiérrez, 26 (1978)
Wild Pitches (Game, 9 innings)	Cecilio Acosta, 6 (June 28, 1979)

Mexican League Rookie of the Year (1937–1988)
(Italics = U.S. major-leaguers)

1937 Alfonso Nieto (Agricultura)
1938 Angel Castro (Tampico)
1939 Epitacio Torres (Monterrey)
1940 Laureano Camacho (Veracruz)
1941 Guillermo Garibay (Union Laguna)
1942 Jesús Díaz (Union Laguna)
1943 Roberto Avila (Puebla)
1944 Jorge Bravo (Mexico City)
1945 Juan Conde (Puebla)
1946 Guillermo Alvarez (Puebla)
1947 Tomás Arroyo (Tampico)
1948 Felipe Montemayor (Monterrey)
1949 Leonard Rodríguez (Union Laguna)
1950 Francisco Ramírez Conde (San Luis)
1951 Fernando García (San Luis)
1952 Jaime Abad (Aguila)
1953 Pecas Serrano (Monterrey)
1954 Alejandro Moreno (Laredo)
1955 Roman Ramos (Aguila)
1956 Jesse Durán (Mexico City Tigers)
1957 Mario Luna (Mexico City Reds)
1958 Alberto Palafox (Mexico City Reds)
1959 Ramón Araño Bravo (Poza Rica and Aguila)
1960 Mauro Ruíz Rubio (Mexico City Tigers)
1961 Pablo Montes de Oca (Aguila)
1962 Héctor Espino (Monterrey)
1963 Vicente Romo (Mexico City Tigers)
1964 Elpidio Osuna (Poza Rica)
1965 Héctor Barnetche (Mexico City Tigers)
1966 Abelardo Balderas (Mexico City Reds)
1967 Francisco Maytorena (Reynosa)
1968 Francisco Campos (Jalisco)
1969 Luís Lagunas (Jalisco)
1970 Ernesto Escarrega (Mexico City Reds)
1971 Miguel Suarez (Mexico City Reds)
1972 Rodolfo Hernández (Jalisco)

Mexican League Rookie of the Year *cont.*

1973	*Francisco Barrios (Jalisco)*
1974	Guadalupe Salinas (Reynosa)
1975	Juan Martínez Cordero (Monterrey)
1976	Alfonso Jiménez (Puebla)
1977	Abraham Rivera (Puebla)
1978	Joel Pérez (Durango)
1979	*Fernando Valenzuela (Yucatán)*
1980	*Teddy Higuera (Ciudad Juarez)*
1981	Matias Carrillo (Mexico City Tigers)
1982	Nelson Matus (Tabasco)
	Jesús Antonio Barrera (Laredo)
1983	Ramón Serna (Ciudad Juarez)
	Jesús Ríos (Mexico City Tigers)
1984	Carlos de los Santos (Cordoba)
1985	Pablo Machiria (Tamaulipas)
	Florentino Vásquez (Monclova)
1986	Eduardo Torres (Saltillo)
	Lorenzo Retes (Mexico City Tigers)
1987	Miguel Angel Valencia (Mexico City Tigers)
1988	Marco Antonio Romero (Jalisco)
	Andres Cruz (Yucatán)

Year by Year in Mexican Pacific League (Winter League) Professional Baseball

(Complete record since 1967-68 season [past 25 years])

Championship Teams and Individual Batting Leaders

Year	Champion	Batting	Home Runs
1967-68	Guaymas	Héctor Espino (.342)	Ron Camacho (18)
1968-69	Los Mochis	Gabriel Lugo (.309)	Rogelio Alvarez (20)
1969-70	Culiacán	Minnie Miñoso (.359)	Two Tied (19)
1970-71	Hermosillo	Héctor Espino (.348)	Héctor Espino (22)
1971-72	Guasave	Héctor Espino (.372)	Bobby Darwin (27)
1972-73	Obregón	Héctor Espino (.415)	Héctor Espino (26)
1973-74	Mazatlán	Jorge Orta (.370)	Roger Freed (20)
1974-75	Hermosillo	Jerry Hairston (.311)	Jack Pierce (14)
1975-76	Hermosillo	Héctor Espino (.319)	Andres Mora (18)
1976-77	Mazatlán	Nick Vázquez (.345)	Charlie Sands (13)
1977-78	Culiacán	Mike Easler (.341)	Willie Aikens (14)
1978-79	Navojoa	Héctor Espino (.344)	Two Tied (15)
1979-80	Hermosillo	Neil Fiala (.364)	Three Tied (11)
1980-81	Obregón	David Green (.321)	Three Tied (14)
1981-82	Hermosillo	Junior Moore (.325)	Mark Funderburk (17)
1982-83	Culiacán	Héctor Espino (.316)	Enrique Aguilar (8)
1983-84	Los Mochis	Jimmy Collins (.314)	Chuckie Canady (14)
1984-85	Culiacán	Roy Johnson (.337)	Three Tied (15)
1985-86	Mexicali	Eddie Brunson (.335)	Carlos Soto (17)
1986-87	Mazatlán	John Kruk (.385)	Willie Aikens (24)
1987-88	Tijuana	Darrell Brown (.360)	Nelson Barrera (16)
1988-89	Mexicali	Nelson Simmons (.353)	Willie Aikens (22)
1989-90	Hermosillo	Dave Hollins (.327)	Alejandro Ortiz (16)
1990-91	Tijuana	Matt Stairs (.330)	Ty Gainey (13)
1991-92	Hermosillo	Ty Gainey (.353)	Ty Gainey (20)

Pitching Leaders

Year	ERA Leader	Winning Percentage Leader
1967-68	Vicente Romo (1.10)	Enrique Romo (15-4, .789)
1968-69	Vicente Romo (1.54)	Don Secrist (15-3, .833)
1969-70	Rene Paredes (1.20)	Salvador Sánchez (11-2, .846)
1970-71	Vicente Romo (1.60)	Max León (7-1, .875)
1971-72	Mark Ballinger (2.13)	Eduardo Acosta (7-2, .778)
1972-73	Saul Montoya (1.89)	Saul Montoya (8-2, .800)
1973-74	Eduardo Acosta (1.51)	Fran Maytorena (8-1, .889)
1974-75	César Díaz (1.40)	Enrique Romo (12-2, .857)
1975-76	Carlos Carrazco (1.45)	Enrique Romo (12-2, .857)
1976-77	Max León (1.47)	Three Tied (9-3, .750)
1977-78	José Peña (1.33)	José Peña (14-1, .933)
1978-79	Byron McLaughlin (1.05)	Angel Moreno (7-1, .875)
1979-80	Max León (0.87)	José Peña (6-1, .857)
1980-81	Alejandro Ahumada (1.42)	Eleno Cuen (14-4, .778)
1981-82	Mike Paul (1.32)	Jaime Orozco (14-2, .875)
1982-83	Salvador Colorado (0.53)	Salvador Colorado (11-3, .786)
1983-84	Ramón Villegas (1.10)	Alfonso Pulido (7-1, .875)
1984-85	Teddy Higuera (1.24)	Arturo González (12-2, .857)
1985-86	Félix Tejada (1.25)	Guillermo Valenzuela (13-3, .813)
1986-87	Vicente Palacios (2.31)	Alfonso Pulido (6-1, .857)
1987-88	Tim Leary (1.30)	Tim Leary (9-0, 1.000)
1988-89	Héctor Heredia (1.43)	Mercedes Esquer (13-3, .813)
1989-90	Narciso Elvira (1.41)	Arturo González (10-1, .909)
1990-91	Derek Livernos (1.21)	Rosario Rodríguez (7-1, .875)
1991-92	Tim Burcham (1.63)	Alfonso Pulido (7-2, .778)

U.S. Pennant Winning Managers

Tim Johnson	(Hermosillo, 1989-90, 1991-92)
Maury Wills	(Hermosillo, 1970-71)
Chuck Goggin	(Navojoa, 1978-79)
Lee Sigman	(Obregón, 1980-81)
Tom Harmon	(Hermosillo, 1981-82)
Dave Machemer	(Mexicali, 1988-89)

APPENDIX F

Latin American Major League Managers and Coaches

Managers

Dominican Republic

(First Dominican major league manager: Felipe Alou [1992]; 2 managers [*interim manager])

Alou (Rojas y Alou), Felipe (**Felipe Alou**) (b. 5-12-1935, Santo Domingo) Debut: 1992 (1992–1993) Team: Montreal (N) Record: 125 G, 70 W, 55 L, .560 Pct.
*Virgil y Pichardo, Osvaldo José (**Ossie Virgil**) (b. 5-17-1933, Montecristi) Debut: 1984 (1984) Team: Montreal (N) Record: 9 G, 4 W, 5 L, .444 Pct.

Cuba

(First Cuban major league manager: Mike González [1938]; 5 managers [*interim manager])

Gómez y Martínez, Pedro (**Pedro "Preston" Gómez**) (b. 4-20-1923, Central Preston) Debut: 1969 (1969–1972, 1973–1974, 1980) Teams: San Diego (N), Houston (N), Chicago (N) Record: 875 G, 346 W, 529 L, .395 Pct.
*González y Cordero, Miguel Angel (**Miguel "Mike" González**) (b. 9-24-1890, Havana; d. 2-19-1977, Havana) Debut: 1938 (1938, 1940) Team: St. Louis (N) Record: 23 G, 9 W, 13 L, .409 Pct.
*Martínez y Oliva, Orlando (**Orlando "Marty" Martínez**) (b. 8-23-1941, Havana) Debut: 1986 (1986) Team: Seattle (A) Record: 1 G, 0 W, 1 L, .000 Pct.
Pérez y Rigal, Atanacio (**Tony Pérez**) (b. 5-14-1942, Camaguey) Debut: 1993 (1993) Team: Cincinnati (N) Record: 44 G, 20 W, 24 L, .455 Pct.
Rojas y Rivas, Octavio Victor (**Cookie Rojas**) (b. 3-6-1939, Havana) Debut: 1988 (1988) Team: California (A) Record: 154 G, 75 W, 79 L, .487 Pct.

Coaches (Alphabetically)

Carlos Alfonso (Cuba) San Francisco Giants (1992)
Sandy Alomar (Puerto Rico) San Diego Padres (1986–1990)
Felipe Alou (Dominican Republic) Montreal Expos (1979–1980, 1984, 1989–1992)
Jesús Alou (Dominican Republic) Houston Astros (1974)
Rubén Amaro (Mexico) Philadelphia Phillies (1980–1981), Chicago Cubs (1983–1986)
Tony Auferio (Cuba) St. Louis Cardinals (1973)

José Cardenal (Cuba) Cincinnati Reds (1993)
Rod Carew (Panama) California Angels (1992–1993)
Leonel Carrión (Venezuela) Montreal Expos (1988–1990)
Bill Castro (Dominican Republic) Milwaukee Brewers (1992–1993)
Orlando Cepeda (Puerto Rico) Chicago White Sox (1980)
Orlando Gómez (Dominican Republic) Texas Rangers (1991–1992)
Preston Gómez (Cuba) Los Angeles Dodgers (1965–1968)
Mike González (Cuba) St. Louis Cardinals (1934*–1940) First Latin American coach
Epy Guerrero (Dominican Republic) Toronto Blue Jays (1981)
Elrod Hendricks (Virgin Islands) Baltimore Orioles (1979–1993)
Louis Issac (Puerto Rico) Cleveland Indians (1988–1991)
Rafael Landestoy (Dominican Republic) Montreal Expos (1989–1991)
Winston Llenas (Dominican Republic) Toronto Blue Jays (1988)
Adolfo Luque (Cuba) New York Giants (1936–1945)
José Martínez (Cuba) Kansas City Royals (1980–1987), Chicago Cubs (1988–1993)
Marty Martínez (Cuba) Seattle Mariners (1984–1986, 1992)
Sam Mejías (Dominican Republic) Seattle Mariners (1993)
Minnie Mendoza (Cuba) Baltimore Orioles (1988)
Minnie Miñoso (Cuba) Chicago White Sox (1976–1981)
José Morales (Virgin Islands) San Francisco Giants (1986–88), Cleveland Indians (1990–93)
Manny Mota (Dominican Republic) Los Angeles Dodgers (1980–1993)
Tony Oliva (Cuba) Minnesota Twins (1976–1991)
Reggie Otero (Cuba) Cincinnati Reds (1959–1965)
Tony Pacheco (Cuba) Cleveland Indians (1974), Houston Astros (1976–1982)
Camilo Pascual (Cuba) Minnesota Twins (1978–1980)
Tony Pérez (Cuba) Cincinnati Reds (1987–1992)
Luís Pujols (Dominican Republic) Montreal Expos (1993)
Ben Reyes (Mexico) Seattle Mariners (1981)
Cookie Rojas (Cuba) Chicago Cubs (1978–1981), Florida Marlins (1993)
Tony Taylor (Cuba) Philadelphia Phillies (1977–1979), Philadelphia Phillies (1988–1989)
Héctor Torres (Mexico) Toronto Blue Jays (1991)
Ossie Virgil (Dominican Republic) San Francisco Giants, San Diego Padres, Montreal Expos, Seattle Mariners (1972–1988)

Bibliography

Annotated Bibliography of Hispanic Baseball's Fifteen Most Important Books

Costas, Rafael. *Enciclopedia Béisbol, Ponce Leones, 1938–1987* (Baseball Encyclopedia, Ponce Lions, 1938–1987). Santo Domingo, Dominican Republic: Editora Corripio, 1989, 344 pp.

The most complete statistical record available for Puerto Rican winter-league baseball. Features year-by-year league leaders in all important individual batting and pitching categories (1939–1987); yearly league standings and playoff results; complete season-by-season batting and pitching records for the Ponce Lions team, all-time Ponce team leaders and individual marks (no-hit games pitched, one-hit games pitched, etc.); career batting and pitching records for most important league players; and much more.

García, Carlos J. *Baseball Forever (Béisbol para Siempre)*. Mexico City, Mexico (self-published volume), 1980. 408 pp. (English and Spanish editions).

An encyclopedic work offering little historical analysis yet providing an immense stockpile of data in terms of chronological outlines, rare black-and-white photographs, and a true hodgepodge of factual nuggets concerning the development of baseball worldwide. Much material on baseball terminology, the origins of major league teams, and North American baseball prehistory is quite pedestrian; yet chronological outlines tracing early history of baseball in Latin America and Europe are invaluable and unparalleled in any other volume.

Jiménez, José de Jesús, Jr. *Archivo de Baseball* (The Baseball Archive). Santiago, Dominican Republic (self-published volume), 1977. 171 pp.

A valuable resource for Spanish-language readers, if only for the dozens of high-quality black-and-white photographs of Latin major league stars and journeymen from the 1940s, 1950s, 1960s and 1970s. Most useful are the first two chapters devoted to brief portraits and career statistics for Latin American pitchers (chapter 1) and nonpitchers (chapter 2). Short career summaries are provided for all Latin major-leaguers active prior to the 1977 season. Two additional chapters cover non–Hispanic big-league outfielders (chapter 3) and first basemen (chapter 4); numerous photos.

Joyce, Gare. *The Only Ticket off the Island*. Toronto, Ontario: Lester and Orpen Dennys, 1990, 229 pp.

Toronto sportswriter (and former Toronto Blue Jays beat writer) spends a winter season traipsing around the Dominican winter-league circuit and pasting together an anecdotal portrait of Caribbean winterball that forces him and his readers to relearn thoroughly the national pastime Dominican-style. A compelling series of portraits of the already famous (George Bell), the once-famous (Rico Carty), the insiders (superscout Epy Guerrero), and the outsiders (ballpark regulars who offer a unique perspective on the game). Gare filters his view of Latin American player development and Latin baseball history with a decided Toronto Blue Jays flavor.

Klein, Alan M. *Sugarball: The American Game, The Dominican Dream*. New Haven, Connecticut: Yale University Press, 1991, 179 pp.

In this most scholarly and sociological approach to the Dominican baseball story, Klein traces the introduction and development of diamond play in a poverty-stricken island nation; provides lively sketches of ballplayers, fans, and stadiums; pursues such fascinating issues as the origin of Dominican baseball academies and growing international competition for Dominican player talent. Here is the best current discussion of just how baseball fosters national pride for Dominicans, spawns competition with the United States, yet at the same time promotes acceptance of a continued North American presence in the Dominican Republic.

Krich, John. *El Béisbol: Travels Through the Pan-American Pastime*. New York: Atlantic Monthly Press, 1989; New York: Prentice-Hall, 1990, 272 pp.

A wacky, wild, opinionated, and always fascinating travelogue across the winter months of baseball in the Pan-American world of primitive diamonds, desperate poverty, hopeless big-league dreams, and a brand of hardball always served up with political flavor. Not much baseball here if one searches only for biographical data about favorite Latin major league stars. Yet there is much of a sociopolitical nature to assist astute readers in grasping those true absurdities so characteristic of Caribbean baseball passions. Krich dances delightfully between myth and history, poetry and politics, rookie prospects and venerated national idols.

Marichal, Juan (as told to Charles Einstein). *A Pitcher's Story*. Garden City, New York: Doubleday, 1967, 215 pp.

Essentially a juvenile biography aimed at teenage readers, yet a book of the same high quality usually associated with those produced by such talented baseball biographers as Charles Einstein, Milton Shapiro, and Gene Schoor during this period. Einstein's ghost-written volume is also further enhanced by its status as the only English-language full-fledged autobiography of Latin America's most famous moundsman. Written at the midpoint of Marichal's illustrious career, the book focuses attention on a proud pitcher's youthful years trapped in Trujillo's Dominican Republic, his sensational big-league debut against the Philadelphia Phillies, and the infamous and controversial John Roseboro incident of the 1966 season. Marichal here offers his own explanation and excuses for the ugly Roseboro affair, an event that unarguably postponed the Dominican Dandy's inevitable Cooperstown election.

Musick, Phil. *Who Was Roberto? A Biography of Roberto Clemente*. Garden City, New York: Doubleday, 1974, 306 pp.

Unrivaled as best among the dozen or so English and Spanish biographies of Puerto Rico's greatest diamond star. Musick consistently offers no-holds-barred treatment of the often controversial Clemente, from his early years on the sandlots through his glory-filled yet often personally disappointing summer seasons in Pittsburgh, to the tragic and mysterious death that eventually finalized the Clemente legend. Even more than the first Latin American Hall-of-Famer or the unrivaled hero of a nation, Roberto Clemente is revealed above all else as a man of contagious enthusiasms whose infectious spirit somehow always managed to overcome his bad press, endless hypochondria, and all-too-frequent diamond frustrations.

Piña Campora, Tony. *Los Grandes Finals* (The Grand Finale). Santo Domingo, Dominican Republic: Editora Colegial Quisqueyana, 1981, 380 pp.

Detailed narrative and statistical summary of the Dominican championship series, beginning with its inaugural match in 1951 and continuing through the 1981 campaign. Each annual historical narrative is followed by line scores or box scores for each series game as well as batting and pitching composites for the entire series. Tables of lifetime series leaders are also provided at the end of the text. Poor-quality black-and-white photos of individual players are offered, but in most cases these are merely photographic reproductions of 1970s-vintage Topps baseball cards.

________. *Presencia Dominicana* (Dominican Presence). Santo Domingo, Dominican Republic (self-published volume), 1990, 153 pp.

Compact summaries of Dominican players active in the big leagues through the 1988 season. The bulk of the book consists of chronologies of important events featuring Dominican players in major league action as well as biographical paragraphs and statistical summaries for each player. Other useful features include such items as a listing of Dominicans hitting major league grand-slam homers, one-hitters by Dominican pitchers, Dominican batters with five hits in a single game, and numerous similar entries.

Ruck, Rob. *The Tropic of Baseball: Baseball in the Dominican Republic*. New York: Carroll and Graf, 1993; Westport, Connecticut: Meckler, 1991, 205 pp.

A rarity in staid academic scholarship, Ruck's book effectively combines a gripping narrative style with thorough research and infectious enthusiasm for this previously untapped subject. No volume better details the historical background of baseball in the Dominican Republic, explains the sport's roots in the cricket play transported from the British West Indies by immigrating sugarcane workers at the turn of the century, or accounts for why this tiny island nation has become the world's leading per capita exporter of major league diamond talent. Ruck leaves no doubt about why baseball has gradually (not overnight, as many believe) become this pauper nation's highest art form as well as an unrivaled touchstone for the entire Caribbean's ambivalent relationship to its Anglo neighbor up north.

Salas H., Alexis. *Los Eternos Rivales, Caracas-Magallanes, Pastora-Gavilanes, 1908–1988* (The Eternal Rivals, Caracas-Magallanes and Pastora-Gavilanes, 1908–1988). Caracas: Grupo Editorial, 1988, 368 pp.

The early history of Venezuelan professional baseball, retold in anecdotal form through accounts of the greatest continuing rivalries in the nation's sporting history. The contemporary rivalry between Caracas and Magallanes (1942–1988), and that from earlier decades between Gavilanes and Pastora (1931–1960), are a central focus, and treatment is in full narrative accounts and box scores for all head-to-head contests. Appendices include summaries (scores, dates, pitchers of record, etc.) for each major rival series.

________. *Momentos Inolvidables del Béisbol Profesional Venezolano, 1946–1984* (Unforgettable Moments from Venezuelan Pro Baseball, 1946–1984). Caracas: Miguel Angel García, 1985, 385 pp.

A full chronology, complete with black-and-white photos, narrative accounts, and relevant box scores for important moments in the history of Venezuelan professional baseball. A truly rare treat is the four-page insert featuring full-color photographs of Venezuelan stars (Luís Aparicio, Alex Carrasquel, Luís Leal, Chico Carrasquel, and others). Highlighted are triumphant moments involving both native Venezuelan heroes and North American big-league imports (Pete Rose, Norm Cash, Negro-leaguer Wilmer Fields), all of whom once excelled during the heyday of Venezuelan winter action.

Senzel, Howard. *Baseball and the Cold War: Being a Soliloquy on the Necessity of Baseball in the Life of a Serious Student of Marx and Hegel from Rochester, New York*. New York: Harcourt Brace Jovanovich, 1977, 298 pp.

Senzel's unique nonfiction fantasy floats somewhere between fictionalized account and documented record of a crucial shaping moment of his baseball childhood. During a 1959 game between the Rochester Red Wings and Havana Sugar Kings played on the eve of Castro's rise to power, gunfire in the grandstand results in the wounding of Rochester third-base coach Frank Verdi. This lost moment of baseball history sets in motion disastrous events that soon rob Castro's Cuba of its pro baseball connection and (Senzel suspects) impact mysteriously on larger issues of hemispheric foreign policy. What follows reads like a highly politicized 1960s novel as Senzel mixes a personal struggle to grasp events controlling his adult world with youthful baseball memories still thoroughly regulating his general outlook on life.

Wagenheim, Kal. *Clemente!* New York: Praeger, 1973, 274 pp.

Wagenheim here provides the only legitimate rival to Phil Musick's landmark Clemente biography. Like Musick, Wagenheim relies heavily upon interviews with former teammates, family members, and business associates to piece together a truly balanced portrait of Clemente the man that sustains and expands more commonplace images of Clemente the ballplayer.

Selected Additional Sources on Latin American Baseball and Hispanic Ballplayers

Aaseng, Nathan. *José Canseco: Baseball's 40–40 Man*. Minneapolis: Lerner, 1989, 56 pp. (juvenile biography).

Alfano, Peter. "Barriers to Advancement Thwart Hispanic Players." *New York Times* (May 4, 1987), 43.

Alou, Felipe. "Latin American Ballplayers Need a Bill of Rights." *Sport* 36 (November 1963): 20–21, 76–79.

________. (told to Herm Weiskopf). *My Life in Baseball*. Waco, Texas: Word Books, 1967, 154 pp. (standard Alou autobiography).

Alvarez Barajes, Rodolfo and Oscar Arango Cadavia. *Alfonso "Chico" Carrasquel, Idolo de siempre* (Alfonso "Chico" Carrasquel, Idol for All Time). Caracas, Venezuela: Ediciones Culturales y Deportivas, 1986.

Angulo Rivera, Rafael, and Jesús M. Ayuso Rosario. *Vida, pasión y muerte del immortal Roberto Clemente* (Life, Passion and Death of the Immortal Roberto Clemente). Carolina, Puerto Rico (self-published volume), 1973.

Arbena, Joseph, editor. *An Annotated Bibliography of Latin American Sport: Pre-Conquest to Present*. Westport, Connecticut: Greenwood Press, 1989 (numerous but incomplete baseball entries).

Aschburner, Steve. "Twins Get Back in Step to the Latin Beat." *Minneapolis Star Tribune*, May 21, 1989, section C.

Atchison, Lewis F. "How Mexican Raids Threatened to Ruin Majors 25 Years Ago." *Baseball Digest* 30:(7) (July 1971): 72–75.

Barnes, Jill. "Baseball's Latin Pioneers." *Vista* 6 (July 1989): 12–13.

Batson, Larry. *Rod Carew*. Mankato, Minnesota: Creative Education, 1977, 31 pp. (juvenile biography).

Benítez, Leo. *Las Grandes Ligas, 1900–1980* (Major Leagues, 1900–1980). Second edition. Caracas, Venezuela: Publicaciones Seleven, 1980 (Venezuelan baseball history and records).

________. *Registro del béisbol profesional de Venezuela, 1965–1985* (Venezuelan Professional Baseball Register, 1965–1985). Caracas: Impresos Urbina, 1986 (Venezuelan baseball history and records).

Berke, Art. "Mike Cuellar." In *Unsung Heroes of the Major Leagues*. New York: Random House, 1976, 92–104.

Bims, Harold J. "Roberto Clemente: Sad End for a Troubled Man." *Ebony* 28 (March 1973): 50–54.

Bisher, Furman. "Major League Minnie." *Sport* 17 (August 1954): 44–47 (Orestes "Minnie" Miñoso).

Bjarkman, Peter C. "Baseball South of the Border: Latin America's Big League Connection." *SABR Bulletin* 19:(3) (June 1989): 6–7 (Society for American Baseball Research).

________. "Caribbean Series Legends: Statistics, Heroic Deeds and Unmatched Diamond Thrills." *Minneapolis Review of Baseball* 9:(2) (Spring 1990): 57–63.

________. "Cuban Blacks in the Majors Before Jackie Robinson." *International Pastime: A Review of Baseball History* 12 (1992): 58–63, edited by Peter C. Bjarkman (Society for American Baseball Research).

________. "Dodgers with a Latin Beat." *Dodgers Magazine* (centennial issue) 3:(4) (July 1990): 24-26, 32-33, 36-37, 48-49, 60-61, 73.
________. "Dolf Luque, Baseball's First Hispanic Star." In *The Perfect Game: A Classic Collection of Facts, Figures, Stories and Characters from the Society of American Baseball Research*, edited by Mark Alvarez. Dallas: Taylor, 1993, 113-122.
________. "First Hispanic Star? Dolf Luque, of Course." *Baseball Research Journal* 19 (1990): 28-32 (Society for American Baseball Research).
________. *Roberto Clemente*. Philadelphia and London: Chelsea House, 1991, 64 pp. (juvenile biography).
________. *The Toronto Blue Jays*. Chapter 6. New York: W. H. Smith, 1990.
Boswell, Thomas. "How Baseball Helps the Harvest, or What the Bay of Pigs Did to the Bigs." In *How Life Imitates the World Series*. Garden City, New York: Doubleday, 1982, 81-96.
Boyle, Robert H. "The Latins Storm Las Grandes Ligas." *Sports Illustrated* 23:(6) (August 9, 1965): 24-30.
Briere, Tom. "Rod Carew, the Complete Ballplayer." *Baseball Digest* 32 (December 1973): 47-52.
Brondfield, Jerry. *Roberto Clemente, Pride of the Pirates*. Champaign, Illinois: Garrard, 1976, 96 pp. (juvenile biography).
Brosnan, Jim. "Orlando Cepeda." In *Great Rookies of the Major Leagues*. New York: Random House, 1966, 189-221.
Brown, Bruce. "Cuban Baseball." *The Atlantic* 253:(6) (June 1984): 109-114.
Brubaker, William. "Hey Kid, Wanna Be a Star? – Latin Players Scouted for the United States Big Leagues." *Sports Illustrated* 55:(3) (July 13, 1981): 64-66.
Burchard, Marshall. *Sports Hero Rod Carew*. New York: Putnam, 1978, 93 pp. (juvenile biography).
Burns, Bud. "Latin Stars Deserve More Recognition in the Majors." *Baseball Digest* 38:(4) (April 1979): 60-63.
Carew, Rod (with Ira Berkow). *Carew*. New York: Simon and Schuster, 1979, 251 pp.
Casas, Edel, Jorge Alfonso and Alberto Pestana. *Viva y en juego* (Alive and at Play). Havana, Cuba: Editorial Científico Técnica, 1986, 41 pp. (Cuban pro baseball history).
Castro, Janice. "Harvesting Baseball Talent." *Time* September 2, 1985, 42 (Dominican big-league talent search).
Castro, Tony. "Something Screwy Going On Here." *Sports Illustrated* 63:(2) (July 8, 1985): 30-37 (Fernando Valenzuela).
Cantwell, Robert Francis. "Invasion from Santo Domingo: Dominican Big Leaguers." *Sports Illustrated* 18:(8) (February 25, 1963), 54-61.
Cepeda, Orlando (with Bob Markus). *High and Inside: Orlando Cepeda's Story*. South Bend, Indiana: Icarus Press, 1984, 160 pp. (Cepeda autobiography).
________, (with Charles Einstein). *My Ups and Downs in Baseball*. New York: Putnam, 1968, 191 pp. (Cepeda autobiography).
Christine, Bill. *Roberto! Número Uno*. New York: Stadia Sports, 1973, 159 pp. (Roberto Clemente biography).
Cohane, Tim. "Luís Aparicio, the Magic Glove." *Look*, August 16, 1960, 65-67.
Cohen, Joel H. *Manny Sanguillen: Jolly Pirate*. New York: Putnam, 1975, 127 pp. (juvenile biography).
Colmenares del Valle, Edgar. *Léxico del béisbol en Venezuela* (Venezuelan Baseball Lexicon). Caracas, Venezuela: Ediciones Centauro, 1977, 266 pp. (Venezuelan baseball history and Spanish baseball terms).
Compton, George, and Adolfo Solorzamo-Diaz. "Latins on the Diamond." *Américas* 3 (June 1951): 9-11, 40-41.
Condon, Dave. "Orestes Miñoso – the Rage of Chicago." *Sport* 12 (February 1952): 22-23.
Condon, David. "Latino Stars in the Majors Still Battle Anonymity." *Baseball Digest* 37:(10) (October 1978): 74-76.
Cope, Myron. "Closeup of Orlando Cepeda." *Sport* 33 (April 1962): 60-68 (unsurpassed Orlando Cepeda portrait).
________. "Where There's Smoke, There's Luis." *Sports Illustrated* 38 (May 7, 1973): 43-44 (Luís Tiant, Jr.).

Cruz, Hector J. *Juan Marichal: La Historia de Su Vida* (Juan Marichal: His Life Story). Santo Domingo, Dominican Republic: Editoria Alfa y Omega, 1983, 270 pp.

Deford, Frank. "Leige Lord of the Latin Hopes: Howie Haak, Pittsburgh Pirate Scout in Latin America." *Sports Illustrated* 39 (August 27, 1973): 24–26.

Delgado, Gabino and Severo Nieto. *Béisbol Cubano, 1878–1955: Records y Estadisticas.* Havana: Editorial Lex, 1955, 186 pp. (rare and complete statistical record of pre-Castro Cuban baseball).

Devaney, John. *Juan Marichal, Mister Strike*. New York: Putnam, 1970, 190 pp.

Dias Rangel, Eleazar, and Guillermo Becerra Myares. *El Béisbol en Caracas, 1895–1966.* Caracas: Edicion del Circulo de Periodistas Deportivos, 1967, 188 pp. (Venezuelan baseball history and anecdotes).

Dowling, Tom. "César Cedeño: The Shot Heard Round the Baseball World." *Sport* 58 (August 1974): 87–98 (Cedeño's off-field problems).

Einstein, Charles. "Juan Marichal at the Crossroads." *Sport* 45 (April 1968): 58–61.

________. "The Juan Marichal Mystery." *Sport* 35 (June 1963): 48–51.

Fabianic, David. "Minority Managers in Professional Baseball." *Sociology of Sport Journal* 1:(2) (1984): 163–171 (continued absence of Latin American big-league managers).

Feldman, Jay. "Baseball in Nicaragua." *Whole Earth Review* (Fall 1987): 40–45.

________. "The Hidden-Ball Trick, Nicaragua, and Me." *National Pastime* (Society for American Baseball Research) 6:(1) (Winter 1987): 2–4.

Fernández Reguero, Victor. *Juan Esteban Vargas Marcano (Tetelo): Su Vida* (Juan Esteban Vargas Marcano (Tetelo): His Life Story). Caguas, Puerto Rico (self-published volume), 1957, 72 pp. (Puerto Rican Hall-of-Famer).

Figueredo, Jorge. "The Day Cristóbal Torriente Outclassed Babe Ruth." *Baseball Research Journal* (Society for American Baseball Research) 11 (1982): 130–32.

Figueroa, Ed, and Dorothy Harshman. *Yankee Stranger*. Smithtown, New York: Exhibition Press, 1982, 215 pp. (Ed Figueroa autobiography).

Frio, Daniel C., and Marc Onigman. "Good Field, No Hit: The Image of Latin American Baseball Players within the American Press, 1871–1946." *Revista-Review Interamericana* 9:(2) (Summer 1979): 192–208 (traces sources of many reigning stereotypes of Latin big league ballplayers).

Gammons, Peter. "Cuba's Next Generation Arrives in Full Force." *Sporting News* 201:(5) (February 3, 1986): 39.

________. "Pleí Bol! – Four Teams Did That at the Caribbean Series." *Sports Illustrated* 70:(8) (February 20, 1989): 16–21.

Gloeckner, Carolyn. *Fernando Valenzuela*. Mankato, Minnesota: Crestwood House, 1985, 48 pp. (juvenile biography).

Gordon, Dick. "Challenge from Latin America." *Baseball Digest* 20:(4) (May 1961): 73–77.

________. "Twin Firsts by a Twin." *Baseball Digest* 23 (December 1964): 67–71 (Tony Oliva becomes first black rookie to win league batting title).

Gutierréz F., Daniel. *50 Años de Big Leaguers Venezolanos, 1939–1989* (Fifty Years of Venezuelan Major Leaguers, 1939–1989). Caracas, Venezuela (self-published volume), 1990, 48 pp.

Gutman, Bill. "César Cedeño." In *New Breed of Heroes in Pro Baseball*. New York: Julian Messner, 1974, 41–55.

________. "Rod Carew." In *More Modern Baseball Superstars*. New York: Dodd, Mead, 1978, 47–66.

Hano, Arnold. "Orlando Cepeda." In *Baseball Stars of 1959*, edited by Charles Einstein. New York: Pyramid, 1959, 25–34.

________. "Orlando Cepeda." In *The Third Fireside Book of Baseball*, edited by Charles Einstein. New York: Simon and Schuster, 1968, 189–194.

________. *Roberto Clemente, Batting King*. New York: Putnam, 1973; New York: Dell, 1973, 192 pp.

________. "Roberto Clemente, Man of Paradox." *Sport* 39 (May 1965): 68–84 (superb Clemente portrait).

Hersch, Hank. "Cat's Meow in Montreal." *Sports Illustrated* 69:(6) (August 8, 1988): 50–52 (Andrés Galarraga).

________. "Our Team Is Pretty Sólido." *Sports Illustrated* 69:(8) (August 22, 1988): 70–71 (Cuban national team and Pan American Games).

Heuer, Robert J. "Luís Aparicio: Breaking Two of Baseball's Barriers." *Nuestro* 8 (March 1984): 46–47.

Hochman, Stan. "Orlando Cepeda – Heavy Bats and Open Arms." *Baseball Digest* 23 (August 1964): 11–14.

Hoekstra, Dave. "Cuban Game Is a Study in Socialism." *Chicago Sun-Times*, February 4, 1990, 20–21, 24 (current Cuban baseball).

Holtzman, Jerome. "Luís Aparicio: A Hall of Famer at Last." *Baseball Digest* 43 (November 1984): 37–41.

Holway, John B. *Blackball Stars: Negro League Pioneers*. New York: Carroll and Graf, 1992; Westport, Connecticut: Meckler, 1988, 400 pp. (Latin American blackball connection).

________. "Cuba's Black Diamond." *Baseball Research Journal* 10 (1981): 139–145.

________. *Voices from the Great Black Baseball Leagues*. New York: Dodd, Mead, 1975, 403 pp. (Latin American blackball stars).

________. "Will the Real Luís Tiant Please Stand Up." *Baseball Digest* 35 (February 1976): 74–79.

Hoose, Philip G. "Hot Blood: The Latin American Baseball Player." In *Necessities: Racial Barriers in American Sports*. New York: Random House, 1989, 90–122.

Hufford, Tim. "Minnie Miñoso: One of the Oldest." *Baseball Research Journal* 6 (1977): 30–36.

Hull, Adrian L. "The Linguistic Accommodation of a Cultural Innovation as Illustrated by the Game of Baseball in the Spanish Language." Ph.D. diss., Columbia University, 1963, 375 pp.

Izenberg, Jerry. "Clemente: A Bittersweet Memoir." In *Great Latin Sports Figures: The Proud People*. Garden City, New York: Doubleday, 1976, 11–25.

________. "Rod Carew." In *Great Latin Sports Figures: The Proud People*. Garden City, New York: Doubleday, 1976, 92–105.

Jamail, Milton. "Astros, Like Others, Look to Latin America for Aid." *Houston Post*, July 22–28, 1990.

________. "An Eye for Winners." *Vista*, February 3, 1990, 6–7, 9 (Latin American scouting).

________. "The Latin Connection." In *Texas Rangers 1992 Official Yearbook*. Westport, Connecticut: Professional Sports, 1992, 56–60.

________. "1990 Hispanic All-Star Baseball Team." *Hispanic* (April 1990): 30–33.

________. "Who Is Rubén Sierra?" *Hispanic* (April 1990): 26–28.

Jordan, Pat. "Clemente and Oliva: Same Ends, Different Means." *Sport* 50 (November 1970): 40–43.

Jupiter, Harry. "Juan Marichal, the Dominican Dandy." *Baseball Digest* 21 (October-November 1962): 27–31.

Kahn, Roger. "The Children of Roberto Clemente." In *A Season in the Sun*. New York: Harper and Row, 1977, 115–126.

________. "Golden Triumphs, Tarnished Dreams." *Sports Illustrated* 45 (August 30, 1976): 35–36 (Roberto Clemente).

Klein, Dave. "César Cedeño." In *Stars of the Major Leagues*. New York: Random House, 1974, 26–39.

Kowet, Don. "Rod Carew, Superloner." *Sport* 57 (June 1974): 62–72.

Kuenster, John. "Latin American Quality Players Abound in the Majors." *Baseball Digest* 42:(7) (July 1983): 17–21.

LaFrance, David G. "A Mexican Popular Image of the United States Through the Baseball Hero, Fernando Valenzuela." *Studies in Latin American Popular Culture* 4 (1985): 14–23.

Lara C., Joaquin. *Historia del Béisbol en Yucatán, I: 1890–1906* (History of Yucatan Baseball, Part I, 1890–1906). Merida, Yucatán (Mexico): Editorial Zamma, 1954, 195 pp.

Lauletta, Michael. "Juan Marichal: A Man in Many Shadows." *Baseball Digest* 29 (June 1970): 31–36.

Leavy, William. "Baseball's Unknown Superstars." *Ebony* 37 (June 1982): 72–74 (Latin American blackball connections).

Leonard, Wilbert M. "Salaries and Race in Professional Baseball: The Hispanic Component." *Sociology of Sport Journal* 5:(3) (September 1988): 278–284.

Lewis, Franklyn. "Sensation from South of the Border." *Saturday Evening Post* 228 (July 16, 1955): 36–37 (Roberto Avila).

Libby, Bill. "Juan Marichal." *Star Pitchers of the Big Leagues*. New York: Random House, 1971, 20–32.

________. *Rod Carew, Master Hitter*. New York: Putnam, 1976, 127 pp. (juvenile biography).

Lidz, Franz. "Wild and Crazy Hombres." *Sports Illustrated* 73 (January 8, 1990): 42–45 (Pascual Pérez, Melido Pérez, and their baseball-playing brothers).

Limardo, Miguel, and Enrique Rodríguez Santiago. *Roberto Clemente: La Cruz sobre las Olas* (Roberto Clemente: The Cross Upon the Waves). El Paso, Texas: Casa Bautista, 1973, 160 pp.

Littlefield, Bill. "A Real World Series at Last?" *World Monitor Magazine* 1:(2) (November 1988): 84–86 (Cuba in world amateur baseball competition).

Mandt, Edward. "Latin American All-Stars: Los Niños de Otoño." *Baseball Research Journal* 17 (1988), 23–24.

Marichal, Juan, with Charles Einstein. *A Pitcher's Story*. Garden City, New York: Doubleday, 1967, 215 pp. (Marichal autobiography).

May, Julian. *Roberto Clemente and the World Series Upset*. Mankato, Minnesota: Crestwood House, 1973, 48 pp. (juvenile biography).

Menton, Seymour. "Mexican Baseball Terminology: An Example of Linguistic Growth." *Hispánia* 37:(4) (December 1954): 478–481.

Mercer, Charles E. *Roberto Clemente*. New York: Putnam, 1974, 58 pp. (juvenile biography).

Mijares, Ruben. *Béisbol por Dentro* (Baseball from Inside). Mérida, Venezuela: Editorial Alfa, 1989, 53 pp. (Venezuelan baseball history).

Miller, Ira, with Foreword by José Torres. *Roberto Clemente*. New York: Grosset and Dunlap, Tempo Books, 1973, 182 pp. (combined English and Spanish text).

Millson, Larry. "The Latin Connection." In *Ballpark Figures: The Blue Jays and the Business of Baseball*. Toronto: McClelland and Stewart, 1987, 208–233 (exploring Toronto Blue Jays Latin scouting).

Miñoso, Orestes Minnie, with Fernando Fernández and Robert Kleinfelder. *Extra Innings: My Life in Baseball*. Chicago: Regnery Gateway, 1983, 205 pp.

Mueser, Anne M. *Picture Story of Rod Carew*. New York: Julian Messner, 1980, 62 pp. (juvenile biography).

Newton, Clarke. "Roberto Clemente." In *Famous Puerto Ricans,* edited by Clarke Newton. New York: Dodd, Mead, 1975, 41–53.

Nightingale, Dave. "Baseball's Secret Treasure." *Sporting News* 200:(8) (August 19, 1985): 24–27.

Núñez, José Antero. *Serie del Caribe, 1988* (The Caribbean Series, 1988). Volume 2. Caracas, Venezuela: Impresos Urbina, 1988, 190 pp. (complete history and records of winterball's Caribbean Series).

________. *Serie del Caribe, 1989* (The Caribbean Series, 1989). Volume 3. Caracas, Venezuela: Impresos Urbina, 1988, 360 pp. (complete history and records of winterball's Caribbean Series).

Nystrom, Duane. "El Béisbol Se Vuelve Interamericano (Baseball Turns Inter-American). *Américas* (Organization of American States) (November–December 1979): 50–52.

Obojski, Robert. "Baseball Latin Style." *Baseball Research Journal* 6 (1977): 104–110.

O'Brien, Jim. "Manny Mota: Baseball's Premier Pinch-Hitter." *Baseball Digest* 38 (September 1979): 86–89.

Oleksak, Michael M., and Mary Adams Oleksak. *Béisbol: Latin Americans and the Grand Old Game*. Grand Rapids, Michigan: Masters Press, 1991, 303 pp.

Oliva, Tony. *Tony O! The Trials and Triumphs of Tony Oliva*. New York: Hawthorn, 1973, 199 pp.

Olsen, James T. *Roberto Clemente, The Great One*. Chicago: Children's Press, 1974 (Mankato, Minnesota: Creative Education Books, 1974), 31 pp. (juvenile biography).

Onigman, Mark. "Historically Speaking: Béisbol Cubanos." *Black Sports* 7 (April 1978): 40–43.

Padura, Leonardo and Raúl Arce. *Estrellas del Béisbol* (Baseball Stars). Havana: Editoria Abril, 1989, 245 pp. (recent vintage Cuban baseball stars).

Peary, Danny. "Vic Power (including interview)." In *Cult Baseball Players: The Greats, the Flakes, the Weird, and the Wonderful*. New York: Simon and Schuster, Fireside Books, 1990, 344–373 (superb Power portrait).

Peebles, Dick. "All Hail the Dominicans." *Baseball Digest* 26 (April 1967): 63–65 (first Dominican big-league invasion).

Peña, Horacio. *Poema a un Hombre Llamado Roberto Clemente* (Poem for a Man Named Roberto Clemente). Managua, Nicaragua: Editorial Union, 1973, 30 pp. (verse biography and homage to Clemente).

Piña Campora, Tony. *Guía del Béisbol Profesional Dominicano* (The Dominican Pro Baseball Guide). Santo Domingo, Dominican Republic (annual publication since 1981, sponsored by the Dominican Republic Professional Baseball League).

Quinn, Tom. "Building a Winner with Well-Chosen Words: Teaching Latin Ballplayers." *Sports Illustrated* 34:(16) (April 19, 1971): 77–78.

Regalado, Samuel. "Baseball in the Barrios: The Scene in East Los Angeles Since World War II." *Baseball History* 1:(2) (Summer 1986): 47–59.

________. "The Minor League Experience of Latin American Baseball Players in Western Communities, 1950–1970." *Journal of the West* 26:(1) (January 1987): 65–70.

________. "The Special Hunger: Latin Americans in American Professional Baseball, 1871–1970." Ph.D. diss., Washington State University, 1987, 227 pp.; Ann Arbor, Michigan: University Microfilms International, order no. 8724322.

Rist, Curtis. "In the City of Shortstops: Dominican Prospects." *New York Newsday*, March 21, 1990, pt. 2, 4–7, 11.

Robinson, Ray. "Luis Aparicio." In *Speed Kings of the Base Paths*. New York: Putnam, 1964, 149–161.

Rodríguez-Mayoral, Luís. *Roberto Clemente: Aun Escucha las Ovaciones* (Roberto Clemente: Now Hear the Applause). Carolina, Puerto Rico: Ciudad Deportiva Roberto Clemente, 1987, 121 pp. (Roberto Clemente biography).

Rogosin, Donn. *Invisible Men: Life in Baseball's Negro Leagues*. New York: Atheneum, 1985, 283 pp. (Latin American blackball connections).

Rosenthal, Harold. "Luís Aparicio, Shortstop." *Sport* 28 (November 1959): 20–21 (early Aparicio portrait).

________. "The War with Mexico." *Baseball Digest* 22:(10) (December 1963–January 1964): 53–56 (Jorge Pasquel's Mexican League of the 1940s).

Ruck, Rob. "Baseball in the Caribbean." In *Total Baseball*, first edition, edited by John Thorn and Pete Palmer. New York: Warner, 1989, 605–611.

________. "Chicos and Gringos of Béisbol Venezolana." *Baseball Research Journal* 15 (1986): 75–78.

________. "The Crisis in Winter Baseball: Can It Survive?" *Baseball America* (February 25–March 9, 1990): 8–10.

________. "Dominican a Real Fan and Talent Hotbed." *Baseball Research Journal* 13 (1984): 3–6.

________. "Hitting Dominican Home Runs." *Americas* 38:(5) (September–October 1986): 20–25.

________. "Juan Marichal: Baseball in the Dominican Republic." In *Baseball History 3: An Annual of Original Baseball Research*, edited by Peter Levine. Westport, Connecticut: Meckler, 1990, 49–70.

Rudeen, Kenneth. *Roberto Clemente*. New York: Crowell, 1974, 34 pp. (juvenile biography).

Russell, David. "Baseball, Hollywood, and Nicaragua." *Monthly Review* 34:(10) (March 1983): 22–29.

Saavedra, Gilda. *Béisbol 70: Guía Oficial Cubana* (Baseball 1970: Official Cuban Guide). Havana, Cuba: Ediciones Deportes, 1971, 392 pp.

Sanchez-Boudy, Jose. "Lenguaje Béisbolero" (Baseball Language). In *El Picuo, El Fisto, El Barrio y Otras Estampas Cubanas*. Miami, Florida: Ediciones Universal, 1977, 134–135 (Cuban baseball terminology).

Santamaria, Enrique. *Remembranzas de Ayer a Hoy* (Remembrances of Yesterday and Today). Ciudad Trujillo, Dominican Republic: Editora Centro, 1952, 61 pp. (Dominican baseball history).

Shaw, Kathryn R. "El Auge de la 'Fernandomania.'" *Américas* (March–April 1982): 54 (Fernando Valenzuela portrait).

Shecter, Leonard. "The Case Against Aparicio." *Sport* 35 (June 1963): 42–45.

Sheer, Harry. "Cuban Ballplayers in the Majors." *Baseball Digest* 30:(11) (November 1971): 72–74.

Smith, Ira L. "Adolfo Luque." In *Baseball's Famous Pitchers*. New York: A. S. Barnes, 1954, 156–160 (rare early Luque portrait).

________. "Minnie Miñoso." In *Baseball's Famous Outfielders*. New York: A. S. Barnes, 1954, 298–302.

Smith, Marshall. "The Senator's Slow-Ball Señor." *Life* 30 (June 11, 1951): 81–82 (Camilo Pascual).

Stump, Al. "Juan Marichal: Behind His Success." *Sport* 38 (September 1964): 84–95.

Sudyk, Bob. "Vic Davalillo's Fight Against Fear." *Baseball Digest* 24 (June 1965): 15–22.

Terzian, James. *The Kid from Cuba: Zoilo Versalles*. Garden City, New York: Doubleday, 1967, 142 pp. (juvenile biography).

Tiant, Luís, and Joe Fitzgerald. *El Tiante: The Luis Tiant Story*. Garden City, New York: Doubleday, 1976, 228 pp.

Torres, Angel. *La Historia del Béisbol Cubano* (The Story of Cuban Baseball). Los Angeles (self-published volume), 1976, 191 pp.

Trenary, Don C. "Those Gay Cubanos!" *Baseball Digest* 20:(3) (April 1961): 47–49 (Cuban big-leaguers of the 1950s).

Triana, Fausto. *Braudillo Vinent, La Fama de la Consistencia* (Braudillo Vinent, the Fame of Consistency). Havana, Cuba: Editorial Científico Técnica, 1985, 112 pp. (biography of 1970s black Cuban pitching star).

Valdez, Tirso A. *Notas Acerca del Béisbol Dominicano del Pasado y del Presente* (Notes Concerning Dominican Baseball of Past and Present). Ciudad Trujillo, Dominican Republic: Editora del Caribe, 1958, 56 pp.

Vass, George. "Clemente: Baseball's Most Complete Player." *Baseball Digest* 29 (May 1970): 41–51.

________. "The Rising Tide of Latin Stars." *Baseball Digest* 32:(2) (February 1973): 16–22.

Vaughn, Gerald F. "Building the Pre-1961 Washington Senators Farm System." Washington, D.C. (unpublished manuscript), 1984.

________. "George Hausmann Recalls the Mexican League of 1946–47." Edited by Peter C. Bjarkman. *International Pastime: A Review of Baseball History* 12 (1992): 9–13.

________. "Jorge Pasquel and the Evolution of the Mexican League." Edited by James Kaplan. *Baseball Research Journal* 19 (1990): 59–63.

Vesilind, Pritt. "Rico Carty Finally Makes It Big." *Baseball Digest* 29 (August 1970): 68–73.

Vicioso, Fernando A., and Alvarez, Mario D. *Béisbol Dominicano, 1891–1967*. Santo Domingo, Dominican Republic (self-published), 1967, 253 pp. (historical and anecdotal accounts of Dominican baseball history).

Wagner, Eric A. "Baseball in Cuba." *Journal of Popular Culture* 18:(1) (Summer 1984): 113–120.

Ward, John J. "González, the Cuban Backstop." *Baseball Magazine* 18 (February 1917): 33–34 (Mike González, first Latin American manager).

Williams, Edgar. "Sandy Amoros—He Got!" *Baseball Digest* 13 (October 1954): 71–78 (Amoros profiled before his glorious 1955 World Series moment).

Wulf, Steve. "Here's a Hot Dog You've Got to Relish." *Sports Illustrated* 58 (January 24, 1983): 28–31 (Joaquín Andújar, the Latin flake).

________. "Standing Tall at Short." *Sports Illustrated* 66:(6) (February 9, 1987): 132–148 (Dominican big-league talent search).

Zanger, Jack. "A Unique View of Juan Marichal." *Sport* 44 (September 1967): 18–21.

Index